Perspectives on Southern Africa

The
South West Africa / Namibia
Dispute

The
South West Africa / Namibia
Dispute

Documents and Scholarly Writings on the

Controversy Between South Africa

and the United Nations

Edited by

John Dugard

Advocate of the Supreme Court of South Africa;
Professor of Law in the University of the Witwatersrand

UNIVERSITY OF CALIFORNIA PRESS

BERKELEY·LOS ANGELES·LONDON

University of California Press
Berkeley and Los Angeles, California
University of California Press, Ltd.
London, England
Copyright © 1973, by
The Regents of the University of California
ISBN: 0-520-01886-9
Library of Congress Catalog Card Number: 76-142052
Printed in the United States of America

For Jane

Contents

Preface

THE POLITICO-LEGAL DISPUTE OVER THE INTERNATIONAL
status of South West Africa, or Namibia,* has featured regularly
on the agenda of the General Assembly since 1946, has been considered annually by the Security Council since 1968, and has been
the subject of six appearances before the International Court of
Justice. Without doubt it has prompted more resolutions, promoted more committees, and produced more judicial decisions
than any other matter to come before the organs of the United
Nations. Together with the question of apartheid, it has been the
focal point of the confrontation between South Africa and the international community over the issues of self-determination and
human rights.

As the international *cause célèbre* of the century, it has inspired a steady flow of scholarly and popular writings, which
include legal analyses of the International Court's decisions and
historical accounts of the evolution of the dispute before the
United Nations. A writer should therefore have some cogent reason for adding to the already profuse literature on this subject.
Unlike existing writings on South West Africa, which are mainly
descriptive and analytical, the present work aims to portray the
dispute through the medium of decisions of the International
Court of Justice, resolutions of and debates in the General Assembly and Security Council, reports of United Nations' Committees,
political addresses, and academic comment. The evolution of the
present stalemate between South Africa and the United Nations
and its historical antecedents are presented in "live" form,

---

* The names South West Africa and Namibia are each used in the editor's
commentary. For historical reasons the former is used when referring to pre-
1968 events. In discussing the territory's subsequent history, the name used
depends on the context in which it appears. The use of one name or the
other should not be construed as a judgment on the status of the territory.

through contemporary documents and comments, so that readers may themselves judge the merits of the respective claims advanced by the United Nations and South Africa. The connecting commentary is deliberately kept to a minimum, as the selected documents and writings speak for themselves.

This collection aims at presenting a picture of the post–World War II dispute before the United Nations and the International Court of Justice. As a correct historical perspective is essential for a true understanding of the present situation, it has been necessary to include chapters on the history of South West Africa under German rule and on the main problems of the League of Nations period (chapters 2 and 4). Here the selection of documents has been most strict: those chosen are intended to do no more than expose the roots of the current conflict. The other chapter (three) dealing with the pre–World War II period describes the creation of the mandates system and is directly relevant to the present situation.

The present study is essentially concerned with the international politico-legal aspects of the South West African question. But the distinction between international and national events is blurred and is impossible to maintain at all times. Many local events, such as the Bondelswarts revolt of 1923 and the "terrorism trial" of 1967, have had important international repercussions, while the South African Government's policy of separate development ceases to be a domestic issue when applied to South West Africa because Article 2 of the Mandate for South West Africa obliges the mandatory to "promote to the utmost the material and moral well-being and the social progress of the inhabitants." The collection therefore includes writings on significant local events and on the more important developments in the application of apartheid to South West Africa. Moreover, chapter one seeks to place the dispute in its geographical and human context. No attempt is made, however, to present a comprehensive picture of South West African internal policies nor of their application in practice.

The main focus falls on the post–World War II period. Here the collected documents and writings are more comprehensive and designed to highlight the most important events in the evolution of the dispute as well as to present differing points of view. Considerations of space have made it impossible to avoid drastic selection. For instance, extracts have been chosen from only eight of the more than sixty scholarly writings on the controversial

1966 decision of the International Court of Justice in the *South West Africa Cases*. Inevitably, fault will be found with the selection. In mitigation, it may be pleaded that errors of selection could only be avoided by producing an unmanageably large volume or a series of volumes on this subject. As both the publisher and the editor believed that this would be unwise, rigorous selection has been unavoidable.

The South West African dispute falls squarely within the concern of the political scientist, the historian, and the lawyer. To the lawyer, however, it has a special appeal, for ever since the inception of the mandates system and the difference of opinion over the location of sovereignty in the mandates, the debate over the status of the territory has been founded on legal concepts and clothed in legal rhetoric. The six decisions of the International Court of Justice on the South West African question have enriched the jurisprudence of the Court and starkly revealed the conflicting approaches to international law among the judges of the Court. A study of these cases is indispensable to an understanding of the international judicial process and of the role of adjudication in the settlement of disputes in the modern world. Because of this "special appeal" to international lawyers many of the documents included are of primary concern to the lawyer. On the other hand, the collection is not intended as a lawyer's compendium. Throughout, every attempt has been made to achieve a fair balance between legal selections and "political" documents and writings. If the former predominate, this is because the South West African question has been largely categorized as a "legal dispute" by politicians.

Although the present work is intended to assist the academic by providing him with a readily accessible collection of source materials for a study of the South West African question, its purpose is more pervasive. South West Africa is a source of potential friction and conflict in the world order. If the "material and moral well-being and the social progress of the inhabitants" of Namibia are to be promoted "to the utmost" and if violent confrontation is to be avoided, realistic therapeutic action must be taken now. This obvious truth is realized by a handful of leaders among the Western Powers and by a limited number of decision-makers in South Africa. These leaders are, at present, operating in a political vacuum with little informed public opinion to guide them. If public opinion is to be rallied on the side of social change in South West Africa the issues posed by the dispute must be more clearly understood. The present work is a modest attempt in this direction. In large measure the prompting to produce this collection of documents and writings came from Mr. William J. McClung of the University of California Press, who convinced the editor of the need to more fully "educate" opinion within the world's community of scholars. The present collection aims to give effect to this vision.

JOHN DUGARD

University of the Witwatersrand,
Johannesburg

Acknowledgments

The idea of a collection of documents and scholarly writings on the international dispute over South West Africa had its origin in discussions with Mr. William J. McClung, then of the Princeton University Press, and Professor Richard A. Falk, Milbank Professor of International Law at Princeton University, during the fall of 1969 when the editor was a visiting Professor at the Woodrow Wilson School of Public and International Affairs. Professor Falk and Mr. McClung, who had a short time before produced a collection of writings on *The Vietnam War and International Law* (edited by Richard A. Falk and published by the Princeton University Press), believed that the time was ripe for a similar work on South West Africa. Later, after Mr. McClung joined the University of California Press, the idea was translated into a project which has now reached fruition. In the first instance, therefore, my thanks are due to Mr. McClung and Professor Falk for their initial encouragement. Since then Mr. McClung has continued his support, both as a publisher and as a friend. Only a well-worn platitude can capture his part in this project: without him it would not have been.

This book is essentially a collection of other men's flowers. My thanks are therefore due to the authors and publishers who have so generously given me permission to reprint their material. Detailed permissions appear below.

My special thanks go to the secretaries of the School of Law, of the University of Witwatersrand, Mrs. M. J. Schlimmer and Mrs. F. Goldman, and to the Law Librarian, Mrs. C. Jaspan, and her assistant, Mrs. P. Farr. They have given unstintingly of their time and assistance and have borne with good humour and patience the heavy demands for secretarial and library services.

Finally, I wish to thank my wife, Jane, for all her help in the preparation of the manuscript; for her acceptance of the inroads made upon family life by this collection; and for her encouragement at all times.

PERMISSIONS

The editor wishes to acknowledge permission given to reprint copyright material by the following authors and publishers:

The American Society of International Law, for permission to reprint from the following articles appearing in the *American Journal of International Law:* John Dugard, "Revocation of the Mandate for South West Africa" (1968) 62 *AJIL* 78; John Dugard, "South West Africa and the 'Terrorist Trial' " (1970) 64 *AJIL* 19; Manley O. Hudson, "The Twenty-Ninth Year of the World Court" (1951) 45 *AJIL* 12; Francis B. Sayre, "Legal Problems arising from the United Nations Trusteeship System" (1948) 42 *AJIL* 263.

Dr. L. J. Blom-Cooper, and the *Modern Law Review,* for permission to reprint from "Republic and Mandate" (1961) 24 *Modern Law Review* 256.

The Cambridge University Press, for permission to reprint from *Cambridge History of the British Empire,* vol. 8 (C. Headlam, "The Race for the Interior").

The Canadian Yearbook of International Law, and Solomon Slonim, for permission to reprint from S. Slonim, "The Origins of the South West Africa Dispute: The Versailles Peace Conference and the Creation of the Mandates System" (1968) 6 *Canadian Yearbook of International Law* 115. (This article now constitutes Chapter I in Solomon Slonim, *South West Africa and the United Nations: An International Mandate in Dispute.* Johns Hopkins Press, 1973.)

The Center on International Race Relations, for permission to reprint from Elizabeth Landis, "Namibia: The Beginning of Disengagement" (1970) 2 *Studies in Race and Nations,* no. 1.

The Columbia Journal of Transnational Law, for permission to reprint from Wolfgang G. Friedmann, "The Jurisprudential Implications of the South West Africa Case" (1967) 6 *Columbia Journal of Transnational Law* 1.

The Comparative and International Law Journal of Southern Africa, and Professor Marinus Wiechers, for permission to reprint from Marinus Wiechers, "South West Africa: The Decision of 16 July 1966 and its Aftermath" (1968) 1 *Comparative and International Law Journal of Southern Africa* 408.

Cornell University, and Dr. Elizabeth Landis, for permission to reprint from the following articles appearing in the *Cornell Law Quarterly:* Elizabeth S. Landis, "South West Africa in the International Court: Act II, Scene 1" (1964) 49 *Cornell Law Quarterly* 179; and Elizabeth S. Landis, "The South West Africa Cases: Remand to the United Nations" (1967) 52 *Cornell Law Quarterly* 627.

The Council on Foreign Relations, Inc., New York, for permission to reprint from the following articles appearing in *Foreign Affairs:* Ernest A. Gross, "The South West Africa Case: What Happened?" (1966) 45 *Foreign Affairs* 36; George F. Kennan, "Hazardous Courses in Southern Africa" (1971) 49 *Foreign Affairs* 218.

Professor Anthony A. D'Amato, for permission to reprint from "Legal and Political Strategies of the South West Africa Litigation" (1967) 4 *Law in Transition Quarterly* 8.

The David Davies Memorial Institute of International Studies, for permission to reprint from D. H. N. Johnson, "The South West Africa Cases (Second Phase)" (1967) 3 *International Relations* 157.

Mr. I. Goldblatt, Q.C., for permission to reprint from I. Goldblatt, *The Conflict between the United Nations and the Union of South Africa in Regard to South West Africa.*

Mr. I. Goldblatt, Q.C., and C. Struik, for permission to reprint from I. Goldblatt, *The Mandated Territory of South West Africa in Relation to the United Nations.*

The Government Printing Works, Pretoria, for permission to reprint extracts from the following official publications reproduced under Government Printer's Copyright Authority 4620 of 8 December 1971: *South West Africa Survey* 1967; Report of the Commission of Enquiry into South West African Affairs (RP 12/1964); Explanatory Memorandum on Background and Objects of the Development of Self-Government for Native Nations in South West Africa (WP 3/1968); Report of the Rehoboth Commission (UG 41/1926); House of Assembly Debates, volumes 52(1945), 56(1946), 60(1947), 66(1949), 5(1963).

Dr. Rosalyn Higgins, for permission to reprint from Rosalyn Higgins, "The International Court and South West Africa: The Implications of the Judgment" (1966) 42 *International Affairs* 573.

Dr. Rosalyn Higgins, and the British Institute of International and Comparative Law, for permission to reprint from Rosalyn

Higgins, "The Advisory Opinion on Namibia: Which UN Resolutions are Binding under Article 25 of the Charter ?" (1972) 21 *International and Comparative Law Quarterly* 270.

The International Court of Justice, for permission to reprint from its pleadings and judgments.

Juta and Company, Ltd., for permission to reprint from the *South African Law Reports,* the *Annual Survey of South African Law,* and from the following articles appearing in the *South African Law Journal:* John Dugard, "South West Africa Cases: Second Phase 1966" (1966) 83 *SALJ* 429; John Dugard, "The Opinion on South-West Africa ('Namibia'): The Teleologists Triumph" (1971) 88 *SALJ* 460; Joseph Nisot, "Advisory Opinion of the International Court of Justice on the International Status of South West Africa" (1951) 68 *SALJ* 274.

Professor Ellison Kahn, for permission to reprint from the following contributions appearing in the *Annual Survey of South African Law:* "Constitutional and Administrative Law" 1964 *Annual Survey of South African Law,* and "Constitutional and Administrative Law" 1968 *Annual Survey of South African Law.*

The *Revue Belge de Droit International,* for permission to reprint from Lyndel V. Prott, "Some Aspects of Judicial Reasoning in the South-West Africa Case of 1962" (1967) 3 *Revue Belge de Droit International* 37.

Round Table, for permission to reprint from "The Sovereignty of South West Africa" (1927–8) 18 *Round Table* 217.

The Royal African Society, and Professor Wm. Roger Louis, for permission to reprint from Wm. Roger Louis, "The South West African Origins of the 'Sacred Trust,' 1914–1919" (1967) 66 *African Affairs* 20.

The South African Institute of Race Relations, for permission to reprint from Ronald B. Ballinger, *South-West Africa: The Case against the Union* (1961), and Muriel Horrell, *South West Africa* (1967).

J. C. Smuts, and Hodder and Stoughton, Ltd., for permission to reprint from J. C. Smuts, *The League of Nations: A Practical Suggestion* (1919).

Stevens and Sons, and Professor Ellison Kahn, for permission to reprint from Ellison Kahn, "The International Court's Advisory Opinion on the International Status of South West Africa" (1951) 4 *International Law Quarterly* 78.

The editors of the *Virginia Journal of International Law,* for permission to reprint from William M. Reisman, "Revision of the

South West Africa Cases" (1966) 7 *Virginia Journal of International Law* 1.

The World Peace Foundation, and Professor Richard A. Falk, for permission to reprint from Richard A. Falk, "The South West Africa Cases: An Appraisal" (1967) 21 *International Organization* 1.

Mrs. Louise Wright, for permission to reprint from Quincy Wright, *Mandates Under the League of Nations* (1930).

A Note on Footnotes and Style

No attempt has been made to provide uniformity of editorial style in the documents and writings in this collection. Instead the style in which the particular extract originally appeared has been retained.

The footnotes in the selected extracts have been retained wherever possible. Where, however, a footnote is unrelated to the present study or refers to a passage in the publication which is not included, it has been omitted. In such a case the footnotes have not been renumbered with the result that there are occasionally gaps in the numbering of footnotes.

Footnotes to the selected extracts appear in numerals. In order to distinguish footnotes in the editor's commentary from those in the selected writings, the former are indicated by letters of the alphabet. In the more lengthy chapters (for example, Chapter 8) it has been necessary to repeat the letters of the alphabet. In such a case, where reference is made to a previous footnote (n.) and there are several such notes identified by the same letter, the page on which the note appears is also provided, for example, "See Smith, n. c (above p. 100)." (An example of such a case is note "a" on page 357.)

Abbreviations

1

The Territory and Its Peoples

GEOGRAPHICAL FEATURES [a]

Counter-Memorial Filed by the Government of South Africa in the South West Africa Cases (1966): [b]

The natural environment of a country not only regulates the size, character and distribution of its population, but also constitutes a major factor in determining the potential pattern and rate of its development. In the context of the present case, however, it is also true that geographical factors and natural resources are relevant and assume importance only to the extent that they can be used by man for his benefit, or that they constitute obstacles to be overcome in developing the Territory.

This survey will indicate that the natural environment of South West Africa is to a large extent unfavourable for man's purposes and that it displays great diversity, resulting in special problems of administration and development. The adverse physical environment places a premium on the role of man in realizing the limited and diverse natural potential of the Territory.

Consequently the two factors of natural environment and human resources, as well as their inter-relationship, are basic to the interpretation of conditions and achievements in South West Africa, and cardinal to the evaluation of any policy of administration and development in the Territory.

LOCATION

I. General

The Territory of South West Africa lies along the Atlantic seaboard in the south-western portion of Africa.

[a] For further reading on this subject, see J. H. Wellington, *South West Africa and Its Human Issues* (1967), part I (pp. 1–128).
[b] International Court of Justice Pleadings, South West Africa, vol. 2, pp. 289–93.

The Territory stretches from the southern border of Angola to part of the northern and north-western border of the Cape Province of the Republic of South Africa; and from the Atlantic Ocean in the west to the western border of [Botswana] in the east. The Tropic of Capricorn divides the Territory into two nearly equal parts. The northern half of South West Africa therefore falls in what is generally known as Tropical Africa.

II. Borders

As in the case of many other territories in Africa, the land boundaries of South West Africa were originally drawn by statesmen who not only had little knowledge of local topographical and ethnic conditions, but were mainly guided by considerations other than local interests and problems of administration. Thus, for instance, the northern boundary intersects the area inhabited by Ovambo tribes so that three tribes fall into Angola, north of the boundary, one tribe is cut in two, while the remainder fall into South West Africa. A similar position obtains in the case of the tribes living on the Okavango River. In such circumstances effective boundary control, e.g., to prevent the spread of human or animal diseases, becomes a virtual impossibility.

The Eastern Caprivi Zipfel presents the same problems arising from the fact that the political boundaries bear no relation to the borders of areas inhabited by particular ethnic groups. In addition its inclusion in the Territory adds to the diversity of the population by bringing portions of tribes living in Rhodesia and [Botswana] into a political unit with the other inhabitants of South West Africa, with whom they have no ethnic or other ties at all, and from whom they are, for practical purposes, almost completely isolated geographically. This factor creates special problems of administration.

AREA

South West Africa has an area of 824,269 sq. km. (318,261 sq. miles) including the area of Walvis Bay (measuring 1,124 sq. km. or 434 sq. miles) which, although part of the Republic of South Africa, is for convenience administered as part of South West Africa.[1]

The Territory is nearly four times the size of the United Kingdom and nearly seven and a half times as large as Liberia. On the other hand, it has less than half the population of Liberia. While the area of South West Africa is virtually the same as that of Nigeria, the latter

[1] *Vide* British Letters Patent dated 14 Dec. 1878, in *British and Foreign State Papers 1878–1879*, Vol. LXX, pp. 495–496, for the British annexation of Walvis Bay. By *Proc.* No. 184 of 1884 (Cape of Good Hope), 7 Aug. 1884, in *The Cape of Good Hope Government Gazette*, No. 6519 (8 Aug. 1884), p. I, it was annexed to the Colony of the Cape of Good Hope. Its administration as part of South West Africa was provided for by sec. I of Act No. 24 of 1922 and *Proc.* No. 145 of 1922 (S.A.), 11 Sept. 1922, in *The Laws of South West Africa 1915–1922*, p. 20 and pp. 56–57.

carries a population 60 times larger than that of South West Africa. The Territory constitutes nearly 3 per cent. of the total area of Africa, while its population of approximately half a million amounts to only about 0.2 per cent. of the total population of Africa. With the exception of [Botswana], which adjoins the Territory, it has the lowest population density in Africa south of the Sahara,[2] and one of the lowest density figures in the world.[3]

From north to south the Territory measures about 1,280 km. (800 miles) and from west to east an average distance of 720 km. (350 miles), which gives it an oblong shape with nearly 80 per cent. of the population concentrated in the northern half of the Territory, that is, north of a line taken just north of Walvis Bay.

TOPOGRAPHY

Topographically, the Territory can be divided into three separate regions, viz., the Namib, the Central Plateau and the Kalahari.

The western marginal area between the escarpment and the coast is known as the *Namib*. It is an extremely arid and desolate desert region stretching along the entire coast-line of the Territory and rising rapidly but evenly inland. The lateral width of the area varies from 80 to 130 km. (50 to 80 miles), and it constitutes more than 15 per cent. of the total land area of South West Africa. It consists mainly of vast plains and seas of constantly moving sand, with occasional low, scattered mountains. Practically the whole population of this region, being less than 6 per cent. of the entire population of South West Africa, is concentrated in four coastal urban areas [Swakopmund, Walvis Bay, Luderitz and Oranjemund].

The *Central Plateau* is the area lying to the east of the Namib. It also stretches all the way from south to north. It varies in altitude between 1,000 and 2,000 m. (3,280 to 6,560 ft.) and in itself offers a diversified landscape of rugged mountains, rocky outcrops, sand-filled valleys and softly undulating plains. It covers slightly more than 50 per cent. of the land area of the Territory.

Finally, the *Kalahari* covers the eastern, north-eastern and northern areas of South West Africa. The dominant feature of this region is its

[2] Both have population densities of less than one person per square kilometre, but the density in Botswana is slightly lower than that of South West Africa—*vide* figures in U.N. *Statistical Yearbook 1962*, pp. 24–25.
[3] The only countries other than South West Africa and Botswana which, according to the figures published in U.N. *Statistical Yearbook 1962*, pp. 21–39, have population densities of less than one person per square kilometre, are Libya, Mauritania, French Southern and Antarctic Territories, a small part of Spanish North Africa, Spanish Sahara, Tristan da Cunha, Greenland, French Guiana, the Falkland Islands, Mongolia, and the Svalbard and Jan Mayen Island (inhabited only during the winter season). For purposes of comparison, the following population densities in persons per square kilometre have been extracted from the same source: Liberia, 12; Ethiopia, 17; United States of America, 20; The Netherlands, 346.

thick cover of terrestrial sands and limestones. This region is often regarded as desert, but, as the rainfall of the northern Kalahari exceeds 600 mm. (24 in.), the Kalahari hardly falls into the same category as the Sahara or the Namib.

In appearance it is mainly an area of level monotonous plains covered with sand dunes, which, in contrast with those of the Namib, have been settled by vegetation. The main problem confronting present and future exploitation is not an inadequate total amount of rainfall or a sparse vegetation—indeed, the Kalahari offers considerable potential for large-stock rearing—but since the rainfall seeps away rapidly through the thick, loose sand and the underlying porous limestone, there is a near total lack of surface water, while ground water is sometimes so deep as to be economically unexploitable.

However, by way of contrast, the eastern section of the Caprivi Strip, which stretches out to the Zambesi and Linyanti (known in its higher reaches as the Kwando and the Chobe) Rivers, exhibits totally different conditions. Because of the extremely low gradients there, nearly one-quarter of the region is annually flooded during the period of peak flow. Floods also occur annually in the eastern part of Ovamboland, which is generally better watered than the rest of this area.

NATURAL RESOURCES

Counter-Memorial Filed by the Government of South Africa in the South West Africa Cases (1966): [e]

WATER RESOURCES

Agricultural and industrial development in South West Africa is seriously hampered by a severe lack of water resources. The effectiveness of the low and unreliable rainfall is diminished by the high rate of evaporation already mentioned. It is estimated that more than 90 per cent. of the average annual rainfall of the Territory is lost directly by evaporation and indirectly through the transpiration of plants. Since the major part of the balance of the rainfall precipitates over the north-eastern sector of the Territory, where there is no surface drainage, it follows that only a small fraction of the total rainfall of the Territory is actually available for utilization.

LAND RESOURCES

The land resources of any country depend basically on its climate, vegetation and soils. . . . [T]he exposition given here is largely an assessment of their significance with respect to agricultural development in South West Africa.

The three major primary industries based on land resources are

[e] International Court of Justice Pleadings, South West Africa, vol. 2, pp. 301–309.

cropping, stock farming and timber exploitation, and the Territory's potentialities in respect of each will be discussed in turn.

(a) *Cropping*

As a result of the low and erratic rainfall, normal dry-land cropping may be practised over only 1.1 per cent. of the Territory's area; possibilities for marginal and sub-marginal dry-land cropping exist over 10 per cent. and 21 per cent. of the area respectively, leaving 67.9 per cent. of the country in which dry-land cropping is precluded. Irrigation potential is best in the north-eastern areas, which are already better off than the rest of the Territory in respect of rainfall; but these favourable conditions are to a certain extent off-set by the low fertility of the Kalahari sands. Over the rest of the Territory too the soil is at best only of moderate fertility. Since South West Africa is situated in the transitional belt between the tropics and the temperate regions, temperature conditions are not really favourable for either tropical or temperate crops.

(b) *Stock Farming*

Stock farming is the predominant type of land use in the Territory. Environmental factors such as vegetation and water supplies lead to a zonal distribution of stock farming in the Territory—small stock in the arid southern areas, mixed small and large stock in the central areas, and large stock in the better watered northern and north-eastern areas. These features cast an interesting light on some aspects of the pre-colonial history of some of the major population groups, viz., the Nama, the Herero, the Ovambo and the Okavango tribes: the agricultural Ovambo and Okavango occupied the sub-tropical north; the Nama, mainly interested in small stock, roamed over the arid steppes of the south and also made use of the mixed grazing offered by the thorn savannahs of the central areas; whereas the cattle-rearing Herero invaded the same savannahs from the north and became engaged in almost continuous warfare with the Nama.

(c) *Timber Exploitation*

The woodland vegetation of the north-eastern portion of the Territory contains some species of trees that could be exploited commercially. It is estimated that the area of exploitable woodland is 20,000 sq. km. in the Ovamboland and Okavango Native Reserves, 10,000 sq. km. in the unoccupied state land in the Grootfontein district, and 5,-000 sq. km. in the Eastern Caprivi Zipfel. Fire belts have had to be cut to divide the forest areas into smaller units and thus to protect them against fires, especially those lit by Bushmen in pursuit of game—a frequent occurrence, e.g., in the Okavango. At present timber is being supplied to the Tsumeb Mine, and two small saw mills are in operation near Grootfontein, but exploitation is hampered by the absence of adequate transport facilities in the uninhabited parts of the northeast and the variety of species of timber occurring in these parts, which necessitates selective exploitation and results in higher costs of labour and transportation.

MINERAL RESOURCES

South West Africa has a great variety of mineral deposits but only a few have proved of real economic importance. There are concentrated occurrences of diamonds, lead/zinc, copper and salt deposits; for the rest the Territory's mineral resources are characterized by rich samples from small quantities widely dispersed over the country.

Diamonds are found in the southern Namib area of South West Africa. The diamond mining at Oranjemund is by far the most profitable of all mining ventures in the territory. Although the prospects for the immediate future are good, diamonds are a dwindling resource. The remaining life expectancy of the Oranjemund fields at present rates of exploitation is put at no more than a few decades. At present dredging for diamonds is taking place off the coast of the Territory, but this type of mining is still in its infancy and it is difficult to say with any certainty what its prospects are. Large-scale mining also takes place at Tsumeb, where various base metals such as lead, copper and zinc are mined. The Oranjemund and Tsumeb mines together account for about 96 per cent. in value of the Territory's total mineral output.

Apart from the two instances mentioned, mineral occurrences in South West Africa are generally of insufficient size to warrant large-scale mining operations. There are a number of small-scale mines in the Territory producing tin, tungsten, copper, etc. On the coast, salt is produced by the evaporation of sea-water.

As far as mineral fuels are concerned, the known coal deposits in the Territory are not worth exploiting, whereas prospecting for petroleum, especially in the northern parts of the Territory, is still in progress.

Deposits of iron ore are to be found at various places in the Territory, but the iron content is generally too low to warrant exploitation. The only really good iron ores occur in a locality where transport difficulties have up to the present not made them an economic proposition, while the absence of known deposits of workable quantities of coal reduces their potential in a local iron and steel industry.

MARINE RESOURCES

In the period after the Second World War South West Africa has emerged as a considerable fish-producing Territory, due to the presence and exploitation of a teeming marine life along the otherwise barren and inhospitable coast. This marine asset is shared by Angola and the Republic of South Africa along the south-western coast of Africa, and calls for close co-operation in research and conservation measures. The marine fishing resources support a pilchard and crawfish industry.

Inland fish resources occur only in the extreme northern and north-eastern parts of the Territory in perennial rivers and swamps. Although these resources are not exploited commercially to any considerable degree, they constitute an important part of the food supply of the local inhabitants.

POPULATION [d]

South West Africa Survey, 1967: [e]

The population of South West Africa is today, and has for centuries been, a heterogeneous one. The main population groups are the following (in the order in which it is proposed to discuss them below)—

(a) The East Caprivi Peoples;
(b) The Okavango Peoples;
(c) The Ovambo;
(d) The Bushmen;
(e) The Dama (also known as Bergdama or Bergdamara or Damara of the Hills);
(f) The Nama (also known as Khoi or Hottentots);
(g) The Herero (also known as Cattle Damara or Damara of the Plains);
(h) The Rehoboth Basters;
(i) The European or White group (mainly of German and South African origin);
(j) The Coloureds;
(k) Others.

THE EAST CAPRIVI PEOPLES

The Caprivi Zipfel (or Caprivi Strip) became a part of South West Africa by a quirk of history. In an agreement of 1st July, 1890, the British Government recognized that the area in question (subsequently named after the German Chancellor, Count von Caprivi) would thenceforth fall within the German sphere of influence, so as to provide access from South West Africa to the Zambesi. In fact the Eastern part of the Caprivi is cut off from the rest of the Territory by large swamp areas.

The western part of the Strip is inhabited only by wandering bands of Bushmen. The inhabitants of the Eastern Caprivi are of Bantu stock, but are not ethnically related to any of the other Bantu clusters found in South West Africa, i.e., the Ovambo and the Okavango peoples or the Herero. Their ethnic relations extend in part northwards

---

[d] See further, Wellington, above, n. a, pp. 129–57; Report of the Rehoboth Commission U. G. 41 of 1926, pp. 4–44; C. H. L. Hahn, H. Vedder, and L. Fourie, *The Native Tribes of South West Africa* (1928).

[e] Published by the Department of Foreign Affairs of the Republic of South Africa, pp. 17–23.

into Zambia and in part southwards into Botswana. The main population groups in the Eastern Caprivi are the Masubia and the Mafuc. Together they constitute almost 88% of the population, small numbers of the Mayeyi, Matotela, Mashi and Mbukushu tribes making up the rest. These small elements have in course of time become incorporated in the Mafue group. . . .

By tradition, the East Caprivi Peoples are agriculturalists and stock farmers, cultivating the land under a system of individual rights of occupation allocated by the tribal authorities. They augment their food supply by hunting, fishing and collecting wild fruits. . . .

According to the 1960 census, the population was 15,840, representing 3.01% of the total population of South West Africa. The estimated 1966 figure was 17,900 or 2.93% of total population. [According to the 1970 census [f] this population group numbers 25,009 of a total population of 746,328.]

THE OKAVANGO PEOPLES

In 1960 the Okavango Peoples numbered 27,871 or 5.30% of the total population of the Territory. The 1966 estimate was 31,500 or 5.18%. They comprise five different tribes, namely the Kuangari, Bunja, Sambiu, Djiriku and Mbukushu, each of which inhabits an area of its own along the southern bank of the Okavango River. The Kuangali language is generally used by the Kuangari, Bunja, Sambiu and Djiriku with local dialectical versions, wheras the Mbukushu have a language of their own.

The traditional economy along the Okavango is mixed agricultural and pastoral, with lands or gardens near the kraals (family villages). Stock consists of cattle and goats. Individual rights of occupation of land for cultivation are granted by the tribal authorities, but grazing is on a communal basis. . . .

Social organization is based on the matrilineal system, children belonging to the lineal group and clan of their mother. The custom is to live in family villages in which the family constitutes the most important socio-economic unit.

The form of government consists of a hereditary chieftainship for each of the five tribes. The Chief, who may be a man or a woman, functions administratively in conjunction with counsellors and ward foremen and is also responsible for the administration of justice. Although each tribe is autonomous, matters of common interest are discussed by the Chiefs at joint meetings under the guidance of an administrative officer.

In addition to utilizing employment opportunities created within the area, some Okavango men enter into employment for limited periods in the Southern part of the Territory. [1970 population: 49,577.]

[f] The 1970 census figures, which are included in brackets, are to be found in *Statistical News Release* (Department of Statistics), 23 September 1971, no. 64.

THE OVAMBO

The Ovambo constitute the largest population group in South West Africa—according to the 1960 census they numbered 239,363 or approximately 45.5% of the total population of the Territory (526,004). The 1966 estimate was 270,900 or 44.4% of the total (610,100). There are eight Ovambo tribes, viz. Ndonga, Kuanyama, Kuambi, Ngandjera, Kualuthi, Mbalantu, Nkolonkati and Eunda, each living in its own area of Ovamboland [renamed Owambo in 1972].

On account of its geographic isolation, being bordered on the south by vast uninhabited stretches, Ovamboland has had very little contact in the past with the groups living in other areas of South West Africa. However, the various Ovambo tribes were in the early days often at war with one another. Thus, on entering the Territory during World War I the South African forces found the Ovambo, in the words of General Smuts, "riddled with witchcraft and engaged in tribal forays in which there was no security for man or beast."

The social organization of the Ovambo peoples is based on the matrilineal system, and the mother's brother is an important person as far as authority and rules of inheritance are concerned. The tribes are subdivided into broad kinship groups or classes, membership of which is hereditary through the mother. The individual family is, however, the most important socio-economic unit.

The political organization of the Ovambo peoples is well developed, with hereditary chieftainships in the case of the Ndonga, Ngandjera and Kualuthi. Chiefs function together with elected headmen as Chiefs-in-Council. In the case of the other tribes, powers of government are exercised by elected Headmen-in-Council. Here, too, the Councils of the various tribes through the encouragement and guidance of South African officials have joint meetings from time to time in order to discuss matters of common interest.

The languages of the different Ovambo tribes belong to the Bantu language family. Although they differ to some extent, they are closely related to one another and are indeed inter-intelligible. The languages of the two largest tribes, the Ndonga and Kuanyama, have been developed into written languages.

The Ovambo are both pastoralists and agriculturalists. They live in family complexes consisting of a number of huts and cattle pens which are surrounded by the cultivated lands where millet, sorghum and beans form the main crops. The land belongs to the tribe, but individual rights of occupation of agricultural land are awarded to individuals for life against payment. Grazing is communal. Many Ovambo men accept employment in the southern part of the Territory for limited periods.

Since 1870 the Ovambo have been strongly influenced by Christian Missionaries, particularly the Finnish Mission which has developed into an independent Ovambokavango Church, with adherents among the Okavango Peoples also. [1970 population: 342,455.]

THE BUSHMEN

In 1960 the Bushmen numbered 11,762 and constituted 2.24% of the total population. The 1966 estimate was 13,300 or 2.18%. They undoubtedly represent the most ancient section of the inhabitants of the Territory. They belong to the Khoisan peoples and are short in stature with a light yellowish-brown skin. In South West Africa the Bushmen consist predominantly of three groups: namely the !Khung, Heikom and Mbarakwengo.

The Bushmen are traditionally a hunting people who used to roam far and wide over the Territory in search of game and edible veld foods. The men did the hunting, for which purpose they mainly used bows with poisoned arrows, while the women looked after the gathering of plant foods.

The social organization of the Bushmen was very primitive and centred around small bands consisting predominantly of kinsfolk. Political organization was virtually non-existent. With the advent in South West Africa of more developed groups such as the Nama and Herero, the Bushmen came to be regarded as a danger to life and property (particularly cattle), and were accordingly exterminated or driven away by the other groups into the more inaccessible desert regions. Even in 1915, General Smuts said, the South African occupation forces found "the roving Bushmen still regarded as little better than wild animals—human vermin of the veld".

The Bushmen have a language of their own, which is different from the Nama and Bantu languages, but shares with the former the phonetic feature of clicks. [1970 population: 21,909.]

THE DAMA OR BERGDAMA

Physically, the Dama are a short statured, negroid type, quite distinct, on the one hand, from the light-skinned Bushmen and Hottentots and, on the other, from the Herero and Ovambo, who belong to the Bantu branch. In 1960 they numbered 44,353 and constituted 8.43% of the total population. The 1966 estimate was 50,200 or 8.23%.

The Dama are also known as the Bergdama or Bergdamara, and are given various names, some with an uncomplimentary meaning, in certain of the native languages of South West Africa.

Very little is known of the origin or early history of the Dama. They were first encountered in historical times as fugitive bands eking out a miserable existence in the more inaccessible areas of the Territory, or as slaves of stronger groups, first the Nama, whose language the Dama had adopted to the complete disappearance of their own, and later the Herero.

By reason of their servile or fugitive existence, the Dama originally possessed no significant political or social organization larger than the individual family, which was often polygamous. However, in 1870, on the urgent representations of missionaries, a tract of land was granted to a number of Bergdama at Okombahe in the Omaruru district. This was later confirmed by the German authorities, and has been maintained ever since. In the Okombahe area the Dama developed a central governing body consisting of a Chief and Councillors.

Modernization has had a strong influence on the Dama. Many are engaged, mainly as employees, in the modern economy, and in the Okombahe area they engage in animal husbandry. [1970 population: 64,973.]

THE HOTTENTOTS OR NAMA

The Hottentots are a relatively short, yellowish brown-skinned people. They are probably of the same original stock as the Bushmen, whom they resemble somewhat in appearance. In 1960 they numbered 34,806 or 6.62% of the population. The 1966 estimate was 39,400 or 6.46%.

It is believed that the Hottentots lived originally somewhere in the region of the Great Lakes of East Africa. Probably as a result of pressure from the north by the Bantu, they gradually moved south-west across Central Africa until they reached the Atlantic. They then turned south, moving down the coast of Africa till well beyond the Cape of Good Hope. At different stages of this migration, sections of the people stayed behind, each of which developed into a separate tribe. Accordingly, there lived in the central and southern parts of South West Africa a number of Hottentot tribes, called Nama, after their language.

These Nama tribes were nomadic pastoralists, dependent on their herds of cattle, sheep and goats. No individual ownership of land existed. In their wanderings with their flocks, they exterminated, enslaved or drove away any Bushmen or Dama they encountered.

The Nama speak one of the four closely related Hottentot languages which have no clear affinities with the other languages of the African Continent, although, as already mentioned, they share the peculiar feature of click sounds with the Bushmen. [1970 population: 32,853.]

THE HERERO

The Herero population of South West Africa is composed of various sections, known as Herero, Mbanderu, Tjimba and Himba. They belong to the southern group of the Bantu peoples, and in 1960 numbered 35,354 or 6.72% of the total population. The 1966 estimate was 40,000 or 6.56%. They are, for the most part, of tall, slender build.

According to Herero tradition, their forebears originally lived in the "land of fountains", west of Lake Tanganyika, whence they emigrated to the south. Eventually they reached the Kaokoveld in South West Africa where they remained for some time, probably till about the end of the eighteenth century. When they continued their southward movement, two sections, the Himba and Tjimba, remained behind in the Kaokoveld. They were later joined by a group of Herero who had returned from the South. The three sections together make up the population of the Kaokoveld which is reserved for them as a homeland.

In 1960 the Kaokovelders numbered 9,234 or 1.75% of the total population. The 1966 estimate was 10,500 or 1.72%. They are mainly herdsmen who often trek with their stock from one watering place to another, leading an exceedingly conservative life, other cultures having made little impression on them. They seldom leave their home areas, and maintain, even in their dress, patterns of the distant past. Their traditional form of government is by headmen and councillors who represent various sections of the people.

The Herero were exclusively pastoral nomads, and did not practise agriculture, their lives being built around their herds and flocks. Primarily they were interested in cattle although they kept sheep and goats as well. Land, which meant grazing, was regarded as belonging to the community.

The social organization of the Herero is unusual in that it is based on a system of double descent, an individual belonging to two social entities, namely, the *oruzo* of his father and the *eanda* of his mother. Both these groups have their rules and regulations.

The Herero system of bilateral descent is unknown amongst the other ethnic groups of South West Africa and Southern Africa. It cannot be widened in scope, and it can only exceptionally be applied to a non-Herero. There is scarcely room for interlopers or new citizens, and so the Herero people can only regenerate itself from within. In this sense it is the perfect model of a "Chosen People": by immutable law, ordained from the beginning, all humanity consists only of Herero and Strangers.

The Herero language belongs to the Bantu family of languages, but differs substantially from other Bantu languages in South West Africa. [1970 population: Herero, 49,203; Kaokovelders, 6,467.]

The Wars between the Herero and the Nama

During 1829 and 1830, the southward movement of the Herero was accelerated by droughts, which forced them to move with thousands of head of cattle into territory claimed by the Nama. Clashes immediately followed, in which the Herero were initially victorious. Consquently the Nama sought the assistance of one Jonker Afrikaner, the Chief of a tribe of Orlam Nama, who was then living in the far south of the Territory. The possession of fire-arms and horses thereupon enabled the Nama to defeat the Herero decisively in a number of battles and minor clashes. In about 1840 Jonker Afrikaner established himself at Windhoek, and for the next twenty years dominated the central part of South West Africa. He kept the Herero in complete subjection. He also carried out successful raids against other Nama tribes and even against the Ovambo in the far north.

By 1860, however, the tide was turning. The Herero, while serving

the Nama, had also come to learn the use of fire-arms. Jonker Afrikaner died in 1861, and shortly afterwards the Herero staged a successful
revolution. The next nine years witnessed continual bloodshed as the
Herero and various Nama tribes fought one another. In 1870 a peace
treaty was signed, through the intervention of missionaries, who on
the whole favoured the Herero. But in 1880 war flared up again, and
after a number of bitter battles, the Herero succeeded in establishing
themselves as the strongest force in the central parts of South West Africa. There were, however, a number of Nama bands who scoured the
country, among them the remnant of the Afrikaner tribe.

The introduction of German rule in South West Africa in 1884, did
not of itself end hostilities in the Territory. . . . [O]ne of the most
difficult tasks the German administration had to tackle was the pacifi-
cation of the country. Hardly had this been accomplished than general
uprisings broke out in the years 1903–1907, involving the Herero and
most of the Nama tribes.

THE BASTERS

During the latter half of the nineteenth century the Basters, persons
of mixed Nama-European descent, left the northern Cape in South Africa and moved northwards into South West Africa. In 1870 they settled at Rehoboth, where they have lived ever since. They numbered in
1960, 11,257, representing 2.14% of the total population. According to
the 1966 estimate the figures were then 13,700 or 2.24%.

The Basters' language is predominantly Afrikaans and their way of
life is similar to that of the Whites. In the Rehoboth Gebiet animal
husbandry is the chief occupation, although a diversified economy has
developed in the township of Rehoboth. Their form of government
consists of a Chief and Councillors and they apply their old patriar-
chal laws. [1970 population: 16,474.]

THE WHITE GROUP

The inhabitants of European descent numbered 73,464 or 13.97% of
the total population in 1960. The 1966 estimate was 96,000 or 15.73%.
They first began to settle in South West Africa during the last century,
even before the establishment of German authority. Most are of South
African or German extraction, and speak Afrikaans, German or English. The European population practises a Western way of life. Its
members are engaging in agriculture, commerce, industry and administration. The economy of the Territory and its administration depend
largely on the knowledge and initiative of this population group. This
was a major factor which induced first the German and, later, the
South African authorities to encourage further settlement of Europeans in the under-populated central and southern parts of the Territory. . . . [1970 population: 90,658.]

COLOUREDS [PEOPLE OF MIXED DESCENT]

The Coloureds numbered 12,708 in 1960, and constituted 2.42% of the total population. The 1966 estimate was 15,400 or 2.52%. For the most part they are relatively recent immigrants from the Republic of South Africa, and speak mainly Afrikaans. They are to be found predominantly in the larger towns such as Windhoek, Walvis Bay, Lüderitz and Keetmanshoop, where they are employed in commerce or industry, or have their own businesses. Many are artisans in the building trade. A small proportion make a livelihood as stock-farmers. [1970 population: 28,275.]

OTHERS

Apart from the above main groups there is an established group of Tswana who live in the Aminuis area and are related to the Tswana peoples of Botswana. Together with various other smaller groups, most of whom speak Bantu languages but are not related to the groups mentioned above, they numbered 9,992 or 1.9% of the total population in 1960. According to the 1966 estimate the figures were then 11,300 or 1.85%. [1970 population: 18,474.]

2

History of the Territory Until the End of German Rule

BRIEF HISTORY OF THE PERIOD

Odendaal Commission Report: [a]

South West Africa has existed as a geographically defined territory in Southern Africa since the closing years of the previous century. It came into being as such under agreements and boundary settlements between the interested powers of the time, Germany, Portugal and Britain. The present political position of the Territory and its connection with the Republic of South Africa, however, are the outcome of a long historical process which . . . need only be given in broad outline.

Although Portuguese navigators such as Diogo Cão (1484), Bartholomeu Dias (1486) and Gasper Vegas (1534), went ashore on their voyages along the coast of the present South West Africa, interest in this part of the Continent was stimulated only after the establishment of the White settlement at the Cape of Good Hope in 1652. The *Grundel* was dispatched by the Cape Governor as early as 1670 to explore the coast of this area. The *Bode,* also from the Cape, followed in 1677. Although both these ships anchored at Angra Pequena and in Sandwich Bay, very little of the interior could be explored owing to the impenetrable nature of the Namib Desert along the coast.

From the beginning of the eighteenth century, however, hunters and explorers began to go northwards through the north-west of the Cape Colony and over the Gariep (later called the Orange River). Two of

[a] Report of the Commission of Enquiry into South West African Affairs, 1962–3, under the Chairmanship of Mr. F. H. Odendaal (R.P. No. 12 of 1964).

the first to visit the Transgariep, or area north of the Orange River, were Willem van Wyk (1738) and Jacobus Coetzee (1760), both farmers from the Cape Colony. Reports reaching the Cape Government through these channels roused considerable interest in the Transgariep. In 1761 a scientific expedition led by Hendrik Hop was sent by the Governor, Ryk Tulbagh, to explore the area. This expedition reached the vicinity of the present Keetmanshoop and mapped part of the area north of the Orange River. In addition, important information concerning the area and its inhabitants was collected during this period by such explorers as Wikar (1775–1779), Patterson (1779), Van Rheenen and Brand (1791–1792).

In the meantime interest continued in the coastal region. French, British and American whalers from time to time called at the landing-places. In 1786 the British ship, the *Nautilus,* explored the coast and anchored at Angra Pequena. However, annexation along this coast did not follow before 1793 when the *Meermin* was sent from the Cape to proclaim Dutch sovereignty over Angra Pequena, Halifax Island and Walvis Bay. When the Cape passed into British hands in 1795, this area along the west coast came under British control. The *Star* was accordingly sent in the same year to hoist the British flag at all the landing-places along the west coast up to Angola.

Important developments affecting the areas north of the Orange River took place during the nineteenth century. From the beginning of that century, already, missionaries were settling in the southern part of the area. They were followed by traders and explorers who gradually penetrated deeper and deeper northwards into the interior. At the same time activities increased along the coast. During the greater part of the nineteenth century the interior north of the Orange River was harassed by continual strife and wars, particularly between the Oorlams, the Nama and the Herero. This led to a direct link between the Cape Authorities and the inhabitants of this area, which was terminated, however, by the eventual creation of the Territory of German South West Africa.

By 1802 the *London Missionary Society* was already active along the Orange River, and in 1807 two mission stations were established north of the river at Warmbad and Blydeverwacht. After Warmbad was destroyed in 1811 by the Oorlams leader, Jager Afrikaander, the activities of the *London Missionary Society* were continued by the *Wesleyan Methodist Missionary Society*. In 1840, however, the *London Missionary Society* transferred its rights to the Rhenish Missionary Society. By this time there were a number of flourishing mission stations throughout the area then known as Namaland and Damaraland.

Although Namaland and Damaraland were therefore well known by the middle of the nineteenth century, the northern parts remained a closed book. The explorations of Sir James Alexander (1836–1837), Sir Francis Galton and Charles John Andersson (1851), James Chapman (1855), Hahn, Rath and Green (1856) and Charles John Andersson (1859–1867), did much, however, to open up the unknown regions. Andersson, in particular, did much to make the sparsely populated northern areas of the Kaokoveld, Ovamboland and the Okavango more generally known. He was also the first person to refer in his writings to the area north of the Orange River as *South West Africa*.

While the interior was being explored, important developments were taking place along the coast. The rich guano deposits on the islands off the coast were being developed from as early as 1842. Between 1861 and 1866 the Cape Government took possession of these uninhabited islands. In the meantime a company, *De Pass, Spence and Company*, started a fishing and fish-oil industry and also established the *Pomona Mining Company*. No authority was actually established along the coast, however, until 1878 when Commander R. C. Dyer on board the British ship, the *Industry*, annexed the area surrounding Walvis Bay in the name of the Queen of Britain. This area was incorporated in the Cape Colony by Act No. 35 of 1884.

During this time the interior of South West Africa continued to be afflicted by incessant wars between the inhabitants at that time. Namaland and Damaraland, in particular, suffered as a result of the struggle between the Oorlams, the Nama and the Herero. Not only was the position of missionaries, traders and explorers unsafe, but the Herero also felt menaced. Maharero, the then leader of a section of the Herero, appealed to the Cape Government for help. In response to this request Dr. William Coates Palgrave was appointed Commissioner Extraordinary for Namaland and Damaraland by the Cape Government on the 16th March, 1876. He was to attempt to restore peace between the indigenous groups and thus also to ensure the safety of the Whites in the area. In 1879 a magistrate, Major Manning, was stationed at Okahandja to act as adviser to Maharero in both internal and external affairs. A justice of the peace was also appointed at Otjimbingwe.

During the period of the Cape Government's representatives in Namaland and Damaraland, the Dorstland Trekkers trekked through the area. After first progressing through the present Bechuanaland to a point west of the Okavango swamps, they turned south via Grootfontein and, proceeding south of the Etosha Pan, entered the Kaokoveld where they remained for some time at places like Otjitundua and Kaoko Otavi. From there they crossed the Kunene River into Angola. A small band returned in 1882 and established the Republic of Upingtonia (Lydensrust) between Grootfontein, Otavi and Waterberg. The representatives of the Cape Government were, however, recalled after the outbreak of the ten years' war between the Herero and the Nama in 1880, and when the Germans arrived on the scene the Dorstland Trekkers relinquished their republic.

It was known in London as early as July, 1883, that a German, Heinrich Vogelsang, had landed at Angra Pequena as an agent for a Bremen merchant, Adolf Lüderitz. Vogelsang succeeded in acquiring an area of approximately 215 sq. miles around Angra Pequena from the Nama Chief of Bethanie, Josef Frederick. The British ship *Boadicea* was thereupon sent to protect the interests of *De Pass, Spence and Company* along the coast. Germany in turn sent the *Nautilus* to protect the Lüderitz area. In April, 1884, the German Consul at the Cape was instructed telegraphically by Bismarck to advise the Cape Government that the area as acquired by Lüderitz had been formally placed under German protection. The German flag was hoisted at Angra Pequena, and the bay was renamed Lüderitzbucht. This actually marked the beginning of the Territory of German South West Africa.

In August, 1884, a German protectorate was formally declared over the area surrounding Lüderitzbucht. This was followed in September of the same year by a protectorate over the coastal area from the Orange River mouth up to Cape Frio, excluding the Territory of Walvis Bay. In October Namaland was also declared a protectorate. In the following year, on the 2nd September, 1885, German agreements followed with the Rooinasie (Red People) (Nama), and on the 15th September with the Basters of Rehoboth. On the 21st October of the same year the Herero accepted German protection.

While Germany was extending its sphere of influence to the interior, Britain in March, 1885, proclaimed a protectorate over Bechuanaland. In the north the Portuguese were already in possession of Angola. The boundaries of the new Territory of German South West Africa were laid down in broad outline by agreements with Portugal in 1886 and with Britain in 1890. The geographical area within these boundaries included not only Namaland and Damaraland, but also the northern areas of the Kaokoveld, Ovamboland, Okavango and the Caprivi. The area around Walvis Bay which had been incorporated in the Cape Colony in 1884, however, retained its *status quo*.

South West Africa remained under German Rule until after the outbreak of the First World War. On the 9th July, 1915, the German troops in the Territory surrendered to the South African Forces who had joined the Allies in the war against Germany. From that date up to the 31st December, 1920, the Territory was under South African military government.

SELECTED READINGS ON THIS PERIOD [b]

1. German Annexation of South West Africa [c]

C. Headlam, "The Race for the Interior," in *Cambridge History of the British Empire:* [d]

[b] I have omitted to include readings on the inter-tribal wars of the nineteenth century. The reader is referred to J. P. van S. Bruwer, *South West Africa: The Disputed Land* (1966), pp. 42–55, and I. Goldblatt, *History of South West Africa from the Beginning of the Nineteenth Century* (1971), Part I, for an account of these wars.

[c] There are a considerable number of detailed studies of this annexation and the German foreign policy that motivated it. See, for example, W. O. Aydelotte, *Bismarck and British Colonial Policy: The Problem of South West Africa, 1883–5* (1937); R. W. Bixler, *Anglo-German Imperialism in South Africa 1880–1900* (1932); Evans Lewin, *The Germans and Africa* (2d ed., 1939), pp. 109 ff.; Wm. Roger Louis, *Great Britain and Germany's Lost Colonies 1914–1919* (1967), chap. 1; A. J. P. Taylor, *Germany's First Bid for Colonies 1884–1885* (1938); M. E. Townsend, *The Rise and Fall of Germany's Colonial Empire, 1884–1918* (1930).

[d] (1963) vol. 8, 2nd ed., pp. 526–28.

The scramble for Africa began. There was now a newcomer among the great colonising nations. In Germany, united now and victorious in Europe, the ambition was growing to assert herself as a World Power with a great colonial empire. Outlets were needed for her increasing population, new markets and the control of resources of raw material for her rapidly growing manufactures. Germany, so the Colonial Party there insisted, must have colonies and a fleet to protect them, and lands for her own people to settle under her own flag. Germany must have a place in the sun. The enterprise and endurance of German traders, missionaries and explorers had already paved the way.

For a quarter of a century the German missionaries in Namaqualand and Damaraland had made frequent complaints of ill-treatment by the Natives and of their internecine wars; but in reply to representations from the German Government, Granville had repeated in 1880, and again in August 1881, the refusal of his predecessors to extend British jurisdiction north of the Orange River outside the narrow circle around Walvis Bay.

At the beginning of 1883, the German Ambassador informed the Foreign Office that Franz Lüderitz, a merchant of Bremen, proposed to establish a factory on the coast between the Orange and Little Fish Rivers, where he had recently purchased lands (November 1882). The German Government desired to know whether Her Majesty's Government exercised any authority in that locality, and would afford him protection in case of need. If not, Germany would extend to the factory the same measure of protection as she gave to her subjects in remote parts of the world, but "without the least design to establish a footing in Africa" (7 February 1883). Granville replied that he must consult the Cape Government (February 23). The Cape Government, however, showed no disposition to occupy the territory south of Walvis Bay.

Neither the murmurs of the missionaries nor the denials of the German diplomats apparently aroused the least suspicion that any acquisition of territory was contemplated. Very few people took the colonial movement in Germany seriously. The Foreign Office and the Cape Ministers alike remained content to defer until their own good time annexations of territory upon which might depend the possibility of a United South Africa.

Lüderitz, however, having been assured of his own Government's protection, sent a ship to Angra Pequeña 280 miles south of Walvis Bay. There his agent concluded a treaty with Frederick, the local Chief, who in return for 2000 marks and a few old muskets assigned to him 215 square miles of land, with his sovereign rights, and ten miles of sea frontage on the bay, which now bears the name of Lüderitzbucht (1 May 1883). Next day the German flag was hoisted for the first time in a German colony. A German gunboat was stationed in the bay (October 15).

Protests were entered on behalf of British concessionaires. H.M.S. *Boadicea* sailed from Cape Town to uphold their rights, but the commander, on being informed on his arrival that he was in German territorial waters, returned to the Cape (November 3). Count Hatzfeldt, in London, then made official enquiry whether the British Government claimed sovereignty over Angra Pequeña and the adjacent territory, and, if so, upon what grounds (November 12).

Granville replied that although the Queen's authority had only been proclaimed at certain points, such as Walvis Bay and the Guano islets opposite Angra Pequeña, yet H. M. Government would regard as an infringement of their rights any claim by a foreign Power to sovereignty or jurisdiction between the Portuguese frontier and that of Cape Colony. Bismarck replied by a despatch on 31 December 1883 in which he insisted on the establishment of some civil and political jurisdiction, and inquired upon what title Great Britain could claim sovereignty over that wide territory, hitherto considered independent, and what steps she had taken to protect German subjects. Trusting to previous assurances that Germany had no desire for territorial acquisitions, Derby at the Colonial Office remained as completely blind as Granville himself to her real intentions. He regarded Bismarck's enquiry as merely a suggestion for British occupation or annexation. The British Government would consent to that, if the Cape Colony would bear the cost; the views of the Colony must therefore first be ascertained. But for some months no answer was received from the Cape.

There a parliamentary crisis had arisen with the defeat of Scanlen's ministry. It was not until May 29 following that a reply was sent by their successors. Thomas Upington, the new Prime Minister, then carried a resolution in favour of annexing the whole coast up to Walvis Bay. The despatch of a warship to Angra Pequeña was suggested, in order that German intervention might not be excused by the absence of British protection. Again, on July 16, the Cape Parliament voted unanimously for the annexation of all territory up to the Portuguese boundary. It was then far too late.

On 24 April 1884, Bismarck had instructed the consul at Cape Town that Lüderitz and his settlement were under the protection of Germany. A German warship patrolled the coast. Yet on May 12, Granville stated in the House of Lords that, so far as he knew, Germany had never claimed sovereignty over any part of the territory in question, and that the subject was under discussion between the two Governments. Bismarck then threatened to make trouble in Egypt, which the British had recently occupied under anomalous conditions. The British Government yielded (June 21), and in August a German protectorate was declared over the whole coast between 26° South latitude and the Portuguese boundary, with the exception of Walvis Bay. The stone which the British builders had rejected became the chief corner-stone of German power in southern Africa.

Subsequently, by the Anglo-German Agreement of July 1890, the inland boundaries of German South-West Africa, embracing 322,450 square miles, were defined, and free access from the protectorate to the Zambesi was conceded by the Caprivi Zipfel, a corridor 20 miles wide.

2. The Nature of the German Protectorate

South West Africa became a German *Schutzgebiet,* or protectorate. The term "protectorate" here is, however, misleading, as it
suggests that Germany did not acquire full sovereignty over the
territory. It is true that, after the annexation, Germany extended
her authority over the territory by the conclusion of treaties of
friendship and protection with the various Herero, Baster, and
Nama chiefs,[e] but these treaties were not protectorate treaties between independent sovereign States, which preserved some of the
sovereign rights of the protected territories.[f] Instead they were
"colonial protectorates," which were simply a disguise for annexation and resulted in the acquisition of full sovereignty by Germany.[g] This was in accordance with international law of the late
nineteenth century, which viewed territory occupied by indigenous peoples as "no man's land" (*territorium nullius*) and therefore subject to the acquisition of sovereignty by occupation by a
European Power.[h] This matter is discussed by Mr. Justice de Villiers in his *Report of the Rehoboth Commision.*[i]

What, then, was the political position of the Rehoboth *Gebiet* as a
Colonial Protectorate of Germany? . . . it is clear that South-West Africa as a whole, or any portion of it, had no international status. According to the view of the Society of States, with the exception perhaps
of the United States of America, a view which was shared by Germany,
the whole of the country included in the *Schutzgebiet* was *territorium
nullius,* and was therefore open to occupation by a civilised power.
That a country in possession of barbarians without an organised
government should be considered as no man's land is not surprising.
But, whatever may be said of the Hereros and the Hottentots, the *Basters,* although a small community, had a settled government, and even
some system of laws. The justification for the view of the civilised Powers is thus put by Westlake: "That civilised states should assume sovereignty over new but not uninhabited countries, on a system which
they arrange among themselves without reference to the natives, can
only be justified by the necessity of a government where whites and

[e] For details of these treaties, see the Report of the Rehoboth Commission
U.G. 41 of 1926, §§ 135–45.
[f] Protected States normally retained certain characteristics of Statehood:
L. Oppenheim, *International Law* (8th ed., by H. Lauterpacht, 1955), vol. 1,
pp. 192–93.
[g] M. F. Lindley, *The Acquisition and Government of Backward Territory in
International Law* (1926), pp. 205–6.
[h] R. Y. Jennings, *The Acquisition of Territory in International Law* (1963),
p. 20.
[i] U.G. 41 of 1926, §§ 169–72.

natives meet, and by the inability of the latter to supply a government adequate to the white men's needs or to their own protection. Accordingly, the modern tendency of thought is to place the original acquisition of title to sovereignty squarely on this basis, and so to furnish the doctrine of effective occupation with a new and solid support."

I am not concerned with whether the views entertained by the civilised Powers, and more especially by Germany, were just or unjust in any individual case. Their view constitutes the law for us, and there can be no doubt that the *Baster* community of Rehoboth were regarded in the same way as the other aboriginal tribes of the country, and, in fact, considered as aborigines. As Germany took possession of *territorium nullius,* it follows that, by virtue of the occupation of the territory with the consent of the various chiefs of the aborigines, Germany obtained the sovereignty over such territory.

The name *Schutzgebiet,* which is merely a translation of the word "Protectorate," when used with regard to territory such as South-West Africa is, therefore, a misnomer. . . . a Protectorate properly so-called can only exist where one sovereign or semi-sovereign state has placed itself under the protection of another sovereign state. As none of the communities of South-West Africa were states, in the sense understood by the Society of Nations, there could be no question of a Protectorate by Germany over any of them.

3. German Rule and Native Policy [j]

The German treatment of the native population of South West Africa was harsh and cruel. Nevertheless, before World War I, humanitarians focussed their attention on Portuguese and Belgian colonial atrocities, and little notice was taken of Germany's performance as a colonial power. Indeed, one writer has stated that "if an opinion poll had been taken in England before August 1914, the result would probably have been that the Germans were regarded as better colonial rulers than any others except the British." [k] During the war and its aftermath, however,

[j] For additional reading, see Wellington, *South West Africa and Its Human Issues,* pp. 225–37; Evans Lewin, *The Germans and Africa* (rev. ed., 1939), pp. 127–48; Helmut Bley, *South-West Africa under German Rule, 1894–1914* (1971); I. Goldblatt, *History of South West Africa,* Part II.

[k] Wm. Roger Louis, *Great Britain and Germany's Lost Colonies, 1914–1919* (1967), p. 35. The prewar British attitude is well illustrated by the following statement by Harry H. Johnston in his *History of the Colonization of Africa by Alien Races* (1899): "It will be seen, I fancy, when history takes a review of the foundation of these African states that the unmixed Teuton— Dutchman or German—is on first contact with subject races apt to be harsh and even brutal, but that he is no fool and wins the respect of the negro or the Asiatic, who admire brute force; while his own good nature in time induces a softening of manners when the native has ceased to rebel and begun to cringe" (258).

the brutality of Germany's presence in South West Africa was fully exposed,[1] with particular emphasis being placed upon her suppression of the Herero uprising of 1904. This exposure was motivated in part by a humanitarian desire to ensure that South West Africa would not be returned to Germany after the war, and in part by a less altruistic desire on the part of South Africa to ensure that the territory was handed over to her. Whatever the motive, however, there can be little doubt as to the correctness of these accounts of German maltreatment of the native population and the unsuitability of Germany as a colonial guardian of the indigenous peoples of South West Africa.

The strongest attack on Germany's colonial rule in South West Africa was contained in the British Government's "Blue Book" on "the Natives of South West Africa and their Treatment by Germany," published in 1918.[m] So vicious were its strictures on German rule that the South African Government later agreed to the book's destruction in order to promote better relations between Germans and South Africans in South West Africa.[n] The following passages give some indication of the general tenor of this report: [o]

As a colonist, the German in South-West Africa, speaking generally, has been a failure. He has never shown the slightest disposition to learn the natives' point of view, to adapt his ideas to the long-established customs and habits of the people, or to fall in with the ways of the country. When he arrived here he found the natives both rich and comparatively numerous. His sole object seemed, as soon as he felt strong enough, to take the fullest advantage possible of the simplicity of these people and despoil them utterly. When the process did not, by

[1] The titles of some of the publications of this period testify to the vehemence of opposition to German colonial rule. See, for example, Africanus, *The Prussian Lash in Africa: A Story of German Rule in Africa* (1918); Frank Maclean, *Towards Extermination: Germany's Treatment of the African Native* (1918).

[m] *Report on the Natives of South West Africa and their Treatment by Germany*, prepared in the Administrator's office in Windhoek and published as a British Government "Blue Book" (cd 9146) in August 1918. This book was condemned by the German authorities as a work of propaganda designed to prevent the return of South West Africa to Germany after the war. Germany sought to counter its effect by publishing a "White Book" which focussed attention on British colonial atrocities: *Die Behandlung der einheimischen Bevölkerung in den Kolonialen Besitzungen Deutschlands und Englands. Eine Erwiderung auf das englishche Blaubuch von August 1918*. See, too, Heinrich Schnee, *German Colonization Past and Future: The Truth about German Colonies* (1926).

[n] Goldblatt, above, n. b, p. 230.   [o] Above, n. m, pp. 9, 52–53.

means of the system of trading that sprang up, which in itself was often but a thinly disguised form of chicanery and knavery, go quickly enough, rapine, murder, and lust were given full play with the disastrous results of which we see evidences every day around us.

This is all the more strange, as in the Cape of Good Hope and Natal German settlers have proved themselves, at all events in years past, adaptable and successful colonists. Possibly the reason may be found in the fact that in those British possessions the German emigrant found a clean-cut line and well-defined understanding between the European element and the aborigines. As a pioneer on his own account in savage lands, and as a colonist left to his own devices without the influence and advice of persons of other nationality who have had longer colonial experience than he has had, he has proved himself, at all events in South-West Africa, to be utterly incapable and unsuitable.

The land here, when colonising was decided on in earnest in Berlin, and after the missions, companies, and traders had been allotted their selected portions, was at first given out, for the most part, to soldiers who had taken their discharges in this country and had expressed a desire to settle here; rough men who, when released from the military organisation under which they had been trained, carried with them to their new possessions the militarist methods and aggressive ideas towards the natives with which they had become imbued during their term of active service here. In their view the native was an out-and-out barbarian, little better than the baboons which frequent the kopjes, and to be treated and disposed of at the sweet will of the master. The police, too, brought up in the same environment and drawn from the same organisation, were no different. If anything they were worse, as they were principally selected from the non-commissioned ranks of an army in which the severity of the sergeant is proverbial.

. . . .

From the point of view of the, at that time, comparatively few German settlers in the country there were far too many Hereros. Once robbed of their land and their cattle, they could not possibly all be employed as farm labourers, and no one seemed to look to the future.

Dr. Karl Dove's "leniency towards the natives is cruelty to the whites" became generally known as proverbial, and it formed the rule of conduct not only of the white settler, soldier, trader, and policeman, but it also actually represented the settled and accepted policy of the Government. Considerations of justice, honesty, and common humanity never arose, or if they did arise were brushed aside by the more brutal demands of convenience and utility. It will be remembered that Leutwein [governor 1898–1904], when referring to the claim that the evidence of seven coloured persons was necessary to outbalance the statement of one white man, said: "in regard to the utility of this I will express no opinion."

Having settled the point of view, it is easy to understand what Dr. Karl Dove is hinting at when he writes:—

While however the single Herero cannot be regarded as a very brave person, he must not be looked upon as harmless. On the contrary the chief danger from them is their numbers and these numbers are a standing menace to our safety.

Therefore the settler who helped to reduce the number of Hereros was performing a public service. There can be no doubt that during the period 1890–1904 very many Hereros were done to death in one way or another or died as the result of brutal floggings and ill-treatment. Despite this, such murders were treated lightly; where possible they were hushed up entirely, and at worst the murderer in his own interests was advised, for fear of reprisals, to leave the country or go to another district. In only four cases during the period 1890–1904 was a German murderer brought to trial, and then the imposition of anything like an adequate or commensurate penalty was unheard of. It was generally endeavoured by the German authorities to compound the offence by allowing the murderer to pay compensation in the shape of a few dozen goats to the relatives of the deceased.

The Herero and Nama Wars of 1904–7.[p]—Most of the criticism directed at Germany's colonial policies in South West Africa arose from the wars of genocide pursued against the Hereros and Namas after they had rebelled in 1904.

The Herero had serious grievances against German rule, chief of which were their exploitation by the traders, which resulted in loss of land and cattle; the indignities visited upon their women by the German settlers; and the racial injustices in the administration of the criminal law. In January 1904, under the leadership of Samuel Maharero, they staged a surprise attack on German farms and outposts in which over a hundred Germans were killed. At the time of this rebellion the bulk of the German forces were engaged in hostilities against the Bondelswarts in the south of the territory, and the Herero were able to keep up a successful offensive until July 1904.

Later, however, reinforcements arrived from Germany, and the relatively enlightened Governor Von Leutwein was replaced by the ruthless General Von Trotha as military commander. In August 1904 the Herero were decisively defeated by the Germans at Waterberg. At this stage Von Trotha issued his infamous extermination order in which he declared:

[p] For accounts of these wars, see Wellington, above, n. j, pp. 204–9; H. Vedder, "The Germans in South West Africa 1883–1914 (The Military Occupation, 1883–1907)," *Cambridge History of the British Empire*, vol. 8, pp. 727–29; Bley, above, n. j. pp. 149–69; Goldblatt, above, n. j. pp. 129–55.

I, the great General of the German soldiers, send this message to the Herero people. Hereros are no longer German subjects. They have murdered and robbed and have cut off the ears and noses and other parts of the body of wounded soldiers, and now out of cowardice they refuse to fight. . . . The Herero people must depart from the country. If they do not, I shall force them to it, with large cannons. Within the German boundaries every Herero, whether found armed or unarmed, with or without cattle, will be shot. I shall not accept any more women and children. I shall drive them back to their people, otherwise I shall order shots to be fired at them. These are my words to the Herero people.[q]

The Herero fled into the barren desert between South West Africa and Bechuanaland. Although many, including Samuel Maharero, reached the haven of Bechuanaland, large numbers died in the attempt. It is estimated that when an armistice was declared in December 1905 only 16,000 Hereros remained of a population of 60,000 to 80,000.[r]

In October 1904 the Namas, under Hendrik Witbooi, also revolted against the German administration. Although Witbooi himself was killed in battle a year later, the Namas continued hostilities against the Germans until 1907. Their losses were heavy. Of the estimated Nama population of 15,000 to 20,000 in 1892, only 9,800 remained in 1911.[s]

German atrocities were not limited to the battlefield. After the Herero-Nama wars prisoner-of-war-cum-labour camps were established in which the conditions were so unhealthy that 45 percent of the inmates died.[t]

It was this legacy of racial dominance and brutality which the victorious Principal Allied and Associated Powers sought to erase in 1920 by placing South West Africa under international tutelage.

[q] Goldblatt, above, n. b, p. 131.   [s] Ibid., pp. 150–51.
[r] Bley, above, n. j, p. 150.   [t] Ibid., p. 151.

3

Transition from Conquered Territory to Mandate

THE PERIOD OF MILITARY GOVERNMENT

Odendaal Commission Report: [a]

With the termination of the German regime in the Territory, all functions of the German Governor and Landesrat fell away. In addition to the Chief Civil Secretary who was already in the Territory, a Military Governor was appointed on the departure of the Officer Commanding the South African forces in the Territory, by Proclamation dated the 11th July, 1915, by the Minister of Defence of the Union of South Africa. In the Proclamation the Territory was designated the South West African Protectorate and the Military Governor was authorised as follows—

. . . subject to any instructions which you may from time to time receive from the Minister of Defence for the said Union, to take all measures, and by proclamation to make such laws, and enforce the same, as you may deem necessary for the peace, order and good government.

The Military Governor and Chief Civil Secretary functioned until October, 1915, when both posts were abolished by Proclamation dated the 28th October, 1915, by the Minister of Defence of South Africa and replaced by that of Administrator. In terms of this Proclamation all the powers, functions and duties previously vested in the Military Governor and the Chief Civil Secretary were transferred to the Administrator appointed in terms of the Proclamation. The powers and functions of the Administrator were more clearly defined in terms of Proclamation dated the 27th November, 1918, by the Minister of Defence as follows—

[a] Report of the Commission of Enquiry into South West African Affairs, R.P. No. 12 of 1964, p. 47.

27

. . . on behalf of the Government of the Union of South Africa, subject to any instructions of that Government which he may from time
to time receive from the Prime Minister of the Union, to take all
such measures and by Proclamation in the official Gazette of the
Protectorate to make such laws, and otherwise to issue therein such
regulations and orders, and enforce the same, as the said Administrator may deem necessary for the peace, order and good government of the Protectorate, while it remains in military occupation by
the Defence Forces of the said Union.

With the termination of the First World War and in terms of Article 119 of the Peace Treaty of Versailles signed on the 28th June, 1919,
Germany relinquished its subject territories including German South
West Africa. Pursuant to the establishment of a C Mandate in respect
of this Territory in terms of Article 22 Part I (Covenant of the League
of Nations) of the said Treaty, the said Mandate for South West Africa
was confirmed by the Council of the League of Nations by resolution
dated the 17th December, 1920, to and in favour of the Government of
the Union of South Africa and its terms defined.

At a special session in September, 1919, the Parliament of South Africa passed the *Treaty of Peace and South West Africa Mandate Act,
1919* (Act No. 49/1919) to give effect to the Mandate for South West
Africa. In terms of that Act legislative and executive powers in respect
of South West Africa were vested in the Governor-General on behalf of
the Government of South Africa. Although the said Act was to remain
in force only up to the 1st July, 1920, it was extended by the *Treaties
of Peace Act,* 1921 (Act No. 32/1921), in accordance with provision
made therein, until such time as it may be repealed by Parliament.

. . . .

Military Government in the Territory was withdrawn as from the
1st January, 1921, in terms of the *Indemnity and Withdrawal of Mar-
tial Law Proclamation, 1920 S.W.A.* (Proclamation No. 76 of 1920),
dated the 31st December, 1920, and signed by the Administrator.

SUGGESTIONS FOR THE FUTURE OF THE TERRITORY

In 1918 General Smuts mooted the idea of a system of international trusteeship for the territories previously under Russian,
Austrian, and Turkish rule in his *The League of Nations: A
Practical Suggestion.* But he was careful to exclude the ex-German colonies from this new order, as he envisaged the incorporation of South West Africa into South Africa.[b]

[b] Pp. 12–15, 21–22. This expectation was shared by George Louis Beer,
Chief of the Colonial Division of the American Delegation to Negotiate
Peace: *African Questions at the Paris Peace Conference* (1923), pp. 60–61,
443.

As a programme for the forthcoming Peace Conference I would . . . begin by making two recommendations:

(1) That in the vast multiplicity of territorial, economic and other problems with which the Conference will find itself confronted it should look upon the setting up of a League of Nations as its primary and basic task, and as supplying the necessary organ by means of which most of those problems can find their only stable solution. Indeed, the Conference should regard itself as the first or preliminary meeting of the League, intended to work out its organization, functions, and programme.

(2) That, so far at any rate as the peoples and territories formerly belonging to Russia, Austria-Hungary and Turkey are concerned, the League of Nations should be considered as the reversionary in the most general sense and as clothed with the right of ultimate disposal in accordance with certain fundamental principles. Reversion to the League of Nations should be substituted for any policy of national annexation.

What are these fundamental principles which must guide the League in its territorial policy as the general heir or successor of the defunct Empires? They have been summed up for the last two years in the general formula of "No annexations, and the self-determination of nations." There is no doubt that behind them is a profound feeling throughout the masses of the European peoples, and any violation of them will meet with stern retribution. It is for the statesmen of Europe to give political form and expression to this deep feeling. I know that these statesmen will be confronted in their colossal task with conflicting considerations. On the one hand they will be greatly tempted to use their unique opportunity for the aggrandisement of their own peoples and countries. Have they not fought and suffered on an unparalleled scale? And must they quixotically throw away the fruits of victory now that the great opportunity has come? They are now in the position to mould the world closer to their heart's desire; why miss the chance which may never come again in history? That is the voice of the Tempter pointing to a fair prospect. On the other hand that prospect lies beyond a very deep abyss and only the most callous and foolhardy political gambler will be prepared for the jump. The horrors and sufferings of this war have produced a temper in the peoples which must be reckoned with as the fundamental fact of the political situation in Europe to-day. The feeling of grief, bitterness, disillusion, despair goes very deep; even in the victorious Entente countries that feeling goes much deeper than the more superficial feeling of joy at the final result. How could it be otherwise? The prolonged horror through which all have passed is a far more real, abiding and fundamental experience than the momentary joy at the end. What has reconciled our Entente peoples to the burdens they were enduring? It was their consciousness of right and their vague hope of a better, fairer world to come which would justify their sacrifices. But if that prospect is rudely blotted out; if the peace really comes, not in the settlement of universal human principles and the dawning of a better order, but in a return of the old policy of grab and greed and partitions, then the bitterness of the disillusion would indeed be complete. Our victory would then become bitterer than Dead Sea fruit. The German battle-front collapsed all the more readily before Foch because the scandalous Brest-Litovsk Treaty had thoroughly disillusioned and demoralised the German home-front. Let Entente statesmen beware of similarly wounding the spirit of their peoples by a peace which gives the final death-blow to their hopes of a better world. For the common people in all lands this war has, however vaguely and dimly, been a war of ideals, a spiritual war. Let not that faith be shattered at the peace. Let the peace be founded in human ideals, in principles of freedom and equality, and in institutions which will for the future guarantee those principles against wanton assault. Only such a peace would be statesmanlike and assure lasting victory. Any other might open the fountains of the deep and overwhelm victor and vanquished alike in the coming flood.

So far I have referred only to territories and peoples split off from Russia, Austria and Turkey. The case of Germany stands on a different footing which is clearly distinguishable in principle. In the first place, if Alsace-Lorraine is annexed to France, that would be a case of disannexation, as it has been put; that is to say, it is a case of restoring to France what was violently and wrongfully taken from her in 1871, against the protests not only of France, but of the population of Alsace-Lorraine speaking through their elected representatives. It is a *restitutio in integrum* on moral and legal grounds, and only in a secondary or consequential sense a territorial annexation. Its restitution to France would therefore satisfy, instead of violating, the moral sense of the world.

In the second place, the German colonies in the Pacific and Africa are inhabited by barbarians, who not only cannot possibly govern themselves, but to whom it would be impracticable to apply any ideas of political self-determination in the European sense. They might be consulted as to whether they want their German masters back, but the result would be so much a foregone conclusion that the consultation would be quite superfluous. The disposal of these Colonies should be decided on the principles which President Wilson has laid down in the fifth of his celebrated Fourteen Points. It is admitted that, like Alsace-Lorraine, this is a special case falling outside the scope of the principles applicable to the European and Asiatic communities we are here discussing. For these reasons I restrict the following general recommendation to the peoples and territories formerly belonging to Russia, Austria and Turkey:

(3) These principles are: firstly, that there shall be no annexation of any of these territories to any of the victorious Powers, and secondly, that in the future government of these territories and peoples the rule of self-determination, or the consent of the governed to their form of government, shall be fairly and reasonably applied.

. . . .

I sum up this discussion in the following recommendation:

(5) That it shall be lawful for the League of Nations to delegate its

authority, control, or administration in respect of any people or territory to some other State whom it may appoint as its agent or mandatary, but that wherever possible the agent or mandatary so appointed shall be nominated or approved by the autonomous people or territory.

The delegation of certain powers to the mandatary State must not, however, be looked upon as in any way impairing the ultimate authority and control of the League, or as conferring on the mandatary general powers of interference over the affairs of the territory affected. For this purpose it is important that in each such case of mandate the League should issue a special Act or Charter, clearly setting forth the policy which the mandatary will have to follow in that territory. This policy must necessarily vary from case to case, according to the development, administrative or police capacity, and homogeneous character of the people concerned. The mandatary State should look upon its position as a great trust and honour, not as an office of profit or a position of private advantage for it or its nationals. And in case of any flagrant and prolonged abuse of this trust the population concerned should be able to appeal for redress to the League, who should in a proper case assert its authority to the full, even to the extent of removing the mandate, and entrusting it to some other State, if necessary. No pegging-out of claims should be allowed under the guise of the mandate. And by keeping in touch with the affairs of the territories concerned through proper liaison, the League should satisfy itself that its mandates are being carried out fairly and properly. It might also call for periodic reports from the mandatary State. I therefore make the following recommendation:

(6) That the degree of authority, control, or administration exercised by the mandatary State shall in each case be laid down by the League in a special Act or Charter, which shall reserve to it complete power of ultimate control and supervision, as well as the right of appeal to it from the territory or people affected against any gross breach of the mandate by the mandatary State.

Ironically, the statesmen charged with the postwar settlement accepted Smuts' notion of a mandates system but insisted on its extension to South West Africa and other ex-German colonies. The shifting views on the future of South West Africa, culminating in its being placed under mandate, are described by Wm. Roger Louis in "The South West African Origins of the 'Sacred Trust,' 1914–1919." [c]

The recent developments in the case before the International Court of Justice and the General Assembly of the United Nations have coincided with the opening for the first time of the British official records of the peace-making at Versailles. It is therefore opportune to re-examine the origins of the South West Africa mandate; to recall that up to the very end of the First World War British as well as South African

[c] (1967) 66 *African Affairs* 20–39.

politicians assumed that the future of the German colony lay in annexation to the Union; but that this assumption proved to be unfounded because of South African statesmanship as well as socialist
and humanitarian influences; and that South West Africa played a
critical part in securing the general acceptance of the mandates system
by the Peace Conference. At the same time it is possible to discern the
determination of South Africa from the outset to accept only a type of
mandatory control that would imply no external interference, whether
from Geneva or London.

South African troops invaded South West Africa on January 14, 1915.
On July 9 the Governor of this, the first German colony, unconditionally surrendered his force of 204 officers and 3,166 men. It had been a
white man's war fought between South Africans and Germans for control of a desert territory larger than Germany. The colony contained a
European population of about 15,000 and an African one estimated at
the time as 80,000. Apart from diamonds, it had yielded the Germans
little in natural resources, and lack of water had hindered the chief industry of stock raising. Nevertheless, it was the only German colony
where, in its temperate areas, white men could settle; for this reason,
among others, the British press interpreted the conquest as a stunning
defeat for German 'imperialism'.[1]

There were three striking features of the campaign: the harmonious
relations between Briton and Afrikaner during the conquest; the significance attached to the victory as an important event of the war; and
the developing determination not to return South West Africa to the
Germans. British attitudes towards the German colonies were no
longer ambivalent. For thirty years there had been a degree of dualism
in British thought about German activities in Africa; on the one hand
—and particularly in the 1880s—Germany had been regarded as a potential partner in the pioneering task of civilizing Africa; on the other
there was the belief that Germany was the leader of an anti-British
conspiracy that existed not only in Africa but the world over.[2] During
the decade before 1914 the latter attitude was in the ascendant—
nowhere more so than in southern Africa, where Germany was associated with Afrikaner opposition, and where the outbreak of war gave
some substance to the fear that her territory there might be used as a
base for a Boer rising. . . .

South Africans and Englishmen alike took it as axiomatic that 'no
greater boon could be conferred upon the native races of Africa than
to relieve them from the abomination of German misgovernment.' Up
to the eve of the war it had been the Belgians and the Portuguese
whom the British humanitarians had chiefly denounced as perpetra-
tors of gross maladministration in Africa; the Germans, despite the
massacre of the Hereros, had practically escaped public censure. But
with the outbreak of hostilities this attitude changed rapidly. The English-speaking South African press was particularly damning:

[1] See for instance *The Times*, 10 July 1915.
[2] This theme is developed more fully in my forthcoming book, *Great Britain
and Germany's Lost Colonies, 1914–1919* (in press).

The German militarist at his worst [observed the *Cape Argus,* June 1, 1915] is a stupid, unteachable brute, and it was to military men of this stamp rather than to experienced men of affairs that the delicate task of governing subject races has generally been entrusted. . . . If instead of the unimaginative numbskulls and military pedants—men devoid alike of any sense of fair play or humanity— Germany could have commanded the services of men of the type of our own magistrates in the native territories, who have a sympathetic consideration of the native standpoint, and above all the desire to do justice, the nameless horrors of the war against the Hereros would never have disgraced the annals of German Colonial history.

The *Cape Times* and the *East London Daily Dispatch* wrote in the same vein.[4] Within a year after the outbreak of the war, the English press in South Africa had concluded that the Germans were brutal and cruel colonizers and unfit to have their colonies returned to them.

. . . .

By the close of 1916 all of the German forces had been conquered except the East African contingent, which Smuts had 'kraaled' in the south of the colony. In July of the next year Smuts joined Lloyd George's War Cabinet. More than any other member he followed developments concerning the German colonies and considered their significance in relation to the general problems of war and peace in Europe. The 'side-show' campaigns, such as those in South West and East Africa, in his view had achieved one of the basic British war aims: the 'destruction of the German colonial system with a view to the future security of all communications vital to the British Empire'. . . .[7]

He attached special importance to South West Africa. As he stated before a committee of the Imperial War Cabinet appointed to consider territorial questions:

. . . retrocession of South-West Africa was absolutely impossible, even in the contingency of a completely unsatisfactory peace. It would mean the submergence of those who had made every sacrifice on behalf of the Empire in South Africa, and would bring other elements to the front whose predominance would jeopardise the whole position in South Africa.[9]

Smuts had no difficulty in carrying his point. His views were shared, not only by the South African and British press, but also by his colleagues in the British government most interested in colonial problems, Lord Curzon, Lord Milner, and the Colonial Secretary, Walter Long. The committee's report, which clearly defined British colonial aims at this stage of the war, contained the following passage: 'the res-

[4] 2 November 1914; 2 June 1915. For similar opinion in the London press, see the *Standard,* 10 July, 1915.

[7] Quoted in David Lloyd George, *War Memoirs* (London, 1934), 1, p. 910.

[9] 'Committee of the War Cabinet on Territorial Desiderata', Secret, 17 April 1917, CAB 21/77, Public Record Office, London.

toration to Germany of South-West Africa is incompatible with the security and peaceful development of the Union of South Africa, and in no circumstances should be contemplated.'[10] The consistently held view of the South African in the innermost circle of the British imperial government—that there could be no alternative to his country's control over South West Africa—was supported heartily by the South African government and press, by most of the members of the British government and parliament, and by the majority of British newspapers.

The logic of that view obviously implied annexation; and the developments in which South West Africa played a key role in the final acceptance of the mandate system constituted at the time a diplomatic defeat for the British hardly less than for the South African government.

The elaboration of the idea of mandates occurred, indeed, in British political circles. . . . The public interest shown in the matter, as well as the need to bring British war aims more into alignment with those of the United States, was probably what led the Prime Minister, Lloyd George, to announce in July that 'the desire and the wishes of the peoples must be the dominant factor' in determining the fate of the German colonies. The following January he declared in his 'British War Aims' speech:

> With regard to the German Colonies, I have repeatedly declared that they are held at the disposal of a Conference whose decision must have primary regard to the wishes and interests of the native inhabitants of such Colonies. None of those territories are inhabited by Europeans. The governing consideration, therefore, in all these cases must be that the inhabitants should be placed under the control of an administration acceptable to themselves, one of whose main purposes will be to prevent their exploitation for the benefit of European capitalists or governments. The natives live in their various tribal organisations under Chiefs and Councils who are competent to consult and speak for their tribes and members and thus to represent their wishes and interests in regard to their disposal. The general principle of national self-determination is, therefore, as applicable in their cases as in those of occupied European territories.[13]

Lloyd George, however, took no chances. To make sure that the indigenous populations would 'self determine' in favour of the British, the Colonial Secretary on the day before Lloyd George's speech, January 4, 1918, had sent secret telegrams to the Governors General of South Africa, Australia, and New Zealand requesting them to provide 'evidence of anxiety of natives' to live under British rule. He received this reply from the Governor General of South Africa:

> I cannot see how the principle of 'national self-determination' could be applied to it [South West Africa] and it will always be more a

[10] Ibid., 28 April 1917.   [13] Lloyd George, *War Memoirs*, II, p. 1515.

European than a native territory, since, thanks to the Germans, there are comparatively few natives.

. . . While the natives, both Ovambos and the rest, would almost all certainly elect to remain under British rule, they could hardly be given a more influential voice than the German inhabitants. If the latter had to vote on the future of the territory the result would scarcely be in doubt, but if the territory were annexed to Union most of Germans would probably remain and become loyal and useful citizens.[14]

A plebiscite for South West Africa was never considered seriously. It was not necessary. The Foreign Office's publication of the 'atrocity Blue Books'[15]—one of which contained photographs of Africans hanged by the Germans—reinforced the conviction that the Germans had committed such atrocious acts that the African population of South West Africa could not help but have a pro-British attitude.

If the wishes of the natives are to have weight, it is beyond question that they are all for British administration . . . native opinion in the colony is unanimously against any idea of its ever being handed back to the tender mercies of Germany, and any suggestion of the possibility of an act of that kind on the part of Great Britain produces the utmost consternation.[16]

The argument of 'self-determination' clearly worked in favour of Britain when applied to South West Africa.

. . . .

Smuts also drove home the importance and urgency of the colonial question to the War Cabinet. It was here that, at the end of a vigorously argued and lengthy memorandum of July 11, 1918, he developed a new and powerful variant on the theme of international co-operation in Africa.

I feel convinced [he wrote] that the lost German Colonies and German Colonial ambitions generally constitute one of the most difficult and important problems which will confront us at the peace . . . Certain Dominions can justly claim that German Colonies lying contiguous or adjacent to their territory and conquered by them should at the peace remain under their control. This probably covers the case of South West Africa so far as the Union of South Africa is concerned. . . . I am clear that its restoration to Germany would damage the Imperial position in South Africa beyond repair.[18]

. . . .

[14] Buxton to Long, Secret telegram, 10 January, 1918, CAB 24/66. See also C.O. 537/1017.

[15] See especially British *Parliamentary Papers*, Cd. 8371, vol. xx, 1916; Cd. 8306, vol. xx, 1916; Cd. 9146, vol. xvii, 1918; Cd. 9210, vol. xlii, 1921.

[16] Buxton to Long, Secret telegram, 10 January 1918, CAB 24/66.

[18] 'The German colonies at the Peace Conference', 11 July 1918, Smuts Papers, Box G., No. 2 A, Cape Town University. I am indebted to Sir Keith Hancock and the Smuts Trustees for allowing me to study these papers. The Public Record Office classification is CAB 29/1/3.

'Security' remained his primary concern. He urged the incorporation of South West Africa into the Union to protect South Africa from aggression and he advocated British control over German East Africa to give the Empire not only continuous land but also air communication from the Cape to Cairo. He envisaged an expanding, vigorous South African dominion as the key to British security in that part of the world. He did not find these ideas incompatible with the conception of a League of Nations and international control in tropical Africa.

> Although the German idea of a Central African Colonial Dominion must be ruled out, there is much to be said for the policy of handling Central African problems on a common basis. Nothing struck me more in that part of the world than the vast difference in development between the colonies of the progressive and the weak nations respectively. More has been done in 25 years in British and GEA than had been accomplished during 400 years of Portuguese rule next door. And yet the Portuguese sit with vast areas of the African Continent, backward, undeveloped, mis-governed or not governed at all.

There was the further danger, he argued, that the Germans, continuing their pre-war policy of economic infiltration, might substitute Portuguese Africa for the old German colonies as a menace to British communications.

> . . . The question arises whether, instead of the German block, it would not be possible after the war to establish some international control over the National Colonies in tropical Africa, which will guarantee their peaceful, non-militaristic exploitation on a common basis for the production of raw materials for the free and common use of the world.
> This Control or Development Board, constituted under an international Convention over the tropical African Colonies at the end of the war, would consist of representatives of the United Kingdom, France, Germany, Belgium and Portugal under the Chairmanship of, say, an American nominee. It would leave the national flags of the colonies alone, would develop the resources of the various colonies with the participation of capital from all the countries represented on the Board, and would control the distribution of raw materials to those countries.

Although the difficulties would be great, so would the advantages.

> The equal development of that immense area for the common good of mankind would be guaranteed and a fruitful source of future international trouble would dry up. And lastly, a foothold would be given to the international system of the future. . . . Central Africa, in fact, might form the beginning of the jurisdiction of the League of Nations.

The scheme did not involve the internationalization of Central Africa, nor the condominium or common ownership and administration by the powers of the existing national African colonies.

It still leaves the colonies national property and under national administration, but for certain defined purposes it establishes the super-control of an International Board. I see no reason why this Board should not be a success on the lines of our Versailles practice, and if successful it would be one of the greatest steps forward from the national jealousies of the past to the international system of the future.

Some such scheme would probably also secure the approval and support of the Government of the United States, and from the British point of view that is a consideration of primary importance.

Support by the United States became increasingly necessary. In the last months of the war and during the period before the Peace Conference, the British government became more and more intent, as Smuts put it, on 'playing up to America, and moving her on to back us up'.[19] The attitude of the United States, along with the attitude of the British left, were the decisive factors in determining the formula of Allied peacemaking in Africa.

Already in December 1916 President Wilson's 'Peace Note' had urged the conclusion of a peace without territorial aggrandizement. In the Allies' reply to the note no mention was made of the German colonies—a fact that was noted with alarm in the southern Dominions of South Africa, Australia and New Zealand. According to the *Cape Times* (January 17, 1917):

If the British Ministry imagined—which we don't for a moment suppose to be the case—that the Union, New Zealand and Australia would consent to give back what they have taken from Germany merely in a spirit of lofty altruism and self-effacement, the British Ministry would be very much mistaken . . . public opinion in the Union will not be in the smallest degree impressed by what reads uncommonly like unctuous balderdash. . . . To restore the Colonies merely in order to demonstrate Britain's disinterestedness would be an act of gratuitous folly.

Lloyd George's 'British War Aims' speech of January 1918, moreover, with its references to self-determination and native welfare, was at least as much directed towards the United States as towards sections of public opinion in Britain. Now Smuts urged that America must not only approve the peace settlement but be drawn into active responsibility for its consequences:

My point is to try and get America on our side. President Wilson is fighting for a League of Nations. If he can go back to the Peace Conference with this point in his favour, he will go a long way to meet us on particular points and help our programme again, and really our programme is an unselfish one. I would try, therefore, to get America into European politics; it is no use her sitting outside. Let her undertake the burden and feel the responsibility.[20]

[19] Eastern Committee Minutes, Secret, 2 December 1918, CAB 27/24.
[20] 'German Colonies at the Peace Conference', CAB 29/1/3.

The responsibility that Smuts had in mind, however, did not involve the German colonies, but the fallen Empires of Eastern Europe and the Middle East. In a broad sense, the League of Nations would step into the shoes of the old Turkish and Russian Empires, but with the purpose of fostering and encouraging local nationalisms. Their component peoples, 'so far as they are of any vitality, would become little autonomous states.' The supervisory role of the League of Nations would be exercised through individual Allied powers, including the United States. 'The result would be, supposing America were to undertake this job, America would keep a large general control over Georgia, but not in her own right, she would do it under a general act of mandate. . . .'[21] He attached supreme importance to getting the United States to assume 'mandatory responsibility'. 'The U.S.A.', he wrote to Lloyd George a few days before the beginning of the Peace Conference, '*must* become a mandatory in some territory of first class importance . . . in return they may be willing to give a free hand in respect of the German Colonies and Turkish possessions claimed by us, either outright or as mandataries.'[22]

One of the territories claimed outright, of course, was South West Africa. Despite his proposal for an International Development Board, Smuts did not wish for the former German territories to become 'mandates'. 'The German Colonies in the Pacific and Africa', he wrote, 'are inhabited by barbarians, who not only cannot possibly govern themselves, but to whom it would be impracticable to apply any ideas of political self-determination in the European sense.' [23]

His own logic, however, put him in an untenable position. If he espoused the general principle that conquered territories should be held in trust, how could he contend that South West Africa deserved to be an exception? Try he did, but the following letter written during the Peace Conference shows that he recognized the flaw in his argument:

> Yesterday we discussed the Dominion claims to the German colonies. I hope I made a good case to South West Africa, but I don't know. My argument was principally that it was a desert, a part of the Kalahari no good to anybody, least of all to so magnificent a body as the League of Nations! It was like the poor sinning girl's plea that her baby was only a very little one! Not that I consider our claim to South West Africa either sinful or wrong.

A few days later he lamely commented that his mandatory idea had 'won its way through . . . and even the German colonies had been brought into the scheme'.[24] Not without reason, a writer for the *Morn-*

---

[21] Eastern Committee Minutes, Secret, 2 December 1918, CAB 27/24. See also Smuts' pamphlet, *The League of Nations; a Practical Suggestion* (London, 1918).

[22] Smuts to Lloyd George, 14 January 1919, Smuts Papers, Vol. 101, No. 64.

[23] Memorandum by Smuts on the League of Nations, War Cabinet Paper, P. 44, Foster Papers, Public Archives of Canada.

[24] Smuts to M. C. Gillett, 25 January 1919, Smuts to A. Clark, 31 January 1919, printed in Selections from the Smuts Papers, IV, 55–6, 58.

ing Post (January 31, 1919) observed that 'General Smuts is hoist by his own petard'.

In his pamphlet he applied this method of disposal to the territories of Russia, Austria and Turkey, but excluded its operation from the captured German Colonies. President Wilson, encouraged by the pamphlet, evidently found no distinction between one set of captured territories and another, and applied to them all the Smutsian rule, to the amazement and disgust of our Dominions.

Smuts ensnared by his own idealism is perhaps a tempting interpretation of the origins of the South West African mandate, but it misses the mark. He himself had supervised the preparation of the British brief on the German colonies to be used at the Peace Conference, and he had made explicitly clear the circumstances and conditions in which Britain would tolerate international control in South West Africa. 'Unconditional annexation of the German Colonies', he wrote to the Colonial Secretary in November 1918, 'should be pressed to the utmost.' He continued:

In case that contention should fail, we should continue to hold them subject to the control of the League of Nations in regard to certain specified subjects (liquor, arms, fortifications, etc.). Such control should be laid down in an Act of a general character, so that the French and others are bound in the same way as ourselves. You will see there is here nothing . . . about joint control, and a small concession is made about the League of Nations which might have the effect of securing the support of the United States to our holding on to these Colonies if our other lines of argument fail.

Our Delegates will, of course, not make this concession until it becomes necessary to carry President Wilson with them.[25]

These tactics were exactly the ones used by the British delegates at the Peace Conference, which convened on January 18, 1919.

On January 24 Lloyd George raised the question of the German colonies before the supreme body of the Peace Conference, the Council of Ten. One of his first comments was that the Germans had deliberately pursued a policy of extermination in South West Africa. President Wilson replied that all were agreed that the colonies should not be returned to Germany. Lloyd George then suggested three possible ways of dealing with them—internationalization, control by the League of Nations, and annexation—and proceeded to put forward the case for annexation in regard to South West Africa. The territory was contiguous to those of the Union of South Africa, and there was no real natural boundary. In the absence of colonization by the Dutch and British population of South Africa, the area would remain a wilderness.

If the Union were given charge of South West Africa in the capacity of a Mandatory there would be, in a territory geographically one,

[25] Smuts to Long (copy), 28 November 1918, Smuts Papers, Vol. 101, No. 49.

two forms of administration. It was questionable whether any advantage would be derived from this division capable of outweighing its practical difficulties.[26]

Following the presentation of Australia's claims to the German islands in the Pacific, Smuts elaborated the Union's case for South West Africa along the same lines as he had throughout the war. South West Africa, he said, was a desert that geographically belonged to the Union. In that way it differed from Germany's valuable and productive colonies in tropical Africa, where the mandatory principle might be more applicable. Germany had exterminated the natives; the Union 'had established a white civilization in a savage continent and had become a great cultural agency all over South Africa'. He hoped that the Conference would 'give' the colony to the Union, and said that he was sure his country's work in that respect 'would be good'.[27]

Partly out of personal respect for Smuts, Wilson was sympathetic towards the Union's case.[28] But for various complicated reasons he did not wish to see South Africa annex the former German colony. If the South Africans were permitted to incorporate South West Africa into the Union, it would be more difficult to resist annexationist claims put forward not only by other British dominions but also by the European powers and—uppermost in Wilson's mind—by Japan. He was determined to avoid the impression that the Peace Conference was dividing up the spoils—to prevent world opinion from thinking 'that the Great Powers first portioned out the helpless parts of the world, and then formed a League of Nations'. On January 27 he explained why mandatory control over South West Africa would be preferable to annexation, and it was in this connection that he first clarified his general ideas about the role of the League of Nations.

The case of South West Africa would be found a most favourable instance to make a clear picture. South West Africa had very few inhabitants, and those had been so maltreated, and their numbers had been so reduced under German administration, that the whole area was open to development that could not yet be determined. Therefore, either it must be attached to its nearest neighbour and so establish what would seem to be a natural union with South Africa, or some institution must be found to carry out the ideas all had in mind, namely, the development of the country for the benefit of those already in it, and for the advantage of those who would live there later. This he assumed to be the principle; it was not intended to exploit any people; it was not intended to exercise arbitrary sovereignty over any people.

The purpose was to serve the people in undeveloped parts, to safeguard them against abuses such as had occurred under German ad-

[26] *Foreign Relations of the United States: the Paris Peace Conference*, III, pp. 719–20.
[27] Ibid., pp. 722–3.
[28] See George Curry, 'Woodrow Wilson, Jan Smuts, and the Versailles Settlement', *American Historical Review*, lxvi (July 1961), 968–86.

ministration and such as might be found under other administrations. Further, where people and territories were undeveloped, to assure their development so that, when the time came, their own interests, as they saw them, might qualify them to express a wish as to their ultimate relations—perhaps lead them to desire their union with the mandatory power.

Should the Union of South Africa be the mandatory of the League of Nations for South West Africa, the mandate would operate as follows:—In the first place, the League of Nations would lay down certain general principles in the mandate, namely, that districts be administered primarily with a view to the betterment of the conditions of the inhabitants. Secondly, that there should be no discrimination against the members of the League of Nations, so as to restrict economic access to the resources of the district. With this limitation, the Union of South Africa would extend such of its laws as were applicable to South West Africa and administer it as an annex to the Union so far as consistent with the interests of the inhabitants.

President Wilson believed that there would be no administrative differences between his scheme and annexation.

The fundamental idea would be that the world was acting as trustee through a mandatory, and would be in charge of the whole administration until the day when the true wishes of the inhabitants could be ascertained. It was up to the Union of South Africa to make it so attractive that South West Africa would come into the Union of their own free will. Should that not be the case, the fault would lie with the mandatory. . . . He would ask: Was this merely camouflage: a means of bringing about the willingness of the people to be united with the Union, to which the Great Powers were not now willing to consent? He would answer, No, as under the mandatory the administration would be so much in the view of the world that unfair processes could not be successfully attempted. If successful administration by a mandatory should lead to union with the mandatory, he would be the last to object.[29]

Following that strong statement by President Wilson, Smuts on the same day began the tactical retreat outlined in his letter to the Colonial Secretary a month earlier. The meeting of the Supreme Council before which Wilson had insisted that all former enemy colonies and dependent territories should be placed under the control of the League of Nations had met at 3.00 p.m. At 6.30 p.m. the British Empire Delegates convened and Smuts reported that he and Lord Robert Cecil (the British delegate charged with the League of Nations question) had agreed to class the problem under three heads—

(1) German Colonies with a British Dominion next door. In these cases there should be annexation. For many reasons it was impossi-

[29] *Foreign Relations,* III, pp. 740–42.

ble to make a Dominion into a mandatory. (2) German Colonies in Central Africa. These were to be distinguished from the first class by the circumstance that the world as a whole was not interested in them. They were cases for a mandatory, but on the basis that the mandatory should be a Power with sovereign rights subject, however, to restrictions in relation to arms, liquor, etc., and the open door. Great Britain and France should be the mandatories in Central Africa, and should bear any expense involved. (3) Other cases where the people of the territories in question could speak for themselves, but where they required assistance in governing and in the development of the country, e.g. Syria and Mesopotamia. At this point the subject became part of the subject of the League of Nations.[30]

Despite the implied division of the occupied territories into three classes (which shortly were to become in inverse order the 'A', 'B' and 'C' mandates) the British Empire Delegation still refused to admit that South West Africa should fall under the influence of the League of Nations.

The next morning, January 28, Wilson insisted in a lengthy conversation with Lloyd George that he 'could not return to America with the world parcelled out by the Great Powers'. That afternoon at a meeting of the Supreme Council, after the presentation of the French claims to Togoland and the Cameroons, the President 'observed that the discussion so far had been, in essence, a negation in detail—one case at a time—of the whole principle of mandatories'. Australia was claiming sovereignty over German New Guinea, and South Africa over German South West Africa, Japan over the German dependencies in the North Pacific; France was claiming a modified sovereignty over the German West African possessions.[31] Lloyd George reported to the British Empire Delegation the next morning, January 29, that 'he feared a deadlock, and that the President would leave the country before an agreement had been reached.' [32] The colonial issue at this stage threatened to disrupt the proceedings of the Peace Conference.

The line taken by the South African delegates at this juncture saved the day for Wilson and the application of the mandate principle to the German colonies. Using all his political ingenuity, Lloyd George persuaded the Prime Ministers of Australia and New Zealand to accept a compromise prepared by Smuts whereby South West Africa and the Pacific Islands would also become mandates, but would be administered as 'integral portions' of the mandatory powers. Nevertheless, on the next day, January 30, the Australian Prime Minister W. M. Hughes collided head-on with President Wilson. After Hughes had represented the strength of Australasian sentiment against the man-

[30] Minutes of the British Empire Delegation, 4, Secret, 27 January, 1919, CAB 29/28/1.
[31] *Foreign Relations*, III, pp. 763–5.
[32] Minutes of the British Empire Delegation, 6, Secret, 29 January 1919, CAB 29/28/1.

dates proposal, Wilson asked whether 'Australia and New Zealand were presenting an ultimatum to the Conference . . .' Hughes replied, 'that's about the size of it, President Wilson'.[33]

At that dangerous point General Botha (who along with Smuts represented South Africa) intervened. The minutes of the meeting include the following paragraph of his speech:

> He appreciated the ideals of President Wilson. They were the ideals of the people of the world, and they would succeed if they all accepted them in the same spirit and supported them in the manner in which they were intended. . . . Personally he felt very strongly about the question of German South West Africa. He thought that it differed entirely from any question that they had to decide in this conference, but he would be prepared to say that he was a supporter [of the mandates proposal] . . . he knew that if the idea fructified, the League of Nations would consist mostly of the same people who were present there that day, who understood the position and who would not make it impossible for the mandatory to govern the country. That was why he would accept it.[34]

Botha's speech carried the day. Wilson feared that if the matter were carried further the powers with annexationist claims might not adhere to the Covenant; he agreed to the compromise. The Australasians intensely disliked the idea of anything less than full sovereignty over the German islands in the southern Pacific; but under great pressure they acquiesced in the mandates proposal. The opposition to the scheme thus did not come from South Africa nor from France (Clemenceau had consented to it on January 28), but from Australia and New Zealand. The following passage of the proposed arrangement, which later became article 22 of the League Covenant, is the one relevant to the 'C' mandate for South West Africa:

> . . . there are territories, such as South-West Africa and certain of the Islands in the South Pacific, which, owing to the sparseness of their population, or their small size, or their remoteness from the centres of civilization, or their geographical contiguity to the mandatory state, and other circumstances, can be best administered as integral portions thereof, subject to the safeguards . . . in the interests of the indigenous population.

On May 7, 1919, South Africa was designated the mandatory power in South West Africa and accepted the responsibility of submitting an annual report to the League of Nations on the territory committed to its charge.

The public response to the creation of the mandates system was one of scepticism in England as well as in South Africa. A few newspapers such as the *Manchester Guardian* and the *Daily Chronicle* gave a luke-

---

[33] This is the version given by Hughes' biographer, L. F. Fitzhardinge, in an unpublished typescript, 'W. M. Hughes and the Treaty of Versailles, 1919'.
[34] *Foreign Relations*, III, pp. 801–2.

warm greeting to the mandates system as a step towards the realization of international idealism, but most of the press commentary was extremely critical. On the political left, such writers as J. A. Hobson denounced it as 'a thin veil for the annexation of enemy countries and the division of the spoil . . .' [35] On the right the conservative newspapers such as the *Globe* (January 30, 1919) attacked the business of 'giving away the empire'. International control, sooner or later, would mean German control, and the war would have been fought to no purpose. Opinion in South Africa ran along somewhat similar lines. *De Burger,* the principal Afrikaner organ, regarded the mandates system —though on nationalist rather than on internationalist grounds—as a hypocritical invention of British imperialism. The *Cape Times* made its opinion clear in the title of one of its leading articles, 'the Mandatory Muddle'. Throughout South African opinion ran the idea that the mandates system would make little difference. According to the *East London Daily Dispatch* (February 3, 1919):

> Now international control is no new thing. . . . In practice [the mandates system] will probably mean that Britain or her Dominions will take over the management of most of Germany's late colonies and administer them in accordance with the well-established British colonial policy.
> Nominally the mandatory power will be the trustee of the League of Nations, but actually she will have a free hand in the administration of the new territories, so long as her system of government is not in conflict with the principles for which the League stands.

The periodical *South Africa* (February 8, 1919) stated the point at the back of everyone's mind more sharply:

> If South-West Africa is not annexed to the Union, we do not know what annexation is. It will remain British 'pink' on our maps. . . . What is a mandate? What is to be the final elucidation of the mandatory theory? We know, and all South Africans know, what it must not mean. It must not mean that the natives of South-West Africa are to have any ground for supposing that if they are dissatisfied at any time with the Union Government some mysterious League across the seas will take up their imaginary grievances. The mandatory theory will have to be very carefully applied to South-West Africa, or it may easily contain the germs of future trouble.

The *Grahamstown Journal* (February 6, 1919) also feared that the mandatory powers might find themselves in an impossible position between the inhabitants on the one hand and the League on the other. Possible international interference lay at the heart of most British reservations about mandatory control.

On what grounds the League could intervene was in fact by no means clear. In the opinion of the *Pall Mall Gazette:* 'A mandate which the League of Nations can give it can also take away.' But did

[35] In a letter in *Common Sense,* 5 March 1919.

the League actually have the authority to do so? To what extent did the League have jurisdiction over South West Africa? These points became of paramount importance in the subsequent debates among international lawyers, so it is important to examine how the founders of the mandates system regarded the question of sovereignty and jurisdiction.

Wilson had no clear answers to these problems.[36] Nor, apart from Smuts (and possibly Balfour) did any of the British leaders. Milner, Colonial Secretary during the Peace Conference, made this revealing comment:

> We are opening a new chapter in International Law. . . . The mandated territories are to be under the supervision of the League of Nations. But actual authority, in each of these territories, will be exercised by one member of that League. I leave it to lawyers to say, where the 'sovereignty' will in any case reside. As it seems to me, there will in all mandated territories be in a sense divided 'sovereignty'. From the practical point of view that does not appear to me to present any great difficulty. What is essential is to get rid of existing sovereignties.[37]

Apart from that fleeting observation, Milner, like most of the statesmen at the Peace Conference, had little time for legal conundrums. Smuts as usual was an exception. Trained in the law, and especially interested in the disposal of the German colonies, he was sensitive to the legal difficulties that might arise.

An important legal question did arise in October 1919 when the Government of New Zealand telegraphed Milner that the administrator of Samoa was anxious to have a clear statement of 'finality' in order to stop rumours that a power other than New Zealand might be given the mandate. The basic issue involved was the granting of authority for New Zealand to rule and legislate. Did that authority derive from the League of Nations or from the King, and if the latter, in what capacity? Milner and his staff proceeded to prepare an Order in Council under the Foreign Jurisdiction Act—implying, in other words, that authority emanated from 'the King in his British Government'. Smuts objected. The South African parliament, he argued, had the power to legislate for South West Africa (a contention that rested ultimately on jurisdiction by conquest). In Smuts' opinion this particular question had nothing to do with the League of Nations. It was a matter that solely concerned British constitutional law. Criticising the proposed Order in Council for Samoa, Smuts telegraphed Milner:

> Mandate over Samoa is given not to United Kingdom, but to New Zealand; that is to say, to His Majesty not in his British Government, but in his Dominion Government. King in his British Gov-

---

[36] See Robert Lansing, *The Peace Negotiations: a Personal Narrative* (Boston, 1928).
[37] Buxton (transmitting message from Smuts) to Milner, Private and personal telegram, 15 November 1919, CAB 24/94.

ernment or Privy Council is not concerned, therefore, and British Order in Council is beside the point. It would only apply where effect is to be given to mandate like GEA which was conferred on His Majesty in his British Government. . . . Any Act purporting to confer jurisdiction over mandated territories like South-West Africa or Samoa must emanate from His Majesty in his Dominion Governor, on whom alone the mandate was conferred. . . .[38]

The Colonial Office submitted the question to the Law Officers of the Crown, who studied the wording of the 'C' mandates. Their opinion, in so far as it concerned South West Africa, was that it was a 'territory over which a mandate is conferred upon His Britannic Majesty for and on behalf of the Government of the Union of South Africa. . . .' The Law Officers, whose views reflected the trends of constitutional law that eventually led to the Statute of Westminster, thus concurred in Smuts' view.

During his long years after 1919 as Prime Minister of South Africa, Smuts did not have to deal in other than a minor way with the question of international intervention in South West Africa. Had he lived to do so perhaps he would have taken the same point of view that he did during the Paris Peace Conference: 'In this great business South West Africa is as dust in the balance compared to the burden now hanging over the civilized world.' [39] For the fact that this former German colony, scantily peopled, poor in resources, came to weigh more heavily in world affairs, he himself was in no small measure responsible.

THE CREATION OF THE MANDATES SYSTEM [d]

S. Slonim, "The Origins of the South West Africa Dispute: The Versailles Peace Conference and the Creation of the Mandates System": [e]

I

The Roots of the South West Africa dispute relate back to the events that took place at the end of World War I and led to the creation of

[d] See further on this subject: D. H. Miller, "The Origin of the Mandates System" (1928) 6 *Foreign Affairs* 276; Wm. Roger Louis, "The United States and the African Peace Settlement" (1963) 4 *Journal of African History* 413; Pittman B. Potter, "Origin of the System of Mandates under the League of Nations" (1922) 16 *American Political Science Review* 572; Quincy Wright, *Mandates under the League of Nations* (1930), pp. 24–63; Norman Bentwich, *The Mandates System* (1930), pp. 1–9.

[e] (1968) 6 *The Canadian Year Book of International Law* 115–43. This article also constitutes Chapter 1 in S. Slonim, *South West Africa and the United Nations: An International Mandate in Dispute*. Johns Hopkins Press, 1973.

[38] Memorandum by Milner on Mandates, Secret, 8 March 1919, CAB 29/9/1.

[39] Smuts to Lloyd George, 4 June 1919, Smuts Papers, Vol. 101, No. 99.

the League of Nations mandates system. More particularly, the conflict between the United Nations and South Africa cannot be understood except by tracing the manner in which South West Africa became a part of that system. The "great compromise" hammered out by President Wilson and the Dominion ministers at the Paris Peace Conference in 1919 produced a three-tiered system of mandates which reflected in a sliding scale a varied balancing of national and international interests. The result of the compromise was a divergency of interpretation that has endured to this day and in considerable measure has fostered and sustained the dispute in its present-day dimensions.

The historical roots of the mandates system undoubtedly stretch back to the concepts and principles enunciated in such earlier international arrangements as the 1885 Treaty of Berlin and the 1906 Algeciras Act.[1] Nonetheless, it is quite clear that the mandates system came about not as a result of organic development in international relations, but rather as a direct result of the diplomatic events of World War I and the Paris Peace Conference.

From 1914 to 1916 Allied leaders, in anticipation of victory, had concluded a series of secret treaties for dividing up colonial spoils severed from Germany and Turkey. Dramatic events in the course of the year 1917, however, caused the Allies to lay increasing emphasis on the moral and liberal goals of their struggle.[3] The Russian Revolution, followed by United States entry into the war, produced a climate that was antagonistic to greedy annexationist schemes such as those formulated in the secret treaties. Now, such progressive ideals as democracy, the right of self-determination of peoples, and protection for minority rights were proclaimed as the true aims of the allied cause. The Bolshevik Revolution confirmed this development and gave cause to the principle of self-determination to be extended to the peoples of Africa and Asia as well as of Europe.

This was the background to the famous Fourteen Points enunciated by President Wilson before a joint session of Congress on January 8,

---

[1] For a review of the historical antecedents of the mandates system, see Pittman B. Potter, "Origin of the System of Mandates under the League of Nations," 16 Am. Pol. Sc. Rev. 563 (1922); Pittman B. Potter, "Further Notes," 20 Am. Pol. Sc. Rev. 842 (1926); Luther H. Evans, "Some Legal & Historical Antecedents of the Mandatory System," 5 *Proceedings of the Southwestern Political Association* 143 (1924); Luther H. Evans, *The Mandates System & the Administration of Territories under C. Mandate,* Part I (unpublished Ph.D. dissertation, Dept. of Political Science, Stanford University); H. W. V. Temperley (ed.), *A History of the Peace Conference of Paris,* Vol. 2, at 236, Vol. 6, Part 4 (1920); Elizabeth Van Maanen-Helmer, *The Mandates System in Relation to Africa & the Pacific Islands* c. 1 & 2 (1929); Wm. Roger Louis, "African Origins of the Mandates Idea," 19 Int'l Organ. 20 (1965); *The Mandates System: Origin, Principles, Application,* League of Nations Publication, Series IV.A, "Mandates" (1945); Quincy Wright, *Mandates Under the League of Nations* c. 1 (1930).

[3] See generally Arno J. Mayer, *Political Origins of the New Diplomacy, 1917–1918,* passim (1959).

1918.[4] Point 5 called for "a free, open-minded, and absolutely impartial adjustment of all colonial claims," based on the principle "that in determining all such questions of sovereignty the interests of the populations concerned must have equal weight with the equitable claims of the government whose title is to be determined."[5] In similar vein, Lloyd George, in the course of an address before the Trade Unions Congress on January 5, 1918, had acknowledged that peoples under Turkish control were entitled to a "recognition of their separate national condition," and that the German colonies should be placed "at the disposal of a conference whose decisions must have primary regard to the wishes and interests of the native inhabitants of such colonies," the principle of self-determination being as "applicable in their cases as in those of occupied European territories."[7]

By early 1918, then, the Allied leaders were basically committed in their peace programme to the right of self-determination of peoples. At the same time, they also envisioned creation of a permanent world organization to preserve peace. They did not, however, at this point relate a solution for the enemy colonies to any such projected international institution. At this stage, the measure of international involvement was to be limited to the deliberations of the Peace Conference which would seek to apply the basic principle of self-determination. No permanent scheme relating to colonies was yet devised. In short, although the principle of self-determination was already enunciated, the effective means for instituting and confirming this right through the provision of international accountability was not yet conceived of.

II

During the course of the year 1918, the original commitment to the principle of self-determination in the disposition of enemy colonies matured gradually into a full scale conception of a League of Nations mandates system. A consensus gradually developed to the effect that the enemy colonies issue could best be resolved by some permanent tie-in with the projected world organization. A review of certain key elements, which progressively contributed to this development, provide the necessary background for an appreciation of the events at Paris.

[4] On the origins and significance of the Fourteen Points, see *ibid.*, 341–44, 352–53; Charles Seymour, *The Intimate Papers of Colonel House*, Vol. 3, at 331 (1928); Seth P. Tillman, *Anglo-American Relations at the Paris Peace Conference of 1919*, at 24–32 (1961). For text, see James Brown Scott (ed.), *Official Statements of War Aims & Peace Proposals, December 1916 to November 1918*, at 234–39 (1921).

[5] Note that this language in Point 5 does not at all refer to mandates. On the contrary, it clearly implies that territories will be annexed, but that the various claims shall be equitably settled, taking into account the interests of the native population as well. Smuts in his initial work on the League of Nations also interpreted Point 5 in this manner. See *infra*. The Commentary to the Fourteen Points, however, did interpret this passage to refer to mandates; see *infra*.

[7] For text see Scott, *op. cit. supra* note 4, at 225–33.

The first (and perhaps most significant) contribution was that of G. L. Beer, a former Columbia University professor, who was a specialist on colonial affairs.[8] At the time of his writing, January 1918, Beer was a member of the Inquiry, that official body of United States experts selected in late 1917 by Colonel House, President Wilson's advisor, to collect data and offer considered opinions on various questions that could be expected to arise at the Peace Conference.[9]

Beer recommended that the "administration of the derelict territories and peoples freed from German and Turkish rule must in general be entrusted to different states acting as mandatories of the League of Nations." This could best "be reached by an arrangement like that of the Six Powers Group in China and that of the Algeciras Act of 1906." Prime attention was to be given to the welfare of native populations; the open door was to be ensured; and provision was to be made for arbitration relating to the mandatories' international obligations.[10]

Beer's outline is the first clear prototype of the mandates system and in fact bears remarkable resemblance to the scheme ultimately adopted. However, it is not fully clear to what extent Beer's work was directly instrumental in guiding President Wilson's thoughts along the path of trusteeship. Nonetheless, before the war was over the President was definitely convinced that some such concept of mandates should be instituted for former enemy territories.

.   .   .   .

The principle of international accountability was more formally expressed in the Official United States Commentary to the Fourteen Points adopted in October 1918. On Point V, the Commentary declared:

> It would seem as if the principle involved in this proposition is that a colonial power acts not as owner of its colonies but as trustees for the natives and for the interests of the society of nations, that the terms on which the colonial administration is conducted are a matter of international concern and may legitimately be the subject of international inquiry and that the peace conference may, therefore, write a code of colonial conduct binding upon all colonial powers.[12]

[8] George Louis Beer, *African Questions at the Paris Peace Conference*, (ed. Louis Herbert Gray, 1923).

[9] For a description of the formation and work of the inquiry, see Sidney Edward Mezes, "Preparations for Peace," in House and Seymour (ed.), *What Really Happened at Paris* I (1921); . . . ; Charles Seymour, *op. cit. supra* note 4, Vol. III, at 168; Lawrence E. Gelfand, *The Inquiry: American Preparations for Peace, 1917–1919* (1963).

[10] Beer, *op. cit. supra* note 8, at 424–25, 431. Beer, however, recommended that South West Africa and New Guinea be annexed by South Africa and Australia respectively: *ibid.*, 453–58.

[12] Seymour, *Intimate Papers*, Vol. IV, at 195. President Wilson confirmed his acceptance of the Commentary as "a satisfactory interpretation of the principles involved" on October 30, 1918: *ibid.*, 153.

The reference in the concluding sentence to "a code binding on all colonial powers" relates only to former enemy colonies; it has no relationship to general colonial policy. See the opening paragraph of the Commentary on this Point. *Ibid.*, 194.

. . . .

In the meantime, the British government was also moving towards acceptance of the mandates idea. In October 1918, Colonel House had met with Lloyd George and had gained British acceptance of the trusteeship principle for all enemy territories, with the exception of South West Africa and the Asiatic islands. These, the British Prime Minister indicated, would have to go to South Africa and Australia respectively, lest he "be confronted by a revolution in those dominions." At this meeting Lloyd George also expressed the hope that the United States would see fit to become trustee for German East African colonies.[14]

In early November 1918, a British Foreign Office memorandum on the League dealt with the mandates issue in the following terms:

> The treaty should give precision to the idea of the responsibility of the civilized states to the more backward peoples. Trusts, or to speak more precisely, charters, should be drawn up for the various territories for whose future government the signatory Powers have to issue a mandate, and particular areas handed over to individual States who would be responsible to the League for the discharge of that mandate. Arrangements of this kind will require to be made for tropical Africa, for the Pacific Islands and for Western Asia.[15]

On November 28, the subject of mandates was fully discussed at a meeting of the Imperial War Cabinet.[16] Lloyd George records that two basic facts emerged from this meeting. Firstly, the Dominions were not prepared to give up any of the colonies conquered by them and contiguous to their own territories. Secondly, Great Britain herself was not desirous of annexing any territory and was fully prepared to accept the former German colonies in the form of mandates.

At a subsequent Cabinet meeting (undated), the distinction between the occupation of a territory in a "possessory" and in a "mandatory" capacity was outlined. The definition adopted is of major significance for the scope of power it concedes to the League and for the dedication to the principle of self-determination that it embodies.

---

[14] House to Wilson, October 30, 1918, Department of State, *Papers Relating to the Foreign Relations of the United States, 1919, The Paris Peace Conference*, Vol. 1, at 407 (1942–1947); hereinafter referred to as Foreign Relations. For a review of the attempts to have the United States assume a mandate under the League Covenant, see Wm. Roger Louis, "The United States & The African Peace Settlement of 1919: The Pilgrimage of George Louis Beer," 4 Journal of African History 413 (1963).

[15] Quoted in Alfred Zimmern, *The League of Nations and the Rule of Law, 1918–1935*, at 202–03 (1936). For the full text of the memorandum, see *ibid.*, 196–208. This memorandum is particularly important since it was to be the starting point for the Smuts draft. It is to be noted, however, that the memorandum does not envisage a regime for South West Africa and the Pacific Islands different from that of the other colonies: see *ibid.*, 209. See also H. Duncan Hall, *Mandates, Dependencies & Trusteeship* 110, n. 13 (1948).

[16] David Lloyd George, *The Truth About the Peace Treaties*, Vol. 1, at 114, (1928).

"Mandatory occupation," it was agreed, would involve "administration by a single power on certain general lines laid down by the League of Nations." These lines would include guarantees for an open door policy, and prohibitions against militarization and fortification.

There would be a right of appeal from the mandatory power to the League of Nations on the part of anyone who considered himself ill-treated or claimed that the conditions laid down by the League of Nations were not being fulfilled. Subject to such appeal, which might involve the League of Nations withdrawing the mandate in the case of deliberate and persistent violation of its conditions, the mandate would be continuous until such time as the inhabitants of the country themselves were fit for self-government.[17]

The mandates doctrine was unanimously accepted by the Cabinet in respect of all enemy territories except South West Africa and the Pacific Islands.[18]

On December 16, 1918, General Jan Smuts published a small pamphlet entitled, "The League of Nations: A Practical Suggestion," which was destined to have a profound influence on the formulation of the mandates system.[19] Almost a third of Smuts' tract was devoted to the subject of mandates. The key point was that the collapse of the old Empires should not be made the occasion for "national annexation" of derelict territories. "Europe," he declared, "is being liquidated, and the League of Nations must be the heir to this great estate." The League of Nations must be made the reversionary, in the broadest sense, of the peoples and territories formerly belonging to Russia, Austria-Hungary and Turkey;[20] the League must be clothed with the right of ultimate disposal in accordance with certain fundamental principles. "These principles," he went on to say, "have been summed up in the formula of 'No annexations and the self-determination of nations'."[21] Since the peoples involved differed in their preparedness for self-government, a scheme of graded mandates was called for. The terms of each mandate would be spelled out in a special

---

[17] *Ibid.*, 118.

[18] *Ibid.*, 123. Smuts appears to have opposed application of the mandates system to any part of Africa, and not just to South West Africa. This would coincide with the viewpoint expressed in his League of Nations pamphlet that Africa was not suited to the institution of mandates. See *infra.*

[19] Jan C. Smuts, *The League of Nations: A Practical Suggestion* (1919).

[20] This reference to the peoples and territories of Russia, Austria-Hungary and Turkey, coupled with exclusion from the plan of the peoples of Africa and the Pacific Islands (as noted below) has been interpreted in some quarters to mean that Smuts' plan, far from being a "plan for the betterment of backward peoples" was rather "something not far removed from a twentieth-century Holy Alliance." Zimmern, *op. cit. supra* note 15, at 212. D. H. Miller likewise considers Smuts' ideas on mandates to have been quite opposite to those of President Wilson: "The Origin of the Mandates System," 6 For. Affairs 281 (1928).

[21] Smuts, *op. cit. supra* note 19, at 10.

charter which would not only reserve ultimate control to the League, but would call for periodic reports, and even allow for appeal against gross breach of the mandate by the people of the mandated territory. Provision would be made for observance of the open door and guarantees against militarization.

Smuts, however, expressly excluded Africa and the Pacific Islands from the mandates principle by declaring:

> The German colonies in the Pacific and Africa are inhabited by barbarians who not only cannot possibly govern themselves but to whom it would be impracticable to apply any idea of political self-determination in the European sense. . . . The disposal of these colonies should be decided on the basis of the principles which President Wilson has laid down in the fifth of his celebrated fourteen points.[22]

Toward the end of December 1918, President Wilson arrived in London and met with Lloyd George. The British Prime Minister presented Wilson with a copy of the Smuts pamphlet and raised the topic of mandates for discussion.[24] There was basic agreement on the principle to be applied. But when Lloyd George presented the case for South African annexation of South West Africa and Australian annexation of the Pacific Islands, the President objected. His objection regarding South West Africa was not serious; he was prepared to recognize some merit, based upon contiguity of territory, in that case. But he was not prepared to accept annexation of the Pacific islands by Australia on grounds of security. . . .

When Lloyd George reported on his meeting with the President to the Imperial Cabinet, Dominion representatives, and particularly Prime Minister Hughes of Australia, were bitterly critical of the President's objections to their plans for annexation. They called upon Lloyd George to "resolutely insist upon such terms of peace as were necessary for the safety of the Empire, through whose sacrifices and efforts victory had been won." Other members of the Cabinet, however, reminded their companions of the over-riding importance of reaching an understanding with the United States.

This dichotomy of interests, as reflected in the Cabinet debates, explains much of the subsequent British conduct towards the mandates issue at the Paris Peace Conference. On the one hand, the British were desirous of co-operating with the United States to the fullest extent possible consistent with their own national interests. Moreover, Great Britain, independently of the United States, had attained a keen appreciation of the responsibilities of mandatory powers, as reflected in the Cabinet discussions and Foreign Ministry memoranda. They were, therefore, fully prepared to accept the mandates system for the territo-

---

[22] *Ibid.,* 12. Wilson's fifth point as noted above made no reference to mandates, and in the words of Hall, "definitely-implied annexation": *op. cit. supra* note 15, at 112. This interpretation of Point V differs of course from the one presented in the Commentary. See *supra.*

[24] David Lloyd George, *op. cit. supra* note 16, at 190.

ries that had come under their own control. On the other hand, Great Britain, the head of a vast British Empire, found itself committed to supporting Dominion claims for annexation, based upon grounds of security and contiguity of territory. Lloyd George resolved that the matter could best be settled by having the Dominion representatives themselves present the issue directly to the President at a session of the Conference.

After his meeting with Lloyd George in London, Wilson returned to Paris and proceeded to draw up a draft Covenant, incorporating therein much of the thought and language of General Smuts.[30] His reliance on Smuts' draft was particularly evident in regard to the mandates section, which was appended as a supplementary agreement to the body of the draft Covenant.[31] The President's plan, however, extended the mandates system, with a clear pledge to the principle of self-determination, to all German colonies—including those in Africa and the Pacific—something which Smuts had specifically excluded. Whereas Smuts had envisaged a mandates system purely as a means of resolving the nationality problem of Eastern Europe and the Near East, the President regarded it as a concept of universal applicability and one that could resolve the colonial problem of Africa and the Pacific as well.[32] This first official American draft of the Covenant was circulated to the Allied governments on January 10, 1919.[33]

On January 25, 1919, David Hunter Miller, the United States legal adviser in Paris, received a British "Draft Convention regarding Mandates" from Lord Cecil, which went into considerable detail regarding the proposed mandates system.[34] Amongst other things, it referred to two categories of mandates—"assisted states" for those mandates close to independence, and "vested territories" for those areas requiring direct administration by the mandatory power. The state placed in charge of a "vested territory" would be "invested with all powers and rights of a sovereign government"; such state would hold the territory "upon trust to afford to the . . . inhabitants peace, order and good government." [35] It also provided for annual reports by the mandatory

---

[30] The President had been deeply impressed by the Smuts plan which he considered "thoroughly statesmanlike in character . . . He was struck by the extraordinary resemblance of General Smuts' views on such subjects as the League of Nations to the American views." Letter from General T. H. Bliss to Newton D. Baker, January 4, 1919, quoted in George Curry, "Woodrow Wilson, Jan Smuts, and the Versailles Settlement," 66 Am. Hist. Rev. 968, 976 (1961).

[31] The extent to which the President drew upon the Smuts draft is analyzed by Potter, "Origin of the System of Mandates under the League of Nations," 16 Am. Pol. Sc. Rev. 563 (1922).

[32] See Quincy Wright, *op. cit. supra* note 1, at 32.

[33] For the text of this first Paris Draft (which was actually Wilson's second draft), see David Hunter Miller, *The Drafting of the Covenant,* Vol. 2, Doc. 7, at 65. . . .

[34] For the text, see Miller, *The Drafting of the Covenant,* Vol. 1, at 106–07.

[35] *Ibid.* It is to be noted that the provisions on "vested territories" contained no reference to independence.

power and included a provision for the creation of a Commission to assist the League in its supervisory role and to receive the annual reports.

In effect, then, there was basic agreement between the United States and Great Britain on the mandates principle. During the course of 1918, both nations had advanced from a simple commitment to the ideal of self-determination to a recognition that this ideal could best be implemented through the creation of a mandates system integrally linked with the League of Nations. The general features of the system were also agreed upon.[37] The main outstanding difference centred on the extent of the mandates system, and particularly the question of exceptions to allow for annexation in certain cases. This issue was to be the chief source of controversy on the topic of mandates at the Paris Peace Conference.

III

The Peace Conference opened in Paris on January 18, 1919. Disposition of colonial territories was the first major issue dealt with by the Conference.

Lloyd George opened the discussion on Friday, January 24, amid early and general concurrence on not returning the colonies to Germany. Great Britain, he declared, was prepared to accept the mandates system for those territories that had come under British control. The mandates system, with its concern for native interest and equality of commercial access was, in essence, already a part of the British colonial system. But the territories conquered by the Dominions, he felt, should be treated differently. South West Africa was a wilderness and could only be developed as an integral part of South Africa upon which it bordered. New Guinea and Samoa likewise could best be administered if they became part of Australia and New Zealand respectively. In these cases, therefore, annexation was advisable.

Each of the Dominion Ministers then stated his case. Hughes argued that control of New Guinea was vital to Australian security. Pointing to a map, he demonstrated that the Pacific islands encompassed Australia like a fortress, and in unfriendly hands constituted a direct menace. Massey of New Zealand likewise emphasized the strategic importance of Samoa for his country; he did not believe the world had seen the last of war. Smuts claimed South West Africa on grounds of contiguity to the Union and the undesirability of a separate administrative system. Borden of Canada endorsed the arguments of his fellow Ministers, pointing out, at the same time, that Canada itself sought no territory. Neither the French, Italians nor Japanese, all of whom were basically opposed to the mandates system, intervened in the debate. Only the Japanese had a really vital stake in the issue, "and they were content to let the British Empire present the case for annexation." [40]

---

[37] The similarity between British and American views was, of course, not due to mere coincidence, but rather to their common derivation from the Smuts plan.

[40] Tillman, *op. cit. supra* note 4, at 91.

At the second meeting on this issue, on Monday, January 27, President Wilson outlined his concept of the mandatory system.[41] The basis of the idea, he said, was world-wide opposition to further annexation. Since it was agreed that the colonies should not be returned to Germany, mandatories acting on behalf of the League would have to take care of the inhabitants of these territories. This guardianship would operate not only to protect the welfare of the people, but also to promote their political development until such time as they were qualified "to express a wish as to their ultimate relations—perhaps [even] lead[ing] them to desire their union with the mandatory power." In case administration of the mandate became a financial burden "it was clearly proper that the League of Nations should bear a proportion of the expense.[42] The fundamental idea would be that the world was acting as a trustee through a mandatory, and would be in charge of the whole administration until the day when the true wishes of the inhabitants could be ascertained. It was up to the Union of South Africa to make it so attractive that South West Africa would come into the Union of their own free will."

Turning to Australia's security arguments, Wilson charged that they were "based on a fundamental lack of faith in the League of Nations." . . .

The Dominion Ministers, however, remained firm in their campaign to obtain the territories outright, without mandatory obligations. Lloyd George pointed out that the President's suggestion for League assumption of ultimate financial responsibility for the mandates, with the possibility of assessments upon members, invited a host of practical difficulties which required careful consideration. At this point the meeting adjourned.[44]

The third meeting on Tuesday, January 28, opened with Lloyd George reiterating British acceptance of the mandate principle.[45] It

[41] Council of Ten, January 27, 1919, 3 p.m., *Foreign Relations, 1919, The Paris Peace Conference,* Vol. 3 at 741–43.

[42] On this point, see Wilson's Third Draft, January 20, 1919, in Miller, *Drafting of the Covenant,* Vol. II, Doc. 9, at 104.

[44] That evening, January 27, Arthur Balfour, British Foreign Minister, presented a memorandum to Lloyd George that seriously questioned the feasibility of the President's proposal regarding finances. The necessity for checking on both expenditures and budget of a mandate, plus the requirement of assessing members, would make for "an almost unworkable fiscal system." He was also critical of that aspect of the President's plan which would empower the League to dispossess a mandatory power upon application of the inhabitants of the mandated territory. Absence of fixity of tenure would seriously weaken the whole system and could well "supply a perpetual incentive to agitation and intrigue." Finally, independent powers of inspection by the League—which Balfour acknowledged was an essential element in any effective mandate system—raised the constant peril of collision between the League and the mandatory power. Lloyd George, *The Truth About the Peace Treaties,* Vol. 1 at 554–57.

[45] Council of Ten, January 28, 1919, 11 a.m., *Foreign Relations, 1919, The Paris Peace Conference,* Vol. 3 at 749–50.

was, he said, not very different from the principles laid down by the
Berlin Conference which had also covered such subjects as the open
door and the prohibition on arms and liquor traffic. The only new
feature was the provision of external machinery for enforcement. With
regard to the Dominion requests, Lloyd George again asked the President to consider them as a special case.

Massey of New Zealand followed through with a dramatic presentation of the case for annexing Samoa. . . .

In the fourth meeting that afternoon, M. Simon, the French Minister for Colonies, in a lengthy memorandum, presented his country's
case for annexation.[48] It was obvious that Wilson was becoming more
and more isolated in his insistence upon universal application of the
mandates principle. Matters became very strained as the President observed that the discussions, so far, had been "a negation in detail—one
case at a time—of the whole principle of mandatories." "It looked," he
said, "as if their roads diverged." There was serious danger that the
Conference might reach an impasse before it had hardly begun. At this
point, Mr. Balfour, in an attempt to iron things out, sought to explain
to the President some of the difficulties which troubled the delegates.
One issue was the problem of League financing of mandated territories. Another was the question of permanency of tenure for the mandatory power. Wilson thereupon acknowledged that practical aspects of
the system had yet to be worked out, but that unless the "quality of
trusteeship was imparted to the League it would be reduced to a
'laughing stock'. The world would say that the Great Powers first portioned out the helpless parts of the world, and then formed a League
of Nations." He bade the delegates to agree on the principle and to
leave resolution of specific problems to the practical determination of
the League.[49]

This passionate plea by the President induced Orlando and Clemenceau to express reserved acceptance of the mandates principle on behalf of their respective countries. Both statesmen, however, acknowledged the merits of the Dominion claims and would allow annexation
in those cases. At this point, Clemenceau, in seeking to clarify the role
of the League in the mandates system, inquired whether the League's
authority over a mandatory power would not really constitute an exercise of legislative-executive power.[50] Lloyd George undertook to define
the true nature of the League's authority. Clemenceau's interpretation,
he said, was unwarranted. The system merely amounted to "general
trusteeship upon defined conditions." Only if conditions were scandal-
ously abused would the League call for an explanation and insist on a
remedy of the abuse. Hitherto diplomatic correspondence between the
Powers had fulfilled this function. Now it would be the task of the
League to ensure compliance.[51] President Wilson assented to this
definition; [52] and the form of the mandates system began to take
shape.

[48] Council of Ten, January 28, 1919, 4 p.m., *Foreign Relations, 1919, The
Paris Peace Conference,* Vol. 3, at 758–63.
[49] *Ibid.,* 765–67.   [50] *Ibid.,* 768–69.   [51] *Ibid.,* 769–70.   [52] *Ibid.,* 769.

Thereupon Lloyd George went a step further and, addressing himself to the President, asked that the selection of mandatories not be delayed. The Council of Ten was practically the League of Nations and acceptance of the principle of trusteeship would resolve the matter now.[53] As the end of the meeting approached, it appeared that a consensus on the mandates principle was being reached. Even Hughes and Massey seemed to be going along on the issue. But Lloyd George's request for immediate designation of the mandatories changed the whole atmosphere, and the previously developing consensus was shattered. President Wilson, as desirous as he was of gaining general acceptance of the mandates principle, was not prepared to settle and finalize the matter there and then; he rejected Lloyd George's request by stating that his difficulty lay in preventing the assignment of mandatories "from appearing to the world as a mere distribution of spoils." [54]

Lloyd George's drive to gain immediate confirmation of the mandatories went far beyond the "acceptance in principle" which the President had sought to achieve; in fact, it might have negated that very principle. The mandate territories would be delivered into the hands of the mandatory powers, free of any international obligations or controls. As one writer comments, "it amounted to the thinnest disguise of annexation. There was as yet no constitution for [Wilson's] League of Nations, much less any formal code of mandatory responsibilities." [55]

By the time the League would come into operation it would be confronted with entrenched powers ruling the new territories as fully annexed provinces of their own countries. The President was not prepared to acquiesce in any such arrangement merely on the basis of a vague pledge to the mandates cause. In fact, Wilson was so displeased and agitated over the course of the discussions, that he considered breaking up the negotiations on the colonial question and bringing the whole issue to the attention of the public.[56] Clearly, he was going to stand firm on the issue. Lloyd George, for one, recognized this only too clearly. His stratagem had failed badly. Apparently he had only been able to persuade the Dominion Ministers to join him in support of the mandates proposal at this session, in the belief that immediate endorsement of the principle would help resolve the whole matter; Wilson would get his mandates system, and the Dominions would still be free to assume full control in their respective territories. But Wilson had foiled the scheme and matters were back where they started.

The next morning, Wednesday, January 29, the Imperial War Cabinet met and "all hell broke loose." [57] Hughes, recognizing now that Wilson was unprepared to acquiesce in any vague arrangement which could amount to an immediate grant of title, free of obligation, reverted to his original demand for outright annexation for New Guinea. No matter what mandatory standards were adopted for other

[53] *Ibid.*, 770.   [54] *Ibid.*, 771.

[55] Paul Birdsall, *Versailles Twenty Years After* at 64 (1941).

[56] Phone conversation with Colonel House, January 28, 1919: see Seymour, *Intimate Papers of Colonel House,* Vol. 4, at 297.

[57] Paul Birdsall, *Versailles Twenty Years After* at 68 (1941).

areas, he was determined that Australia should receive its Pacific possessions unencumbered by international controls.

. . . .

Lloyd George warned his fellow cabinet members of the danger of a deadlock, with the possibility that President Wilson might leave the country before an agreement could be reached, and called upon them to endorse a draft resolution which had been worked out in the interval by General Smuts.[59]

The draft resolution was heavily predicated on the earlier British

---

[59] General Smuts, after formulating the draft resolution, had consulted with Colonel House who approved of the document as a "fair compromise": Seymour, *Intimate Papers of Colonel House,* Vol. IV, at 298. Parenthetically, it is noteworthy that Colonel House intimated in conversation with Lord Cecil (with Wiseman and Miller also present) that, if the Dominions would be willing to accept the colonies as mandates for the meanwhile, they would probably be able to annex them in a short time. In the light of subsequent developments this trend of thought is rather significant, more particularly since the idea is attributed to President Wilson. The accuracy of this House-Cecil conversation is confirmed from various sources. In a Wiseman Memorandom dated January 27, 1919, it is reported as follows: "House argues that the League of Nations must reserve the right to cancel the mandate in cases of gross mismanagement, but says the President would agree that the peoples concerned should be able at any time to vote themselves part of Australia and South Africa, thereby cancelling the mandate": Seymour, *Intimate Papers of Colonel House,* Vol. IV, at 294. In the House diary the concluding thought is expressed in the following manner: "I convinced him that it was best for Great Britain as a whole to take what we had proposed rather than what the Dominions proposed. The result I thought would be presumably the same and in the end the Mandatory Power would in a short time persuade the colony to annex itself": *ibid.,* 296. Similarly, in David Hunter Miller's diary the entry for January 27, 1919, reads: "Colonel House said . . . that the President's plan was that the Colonies should not go back to Germany but that they should be held by Australia, New Zealand, South Africa, Great Britain, France, etc., with a provision permitting them to be annexed when the inhabitants so wished. He thought this would result in annexation in a few years of good management." In a footnote, Miller comments: "This reads like a very free translation of the President's ideas": David Hunter Miller, *My Diary at the Conference of Paris,* Vol. 1, at 94, 341. Later in London, during the Milner Commission discussion on the Mandate Agreements, a draft C Mandate agreement was submitted on July 9 (origin not clear), which would have permitted the natives of a mandated territory to express a desire to be united to the mandatory Power and would have permitted incorporation of the Mandate into the territory of the mandatory Power. As a result of French opposition the proposal was not adopted: see *Conference de la Paix 1919–1920, Recueil des Actes de la Conference,* Partie 4B(1), at 354–56 (1934). The idea for such a proposal arose, no doubt, out of the discussions that had taken place at this stage of the Paris negotiations.

The Smuts resolution, with minor modifications, was ultimately adopted as Article 22 of the Covenant. . . . The text of the Smuts resolution may be found in Miller, *The Drafting of the Covenant,* Vol. 1, at 109–10; *Foreign Relations, 1919, The Paris Peace Conference,* Vol. 3 at 795–96; Lloyd George, *The Truth About the Peace Treaties,* Vol. 1, at 538–41.

Draft Convention, which in turn had been developed from the original Smuts plan. But in contrast to that plan, no explicit reference was made to the principle of self-determination, nor was the League classified as the ultimate reversionary. The purpose of the Mandates was couched in broad general terms. As a compromise proposal it was designed, on the one hand, to meet the President's demands by defining specific international obligations to be assumed by the mandatory power. On the other hand, it would not impose a uniform set of standards upon all mandatories indiscriminately. The degree of obligation would vary in accordance with the type of mandate. Three categories of mandates were designated, depending upon the stage of development attained. The first, covering the territories severed from the Turkish Empire, were deemed to have reached a stage of provisional independence, so that the rule of the mandatory power would be limited to "the rendering of administrative advice and assistance" [60] until such time as the mandate would be able to stand alone. The second category, made up of former German colonies in Central Africa, would require the mandatory to be responsible for administration, subject to conditions guaranteeing preservation of the open door as well as prohibition of the slave trade, traffic in arms and liquor, militarization and fortification. The third group, consisting of such territories as South West Africa and the islands of the South Pacific were, "owing to the sparseness of their population, or their small size, or their remoteness from the centers of civilization" to be "administered under the laws of the mandatory state as integral portions thereof subject to the safeguards above mentioned in the interests of the indigenous population." [61]

Despite the fact that the gradations within the mandates system were attributed primarily to the different stages of development attained by the respective territories, it is obvious that they reflected, more significantly, different degrees of national interest in annexing the territories concerned. Thus, an inverse relationship existed between national interest in annexation and the measure of international involvement to be introduced. In the case of the Class C mandates, the Dominions' interest in annexation would result in a minimal measure of obligation to the international community of states and maximal concession to national authority. The principle of international accountability, however, was to be retained throughout.

Lloyd George told the Dominion Ministers that "if they persisted in asking for more than this compromise, they must go on without the help of the British government with all that this implied." [62] The Australian Prime Minister was still deeply dissatisfied; he felt that Australia's security was imperilled. Lloyd George devoted considerable efforts

[60] Clause 6.
[61] Clause 8. The principal obligation omitted from the Class C group was the open door requirement. Most writers credit General Smuts with exclusive authorship of this compromise resolution.
[62] Ernest Scott, *Australia During the War*, in XI *The Official History of Australia in the War of 1914–1918* at 784 (1936).

to convincing him that a Class C mandate for New Guinea was tantamount to Australian ownership of the island, subject only to certain conditions on behalf of the natives.[63] Finally, Mr. Hughes asked: "Is this the equivalent of a 999 years' lease as compared with a freehold?" Assured that it was, Hughes notified Lloyd George in writing of his acceptance of the draft, and the British Prime Minister prepared to present it to the Conference the next morning, Thursday, January 30.[64]

At this fifth meeting, Lloyd George introduced the Smuts resolution by noting that although it did not represent the "real views" of the Dominions, "they had agreed to this compromise rather than face the catastrophe of a break-up." [65]

In reply, President Wilson indicated that he considered it a very gratifying paper. He was prepared to accept it "as a precursor of agreement, [but] it did not constitute a rock foundation, as the League of Nations had not yet been fixed, on which this superstructure should rest. What would [a mandate] involve? No one could . . . answer. . . . In every instance the mandate should fit the case as the glove fits the hand." [66]

The President was obviously not going to be pressured. He had defeated Lloyd George's original thrust for distributing mandates free of international commitment. Nor was he now willing to accede to an immediate allotment merely because certain international obligations had been spelled out in the mandates draft. In his eyes, the Smuts plan was rather more in the nature of a working paper than a finalized document. Clearly, in the President's view, neither the list of mandatory powers nor the terms upon which they would assume their mandates had been really determined. This spelt particular "danger" for the vague obligations referred to in Clause 8, dealing with Class C mandates.

Mindful of the apprehensions of the Dominion Ministers, Lloyd George remarked that the words of the President "filled him with despair." He candidly admitted that only with the greatest difficulty had the Ministers been prevailed upon to accept the Smuts draft, even provisonally; postponement of the mandates issue until the League was established would signify that no final decision could ever be reached on this or any other question; he strongly appealed for provisional acceptance of the resolution.[67]

---

[63] In the course of the discussion this dialogue resulted. Lloyd George: "Did Mr. Hughes object to the prohibition of both slavery and the sale of strong drink to the natives?" No, Mr. Hughes did not object. "Are you prepared to receive missionaries?" "Of course," replied Hughes, "the natives are very short of food and for some time past they have not had enough missionaries to eat." See *Lord Riddell's Intimate Diary of the Peace Conference and After, 1918–1923*, at 17 (1933). . . .

[64] Ernest Scott, *op. cit. supra* note 62, at 784.

[65] *Ibid.*, 541; Council of Ten, January 30, 1919, 11 a.m. *Foreign Relations, 1919, The Paris Peace Conference*, Vol. 3, at 785–94.

[66] Council of Ten, *op. cit. supra*, 788–89.   [67] *Ibid.*, 789–90.

In response, Wilson agreed to accept the Smuts scheme as a provisional arrangement, with the League acting as a final court of appeal on this as on other issues.[68] This was a significant concession on the part of the President to meet Lloyd George's wishes.

Hughes, however, was not satisfied. Provisional acceptance did not by any means amount to a definite confirmation of the mandates on the limited terms outlined in the plan. He wanted this Conference—which amounted to a *de facto* League—to act as an executive and assign the mandates. What settlement was there, he asked, if all they knew was that "the arrangements would be such that the scheme would fit like a glove to the hand?" Hughes and Wilson were fast moving to a showdown.

That afternoon matters came to a head in a sharp clash. Massey of New Zealand was the first to speak. He cited the specific international obligations which related to Class C mandates and called upon the President to confirm that this would be the sum total of obligation. Basically, said Massey, he favoured annexation; but if he were to accept the Smuts plan, he at least awaited a clear word from the President on the finality of Clause 8.[69] This statement by Massey provoked the President to anger. He demanded to know whether New Zealand and Australia had presented an ultimatum to the Conference; was he to understand the Clause 8 was the most that they were prepared to concede "and if that was not conceded definitely now, they could not take part in any agreement at all?" At this peremptory challenge, Massey backed down somewhat and indicated that he had not meant anything in the nature of an ultimatum. Hughes, however, remained quite undismayed. He did not hear the question clearly and the President repeated it to him in the following terms, "And do you mean Mr. Hughes that in certain circumstances Australia would place herself in opposition to the whole civilized world?"; to which Hughes replied, "Very well put, Mr. President, you have guessed it. That's just so!" [70]

At this critical juncture, Botha of South Africa delivered an eloquent address appealing to both sides to strive toward "the higher ideal." He expressed appreciation of the ideals of President Wilson, which, he said, "were the ideals of the people of the world," and which would succeed.

> Personally he felt very strongly about the question of German South West Africa. He thought that it differed entirely from any question they had to decide in this conference, but he would be prepared to say that he was a supporter of the document handed in that morning, because he knew that, if the idea fructified, the League of Nations would consist mainly of the same people who were present

---

[68] *Ibid.*, 791.

[69] Council of Ten, January 30, 1919, 3:30 p.m., *Foreign Relations, 1919, The Paris Peace Conference*, Vol. 3 at 797–802; Miller, *The Drafting of the Covenant*, Vol. 2 at 206–15; Lloyd George, *The Truth About the Peace Treaties*, Vol. 1 at 542–46.

[70] Ernest Scott, *op. cit. supra* note 62, at 786, n. 56.

there that day, who understood the position and who would not make it impossible for any mandatory to govern the country. That was why he said he would accept it.

He called for a spirit of co-operation and compromise and sincerely hoped that the President would see fit to support Lloyd George's resolution which was the result of long and serious efforts.[71] Botha's conciliatory speech made a deep and memorable impression upon the President,[72] and the situation eased considerably.

Matters now moved rapidly toward agreement. Massey offered renewed assurances that he had not implied anything in the nature of a threat. Lloyd George then modified his earlier request that the President accept the Smuts resolution at once without qualification, and so commit himself to immediate distribution of the mandates upon the terms specified. Instead, he now proposed that this be taken as a provisional decision "subject to the right of reconsideration if the Covenant of the League as finally drafted did not fit in." [73] No formal vote was taken on the resolution, but at the suggestion of President Wilson it was agreed that a communique be issued stating that the Conference had arrived at a satisfactory provisional arrangement with regard to dealing with the German and Turkish territory outside Europe.[74] Implicitly, then, it was agreed that the Dominions would receive the territores in question as Class C mandates upon the terms specified.

At a subsequent meeting early in May, President Wilson confirmed that the tacit arrangement had settled the matter "to all intents and purposes . . . the mandate for German South-West Africa should be given to South Africa, for New Guinea and the adjacent islands to Australia, for Samoa to New Zealand." [75] A formal resolution presented by Great Britain confirming these and the other mandates was adopted and published (with minor changes) on May 7, 1919.[76]

IV

Wilson's acceptance of the Class C compromise in the Council of Ten ensured that the principle of international accountability would have universal application in the post-war colonial settlement. This

---

[71] Council of Ten, January 30, 1919, 3:30 p.m., *Foreign Relations, 1919, The Paris Peace Conference,* Vol. 3, at 800–02. South Africa repeatedly cited Botha's statement in the pleadings on the South West Africa case, as an indication of the restricted nature of the commitment undertaken by South Africa: see 1 *South West Africa Case—I.C.J. Pleadings* 222 (1966) (hereinafter cited as *SWA Pleadings*).

[72] Lloyd George, *The Truth About the Peace Treaties,* Vol. 1, at 546.

[73] *Ibid.,* 546; Council of Ten, January 30, 1919, 3:30 p.m. *Foreign Relations, 1919, The Paris Peace Conference,* Vol. 3, at 802; Miller, *The Drafting of the Covenant,* Vol. 2, at 215. . . .

[74] Council of Ten, *Foreign Relations, 1919, The Paris Peace Conference,* Vol. 3, at 816.

[75] Council of Four, May 5, 1919, 11 a.m., *Foreign Relations, 1919, The Paris Peace Conference,* Vol. 5, at 472–73. . . .

[76] Council of Four, May 7, 1919, 4:15 p.m., *ibid.,* 507–08.

principle was confirmed for even the most backward areas of the globe, with no exceptions allowed for considerations of contiguity, security, common economic interest or advantages of administrative unity. In this respect the mandates system represented a new creation of a genre previously unknown in international relations. As Beer records in Temperley, "The experience of the past affords no counterpart to the Mandatory System. . . . What sharply distinguishes the Mandate System from all such international arrangements of the past, is the unqualified right of intervention possessed by the League of Nations." [77] All previous commitments undertaken by states with reference to colonial areas simply amounted to pious declarations of intention. There was no set procedure or form for checking on violations of the commitments, and only other states, parties to the original agreement, were individually entitled under international law to raise the matter with the offending state. The mandates system was unique in that it associated defined standards in international law with a continuing international organization which acted on behalf of the world community to ensure that these standards were faithfully observed.

The compromise agreement firmly established the principle of international accountability, but the question remained to what extent had it actually incorporated the principle of self-determination and how far had it gone in barring future annexation of the respective territories.

The compromise document itself did not (in contrast to previous formulations) enunciate the principle of self-determination in any clear or categorical terms. It certainly did not postulate independence as the definite goal of all mandates. Only paragraph 4 contained a reference to independence, by describing the A mandates as having "reached a stage of development where their existence as independent nations can be provisionally recognized." Otherwise, the purpose or design of the mandates system was dealt with in a series of broad rhetorical and imprecise phrases, such as: "peoples not yet able to stand by themselves"; "the well-being and development of such peoples form a sacred trust of civilization"; "securities for the performance of this trust," and so on. Nor was the provision in the Class C mandates allowing administration as "integral portions of [the Mandatory's] territory" clearly defined. It was evident that the draftsman had purposely avoided using any precise legal language for fear that too much or too little might be committed. The vague phraseology allowed for a variety of different, and even conflicting, interpretations. Whereas to some it represented a pledge to promote self-government for all peoples, black as well as white, to others it merely instituted a more effective device for protecting the native welfare from specific abuses. The latter restricted concept of the mandates system was frequently expressed by Lloyd George during meetings of the Council of Ten. In his view it would not amount to much more than the international obligations already incumbent upon colonial powers as a result of earlier international trea-

[77] Temperley, *op. cit. supra* note 1, Vol. 2, at 236.

ties. He did not consider that involvement of the League would very radically affect the colonial set-up; in fact, he frequently declared that the mandates system was already basically in effect in British colonial practice, with its enlightened outlook regarding native welfare. The final version of Article 22 did nothing to clarify the matter since the ambiguous phraseology was faithfully preserved throughout all discussions.

The compromise document accepted provisionally on January 30, 1919, was taken up on February 8 by the Commission on the League of Nations for insertion in the Covenant.[79] The draft introduced by General Smuts was identical with the text of the compromise document, except for the elimination of two introductory paragraphs and the addition of two supplementary paragraphs at the end. The latter two were what later became paragraphs 8 and 9 of Article 22. The first of these paragraphs empowered the League Council to define "the degree of authority, control, or administration" of the Mandatory if this was not "previously agreed upon by the High Contracting Parties." [80] The second paragraph provided for the establishment of "a Mandatory Commission to receive and examine the annual reports . . . and to assist the League in ensuring the observance of the terms of all Mandates." [81]

The deliberations in the Commission on the League of Nations reveal that Wilson and the British Empire delegates were primarily con-

[79] See Miller, *Drafting of the Covenant,* Vol. I, at 185–90; Vol. II, at 271–76.

[80] *Ibid.,* 275. Subsequently, the terms, "High Contracting Parties" was replaced by "Members of the League"; *ibid.,* 680. Whether or not this change signified a substantive change in meaning was an issue of major contention in the subsequent 1962 and 1966 Judgments.

[81] Miller, *Drafting of the Covenant,* II, 275. The latter part of this draft provision was retained intact throughout all the readings of the Covenant, but was changed by Hurst and Miller in the text which they presented to the Drafting Committee on March 31, 1919, to read: "and to advise the Council on all matters relating to the observance of the mandates" (the final form). No explanation is given for this substitution; but by its terms the revised text modifies the power of the Commission and tones down the spirit of compulsion in supervision, which the previous version seemed to reflect. This writer has not found any reference to the significance of this modification in any of the judgments or separate opinions in the 1962 or 1966 *South West Africa Cases,* nor in the extensive pleadings in the case. Curiously enough, South Africa even while adverting to the text of the relevant basic instruments as evidence against the alleged authority of the supervisory body to set binding standards for the administration of the mandate (see, e.g., *SWA Pleadings,* IX, 591–597), failed to make anything of the above-mentioned drafting change (or even to make any reference at all to paragraph 9 of Article 22).

In any event, the modification in wording would appear to lend some weight to the view of the 1966 Court that the idea of compulsion was quite alien to the constitution and operation of the mandate system, and would tend to confirm the view of that Court, that the provision for an adjudicatory clause in the Mandates was not designed to impart compulsory supervisory power to the Court.

cerned with one thing—preserving intact both the substance and form of the compromise agreement concluded in the Council of Ten. When Mr. Orlando and Mr. Bourgeois suggested certain amendments to the text, President Wilson (supported by Lord Cecil) emphasized that General Smut's text was based upon a decision of the Conference of the Five Powers.[82] The only significant (if small) changes that were accepted were designed to restore the original compromise to its exact earlier text. The word "yet" which Smuts had now dropped from the phrase "peoples not *yet* able to stand for themselves" was reinserted.[83] And the word "if" which Smuts had now included into the phrase "as *if* integral portions" (of the Mandatory's territory) was dropped from the Class C paragraph, since it was said that it had not figured there in the original agreement and, in effect, modified it.[84] At the same time, an amendment proposed by Mr. Vesnitch, the Serbian representative, designed expressly to facilitate the complete emancipation of the mandated peoples and their admission to the League was not accepted.[85]

The Commission was obviously not prepared to accept any changes which would either strengthen or weaken the ideals incorporated in the text or that might even attempt to spell them out. The vague general ideals enunciated in the compromise agreement satisfied all parties and it would be a precarious undertaking to introduce any modifications. As Smuts is reported to have said to Makino, "If you pull out a single plank, the whole edifice, miserable as it is, will come crashing down." [86] This warning was heeded by the Commission and the compromise document was confirmed.

In summary, then, Article 22 of the League of Nations Convenant establishing the mandates system passed through the following stages until it reached its final form in 1919. In early 1918, Wilson and Lloyd George postulated the principle of self-determination in the settlement of the colonial problem. They did not, however, link that principle with the proposed League, and so the concept of international account-

[82] *Ibid.*, Vol. II, at 272.   [83] *Ibid.*, 306.   [84] *Ibid.*, Vol. I, at 190; Vol. II at 273.
[85] *Ibid.*, Vol. I, at 188–90; Vol. II, at 273. The text of the amendment read as follows: "The Mandatory Commission may also, when it shall deem the time proper, suggest that the independence of any such people may be proclaimed and recognized with a view to the eventual admission of such people as a member of the League": *ibid.*, Vol. I at 188.
[86] Stephen Bonsal, *Unfinished Business* 36 (1944). Bonsal's is the only verbatim record of that meeting in existence, since Miller's record merely presents the minutes. According to Bonsal, Smuts, in presenting the mandates draft article, apologized for the ambiguity and lack of clarity, saying, "We admit that the original purpose with which we set out upon our task is not easily recognizable, but upon patient scrutiny you will find that it is there and that while it may not be an ideal solution, it is, I can assure you, the best that your delegates will agree to at this juncture in world history": *ibid.*, 35. Bonsal notes that Wilson was quite pleased with Smuts' performance: "He is not so insistent now upon details as he was a few weeks ago. He is pinning his faith to the cooling-off influences of time and the interpretive work of the League": *ibid.* 36.

ability was not yet born. Smuts and Beer did, however, link self-determination with a going world-organization, and proposed a system of mandates to be supervised by the League. Theirs was the first clear enunciation of the principle of international accountability. Smuts, however, (and Beer to an extent,) did not regard the system as one of-universal application. Smuts, in fact, expressly excluded the African colonies from the proposed mandates system, since he considered the inhabitants of those territories completely remote from the exercise of self-determination. Wilson adopted the Smuts plan, but universalized it—with confirmation of the principle of self-determination for even the most backward colony. Smuts and the other Dominion ministers then recognized that they could not obtain their respective territories totally free of international obligations. But if the mandates principle was to be universalized, it would have to have a variable content with a graded system of mandates, in which the Class C mandate would be as close to annexation as one can go without formal annexation. Moreover, the goals and purposes would have to be so worded that for the Class A mandates independence would be assured, whilst for the Class C mandates a process of ultimate absorption into the metropolitan country would be envisaged. This meant that the mandates article could no longer postulate the principle of self-determination as a definitive goal. The earlier reference to self-determination would have to be omitted. A skilfully drafted document, which was to imply different things for different situations, was what finally emerged as Article 22. Starting off with self-determination without international accountability, it had finished up as international accountability without self-determination (as an express goal).

Article 22 had gone through a process, aptly described by Hudson, as one in which "it is sometimes less profitable to seek clarity than to arrive at acceptable ambiguity." [87] The resultant wording could satisfy annexationists and internationalists simultaneously; indeed, this was its purpose. As a result, to Hughes, Australia was obtaining a 999 year lease on New Guinea; [88] and to Smuts, "in effect the relations between the South-West Protectorate and the Union amount to annexation in all but name"; [89] whilst to President Wilson the mandates system represented the universal application of a principle . . . of Colonies

[87] Manley O. Hudson, *The Permanent Court of International Justice, 1920–1942*, at 229 (1943).

[88] See *supra*. In a memorandum dated May 5, 1919 to Colonel House, Hughes, referring to the differences between the various Mandates, said: "Whereas a Mandate under Class 1 looks to the mandated country being ultimately 'able to stand alone', the Mandate under Class 3 provides for the mandated territory being administered as an 'integral portion of the territory' of the Mandatory, and looks to its ultimate incorporation by the free will of its inhabitants"; see David Hunter Miller, *Diary*, Doc. 936.

[89] *P.M.C., Min.,* Annex 6, at 92 (1922). In similar vein, Lord Balfour subsequently referred to mandates as "self imposed limitations by the conquerors on the sovereignty which they obtained over conquered territory": cited in Quincy Wright, *op. cit. supra* note 1, at 62 n. 115.

[being] lifted into the sphere of complete self-government." [90] It was this divergency of interpretation that laid the groundwork for the subsequent South West Africa dispute.

THE MANDATES SYSTEM [f]

1. Article 22 of the Covenant of the League

1. To those colonies and territories which as a consequence of the late war have ceased to be under the sovereignty of the States which formerly governed them and which are inhabited by peoples not yet able to stand by themselves under the strenuous conditions of the modern world, there should be applied the principle that the well-being and development of such peoples form a sacred trust of civilization and that securities for the performance of this trust should be embodied in this Covenant.

2. The best method of giving practical effect to this principle is that the tutelage of such peoples should be entrusted to advanced nations who, by reason of their resources, their experience or their geographi-

[f] See, generally, Quincy Wright, *Mandates under the League of Nations;* N. Bentwich, *The Mandates System* (1930); E. van Maanen-Helmer, *The Mandates System in Relation to Africa and the Pacific Islands* (1929); N. Macaulay, *Mandates* (1937); F. White, *Mandates* (1926); J. C. Hales, "The Creation and Application of the Mandate System" (1939) 25 *Transactions of the Grotius Society* 185; H. Duncan Hall, *Mandates, Dependencies and Trusteeship* (1948); R. N. Chowdhuri, *International Mandates and Trusteeship Systems* (1955).

[90] Plenary Sess., February 14, 1919, *Foreign Relations, 1919, The Paris Peace Conference,* Vol. 3 at 214. See also Miller, *Drafting of the Covenant,* Vol. II, at 564. At a subsequent meeting of the Council of Four, Wilson said: "The whole theory of mandates is not the theory of permanent subordination. It is the theory of development, of putting upon the mandatory the duty of assisting in the development of the country under mandate, in order that it may be brought to a capacity for self-government and self-dependence, which for the time being it has not reached, and that therefore the countries under mandate are candidates, so to say, for full membership in the family of nations": Council of Four, May 17, 1919, 4:30 p.m., *Foreign Relations, 1919, The Paris Peace Conference,* Vol. 5 at 700.

Notwithstanding the thesis presented in the text regarding the nature of the mandates compromise ultimately worked out, it may be noted that Smuts is reported by Bonsal to have presented the compromise to the Conference in the following very Wilsonian terms: "If you give your sanction to our work you will demonstrate that world public opinion is in favor of the ultimate self-government of all peoples, without distinction as to race, religion, or color, or previous condition of servitude. It also provides for a careful supervision and scrutiny as to the way in which the mandates are exercised." *Op. cit.,* p. 35. Remarkably enough, Ethiopia and Liberia, in presenting their case against the application of apartheid to South West Africa before the International Court in the *South West Africa Cases,* made no reference to the foregoing statement.

cal position, can best undertake this responsibility, and who are willing to accept it, and that this tutelage should be exercised by them as Mandatories on behalf of the League.

3. The character of the mandate must differ according to the stage of the development of the people, the geographical situation of the territory, its economic conditions and other similar circumstances.

4. Certain communities formerly belonging to the Turkish Empire have reached a stage of development where their existence as independent nations can be provisionally recognized subject to the rendering of administrative advice and assistance by a Mandatory until such time as they are able to stand alone. The wishes of these communities must be a principal consideration in the selection of the Mandatory.

5. Other peoples, especially those of Central Africa, are at such a stage that the Mandatory must be responsible for the administration of the territory under conditions which will guarantee freedom of conscience and religion, subject only to the maintenance of public order and morals, the prohibition of abuses such as the slave trade, the arms traffic and the liquor traffic, and the prevention of the establishment of fortifications or military and naval bases and of military training of the natives for other than police purposes and the defence of territory, and will also secure equal opportunities for the trade and commerce of other members of the League.

6. There are territories, such as South West Africa and certain of the South Pacific islands, which, owing to the sparseness of their population or their small size, or their remoteness from the centers of civilization, or their geographical contiguity to the territory of the Mandatory, and other circumstances, can be best administered under the laws of the Mandatory as integral portions of its territory, subject to the safeguards above mentioned in the interests of the indigenous population.

7. In every case of mandate, the Mandatory shall render to the Council an annual report in reference to the territory committed to its charge.

8. The degree of authority, control or administration to be exercised by the Mandatory shall, if not previously agreed upon by the Members of the League, be explicitly defined in each case by the Council.

9. A permanent Commission shall be constituted to receive and examine the annual reports of the Mandatories, and to advise the Council on all matters relating to the observance of the mandates.

2. *The Establishment of the System*

Article 22 of the Covenant of the League contemplated the division of the mandated territories into three classes, A (referred to in Article 22 [4]), B (22 [5]) and C(22 [6]). The "A" Mandates and their mandatories (in parentheses) were: Iraq (Great Britain); Palestine and Transjordan (Great Britain); Syria and Lebanon (France). The "B" Mandates and their mandatories were: British Cameroons (Great Britain); French Cameroons (France); British Togoland (Great Britain); French Togoland (France); Tanganyika (Great Britain); Ruanda Urundi (Belgium). The "C" Mandates and their mandatories were: South West Africa (Union of South Africa); Samoa (New Zealand); Nauru (Great Britain, Australia, and New Zealand jointly); other Pacific Islands south of the Equator (Australia); Pacific Islands north of the Equator (Japan). The manner in which mandatories were appointed is described in the League of Nations publication, *The Mandates System*.[g]

Article 22 of the Covenant did not specify which the mandatory Powers were to be or how the mandated territories were to be distributed between them. These points were decided by the Supreme Council of the Allied Powers.

The German colonies in Africa and the Pacific were handed over, not to the League of Nations, but to the Principal Allied and Associated Powers. According to Article 119 of the Treaty of Versailles, "Germany renounces in favour of the Principal Allied and Associated Powers all her rights and titles over her overseas possessions". Article 132 of the Treaty of Sèvres of 1920 contained a similar clause whereby Turkey renounced in favour of the Principal Allied and Associated Powers all rights and titles over her territories outside Europe "which are not otherwise disposed of by the present Treaty". As a result, however, of subsequent events, the Treaty of Sèvres never came into force; it was replaced by the Treaty of Lausanne of July 24th, 1923. Under Article 16 of the latter Treaty, Turkey renounced all rights and title over the territories situated outside the frontiers recognised and laid down in this Treaty. Article 16 also provided that the future of such territories was being or would be settled by the parties concerned.

Thus, under the terms of the Treaties of Peace, it was for the Supreme Council of the Allied Powers, and not the League of Nations, to select the mandatory Powers.

On May 7th, 1919, the Supreme Council took the following decisions on this subject:

It allotted the Mandates for *Togoland* and the *Cameroons* to France and Great Britain, requesting them to present a joint recommendation regarding the status of these territories to the League of Nations.[1] The Mandate for *German East Africa* (Tanganyika Territory) was allotted to Great Britain, that for *South West Africa* to the Union of South Af-

[g] Series of League of Nations Publications VI. A. Mandates 1945, pp. 18–21.
[1] An Agreement regarding the delimitation of the portions of the Cameroons and of Togoland under British and French Mandates respectively was concluded between France and Great Britain on July 10th, 1919, and communicated to the League of Nations.

rica, that for *Western Samoa* to New Zealand, and that for the Island of *Nauru* to the British Empire [2]; the other German possessions in the Pacific south of the Equator (that is to say, *German New Guinea* and the adjacent islands) were allotted to Australia, and the *German islands north of the Equator* to Japan. As a result of subsequent negotiations, the north-western part of Tanganyika Territory (the provinces of *Ruanda* and *Urundi*) was placed under Belgian Mandate by a decision of the Supreme Council dated August 21st, 1919.

The Mandatories for Syria, Palestine and Mesopotamia (Iraq) were designated by the Supreme Council at San Remo on April 25th, 1920. France was entrusted with the administration of *Syria* and Great Britain with that of *Palestine* and *Iraq*.

Though the League of Nations played no part in the designation of the mandatory Powers, it was the League which, by means of a series of legal instruments, specified the degree of authority, supervision or administration to be exercised by the selected Mandatories. These "charters", drawn up in respect of each of the territories, specified the conditions governing the various mandates and to be observed by the Mandatories.

According to Article 22 of the Covenant, "the degree of authority, control or administration to be exercised by the Mandatory shall, if not previously agreed upon by the Members of the League, be explicitly defined in each case by the Council". The interpretation and application of this clause gave rise to some difficulty. It would seem that the authors of the Covenant had at first intended to insert the terms of the mandates in the Treaties of Peace; this idea was, however, subsequently abandoned. In July 1919, a Committee composed of experts in colonial questions belonging to the Principal Allied and Associated Powers met in London, under the chairmanship of Lord Milner, in order to frame the charters for the mandated territories in Africa and the Pacific; no agreement, however, was reached because some of the Governments concerned had made important reservations.

Subsequently, the Principal Allied and Associated Powers submitted to the Council a number of draft mandates which the latter adopted with slight amendments, after satisfying itself that they were in conformity with the terms of the Covenant.

In this way, the Council on December 17th, 1920, confirmed the mandates for South West Africa, New Guinea, Nauru, Samoa and the Islands north of the Equator (the "C" Mandates).

With regard, however, to the remaining African mandates (the "B" Mandates) and the mandates for the Near-Eastern territories (the "A" Mandates), which were to have been confirmed in February 1921, a considerable delay occurred, owing chiefly to the

[2] The administration of the Island of Nauru was entrusted to the Governments of the United Kingdom, Australia and New Zealand. These three Governments handed over the administration of the island to the Australian Governmemt for the first five years, but had to come to an agreement in regard to all fundamental questions. The arrangement made with the Australian Government has since been several times renewed.

intervention of the United States. During its session in February 1921, in fact, the Council received a note from the Government of that country requesting that the draft mandates should first be communicated to it for consideration. The Council, which, before the receipt of the communication from the United States Government, had already postponed examination of the draft "A" Mandates, decided also to defer consideration of the draft "B" Mandates, in order to comply with the wishes of that Government. In the course of the following eighteen months negotiations took place between the United States and the various mandatory Powers regarding the terms of these mandates.

Finally, on July 20th, 1922, the various mandatory Powers and the United States having in the meantime reached agreement, the Mandates for the Cameroons, Togoland, Tanganyika, Ruanda-Urundi (the "B" Mandates) were confirmed by the Council and at once came into force.

The two Mandates for Palestine and Transjordan and for Syria and Lebanon were approved by the Council a few days later, on July 24th, 1922, subject to the proviso that they should not come into force until the French and Italian Governments should have notified the President of the Council that the negotiations proceeding between them regarding certain special points of the Mandate for Syria had been concluded and complete agreement reached. On September 29th, 1923, the representatives of France and Italy announced that this agreement had been reached and the Council noted that the mandates for Syria and Lebanon and for Palestine and Transjordan would in consequence enter into force automatically and at the same time.

A variety of causes delayed the confirmation and entry into force of the mandate for Iraq for several years. The British Government, which, in 1920, had submitted to the Council a draft mandate, announced on November 17th, 1921, through its representative on the Council that political developments in Iraq—the people of which had manifested a desire to have a national Government under an Arab ruler—had led them to the conclusion that their obligations vis-à-vis the League could be most effectively discharged if the principles on which they rested were embodied in a Treaty to be concluded between Great Britain and the King of Iraq. This Treaty was concluded on October 10th, 1922, and communicated to the League of Nations. It was supplemented by a Protocol signed on April 30th, 1923, and by four subsidiary agreements dated March 25th, 1924. These instruments were summarised and supplemented by the mandatory Government in a communication defining its own obligations towards the League of Nations with regard to the application of Article 22 of the Covenant. On September 27th, 1924, the Council approved the terms of this communication as giving effect to the provisions of Article 22 of the Covenant. A similar decision was taken by the Council on March 11th, 1926, respecting a new Treaty concluded between the mandatory Power and Iraq on January 13th, 1926.

In the last place, in order to ensure the working of the mandates system, the Commission contemplated by paragraph 9 of the Article 22 of the covenant had to be constituted. On December 1st, 1920, after prolonged discussion, the Council approved the constitution of the Permanent Mandates Commission, which has undergone no essential modification since that time. The members of the Commission were appointed on February 22nd, 1921, and the Commission held its first meeting on October 4th, 1921.

3. *The Mandate for South West Africa*

The Council of the League of Nations:

Whereas by Article 119 of the Treaty of Peace with Germany signed at Versailles on 28 June, 1919, Germany renounced in favour of the Principal Allied and Associated Powers all her rights over her oversea possessions, including therein German South West Africa; and

Whereas the Principal Allied and Associated Powers agreed that, in accordance with Article 22, Part 1 (Covenant of the League of Nations) of the said Treaty, a Mandate should be conferred upon His Britannic Majesty to be exercised on his behalf by the Government of the Union of South Africa to administer the territory aforementioned, and have proposed that the Mandate should be formulated in the following terms; and

Whereas His Britannic Majesty, for and on behalf of the Government of the Union of South Africa, has agreed to accept the Mandate in respect of the said territory and has undertaken to exercise it on behalf of the League of Nations in accordance with the following provisions; and

Whereas by the aforementioned Article 22, paragraph 8, it is provided that the degree of authority, control or administration to be exercised by the Mandatory, not having been previously agreed upon by the Members of the League, shall be explicitly defined by the Council of the League of Nations:

Confirming the said Mandate, defines its terms as follows:

Article 1

The Territory over which a Mandate is conferred upon His Britannic Majesty for and on behalf of the Government of the Union of South Africa (hereinafter called the Mandatory) comprises the territory which formerly constituted the German Protectorate of South West Africa.

Article 2

The Mandatory shall have full power of administration and legislation over the territory subject to the present Mandate as an integral portion of the Union of South Africa, and may apply the laws of the Union of South Africa to the territory subject to such local modifications as circumstances may require.

The Mandatory shall promote to the utmost the material and moral well-being and the social progress of the inhabitants of the Territory subject to the present Mandate.

Article 3

The Mandatory shall see that the slave trade is prohibited and that no forced labour is permitted, except for essential public works and services, and then only for adequate remuneration.

The Mandatory shall also see that the traffic in arms and ammunition is controlled in accordance with principles analogous to those laid down in the Convention relating to the control of the arms traffic signed on 10 September, 1919, or in any Convention amending the same.

The supply of intoxicating spirits and beverages to the natives shall be prohibited.

Article 4

The military training of the natives, otherwise than for purposes of internal police and the local defence of the territory, shall be prohibited. Furthermore, no military or naval base shall be established or fortifications erected in the territory.

Article 5

Subject to the provisions of any local law for the maintenance of public order and public morals, the Mandatory shall ensure in the territory freedom of conscience and the free exercise of all forms of worship, and shall allow all missionaries, nationals of any State Member of the League of Nations, to enter into, travel and reside in the territory for the purpose of prosecuting their calling.

Article 6

The Mandatory shall make to the Council of the League of Nations an annual report to the satisfaction of the Council, containing full information with regard to the territory, and indicating the measures taken to carry out the obligations assumed under Articles 2, 3, 4 and 5.

Article 7

The consent of the Council of the League of Nations is required for any modification of the terms of the present Mandate.

The Mandatory agrees that, if any dispute whatever should arise between the Mandatory and another Member of the League of Nations relating to the interpretation or the application of the provisions of the Mandate, such dispute, if it cannot be settled by negotiation, shall be submitted to the Permanent Court of International Justice provided for by Article 14 of the Covenant of the League of Nations.

The present Declaration shall be deposited in the archives of the League of Nations. Certified copies shall be forwarded by the Secretary-General of the League of Nations to all Powers Signatories of the Treaty of Peace with Germany.

Made at Geneva on the 17th day of December, 1920.

4

South West Africa Under the League of Nations, 1920–1946

It is not the aim of this chapter to provide a comprehensive account of the history of South West Africa during the League of Nations period. For this purpose the reader should consult one of the general studies of South West African history.[a] Attention is focused only on two issues which relate to the subsequent dispute between South Africa and the United Nations, namely the debate over the nature of South Africa's legal title to the territory, and the treatment of the native population.

THE NATURE OF SOUTH AFRICA'S LEGAL TITLE

Neither the mandate agreements nor Article 22 of the Covenant of the League of Nations defined the exact legal nature of a mandatory's powers or dealt with the location of sovereignty in respect of mandated territories. This resulted in several theories being advanced by international lawyers, which are briefly described by Francis B. Sayre:[b]

[a] For example, Goldblatt, *History of South West Africa*, Part III; Wellington, *South West Africa and Its Human Issues*, pp. 270–320; C. Dundas, *South-West Africa: The Factual Background* (1946); L. H. Wessels, *Die Mandaat vir Suidwes-Afrika* (1938).
[b] "Legal Problems arising from the United Nations Trusteeship System" (1948) 42 *AJIL* 263 at 268–70. For a more detailed discussion of these theories, see Wright, *Mandates under the League of Nations*, pp. 319–39.

One of the most perplexing legal questions arising out of the mandates system was that of the location of sovereignty of the territories under mandate. It has been the subject of extended treatment by writers on international law.

The difficulty of assigning a precise locus of sovereignty for the mandated territories arose because of the unique character of the mandates system itself which departed widely from accustomed patterns. The mandates system involved an inter-relationship of (a) the Principal Allied and Associated Powers, which allocated the territories to be placed under mandate among the several Mandatory Powers; (b) the League of Nations, which exercised supervisory functions with respect to the mandates; and (c) the Mandatory Powers, which were the states actually administering the mandated territories. Since with respect to the mandated territories all three of these exercised certain powers usually attributed to sovereignty which had been formerly exercised by Germany and Turkey, the question of the location of sovereignty became unavoidably clouded after Germany had renounced sovereignty in the Treaty of Versailles and Turkey in the Treaty of Lausanne.

The question became the subject of a considerable division of opinion among writers on international law. It has never been decided by an International Court, by decision of the League of Nations, by vote of the United Nations, or by agreement among the interested states.

The four leading theories variously put forward with respect to the location of title to the mandated territories are as follows:

(1) *Title in the Principal Allied and Associated Powers.* Under Article 119 of the Treaty of Versailles, Germany renounced in favor of the Principal Allied and Associated Powers all her rights and titles over her overseas possessions. The view has therefore been advanced and strongly maintained by many that sovereignty at least over the "B" and "C" mandates must rest in the Principal Allied and Associated Powers. In the case of the former Turkish territories, which became the "A" mandates, a similar renunciation was contained in the Treaty of Sevres. This treaty did not come into effect. However, Article 16 of the Treaty of Lausanne gave effect to the allocation of these territories. By the time this treaty came into force, the "A" territories had already been allocated by the Principal Allied Powers. All in all, this theory of title resting in the Principal Allied and Associated Powers would seem to be the strongest case legally.

(2) *Title in the League of Nations.* There is no treaty provision which specifically vests title to any of the mandated territories in the League of Nations. Those supporting this view, however, point to the clause in the preamble of the mandates which refers to the exercise of the mandate by the Mandatory Power "on behalf of the League of Nations." Others have based their arguments on the general responsibilities of the League of Nations with respect to the mandates system.

(3) *Title in the Mandatory Powers.* The one point in this highly controversial question of title on which there was almost unanimous agreement was that title does not reside in the Mandatory Powers. Ar-

ticle 22 of the League Covenant provided that territories of the "C" mandate category "could be best administered under the laws of the Mandatory as integral portions of its territory" and thus afforded perhaps some slight color to the claim of title in the "C" Mandatory Powers. However, the clear view of the organs of the League of Nations concerned with Mandates—the Permanent Mandates Commission and the League Council—was that sovereignty, even as regards the "C" Mandates, did not reside with the Mandatory Powers.[18] Japan, formerly one of the "C" Mandatory Powers, also declared in unequivocal terms that the Japanese Government "have never entertained the view that those islands (mandated to Japan) are Japanese territory." [19]

(4) *Title in the Inhabitants of the Mandated Territories.* This theory rests upon the general argument that sovereignty over any territory rests in the inhabitants of the territory. This conception rests upon a somewhat different meaning attributed to the word, sovereignty. The three preceding theories refer to sovereignty in the sense of a state or body having the right to dispose of the territory. The conception that sovereignty is located in the people of the mandated territories, on the other hand, refers perhaps more to the ultimate location of political authority over the territory. While such a theory might be plausibly applied to the "A" mandates, described by Article 22 of the Covenant as having "reached a stage of development where their existence as independent nations may be provisionally recognized subject to the rendering of administrative advice and assistance by a Mandatory until such time as they are able to stand alone," it was clearly inapplicable to the "B" and "C" mandates.

Despite the rejection of the theory that sovereignty vested in the mandatory power by most international lawyers, the South African Government and courts persistently maintained that, at least for internal purposes, sovereignty over South West Africa vested in the South African Government. The nature of this assertion appears from an anonymous contemporaneous comment in *Round Table:* [c]

The Treaty of Versailles and the League of Nations have often been attacked for putting a hypocritical cloak over the annexation of the German oversea possessions by the specious device of the mandatory system.

[c] "The Sovereignty of South-West Africa" (1927–28) 18 *Round Table* 217–22.
[18] See Quincy Wright, *op. cit.*, pp. 121–324 ff., and 446–47 and the League documents there cited. For an analysis of particular interest see the report to the Permanent Mandates Commission by M. van Rees on "The System of State Lands in B and C Mandated Territories," Minutes of the Third Session of the Permanent Mandates Commission, pp. 216 ff.
[19] Statement of Japanese Minister of Foreign Affairs to the Diet on February 22, 1934.

The question was raised in a concrete form by the terms of the treaty between the Union and Portugal defining the boundary between Angola and South West Africa. The preamble to this treaty states:—

Whereas under a mandate issued by the Council of the League of Nations in pursuance of Article 22 of the Treaty of Versailles, the Government of the Union of South Africa, subject to the terms of the said mandate, possesses sovereignty over the territory of South West Africa, lately under the sovereignty of Germany.

The Mandates Commission met in November 1926, and took exception to the words "possesses sovereignty" and unanimously expressed the opinion that mandatory Powers had no right of sovereignty over mandated territories. The Commission's report to the Council stated that "it doubted whether the expression 'possesses sovereignty' can be held to define correctly, having regard to the terms of the Covenant, the relations existing between the mandatory Power and the territory placed under its mandate."

In July 1927 the Mandates Commission asked the Union Government to explain whether in its view the term "possesses sovereignty" expressed only the right to exercise full powers of administration or whether it implied that the Government of the Union regarded itself as being sovereign over the territory itself.

The Union representative at Geneva maintained the point of view of his Government that the sovereignty over South West Africa resides in the Union Government. The Prime Minister had previously on March 11 expressed the same view in Parliament in answer to a question. In October 1927 the Assembly of the League approved of a report from the Permanent Mandates Commission already adopted by the Council. The Commission took the view that the actual nature of the legal relations existing between a mandatory Power and its mandated territory was determined and defined, for all practical purposes, by the sum total of the effects of the rights and obligations conferred and imposed on the mandatory Power by the terms of its mandate. An examination of the terms and their cumulative effect led the Commission to the conclusion that the condition thus produced was something new to international law, something *sui generis*. That being so certain technical terms of international law were inapplicable to mandates and their use in respect of mandates had naturally resulted in misunderstandings.

This formula escapes from, but does not solve the difficulty. The Commission does not say in whom the sovereignty is vested, nor if they hold that there is no sovereign do they distinguish the powers of the mandatory from those of a possessor. No statement has since been made by the Union Government showing whether its original opinion has been in any way modified.

In expressing the view which led to this controversy the Union Government relied on the opinion of the judges of the Appellate Division of the Supreme Court as given in the judgments in the case of *Rex v.*

Christian in 1924. Christian was a leader of the Bondelzwart Hottentots who rebelled in 1922. After the suppression of the rising, he was found guilty of engaging in active hostilities against the forces of the mandatory Power. The case went on appeal on the question of whether this amounted to treason or not.

Under the Roman-Dutch law—which by proclamation now forms the common law of the territory and which in this respect is pure Roman law—treason (*perduellio*) is a particular case of *crimen læsæ majestatis* and can only be committed against a person or persons in possession of *majestas* or sovereignty. Consequently, it was necessary for the Court to find as a question of fact whether the Union Government possessed *majestas* in respect of South West Africa. The judgments are complex and lengthy, but the main points may be summarised.

Article 119, read in conjunction with Article 22 of the Peace Treaty, shows that Germany was divested of her overseas possessions in favour of the Principal Allied Powers who were to allow the Council of the League of Nations to direct the disposal of them to mandatory Powers. In other words, the treaty takes the possessions from Germany but does not give them to anyone; the giving is to be done not by the allies, but by a third party, the Council of the League. The mandate for South West Africa was decided on in May 1919—before the treaty was signed—and the terms of the mandate were settled in December 1920. This was a mandate of the "C" type and its juridical effects were totally different from those of the "A" and "B" types.

The term "mandate" is a misnomer as it bears no analogy at all to the contract of mandate or agency but is more analogous to a trust in which the inhabitants of the mandated territories are the *cestuis-qui-trustent*. The terms of the mandate are: that the mandatory is to have full power of administration and legislation over the territory as an integral portion of the Union and may apply the laws of the Union subject to local modifications; it is to promote the moral and material well being and the social progress of the inhabitants and to observe the prohibitions contained in Article 22 of the Treaty relating to the slave trade, the traffic in arms and liquor, the military training of natives and the establishment of military and naval bases and fortifications; freedom of conscience and of religious worship is to be ensured; the annual report under Article 22 is required by the mandate to be to the satisfaction of the Council and to indicate the measures taken to carry out the obligations assumed by the mandatory. Finally, the consent of the Council is required to any modification of the mandate, and any dispute relating to the application or interpretation of the mandate which cannot be settled by negotiation is to be referred to the Permanent Court of International Justice. No limit is placed on the duration of the mandate and no sanction is provided for a breach of its terms.

The Court adopted two lines of reasoning. Sovereignty must be vested in some ultimate authority, otherwise an organised government could not be maintained as its acts could be flouted with impunity. The actual administration of the territory is *ex hypothesi* a subordinate authority. The League of Nations is not a State; it has no territory or subjects; it is an association of nations with common objects, the mandated territories have never been vested in the League; it cannot, and does not exercise sovereign powers; the Principal Allied Powers are not the sovereign as they do not even purport to exercise authority in mandated territories; the British Empire is in a similar position; the only authority which does exercise any power is the Government of the Union. Therefore the Union must have the sovereign power.

The other line of reasoning was to consider the actual powers of the Union and its limitations. These limitations are not inconsistent with the retention of sovereignty by the Union as no other sovereign power has been recognised. Cases of voluntary restriction of sovereign rights are well known.

De Villiers, J.A., sums up the position:—

> I have come to the conclusion that *majestas* or sovereignty over South West Africa resides neither in the Principal Allied and Associated Powers, nor in the League of Nations, nor in the British Empire, but in the Government of the Union of South Africa which has full powers of legislation and administration (only limited in some respects by the mandate) and does not recognise the sovereignty of any person or body in the territory.

This paragraph was cited in Parliament by the Prime Minister who stated that the Government adhered to it.

Sovereignty is a necessarily judicial conception. Without an ultimate authority no State can exist. But as a matter of practice sovereignty may be so divided as to be unrecognisable. The recognition of an authority as a sovereign Power is not a matter of law but one of fact; the recognition may be dictated by political or commercial expediency rather than by the fulfilment of theoretical requirements in a governing body.

It is more useful in practice to consider the powers habitually exercised by the mandatory and to compare these with the powers habitually exercised by other Powers over their dependencies. If this is done the powers exercised by the Union over South West Africa would appear to differ in their extent rather than in their nature from those exercised by the United Kingdom over Ceylon or by the United States over the Philippines. From this point of view the mandate is in effect a Bill of Rights in favour of the inhabitants of the mandated territory. These rights are more secure than any provision in a constitution as their observance is secured by the necessity for reports to the League, and the mandatory cannot by the exercise of its majority strength deny the rights due to a minority, that is, the inhabitants of the mandated territory, without unfavourable international comment. The real sovereign, as always, is public opinion; publicity is its instrument, and the League exists to guarantee that the instrument is real.

The reasoning of the South African Appellate Division in *Rex v Christian*[d] is well illustrated by the separate judgment of Mr. Justice Wessels:

The question for our determination is whether the Union of South Africa as the mandatory power over South-West Africa possesses that *majestas* in South-West Africa which if offended gives rise to the *crimen laesae majestatis*.

Now by the Treaty of Versailles Germany has renounced all right to the territory known as South-West Africa. There is, therefore, no German sovereignty any longer in that territory. What has replaced the German sovereignty? It can only be either the associated powers of the Treaty of Versailles or the League of Nations or the Union of South Africa.

The associated powers do not constitute a State or a sovereign power. It is neither a *Staten bund* nor a *bundes Staat*. The associated powers are only certain sovereign States which have mutually agreed to recognise certain political conditions created by the Treaty of Versailles. They have no combined sovereign power or *majestas* and a resident of South-West Africa owes them no allegiance and cannot be indicted as having committed treason against them or as having offended their *majestas*. There is no *majestas* according to our law in independent States bound together by treaty. Does the sovereignty in South-West Africa lie in the League of Nations? Whatever the League of Nations may be it is not a State. It has none of the attributes of a sovereign power. It does not govern and it makes no laws. The council of the League of Nations is not the parliament or executive power of the League of Nations. By the Treaty of Versailles, the council merely acts as an intermediary between the associated powers and any particular power as for instance a mandatory power. As it exercises no sovereign power it has no *majestas* and therefore the *crimen laesae majestatis* cannot be committed against the League of Nations or its Council. It is unnecessary to determine the exact docket in Constitutional or International law in which the League of Nations must be placed, it is sufficient to say that as a political institution it is *sui generis;* but whatever it may be it certainly is not a State and according to our law the *crimen laesae majestatis* can only be committed against a State. The League of Nations has no *imperium* whatever in the true sense over South-West Africa.

This leaves us with the mandatory power. Now although the term mandatory power seems to imply that the mandatory acts as the agent of the League of Nations or of the associated powers yet in fact that is not so. Neither by the Treaty of Versailles nor by the mandate of the League of Nations has the Union of South Africa been appointed as a mere agent. There is no question here of *respondeat superior*. Once having elected to hand over South-West Africa to the Union of South Africa the League of Nations as such has no right or power to dictate

[d] 1924 *South African Law Reports (Appellate Division)* 101 at 136–37.

to the mandatory power what laws are to be established in South-West Africa and how it has to be governed. The associated powers through the League of Nations have by treaty between themselves entrusted the complete Government of South-West Africa to His Britannic Majesty through the Union as an integral part of its territory. The Union of South Africa determines by what laws South-West Africa is to be governed and how these laws are to be enforced. It has the right to impose its civil and criminal law in South-West Africa and in doing so the Union must have the right to demand from all residents of that territory respect for the laws of the Union and for its *majestas* in the protection of the territory and in the enforcement of law. There is no other power which can safeguard the territory or enforce law and order there. Our law considers it essential that the highest power which gives law to South-West Africa and which governs it should have the right to suppress treason by punishing persons guilty of it according to our laws and the only power capable of doing so and entitled to do so is the mandatory power.

The fact that the associated powers have mutually agreed that the mandatory should report to the League of Nations what its political action is in the mandated territory makes no difference. It is a mere treaty obligation which does not affect its independence or its *summum imperium*.

South Africa's attitude towards the question of sovereignty had important political implications and resulted in the widely held view that the conferment of the Mandate was simply a pretext for annexation. This in turn was largely responsible for the demand for the incorporation of the territory into the Union as a fifth province, which was a feature of white politics in South West Africa in the League period.[e]

THE TREATMENT OF THE NATIVE POPULATION [f]

The League period was not marked by the bitter confrontation between South Africa and the international community over the treatment of South West Africa's native population that has been a feature of the United Nations era. In large measure this was due, first, to the spirit of compromise which prevailed in the League and, second, to the fact that the League was essentially Eurocentric in outlook and not as concerned about human rights and self-determination in colonial territories as the United Na-

[e] Goldblatt, above, n. a, pp. 233–36; Wessels, above, n. a, chap. 4.
[f] For detailed accounts of this subject, see Goldblatt, above, n. a; Wellington, above, n. a; and Arnold J. Toynbee, *Survey of International Affairs 1920–1923* (1927), pp. 397–417.

tions. The absence of such a confrontation could not, however, be interpreted as approval of South Africa's racial policies in her mandated territory by the organs of the League. This is clear from the debates of the Permanent Mandates Commission, and sometimes of the Council and Assembly, on South Africa's annual reports on her administration of South West Africa.

From the outset South Africa placed the interests of the White minority above those of the native peoples. White immigration from the Union of South Africa was actively promoted,[g] and limited self-government was conferred on the White population in 1925.[h] Throughout the League period the mandatory power was more concerned with maintaining harmonious relations between the German settlers and the White South African settlers than with promoting just relations between White and Non-White and advancing the well-being of the indigenous inhabitants.[i] The failure of the South African administration to view its prime responsibility as the promotion of the welfare of the native peoples was tragically illustrated by the Bondelswarts incident of 1922, when a rebellion on the part of the small Bondelswarts tribe was ruthlessly suppressed by the dropping of bombs on the rebels with considerable loss of life.[j] This action was censured by the Permanent Mandates Commission, and this censure was probably responsible for the more restrained attitude adopted by the mandatory power towards the Rehoboth Basters when they rebelled against the administration in 1925.[k]

In short, the policy of white supremacy first introduced into South West Africa by the Germans was permitted to continue albeit in the more moderate South African form. The pattern of race relations which was to result in the acrimonious dispute between South Africa and the United Nations in later years was already established in the early days of the League period. That the

---

[g] Goldblatt, above, n. a, p. 226.

[h] By the South West Africa Constitution Act, No. 42 of 1925.

[i] In 1936 the South West Africa Commission (under the Chairmanship of Mr. Justice van Zyl), appointed by the South African Government to inquire into the effectiveness of the constitutional structure of the territory, drew attention to the inadequate efforts made by the mandatory power to advance the well-being of the native inhabitants: Report of the South West Africa Commission U.G. 26 of 1936, §§ 382–86.

[j] For general accounts of this incident, see Goldblatt, above, n. a, pp. 215–18; Wellington, above, n. a, pp. 284–89. For more specific studies, see R. Freislich, *The Last Tribal War* (1964), and A. M. Davey, *The Bondelzwarts Affair: A Study of the Repercussions 1922–1959* (1961).

[k] Goldblatt, above, n. a, pp. 222–25.

Permanent Mandates Commission was aware of South Africa's shortcomings as a mandatory power is clear from Quincy Wright's analysis of the situation, which appeared in his *Mandates under the League of Nations* published in 1930: [1]

> Among the C mandatories South Africa has contended with the difficult problem of reconciling the interests of a considerable white population, half of it disgruntled ex-German farmers, with those of the natives in the vast dry region of Southwest Africa.
>
> . . . .
>
> The policy of segregating blacks on reserves where it is not certain that the "civilizing influence" of the mandatory will penetrate; the policy of compelling missionaries to be propagandists of loyalty to Union policies and of the native duty to labor; and the apparent assumption by the white population that "natives exist chiefly for the purpose of labor for the whites" have all caused the Commission grave concern.[50]

In its third report made after the Bondelzwart incident we read:

> The commission deplores the unfortunate relations which the report discloses between the white population and a large proportion of the natives of the mandated territory. It trusts that the administration will resist the influence of these deplorable relations which are largely the heritage of past events in Southwest Africa and which are so much opposed to the essential principles of Article 22 of the Covenant. It hopes that future reports will be able to disclose better relations between the two races.[51]

The Bondelzwart insurrection of 1922 called forth resolutions from the Assembly, stimulated by the remarks of M. Bellegarde of Haiti, which hoped that the Commission would consider the question and that the mandatory would remedy conditions, while expressing "profound satisfaction" with the South African representative's statement that a full and impartial inquiry into all the facts would be made.[52] The results of this investigation were regarded as inadequate by the Mandates Commission because the South African government did not assume responsibility for any of the conflicting reports which it submitted. Nevertheless, after cross-questioning the accredited representative, a majority of the Commission (five out of eight present) agreed that the trouble was due fundamentally to native grievances arising in part from legislative and administrative action in behalf of the white settlers and immediately to mistakes of the administrator after the situation had become serious. Though not criticizing the severe measures of repression, the majority of the Commission indicated the inadequacy of remedial measures by quoting the replies to questions of the accredited representative. M. d'Andrade, though admitting that the natives had cause for grievance, was less critical of the administration; M. Van Rees thought the evidence was not sufficient to reach any con-

[1] Pp. 208–12, 240–42.
[50] *P.M.C., Min.,* III, 292; XI, 95, 97–100.
[51] *Ibid.,* III, 325; Rep., sess. IV, *O.J.,* V, 1412.   [52]*Ibid.,*

clusion; and the chairman, Marquis Theodoli, insisted that while the mandatory's first duty should be to the natives, in this case it had "pursued a policy of force rather than of persuasion and further that the policy has always been conceived and applied in the interests of the colonists rather than in the interests of the natives." [53]

In the Council M. Branting thought in view of the division in the Commission the Council "could not express any final opinion on the essence of the dispute" though apparently the ultimate causes lay in the unstable conditions among the native population "subjected for years to a harsh régime" and the lack of comprehension between the two elements of the population. He passed lightly over the "administrative measures which may have contributed to the outbreak of discontent" and followed the Commission in reserving judgment on the measures of repression, though he thought the mandatory should note the Commission's remark on the inexpediency of allowing the administrator himself to lead the troops engaged in this work, thus depriving the natives of appeal to him as an impartial authority, in case of excesses. M. Branting proposed a mild resolution which, however, was criticized by Sir Edgar Walton, representative of South Africa, because it failed to mention the "great efforts to improve the situation of the Bondelzwarts" made by his government and "might appear to contain an unjustifiable censure" of his government "which was anxious to collaborate with the League of Nations in every possible manner." By the resolution, as amended on motion of Lord Robert Cecil, to note the "efforts" of the mandatory, the Council expressed the hope that in its annual reports the mandatory government might be able to record a satisfactory result of its efforts on behalf of the Bondelzwart people and a steady and continuous advancement in civilization and in moral and material well being.[54]

The Rehoboth community of half-breeds in the center of Southwest Africa, like the Druses of Syria, had been granted a high degree of autonomy by the administration soon after the war. They petitioned the League in 1924 when they thought these privileges were being encroached upon, but before the Commission considered the petition they prepared for armed resistance and in the spring of 1925 the administrator sent out a large military force. Profiting by the Bondelzwart experience, active hostilities were delayed and the Rehoboth's finding themselves outnumbered surrendered without bloodshed. The Commission answered the petition by approving the mandatory's policy of negotiating a new agreement after the Rehoboth leaders had regularized their position by an election. Concern was expressed for the Rehoboth prisoners taken, and at the ninth session the Commission noted the accredited representative's promise to furnish the report of an inquiry into their situation. The delay of this report under prepa-

---

[53] *P.M.C., Min., III, 293, 296.*
[54] L. of N., Council, Min., sess. XXVII, *O.J.*, IV, 341, 393. In agreeing to the resolution M. Quinones de Leon of Spain "wished to testify to the great zeal and efficiency of the commission, which enjoyed the entire confidence of the council. Nothing should be done to impair or limit its valuable work."

ration by Justice de Villiers was noted during the tenth and eleventh sessions, and when it was finally received at the twelfth session action was impossible because the mandatory's attitude toward it and toward a new petition received from the Rehoboths in November, 1926, was not made clear. The Commission indicated considerable irritation at these long delays by the mandatory but was satisfied with the mandatory's detailed statement of policy toward the Rehoboths considered at the fourteenth session.[55]

The usual African mandate problems of land tenure, forced labor, suppression of slavery and liquor traffic, development of education, and public-health service have arisen in Southwest Africa in aggravated form. The Commission has inquired into the reason for the very high mortality of native labor in the diamond mines and for the unrest and desertion among the Xoxas tribe. It has intimated that an insufficent proportion of the revenue received from the natives is spent for their welfare. The Commission has also had difficulty in assuring itself, in view of the union of the customs, railway, and harbor system of the territory with those of South Africa, that a proper proportion of the receipts from these public works and customs were credited to the territory.[56] In its sixth report the Commission commented on the proposal to transform the advisory council into a legislative council elected in part by the British subjects (most of the white population since the Germans have been naturalized) in the area. This action, it insisted, could not derogate from the undivided responsibility of the mandatory toward the League. It is quite probable that the resident whites when in authority will be even less considerate of the natives than the Union government. Because of this white minority, and the temperate climate of Southwest Africa which makes possible its increase, the League's problem in protecting the natives in this area is likely to become even more difficult as time goes on.

.   .   .   .

In some mandated areas, especially Southwest Africa, the inhabitants at the time the system went into effect included both natives and white settlers. The Commission seems to agree that both types of inhabitants are entitled to protection, but is there a difference in the degree? The Covenant refers to "people not yet able to stand by themselves," "communities formerly belonging to the Turkish empire," "peoples of central Africa," and "indigenous populations" of Southwest Africa and the Pacific islands. M. Yanaghita seemed to think that this gave the "least developed or weakest peoples" the greatest protection, and M. Rappard insisted that "it was the first duty of the commission to look after the welfare of the natives." [36] During the discussion of the Bondelzwart rebellion in Southwest Africa the question aroused acute

[55] P.M.C., Min., VI, 181; IX, 220; X, 86; XI, 217–18; XII, 195; XIV, 243, 277.
[56] See especially P.M.C. Rep., II, 11; Min., II, 325; Rep., sess. IV (O.J., V, 1412); Min., VI, 178; IX, 220; XI, 100 f. and 205.
[36] Ibid., II, 280; VI, 48.

discussion. The Marquis Theodoli, chairman of the Commission, expressed the conviction that the mandate system marked an innovation in colonial policy in that it required the interest of the natives to take precedence of that of the whites." To this M. Orts took exception, pointing out that the Covenant or mandates made no such distinction but referred to all peoples of the territory.

> What were the actual words of the Covenant: "the well-being and development of such peoples form a sacred trust of civilization." Nothing more. As to the mandate for Southwest Africa, it confined itself to defining as follows the duty of the mandatory Power as regards the natives: "The mandatory shall promote to the utmost the material and moral well-being and the assured progress of the inhabitants of the territory subject to the present mandate." The Commission should beware of stating opinions not justified by existing texts, otherwise the mandatory Power could say with justice: "Where did you find that? Did you find it in the Covenant, the only document which, together with mandates, you are justified in indicating? Or have you found any provision whatever which would allow you to state that in the territories in question the whole preoccupation of the administration should be in the first instance for the blacks, and that care for the prosperity of the European community should only be a secondary consideration?"

MM. Beau and Van Rees agreed with this but the Marquis Theodoli "maintained his point of view."

> It was inconceivable that the illustrious authors of the covenant had produced a work which was anything but an entire departure from precedent. The spirit of the mandates required as a fundamental principle the material and moral progress of the natives; the white population ought only to be considered in so far as it assisted in achieving this progress.

Inasmuch as his colleagues would not agree to this principle or to the deductions he drew from it in reference to the handling of the Bondelzwart affair by the South African government, he refused to associate himself with the report on that subject and withdrew from further meetings of that session of the Commission.[37] The decision on this question is clearly fundamental for determining both the policy of immigration and the proper native policy in mandated areas where there are whites, or where whites have been permitted to migrate. . . . In regard to the relations of domiciled whites and natives the policy of assimilation has been opposed to the policy of segregation through native reserves. M. d'Andrade wrote:

> There is no question of forming separate organizations of natives and whites; a complete amalgamation of the two races would be the best means of furthering the development and well-being of such

---

[37] *Ibid.*, III, 204–7. M. Orts, interpretation of the term "peoples" in article 22 of the Covenant is doubtful (see *supra*, n. 36).

peoples. . . . So far from creating a number of small organizations living side by side in mutual rivalry and detestation, it is desirable to endeavour to secure the co-operation of all and the amalgamation of the various interests in order to make the peoples capable of self government.

To which replied Sir Frederick Lugard:

Why should communities living side by side "detest" each other? The rivalry may be entirely wholesome and lead to progress. Natural causes will no doubt lead in many cases to the absorption of less virile tribes by others but I see no reason why it should be an object of policy to hasten the process.[38]

---

[38] *Ibid.*, VII, 201, 204, 206. The policy of confining the natives to reserves has been farthest developed in Southwest Africa, where the Commission has watched it with some concern (*ibid.*, IV, 62; IX, 36). It has also been discussed in connection with Tanganyika (*ibid.*, IV, 91).

5

The Mandate, the Dissolution of the League of Nations, and the Creation of the United Nations, 1945–1949

1. South Africa Reserves Her Position

During the 1930s and early 1940s proposals were made within South Africa and South West Africa for the incorporation of the territory into the Union as a fifth province,[a] but no steps were taken to give effect to these proposals until the end of World War II. In 1945 at the San Francisco Conference, when the Charter of the United Nations was being drafted, South Africa first served notice on the international community of her intention to request incorporation of South West Africa into the Union. When the provisions of the Charter relating to the proposed trusteeship system were discussed, the South African representative made the following statement:[b]

(d) For twenty-five years, the Union of South Africa has governed and administered the Territory as an integral part of its own Territory and has promoted to the utmost the material and moral well-being and the social progress of the inhabitants.

[a] *GAOR*, 1st session (2nd part), Fourth Committee, Part 1, pp. 231–32 (Doc. A/123 §§ 153–54). See, too, Michael Scott, *The Orphans' Heritage* (1958), pp. 11–12.
[b] *GAOR*, 1st session (2nd part), Fourth Committee, Part 1, pp. 200–201 (Doc. A/123 § 1).

It has applied many of its laws to the Territory and has faithfully performed its obligations under the mandate.

(e) The Territory is in a unique position when compared with other Territories under the same form of mandate.

(f) It is geographically and strategically a part of the Union of South Africa, and in World War I a rebellion in the Union was fomented from it, and an attack launched against the Union.

(g) It is in large measure economically dependent upon the Union, whose railways serve it and from which it draws the great bulk of its supplies.

(h) Its dependent Native peoples spring from the same ethnological stem as the great mass of the Native peoples of the Union.

(i) Two-thirds of the European population are of Union origin and are Union Nationals, and the remaining one-third are enemy Nationals.

(j) The Territory has its own Legislative Assembly granted to it by the Union Parliament, and this Assembly has submitted a request for incorporation of the Territory as part of the Union.

(k) The Union has introduced a progressive policy of Native administration, including a system of local government through Native councils giving the Natives a voice in the management of their own affairs; and under Union administration Native Reserves have reached a high state of economic development.

(l) In view of contiguity and similarity in composition of the Native peoples of South West Africa the Native policy followed in South West Africa must always be aligned with that of the Union, three-fifths of the population of which is Native.

(m) There is no prospect of the Territory ever existing as a separate State, and the ultimate objective of the mandatory principle is therefore impossible of achievement.

(n) The delegation of the Union of South Africa therefore claims that the mandate should be terminated and that the Territory should be incorporated as part of the Union of South Africa.

(o) As territorial questions are however reserved for handling at the later Peace Conference, where the Union of South Africa intends to raise this matter, it is here only mentioned for the information of the Conference in connexion with the mandates question.

This reservation was later stressed by General Smuts in a statement before the Fourth Committee of the General Assembly of the United Nations in 1946: [e]

In the latter stages of the war, the consideration being given to the manner and form of the general peace settlement again stimulated discussion in South West Africa as to the desirability of securing a final

---

[e] *Ibid.,* pp. 238–39 (Doc. A/C. 4/41). See further on South Africa's reservations, Richard Dale, "The Evolution of the South West African Dispute before the United Nations 1945–1950" (Princeton University Ph.D., 1962, University Microfilms, Ann Arbor, Michigan), pp. 109–111.

settlement of the status of the mandated Territory. The view of the European population, unanimously expressed through the medium of the South West African Legislature, was clearly in favour of terminating the mandate. This view was emphatically and repeatedly represented to the Union Government. The Union Government clearly understood, however, that its international responsibility precluded it from taking advantage of the war situation by effecting a change in the status of South West Africa without proper consultation either of all the peoples of the Territory itself or with the competent international organs. The correctness of this attitude is perhaps in contrast to the action taken in another part of the world where three border states were incorporated into a larger union without any consultation whatsoever with the comity of nations.

It was nevertheless incumbent on the Union Government as trustee of the interests of the people of South West Africa to ensure that, when the proper time arrived for consideration of any change in the status of the Territory, such consideration should not be prejudiced by any prior commitment on the part of the Union Government by virtue of its membership of any organization which might replace the League of Nations. Accordingly, in May 1945, when questions relating to trusteeship were under consideration by the San Francisco Conference, the Union Government entered a reservation designed to ensure that the future status of South West Africa and the desirability of its incorporation in the Union should not be prejudiced by any proposals adopted by the Conference in regard to the future of mandated Territories.

2. The Trusteeship System

The United Nations Charter made no clear provision for the future of mandated territories, as it was confidently expected that mandatory States would place their mandated territories under the new system of international tutelage, the trusteeship system. The trusteeship system [d] was created by Chapters XII and XIII of the United Nations Charter, while Chapter XI provided for a limited form of international accountability in respect of Non-Self-Governing Territories.

[d] For brief comments on the trusteeship system and Chapter XI, see D. W. Bowett, *The Law of International Institutions*, 2nd ed. (1970), pp. 66–79; H. Duncan Hall, "The Trusteeship System" (1947) 24 *British Year Book of International Law* 33; and Francis B. Sayre, "Legal Problems Arising from the United Nations Trusteeship System" (1948) 42 *AJIL* 263. For more detailed accounts, see H. Duncan Hall, *Mandates, Dependencies and Trusteeship* (1948); James N. Murray, Jr., *The United Nations Trusteeship System* (1957); Charmian Edwards Toussaint, *The Trusteeship System of the United Nations* (1956); and R. N. Chowdhuri, *International Mandates and Trusteeship Systems* (1955).

CHAPTER XII

International Trusteeship System

Article 75

The United Nations shall establish under its authority an international trusteeship system for the administration and supervision of such territories as may be placed thereunder by subsequent individual agreements. These territories are hereinafter referred to as trust territories.

Article 76

The basic objectives of the trusteeship system, in accordance with the Purposes of the United Nations laid down in Article 1 of the present Charter, shall be:

    a. to further international peace and security;

    b. to promote the political, economic, social, and educational advancement of the inhabitants of the trust territories, and their progressive development towards self-government or independence as may be appropriate to the particular circumstances of each territory and its peoples and the freely expressed wishes of the peoples concerned, and as may be provided by the terms of each trusteeship agreement;

    c. to encourage respect for human rights and for fundamental freedoms for all without distinction as to race, sex, language, or religion, and to encourage recognition of the interdependence of the peoples of the world; and

    d. to ensure equal treatment in social, economic, and commercial matters for all Members of the United Nations and their nationals, and also equal treatment for the latter in the administration of justice, without prejudice to the attainment of the foregoing objectives and subject to the provisions of Article 80.

Article 77

1. The trusteeship system shall apply to such territories in the following categories as may be placed thereunder by means of trusteeship agreements:

    a. territories now held under mandate;

    b. territories which may be detached from enemy states as a result of the Second World War; and

    c. territories voluntarily placed under the system by states responsible for their administration.

2. It will be a matter for subsequent agreement as to which territories in the foregoing categories will be brought under the trusteeship system and upon what terms.

Article 78

The trusteeship system shall not apply to territories which have become Members of the United Nations, relationship among which shall be based on respect for the principle of sovereign equality.

Article 79

The terms of trusteeship for each territory to be placed under the trusteeship system, including any alteration or amendment, shall be agreed upon by the states directly concerned, including the mandatory power in the case of territories held under mandate by a Member of the United Nations, and shall be approved as provided for in Articles 83 and 85.

Article 80

1. Except as may be agreed upon in individual trusteeship agreements, made under Articles 77, 79, and 81, placing each territory under the trusteeship system, and until such agreements have been concluded, nothing in this Chapter shall be construed in or of itself to alter in any manner the rights whatsoever of any states or any peoples or the terms of existing international instruments to which Members of the United Nations may respectively be parties.

2. Paragraph 1 of this Article shall not be interpreted as giving grounds for delay or postponement of the negotiation and conclusion of agreements for placing mandated and other territories under the trusteeship system as provided for in Article 77.

Article 81

The trusteeship agreement shall in each case include the terms under which the trust territory will be administered and designate the authority which will exercise the administration of the trust territory. Such authority hereinafter called the administering authority, may be one or more states or the Organization itself.

Article 82

There may be designated, in any trusteeship agreement, a strategic area or areas which may include part or all of the trust territory to which the agreement applies, without prejudice to any special agreement or agreements made under Article 43.

Article 83

1. All functions of the United Nations relating to strategic areas, including the approval of the terms of the trusteeship agreements and of their alteration or amendment, shall be exercised by the Security Council.

2. The basic objectives set forth in Article 76 shall be applicable to the people of each strategic area.

3. The Security Council shall, subject to the provisions of the trust-

eeship agreements and without prejudice to security considerations, avail itself of the assistance of the Trusteeship Council to perform those functions of the United Nations under the trusteeship system relating to political, economic, social, and educational matters in the strategic areas.

Article 84

It shall be the duty of the administering authority to ensure that the trust territory shall play its part in the maintenance of international peace and security. To this end the administering authority may make use of volunteer forces, facilities, and assistance from the trust territory in carrying out the obligations towards the Security Council undertaken in this regard by the administering authority, as well as for local defence and the maintenance of law and order within the trust territory.

Article 85

1. The functions of the United Nations with regard to trusteeship agreements for all areas not designated as strategic, including the approval of the terms of the trusteeship agreements and of their alteration or amendment, shall be exercised by the General Assembly.

2. The Trusteeship Council, operating under the authority of the General Assembly, shall assist the General Assembly in carrying out these functions.

CHAPTER XIII

The Trusteeship Council

Composition

Article 86

1. The Trusteeship Council shall consist of the following Members of the United Nations:
    a. those Members administering trust territories;
    b. such of those Members mentioned by name in Article 23 as are not administering trust territories; and
    c. as many other Members elected for three-year terms by the General Assembly as may be necessary to ensure that the total number of members of the Trusteeship Council is equally divided between those Members of the United Nations which administer trust territories and those which do not.

2. Each member of the Trusteeship Council shall designate one specially qualified person to represent it therein.

Functions and Powers

Article 87

The General Assembly and, under its authority, the Trusteeship Council, in carrying out their functions, may:

a. consider reports submitted by the administering authority;

b. accept petitions and examine them in consultation with the administering authority;

c. provide for periodic visits to the respective trust territories at times agreed upon with the administering authority; and

d. take these and other actions in conformity with the terms of the trusteeship agreements.

Article 88

The Trusteeship Council shall formulate a questionnaire on the political, economic, social, and educational advancement of the inhabitants of each trust territory, and the administering authority for each trust territory within the competence of the General Assembly shall make an annual report to the General Assembly upon the basis of such questionnaire.

Voting

Article 89

1. Each member of the Trusteeship Council shall have one vote.

2. Decisions of the Trusteeship Council shall be made by a majority of the members present and voting.

Procedure

Article 90

1. The Trusteeship Council shall adopt its own rules of procedure, including the method of selecting its President.

2. The Trusteeship Council shall meet as required in accordance with its rules, which shall include provision for the convening of meetings on the request of a majority of its members.

Article 91

The Trusteeship Council shall, when appropriate, avail itself of the assistance of the Economic and Social Council and of the specialized agencies in regard to matters with which they are respectively con-concerned.

CHAPTER XI

Declaration Regarding Non-Self-Governing Territories

Article 73

Members of the United Nations which have or assume responsibilities for the administration of territories whose peoples have not yet attained a full measure of self-government recognize the principle that the interests of the inhabitants of these territories are paramount, and accept as a sacred trust the obligation to promote to the utmost, within the system of international peace and security established by the

present Charter, the well-being of the inhabitants of these territories. and, to this end:

a. to ensure, with due respect for the culture of the peoples concerned, their political, economic, social, and educational advancement, their just treatment, and their protection against abuses;

b. to develop self-government, to take due account of the political aspirations of the peoples, and to assist them in the progressive
development of their free political institutions, according to the particular circumstances of each territory and its peoples and their varying stages of advancement;

c. to further international peace and security;

d. to promote constructive measures of development, to encourage research, and to co-operate with one another and, when and
where appropriate, with specialized international bodies with a view
to the practical achievement of the social, economic, and scientific
purposes set forth in this Article; and

e. to transmit regularly to the Secretary-General for information
purposes, subject to such limitation as security and constitutional
considerations may require, statistical and other information of a
technical nature relating to economic, social, and educational conditions in the territories for which they are respectively responsible
other than those territories to which Chapters XII and XIII apply.

Article 74

Members of the United Nations also agree that their policy in respect of the territories to which this Chapter applies, no less than in
respect of their metropolitan areas, must be based on the general principle of good neighbourliness, due account being taken of the interests
and well-being of the rest of the world, in social, economic, and commercial matters.

3. The Dissolution of the League of Nations

The Charter of the United Nations came into force on 24 October 1945. In April 1946 the League of Nations was voluntarily
dissolved. At its last meeting the Assembly of the League of Nations adopted the following resolution, which was supported by
South Africa.

The Assembly:

Recalling that Article 22 of the Covenant applies to certain territories placed under mandate the principle that the well-being and development of peoples not yet able to stand alone in the strenuous conditions of the modern world form a sacred trust of civilization:

1. Expresses its satisfaction with the manner in which the organs of
the League have performed the functions entrusted to them with respect to the mandates system and in particular pays tribute to the
work accomplished by the Mandates Commission;

2. Recalls the role of the League in assisting Iraq to progress from its status under an 'A' mandate to a condition of complete independence, welcomes the termination of the mandated status of Syria, the Lebanon and Transjordan, which have, since the last session of the Assembly, become independent members of the world community;

3. Recognizes that, on the termination of the League's existence, its functions with respect to the mandated territories will come to an end, but notes that Chapters XI, XII and XIII of the Charter of the United Nations embody principles corresponding to those declared in Article 22 of the Covenant of the League;

4. Takes note of the expressed intentions of the members of the League now administering territories under mandate to continue to administer them for the well-being and development of the peoples concerned in accordance with the obligations contained in the respective mandates until other arrangements have been agreed between the United Nations and the respective mandatory powers.

At the time of the dissolution of the League of Nations, and at the inception of the United Nations, South African delegates entered reservations concerning South Africa's position in respect of the future of South West Africa. Although the intention to request incorporation was made clear, it was not clearly stated what South Africa's attitude would be in the event of the rejection of such a request. Undertakings given to maintain the status quo, and to submit reports on the territory to the United Nations in such an event, not surprisingly gave rise to the belief that South Africa had accepted the United Nations as the successor to the League of Nations in the matter of international accountability. South Africa's equivocal attitude on the international front is illustrated by the statement made by Mr. Leif Egeland before the Assembly of the League of Nations in April 1946: [e]

Since the last League meeting, new circumstances have arisen obliging the mandatory Powers to take into review the existing arrangements for the administration of their mandates. As was fully explained at the recent United Nations General Assembly in London, the Union Government have deemed it incumbent upon them to consult the peoples of South West Africa, European and non-European alike, regarding the form which their own future Government should take. On the basis of those consultations, and having regard to the unique circumstances which so signally differentiate South West Africa—a territory contiguous with the Union—from all other mandates, it is the intention of the Union Government, at the forthcoming session of the United Nations General Assembly in New York, to formulate its case for according South West Africa a status under which it would be internationally recognized as an integral part of the Union. As the As-

[e] *League of Nations Official Journal,* 21st Assembly, 32–33 (Plenary, 1946).

sembly will know, it is already administered under the terms of the Mandate as an integral part of the Union. In the meantime, the Union will continue to administer the territory scrupulously in accordance with the obligations of the Mandate, for the advancement and promotion of the interests of the inhabitants, as she has done during the past six years when meetings of the Mandates Commission could not be held.

The disappearance of those organs of the League concerned with the supervision of mandates, primarily the Mandates Commission and the League Council, will necessarily preclude complete compliance with the letter of the Mandate. *The Union Government will nevertheless regard the dissolution of the League as in no way diminishing its obligations under the Mandate, which it will continue to discharge with the full and proper appreciation of its responsibilities until such time as other arrangements are agreed upon concerning the future status of the territory.* [Italics added.]

On the home front the same confusion prevailed. On 20 March 1945 the Prime Minister, General Smuts, suggested that he was prepared to account to a new world organisation in respect of South West Africa when he stated in the House of Assembly: [f]

If the League of Nations lapses, then the mandatory system also lapses. That is an uncertain matter. It is something that must be gone into at the conference at San Francisco. If a decision is taken for a new world organisation it must be stated what should happen with those organisations that were the outcome of the League of Nations, and there must be some arrangement in connection with the mandates. My own opinion is that the best solution will be to get rid of the mandatory system and to attend to the matter in a different way, even though we have to send a report to another organisation. The mandate will have to be abolished, and the territory can be incorporated as a province of the Union under a special provision. I do not think that the existing provincial arrangement as it stands in relation to the four provinces of the Union, will be applicable in all respects to a territory like South-West Africa. The circumstances are different.

This approach was again apparent a year later when General Smuts replied to a motion by Mr. Eric Louw [g] urging the Government to "take the necessary steps for the incorporation of the Territory of South West Africa as a Province of the Union . . . subject solely to the sovereign power of the Union of South Africa in regard to both external and internal affairs." [h] On this occasion he stated: [i]

[f] *House of Assembly Debates,* vol. 52, col. 3752.
[g] Later chief spokesman on international affairs under the National Party Government.
[h] *House of Assembly Debates,* vol. 55, cols. 2382–83 (26 February 1946).
[i] *Ibid.,* vol. 56, cols. 3675–76; 3677–80; 3681–82 (15 March 1946).

What is the position under the United Nations Organisation? It is a new position. The United Nations Organisation, and the Charter as it stands now, deals with this question anew. There is no derivation of authority from the League of Nations that would have raised, and that does raise again, all sorts of legal questions. Had the League of Nations the power to give transfer of this territory? Had it the authority to transfer? The United Nations Organisation, therefore, in its conference at San Francisco sidetracked this whole question about transfer and dealt with the position anew. And what does it say? The settlement it came to is this; it is embodied in sections 79 and 80 of the Charter. In section 79 it says a mandatory can come under the Trusteeship Council, that is under the United Nations Organisation, by agreement with those concerned, which means first and foremost the mandatory power. There must be a new agreement; they did not go back to what was done at Paris in 1919. They say there must be a new agreement between the mandatory powers and the others concerned. That is the one stipulation it makes. Then it goes further and in section 80 says this, that until a new agreement is made the status quo under the old mandate shall be maintained. These are the two terms. You see therefore, Mr. Speaker, that the new position under UNO is also perfectly clear. There must be an agreement between the parties concerned, and the principal party is the holder of the mandate; and until such an agreement has been concluded the old position holds, the status quo remains.

MRS. BALLINGER: To whom is a report to be made?

THE PRIME MINISTER: The question of to whom a report is to be made may be one of detail, because Article 80 deals with the rights of the people, the rights of the mandatories and so on.

MR. LOUW: Does that mean you are obliged to enter into an agreement?

THE PRIME MINISTER: You are a free agent. There is no compulsion.

MR. LOUW: But sub-section (2) states that nothing in paragraph 1 of the article shall be interpreted as grounds for the delay or the postponement of an agreement.

THE PRIME MINISTER: That was to prevent a situation where the mandatory says: I do not want to make an agreement at all. It is very much the position held by the hon. member for Beaufort West [Mr. Louw]. He takes this position, that the League of Nations having disappeared we are now free, that we can do what we like.

MR. LOUW: Yes.

THE PRIME MINISTER: Yes; that position is in conflict with Article 80, sub-section (2).

MR. LOUW: That means you must enter into an agreement.

THE PRIME MINISTER: No, you must take steps to enter into an agreement. You must be serious about it, but there is no compulsion laid on you to accept the terms. To my mind the position is quite simple. What sub-section (2) of Article 80 was intended to prevent was that a mandatory should say: The League of Nations is dead; I am in this position, I do not want to come under UNO at all, and I do not want to come under the Trusteeship Council at all. That position is precluded. That is how I understand it.

MR. LOUW: The mandatory proceeds to say: All right, I will enter into an agreement. But he later refuses to enter into an agreement afterwards. What then?   .

THE PRIME MINISTER: That question is dealt with here.

MR. J. G. STRYDOM: Is it merely a moral obligation to take steps?

THE PRIME MINISTER: You are morally bound not to take up a recalcitrant and non-possumus attitude, and say: I am not going to make an agreement with UNO, I am not going under the Trusteeship Council. That was the object of sub-section (2) being introduced, that there might be Powers who would take up that attitude. We never took that attitude. We entered into this charter wholeheartedly. We supported the United Nations Organisation. We looked upon the United Nations Organisation as a safeguard for the future peace of the world, and we are quite frank and quite clear about it. We want to come to an agreement. Of course, we are going to negotiate as free agents. We are not going to be forced into accepting an agreement of which we disapprove.

MR. LOUW: Once you enter into an agreement you have submitted to the authority of UNO.

THE PRIME MINISTER: Yes, once you have done it you submit to UNO on the terms of your agreement; it depends on the agreement.

.   .   .   .

The third question I want to raise is this: What are the plans of the Government? The plans of the Government are as follows: At San Francisco the Union Government gave notice to the New Organisation that they were going to plead their case, and in the meantime they were preserving their case for full incorporation of the territory of South-West Africa into Union territory. That is the reservation that the hon. member for Cape Eastern refers to. Our reservation was this, that we claimed in the interests of the Union and in the interests of South-West Africa that it should be incorporated as part and parcel of Union territory and that we are going to plead that case. We were not going to act unilaterally, off our own bat, and we were going to argue the case.

MRS. BALLINGER: What more does it involve than the powers we had under the mandate system?

THE PRIME MINISTER: Under the mandate system it was quite a question whether we could annex the territory. I am very doubtful whether under the terms of the old mandate . . .

MRS. BALLINGER: We could incorporate.

THE PRIME MINISTER: The word "incorporate" is a vague term. The hon. member has used the word "annexation." I am doubtful whether in terms of the mandate we had from the principal Allied and Associated Powers we could annex the country because annexation would mean at once that there would be no necessity to report in future.

MR. LOUW: I agree. But what is the position today?

THE PRIME MINISTER: He has held that we have had sovereignty in the sense that we could annex the territory and the mandate, but I am doubtful about it because I think the chances are the other way. But now under the new system we have reserved our right to plead before UNO for full incorporation and annexation. That is the whole point. So that if this plea succeeds, then in future we shall be absolved from the duty of reporting to UNO as we have been making reports to the League. That is the matter we are going to argue. We are not going to act unilaterally as if we can dispose of the matter whichever way we want to. We will argue it, and I hope we shall be able to make out a very strong case indeed for complete annexation.

MR. LOUW: And if your case is not accepted?

THE PRIME MINISTER: I will come to that. I think that we have the strongest case for it. If ever there were a territory which was part of the Union from every point of view, it is South-West. It is not a distant island or some outlying portion over which we want to exercise authority. The Orange River does not divide it from the Union. The territory is united, and it was only the neglect of the old Cape Government which left the door open for the Germans to step in at Walvis Bay. It was really the territory of the old Cape. Both historically and from the point of view of the defence of South-West Africa, it is an integral portion of South Africa. We have twice had to fight wars for South-West, and although there was a dispute in the House over the rights and wrongs, there is no doubt that we were in grave danger in both cases, because we had no real authority in South-West. From the defence point of view it is part and parcel of our whole system here, and from the administrative point of view there is no question about it at all. Administratively it is already a part of the Union. We have such a strong case that I am prepared to plead it to the best of my ability, and I hope to succeed. If I do not succeed I shall fall back on the status quo. The status quo is here, and unless a reasonable agreement can be come to, unless the conference recognises that it is essential to the Union to incorporate this territory, I will think that they are acting unreasonably and I will say that I stick to the status quo; I do not want to flout them, and I am prepared to make an agreement, but in that agreement I want to stick to the status quo and continue as before to make my reports, in the same way as I used to make them. I will stick to the position as laid down in article 80. If my friends in UNO agree that the Union has an exceptional case, a case quite unlike that of any other mandated territory, then we can come to an agreement. Even then one may be prepared to render reports. The British Government has informed UNO that they are prepared in respect of their Crown Colonies, to render reports as to what they are doing to develop the territories, even though they do not come under UNO or the trusteeship system, and I am prepared in the interests of this country, if I can carry the incorporation of South-West, to tell UNO that I will give them all the information as we gave it to the League about the progress of the territory, and the steps taken for improvement. But it will not be a matter of contractual obligation; it will be a matter which we freely undertake to do as our contribu-

tion to the new system. That is the position. There are two alternatives. Either UNO may agree to our annexation of the territory as an essential part of the Union with full freedom on our part to govern it as part of the Union in which case I may be prepared to give them reports . . .

MR. LOUW: Why give them reports? It detracts from our sovereignty.

THE PRIME MINISTER: They may not accede to my proposition at all. I wish my hon. friend had been at UNO, at the first meeting in London, and had been in the shoes of our High Commissioner there. No, it will be a difficult and tough business, a rough fight. I am very anxious indeed to have complete incorporation and annexation of this territory.

MR. S. E. WARREN: What obligations will you accept, apart from reporting, if they are not satisifed?

THE PRIME MINISTER: I am only bound to stick to the status quo in the absence of our coming to an agreement.

MR. LOUW: A status quo minus the old League?

THE PRIME MINISTER: Yes, we had an obligation under the League to render reports, and if no agreement can be come to, then under Article 80 it is our obligation to continue to render reports.

MR. LOUW: Does not your reference to a status quo rather suggest that the League still exists? Do you mean a status quo without a League?

THE PRIME MINISTER: Yes.

.   .   .   .

MR. LOUW: Can we take it that the use of the term "continuance of the status quo" is equivalent in your mind with annexation?

THE PRIME MINISTER: No, it is a continuance of the present regime, of our full government and administrative and legislative power plus the obligation to render annual reports.

MR. LOUW: To whom?

THE PRIME MINISTER: To UNO. UNO is the only authority to which reports can be made.

MR. LOUW: Does that mean that as under the old mandatory system the people of the territory can send petitions to UNO? In other words, can the natives there send petitions to UNO?

THE PRIME MINISTER: Yes.

MR. LOUW: Are you agreeable to that?

THE PRIME MINISTER: Yes, I am because the word "peoples" is specially mentioned.

MR. LOUW: Then you are willing to submit to petitions being sent to UNO by the natives of South-West Africa?

THE PRIME MINISTER: Yes, in this sense that we make the reports which were customarily put before the League of Nations to UNO.

MR. LOUW: And what about Article 87 (c) which provides for ". . . periodic visits to the respective trust territories at times agreed upon with the administering authority."

Does it mean that UNO can send out people to inspect the territory?

THE PRIME MINISTER: That is not the status quo. That breaks new ground.

In withdrawing his motion in order not to embarrass the United Party Government at the United Nations, Mr. Louw highlighted the equivocal and fluctuating attitude of the Prime Minister: [j]

I said at the beginning of my speech that the striking characteristic of the Prime Minister's speech was that he did not keep to his standpoint. He said one thing and within a few minutes he again said something else. He said: "There will be no need to make the usual reports". Then I was perfectly satisfied. That was the very thing, annexation in the fullest sense of the word! He also said: "We are going to argue the right of annexation". He did not speak of incorporation". "Annexation" was the word he used. There would then be no necessity for submitting reports. I was then delighted. I thought that all was well. He was going to fight for consent to annexation, and if he did not get his way, then he would simply go over to annexation. But then it seemed as though a thought struck the Prime Minister. He suddenly said: "But all the same we are prepared to make a report". Within ten minutes he had this new idea of making a report. That is the unsatisfactory portion of the Prime Minister's speech. I said that at the beginning I appreciated the Prime Minister's attitude. I was glad to see him displaying a certain tendency which coincided with our attitude. But then it was disappointing to see how he adopted one standpoint, and then departed from it within a few minutes.

The standpoint of the Prime Minister was further that if he could not persuade the UNO to give us a free hand, then he would keep to the status quo. He will remember that I asked by way of interjection not once, but three or four times, what he meant by the status quo? I asked: "Do you mean the status quo minus the League?" And first he said: "Yes" and then again: "No". It was very difficult to obtain an explicit statement from the Prime Minister of exactly what he meant by the words "status quo". And then apparently, while he was speaking, other thoughts began to occur to him. I asked whether South Africa would still stand under the authority of the UNO with relation to South-West; "whether there still will be submission to UNO?" He said: "Yes", and then all the wonderful expectations which the Prime Minister had created, that if he could not come to an agreement, he would go over to annexation, were gone with the wind. What is the status quo going to mean if it must be under the authority of the UNO? He also said that the UNO would then take the place of the League of Nations. Where are we then? We want to know where we will be then, and my supposition is that we are then going to be much worse off. If he places the UNO in the place of the League of Nations

[j] *Ibid.*, cols. 3697–98 (15 March 1946). For comment on this debate, see E. F. W. Gey Van Pittius, "Whither South-West Africa?" (1947) 23 *International Affairs* 202; and Dale, above, n. c, pp. 176–193.

and he acknowledges the authority of the UNO in respect of South-West Africa, then I say with all due deference, but emphatically, that as soon as we acknowledge the authority of UNO, we are subject to the trusteeship provisions to which I referred. The Prime Minister can argue this way or that way, but as soon as he acknowledges that we are subject to the authority of the UNO in relation to South-West Africa, then we are also subject to Articles 75, 76, 79, 80, and also to parts of other articles, such as 87 and 88. The Prime Minister will remember that I made an interjection when he discussed this point. I thought that I would put him to the real test. I put the question to the Prime Minister as to whether the inhabitants of South-West Africa could then send petitions to the UNO, and he replied that they would most certainly be able to send petitions to the UNO. I must admit that I was disappointed towards the end with the Prime Minister's attitude. If the position is that there will be a submission to the authority of the UNO, in case he does not get his way, where are we then? Then it amounts to this. Even should they say that we can incorporate South-West Africa as a fifth province, but that we must still make reports and stand under the authority of the UNO, then I say emphatically here today, and I hope the Prime Minister will remember it, that our last position is worse than the first.

4. The "Consultation" of the Peoples of South West Africa

In 1946 the South African Government "consulted" the people of South West Africa on their attitude to incorporation. While the White inhabitants of the territory expressed their wishes through elected representatives in the Legislative Assembly, the Non-White people were "consulted" through their tribal leaders. Having obtained a mandate for incorporation from this "consultation," the South African Government approached the General Assembly of the United Nations for permission to incorporate the territory. This request, together with an explanation of the way in which the people were consulted, appears in the official communication to the Fourth Committee.[k]

150. The Union Government, as Mandatory, has governed the mandated Territory of South West Africa for over a quarter of a century. The results of that period of government, it is submitted, are satisfactory, for the development of the country and its people has been considerable, and, what is more significant, the indigenous population is more contented than ever before in its history. That the Mandatory is satisfied that its duties under the mandate have been faithfully carried

k *GAOR*, 1st session (2nd part) Fourth Committee, Part 1, pp. 231–35 (Doc A/123). See, too, *ibid.*, pp. 239–44, and *South West Africa and the Union of South Africa: History of a Mandate* (1946) pp. 80–94. See the note by Martin Wight in (1947) 23 *International Affairs* 209; and the speech by S. Kahn, M. P. in *House of Assembly Debates*, vol. 66, cols. 1626–27 (23 February 1949).

out is justified by the fact that the Permanent Mandates Commission, while always characteristically critical, has given ample indication of its confidence in the Union's mandatory policy and administration.

151. Yet the Union Government, considering the fruits of its efforts in the Territory and the task which lies ahead, shares with the people of South West Africa the conviction that the Mandates System is inapplicable to the Territory. This conviction rests upon three main considerations, namely:

(a) The fundamental principle of the Mandates System and its successor the Trusteeship System is ultimate political self-government and separate statehood. The low economic potential of the Territory and the backwardness of the vast majority of the population render this impossible of achievement.

(b) The immediate aim of the mandate is the development of the Territory and its people. This development can be satisfactorily carried on only at an expense to the Mandatory which, in the nature of things, it cannot undertake.

(c) The uncertainty as to the ultimate future of the Territory inevitably militates against racial tranquillity and the optimum development of the country.

152. As already declared by the Union High Commissioner before the General Assembly of the United Nations Organization, when trusteeship matters were being considered, the Union Government regards it as implicit in the Mandates System that no change shall be introduced into the form of government of a mandated Territory except with the specific consent of the people of that Territory and in accordance with their wishes. The European population having already signified its wishes in the matter, the Union Government therefore caused the non-European inhabitants of South West Africa to be consulted.

153. The European section of the population of South West Africa has repeatedly given expression to its wish that the mandate over the Territory be terminated and that the Territory be incorporated in the Union of South Africa. This desire has been expressed in the Press, in public utterances by representative leaders, and in two resolutions unanimously adopted by the Legislative Assembly of South West Africa. The first of these resolutions, adopted on 14 May 1943, was in the following terms:

"That this House respectfully requests His Honour the Administrator forthwith to urge upon the Government of the Union of South Africa that the time has arrived for the termination of its mandate over the Territory of South West Africa, and that it is the earnest desire of the inhabitants of this Territory that upon such termination of the mandate, the Territory of South West Africa be formally annexed to and incorporated in the Union of South Africa upon such terms as to financial relations and political representation as may be mutually agreed upon between the Government of the Union of South Africa and representatives nominated by this House."

On 8 May 1946, the Legislative Assembly unanimously adopted a similar resolution, the Chairman directing that his vote also be recorded in favour of the resolution.

154. German nationals in the Territory have also made various representations to the Assembly in favour of incorporation and recently offered to get a petition signed in favour of incorporation by non-enfranchised Germans who have no voice in the Legislative Assembly.

155. The consultation of the non-Europeans necessarily presented certain difficulties, as it was essential that they should clearly understand the implications of the question at issue and that their differing tribal customs should be observed. It was therefore decided to entrust consultation to officials who had the necessary experience in Native affairs and who enjoyed the confidence of the non-Europeans. Moreover, having regard to Native custom and susceptibilities, it was arranged to consult the different tribes as units and not as individuals.

156. The officials specially selected were the Native Commissioners and certain Magistrates (who are also local Native Commissioners) who were instructed to emphasize the fact that the Natives are a free people and therefore have the right to express their views without fear. It was also arranged that, in so far as tribal considerations permitted, similar terms should be employed in both the address and in the different memorials to be submitted for signature.

157. Following are quotations from the address delivered to the tribal meetings:

"I have asked you all to attend this meeting as I wish your answer to be the voice of all the people who live in this Reserve. You must understand that you are free people and can always express your views, whatever they are, without fear. Similar meetings are being held in all the Native Reserves and these meetings are being addressed by Native Commissioners (Magistrates) of the districts concerned. They are using the same words as I will use today so that all the people will understand this big question fully and so that there can be no misunderstanding among the people of the various Reserves."

158. The memorial read as follows:

"We, the undersigned, Chiefs, Headmen or Board Members of the people of the . . . tribe, who live in the . . . Reserve in this mandated Territory of South West Africa, acting with full authority of the people of the tribe of the . . . Reserve, wish to say that we have heard that the people of the world are talking about the administration of countries such as ours and that the administration of these countries may be changed.

"We and our people wish the following matters to be known to the peoples of the world:

(a) That our people have been happy and have prospered under the rule of the Government of the Union of South Africa and that we should like that Government to continue to rule us;

(b) That we do not wish any other Government or people to rule us; and

(c) That we would like our country to become part of the Union of South Africa."

159. Following is a detailed summary showing the results of the consultations and the numbers of those who were so consulted:

Territory or Reserve *Territoire ou Réserve*	Tribe *Tribu*	Population (To nearest 10) *(Chiffres arrondis à 10)*
	IN FAVOUR *VOTENT POUR*	
OVAMBOLAND	Ondonga Ukusnyama Ukuambi Okandjera Okolankathi Ukualuthi Ombalantu Eunda	129,760
OKAVANGO and WESTERN CAPRIVI ZIPFEL *OKAVANGO et CAPRIVI ZIPFEL OCCIDENTAL*	Ukuangari Bunja Sambio Diriko Nbukushu	25,540
POLICE ZONE *ZONE DE POLICE*	Ovambo and Okavango tribesmen (not specially consulted) *Ovambos et Okavangos indigènes (pas spécialement consultés)*	21,750
KAOKOVELD	Ovahimbas Ovatjimbas Hottentots	5,990
REHOBOTH BASTER GEBIET and elsewhere throughout Police Zone *REHOBOTH BASTER GEBIET et ailleurs dans la Zone de police*	Basters and Coloureds *Basters et hommes de couleur*	19,450
BONDEIS KRANZFONTEIN HOACHANAS FRANZPLAATS and other Reserves *FRANZPLAATS et autres Réserves*	Hottentots	1,320
OKOMBAHE OTJIMBINGWE and other Reserves *OTJIMBINGWE et autres Réserves*	Damaras	3,090

Territory or Reserve *Territoire ou Réserve*	Tribe *Tribu*	Population (To nearest 10) *(Chiffres arrondis à 10)*
	IN FAVOUR *VOTENT POUR*	
RESERVES IN POLICE ZONE *RESERVES DANS LA ZONE DE POLICE*	Other unspecified tribes ⎫ *Autres tribus non spécifiées* ⎬ ⎭	1,950
		‾‾‾‾‾‾‾ 208,850
	AGAINST *VOTENT CONTRE*	
BERSEBA SOROMAS and other Reserves *SOROMAS et autres Réserves* ⎫⎬⎭	Hottentots	2,810
AUKEIGAS and other Reserves *AUKEIGAS et autres Réserves* ⎫⎬⎭	Damaras	1,690
ALL TERRITORY *TOUT LE TERRITOIRE* ⎬	Hereros	27,350
RESERVES IN POLICE ZONE *RESERVES DANS LA ZONE DE POLICE*	Other tribes ⎫ *Autres tribus* ⎬	1,670
		‾‾‾‾‾‾ 33,520
	NOT CONSULTED *NON CONSULTES*	
POLICE ZONE *ZONE DE POLICE* ⎧⎪⎨⎪⎩	Bushmen	9,330
	Hottentots	19,100
	Damaras	25,560
	Other tribes ⎫ *Autres tribus* ⎬	2,800
		‾‾‾‾‾‾ 56,790
	GRAND TOTAL ⎫ *TOTAL GENERAL* ⎬	299,160

160. As will be noted, a number of Bushmen, Hottentots, Damaras and a few other Natives were not consulted. This was due to the fact that they are scattered on farms over the whole Territory and because of the absence of authorized tribal Headmen.

161. It will also be observed that the Natives against the incorporation of the Territory with the Union are, in the main, Hereros. In

fact, apart from some 994 in the Kaokoveld and 1,574 in the Otjituo Reserve, all the Hereros are against incorporation. This, it is believed, is due to the traditional grievance of the Hereros that their country was not returned to them after the defeat of Germany in World War I. Any form of government limiting their independence would be equally objectionable to them.

162. However, the result of consultation is briefly: *for,* 208,850, *against,* 33,520, *not consulted,* 56,790.

These figures, it is submitted, speak for themselves; and when one considers the terms in which many of the replies by Headmen and others in authority were couched there can be no doubt as to the feelings of the non-Europeans. Indeed, the words of Councillor-Headman Shitala Namangangala of Ovamboland that "we are like man who has lived a long time with a good wife . . . a man who likes his first wife does not get rid of her . . . it is so with this Government of ours . . .", constitute a clear and unequivocal reply to President Wilson's remark at Versailles that "if South Africa managed South West Africa as well as she had managed her own country then she would be *married* to South West Africa".

163. Since therefore the people of South West Africa have freely and unequivocally expressed themselves in favour of a status which would make their country part of the Union;

Since furthermore

A. Doubts originally existed as to the applicability of the Mandates System to the Territory;

B. Experience of more than a quarter of a century has shown that the unique circumstances of the Territory do not permit of satisfactory government under the mandates or any analogous system;

C. The territories of the Union and South West Africa should, for geographic reasons, constitute a single unit;

D. The Territories of the two countries should, in the interests of national security and world peace, constitute a strategic unit;

E. The people of the Territory have a close ethnological and national affinity with the people of the Union;

F. The Territory is economically dependent on the Union;

G. The administration of the Territory has already been integrated partially with that of the Union, and should, in the general interests of the country and its population, be further integrated;

The Government of the Union of South Africa considers that the interests of the peoples of South West Africa would best be served by the speedy implementation of the wishes they have fully and freely expressed regarding the future status of their country.

The validity of this consultation was seriously questioned both inside South Africa and outside, particularly by the Reverend Michael Scott, whose endorsement of the cause of the Non-White people of South West Africa was to become a feature of the South West Africa dispute. In 1947 he transmitted a lengthy memorandum to the Fourth Committee on the injustices of the South African administration of South West Africa in which he also refuted the "consultation" of the Non-White people.[1] His views on this subject are briefly set out in an article in *The British Africa Monthly* of 1948.[m]

The whole notion of a referendum was ill-conceived. In the first place the great majority of the Native people were neither sufficiently educated nor instructed in the issues at stake to be in a position to express any opinion. Such was the conclusion reached by Mr. Justice Van Zyl when, some time previously, he had been asked by the Union Government to report on this question:

> If one considers the backwardness of the indigenous population (i.e. South-West African Natives) it becomes clear that there is no reasonable expectation of their acquiring those mental, moral and civic qualities which would justify their being taken seriously into consideration before a point of time so remote as hardly to merit present consideration.

. . . .

That the Chiefs should have been asked to give, after three and a half hours' consideration, the answer of their people to questions which would affect the whole future of their country is an index of the trustworthiness of the referendum. But then it was not revealed, as it can be now, that in the form of words used in the question no attempt was made to explain what the United Nations Organization is, nor what the implications of Trusteeship or incorporation were. Nor was it explained that there was a great difference between being under the British flag and being under the Union flag, the Native policy of the British Government being vastly different from that of the Union Government. Yet it was admitted in the Union Government's report that many of the Native Tribes' spokesmen, before they would give any answer at all on the question of incorporation wanted to know "whether any change in the administration of the Territory would remove them from under the shadow of the Crown of King George of England."

Once assured that the change implied no departure from South Africa's partnership in the British Commonwealth of Nations, the Natives declared themselves fully satisifed on this point. (Page 84 "History of a Mandate.")

[1] *GAOR,* 2nd session, Fourth Committee, pp. 139–93 (Doc. A/C 4/95). For the South African Government's reply, see, *ibid.,* pp. 193–97 (Doc. A/C 4/118). For further criticism of this "consultation," see *GAOR,* 4th session, Fourth Committee, Annex pp. 34–35 (DOC. A/C 4/L.66); and Dale, above, n. c, pp. 111–54.

[m] Vol. 1, No. 12, August 1948, pp. 13–15. See further by Michael Scott on this subject: "The International Status of South West Africa" (1958) 34 *International Affairs* 318 at 324–26; *The Orphan's Heritage* (1958), pp. 12–16; *Shadow over Africa* (1950).

That an assurance of such a kind could be given in face of the facts that the Opposition in the Union Parliament (now the Government), had declared their aim to be a Republic affords some indication of the honesty of the Referendum.

5. *The General Assembly Rejects Incorporation*

On 14 December 1946, the General Assembly considered South Africa's request but resolved that it was unable to grant it. Instead it recommended that South West Africa be placed under trusteeship.
Resolution 65(1):

The General Assembly,
Having considered the statements of the delegation of the Union of South Africa regarding the question of incorporating the mandated territory of South West Africa in the Union:
Noting with satisfaction that the Union of South Africa, by presenting this matter to the United Nations, recognizes the interest and concern of the United Nations in the matter of the future status of territories now held under mandate;
Recalling that the Charter of the United Nations provides in Articles 77 and 79 that the trusteeship system shall apply to territories now under mandate as may be subsequently agreed;
Referring to the resolution of the General Assembly of 9 February 1946, inviting the placing of mandated territories under trusteeship;
Desiring that agreement between the United Nations and the Union of South Africa may hereafter be reached regarding the future status of the mandated territory of South West Africa;
Assured by the delegation of the Union of South Africa that, pending such agreement, the Union Government will continue to administer the territory as heretofore in the spirit of the principles laid down in the mandate;
Considering that the African inhabitants of South West Africa have not yet secured political autonomy or reached a stage of political development enabling them to express a considered opinion which the Assembly could recognize on such an important question as incorporation of their territory:
The General Assembly, therefore,
Is unable to accede to the incorporation of the territory of South West Africa in the Union of South Africa; and
Recommends that the mandated territory of South West Africa be placed under the international trusteeship system and invites the Government of the Union of South Africa to propose for the consideration of the General Assembly a trusteeship agreement for the aforesaid territory.

This Resolution was adopted by thirty-seven votes to none with nine abstentions. In view of subsequent allegations that opposi-

tion to South Africa's stance on South West Africa is largely inspired by the Afro-Asian States, it should be recalled that those
States which voted for this first resolution on South West Africa
included Belgium, Canada, and the United States.

6. South Africa's Response

Following this rebuff South Africa continued to submit reports to
the United Nations on her administration of South West Africa,
but refused to enter into a trusteeship agreement. She now declared that her policy was "to administer the Territory in the
spirit of the existing Mandate": [n]

NOTE BY THE SECRETARY-GENERAL

The following letter dated 23 July 1947 has been received from the
Legation of the Union of South Africa at Washington, D.C.:
Sir,
In your letter No. 1204-4-17/PCK of the 15th May, 1947, you were
good enough to refer to resolution 65 (I) adopted by the General Assembly on 14 December 1946, concerning the future status of South
West Africa, and to enquire of any action taken or any steps being
considered by the Government of the Union of South Africa in implementation of the recommendation contained in that resolution.
I have the honour to inform you by direction that the resolution has
been duly considered by the Union Government, and was discussed in
the Union Parliament, when a resolution in the following terms was
adopted:

> Whereas in terms of the Treaty of Versailles, full power of legisla-
> tion and administration was conferred on the Union of South Africa
> in respect of the Territory of South West Africa, subject only to the
> rendering of reports to the League of Nations; and
> Whereas the League of Nations has since ceased to exist and was
> not empowered by the provisions of the Treaty of Versailles or of
> the Covenant to transfer its rights and powers in regard to South
> West Africa to the United Nations Organization, or to any other in-
> ternational organization or body, and did not in fact do so; and
> Whereas the Union of South Africa has not by international
> agreement consented to surrender the rights and powers so acquired,
> and has not surrendered these by signing the Charter of the United
> Nations Organization and remains in full possession and exercise
> thereof; and
> Whereas the overwhelming majority of both the European and
> non-European inhabitants of South West Africa have expressed
> themselves in favour of the incorporation of South West Africa with
> the Union of South Africa;

[n] *GAOR,* 2nd session, Fourth Committee 134–35. (Doc. A/334).

Therefore this House is of opinion that the Territory should be represented in the Parliament of the Union as an integral portion thereof, and requests the Government to introduce legislation, after consultation with the inhabitants of the Territory, providing for its representation in the Union Parliament, and that the Government should continue to render reports to the United Nations Organization as it has done heretofore under the Mandate.

In this connexion I am also requested to recall that the Union Government, in submitting their statement to the last General Assembly regarding the outcome of the consultations with the peoples of South West Africa and the future of the mandated Territory, suggested that the interests of those peoples would be best served by the speedy implementation of their wish to see the Territory incorporated in the Union, for the reasons fully stated in the memorandum included in that statement.

The Union Government had hoped that the General Assembly would approve of that suggestion. Instead, however, a resolution was adopted which expressed the inability of the General Assembly to accede to the incorporation of South West Africa in the Union. The Union Government have therefore decided not to proceed with the incorporation of the Territory desired by its inhabitants. In this respect therefore the Union Government's decision fully agrees with the terms of the General Assembly's resolution.

The General Assembly, in the resolution, added a recommendation that South West Africa be placed under the trusteeship system and that the Union Government submit a trusteeship agreement in respect of the Territory. In this connexion the Union Government desire to reiterate their view that it is implicit in the mandate system and in the Mandate for South West Africa that due regard shall be had to the wishes of the inhabitants in the administration of the Territory. The wish, clearly expressed by the overwhelming majority of all the native races in South West Africa and by unanimous vote on the part of the European representatives of the Territory that South West Africa be incorporated in the Union therefore debars the Union Government from acting in accordance with the resolution of the General Assembly, and thereby flouting the wishes of those who under the Mandate have been committed to their charge. In the circumstances the Union Government have no alternative but to maintain the *status quo* and to continue to administer the Territory in the spirit of the existing Mandate.

The Union Government are mindful of the fact that the General Assembly, in passing the recommendation, was mainly concerned about the welfare of the inhabitants of the Territory—especially the non-Europeans. This concern the Union Government naturally shares. It will however be recalled that the interests of the native inhabitants were fully provided for with specific safeguards under the Mandate and that the administration of South West Africa and the implementation of those safeguards have been uniformly satisfactory ever since the inception of the mandatory system. They feel confident, therefore, that their continued administration of the Territory in the spirit of the Mandate will equally merit the satisfaction of the United Nations.

To that end the Union Government have already undertaken to submit reports on their administration for the information of the United Nations.

When pressed to clarify the basis on which these reports were submitted, the South African delegate stated that [o]

the annual report which his Government would submit on South West Africa would contain the same type of information on the Territory as is required for Non-Self-Governing Territories under Article 73 (e) of the Charter. It was the assumption of his Government, he said, that the report would not be considered by the Trusteeship Council and would not be dealt with as if a trusteeship agreement had in fact been concluded. He further explained that, since the League of Nations had ceased to exist, the right to submit petitions could no longer be exercised, since that right presupposes a jurisdiction which would only exist where there is a right of control or supervision, and in the view of the Union of South Africa no such jurisdiction is vested in the United Nations with regard to South West Africa.

The South African Government's vulnerability on this score was not limited to the United Nations. On the home front General Smuts was criticized when Mr. Eric Louw introduced a motion in the House of Assembly requesting the Government "to provide for the integration of South West Africa with the Union . . . without any responsibility whatsoever, as regards the administration of the Territory, to the United Nations Organisation." [p] Mr. Louw skilfully exposed the Government's vacillations in the following attack: [q]

What are the statements of the Prime Minister? In New York, after the adverse decision of the United Nations Assembly, the Prime Minister stated that the Union would continue to administer South-West Africa in the terms and in the spirit of the mandate. I notice that the representative of South Africa at the burial ceremony of the League made a similar statement. He there stated that it was the intention of the Prime Minister to formulate his case at New York for according to South-West Africa an international status under which it would be administered as an integral part of the Union. But he said that South Af-

[o] *Ibid.*, Plenary Mtgs., Vol. 11, pp. 1538 (DOC. A/422). See, too, *GAOR* 1st session (2nd part), Part 1, p. 102. See generally on this phase, H. Duncan Hall, "The Trusteeship System and the Case of South-West Africa" (1947) 24 *British Year Book of International Law* 385.
[p] *House of Assembly Debates*, vol. 60, col. 1319 (19 March 1947). See further, Dale, above, n. c, pp. 195–209.
[q] *Ibid.*, cols. 1336–43.

rica would continue to administer the territory scrupulously in accordance with the obligations of the mandate. I repeat: "in accordance with the obligations of the mandate." What are the obligations of the mandate, the mandate which no longer exists? The obligations of the mandate include amongst other things the rendering of annual reports, and also to permit the people of the territory, more particularly the native people, to submit petitions to the League of Nations. In the past they submitted their petitions to the League. If the Rt. Hon. the Prime Minister intends pursuing this idea of his, it is quite obvious that he cannot submit annual reports to the League. The reports under these circumstances can only be submitted to UNO. If there were any doubt as to the Prime Minister's intentions on the question of submitting reports, then these doubts are removed by certain statements he made in the House last year when he said, "I am very anxious indeed to have complete incorporation and annexation of the territory." And he added he was going "to maintain the status quo." I asked a question, "A status quo minus the old League?" The Prime Minister replied, "Yes, we had an obligation under the League to render reports, and if no agreement can be come to, then under Article 80 it is our obligation to continue to render reports." I think Article 80 in the Hansard report must be a misprint. It has nothing to do with it. Then later on I asked the Prime Minister this question, "Can we take it that the use of the term 'continuance of the status quo' is equivalent in your mind with annexation?" The Prime Minister replied, "No, it is a continuance of the present regime, of our full government and administration and legislative power plus the obligation to render annual reports."

MR. LOUW: To whom?

THE PRIME MINISTER: To UNO. UNO is the only authority to which reports can be made.

MR. LOUW: Does that mean that as under the old mandatory system the people of the territory can send petitions to UNO? In other words, can the natives there send petitions to UNO?

THE PRIME MINISTER: Yes.

MR. LOUW: Are you agreeable to that?

THE PRIME MINISTER: Yes, I am, because the word "peoples" is specially mentioned.

MR. LOUW: Then you are willing to submit to petitions being sent to UNO by the natives of South-West Africa?

THE PRIME MINISTER: Yes, in this sense, that we make the reports which were customarily put before the League of Nations to UNO.

Those are the statements made by the Rt. Hon. the Prime Minister last year. I hope the hon. member for Hospital (Mr. Barlow) is now satisfied, as I think I satisfied him in the previous part of my speech.

What is the Prime Minister's attitude today? We have this interesting development, that the Prime Minister recently repeated the statement regarding the rendering of reports, when this matter was raised

by the Leader of the Opposition in January of this year. But the
Prime Minister has now shifted his position. He is still willing to submit reports, but not in the manner of last year, when he said it was an
obligation resulting from the Mandate. Now the Rt. Hon. the Prime
Minister has a new idea. His idea now is not to submit reports under
Chapter XII of the Charter. He told the House in January last that he
is going to submit reports under Chapter XI, and he says it will be
purely for the information of UNO. Let us look at Chapter XI, and I
hope I will satisfy the hon. member for Hospital. This is what the
Prime Minister said in January of this year. I quote from Hansard—

> The question has been asked whether we are going to submit re-
> ports. In that respect my opinion is that there are two types of terri-
> tories under the Charter. There are subordinate States which do not
> come under trusteeship; I refer to the colonies.

You see, Mr. Speaker, the Prime Minister has now discarded his previous plea of submitting reports in terms of the Mandate. He has now
decided that South-West Africa is a different type of territory—

> The colonies of the various countries which are not mandated terri-
> tories also fall under the Charter, but not under the trusteeship sys-
> tem, and as far as they are concerned, it was laid down that they can
> submit reports to UNO for information.

I was rather surprised to hear about this new idea, so I asked, "Where
is that provision?"
The Prime Minister replied:

> In Chapter XI, which deals with non-self-governing nations. There
> it will be seen that regulations were promulgated in connection with
> such countries. Colonial Powers, which will not come under the
> trusteeship system, can submit reports for the sake of social co-opera-
> tion with the world, for the sake of furnishing information, and my
> opinion is that that is what we ought to do.

> MR. LOUW: That does not relate to mandated territories.
> THE PRIME MINISTER: South-West is no longer a mandated terri-
> tory.

That is another shift of position, because in his own White Paper the
Prime Minister speaks of "the termination of the Mandate", and asks
that the Mandate be terminated. It is necessary to quote chapter and
verse, in order to make the position quite clear. In his own White
Paper he says: "The delegation of the Union of South Africa therefore
claims that the Mandate should be terminated. . . ."
But now he tells us that the mandates no longer exist! And because
the mandates no longer exist, we have to submit our reports under
Chapter XI. The Prime Minister said further, in reply to my questions
in January: "I should rather associate our position with that of colonial territories, which do not fall under trusteeship, but under the colonial system. In my opinion, that is what we should do. It is a conces-

sion . . ." I unfortunately interjected at this point and stopped the train of the Prime Minister's thoughts, which were probably very interesting. I asked, "What do you understand by 'non-self-governing' territories?"

THE PRIME MINISTER: One must look at this matter more from the point of view of South-West Africa, and not from the point of view of South Africa.

MR. LOUW: Is South-West Africa not self-governing? It falls under the Union; it is an integral portion of the Union?

THE PRIME MINISTER: Do not look at the matter from the point of view of South Africa, but rather from the point of view of South-West Africa.

I asked, "South-West is part of the Union?"

MR. SWART: In other words, a colony?

THE PRIME MINISTER: It can be likened more to the colonial conception. It is not a colony, but it is almost tantamount to that; it is more in the nature of a colony.

There is a shift of position again. It is first "a mandated territory", then "a colonial possession", and in the same breath it is "not a colony"—"It is not a colony, but it is almost tantamount to that. . . ." Then he says, "We can furnish this information, and they can do with it as they please; but it is being done voluntarily, and not as the result of any obligation."

I said, "Chapter XI (e) stipulates that you must report. It imposes quite a number of obligations."

THE PRIME MINISTER: These are ordinary reports and I cannot see any objection to furnishing that information.

Let us take the matter a little further. The Prime Minister has now shifted from Chapter XII to Chapter XI. I hope the Prime Minister will not take it amiss if I say that this looks very suspiciously like splitting of hairs. Or to change the metaphor, he is trying to sit on two stools.

THE PRIME MINISTER: Splitting of hairs by whom, by you or by me?

MR. LOUW: By the Rt. Hon. the Prime Minister in first describing South-West Africa as a mandated territory, then calling it a colony, then saying it was not quite a colony, and then again that it was tantamount to a colony. What has obviously happened, is that the Prime Minister since this matter was discussed here last year, has realised that reports under Chapter XII would be an acknowledgment of UNO's authority. The Prime Minister has realised that, and I am very glad he has realised it; it is all to the good. So the Prime Minister decides to side-step the issue, to side-step Chapter XII, and to try to get in under Chapter XI. Obviously, the Prime Minister for fear of perhaps annoying UNO, or what not, wants to do something. He wants to give them something, so he decides to cut out Chapter XII and to give them the reports under Chapter XI. I want to say frankly that it is a very ingenious idea, but I am afraid it will not deceive anybody, certainly not Mr. Vishinsky or Mr. Molotov. And what is even more important is that the ultimate result will be exactly the same, whether you submit the report under Chapter XII or under Chapter XI. The ultimate result is going to be exactly the same.

.   .   .   .

Then there is a final reason why Chapter XI cannot apply to South-West Africa. The Prime Minister wishes South-West Africa to maintain some sort of connection with UNO. That is obviously what he has in mind. He wants to incorporate the territory in the Union, but he also wants to satisfy UNO in some way or another. If he wants to maintain South-West Africa's connection with UNO, I submit it can only be done under Chapter XII, quite apart from the fact as to whether he is prepared to accept the conditions attached to Chapter XI. South-West Africa was a mandated territory, and Chapter XII, Article 77, deals with "territories now held under mandate." When the Rt. Hon. the Prime Minister signed the Charter, South-West Africa was a territory previously held under mandate. How can he now, for purposes of his own policy, take South-West Africa out of Chapter XII, which deals with territories held under mandate, and say: "I am going to put it under Chapter XI." It cannot be done. The idea is an ingenious one, but he cannot carry it out. And I suggest that it will satisfy no one. You cannot drag in Chapter XI. As far as South-West Africa is concerned, if the Prime Minister wants to maintain the connection with UNO, it is Chapter XII or nothing. And our attitude is that it must be nothing.

I come to the matter of the submission of reports, be it in terms of the mandate, or in terms of Chapter XI or in terms of Chapter XII. What does it imply, under whichever chapter it is done? What are going to be the consequences of submitting annual reports to UNO? Mr. Speaker, I can speak from personal experience, having on two occasions had the honour of submitting the South-West Africa report to the League of Nations Mandates Commission. And, Mr. Speaker, let me say this, that the Mandates Commission of those days was a body of sympathetic affable gentlemen. And yet, on each occasion I was examined and cross-examined for two full days by the Commission. I was cross-examined very closely on the Union's administration of South-West Africa. But I suggest that when these reports of the Rt. Hon. The Prime Minister go to UNO, it is going to be a very different story. The examination of the Union by the UNO Trusteeship Committee will be very different from what it was in the days of the old League of Nations, because the old League, with possibly half a dozen exceptions, was a white organisation, an organisation of predominantly European powers.

Mr. Barlow: What about the Japanese?

Mr. Louw: I said with some exceptions. [Interruption.] But UNO is a horse of a very different colour, because UNO is predominantly coloured; it consists of predominantly coloured and Asiatic nations, and of off-colour nations. A considerable number of South and Central American nations are predominantly of mixed blood. And the position is going to be very different when our representative—I pity the poor man—turns up to submit his report on South-West Africa, to UNO as at present constituted.

Although Mr. Louw's resolution was rejected in favour of one supporting the Government's policy,[r] it is interesting to recall that during this debate the Labour Party urged the Government to recognize the United Nations as successor to the League[s] and one of the Native representatives in the House argued that South Africa was in law obliged to place the territory under trusteeship.[t]

7. The National Party's Approach to South West Africa

In 1948 the National Party was elected to office on the platform of apartheid. On 11 July 1949 the new Government informed the United Nations that it would discontinue its reports:[u]

The recommendation of the General Assembly that the Union should continue to supply information on its administration of South West Africa has been given most careful consideration.

It will be recalled, however, that the Union Government have at no time recognized any legal obligations on their part to supply information on South West Africa to the United Nations, but in a spirit of goodwill, co-operation and helpfulness offered to provide the United Nations with reports on the administration of South West Africa, with the clear stipulation that this would be done on a voluntary basis, for purposes of information only and on the distinct understanding that the United Nations has no supervisory jurisdiction in South West Africa. In this spirit a report was submitted in 1947, and in 1948 detailed replies were furnished to a subsequent questionnaire formulated by the Trusteeship Council. It was emphasized at the time that the forwarding of information on policy should not be regarded as creating a precedent, or construed as a commitment for the future or as implying any measure of accountability to the United Nations on the part of the Union Government. The Union Government also expressed their confidence that the Trusteeship Council would approach its task in an entirely objective manner and examine the report in the same spirit of goodwill, co-operation and helpfulness as had motivated the Union in making the information available.

These hopes have not been realized. Instead, the submission of information has provided an opportunity to utilize the Trusteeship

[r] Ibid., col. 2624 (14 April 1947). The resolution adopted appears above, p. 112.

[s] Ibid., col. 1371 (19 March 1947).

[t] Mr. Molteno, M. P., ibid., cols. 2607–8 (11 April 1947).

[u] GAOR, 4th session, Fourth Committee, Annex to the summary records of meetings of 1949, pp. 7–8 (Doc. A/929).

Council and the Trusteeship Committee as a forum for unjustified criticism and censure of the Union Government's administration, not only in South West Africa but in the Union as well. Inferences and deductions have been drawn from the information submitted which are quite inconsistent with facts and realities. The misunderstandings and accusations to which the United Nations discussions of this subject have given rise have had repercussions both in the Union and in South West Africa, with deleterious effects on the maintenance of the harmonious relations which have hitherto existed and are so essential to successful administration. Furthermore, the very act of submitting a report has created in the minds of a number of Members of the United Nations an impression that the Trusteeship Council is competent to make recommendations on matters of internal administration of South West Africa and has fostered other misconceptions regarding the status of this Territory.

In these circumstances the Union Government can no longer see that any real benefit is to be derived from the submission of special reports on South West Africa to the United Nations, and have regretfully come to the conclusion that in the interests of efficient administration no further reports should be forwarded. In coming to this decision the Union Government are in no way motivated by a desire to withhold from the world factual and other information regarding South West Africa, published in accordance with the customary practice of democratic nations, and information of this nature previously embodied in annual reports to the League of Nations or the United Nations will continue to be made available to the general public in the form of statistics, departmental reports, reports by the Administrator to the South West African Legislature, blue books, and other governmental publications.

In the same year the Government introduced the controversial South West Africa Affairs Amendment Act 23 of 1949, which provided for closer association with South Africa. The scope of this statute appears from a memorandum submitted to the United Nations.[v]

The Act gives South West Africa six representatives in the Union House of Assembly all of whom will be elected, and four in the Senate, two of whom will be elected and the other two nominated by the Governor-General. One of the nominated senators will be selected mainly on the ground of his thorough acquaintance, by reason of his official experience or otherwise, with the reasonable wants and wishes of the coloured races of the Territory.

The South West Africa Legislative Assembly, in terms of the Act, will consist of eighteen members elected by the registered voters of the Territory. At present the Assembly has twelve elected members and six nominated members.

[v] *Ibid.*, pp. 11–12. See further, Dale, above, n. c, pp. 214–27.

. . . .

As far as is practicable, the Governor-General in appointing an Administrator for South West Africa, will give preference to persons who live or have lived there and have special knowledge of the Territory.

South West Africa will not come under the Union's taxation system. The Act specifically provides that no Act of the Union Parliament, other than the laws relating to customs and excise, which imposes a tax, duty, charge or burden on the people of the Union, shall be of force in the Territory. South West African representatives in the Union Parliament will, however, have all the rights, powers, privileges and immunities of other members of Parliament. The position will thus be created that while the representatives of South West Africa in the Union Parliament have both a voice and vote on measures imposing taxation on the people of the Union, the Union members of Parliament have no say in regard to the taxation of the people of South West Africa.

. . . .

The following matters are reserved from legislation by the South West Africa Legislative Assembly but provision exists in terms whereof the Assembly may make Ordinances on these matters subject to the consent of the Governor-General previously having been obtained:

(a) Native affairs or any matters specially affecting Natives, including the imposition of taxation upon the person's land, habitations or earnings of Natives. Whenever any Ordinance of the Assembly imposes taxation upon persons, lands, habitations, or incomes or earnings generally, Natives and their lands, habitations and earnings shall be exempt from its provisions;

. . . .

The Act declares that nothing contained in it shall be construed as in any manner abolishing, diminishing or derogating from the full powers of administration and legislation over the Territory as an integral part of the Union which have hitherto been vested in the Union.

. . . .

An Ordinance made by the Legislative Assembly shall, though promulgated, have effect in and for the Territory so long as and as far only as it is not repugnant to or inconsistent with an Act of Parliament applicable to the Territory.

The members of the Union House of Assembly to be elected under the Act will be chosen by the duly registered voters of the Territory for the electoral divisions delimited for the purpose under the South West Africa Constitution Act.

A member of the House of Assembly to be elected under the Act must:

(a) Be qualified to be registered as a voter for the election of members of the House of Assembly in one of the provinces, or in the Territory;

(b) Have resided for five years in the Union or the Territory;

(c) Be a Union national of European descent.

A nominated senator will hold his seat for ten years. If his seat becomes vacant, the Governor-General will nominate another person to be senator, who will also hold his seat for ten years.

The elected senators will be chosen by the members of the Legislative Assembly of the Territory together with the members of the House of Assembly, according to the principles of proportional representation as is the case with elected senators in the Union. An elected senator will hold his seat for ten years unless the Senate is sooner dissolved. If the seat of an elected senator becomes vacant, another may be elected for the unexpired part of the ten years.

A senator to be nominated or elected must:

(a) Be not less than thirty years of age;

(b) Be qualified to be registered as a voter for the election of members of the House of Assembly in one of the provinces or in the Territory;

(c) Have resided for five years in the Union or the Territory;

(d) Be a Union national of European descent;

(e) In the case of an elected senator, he must be the registered owner of immovable property within the Union or the Territory to the value of not less than five hundred pounds over and above any special mortgage thereon.

. . . .

In effect the Act gives the Territory of South West Africa representation in the Union Parliament without in any way curtailing its existing powers of self-government or interfering with its fiscal autonomy. . . . so far from conferring additional powers on the Union Government, the Act provides that certain powers, previously exercised by the Union Government, should now be exercised by the South West Africa Legislature. The position regarding Native interests will, however, remain unaltered. The arrangement will continue under which it is *not* competent for the South West Africa Legislature to make any Ordinance on Native affairs or any matters specially affecting Natives, including the imposition of taxation upon the persons, land, habitations, or earnings of Natives. The obligations of the Union Government vis-à-vis the Natives, which derive from the mandate and are embodied in the original Act, thus remain in full force.

Although the South African Government denied that this constituted an act of annexation, it clearly envisaged a situation which was close to annexation. In the Parliamentary debate on this legislation Prime Minister Malan stated: [w]

We will continue to refuse to place South-West Africa under the Trusteeship Council. Then the question arose what we had to do in such circumstances. Should the same thing be repeated which we experienced in regard to the future of South-West Africa, namely, when, at three annual meetings at least, I think, of UNO year after year the future of South-West Africa was a subject for discussion? If that were to

[w] *House of Assembly Debates*, vol. 66, col. 1275 (17 February 1949).

be repeated year after year, there would never be any peace or certainty for the future in connection with this matter. Therefore a course had to be adopted in order to try to bring the matter to a conclusion in some way or another. There is as far as I can see—to me at least it was very evident—only one way to do so and that way is: Place South-West Africa in a position where it will be invulnerable against that type of propaganda and incitement. Knit South-West Africa and the Union together in such a manner, knit them together constitutionally in such a way that the two areas will in future be inseparably bound together. In order to achieve this, let us make use of the unquestionable right which South Africa possesses, the right which South Africa also possessed when the mandate was still in existence and the principal in regard to the mandate had not yet disappeared, and bring about a position of closer affiliation of the two territories, the Union and South-West Africa, even if, at least, for the present, we do not go as far as the ultimate limit of incorporating South-West Africa in the Union. Even if we do not go to that limit of incorporating South-West Africa in our country, we can still knit South-West Africa and the Union so closely together constitutionally that they can never again be separated. In consequence of this Bill South-West Africa would cease to be a territory administered from outside, a territory with an overlord, and a territory which, being outside the Union and having an overlord might easily at least in the opinion of some people be transferred from one overlord to another. For that reason I felt that we should first of all grant South-West Africa self-government as far as its internal matters are concerned, which will mean much more freedom; the second concession we give, externally, is that every measure and every Act which is passed and which is also to be applied to South-West Africa, will be passed by South-West Africa in participation with the whole Union, or as I expressed it before—do not only make South-West Africa a mandated country—if we can still use the term "mandate"—but make South-West Africa, together with the Union as a whole, a co-mandatory of its own territory.

It is frequently contended that the National Party's approach to South West Africa was fundamentally different from that of the United Party and that this accounted for the new stance at the United Nations. This argument is examined by R. B. Ballinger: [x]

It has frequently been argued that the Nationalist Party victory of 1948, which brought Dr. Malan's government into office, saw a radical change in the Union's attitude and policy towards the United Nations.[42] As evidence it is pointed out, first, that there is the break with the previous government in the matter of annual reports; secondly,

[x] *South West Africa. The Case Against the Union* (1961), pp. 18–22. See, too, Dale, above, n. c. pp. 195–214.
[42] For the most recent expression of this view, see *South Africa and the Rule of Law*, International Commission of Jurists (Geneva, 1960), 85.

that in the same year the Nationalist Government took a further step towards the incorporation—or annexation—of the territory, by giving its white inhabitants representation in the Union Parliament. Moreover, it would appear that the first actual assertion by the Union in the United Nations that the Mandate had lapsed, was made by Mr. Louw in the Fourth Committee discussions, November 9, 1948. He referred to *"the previous mandate since expired"*. And it might also be added that an examination of the debates on South-West Africa in Parliament during the years 1946–1949, and particularly in 1947, reveals a much greater caution and flexibility on the part of Field-marshal Smuts and his colleagues than was evident in the speeches of the Nationalist Party members. To take one example, Mr. Louw in support of his own motion to incorporate South-West Africa as a fifth province within the Union without further reference to any international body, said in March 1947:

> South Africa's case is good. The grounds on which we base our case are sound. They are sound juridically. They are sound factually, and I say let us not hesitate. I believe that in this matter we have hesitated too long. Already there has been some talk of sanctions. I think it was raised as an interjection about five weeks ago. May I suggest that we must not allow ourselves to be scared by talk of sanctions, nor to be deflected from our course by any such suggestions. We saw what happened in the case of Italy some years ago. May I add that South Africa is too valuable an export market for the United States of America, for Great Britain, for France, for the West European countries, to encourage the imposition of economic sanctions on South Africa. In any case let us remain master in our own house. To remain master in our own house and to maintain white civilization in this country is of greater importance than the maintenance of trade relations.[43]

And he appealed to Smuts not to send reports to the United Nations. In reply Field-marshal Smuts, as Prime Minister, agreed that the Union case was a sound and a strong one but contended that this was no reason for adopting

> language which looks like a challenge which may appear provocative and which may put the bristles up of stronger nations than ourselves and make our case more difficult. It is not wisdom to use language which looks like a challenge. We are at the beginning of what may be a difficult phase for this country.[44]

Smuts thought it would be wiser to continue sending reports to the United Nations. But when asked by Mr. Louw whether this was not an acknowledgement of its authority—as the Nationalists had held the

[43] Union White Paper, South-West Africa, 1947–8. Annexure 3, for text of Mr. Louw's opening speech, p. 17; House of Assembly Debates, March 19, 1947, Vol. 60, Cols. 1346–7.
[44] *Ibid.*, Col. 1360.

original approach over incorporation to appear to be—he replied that it was not since there was no such authority, and he was assuming no obligation. It was simply a way of easing tension, a wise concession to make. He held that under the Mandate the Union had always had the power and the authority to give South-West Africa representation in Parliament only *"we did not seem to have the opportunity and nobody bothered. But the time is ripe now and we are going to do it"*.[45] He went on to say that he did not think there was any fundamental difference between the parties on the issue. And Mr. Louw agreed, maintaining that the only difference *"was of machinery . . . I ask for a fifth province and the Prime Minister asks for direct representation in Parliament. The principle is the same"*.[46]

With that conclusion it is difficult to quarrel. Despite the apparent differences of attitude towards the United Nations between the two major parties, and the obvious reluctance on the part of Smuts and his followers to formulate their legal standpoint with any precision, the basic agreement between the two parties on the vital questions at issue was far more striking than differences about the wisdom or unwisdom of these or those words. Neither Smuts, when Prime Minister, nor his party liked the cold hard logic of Mr. Louw's rigid legalistic approach. *"My submission, therefore, is,"* said Mr. Louw in March 1947,

> that with the passing of the League, and with the removal of League supervision, the Union of South Africa thereby, in addition to *de facto* possession, also acquired *de jure* possession. I may put it this way, that the nine points of law arising from possession now become the ten points of the law in the full sense of the term.[47]

But earlier in the year, Smuts himself had declared that there was no longer a Mandate and spoke of a relationship similar to that of a colonial possession.[48] Although the United Party speakers might accuse the Nationalists of being over-ready to flout the United Nations or to disregard international opinion, Mr. D. Molteno—who disagreed with Smuts—was right when he said:

> So on that vital question of the authority of UNO, which is really at issue in this debate, the hon. member for Beaufort West (Mr. Louw)

[45] *Ibid.*, Col. 1361. See also March 19, 1947, Cols. 1354, 1357, and April 11, Col. 2611.

[46] *Ibid.*, Vol. 60, April 11, 1947, Col. 2592.

[47] *Ibid.*, Vol. 60, March 19, 1947, Col. 1327.

[48] In the debate on April 11, 1947, in the House of Assembly, Colonel Stallard said, after maintaining that in substance the Prime Minister's position was substantially the same as Mr. Louw's: "I cannot help accompanying that resolution with a speech which the Prime Minister delivered earlier in the year in this House though in the other session, in which he declared categorically there was no longer a mandate. He then proceeded to develop the theory that the relationship between South-West Africa and the Union more nearly approximated to that of a colonial possession than anything else." Vol. 60, Col. 2588. For Field-marshal Smuts's statement see House of Assembly Debates, January 21, 1947, Vol. 59, Cols. 10916–7.

and the Prime Minister are *ad idem*. That is really the issue in this debate. As I see it, it is the question of whether or not there is any international obligation subject to which our policy and our administration of South-West Africa must be pursued.[49]

The answer to that question, of course, was: No. On this, as on their outright rejection of the trusteeship system, Smuts and his opponents were agreed. Thus the full case for the total lapse of the mandate, presented to the International Court of Justice in 1950, was already foreshadowed here. The similarities go further. In the event, the Nationalist Government, when it implemented the motion passed by its predecessor *"that the territory should be represented in the Parliament of the Union as integral portion thereof"*, followed the Smuts approach.

This leaves only the question of the reports. Here the Nationalist leaders could not follow the logic of Smuts. Their attitude was clear, and given the premises—on which as we have seen there was a large measure of agreement—the logic was unassailable. Logic, however, is one thing, experience another. Smuts, after six years of war and his experience in the creation of the United Nations Organization, had a greater understanding of the problems and the international climate of opinion which now faced the Union. The logic of a legal case was less important to him than the reactions of the international community to South Africa's special problems. His reluctance to stress the legal aspects of the Union's case and the claims which, clearly, he thought stemmed from them, was due to a desire, a determination not to lose friends at United Nations—even if he could win none.[50]

It is possible to argue, of course, that with his greater flexibility of approach, Smuts would have found a compromise solution. But after the Advisory Opinion of 1950, this would have been possible only by acknowledging international obligations to the United Nations. There is little evidence that this would have been welcome to any considerable body of opinion in the country. Equally, however, it could be argued that the logic of the Union's position and the requirements of its legal stand, might have forced a United Party Government to discontinue the reports. In this connection, it is worth recalling that the United States Government, in its written statement of December 6, 1949, to the International Court of Justice, contended that the submission of reports by the Union constituted a request to the United Nations to assume functions formerly belonging to the League, and a recognition that the Mandate was still in force.[51] Such requests were provided for in a General Assembly resolution of February 1946.* The

---

* General Assembly Resolution XIV-1 (i), February 12, 1946, which provided that the General Assembly could consider assuming certain League functions, including those relating to Mandates, if any remained to be attended to, on "any request from the parties."

[49] House of Assembly Debates, April 11, 1947, Vol. 60, Col. 2599.

[50] See especially his speech, March 19, 1947, *Ibid.*, Vol. 60, Col. 1362.

[51] I.C.J. International Status of South-West Africa, Pleadings, Oral Arguments, Documents, 1950, 108–111.

same statement saw in Mr. Louw's reminder, during the third session of the General Assembly, 1948, that the submission of reports was on a voluntary basis and not *"an admission of accountability for the administration of South-West Africa"*, a breach with the earlier statements and conduct of the Union *"from 1946 up to that time in regard to South-West Africa"*.[52] Since Field-marshal Smuts had been explicit, both as to the voluntary nature of the Union's action, in the absence of any legal obligation, and the Article of the Charter in terms of which they were transmitted, only one explanation seems possible. The United States Government's legal advisers must have found the logic of his position no easier to follow than did Mr. Louw. It was frequently contended by Members, then and on many occasions afterwards, that the Union's action was evidence of the continuance of the Mandate.

The decision of the South African Government to refuse to submit reports was "regretted" by the General Assembly in December 1949 in Resolution 337(IV). Thus by 1949 a deadlock had been reached on the status of South West Africa and South Africa's obligations towards the United Nations. The stage was set for the beginning of the legal drama.

[52] *Ibid.*, 110–1.

6

The Dispute Grows, 1950–1960 [a]

1. The 1950 Advisory Opinion

In December 1949 the General Assembly decided to seek clarity on the legal status of South West Africa by asking for an advisory opinion from the International Court of Justice. Resolution 338(IV), adopted by forty votes in favour, seven against, and four abstentions, declared:

> *The General Assembly,*
>
> *Recalling* its previous resolutions 65 (I) of 14 December 1946, 141 (II) of 1 November 1947 and 227 (III) of 26 November 1948 concerning the Territory of South West Africa,
>
> *Considering* that it is desirable that the General Assembly, for its further consideration of the question, should obtain an advisory opinion on its legal aspects,
>
> 1. *Decides* to submit the following questions to the International Court of Justice with a request for an advisory opinion which shall be transmitted to the General Assembly before its fifth regular session, if possible:
>
> What is the international status of the Territory of South West Africa and what are the international obligations of the Union of South Africa arising therefrom, in particular:

---

[a] For general studies of this period, see I. Goldblatt, Q.C., *The Mandated Territory of South West Africa in Relation to the United Nations* (1961); Ronald B. Ballinger, *South-West Africa: The Case against the Union* (1961); Faye Carroll, *South West Africa and the United Nations* (1967), chap. 6; R. W. Imishue, *South West Africa: An International Problem*, chaps. 5 and 6; Solomon Slonim, *South West Africa and the United Nations: An International Mandate in Dispute* (1973).

(*a*) Does the Union of South Africa continue to have international obligations under the Mandate for South West Africa and, if so, what are those obligations?

(*b*) Are the provisions of Chapter XII of the Charter applicable and, if so, in what manner, to the Territory of South West Africa?

(*c*) Has the Union of South Africa the competence to modify the international status of the Territory of South West Africa, or, in the event of a negative reply, where does competence rest to determine and modify the international status of the Territory?

2. *Requests* the Secretary-General to transmit the present resolution to the International Court of Justice, in accordance with Article 65 of the Statute of the Court, accompanied by all documents likely to throw light upon the question.

The Secretary-General shall include among these documents, the text of article 22 of the Covenant of the League of Nations; the text of the Mandate for German South West Africa, confirmed by the Council of the League on 17 December 1920; relevant documentation concerning the objectives and the functions of the Mandates System; the text of the resolution adopted by the League of Nations on the question of Mandates on 18 April 1946; the text of Articles 77 and 80 of the Charter and data on the discussion of these Articles in the San Francisco Conference and the General Assembly; the report of the Fourth Committee and the official records, including the annexes, of the consideration of the question of South West Africa at the fourth session of the General Assembly.

Written statements were submitted by Egypt, South Africa, the United States, India, and Poland, while oral statements were made on behalf of the Secretary-General of the United Nations, the Philippines, and South Africa.[b] South Africa was represented by Dr. L. C. Steyn, K. C., who later became Chief Justice of South Africa.

Academic views expressed before the Court handed down its Opinion were evenly divided on the legal aspects of the dispute. These views are summarized by Ellison Kahn: [c]

Before setting out and analysing the conclusions of the judges of the International Court, it might be of interest to show the diversity of opinion amongst the leading writers, and the attitude of the Union Government. The views swing from pole to pole—from placing the United Nations as far as possible in the stead of the League, asserting that the mandate continues and that the Union is obliged to place South-West Africa under trusteeship, to holding that the mandate is

[b] For an account and analysis of the arguments presented to the Court, see J. F. L. van Essen, "Zuid-West Afrika voor het Internasionale Hof van Justisie" (1950) 13 *Tydskrif vir Hedendaagse Romeins-Hollandse Reg* 187.

[c] "The International Court's Advisory Opinion on the International Status of South-West Africa" (1951) 4 *International Law Quarterly* 78 at 84–86.

ended and the Union is under no obligation whatsoever to the United Nations and may incorporate South-West Africa.

The one extreme may be exemplified by Quincy Wright, who made out a case for 'the theory that the League of Nations was sovereign of the areas and on its demise the United Nations as its *de facto* successor was competent to dispose of these rights'.[16]

Intermediate positions were adopted by Brierly and Duncan Hall. Brierly says [17] :

> Under its mandate for [the] territory the Union of South Africa has hitherto administered it as "an integral portion" of its own territory, and in those circumstances its annexation, which the Union now desires to carry out, would be little more than a formal change. The General Assembly, however, has called upon the Union to submit a trust agreement for the territory, but there is nothing in the Charter which compels the Union to do this, nor can the General Assembly compel it to do so. The present position is therefore that the mandate continues, but as the only responsibility of the mandatory is to the League of Nations, which is defunct, it is for practical purposes at an end.

Duncan Hall, too, was of opinion that there was no obligation on the Union to submit to a trusteeship agreement. In his view sovereignty vests in the mandatory, South Africa, subject to 'the servitude imposed by Article 22 of the Covenant and the text of the Mandate'.[18]

The other extreme view is expressed by Kelsen and the Union Government. In his latest work, *The Law of the United Nations,* which appeared while the International Court was still engaged in its deliberations, Kelsen, applying his own notions of interpretation of written instruments, and his concept of 'pure legal science' reaches conclusions almost identical with those put forward by the Union Government when presenting its case before the General Assembly [19] and later the International Court. According to Kelsen there is no competency in the United Nations to place mandated territories under the trusteeship system; this would have required a valid agreement between the United Nations and the League, but no such agreement was concluded, or, indeed, could have been concluded in conformity with the Covenant of the League. The consent of the mandatory is necessary for placing 'mandated' territories under trusteeship. The mandates came to an end with the demise of the League, for the latter's existence was essential to the continuance of the mandate agreement, to which it was a contracting party. Thus while the Union is under the obligation it has voluntarily assumed under Articles 73 and 74 of the

---

[16] 62 Harvard Law Review (1948–9), 1425.

[17] *The Law of Nations,* 4th ed. (1949), 155, n. 1.

[18] *Mandates, Dependencies and Trusteeship,* 274.

[19] See, *e.g.,* the opening speech of Mr. Eric Louw before the Fourth (Trusteeship) Committee of the Third Session of the General Assembly on November 9, 1948. (Full text in Union White Paper, 1947–8, 16–19.)

Charter, South-West Africa no longer has the status of a mandated territory. Kelsen is prepared to say that extension by the Union of its sovereignty over South-West Africa, amounting to annexation, is certainly possible without any violation of the Covenant—which has ceased to be in force—or of the Charter.[21]

The attitude of the Union Government is that its past submission of reports was not an acknowledgement of accountability to the United Nations. It is under no legal or moral obligation to place South-West Africa under trusteeship and retains its powers of control and administration over South-West Africa as an integral part of the Union. The territory must not be taken to have been incorporated into the Union, or to be in the position of a fifth province. Nevertheless the mandate is at an end, and sovereignty is vested in the Union.[22] As to the present juridical status of South-West Africa, all that can be said is that it is *sui generis.*

The Court's Opinion on the *International Status of South-West Africa* was handed down on July 11, 1950 [d]:

The request for an opinion begins with a general question as follows:

What is the international status of the Territory of South-West Africa and what are the international obligations of the Union of South Africa arising therefrom?

The Court is of opinion that an examination of the three particular questions submitted to it will furnish a sufficient answer to this general question and that it is not necessary to consider the general question separately. It will therefore begin at once with an examination of the particular questions.

[d] 1950 ICJ Reports 128 at 131–44.

[21] *The Law of the United Nations* (1950), 571, 575, 596 ff.

[22] These views were put forward by Dr. D. F. Malan, Prime Minister of the Union, in the course of the debate on South-West Africa Affairs Amendment Bill. See *Senate Debates,* April 5, 1949, cols. 1277–8, 1286; *House of Assembly Debates,* February 16, 1949, col. 1172. See also the statements of the Minister of the Interior, Dr. T. E. Dönges, *House of Assembly Debates,* February 21, 1949, cols. 1476 ff. The Prime Minister has stated that the mandate is at an end (*House of Assembly Debates,* March 30, 1949, col. 3022); but on other occasions has remarked that if one still desired to use the term 'mandate' then South-West Africa 'has become jointly with the Union the mandatory over itself' (*House of Assembly Debates,* February 16, 1949, col. 1172; *Senate Debates,* April 5, 1949, cols. 1273–4). It is difficult to follow the meaning of these statements. It is interesting to observe that all reference to the establishment of the mandate for South-West Africa made in the preamble to the South-West Africa Constitution Act, 1925, has been removed by the South-West Africa Affairs Amendment Act, 1949; so, too, the word 'mandated' in the phrase 'mandated territory of South-West Africa' in the long title of the 1925 Act. The Union Government apparently is guarding itself against a plea of estoppel, waiver or admission.

Question (a): Does the Union of South Africa continue to have international obligations under the Mandate for South-West Africa and, if so, what are those obligations?

The Territory of South-West-Africa was one of the German overseas possessions in respect of which Germany, by Article 119 of the Treaty of Versailles, renounced all her rights and titles in favour of the Principal Allied and Associated Powers. When a decision was to be taken with regard to the future of these possessions as well as of other territories which, as a consequence of the war of 1914–1918, had ceased to be under the sovereignty of the States which formerly governed them, and which were inhabited by peoples not yet able to assume a full measure of self-government, two principles were considered to be of paramount importance: the principle of non-annexation and the principle that the well-being and development of such peoples form "a sacred trust of civilization".

With a view to giving practical effect to these principles, an international régime, the Mandates System, was created by Article 22 of the Covenant of the League of Nations. A "tutelage" was to be established for these peoples, and this tutelage was to be entrusted to certain advanced nations and exercised by them "as mandatories on behalf of the League".

Accordingly, the Principal Allied and Associated Powers agreed that a Mandate for the Territory of South-West Africa should be conferred upon His Britannic Majesty to be exercised on his behalf by the Government of the Union of South Africa and proposed the terms of this Mandate. His Britannic Majesty, for and on behalf of the Government of the Union of South Africa, agreed to accept the Mandate and undertook to exercise it on behalf of the League of Nations in accordance with the proposed terms. On December 17th, 1920, the Council of the League of Nations, confirming the Mandate, defined its terms.

In accordance with these terms, the Union of South Africa (the "Mandatory") was to have full power of administration and legislation over the Territory as an integral portion of the Union and could apply the laws of the Union to the Territory subject to such local modifications as circumstances might require. On the other hand, the Mandatory was to observe a number of obligations, and the Council of the League was to supervise the administration and see to it that these obligations were fulfilled.

The terms of this Mandate, as well as the provisions of Article 22 of the Covenant and the principles embodied therein, show that the creation of this new international institution did not involve any cession of territory or transfer of sovereignty to the Union of South Africa. The Union Government was to exercise an international function of administration on behalf of the League, with the object of promoting the well-being and development of the inhabitants.

It is now contended on behalf of the Union Government that this Mandate has lapsed, because the League has ceased to exist. This contention is based on a misconception of the legal situation created by

Article 22 of the Covenant and by the Mandate itself. The League was not, as alleged by that Government, a "mandator" in the sense in which this term is used in the national law of certain States. It had only assumed an international function of supervision and control. The "Mandate" had only the name in common with the several notions of mandate in national law. The object of the Mandate regulated by international rules far exceeded that of contractual relations regulated by national law. The Mandate was created, in the interest of the inhabitants of the territory, and of humanity in general, as an international institution with an international object—a sacred trust of civilization. It is therefore not possible to draw any conclusion by analogy from the notions of mandate in national law or from any other legal conception of that law. The international rules regulating the Mandate constituted an international status for the Territory recognized by all the Members of the League of Nations, including the Union of South Africa.

The essentially international character of the functions which had been entrusted to the Union of South Africa appears particularly from the fact that by Article 22 of the Covenant and Article 6 of the Mandate the exercise of these functions was subjected to the supervision of the Council of the League of Nations and to the obligation to present annual reports to it; it also appears from the fact that any Member of the League of Nations could, according to Article 7 of the Mandate, submit to the Permanent Court of International Justice any dispute with the Union Government relating to the interpretation or the application of the provisions of the Mandate.

The authority which the Union Government exercises over the Territory is based on the Mandate. If the Mandate lapsed, as the Union Government contends, the latter's authority would equally have lapsed. To retain the rights derived from the Mandate and to deny the obligations thereunder could not be justified.

These international obligations, assumed by the Union of South Africa, were of two kinds. One kind was directly related to the administration of the Territory, and corresponded to the sacred trust of civilization referred to in Article 22 of the Covenant. The other related to the machinery for implementation, and was closely linked to the supervision and control of the League. It corresponded to the "securities for the performance of this trust" referred to in the same article.

The first-mentioned group of obligations are defined in Article 22 of the Covenant and in Articles 2 to 5 of the Mandate. The Union undertook the general obligation to promote to the utmost the material and moral well-being and the social progress of the inhabitants. It assumed particular obligations relating to slave trade, forced labour, traffic in arms and ammunition, intoxicating spirits and beverages, military training and establishments, as well as obligations relating to freedom of conscience and free exercise of worship, including special obligations with regard to missionaries.

These obligations represent the very essence of the sacred trust of civilization. Their *raison d'être* and original object remain. Since their fulfilment did not depend on the existence of the League of Nations, they could not be brought to an end merely because this supervisory organ ceased to exist. Nor could the right of the population to have the Territory administered in accordance with these rules depend thereon.

This view is confirmed by Article 80, paragraph 1, of the Charter, which maintains the rights of States and peoples and the terms of existing international instruments until the territories in question are placed under the Trusteeship System. It is true that this provision only says that nothing in Chapter XII shall be construed to alter the rights of States or peoples or the terms of existing international instruments. But—as far as mandated territories are concerned, to which paragraph 2 of this article refers—this provision presupposes that the rights of States and peoples shall not lapse automatically on the dissolution of the League of Nations. It obviously was the intention to safeguard the rights of States and peoples under all circumstances and in all respects, until each territory should be placed under the Trusteeship System.

This view results, moreover, from the Resolution of the League of Nations of April 18th, 1946, which said:

> Recalling that Article 22 of the Covenant applies to certain territories placed under Mandate the principle that the well-being and development of peoples not yet able to stand alone in the strenuous conditions of the modern world form a sacred trust of civilization:
>
> . . . .
>
> 3. Recognizes that, on the termination of the League's existence, its functions with respect to the mandated territories will come to an end, but notes that Chapters XI, XII and XIII of the Charter of the United Nations embody principles corresponding to those declared in Article 22 of the Covenant of the League;
>
> 4. Takes note of the expressed intentions of the Members of the League now administering territories under Mandate to continue to administer them for the well-being and development of the peoples concerned in accordance with the obligations contained in the respective Mandates, until other arrangements have been agreed between the United Nations and the respective mandatory Powers.

As will be seen from this resolution, the Assembly said that the League's functions with respect to mandated territories would come to an end; it did not say that the Mandates themselves came to an end. In confining itself to this statement, and in taking note, on the other hand, of the expressed intentions of the mandatory Powers to continue to administer the mandated territories in accordance with their respective Mandates, until other arrangements had been agreed upon between the United Nations and those Powers, the Assembly manifested its understanding that the Mandates were to continue in existence until "other arrangements" were established.

A similar view has on various occasions been expressed by the Union of South Africa. In declarations made to the League of Nations, as well as to the United Nations, the Union Government has acknowledged that its obligations under the Mandate continued after the disappearance of the League. In a declaration made on April 9th, 1946, in the Assembly of the League of Nations, the representative of the Union Government, after having declared his Government's intention to seek international recognition for the Territory of South-West Africa as an integral part of the Union, stated: "In the meantime, the Union will continue to administer the Territory scrupulously in accordance with the obligations of the Mandate for the advancement and promotion of the interests of the inhabitants as she has done during the past six years when meetings of the Mandates Commission could not be held." After having said that the disappearance of the Mandates Commission and of the League Council would "necessarily preclude complete compliance with the letter of the Mandate", he added: "The Union Government will nevertheless regard the dissolution of the League as in no way diminishing its obligations under the Mandate, which it will continue to discharge with the full and proper appreciation of its responsibilities until such time as other arrangements are agreed upon concerning the future status of the Territory."

In a memorandum submitted on October 17th, 1946, by the South-African Legation in Washington to the Secretary-General of the United Nations, expression was given to a similar view. Though the League had at that time disappeared, the Union Government continued to refer to its responsibility under the Mandate. It stated: "This responsibility of the Union Government as Mandatory is necessarily inalienable." On November 4th, 1946, the Prime Minister of the Union, in a statement to the Fourth Committee of the United Nations General Assembly, repeated the declaration which the representative of the Union had made previously to the League of Nations.

In a letter of July 23rd, 1947, to the Secretary-General of the United Nations, the Legation of the Union referred to a resolution of the Union Parliament in which it was declared "that the Government should continue to render reports to the United Nations Organization as it has done heretofore under the Mandate". It was further stated in that letter: "In the circumstances the Union Government have no alternative but to maintain the *status quo* and to continue to administer the Territory in the spirit of the existing Mandate."

These declarations constitute recognition by the Union Government of the continuance of its obligations under the Mandate and not a mere indication of the future conduct of that Government. Interpretations placed upon legal instruments by the parties to them, though not conclusive as to their meaning, have considerable probative value when they contain recognition by a party of its own obligations under an instrument. In this case the declarations of the Union of South Africa support the conclusions already reached by the Court.

. . . .

The Court will now consider the above-mentioned second group of obligations. These obligations related to the machinery for implementation and were closely linked to the supervisory functions of the League of Nations—particularly the obligation of the Union of South

Africa to submit to the supervision and control of the Council of the League and the obligation to render to it annual reports in accordance with Article 22 of the Covenant and Article 6 of the Mandate. Since the Council disappeared by the dissolution of the League, the question arises whether these supervisory functions are to be exercised by the new international organization created by the Charter, and whether the Union of South Africa is under an obligation to submit to a supervision by this new organ and to render annual reports to it.

Some doubts might arise from the fact that the supervisory functions of the League with regard to mandated territories not placed under the new Trusteeship System were neither expressly transferred to the United Nations nor expressly assumed by that organization. Nevertheless, there seem to be decisive reasons for an affirmative answer to the above-mentioned question.

The obligation incumbent upon a mandatory State to accept international supervision and to submit reports is an important part of the Mandates System. When the authors of the Covenant created this system, they considered that the effective performance of the sacred trust of civilization by the mandatory Powers required that the administration of mandated territories should be subject to international supervision. The authors of the Charter had in mind the same necessity when they organized an International Trusteeship System. The necessity for supervision continues to exist despite the disappearance of the supervisory organ under the Mandates System. It cannot be admitted that the obligation to submit to supervision has disappeared merely because the supervisory organ has ceased to exist, when the United Nations has another international organ performing similar, though not identical, supervisory functions.

These general considerations are confirmed by Article 80, paragraph 1, of the Charter, as this clause has been interpreted above. It purports to safeguard, not only the rights of States, but also the rights of the peoples of mandated territories until Trusteeship Agreements are concluded. The purpose must have been to provide a real protection for those rights; but no such rights of the peoples could be effectively safeguarded without international supervision and a duty to render reports to a supervisory organ.

The Assembly of the League of Nations, in its Resolution of April 18th, 1946, gave expression to a corresponding view. It recognized, as mentioned above, that the League's functions with regard to the mandated territories would come to an end, but noted that Chapters XI, XII and XIII of the Charter of the United Nations embody principles corresponding to those declared in Article 22 of the Covenant. It further took note of the intentions of the mandatory States to continue to administer the territories in accordance with the obligations contained in the Mandates until other arrangements should be agreed upon between the United Nations and the mandatory Powers. This resolution presupposes that the supervisory functions exercised by the League would be taken over by the United Nations.

The competence of the General Assembly of the United Nations to exercise such supervision and to receive and examine reports is derived from the provisions of Article 10 of the Charter, which authorizes the General Assembly to discuss any questions or any matters within the scope of the Charter and to make recommendations on these questions or matters to the Members of the United Nations. This competence was in fact exercised by the General Assembly in Resolution 141 (II) of November 1st, 1947, and in Resolution 227 (III) of November 26th, 1948, confirmed by Resolution 337 (IV) of December 6th, 1949.

For the above reasons, the Court has arrived at the conclusion that the General Assembly of the United Nations is legally qualified to exercise the supervisory functions previously exercised by the League of Nations with regard to the administration of the Territory, and that the Union of South Africa is under an obligation to submit to supervision and control of the General Assembly and to render annual reports to it.

The right of petition was not mentioned by Article 22 of the Covenant or by the provisions of the Mandate. But on January 31st, 1923, the Council of the League of Nations adopted certain rules relating to this matter. Petitions to the League from communities or sections of the populations of mandated territories were to be transmitted by the mandatory Governments, which were to attach to these petitions such comments as they might consider desirable. By this innovation the supervisory function of the Council was rendered more effective.

The Court is of opinion that this right, which the inhabitants of South-West Africa had thus acquired, is maintained by Article 80, paragraph 1, of the Charter, as this clause has been interpreted above. In view of the result at which the Court has arrived with respect to the exercise of the supervisory functions by the United Nations and the obligation of the Union Government to submit to such supervision, and having regard to the fact that the dispatch and examination of petitions form a part of that supervision, the Court is of the opinion that petitions are to be transmitted by that Government to the General Assembly of the United Nations, which is legally qualified to deal with them.

It follows from what is said above that South-West Africa is still to be considered as a territory held under the Mandate of December 17th, 1920. The degree of supervision to be exercised by the General Assembly should not therefore exceed that which applied under the Mandates System, and should conform as far as possible to the procedure followed in this respect by the Council of the League of Nations. These observations are particularly applicable to annual reports and petitions.

According to Article 7 of the Mandate, disputes between the mandatory State and another Member of the League of Nations relating to the interpretation or the application of the provisions of the Mandate, if not settled by negotiation, should be submitted to the Permanent Court of International Justice. Having regard to Article 37 of the Statute of the International Court of Justice, and Article 80, paragraph 1, of the Charter, the Court is of opinion that this clause in the Mandate is still in force and that, therefore, the Union of South Africa is under an obligation to accept the compulsory jurisdiction of the Court according to those provisions.

. . . .

Reference to Chapter XI of the Charter was made by various Governments in written and oral statements presented to the Court. Having regard to the results at which the Court has arrived, the question whether the provisions of that chapter are applicable does not arise for the purpose of the present Opinion. It is not included in the questions submitted to the Court and it is unnecessary to consider it.

. . . .

Question (b): Are the provisions of Chapter XII of the Charter applicable and, if so, in what manner, to the Territory of South-West Africa?

Territories held under Mandate were not by the Charter automatically placed under the new International Trusteeship System. This system should, according to Articles 75 and 77, apply to territories which are placed thereunder by means of Trusteeship Agreements. South-West Africa, being a territory held under Mandate (Article 77 *a*), may be placed under the Trusteeship System in accordance with the provisions of Chapter XII. In this sense, that chapter is applicable to the Territory.

Question (*b*) further asks in what manner Chapter XII is applicable to the Territory. It appears from a number of documents submitted to the Court in accordance with the General Assembly's Resolution of December 6th, 1949, as well as from the written and the oral observations of several Governments, that the General Assembly, in asking about the manner of application of Chapter XII, was referring to the question whether the Charter imposes upon the Union of South Africa an obligation to place the Territory under the Trusteeship System by means of a Trusteeship Agreement.

Articles 75 and 77 show, in the opinion of the Court, that this question must be answered in the negative. The language used in both articles is permissive ("as may be placed thereunder"). Both refer to subsequent agreements by which the territories in question may be placed under the Trusteeship System. An "agreement" implies consent of the parties concerned, including the mandatory Power in the case of territories held under Mandate (Article 79). The parties must be free to accept or reject the terms of a contemplated agreement. No party can impose its terms on the other party. Article 77, paragraph 2, moreover, presupposes agreement not only with regard to its particular terms, but also as to which territories will be brought under the Trusteeship System.

It has been contended that the word "voluntarily", used in Article 77 with respect to category (*c*) only, shows that the placing of other territories under Trusteeship is compulsory. This word alone cannot, however, over-ride the principle derived from Articles 75, 77 and 79 considered as a whole. An obligation for a mandatory State to place the Territory under Trusteeship would have been expressed in a direct manner. The word "voluntarily" incorporated in category (c) can be explained as having been used out of an abundance of caution and as an added assurance of freedom of initiative to States having territories falling within that category.

It has also been contended that paragraph 2 of Article 80 imposes on mandatory States a duty to negotiate and conclude Trusteeship Agreements. The Court finds no justification for this contention. The paragraph merely states that the first paragraph of the article shall not be interpreted as giving grounds for delay or postponement of the negotiation and conclusion of agreements for placing mandated and other territories under the Trusteeship System as provided for in Article 77. There is nothing to suggest that the provision was intended as an exception to the principle derived from Articles 75, 77 and 79. The provision is entirely negative in character and cannot be said to create an obligation to negotiate and conclude an agreement. Had the parties to the Charter intended to create an obligation of this kind for a mandatory State, such intention would necessarily have been expressed in positive terms.

It has further been maintained that Article 80, paragraph 2, creates an obligation for mandatory States to enter into negotiations with a view to concluding a Trusteeship Agreement. But an obligation to negotiate without any obligation to conclude an agreement can hardly be derived from this provision, which expressly refers to delay or postponement of "the negotiation and conclusion" of agreements. It is not limited to negotiations only. Moreover, it refers to the negotiation and conclusion of agreements for placing "mandated and other territories under the Trusteeship System as provided for in Article 77". In other words, it refers not merely to territories held under Mandate, but also to the territories mentioned in Article 77 (b) and (c). It is, however, evident that there can be no obligation to enter into negotiations with a view to concluding Trusteeship Agreements for those territories.

It is contended that the Trusteeship System created by the Charter would have no more than a theoretical existence if the mandatory Powers were not under an obligation to enter into negotiations with a view to concluding Trusteeship Agreements. This contention is not convincing, since an obligation merely to negotiate does not of itself assure the conclusion of Trusteeship Agreements. Nor was the Trusteeship System created only for mandated territories.

It is true that, while Members of the League of Nations regarded the Mandates System as the best method for discharging the sacred trust of civilization provided for in Article 22 of the Covenant, the Members of the United Nations considered the International Trusteeship System to be the best method for discharging a similar mission. It is equally true that the Charter has contemplated and regulated only a single system, the International Trusteeship System. It did not contemplate or regulate a co-existing Mandates System. It may thus be concluded that it was expected that the mandatory States would follow the normal course indicated by the Charter, namely, conclude Trusteeship Agreements. The Court is, however, unable to deduce from these general considerations any legal obligation for mandatory States to conclude or to negotiate such agreements. It is not for the Court to pronounce on the political or moral duties which these considerations may involve.

For these reasons, the Court considers that the Charter does not impose on the Union an obligation to place South-West Africa under the Trusteeship System.

. . . .

Question (c): Has the Union of South Africa the competence to modify the international status of the Territory of South-West Africa, or, in the event of a negative reply, where does competence rest to determine and modify the international status of the Territory?

The international status of the Territory results from the international rules regulating the rights, powers and obligations relating to the administration of the Territory and the supervision of that administration, as embodied in Article 22 of the Covenant and in the Mandate. It is clear that the Union has no competence to modify unilaterally the international status of the Territory or any of these international rules. This is shown by Article 7 of the Mandate, which expressly provides that the consent of the Council of the League of Nations is required for any modification of the terms of the Mandate.

The Court is further requested to say where competence to determine and modify the international status of the Territory rests.

Before answering this question, the Court repeats that the normal way of modifying the international status of the Territory would be to place it under the Trusteeship System by means of a Trusteeship Agreement in accordance with the provisions of Chapter XII of the Charter.

The competence to modify in other ways the international status of the Territory depended on the rules governing the amendment of Article 22 of the Covenant and the modification of the terms of the Mandate.

Article 26 of the Covenant laid down the procedure for amending provisions of the Covenant, including Article 22. On the other hand, Article 7 of the Mandate stipulates that the consent of the Council of the League was required for any modification of the terms of that Mandate. The rules thus laid down have become inapplicable following the dissolution of the League of Nations. But one cannot conclude therefrom that no proper procedure exists for modifying the international status of South-West Africa.

Article 7 of the Mandate, in requiring the consent of the Council of the League of Nations for any modification of its terms, brought into operation for this purpose the same organ which was invested with powers of supervision in respect of the administration of the Mandates. In accordance with the reply given above to Question (a), those powers of supervision now belong to the General Assembly of the United Nations. On the other hand, Articles 79 and 85 of the Charter require that a Trusteeship Agreement be concluded by the mandatory Power and approved by the General Assembly before the International Trusteeship System may be substituted for the Mandates System. These articles also give the General Assembly authority to approve alterations or amendments of Trusteeship Agreements. By analogy, it can be inferred that the same procedure is applicable to any modification of the international status of a territory under Mandate which would not have for its purpose the placing of the territory under the Trusteeship System. This conclusion is strengthened by the action taken by the General Assembly and the attitude adopted by the Union of South Africa which is at present the only existing mandatory Power.

On January 22nd, 1946, before the Fourth Committee of the General Assembly, the representative of the Union of South Africa explained the special relationship between the Union and the Territory under its Mandate. There would—he said—be no attempt to draw up an agreement until the freely expressed will of both the European and native populations had been ascertained. He continued: "When that had been done, the decision of the Union would be submitted to the General Assembly for judgment."

On April 9th, 1946, before the Assembly of the League of Nations, the Union representative declared that "it is the intention of the Union Government, at the forthcoming session of the United Nations General Assembly in New York, to formulate its case for according South-West Africa a status under which it would be internationally recognized as an integral part of the Union".

In accordance with these declarations, the Union Government, by letter of August 12th, 1946, from its Legation in Washington, requested that the question of the desirability of the territorial integration in, and the annexation to, the Union of South Africa of the mandated Territory of South-West Africa, be included in the Agenda of the General Assembly. In a subsequent letter of October 9th, 1946, it was requested that the text of the item to be included in the Agenda be amended as follows: "Statement by the Government of the Union of South Africa on the outcome of their consultations with the peoples of South-West Africa as to the future status of the mandated Territory, and implementation to be given to the wishes thus expressed."

On November 4th, 1946, before the Fourth Committee, the Prime Minister of the Union of South Africa stated that the Union clearly understood "that its international responsibility precluded it from taking advantage of the war situation by effecting a change in the status of South-West Africa without proper consultation either of all the peoples of the Territory itself, or with the competent international organs".

By thus submitting the question of the future international status of the Territory to the "judgment" of the General Assembly as the "competent international organ", the Union Government recognized the competence of the General Assembly in the matter.

The General Assembly, on the other hand, affirmed its competence by Resolution 65 (I) of December 14th, 1946. It noted with satisfaction that the step taken by the Union showed the recognition of the interest and concern of the United Nations in the matter. It expressed the desire "that agreement between the United Nations and the Union of South Africa may hereafter be reached regarding the future status of the Mandated Territory of South-West Africa", and concluded: "The General Assembly, therefore, is unable to accede to the incorporation of the Territory of South-West Africa in the Union of South Africa."

Following the adoption of this resolution, the Union Government decided not to proceed with the incorporation of the Territory, but to maintain the *status quo*. The General Assembly took note of this decision in its Resolution 141 (II) of November 1st, 1947.

On the basis of these considerations, the Court concludes that competence to determine and modify the international status of South-West Africa rests with the Union of South Africa acting with the consent of the United Nations.

For these reasons,

The Court is of opinion,

On the General Question:

unanimously,

that South-West Africa is a territory under the international Mandate assumed by the Union of South Africa on December 17th, 1920;

On Question (a):

by twelve votes to two,

that the Union of South Africa continues to have the international obligations stated in Article 22 of the Covenant of the League of Nations and in the Mandate for South-West Africa as well as the obligation to transmit petitions from the inhabitants of that Territory, the supervisory functions to be exercised by the United Nations, to which the annual reports and the petitions are to be submitted, and the reference to the Permanent Court of International Justice to be replaced by a reference to the International Court of Justice, in accordance with Article 7 of the Mandate and Article 37 of the Statute of the Court;

On Question (b):

unanimously,

that the provisions of Chapter XII of the Charter are applicable to the Territory of South-West Africa in the sense that they provide a means by which the Territory may be brought under the Trusteeship System;

and by eight votes to six,

that the provisions of Chapter XII of the Charter do not impose on the Union of South Africa a legal obligation to place the Territory under the Trusteeship System;

On Question (c):

unanimously,

that the Union of South Africa acting alone has not the competence to modify the international status of the Territory of South-West Africa, and that the competence to determine and modify the international status of the Territory rests with the Union of South Africa acting with the consent of the United Nations.

2. Analysis of the Opinion

The Court's Opinion, together with the separate concurring opinions of Judges McNair and Read and dissenting opinions of Judges Alvarez, de Visscher, and Krylov, was analysed by the South African jurist Ellison Kahn: [e]

THE OPINION OF THE INTERNATIONAL COURT [23]

On the general question as to the international status of South-West Africa, the Opinion was unanimous

that South-West Africa is a territory under the international Mandate assumed by the Union of South Africa on December 17, 1920.[24]

Question (a).

On question (a), there was a division of opinion. By a majority of twelve to two (Judges Sir Arnold McNair and Read), the court found

that the Union of South Africa continues to have the international obligations stated in Article 22 of the Covenant of the League of Nations and in the Mandate for South-West Africa as well as the obligation to transmit petitions from the inhabitants of that Territory, the supervisory functions to be exercised by the United Nations, to which the annual reports and the petitions are to be submitted, and the reference to the Permanent Court of International Justice to be replaced by a reference to the International Court of Justice, in accordance with Article 7 of the Mandate and Article 37 of the Statute of the Court.[25]

[e] Above, n. c, 86–99.
[23] President Basdevant (France); Vice-President Guerrero (El Salvador); Judges Alvarez (Chile), Hackworth (U.S.A.), Winiarski (Poland), Zoričić (Yugoslavia), de Visscher (Belgium), Sir Arnold McNair (U.K.), Klaestad (Norway), Badawi Pasha (Egypt), Krylov (U.S.S.R.), Read (Canada), Hsu Mo (China), Azevedo (Brazil).
[24] I.C.J. Reports, 1950, p. 143.   [25] P. 143.

Judges Sir Arnold McNair and Read could not agree with the majority as to accountability and report to, and supervision by, the United Nations, and the right of petition. These rights and obligations, they considered, were at an end. They agreed with the majority finding [26] in other respects, including the compulsory jurisdiction of the International Court in the place of the former Permanent Court of International Justice. Judge Alvarez in his so-called dissenting opinion, whilst concurring with the majority finding, in passing made certain remarks which go even farther than the majority were prepared to.

The answer to Question (a) may thus be analysed in two parts: firstly, that part agreed to by all members of the court, Judges Sir Arnold McNair and Read giving separate reasons; and secondly, that part in which the latter two judges, and to some extent Judge Alvarez, come to different conclusions from the majority.

That part of the answer to Question (a) on which the opinion was unanimous.—The Main Opinion [27] holds that the mandate continues, and the submission of the Union Government, that it has lapsed with the demise of the mandator, is rejected. This submission, runs the Opinion, arises out of confusion resulting from analogies drawn from the concept of mandate in certain 'national' laws; but no such analogy should be drawn. The mandate was created as an international institution with the object of a sacred trust of civilisation, and the rules regulating the mandate constituted an international status for the territory. If the Union Government's contention were correct, it means that that Government's authority, derived from the mandate, must also have lapsed.

The obligations of the Union under Article 22 of the Covenant and Articles 2 and 5 of the mandate, the Opinion states, represent the very essence of this sacred trust, and their existence is independent of that of the League. Article 80 (1) of the Charter is used as a support for this conclusion, but, as Sir Arnold McNair points out, this Article merely says that nothing in Chapter XII of the Charter shall be construed to alter rights under existing international instruments, and it is difficult to see its relevance. The Main Opinion refers to the dissolution resolution of the League Assembly of April 18, 1946, by which the Assembly 'manifested its understanding that the Mandates were to continue in existence until "other arrangements" were established'. It goes on to state that on divers occasions the Union Government has expressed a similar view, but with respect it is submitted that it is impossible to draw a clear inference from the statements of the Union Government that it recognised that legally its obligations under the mandate continued. This, however, is of little moment, as the court

---

[26] That is, the opinion of the court as a whole. There are 'separate opinions' by Judges Sir Arnold McNair and Read, and 'dissenting opinions' by Judges Alvarez, de Visscher and Krylov. The distinction between a 'separate' and a 'dissenting' opinion is not always apparent.

[27] Pp. 131–8.

did not rely on the statement made by South African representatives as more than buttressing the conclusion the court had already reached.

Finding that the mandate continues, the Main Opinion comes to the conclusion that the degree of supervision to be exercised by the General Assembly should not exceed that applied under the mandates system, and should conform as far as possible, and especially in respect of reports and submissions, to the procedure followed by the League Council. It is not clear, however, what the majority view is on the jurisdiction of the International Court, which all agree has been vested by Article 37 of its Charter with the former compulsory jurisdiction of the Permanent Court in matters of dispute between the mandatory and another member of the League. Is it only in respect of former members of the League that this jurisdiction exists (as Sir Arnold McNair contends), or any member of the United Nations, even though it was not a member of the League?

Certain of Sir Arnold McNair's views have already been touched on, but it would be best to look at his valuable opinion [28] as a whole. In rejecting the Union's contention that the demise of the League put an end to the mandate, he subjects the term 'mandate', newly applied in international law after World War I, to a very close analysis. When 'confronted with a new legal institution', says Sir Arnold in a noteworthy passage, 'the duty of international tribunals . . . is to regard any features or terminology which are reminiscent of the rules and institutions of private law as an indication of policy and principles rather than as directly importing these rules and institutions'.[29] Applying this test to the Mandate, he cites with approval Brierly's thesis [30] and certain passages from the South African case of *R.* v. *Christian* [31] and the Australian case of *Ffrost* v. *Stevenson,*[32] that the governing principle of the mandates system is to be found in the trust, not in mandate or agency.

Sir Arnold's second ground for finding that the mandates system still exists, is that it was a case of creation 'by a multipartite treaty [of] some new international regime or status, which soon acquires a degree of acceptance beyond the limits of the actual contracting parties, and giving it an objective existence'.[33] The difficulty produced by the dissolution of the League is only the 'mechanical' one that the obligations of the mandatory to the League itself have ended; but the obligations owed to the members of the League at the time of its dissolution subsist, save those which in their performance would require the League's co-operation.

The third ground advanced by Sir Arnold is that the mandate created two types of rights and duties: personal rights and obligations, arising out of a contractual obligation of the mandatory to furnish reports, obtain consent of the League Council for modification of the

---

[28] Pp. 146–163, and in this connection especially pp. 146–158.   [29] At 148.
[30] 16 B.Y.I.L. (1929), 217–9.   [31] [1924] A.D. 101 at 121 and 136.
[32] 58 Commonwealth L.R. (1937), 528; *Annual Digest, 1935–7,* Case No. 29.
[33] P. 153.

mandate and to submit disputes to the Permanent Court; and real rights and obligations arising from the transfer to the mandatory, on specified terms, of certain rights of possession and government of South-West Africa, valid against the world. The dissolution of the League put an end to the personal, but not the real rights, which provided that element of permanence which gave South-West Africa a status independent of the existence of the League. There is a difficulty in the way of acceptance of this ingenious analysis, however: can one conceive of the Union as a trustee in respect of South-West Africa and at the same time vested with rights yielding beneficial enjoyment over her?

Judge Read in his Separate Opinion [34] also concludes that the legal rights and interests, under the mandate, of the members of the League, including those not members of the United Nations, continue. Only action by the League itself, or consent of its members, could have ended them, and this did not occur.

That part of the answer to Question (a) on which opinion was divided.—All the members of the court, save Sir Arnold McNair and Judge Read, hold that the 'secondary' or 'auxiliary' obligations of the mandatory—report, accountability, supervision and petition—continue. This finding is of very considerable importance. These obligations afford the main practical means of bringing the mandatory's actions before the judgment of other nations. Judge Read stresses the value of the compulsory jurisdiction of the International Court and the powers of the General Assembly under Article 10 (the 'discussion clause' of the Charter), but it may well be doubted whether in practice they would prove an effective means of controlling the mandatory. On the other hand, should the General Assembly accept the majority decision, against the clear wishes of the Union Government but in accordance with past practice, a serious deterioration in the relationship of the Union with the United Nations may be expected.

The difference in the views of the members of the court rests fundamentally on a difference in approach to the construction of the relevant international instruments. Judges Sir Arnold McNair and Read construe them more strictly than the other judges.

The foundation of the majority Opinion [35] is that the performance of these duties is necessary for the efficient performance of 'the sacred trust of civilisation'. Therefore, despite the fact that the League's supervisory functions were not expressly transferred to or assumed by that body, the obligation of the Union to submit to international supervision remains. The obligation is owed to the United Nations, which, through the Trusteeship Council, has an organ performing similar functions to the now defunct Permanent Mandates Commission. The comment might be made that the composition of the bodies is very different, particularly in that the Mandates Commission was 'non-political' while the Trusteeship Council is representative of governments. Three grounds are adduced in the Main Opinion for find-

[34] Pp. 164–173.   [35] Pp. 136–8.

ing that the United Nations is legally qualified to exercise the supervisory functions. Firstly, the purpose of Article 80 is to provide proper protection for the rights of the inhabitants of mandated territories until trusteeship agreements have been concluded, which requires international supervision. Secondly, Article 10 grants this competence, for it empowers the General Assembly to discuss any matter within the scope of the Charter. Thirdly, the League's winding-up resolution 'presupposes that the supervisory functions exercised by the League would be taken over by the United Nations'.

The majority find, too, that the right of petition is maintained by Article 80 (1) of the Charter, and that the examination of petitions is part of the supervisory functions of the United Nations.

It is submitted that the finding of the majority is untenable, and that the views of Judges Sir Arnold McNair [36] and Read [37] are to be preferred. They arrive at the same result for much the same reasons, and it is proposed to look only at the judgment of the former. He rejects the contention that the United Nations succeeded to the supervisory rights and functions of the League, as 'pure inference'. Sir Arnold, indeed, finds that there is a significant omission in the Charter which points in the other direction—the omission to provide for the succession of the United Nations in this regard, although in the case of the International Court its succession was expressly provided for in its Charter, and although at the San Francisco Conference, when the Charter of the United Nations was being drafted, the Union Government gave public notice that it would claim that South-West Africa be incorporated in the Union. It has already been shown that Sir Arnold rejected the reference to Article 80 (1) on the ground that it was irrelevant. Nor can he find in the statements of the Union Government 'adequate evidence that [she] has either assented to an implied succession by the United Nations to the administrative supervision [formerly] exercised by the League . . . or has entered into a new obligation towards the United Nations to revive the pre-war system of supervision'. The dissolution resolution of the League, he says, cannot be interpreted as imposing a legal obligation on the Union to make annual reports to the United Nations. The General Assembly, Sir Arnold agrees, can discuss the South-West Africa mandate and make recommendations under Article 10 (the so-called 'discussion clause' of the Charter), but this rests on the terms of the Charter itself and not on any theory of implied succession. (It might be added that the reasoning of the majority that Article 10 grants competency to the United Nations to exercise the supervisory functions, is a *petitio principii*.)

There remains to consider Judge Alvarez' Dissenting Opinion. It has already been pointed out that it suffers from an internal antinomy. Judge Alvarez' final conclusion on Question (*a*) [38] is the same as that expressed in the Main Opinion, *i.e.*, that the Union has the same international obligations which she had under the mandate and Article 22 of the Covenant. Within the body of his Opinion, however, he goes

[36] At 159–162.   [37] At 166–173.   [38] Pp. 184–5.

much further, stating that the Union's duty of report on, and the United Nations' control and supervision over, South-West Africa extend beyond the mandate to Articles 87 and 88 of the Charter. These Articles give the General Assembly and Trusteeship Council authority to consider reports, accept petitions, provide for visits to trust territories, and require the Trusteeship Council to formulate a questionnaire which must be answered by the administering authority. Obviously in so stating M. Alvarez travels beyond the Main Opinion which provides that 'the degree of supervision to be exercised by the General Assembly should not . . . exceed that which applied under the Mandates System, and should conform as far as possible to the procedure followed in this respect by the Council of the League of Nations'.[39]

With all due respect to so eminent a jurist as M. Alvarez, it is not surprising that inconsistencies appear in his Opinion, when regard be had to his unorthodox approach to problems of international law. The very commencement of his Opinion, in which he states that the questions propounded for decision are 'of great importance not only from the point of view of international law, but also from the social, economic and international political points of view',[40] gives the reader cause for belief that unusual views are to be expounded; nor is he disappointed, for he is at once thrust into a dissertation on the 'new international law'. It is best to let the learned judge's words speak for themselves. The mandate and trusteeship systems exemplify, he says, this 'new international law', which has arisen from the transformation of the community of states, hitherto anarchical, into an organised international society. 'It rests on the basic reconstruction of fundamental principles of classical international law, and brings them into harmony with the new conditions of the life of peoples; finally, it is based on the new social régime which has appeared, *the régime of interdependence,* which is taking the place of the individualistic régime. . . . This new régime has given rise to what may be called *social interdependence* which is taking the place of traditional *individualism.*' [41]

The new international law, says Judge Alvarez, has as its object international social justice, and thus must lay stress on the obligations of states towards the international community, requiring the limitation of the absolute international sovereignty of states. The obligations are not only legal obligations, but also moral obligations and obligations of a political international character. This new law is in the course of formation and it is for the International Court and the jurists to develop it. The exact function of the court does not appear clear:

> . . . it may be said that the court *creates* the law; it creates it by modifying classical law; in fact it merely *declares* what is the law today.

With the aid of what rules of construction does M. Alvarez propose to create, or if you will, expound the new international law? In a passage with which the majority of international lawyers may not agree,

---

[39] P. 138.   [40] P. 174.   [41] P. 175.

he condemns the 'traditional line' of interpretation of texts, the 'juridical technique' of searching for the 'strictly literal sense of the text', with the aid of *travaux préparatoires* and the postulates, axioms and precepts of 'general law' (especially Roman law, and even natural law), and of classical international law.

> Extreme logic, dialectics and exclusively juridical technique must also be banished. Reality, the requirements of the life of nations, the common interest, social justice, must never be forgotten.[43]

Certainly the common reproach could not be levelled that law lags behind social and political needs and realities, were M. Alvarez' views to be generally adopted.[44] But it is believed that their application would eliminate the disease by killing off the patient. For their underlying assumption surely is that it is not possible to distinguish a legal from a purely moral or social or political obligation. If this be so, what need for international *law*? In an address delivered some years ago, Sir Arnold McNair put into express terms his criticism of the school to which M. Alvarez belongs, a criticism which is implicit in his Separate Opinion. 'The sphere of operation of Public International Law', he said, 'is the legal relations between states, not their political or economic or moral relations, just as English law regulates our legal relations, and not our social relations, such as a dinner engagement, or our moral relations, such as the duty of charity or of being a good neighbour'.[45]

Question (b).

The opinion of the judges was unanimous 'that the provisions of Chapter XII of the Charter are applicable to the Territory of South-West Africa in the sense that they provide a means by which the Territory may be brought under the Trusteeship System'.[46]

Whether the Union is under a legal obligation to place South-West Africa under the trusteeship system, however, promoted the sharpest of the division of views of the court. Eight [47] held she was not. Of the other six members of the court, five [48] were of the opinion that the Union was under a legal obligation 'to enter into negotiations with a view to concluding a Trusteeship Agreement' [49]; Judge Alvarez went somewhat further than the other minority judges, and his views will be analysed later.

The reasoning in the Main Opinion [50] is simple and in accordance

---

[43] P. 178.

[44] He expounds similar views in an article entitled 'The Reconstruction and Codification of International Law', 1 I.L.Q. (1947), 469.

[45] 1 I.L.Q. (1947), 4.   [46] P. 144.

[47] President Basdevant, Judges Hackworth, Winiarski, Sir Arnold McNair, Klaestad, Read, Hsu Mo and Azevedo.

[48] Vice-President Guerrero, Judges Zoričić, de Visscher, Badawi Pasha, Krylov.

[49] See pp. 144–5, 186 ff., 191–2.   [50] Pp. 138–140.

with the view expressed by the preponderance of legal opinion in the past. Articles 75 and 77 are both permissive in character. The fact that Article 77 (1) paragraph (c) used the word 'voluntarily' ('territories voluntarily placed under the [trusteeship] system'), whereas the word was not used in paragraph (a) ('territories now held under mandate') or paragraph (b) ('territories which may be detached from enemy states') does not go to show that there is a legal obligation to place territories falling under the latter two categories under the trusteeship system. The word 'voluntarily' was used *ex abundanti cautela*. Article 80 (2) is entirely negative in character, and had it been intended to impose a duty on mandatories to negotiate and conclude trusteeship agreements it would have been couched in positive terms. Nor could that Article have been intended to create an obligation on mandatories to 'enter into negotiations with a view to concluding a trusteeship agreement', for it refers also to territories covered by Article 77 (1) (b) and (c), in respect of which there obviously could be no such intention.

It is true, runs the Main Opinion, that the Charter contemplated and made provision for only one system, the trusteeship system; and that it was anticipated that mandatories would conclude trusteeship agreements. But, it goes on to say, it is not possible to conclude from this that there is a legal obligation on mandatories to do so.

There are three minority Opinions on this issue. Judge de Visscher's Opinion is concurred in by Vice-President Guerrero and Judges Zoričić and Badawi Pasha. Judges Alvarez and Krylov wrote separate dissenting Opinions.

Judge de Visscher [51] concedes that the provisions of Chapter XII of the Charter ('International Trusteeship System') 'do not impose on the Union of South Africa a legal obligation to conclude a Trusteeship Agreement, in the sense that the Union is free to accept or to refuse the particular terms of a draft agreement'. But he does consider that that Chapter imposes on the Union 'an obligation to take part in negotiations with a view to concluding an agreement'. This conclusion (the practical effect of which the present writer does not profess to understand) is reached by the learned judge from a consideration of the relevant Articles of the Charter from the viewpoint that, as far as possible, they ought to be interpreted as imposing an obligation on the mandatory to conclude a trusteeship agreement, for to hold otherwise would be to allow the perpetual existence of the mandates system, not governed by the Charter and inconsistent with the objects of Chapter XII. Since by the clear wording of Articles 75, 77 and 79 the mandatory is not compelled to accept the terms of a proposed agreement, Judge de Visscher is constrained to conclude that there is a lesser legal obligation, 'to be ready to take part in negotiations' and to conduct them 'in good faith with a view to concluding an agreement'. He says that his conclusion is fortified by the use of the word 'voluntarily' in Article 77 (1) paragraph (c) only, and not in paragraphs (a) and (b),

[51] See pp. 186–190.

referring to mandated territories and territories detached from enemy states. It is only in respect of territories falling under paragraph (c) that there is no obligation to enter into negotiations with a view to concluding a trusteeship agreement. But Judge de Visscher makes no effort to answer the point of the majority that Article 80 (2) refers to territories mentioned in this paragraph (c). This is the fundamental weakness of his analysis, and, it is believed, warrants the rejection of his conclusion.[52]

Judge Alvarez is more explicit in his decision on the legal duty of the Union, for he finds that not only is it under a duty to negotiate a trusteeship agreement, but also to conclude it.[53] He derives this conclusion 'from the spirit of the Charter, which leaves no place for the future co-existence of the Mandates System and the Trusteeship System'. But then follows a passage in his Opinion which bears out the criticism already made of his general approach:

> Even admitting that there is no legal obligation to conclude an agreement, there is, at least, a political obligation, a duty which derives from social inter-dependence and which can be sanctioned by the Assembly of the U.N.[54]

What would take place if no agreement could be reached, is not clear from M. Alvarez' Opinion. In the course of his analysis of the issue, he says: 'It then becomes necessary to refer to arbitration. . . . One would then have to seek an amicable solution, or to submit the case to the International Court of Justice'.[55] In his final answers to the questions propounded, he says in one passage that the case must be referred to arbitration, and in another that 'the United Nations must then take the appropriate measures which it is empowered to take under Article 10 of the Charter'.

Question (c).

> The Court was of the unanimous opinion [56] 'that the Union of South Africa acting alone has not the competence to modify the international status of the Territory of South-West Africa, and that the competence to determine and modify the international status of the Territory rests with the Union of South Africa acting with the consent of the United Nations'.

Two grounds are given for this conclusion:
(a) the powers of supervision over mandates are now vested in the General Assembly of the United Nations (answer to Question (a));
(b) the power to substitute the trusteeship system for the mandates system is vested in the General Assembly by its approving of a proposed trusteeship agreement; and it also has power to approve amendment of such agreement.[57]

[52] And also that of Judge Krylov, who, in a very short dissenting opinion (pp. 191–2) comes to the same conclusion for much the same reasons.
[53] P. 183.   [54] P. 184.   [55] P. 184.   [56] P. 144.
[57] Articles 79 and 85 of the Charter.

By analogy, it can be inferred that the same procedure is applicable to any modification of the international status of a territory under mandate which would not have for its purpose the placing of the territory under the Trusteeship System.[58]

The court considered that its conclusion was strengthened, firstly by the attitude of the Union Government, which has recognised the competence of the General Assembly in the matter; and secondly, by the affirmation by the General Assembly of its competence in the matter, through its resolution of December 14, 1946. It may be doubted, however, if either of these facts affords any support in *law* for the court's conclusion.

It is submitted that the reasoning of Sir Arnold McNair [61] is to be preferred to that in the Main Opinion. He points out that the first paragraph of Article 7 of the Mandate, by which the consent of the League Council was required for any modification of the mandate, has lapsed owing to the disappearance of the League and the Council. The League and its then existing members, through paragraphs (3) and (4) of the winding-up resolution of the League, on April 18, 1946, granted its consent to any future change in the terms of the mandate through agreement between the Union and the United Nations.

Judge Alvarez once again goes further in the body of his Opinion [63] than in his final conclusions.[64] The latter is in the same terms as the Main Opinion. In the course of his analysis, however, he states that if the mandatory does not perform its obligations under the mandate, the General Assembly has the right, under Article 10 of the Charter, to make admonitions, and if necessary, revoke the Mandate. It is difficult to see how, even under the dispensation of the new international law, Article 10, the 'discussion clause' of the Charter,[65] can be construed to give this executive power. It is equally difficult to follow the legal basis for, and indeed at times the true meaning of, the other conclusions M. Alvarez arrives at: that the General Assembly may terminate a mandate if the local population is capable of governing itself, despite contrary opinion of the mandatory; that the General Assembly 'may also terminate a mandate for political considerations. . . . In so doing, however, it must not abuse its right'; and finally, that where the mandatory reports that the local population of the mandated territory 'will never be able, for anthropological or other reasons', to attain 'a sufficient degree of civilisation to become capable of self-government', the General Assembly should institute an inquiry, and if the statement be proved true, authorise the mandatory to annex the territory, 'for it cannot remain without a protector or guide' (it might have been thought that this was just the purpose the mandatory was supposed to have served).

[58] P. 142.   [61] Pp. 162–3.   [63] Pp. 182–3.   [64] P. 185.
[65] See Goodrich and Hambro, *Charter of the United Nations, ad loc.*

SOVEREIGNTY

One very interesting question, not yet touched on in this review, was dealt with in passing by the judges of the International Court—the seat of sovereignty in the C Mandates. Quincy Wright in 1930 had discovered 'some fifty juristic discussions' [66] and, as Latham C.J. pointed out in *Ffrost* v. *Stevenson*,[67] there have been many discussions since. At least eight different views were held.[68] Some writers found that sovereignty resided in the mandatory [69]; others in the mandatory *pro tem* [70]; yet others in the mandatory acting with the consent of the League Council.[71] Another school favoured the view that sovereignty vested in the Principal Allied and Associated Powers.[72] The League of Nations was put forward by other jurists,[73] but was decisively rejected by the Appellate Division of the Union in *R.* v. *Christian*.[74] A variation of the latter thesis was that sovereignty vested in the League but was exercised by the mandatory. Finally, there was the claim that sovereignty resided in the inhabitants of the mandated territory, but was temporarily in suspense.[75] Quite another type of approach was followed by those who considered that nothing was to be gained by trying to apply the concept of sovereignty to the juridical status of a mandated territory, which was something *sui generis*.[76]

Several interesting statements were made by the International Court in the Opinion under review. In the Main Opinion,[77] and also in Judge Read's separate opinion,[78] it is categorically stated that the creation of the mandates system did not involve a transfer of sovereignty to the Union. Sir Arnold McNair states that this system was 'a new species of international government, which does not fit into the old concept of sovereignty and which is alien to it. The doctrine of sover-

[66] *Op. cit.*, 319, n. 18.   [67] *Supra*.

[68] See, generally, McNair, 3 Cambridge Law Journal (1928), 149; Oppenheim, *op. cit.*, 202 n.; Wright, *op. cit.*, 319 ff.

[69] *E.g.*, Keith, with modifications, *Journal of Comparative Legislation*, 3rd series, Vol. 7 (1925), 279–280; Vol. 10 (1928), 121–2; de Villiers and Wessels, JJ.A., in *R.* v. *Christian* (*supra*).

[70] *E.g.*, Rosenow, 3 *Tydskrif vir Hedendaagse Romeins-Hollandse Reg* (1939), 229 ff.

[71] *E.g.*, McNair, *op. cit.*; Wright, 17 A.J.I.L. (1923), 681 ff.; 18 A.J.I.L. (1924), 306 ff.; 20 A.J.I.L. (1926), 768 ff.

[72] See Wright, 319, n. 20; Hall, 22 *International Affairs* (1946), 205.

[73] See authorities cited in Oppenheim, *loc. cit.*   [74] *Supra*.

[75] Stoyanovsky, *La théorie générale des mandats internationaux* (1925); Wessels, *op. cit.* Cf. the view of van den Heever J. in *Verein Für Schutzgebiedsanleinen E.V.* v. *Conradie, N.O.*, reported in [1937] A.D. 113 ff., that sovereignty, wherever it might then be residing, was held 'in trust for the future State to emerge from its present chrysalis or into which the present Mandated Territory will emerge' (at 121).

[76] Brierly, 16 B.Y.I.L. (1929), 217, and *The Law of Nations* (4th ed., 1949), 157–9; *Ffrost* v. *Stevenson* (*supra*).

[77] P. 132.   [78] P. 168.

eignty has no application to this new system. Sovereignty over a Mandated Territory is in abeyance; if and when the inhabitants of the territory obtain recognition as an independent State . . . sovereignty will revive and vest in the new State'.[79] Somewhat similar sentiments were expressed by Judge Alvarez.[80] As South-West Africa is the only one of the former mandated territories which has not become an independent state or the subject of a trusteeship agreement, the search for the location of sovereignty in a mandated territory, on which considerable effort has been expended, yielding much heat but little light, might well now be abandoned.

3. Judge McNair's Separate Opinion

Judges McNair and Read found that, although the Mandate remained in force, South Africa was not obliged to submit to the supervision of the United Nations in respect of her administration of the territory. On the other hand, they held that the judicial supervision of the Mandate remained and that this was to be exercised by the International Court of Justice—a finding which was to be rejected by the International Court in 1966. The following is an extract from Judge McNair's separate opinion: [f]

The Mandate for South-West Africa was never formally terminated, and I can find no events which can be said to have brought about its termination by implication. Paragraph 3 of the Resolution of the Assembly of the League regarding the Mandates, dated April 18, 1946, does not say that the Mandates come to an end but that, "on the termination of the League's existence, its functions with respect to the Mandated Territories will come to an end".

Which then of the obligations and other legal effects resulting from the Mandate remain to-day? The Mandatory owed to the League and to its Members a general obligation to carry out the terms of the Mandate and also certain specific obligations, such as the obligation of Article 6 to make an annual report to the Council of the League. The obligations owed to the League itself have come to an end. The obligations owed to former Members of the League, at any rate, those who were Members at the date of its dissolution, subsist, except in so far as their performance involves the actual co-operation of the League, which is now impossible. (I shall deal with Article 6 and the first paragraph of Article 7 later.) Moreover, the international status created for South-West Africa, namely that of a territory governed by a State in pursuance of a limited title as defined in a Mandate, subsists.

Although there is no longer any League to supervise the exercise of the Mandate, it would be an error to think that there is no control over the Mandatory. Every State which was a Member of the League

[f] 1950 ICJ Reports, 157–59. For Judge Read's views on this subject, see *ibid.*, 164–73.
[79] P. 150.   [80] P. 180.

at the time of its dissolution still has a legal interest in the proper exercise of the Mandate. The Mandate provides two kinds of machinery for its supervision—*judicial,* by means of the right of any Member of the League under Article 7 to bring the Mandatory compulsorily before the Permanent Court, and *administrative,* by means of annual reports and their examination by the Permanent Mandates Commission of the League.

The *judicial supervision* has been expressly preserved by means of Article 37 of the Statute of the International Court of Justice adopted in 1945:

> Whenever a treaty or convention in force provides for reference of a matter to a tribunal to have been instituted by the League of Nations, or to the Permanent Court of International Justice, the matter shall, as between the parties to the present Statute, be referred to the International Court of Justice.

This article effected a succession by the International Court to the compulsory jurisdiction conferred upon the Permanent Court by Article 7 of the Mandate; for there can be no doubt that the Mandate, which embodies international obligations, belongs to the category of treaty or convention; in the judgment of the Permanent Court in the *Mavrommatis Palestine Concessions (Jurisdiction)* case, Series A, No. 2, p. 35, the Palestine Mandate was referred to as an "international agreement"; and I have endeavoured to show that the agreement between the Mandatory and other Members of the League embodied in the Mandate is still "in force". The expression "Member of the League of Nations" is descriptive, in my opinion, not conditional, and does not mean "so long as the League exists and they are Members of it"; their interest in the performance of the obligations of the Mandate did not accrue to them merely from membership of the League, as an examination of the content of the Mandate makes clear. Moreover, the Statute of the International Court empowers it to call from the parties for "any document" or "any explanations" (Article 49); and to entrust any "individual, body, bureau, commission or other organization that it may select, with the task of carrying out an enquiry. . . ." (Article 50). Article 94 of the Charter empowers the Security Council of the United Nations to "make recommendations or decide upon measures to be taken to give effect to the judgment" of the Court, in the event of a party to a case failing to carry out a judgment of the Court. In addition, the General Assembly or the Security Council of the United Nations may request the Court to give an advisory opinion on any legal question (Article 96 of the Charter).

On the other hand, the *administrative supervision* by the Council of the League, as advised by the Permanent Mandates Commission, has lapsed, including the obligation imposed by Article 22 of the Covenant and Article 6 of the Mandate to make, in the words of the Mandate, "to the Council of the League of Nations an annual report to the satisfaction of the Council. . . .". This supervision has lapsed because the League and its Council and Permanent Mandates Commission—

the organs which were designated (i) to receive the reports, (ii) to be satisfied with them and (iii) to examine and advise upon them—no longer exist, so that it has become impossible to perform this obligation. (When a particular Mandate was under discussion by the Council, the Mandatory, if not a Member of the Council, was invited to sit with the Council, with full power of speaking and voting.)

4. Academic Criticism of the Opinion

Academic opinion was critical of the Court's finding that the United Nations had succeeded to the supervisory powers of the League of Nations. Manley O. Hudson commented: [g]

The supervisory functions of the League of Nations were based upon Article 22 of the Covenant and Article 6 of the Mandate for South West Africa. Article 22 (7) required each Mandatory to render to the Council an annual report in reference to the mandated territory, and Article 22 (9) provided for a permanent commission to receive and examine the annual reports and to advise the Council on all matters relating to the observance of the Mandates. Article 6 of the Mandate required the Mandatory to make to the Council "an annual report to the satisfaction of the Council, containing full information with regard to the territory, and indicating the measures taken to carry out the obligations assumed" in certain articles of the Mandate. The Court took the view that the obligation to submit to such supervision did not disappear when the Council of the League of Nations ceased to exist.

To support its additional conclusion that the Union of South Africa is obliged to submit to the supervision of, and to render annual reports to, the United Nations, the Court relied upon a resolution adopted by the final Assembly of the League of Nations on April 18, 1946, which was said to presuppose "that the supervisory functions exercised by the League would be taken over by the United Nations." This is hardly borne out by the text of the resolution, however. Nor is the succession of the General Assembly a necessary consequence of its competence under Article 10 of the Charter to which the Court refers.

The Court referred to an "innovation" by which "the supervisory function of the Council was rendered more effective." This was the resolution adopted by the Council of the League of Nations on January 31, 1923, by which the Council decided that a certain "procedure shall be adopted in respect of petitions regarding inhabitants of mandated territories." No reference was made to the power which the Council of the League of Nations must have had to change the procedure, or to abolish it altogether. Yet the establishment of this procedure was found to have bestowed a "right" on the inhabitants of South West Africa, and the right "which the inhabitants of South West Africa had thus acquired" was found to have been "maintained" by Article 80 (1)

[g] "The Twenty-Ninth Year of the World Court" (1951) 45 *AJIL* 12–16.

of the Charter. The Court proceeds to say that the "dispatch and examination of petitions form a part" of the supervision to be exercised by the United Nations, concluding that the Government of the Union of South Africa is obliged to transmit petitions to the General Assembly of the United Nations.

The Court referred in some detail to action taken by the Government of the Union of South Africa. In a declaration to the Assembly of the League of Nations, that government stated its intention to continue to administer the territory in accordance with the obligations of the Mandate; and to regard such obligations as not diminished by the dissolution of the League, even though that fact would "necessarily preclude complete compliance." In declarations made to the United Nations, that government had stated its intention to render reports to the United Nations, though a contrary intention was later expressed. These declarations give scant support to the Court's conclusion that the Mandatory has an obligation to render reports to the General Assembly.

The Court seems to have placed emphasis on the competence of the General Assembly to exercise supervision and to receive and examine reports. Such competence can hardly be doubted. Yet it does not follow from the conclusion that the General Assembly "is legally qualified to exercise the supervisory functions previously exercised by the League of Nations," that the Union of South Africa is under an obligation to submit to supervision and control by the General Assembly, or that it is obligated to render annual reports to the General Assembly.

Having concluded that the supervisory functions of the Council of the League of Nations have devolved upon the General Assembly of the United Nations, the Court found it necessary to state a qualification. It said that

> South West Africa is still to be considered as a territory held under the Mandate of December 17, 1920. The degree of supervision to be exercised by the General Assembly should not therefore exceed that which applied under the Mandates System, and should conform as far as possible to the procedure followed in this respect by the Council of the League of Nations.

It was added that "those observations are particularly applicable to annual reports and petitions." As the Council of the League of Nations was free to change its procedure at any time, the restriction may tend to freeze a procedure which experience would not justify.

Article 80 (1) of the Charter seems to be the principal basis of the Court's conclusion that the Union of South Africa must report to the General Assembly. This article provided that, until the conclusion of Trusteeship Agreements, nothing in Chapter XII of the Charter should "be construed *in or of itself* to *alter in any manner the rights whatsoever of any states or any peoples* or the terms of existing international instruments" (italics supplied). The text clearly shows an intention that Chapter XII should not effect any alteration of rights or terms. This intention was "entirely negative in character." The provision served an obvious purpose when Chapter XII of the Charter was drawn up: the Mandate was still in force at that time; as the League of Nations had not then been dissolved, any alteration of the existing situation was a matter for its consideration. Article 80 (1) was a precautionary provision designed to negative the accomplishment of any change in the existing situation by reason of Chapter XII "in or of itself." It is not surprising that Judge McNair found it "difficult to see the relevance of this article."

Yet the Court gave an affirmative effect to Article 80 (1), turning it into a positive "safeguard" for maintaining the rights of states and the rights of the peoples of the mandated territory. This is the more notable because at a later stage the Court stressed the "entirely negative" character of Article 80 (2), declining to say that the latter imposed a positive obligation on the Mandatory even to negotiate with a view to the conclusion of a Trusteeship Agreement.

No attention was paid by the Court to the fact that certain states, which as Members of the former League of Nations may have "rights" under Article 22 of the Covenant and under the Mandate itself, had no responsibility for the Charter and have never become Members of the United Nations. For example, Finland, Ireland and Portugal, which were represented at the final session of the Assembly of the League of Nations in 1946, are in this category. If their rights are "maintained" by Article 80 (1) of the Charter, they have no voice in the supervision to be exercised by the General Assembly.

Joseph Nisot was equally critical: [h]

(a) The reasoning of the Court rests essentially on its interpretation of Article 80, paragraph 1, of the Charter, the terms of which must be recalled here:

Except as may be agreed upon in individual trusteeship agreements, made under Articles 77, 79 and 81, placing each territory under the trusteeship system, and until such agreements have been concluded, nothing in this Chapter shall be construed in or of itself *to alter in any manner the rights whatsoever of any States or any peoples or the terms of existing international instruments to which Members of the United Nations may respectively be parties.*

(b) The Court, for the needs of its demonstration, contends that this article 'maintains' the rights of States and peoples resulting from the Mandate and the Covenant.

This expression (*maintains*) is likely to lead to a misconception as to what Article 80, interpreted in accordance with its wording and spirit, really means. The only purpose of the Article is to prevent Chapter XII of the Charter from being construed as in any manner affecting or

[h] "The Advisory Opinion of the International Court of Justice on the International Status of South West Africa" (1951) 68 *SALJ* 274 at 278–81. See, too, K. Steinberg in (1950) 67 *SALJ* 422.

altering the rights whatsoever of States and peoples, as they stand pending the conclusion of trusteeship agreements. Such rights draw their judicial life from the instruments which created them; they remain valid in so far as the latter are themselves still valid. If they are maintained, it is by virtue of those instruments, not by virtue of Article 80, which confines itself to providing that the rights of States and peoples—whatever they may be and to whatever extent they may subsist—are left untouched by Chapter XII.

(c) As stated above, in so far as they correspond to the obligations of the second group, the rights of peoples find, according to the Court, their concrete expression in the right to have the territory administered under international supervision and control, the mandatory Power being bound to render annual reports and the inhabitants being entitled to send petitions.

These rights, the Court holds, continue to exist, since they have been maintained by Article 80.

But, even supposing it did maintain anything, Article 80 could only maintain whatever existed. It could neither resurrect extinct rights nor create new ones.

Now, what, in actuality, were the rights derived by peoples from the Mandate and from Article 22 of the Covenant? They were not rights to the benefit of abstract supervision and control. They consisted of the right to have the administration supervised and controlled by the *Council of the League of Nations,* and, in particular, the right to ensure that annual reports were rendered by the mandatory Power to the *Council of the League of Nations,* as it was, and the right to send petitions to the *Secretariat of the League of Nations.* What has become of these rights? They have necessarily disappeared as a result of the disappearance of the organs of the League (Council, Permanent Mandates Commission, Secretariat).

The Court could not correctly conclude that such rights had been maintained by Article 80, except by contending at the same time that, for the purposes of the Mandate for South-West Africa, the said organs had survived the dissolution of the League.

(d) Being unable, and for good reasons, so to contend, the Court creates *new* rights. To the Court, the right of peoples 'maintained' by Article 80 is linked to the *United Nations Organization.* It is a right to supervision and control by the *United Nations,* to which annual reports and petitions are, in consequence, to be rendered and addressed.

Lacking any other available provision in the Charter, the Court founds such a conclusion on Article 80. According to its thesis, it is because Article 80 'maintains' the rights of peoples that these, though linked to the League, must now be deemed linked to the United Nations! To infer this from a text worded as is Article 80 amounts to assuming that, with respect to the mandates system, the United Nations stands as the legal successor of the League, an assumption inconsistent with the discussions of San Francisco and with the very fact that the Charter provides for the conclusion of trusteeship agreements.

(e) However, the court also invokes, as supporting its conclusions, the resolution of 18th April, 1946, whereby the Assembly of the League of Nations 'recognizes that, on the termination of the League's existence, its functions with respect to the mandated territories will come to an end, but notes that Chapters XI, XII and XIII of the Charter of the United Nations embody principles corresponding to those declared in Article 22 of the Covenant of the League'.

But one fails to see how this statement can provide any support for a suggestion that it was the Assembly's opinion that a mandatory Power, though not bound by a trusteeship agreement, was under an obligation to submit to supervision and control by the United Nations.

This was no more the opinion of the Assembly of the League of Nations than that of the General Assembly of the United Nations, which, by its resolution of 9th February, 1946, urged the conclusion of trusteeship agreements, implying that no implementation of the principles of the trusteeship system—therefore, no supervision or control—was possible in the absence of such agreements.

(f) Lastly, the Court avails itself to certain public declarations made by the Government of the Union of South Africa.

However, these declarations, which are in the aggregate contradictory and inconsistent, cannot be considered as adequately evidencing that the Union has either recognized a succession by the United Nations to the supervisory functions exercised by the League, or has assumed a new obligation towards the United Nations to revive the prewar system of supervision.

(g) The Court, as has been seen, makes the following admission: '. . . the Charter has contemplated and regulated only a single system, the International Trusteeship System. It did not contemplate or regulate a co-existing Mandates System.' Yet, the Court advocates a solution implying the co-existence under the Charter, of the two systems; it suggests that it is for the United Nations to provide for such adjustments as would permit the functioning, in the framework of the Charter, of the Mandate for South-West Africa, which, in the Court's view, would still remain a mandate.

Concerning these adjustments, the Court declares: 'The degree of supervision to be exercised by the General Assembly should not therefore exceed that which applied under the Mandates System, and should conform as far as possible to the procedure followed in this respect by the Council of the League of Nations.' This may call for the enactment of a set of new provisions.

(h) To which organ of the United Nations does the Court assign competence in the matter?

The Charter does not, in this special connection, mention any organ, which is understandable, since it neither contemplates nor regulates a mandates system. Hence the necessity in which the Court found itself to have recourse to Article 10, which empowers the General Assembly to make recommendations on any question within the scope of the Charter.

But the resolutions of the General Assembly, mere recommendations, will fail to bind the Union of South Africa. In practice, therefore, the carrying out of the Court's solution may prove juridically contingent to a large extent on the consent of the Union.

(*i*) The foregoing considerations lead us to the conclusion that, as matters now stand, the Union is under no obligation to submit to supervision and control by the United Nations. This, however, does not, in our opinion, deprive the status of South-West Africa of its contractual character. We, indeed, believe that, apart from the duty to submit to international supervision and control, the obligations imposed upon the Union still subsist, as it is clear that the contracting parties had not intended to make them contingent on the longevity of the League of Nations. Among the surviving obligations, those involved in the principle of non-annexation and the principle that the well-being and development of the peoples of South-West Africa form 'a sacred trust of civilization' are undoubtedly paramount.

The negotiators of San Francisco were confident that all the mandatory Powers would resort to the conclusion of trusteeship agreements. Therefore, although knowing this latter course to be optional, they failed to provide for international supervision with respect to the obligations incumbent on a mandatory State, should it elect not to conclude such an agreement. This lack of foresight has resulted in the present situation, which the Court attempts itself to redress, stepping out of its role as interpreter of the law to assume that of legislator.

Hudson did, however, add the following important qualification to his criticism of the decision, a qualification which is frequently overlooked by those who invoke his views against this Opinion: [1]

If one finds some difficulty in following the reasoning offered by the Court for its conclusion that the United Nations is the successor to the League of Nations with respect to the latter's supervisory functions under the "Mandate System," he may nevertheless be gratified that the Court was able to build a bridge of historical continuity between the League of Nations and the United Nations. The conclusion is hardly consistent with the caution manifested by the General Assembly itself in its resolution of February 12, 1946, concerning the transfer to the United Nations of certain functions of the League of Nations. In that resolution it was stated that

the General Assembly will itself examine, or will submit to the appropriate organ of the United Nations, any request from the parties that the United Nations should assume the exercise of functions or powers entrusted to the League of Nations by treaties, international conventions, agreements and other instruments having a political character.

Nor can the historical continuity be said to have been a moving *desideratum* with most of the statesmen who labored in the Conference at San Francisco in 1945; they were actuated rather by a desire for a decided break with the experience of the past, and this disposition left

[1] Above, n. g, 19. See, too, J. H. W. Verzijl, *The Jurisprudence of the World Court*, 2 (1966):47 ff.

unfortunate traces in the Charter. All the better it would seem to be, if the Court, acting as in this case within the bounds of judicial restraint, can escape some of the consequences of their limited vision.

5. The Response of the United Nations and of South Africa to the Opinion

Despite the fact that the Court rejected the main contention of the General Assembly that South Africa was obliged to place South West Africa under Trusteeship, the General Assembly accepted the Court's Advisory Opinion in Resolution 449A(V) and established an *Ad Hoc* Committee to confer with South Africa on the implementation of the Opinion. At the same time, however, the General Assembly reiterated its request that the territory be placed under Trusteeship in Resolution 449B(V).

The General Assembly,

. . . .

Considering that in accordance with Articles 75, 77, paragraph 1a, 79 and 80, paragraph 2, of the Charter of the United Nations the Trusteeship System has been applied to all mandated territories which have not achieved independence, with the sole exception of the Territory of South West Africa,

Considering that, under the terms of the Charter of the United Nations, it is clear that the International Trusteeship System takes the place of the former Mandates System instituted by the League of Nations and, further, that there is no specific provision indicating the permanent co-existence of the Mandates System with the International Trusteeship System,

1. *Reiterates* its resolutions 65 (I) of 14 December 1946, 141 (II) of 1 November 1947, 227 (III) of 26 November 1948 and 337 (IV) of 6 December 1949 to the effect that the Territory of South West Africa be placed under the International Trusteeship System;

2. *Reiterates* that the normal way of modifying the international status of the Territory would be to place it under the Trusteeship System by means of a Trusteeship Agreement in accordance with the provisions of Chapter XII of the Charter.

Although an advisory opinion is not legally binding upon States, it does constitute a statement of the law by the most authoritative international tribunal, with the result that it differs little from a judgment in a dispute between States. This point is stressed by Advocate I. Goldblatt, Q. C. of the South West African Bar: [j]

---

[j] *The Mandated Territory of South West Africa in Relation to the United Nations*, p. 34. See further, Shabtai Rosenne, *The Law and Practice of the International Court* 2 (1965):744–47.

In view of the oft heard argument that this is "merely an advisory opinion", it should at this stage be explained what an advisory opinion of the International Court of Justice is, and in what respects an advisory opinion differs from a compulsory opinion (judgment).

In the case of a compulsory judgment, there is a dispute between two states as to their respective rights and obligations in regard to a particular matter.

The Court decides the law in the matter and pronounces a judgment in favour of the successful party.

Now, in International Law there are ordinarily no means of carrying into effect a judgment of an International Court, if the losing party decides not to abide by it.

However, in terms of Article 94 (2) of the Charter, the Security Council is given power if called upon to take steps to ensure that the judgment of the International Court is carried into effect.

But let it be noted that what the Court does in the case of a compulsory judgment, whether unanimous or by majority vote, is
(1) To decide what the legal obligations and rights are of the parties;
(2) To order the losing party to do something.

In other words, it lays down the law, and gives its order on the law as laid down. And the law as laid down is taken as a precedent for subsequent cases before the International Court of Justice and serves the purpose of developing International Law.

In the case of an advisory opinion, there is no dispute between states. The General Assembly and certain subordinate organs of the United Nations have been specifically given the right by Article 96 of the Charter, to submit for the opinion of the International Court of Justice any questions of law arising out of the performance of their functions.

For example, the question may be the interpretation of an Article of the Charter itself.

The necessity for such an opinion may arise because of a difference of opinion or a dispute amongst delegates in the General Assembly or subordinate organisations, and the purpose of obtaining an opinion from the International Court of Justice, is to settle the question of law which has given rise to the difference of opinion or dispute.

Certain specific legal questions would thereupon be submitted to the International Court.

Exactly as in the case of a compulsory judgment, the Court examines documents, records, the Charter, hears argument on both sides, applying principles of International Law, lays down the law applicable to the particular dispute, and gives its answers to the questions put, in accordance with the law as laid down.

But it pronounces no judgment and it makes no order. The difference between the compulsory and the advisory opinion is in the fact that in the one an order is made upon the losing party and in the other no order is made.

But in both cases, the Court declares the law applicable to the case and either explicitly or impliedly declares, where necessary, the legal rights and obligations that flow from the law so laid down.

The advisory opinion is not binding upon the General Assembly, but the law as pronounced by the Court cannot be wiped out of existence, even if for political reasons the General Assembly decides not to give effect to it, and in International Law it is of exactly the same value as the law as laid down in a compulsory judgment.

By refusing to give effect to it, the General Assembly or any other organ, cannot declare that the law as laid down by the Court is not the law, for the Court is the only body to declare the law.

South Africa refused to accept the Court's Opinion on the grounds that there was certain vital information relating to the dissolution of the mandates system which had not been placed before the Court. The nature of this information was referred to by the South African delegate, Dr. T. E. Dönges, in the Fourth Committee. [k]

47. The International Court, by a vote of 12 to 2, had decided that, in view of the necessity of continuing supervision, the obligation to submit reports persisted, and that, because the United Nations had succeeded to the rights and functions of the League in that respect, the reports were to be submitted to the United Nations. The South African delegation believed, however, that in formulating its opinion the Court had been unaware of the circumstances surrounding the adoption of the League's final resolution of 18 April 1946, on which that part of its opinion had largely been based. Mr. Dönges was convinced that if the additional information which had now been discovered had been available to the Court, it would have accepted the minority view that there had been no transfer of the functions of the League to the United Nations.

48. The governments represented at the final meeting of the League of Nations had generally recognized that the future of the Mandates System was a complex and delicate problem on which it would eventually be necessary for the League to pronounce an opinion. There had not been time for discussion of the question in the appropriate committee at the last session of the Assembly of the League in April 1946; but private discussions had been initiated between governments, and each Mandatory Power had made a statement of its intentions regarding its mandated territories. The Union of South Africa had stated at that time that it intended to discharge its obligations in accordance with the procedure it had followed during the preceding six years.

49. The Chinese delegation to the League of Nations had raised the question of the Mandates System in the First Committee on 9 April 1946, and had presented a draft resolution recommending that the Mandatory Powers should submit reports to the United Nations and

[k] *GAOR*, Fifth Session, Fourth Committee, 196th Mtg, §§ 47–52. The full text of this speech appears in A/C 4/185 and in the South African WPD of 1951 (South West Africa: Discussion and Proceedings in the United Nations, 1949–50), pp. 46–53.

should submit to inspection by the United Nations until such time as the Trusteeship Council should be constituted. No discussion of the substance of the proposal had taken place, since it had been ruled that the resolution was not relevant to the question under discussion. Private discussions had subsequently taken place between the delegations of the governments directly concerned, with a view to reaching amicable agreement on the question and producing a resolution which could be unanimously adopted by the Council of the League. Agreement had finally been reached on a text introduced by the Chinese delegation on 12 April 1946, which omitted any reference to the transfer of the League's supervisory functions to the United Nations, or to inspection of mandated territories or submission of reports; that text had differed widely from the original Chinese proposal. In these circumstances, neither the South African delegation nor any of the delegations with whom the matter had been discussed understood the proposal to contemplate any transfer of supervisory functions; indeed, it had been introduced and adopted with the very object of avoiding any such transfer. Otherwise the Union of South Africa would have opposed the resolution, since that government had clearly stated its intention of formulating, at the following sessions of the United Nations, its case for according a new status upon South West Africa by which it would become an integral part of the Union. In that case, the resolution would have been rejected, since it would not have secured the unanimous vote of the League Assembly as required by Article 5 of the Covenant and rule 19 of that Assembly's rules of procedure.

50. Mr. Dönges pointed out that although there had been a considerable lapse of time between dissolution of the League of Nations and the conclusion of the first trusteeship agreements, no reports on mandated territories had been submitted to the United Nations during that time by the Mandatory Powers, nor had such reports been requested. That situation further confirmed the general assumption that there was to be no transfer of supervisory functions.

51. Furthermore, the United Nations, in its resolution 24 (I) adopted on 12 February 1946, had decided that in respect to functions and powers under treaties, international conventions, agreements and other instruments having a political character, the General Assembly would itself examine, or submit to an appropriate organ of the United Nations, any request from the parties concerned that the United Nations should assume the exercise of functions of powers entrusted to the League of Nations by treaties or other instruments having a political character. It was not likely, therefore, that the League, faced with that resolution of the United Nations, would have adopted a resolution two months later whereby the supervisory functions of the League in respect of mandates should be transferred to the United Nations.

52. The researches which had brought to light those new and material facts had only recently been concluded, and the discovery represented a new development which the South African Government would weigh carefully, together with whatever resolution the General Assembly might eventually adopt in considering the appropriate way of han-

dling the new situation. Until all aspects of the problem had been fully and carefully examined, Mr. Dönges could not make any statement which might be interpreted as binding upon his government in any way.

South Africa's failure to disclose this information until after the Court's Opinion is disquieting, as it is difficult to see how the South African legal advisers could originally have overlooked the point.[1] South Africa's decision to reject the Opinion was strongly criticized by the South West African jurist I. Goldblatt: [m]

The Court heard argument on the question in open Court, for and against. The Union Government was represented by its Senior Legal Adviser, Dr. L. C. Steyn, Q.C. (at present Chief Justice of the Union of South Africa), and the argument advanced by the Union that the disappearance of the League of Nations had resulted in the extinction of the Mandate, was thoroughly examined and unanimously rejected by all the Judges.

It passes all comprehension that one should thereafter hear from people—from Prime Minsters downwards—unqualified in International Law—the view expressed that the International Court of Justice was wrong in a matter exclusively involving International Law.

And, in so far as the Union Government is concerned, while it is true that in an advisory opinion the Court makes no binding order upon anyone, it does, however, declare what the law is.

The Union Government's refusal, therefore, to abide by the Court's view does not deprive the Court's opinion of its full legal value, but merely means that the Union Government relies upon the fact that there is no machinery for giving effect to that decision.

6. United Nations' Attempts to Implement the Opinion

In 1951 the *Ad Hoc* Committee held several meetings with the representative of the South African Government in an attempt to settle the dispute. But with the Committee obliged to negotiate on the basis of the 1950 Advisory Opinion and South African unwilling to accept the authority of the United Nations over South West Africa no agreement was possible. South Africa's suggestion that she conclude a new agreement with the Principal Allied and Associated Powers of World War I (the United Kingdom, France, and the United States of America) was rejected by the Committee, as it was incompatible with the Court's Opinion. The different stances of the two parties appear from the Report of the *Ad Hoc* Committee in 1951.[n]

[1] See the comment of the Chinese delegate on this argument: *Ibid.*, § 63–64.
[m] *The Conflict between the United Nations and the Union of South Africa in regard to South West Africa* (1960), p. 15.
[n] *GAOR*, Sixth Session, Annexes (Agenda Item 38) pp. 2–8 (A/1901).

14. The representative of the Union of South Africa stated that it was his Government's proposal that it should reassume its international obligations under the Mandate by negotiating a new international instrument with the three remaining members of the Principal Allied and Associated Powers of the First World War with a direct legal obligation of the South African Government to the three Powers. In making that proposal the representative of the Union of South Africa explained that the original Mandate had been conferred upon the Union of South Africa by the Principal Allied and Associated Powers and was confirmed by the League of Nations. The League no longer existed and neither did the original Principal Allied and Associated Powers as a group. Italy had been disassociated from the Mandates System in the Treaty of Peace (article 40) and the same would probably be the case of Japan. However, three of the original group remained —France, the United Kingdom and the United States—if not as a group at least as individual States. He explained that both the United Nations and the South African Government wanted to continue the sacred trust, and in the opinion of his Government the only method of doing that was to negotiate a new instrument to reassume the fundamental obligations inherent in its sacred trust. As unilateral action was inadequate, a second party with whom to conclude an agreement was necessary. That party had not been chosen at random, but rather on the basis of historical association.

15. The senior law adviser of the Union of South Africa stated in that connexion that in his Government's opinion, the three remaining members of the Principal Allied and Associated Powers were in a special position since they had conferred the original Mandate. He added, however, that there were no legal obligations subsisting towards those Powers since the part that they had originally played was simply that of an intermediary. Once the Mandate had been confirmed by the League of Nations, they had passed out of the picture and the South African Government had assumed its legal obligations towards the League of Nations. It was not because the South African Government felt that it had any legal obligations towards the Principal Allied and Associated Powers that it was proposing to negotiate a new agreement with them, but simply because those Powers had been connected with the original Mandate. He also stated that although the Court stated in its advisory opinion that the obligations assumed by the Union of South Africa under the Mandate were still in force, it did not mention the party to whom the Union Government owed those obligations. There was some indication on that point in the separate opinions of Judge Read and Sir Arnold McNair, but the majority opinion did not deal with the subject at all, thus giving the impression that the majority did not agree with the views of the minority on the point.

16. In the course of the 3rd meeting, the representative of the Union of South Africa stated that the United Nations would have to find out if the three Powers concerned were willing to become the other party to the new contractual agreement. If they were willing, the United Nations would then call upon them to negotiate the instrument and the Union of South Africa would be directly responsible to

them and not to the United Nations. He explained further that his Government did not contemplate that the United Nations must be in some way connected with the new arrangement, or would have to remain the final authority and that the three Powers would simply become an agency of the United Nations. But in the course of the 7th meeting the representative of the Union of South Africa stated that his delegation had originally stated that an agreement could be negotiated at the request and with the specific approval of the United Nations. In an effort to meet the wishes of the United Nations, the South African Government was now prepared to agree to final confirmation of the new instrument by the United Nations.

17. With reference to the obligations which the Union of South Africa would assume under the new agreement, the representative of the Union of South Africa stated that his Government had suggested that it should negotiate an instrument with the three remaining members of the Principal Allied and Associated Powers to safeguard the fundamental principles of the sacred trust described in the original Mandate. He further stated that the actual details of the new agreement would have to be settled by negotiations between the three Powers concerned and the South african Government. The three Powers would have to satisfy themselves that the new arrangement would achieve the basic purpose of the Mandate and at the same time they would have to meet the essential requirements of the South African Government.

18. Concerning the question relating to the machinery of implementation, the representative of the Union of South Africa stated, in the course of the 5th meeting, that if it were desired that the proposed instrument should include provisions relating to implementation, the South African Government would be prepared to consider the matter provided it was made clear beforehand how implementation was to be brought about. In the course of the 7th meeting, after the *Ad Hoc* Committee had submitted to the representative of the Union of South Africa certain fundamental principles (see para. 19 below), the representative of the Union of South Africa stated *inter alia;*

> Articles 6 and 7 of the Mandate provided for implementation in respect of the principles of the sacred trust. The Union Government had therefore referred to those provisions as auxiliary. Article 6 of the Mandate provided for League supervision while article 7 provided for judicial supervision. In the former case, it was significant to note that the League of Nations had disappeared and that no other international organization had assumed the League function in question. In the Union's view the position that that function had been transferred to the United Nations was untenable for reasons which would be explained at a later stage. Since, in the Union's view, no other organization could legally claim to have assumed the League supervision, South Africa was not required to renew article 6 of the Mandate.
> At the outset the Union of South Africa had voluntarily sub-

mitted reports on South West Africa but had been obliged to discontinue those reports because of compelling reasons which had been explained repeatedly. In the absence of the trusteeship agreement or other agreement obliging the Union Government to carry out the sacred trust, the United Nations had considered reports on South West Africa as the only means of showing its concern and interest in the territory. The controversy about the reports had led to exaggeration of their importance. As the reports had led to conditions endangering the fulfilment of the Government's sacred trust under the Mandate, the Union Government did not wish under the new agreement to assume obligations which it felt were unnecessary and unsound for South West Africa, a territory which was unique.

The Union delegation was conscious of the fact that the Committee regarded implementation as essential and that any formula failing to make provision for implementation would be unacceptable. It felt, however, that the requirement of implementation could be met without the system of supervision as envisaged in article 6 of the Mandate. The same results could be achieved by judicial supervision as outlined in article 7, with the Court rendered competent and given compulsory jurisdiction. The United Nations would continue to be competent to deal with any dispute which, within the compass of the Charter, might be referred to it. In the Union view, adequate safeguards would thus be provided for implementation of the agreement. Moreover the Court itself had recognized that continuation of the sacred trust was not dependent on the continuation of the implementation measures under the Mandate but that that aim could be effected by other means.

19. In the course of its 6th meeting the *Ad Hoc* Committee discussed the proposal of the Union of South Africa and drew up a statement of three fundamental principles which it considered essential. At its 7th meeting the Committee submitted those principles to the representative of the Union of South Africa. They were as follows:

(1) An agreement could be negotiated which would be entered into under the authority of the United Nations.

(2) The agreement should embody obligations contained in the Mandate as exercised under the League of Nations, including the sacred trust and the handling of annual reports and petitions.

(3) The agreement could take into consideration modifications in the provisions of the Mandate dictated by changed conditions, as, for example, military provisions.

20. In the course of the 7th meeting the representative of the Union of South Africa expressed his views of the Committee's principles.

21. Concerning the first point, he stated:

As the first point was vaguely worded, the Union delegation was obliged to give its interpretation before accepting. The opening words showed that the formula permitted negotiation of a new instrument. Since the test was silent in the manner of identifying the other party, it was the Union delegation's view that the negotiation of a new instrument with the three Powers it had proposed was not excluded. The first five words thus interpreted were therefore acceptable.

The remainder of the first point required clarification. The Union delegation had originally stated that an agreement could be negotiated at the request and with the specific approval of the United Nations. In an effort to meet the wishes of the United Nations, the Union Government was now prepared to agree to final confirmation of the new instrument by the United Nations. It was the Union Government's understanding that the requirements of the first point would thereby be fulfilled. If that understanding was correct, the Union delegation was prepared to accept the first point.

22. Concerning the second point he stated that the South African Government would wish the text of point two to be changed so as to read: "The agreement should embody obligations similar to those provided for in article 2, 3, 4, 5, and 7 of the Mandate." (see also para. 18, above.)

23. Concerning the third point, the representative of the Union of South Africa found it satisfactory.

24. In the course of the 7th meeting the senior law adviser of the Union of South Africa stated that from a strictly legal point of view the Union of South Africa did not feel obliged to submit to supervisory functions by the United Nations but that the South African Government nevertheless had expressed its willingness to submit to judicial supervision by the International Court of Justice.

25. The representative of the Union of South Africa summarized the attitude which his Government had taken in the negotiation as follows:

(a) The South African representative indicated that notwithstanding his country's legal position, the Government of the Union South Africa, in deference to the wishes of the United Nations, would be prepared to accept afresh international responsibility in regard to South West Africa;

(b) He explained that in that spirit the South African Government would be prepared to negotiate a new agreement with the three remaining members of the Allied and Associated Powers (France, the United Kingdom and the United States);

(c) While the South African Government itself did not see the need for any provision relating to implementation, it was willing to go further in its efforts to meet the Committee's point of view by proposing judicial supervision;

(d) Since the Committee felt that the proposal of the Union of South Africa did not give the United Nations a sufficient role, the South African representative indicated that after further consideration his Government was prepared to accept a compromise whereby the idea of negotiating a fresh agreement with the three Powers should first be sanctioned by the United Nations;

(*e*) As that still did not satisfy the Committee, he intimated that the South African Government would be willing to have the agreement referred back to the United Nations for confirmation;

(*f*) The South African representative indicated that if the Committee considered his proposal as falling outside its terms of reference he would be glad to submit to his Government any suggestion that the Committee might wish to put forward indicating how the proposal could be brought within the Committee's competence.

26. In the course of the 8th meeting the Chairman of the *Ad Hoc* Committee informed the representative of the Union of South Africa that the Committee was bound by its terms of reference under the Assembly's resolution to implement the explicit Court opinion requiring the submission of annual reports and expressly stating that the United Nations should supervise the discharge by the South African Government of at least one group of its obligations. The South African suggestion for the procedure eliminating reports could not, therefore, be considered as within the Committee's terms of reference.

27. In the course of its 9th and 10th meetings the *Ad Hoc* Committee considered the proposal of the Union of South Africa and found it to be unacceptable because it did not allow for a full implementation of the advisory opinion of the International Court of Justice which had been accepted by the General Assembly. The Committee noted particularly that the Union of South Africa was not considering as part of its proposal any provision for the supervision of the administration of the Territory of South West Africa by the United Nations as had been foreseen in the advisory opinion of the International Court of Justice. Therefore the Committee discussed and adopted for submission to the Government of the Union of South Africa a counter-proposal. . . .

29. By letter, dated 11 July 1951, the Chairman of the *Ad Hoc* Committee transmitted the Committee's counter-proposal to the representative of the Union of South Africa. The letter read as follows:

. . . The Committee is glad to learn that much common ground exists between itself and the Union. In particular, it is manifest that both conferring groups are agreed that the question of South West Africa should be regulated by means of an agreement, but this agreement should make provisions for its implementation, and that the agreement might contain certain modifications in the provision of the mandate, particularly as regards military provision, having regard to the new obligations of United Nations Members flowing from the Charter.

The Committee carefully examined certain concrete proposals made by the Union representatives suggesting, in particular, an agreement based on Article 2–5 of the Mandate, which would be negotiated and contracted between the Union and the remaining Principal Allied and Associated Powers (France, the United Kingdom and the United States) and confirmed by the United Nations. The proposal included a suggestion for implementation by means of 'judicial supervision' through access to the Court in cases of alleged non-compliance.

The Committee, while appreciative of this effort on the part of the Union, feels that an agreement on this basis not only would go beyond its terms of reference but would in its substance be unlikely to gain the desired acceptance of the General Assembly, with the result that the question would remain unsettled.

The Committee consequently feels it its duty to submit a counter-proposal for the consideration of representatives of the Union which it most earnestly hopes will gain the approval of the Union Government.

The principal feature of this counter-proposal is in its provision for implementation which would be through the United Nations by a procedure as nearly as possible analogous to that which existed under the League of Nations, thus providing terms no more extensive or onerous than those which existed before.

. . . .

32. By letter, dated 20 September 1951, the deputy permanent representative of the permanent delegation of the Union of South Africa to the United Nations informed the Chairman of the Committee as follows:

. . . .

4. In spite of the Committee's rejection of the Union's proposal, the Union Government have given most careful consideration to the Committee's counter-proposal put forward as a basis for discussion. It would seem, however, that this proposal does not give due weight to the viewpoint of the Union Government as explained by the Union Government's representatives in the discussions with the Committee. The Union representatives endeavoured to make it clear that there were certain basic requirements which the Union, as administering Power, considered essential to the achievement of a satisfactory solution. If these were recognized, the Union would not be unwilling to concede certain basic requirements in the standpoint adopted by the United Nations such as the principle of international accountability and recognition of the necessity for United Nations approval for any change in the international status of the territory (subject of course to the provisions of article 2 of the Mandate). It would also appear that the Committee's proposal would have the effect of imposing on the Union obligations even more extensive than those implicit in the mandates system, notwithstanding the reference in Your Excellency's letter to 'terms no more extensive or onerous than those which existed before'. Instances were brought to the notice of the Committee at the discussions with Union representatives, but to give one example, I would mention that the Committee's proposals would confer certain rights in respect of South West Africa on states now members of the United Nations which had no such rights under the League of Nations.

5. In regard to the question of submission of reports on the territory, I am to state that the Union Government are unable to accept this principle. It will be recalled that they informed the Secretary-General of the United Nations in their letter of 11th July, 1949, that they would not be able to submit further reports. On that occasion the Union Government explained that while they had submitted a report in a spirit of goodwill, co-operation and helpfulness, this report had been utilized as a basis for unfounded and unjustified criticism and censure of the Union Government's administration. Not only did this cause much resentment but the misunderstandings to which it gave rise in the Union and South West Africa undermined the harmonious relations which had hitherto existed and which were so essential to successful administration. There is always available, however, essential information on the territory in the form of statistics, departmental reports, records of the South West African Legislature, blue books and other governmental publications.

6. In these circumstances the Union Government feel they have no alternative, in reply to the Committee's counter-proposal, but to reiterate their willingness to conclude an agreement on the lines explained to the Committee. . . .

While the *Ad Hoc* Committee was busy with its attempts to reach a settlement, relations between South Africa and the Fourth Committee were exacerbated by the decision of that Committee to grant oral hearings to petitioners.° South Africa's objections to this procedure were voiced by Dr. T. E. Dönges in the General Assembly: ᴾ

159. The resolution of 16 November in terms of which the Fourth Committee decided to hear oral petitions from certain Herero Chiefs, is clearly irregular and unconstitutional. The grounds for this contention are set out briefly in my letters to you, Mr. President, which I desire to be regarded as incorporated herein, but which need not be repeated here. For the purpose of refreshing the memories of my fellow representatives I merely summarize them shortly. It was contended that this resolution:

(*a*) is in conflict with the Charter of the United Nations which provides only for the hearing of petitions concerning Trust Territories, and as South West Africa is not a Trust Territory no oral petitions can be received by the Fourth Committee in terms of the Charter;

(*b*) flouts resolution 449 (V) of the General Assembly of last year in terms of which an *ad hoc* committee was appointed to examine petitions and any other matters relating to South West Africa as far as possible in accordance with the procedure of the former Mandates System. In conflict with this resolution of the General Assembly, the Fourth

° *Ibid.*, pp. 16–32. For an account of this matter, see Goldblatt, *The Mandated Territory of South West Africa*, pp. 39–49.
ᴾ *GAOR*, Sixth Session, Plenary, 361st Mtg. § 159.

Committee usurped the functions of the special committee and proceeded itself to deal with petitions concerning South West Africa in a
manner in conflict with that prescribed by the General Assembly last
year;

(c) is contrary to the procedure adopted under the old Mandates
System which never allowed oral petitions, a procedure which the Advisory Opinion of the International Court of Justice, whether rightly
or wrongly, specifically enjoined.

The sponsors of the resolution of 16 November to hear oral petitions,
and those who voted in its favour, are among those who have accepted
that Advisory Opinion.

Although the *Ad Hoc* Committee was reconstituted in 1952 [q]
and 1953, [r] it was unable to reach any agreement with the South
African Government, for the same reasons as before. Consequently, in 1953 a permanent Committee on South West Africa
was established by Resolution 749A(VIII). At the same time the
General Assembly reiterated its recommendation that the territory be placed under Trusteeship. The terms of reference of the
Committee appear from the Resolution.

The General Assembly,
. . . .
12. *Establishes,* until such time as an agreement is reached between
the United Nations and the Union of South Africa, a Committee on
South West Africa, consisting of seven Members, and requests this
Committee to:

(a) Examine, within the scope of the Questionnaire adopted by the
Permanent Mandates Commission of the League of Nations in 1926,
such information and documentation as may be available in respect of
the Territory of South West Africa;

(b) Examine, as far as possible in accordance with the procedure of
the former Mandates System, reports and petitions which may be submitted to the Committee or to the Secretary General;

(c) Transmit to the General Assembly a report concerning conditions in the Territory taking into account, as far as possible, the scope
of the reports of the Permanent Mandates Commission of the League
of Nations;

(d) Prepare, for the consideration of the General Assembly, a procedure for the examination of reports and petitions which should conform as far as possible to the procedure followed in this respect by the
Assembly, the Council and the Permanent Mandates Commission of
the League of Nations;

13. *Authorizes* the Committee to continue negotiations with the
Union of South Africa in order to implement fully the advisory opin-

[q] General Assembly Resolution 570(VI).
[r] General Assembly Resolution 651(VII).

ion of the International Court of Justice regarding the question of South West Africa;

14. *Requests* the Committee to submit reports on its activities to the General Assembly at its regular sessions.

The Committee on South West Africa was as unsuccessful as its predecessor in its attempt to implement the 1950 Advisory Opinion. This appears from the Report of the Committee submitted in 1954: [8]

9. Pursuant to paragraph 13 of General Assembly resolution 749 A(VIII), the Committee, at the closed part of its 2nd meeting on 21 January 1954, requested the Chairman to inform the Government of the Union of South Africa that the Committee had been formally constituted and was ready to continue negotiations in order to implement fully the advisory opinion of the International Court of Justice regarding the question of South West Africa. The Committee therefore invited the Union Government to designate a representative to confer with it, in the earnest hope that, through new negotiations, satisfactory and positive results might be attained. . . .

10. By a letter dated 25 March 1954, the Permanent Representative of the Union of South Africa to the United Nations transmitted a reply from the Minister of External Affairs. . . . This reply, *inter alia,* reviewed the position of the Union Government with respect to earlier negotiations with the *Ad Hoc* Committee on South West Africa. The *Ad Hoc* Committee, it was recalled, had been informed of the standpoint of the Union Government regarding South West Africa in a letter dated 4 September 1953, namely:

(*a*) The Union Government maintain that the Mandate in respect of South West Africa has lapsed and that while they continue to administer the Territory in the spirit of the trust they originally accepted, they have no other international commitments as a result of the demise of the League [of Nations]. Nevertheless, in order to find a solution which would remove this question from the United Nations, they are prepared to enter into an arrangement with the three remaining Allied and Associated Powers, namely France, the United Kingdom and the United States.

(*b*) The Union Government's responsibilities in regard to South West Africa should not in any way exceed those which they assumed under the Mandate.

The letter pointed out that, despite lengthy discussions, it had not been possible to reach agreement. The proposals of the Union Government were not acceptable to the *Ad Hoc* Committee "because it did not consider that they provided means whereby the advisory opinion of the International Court of Justice could be implemented and because the proposals did not recognize the principle of supervision of

[8] *GAOR*, Ninth Session, Suppl. No. 14 (A/2666) at pp. 1–2.

the administration of South West Africa by the United Nations". On the other hand, the letter stated, the Union Government was not prepared to consider proposals which did not meet its basic requirements.

11. With respect to the present Committee, paragraph 5 of the reply of the Union Government stated:

> As the terms of reference of your Committee appear to be even more inflexible than those of the *Ad Hoc* Committee the Union Government are doubtful whether there is any hope that new negotiations within the scope of your Committee's terms of reference will lead to any positive results.

12. The letter from the Permanent Representative of the Union of South Africa to the United Nations was discussed by the Committee on 1 April 1954, during its 16th and 17th (closed) meetings. The Committee replied to the Permanent Representative by letter dated 1 April 1954. . . . The Committee stated that it regretted that it could only interpret the Union Government's reply and its failure to appoint a representative to confer with the Committee as a refusal to cooperate for the present in the resumption of negotiations. In this connexion, the Committee found the standpoint of the Union, as given in paragraph (a) of the letter of 4 September 1953, to be not only incompatible with the advisory opinion of the Court but also with General Assembly resolution 749 A (VIII). The Committee informed the Union Government, however, that it remained ready, in accordance with its terms of reference as stated in that resolution, to continue negotiations concerning the question of South West Africa if the Union Government should be willing to negotiate with a view to implementing fully the advisory opinion of the International Court on the question.

13. By a letter dated 2 April 1954 . . . the Permanent Representative acknowledged receipt of this letter and informed the Committee that its contents were being transmitted to the Union Government.

14. As at 25 June 1954, the date of the adoption of the present report, the Committee had received no reply from the Union Government to its letter of 1 April.

7. *The 1955 Advisory Opinion*

Owing to South Africa's refusal to submit reports on her administration of the territory, the Committee was obliged to obtain such information itself for the compilation of its report. Despite South Africa's lack of co-operation, the Committee managed to compile a report based largely on official information issued by the South African Government in which it examined political, economic, social, and educational conditions in the territory.[t] In terms of the proposed procedure for the examination of these reports by the

[t] *Ibid.*, pp. 14–31 (Annex V).

General Assembly, decisions of the Assembly on this subject were considered to be important questions within the meaning of Article 18(2) of the Charter, requiring a two-thirds majority vote.[u] As South Africa contended that this constituted a greater degree of supervision than that prevailing under the League of Nations, where a unanimous vote was required (including that of the mandatory) for any resolution affecting a mandatory State, the General Assembly resolved to refer the question whether the two-thirds majority voting rule was compatible with the Court's 1950 Advisory Opinion to the International Court of Justice for a second Advisory Opinion. In 1955, in the *Voting Procedure Case,* the Court ruled in favour of the two-thirds majority voting rule.[v]

By Resolution 904 (IX) of December 23rd, 1954, the General Assembly

> Requests the International Court of Justice to give an advisory opinion on the following questions:
>
> (*a*) Is the following rule on the voting procedure to be followed by the General Assembly a correct interpretation of the advisory opinion of the International Court of Justice of 11 July 1950: 'Decisions of the General Assembly on questions relating to reports and petitions concerning the Territory of South-West Africa shall be regarded as important questions within the meaning of Article 18, paragraph 2, of the Charter of the United Nations'?
>
> (*b*) If this interpretation of the advisory opinion of the Court is not correct, what voting procedure should be followed by the General Assembly in taking decisions on questions relating to reports and petitions concerning the Territory of South-West Africa?

The rule quoted in this Request for an Advisory Opinion is Rule F, which is set out in Resolution 844 (IX) adopted by the General Assembly on October 11th, 1954. This Rule prescribes a voting system to be followed by the General Assembly.

The General Assembly asks, in the first place, whether this Rule is a correct interpretation of the Advisory Opinion given by the Court on July 11th, 1950. This is the first question to be considered. The second question arises only in the event that the Court expresses the opinion that Rule F is not a correct interpretation of the Advisory Opinion of 1950.

[u] *Ibid.,* p. 13 (Special rule F). Adopted by the General Assembly in Resolution 844(IX).
[v] 1955 ICJ Reports 67, 70–78. For academic comment on and criticism of this decision, see R. Y. Jennings, "The International Court's Advisory Opinion on the Voting Procedure on Questions Concerning South-West Africa" (1956) 42 *Transactions of the Grotius Society* 85; Manley O. Hudson in (1956) 50 *AJIL* 5–9; J. H. W. Verzijl, *The Jurisprudence of the World Court,* 2:218–29.

By Resolution 449 (V) A of December 13th, 1950, the Opinion of 1950 was adopted by the General Assembly as the basis for the supervision of the administration of the mandated Territory of South-West Africa. There followed prolonged and unfruitful negotiations between representatives of the Government of the Union of South Africa and an *ad hoc* Committee of the General Assembly.

At the Eighth Session, the General Assembly, by Resolution 749 (VIII) of November 28th, 1953, established a Committee on South-West Africa. It was requested to:

> (*a*) Examine, within the scope of the Questionnaire, adopted by the Permanent Mandates Commission of the League of Nations in 1926, such information and documentation as may be available in respect of the Territory of South-West Africa;
>
> (*b*) examine, as far as possible, in accordance with the procedure of the former Mandates System, reports and petitions which may be submitted to the Committee or to the Secretary-General;
>
> (*c*) transmit to the General Assembly a report concerning conditions in the Territory taking into account, as far as possible, the scope of the reports of the Permanent Mandates Commission of the League of Nations;
>
> (*d*) prepare, for the consideration of the General Assembly, a procedure for the examination of reports and petitions which should conform as far as possible to the procedure followed in this respect by the Assembly, the Council and the Permanent Mandates Commission of the League of Nations.

Acting under this authority, the Committee on South-West Africa prepared two sets of rules. One set of rules relates to its own procedure, and to the examination of reports, petitions and other information concerning the Territory of South-West Africa. The procedure was designed to be analogous to that which was followed by the Permanent Mandates Commission under the League of Nations. Provision was made for obtaining the views of the Mandatory Power and for the submission of reports and observations by the Committee to the General Assembly. The other set of rules prepared by the Committee prescribed the procedure to be followed by the General Assembly in its consideration of the reports and observations of the Committee on South-West Africa. The rules covered such matters as reports, petitions, and private meetings, as well as the way in which decisions of the General Assembly with regard to reports and petitions were to be made, the last-mentioned matter being dealt with in Rule F.

It appears that Rule F is part of a regime established by Resolutions of the General Assembly of November 28th, 1953, and October 11th, 1954, in which the expressed intention of the General Assembly was to conform to the Opinion of 1950.

The scope of Question (*a*) is thus limited by the wording used and by the reference to the General Assembly's acceptance of the Opinion previously given by the Court. It is therefore essential that the Court should keep within the bounds of the question put to it by the General Assembly.

. . . .

In the question submitted to the Court there is a slight difference between the wording of the English and the French texts. The French version seems to express more precisely the intention of the General Assembly in submitting the matter to the Court for its Opinion. It asks whether Rule F corresponds to a correct interpretation of the previous Opinion. It refers generally to the previous Opinion, but the debates in the Fourth Committee and in the General Assembly indicate that the latter was primarily concerned with the question whether the rule as to the system of voting corresponds to a correct interpretation of the following passage:

> The degree of supervision to be exercised by the General Assembly should not therefore exceed that which applied under the Mandates System, and should conform as far as possible to the procedure followed in this respect by the Council of the League of Nations.

At this stage consideration will be given to the first part of this passage, namely, the statement that "The degree of supervision to be exercised by the General Assembly should not therefore exceed that which applied under the Mandates System. . . ." The task of the Court is to establish the true meaning of this statement. The question is whether this statement may properly be construed as including the system of voting to be followed by the General Assembly.

The function of supervision exercised by the General Assembly generally takes the form of action based on the reports and observations of the Committee on South-West Africa, whose functions are analogous to those exercised by the Permanent Mandates Commission. The words "the degree of supervision" relate to the extent of the substantive supervision thus exercised, and not to the manner in which the collective will of the General Assembly is expressed.

Accordingly, these words, if given their ordinary and natural meaning, should not be interpreted as relating to procedural matters. They relate to the measure and means of supervision. They comprise the means employed by the supervising authority in obtaining adequate information regarding the administration of the Territory and the methods adopted for evaluating such information, maintaining working relations with the Mandatory, and otherwise exercising normal and customary supervisory functions. The statement that the degree of supervision to be exercised by the General Assembly should not exceed that which was applied under the Mandates System means that the General Assembly should not adopt such methods of supervision or impose such conditions on the Mandatory as are inconsistent with the terms of the Mandate or with a proper degree of supervision measured by the standard and the methods applied by the Council of the League of Nations.

Consequently, the action of the General Assembly in adopting Rule F, which prescribes the two-thirds majority rule, cannot be regarded as relevant to the "degree of supervision". It follows that this Rule cannot be considered as instituting a greater degree of supervision than that which was envisaged by the previous Opinion of the Court.

. . . .

This interpretation of the words used is confirmed by an examination of the circumstances which led to their use.

The Court, in the previous Opinion, was answering the question: "Does the Union of South Africa continue to have international obligations under the Mandate for South-West Africa and, if so, what are those obligations?" It was dealing with two kinds of international obligations assumed by the Union of South Africa under the Mandate.

The first kind of obligation was directly related to the administration of the Territory and corresponded to the sacred trust of civilization referred to in Article 22 of the Covenant. The Court found that these obligations did not lapse on the dissolution of the League of Nations.

The second kind of obligations related to the supervision of the administration of the mandated Territory by the League. The Court, taking into account the Resolution of the Assembly of the League of Nations of April 18th, 1946, and the provisions of Articles 10 and 80 of the Charter, recognized that the General Assembly was legally qualified to exercise the supervisory functions which had previously been exercised by the Council of the League. It was necessary for the purpose of defining the international obligations of the Union to indicate the limits within which it was subject to the exercise of supervision by the General Assembly.

In order to indicate those limits, it was necessary to deal with the problem presented by methods of supervision and the scope of their application. The General Assembly was competent, under the Charter, to devise methods of supervision and to regulate, within prescribed limitations, the scope of their application. These were matters in which the obligations could be subjected to precise and objective determination, and it was necessary to indicate this in a clear and unequivocal manner. This was done when it was said in the previous Opinion that: "The degree of supervision to be exercised by the General Assembly should not therefore exceed that which applied under the Mandates System."

On the other hand, in marking out those limits, the Court did not need to deal with the system of voting. In recognizing that the competence of the General Assembly to exercise its supervisory functions was based on the Charter, the Court also recognized implicitly that decisions relating to the exercise of such functions must be taken in accordance with the relevant provisions of the Charter, that is, the provisions of Article 18. If the Court had intended that the limits to the degree of supervision should be understood to include the maintenance of the system of voting followed by the Council of the League of Nations, it would have been contradicting itself and running counter to the provisions of the Charter. It follows that the statement that "The degree of supervision to be exercised by the General Assembly should not therefore exceed that which applied under the Mandates System" cannot be interpreted as extending to the voting system of the General Assembly.

Accordingly, the Court finds that the statement in the Opinion of
July 11th, 1950, that "The degree of supervision to be exercised by the
General Assembly should not therefore exceed that which applied
under the Mandates System", must be interpreted as relating to substantive matters, and as not including or relating to the system of voting followed by the Council of the League of Nations.

. . . .

In the course of the proceedings in the General Assembly and Committees of the United Nations, it was contended by representatives of
the Union of South Africa that Rule F would not correspond to a correct interpretation of the previous Opinion. It was argued that the
rule of unanimity governed the proceedings in the Council of the
League of Nations, in which the mandatory Power was entitled to participate and vote; and that Rule F, by substituting a two-thirds majority rule, would lead to a degree of supervision exceeding that which
applied under the Mandates System.

These contentions were questioned by representatives of other Governments and also in the written statements submitted to the Court in
the present proceedings.

In view of the finding of the Court that the statement in the Opinion of 1950 that "The degree of supervision to be exercised by the
General Assembly should not therefore exceed that which applied
under the Mandates System" does not include or relate to the system
of voting, it is unnecessary to deal with the issues raised by these contentions or to examine the extent and scope of the operation of the
rule of unanimity under the Covenant of the League of Nations.

. . . .

The Court will now consider whether Rule F is in accord with the
statement in the Opinion of 1950, that the supervision to be exercised
by the General Assembly "should conform as far as possible to the procedure followed in this respect by the Council of the League of Nations".

While, as indicated above, the statement regarding the degree of supervision to be exercised by the General Assembly over the Mandate
of South-West Africa, relates to substantive matters, the statement requiring conformity "as far as possible" with the procedure followed in
the matter of supervision by the Council of the League of Nations, relates to the way in which supervision is to be exercised, a matter which
is procedural in character. Thus, both substance and procedure are
dealt with in the passage in question and both relate to the exercise of
supervision. The word "procedure" there used must be understood as
referring to those procedural steps whereby supervision is to be effected.

The voting system of the General Assembly was not in contempla-
tion when the Court, in its Opinion of 1950, stated that "supervision
should conform as far as possible to the procedure followed in this respect by the Council of the League of Nations". The constitution of an
organ usually prescribes the method of voting by which the organ arrives at its decisions. The voting system is related to the composition

and functions of the organ. It forms one of the characteristics of the constitution of the organ. Taking decisions by a two-thirds majority vote or by a simple majority vote is one of the distinguishing features of the General Assembly, while the unanimity rule was one of the distinguishing features of the Council of the League of Nations. These two systems are characteristic of different organs, and one system cannot be substituted for the other without constitutional amendment. To transplant upon the General Assembly the unanimity rule of the Council of the League would not be simply the introduction of a procedure, but would amount to a disregard of one of the characteristics of the General Assembly. Consequently the question of conformity of the voting system of the General Assembly with that of the Council of the League of Nations presents insurmountable difficulties of a juridical nature. For these reasons, the voting system of the General Assembly must be considered as not being included in the procedure which, according to the previous Opinion of the Court, the General Assembly should follow in exercising its supervisory functions.

. . . .

There is, however, another aspect of this question. Rule F is contained in a group of six special rules, which were adopted by the General Assembly in Resolution 844 (IX) of October 11th, 1954. They were designed to apply "as far as possible, and pending the conclusion of an agreement between the United Nations and the Union of South Africa, the procedure followed in that respect by the Council of the League of Nations". It seems to be clear that, both in adopting Rule F and in referring Question (*a*) to the Court, the General Assembly was proceeding upon the assumption that the word "procedure", as used in the second part of the passage in question, includes the voting system. It is also necessary to examine the question on the basis of that assumption. Looking at the matter from that point of view, there is equally no incompatibility between Rule F and the previous Opinion.

It is to be recalled that the Court, in its previous Opinion, stated that "The competence of the General Assembly of the United Nations to exercise such supervision and to receive and examine reports is derived from the provisions of Article 10 of the Charter, which authorizes the General Assembly to discuss any questions or any matters within the scope of the Charter and to make recommendations on these questions or matters to the Members of the United Nations". Thus, the authority of the General Assembly to exercise supervision over the administration of South-West Africa as a mandated Territory is based on the provisions of the Charter. While, in exercising that supervision, the General Assembly should not deviate from the Mandate, its authority to take decisions in order to effect such supervision is derived from its own constitution.

Such being the case, it follows that the General Assembly, in adopting a method of reaching decisions in respect of the annual reports and petitions concerning South-West Africa should base itself exclusively on the Charter. Article 18 of the Charter authorizes the General

Assembly to decide whether decisions of this nature involve "important questions" or "other questions". The General Assembly has concluded that decisions by it on questions relating to reports and petitions concerning the Territory of South-West Africa shall be regarded as decisions on important questions to which the two-thirds majority rule should apply. It is from the Charter that the General Assembly derives its competence to exercise its supervisory functions; and it is within the framework of the Charter that the General Assembly must find the rules governing the making of its decisions in connection with those functions. It would be legally impossible for the General Assembly, on the one hand, to rely on the Charter in receiving and examining reports and petitions concerning South-West Africa, and, on the other hand, to reach decisions relating to these reports and petitions in accordance with a voting system entirely alien to that prescribed by the Charter.

When the Court stated in its previous Opinion that in exercising its supervisory functions the General Assembly should conform "as far as possible to the procedure followed in this respect by the Council of the League of Nations", it was indicating that in the nature of things the General Assembly, operating under an instrument different from that which governed the Council of the League of Nations, would not be able to follow precisely the same procedures as were followed by the Council. Consequently, the expression "as far as possible" was designed to allow for adjustments and modifications necessitated by legal or practical considerations.

In the matter of determining how to take decisions relating to reports and petitions concerning the Territory of South-West Africa, there was but one course open to the General Assembly. It had before it a text, Article 18 of the Charter, which prescribes the methods for taking decisions. The Opinion of 1950 left the General Assembly with Article 18 of the Charter as the sole legal basis for the voting system applicable to decisions in connection with its supervisory functions. It was on that basis that Rule F was adopted. In adopting that Rule, the General Assembly acted within the bounds of legal possibility.

There is thus no incompatibility between Rule F and the Opinion of 1950 in which the Court stated that the supervision to be exercised by the General Assembly should conform as far as possible to the procedure followed in this respect by the Council of the League of Nations.

.   .   .   .

The Court therefore considers that Rule F, recited in Question (*a*) of Resolution 904 (IX) of the General Assembly of November 23rd, 1954, is in accord with the passage contained in the Court's previous Opinion, namely, that "The degree of supervision to be exercised by the General Assembly should not . . . . exceed that which applied under the Mandates System, and should conform as far as possible to the procedure followed in this respect by the Council of the League of Nations". Accordingly, the Court concludes that Rule F corresponds to a correct interpretation of its Advisory Opinion of 1950.

Question (*a*) having been answered in the affirmative, it is not necessary to consider Question (*b*).

For these reasons,

THE COURT IS UNANIMOUSLY OF OPINION

with regard to Question (*a*):

> "Is the following rule on the voting procedure to be followed by the General Assembly a correct interpretation of the advisory opinion of the International Court of Justice of 11 July 1950:
>
> 'Decisions of the General Assembly on questions relating to reports and petitions concerning the Territory of South-West Africa shall be regarded as important questions within the meaning of Article 18, paragraph 2, of the Charter of the United Nations'?"

that the said rule is a correct interpretation of the Advisory Opinion of July 11th, 1950.

8. Judge Lauterpacht's Separate Opinion

In a separate opinion Judge Lauterpacht of the United Kingdom examined the question whether the rule of unanimity did in fact prevail in the Council of the League of Nations. This part of his opinion [w] is included because the question later became relevant in connection with the procedure adopted for revoking the Mandate.

Did the Rule of Absolute Unanimity obtain in the Council of the League acting as a Supervisory Organ of the Mandates System?

I now come to the first of the three principal legal issues with which the Court must properly be deemed to be confronted in the present case: Does the contemplated Rule F correctly interpret the Opinion of the Court inasmuch as it replaces by a less stringent system the rule of absolute unanimity which, according to the contention of the Government of South Africa, obtained in the Council of the League of Nations in respect of its supervisory functions under the Mandates System? Did any such rule obtain in the Council of the League of Nations?

With regard to this question, I am unable to accept the contention advanced by the Government of the Union of South Africa that there is an inconsistency between the proposed Rule F and the procedure followed by the Council of the League of Nations for the alleged reason that the latter was based on the rule of absolute unanimity, including the vote of the Mandatory State concerned. This has been the principal view put forward by the Government of South Africa in the matter. I have given reasons why it was desirable that the Court should examine it in all its aspects.

[w] 1955 ICJ Reports 98–106.

Admittedly, the procedure of the Council of the League of Nations was governed by the principle of unanimity not only of the Members of the Council but of States who, though not ordinarily Members thereof, were invited to sit at its table in connection with a matter under its consideration—a rule which applied also to the representatives of the Mandatory State invited to take part in the proceedings of the Council. However, having regard both to principle and practice, as I interpret them, the ruling of the Court given in its Twelfth Advisory Opinion on the *Interpretation of the Treaty of Lausanne* must be held to apply also to the question with which the Court is now concerned. In that case, the Court held that the principle which was enshrined in Article 15 of the Covenant and which excluded the vote of the parties to the dispute from the requirement of unanimity as a condition of the validity of a recommendation made by the Council, was of general application in so far as it embodied the "well-known rule that no one can be judge in his own suit" (Series B, No. 12, p. 32). That "well-known rule", henceforth sanctioned by a pronouncement of the Permanent Court of International Justice, must be held to apply to the case in which an international organ, even when acting otherwise under the rule of unanimity, judges in a supervisory capacity the legal propriety of the conduct of a State administering an international mandate or trust. The supervisory organ may do so either directly by pronouncing a verdict upon the conformity of the action of the administering State with its international obligations or indirectly by calling upon it to adopt—or desist from—a certain line of action.

In the absence of cogent proof to the contrary, there is no justification for rendering legally permissible a situation in which a State, bound by virtue of solemn international obligations to observe a definite rule of conduct and to submit to the international supervision of its observance, is at the same time entitled to render, by its adverse vote, such supervision nominal and ineffective. Undoubtedly, international practice knows instances of States reserving for themselves the right to determine the extent of their own obligation and, in a sense, to remain judges in their own case. However, unless such right is reserved in explicit terms, States which thus attempt to avail themselves of their contractual capacity for purposes alien to its primary purpose —which is the creation of binding obligations—act at their peril. Such express reservation of this exceptional right, obnoxious to legal principle and to tenets of good faith, cannot be conclusively inferred from the mere fact that the basic instrument provides for the rule of unanimity. It could not, in particular, be inferred from the rigid wording of Article 5 of the Covenant, which laid down that, unless expressly provided to the contrary, the rule of unanimity should obtain. For, in the absence of a clear provision to the contrary, that rule is in itself qualified by the principle laid down by the Permanent Court of International Justice in the Advisory Opinion on the *Interpretation of the Treaty of Lausanne*. In that Opinion the Court considered this rule to be of general application for the decisions of the Council when acting in a judicial or arbitral capacity. Its ruling was not limited to cases brought before it by virtue of an extraneous treaty.

It must be conceded that the application of the principle *nemo judex in re sua* to what is in essence a controversy between the mandatory and the otherwise unanimous Council constitutes an extension of that principle as laid down by the Court. However, the extension is more apparent than real. For the reasons stated above, there does not seem to exist any solid ground for distinguishing between decisions taken in pursuance of the supervisory functions of an international organ and decisions of a judicial or arbitral nature such as that with which the Council of the League was confronted in the matter of the determination of the boundary between Turkey and Iraq. In all cases in which there is a difference of opinion, brought to the point of a formal discordant vote, between the supervising organ and the administering authority as to the conformity of the conduct of the latter with its international obligations, such difference has the essential elements of a dispute as to the application of a binding international instrument. In any such controversy the principle that no one is judge in his own cause must be deemed to apply. To put it differently, there is no valid reason for distinguishing, in connection with the applicability of the principle that no one is judge in his own cause, between the judicial and the supervisory organs. Both administer, in different ways, a system of binding rules of conduct.

. . . .

I will now turn from principle to practice. The practice, as I read it, of the League of Nations, does not conclusively support the view that there was an invariable, or even predominant, tendency—in cases in which a Member of the Council was itself a party to the dispute—to attach literal importance to the seemingly rigid or exhaustive provisions of Article 5 of the Covenant in the matter of unanimity. On occasions, the principle of absolute unanimity, including the votes of the parties to the dispute, was acted upon with some rigidity. This occurred in two cases in connection with the application of Article 11 of the Covenant, namely, in the dispute between Poland and Lithuania in 1928 (*Official Journal of the League of Nations,* 1928, p. 896), and, in particular, in the course of the Sino-Japanese dispute in 1931 (*Official Journal of the League of Nations,* 1931, p. 2358). In both cases a resolution of the Council, assented to by all its Members save one of the parties to the dispute, was formally stated not to be binding. It may be observed that with regard to the latter case, Professor Brierly, a writer of authority noted for his restraint, stated that the interpretation of Article 11 then adopted was "unexpected and doubtfully correct" (*The Covenant and the Charter,* 1947, p. 15). Apart from these rare cases, the tendency was either in the direction of an express amendment of these provisions of the Covenant which, on the face of it, left room for the frustration of an otherwise unanimous decision by a vote of an interested party or in the direction of regarding such amendment as unnecessary and of acting on the view that the principle *nemo judex in re sua* was already an integral part of the Covenant. Thus, in 1921, the Assembly recommended that, pending the ratification of an express amendment of the Charter to that effect, the votes of the parties to the dispute should be excluded in the voting on the question whether a Member of the League had gone to war in breach of the Covenant (*Records of the Second Assembly, Plenary Meeting*, p. 806). In 1922, the Council seems to have proceeded in two cases on the view that when acting in an arbitral or semi-judicial capacity it was bound to exclude the votes of the parties for the purpose of ascertaining the unanimity required by the Covenant. The first of these cases concerned the claim of India to be included among the eight States of chief industrial importance in connection with representation on the Governing Body of the International Labour Organisation. In that case, the Council endorsed and acted on the legal opinion submitted to it by the Secretariat to the effect that "the Council would act in this affair as arbitrator, and that India could not be both judge and party to the case" (*Official Journal*, 1922, p. 1160). The case is of special importance in the present connection inasmuch as the Council acted in an administrative rather than judicial capacity. In the acute Greco-Bulgarian dispute in 1925, the Council, acting in a private meeting in the absence of the representatives of the two parties, prepared what was described as a "dictatorial request" for acceptance by the parties who declared themselves ready to accept the *decision* of the Council thus subsequently sanctioned by a unanimous vote (*Official Journal*, 1925, p. 1700). In the same year, in the Hungarian Optants dispute between Hungary and Roumania, which came before it under Article 11, paragraph 2, of the Covenant, the Council accepted a recommendation by a unanimous vote exclusive of the representatives of the parties after the President of the Council stated that, in inviting the Council to pronounce itself on the recommendation contained in the report, he "deliberately excepted two members of the Council who are parties to the dispute" (1927, p. 1413).

It would thus appear that the Twelfth Advisory Opinion of the Court, in addition to being based on a general principle of law of cogent application, was not without support in the practice of the League, both prior and subsequent to the time when it was rendered. It may be useful in this connection to draw attention to the official publication of the Secretariat of the League of Nations, entitled "The Council of the League of Nations, 1920–1938", in which, on page 69, according to the view of the Secretariat, on the question of the inclusion of the votes of the parties in determining unanimity "there is a certain division of opinion as to whether the votes of the parties should or should not be counted".

It has been maintained that whatever may have been the practice of the Council of the League of Nations in the matter of international disputes, in other spheres it strictly adhered to the principle of absolute unanimity. From this the conclusion is drawn that the Mandatory State enjoyed a power of veto with regard to the supervisory function of the Council. I am not persuaded of the accuracy either of what is supposed to be the factual premise or of the conclusion which is being drawn from it. An account of some of the practice of the Council in this sphere is given in a paper prepared by the Secretariat of the

United Nations for the working group of the Committee on South Africa and included as No. 39 in the file of documents put at the disposal of the Court. There are other cases to which reference will be made presently. My reading of the practice as recorded is that, while there is no instance of a resolution of the Council being formally declared adopted as against the opposing vote of the mandatory State, there is, on the evidence, no authentic and recorded instance of a contemplated resolution of the Council being frustrated as the result of the adverse vote of the mandatory State. A study of these cases, which were concerned with the mandated territory of South-West Africa, shows that while in no instance a resolution was adopted contrary to the express attitude of the Government of South Africa, this was not necessarily so because of any threatened exercise of the power of veto. In some of these cases, that Government, after having stated its doubts or objections, did not insist on them; in two other cases the Council modified an alternative text submitted by the representative of South Africa; in the sixth case the Government of South Africa eventually decided not to be represented at the resumed discussion of the issue in question. The same solution was adopted by the South African Government in some other cases, of which one relating to the status of the South African Mandate calls for special mention. In its Report, made in 1935, the Mandates Commission noted that it had been informed by the Mandatory Power that the latter had appointed a special Committee to study certain constitutional problems raised by a motion of the Legislative Assembly of the territory aiming at its incorporation as "a fifth province of the Union". The Report concluded with the following passage: "As the guardian of the integrity of the institution of Mandates, the Commission therefore expects to be informed of the Mandatory Power's views on the question, which it will not fail to subject to that careful examination that its international importance demands. The Commission wishes, on this occasion, to draw attention to the Mandatory Power's fundamental obligation to give effect, not only to the provisions of the Mandate, but also to those of Article 22 of the Covenant." (*League of Nations Official Journal*, 1935, p. 1235.) The Report of the Commission on this and other matters was adopted by the Council which instructed the Secretary-General to communicate to the Mandatory Powers the observations of the Commission and to request them to take the action asked for by the Commission (*ibid.*, p. 1148). The Government of South Africa informed the Secretary-General that it would not be represented at the meeting of the Council. It may or may not be profitable to enquire into the reasons which prompted abstention from participation in a decision which had a distinct bearing on an important issue touching upon an essential aspect of the rights and duties of the mandatory. At least on six other occasions the Government of South Africa was not represented at meetings of the Council at which Resolutions were adopted or discussions took place concerning South-West Africa.

The fact which thus emerges with some clarity from a survey of the practice of the Council of the League of Nations on the subject is that it supplies no conclusive or convincing evidence in support of the view that as a matter of practice the rule of unanimity operated and was interpreted in a manner substantiating any right of veto on the part of the mandatory Power. It would probably be more accurate to say that, assuming that it existed during the initial period of the functioning of the League, that right fell into desuetude and lapsed as the result. Undoubtedly, importance was attached to securing the concurring vote of the Mandatory Power by patient efforts at compromise and accommodation, especially with respect to the language of the Resolutions of the Council. It is therefore probable that a case, repeatedly—though rather vaguely—referred to in the argument of the Government of South Africa before the United Nations, in which the Council of the League of Nations desisted in deference to the attitude of South Africa from a proposed course of action, is not wholly apocryphal. There were bound to be a number of cases of that nature. However, these do not tell the whole story. In other—and probably more frequent—cases unanimity was achieved for the reason that the Mandatory Power adapted its attitude to the general sense of the Council, or, in some cases, for the reason that it decided not to participate in the meeting at which the Council accepted the Resolution. It is probable—we cannot put it higher than that—that it adopted that course because it deemed it preferable to open disagreement with an otherwise unanimous Council or to a public debate before an antagonistic and practically unanimous Assembly. From this point of view there is a distinct measure of unreality in the insistence on the absolutely unanimous vote in the Council. The Council was not a mere voting machine.

It is of interest to note that Professor Quincy Wright, in the most exhaustive treatise on the subject of mandates, comes to the following conclusion: "Thus it is possible that a resolution dealing with a particular mandatory might be effective over the adverse vote of that mandatory. On the other hand, it may be thought that the Council in dealing with mandates acts in an administrative rather than a quasi-judicial character, in which case absolute unanimity might be required. It is probable that the character of the particular question before the Council would determine the matter but up to date there has always been absolute unanimity." (*Mandates under the League of Nations* (1930), p. 132. A similar view is expressed on p. 522.) However, as already suggested, the Council, in passing resolutions on mandates, acted essentially in a quasi-judicial capacity. Apart from procedural safeguards, there is probably no basic difference between the judicial and the administrative application of the law. As shown, the circumstance that resolutions had in fact been accepted by absolute unanimity throws no decisive light on the legal position here examined. When Professor Wright stated—a statement subsequently repeated by other well-informed commentators (see Duncan Hall, *Mandates, Dependencies and Trusteeship* (1948), p. 175)—that as a matter of fact decisions of the Council in the matter of mandates were unanimous, the statement, if we disregard the occasional abstention of the Mandatory Power from participation in the meetings, was on the face of it correct. But, as shown, it was clearly intended only as a statement of fact, not of law. That fact is open to varying—and divergent—legal construction.

There is thus in the practice of the Council no conclusive factor which is apt to override the basic legal considerations to which I have referred above, namely, that in an instrument such as the Covenant of the League of Nations the general requirement of unanimity is not in itself sufficient to displace the principle that a party cannot be judge in its own case: that the requirement of unanimity, however expressly stated, is implicitly qualified by the latter principle; and that nothing short of its express exclusion is sufficient to justify a State in insisting that it should, by acting as judge in its own case, possess the right to render inoperative a solemn international obligation to which it has subscribed. This principle ought to be kept prominently in mind when it is a question of the supervised State claiming the right to frustrate by its own vote the legal efficacy of the supervision. The effectiveness of international obligations may not be the only governing consideration in the interpretation of treaties seeing that the parties occasionally intend to render them less effective than is indicated by their apparent purpose. But it is a consideration which cannot be ignored. In so far as the principle *nemo judex in re sua* is not only a general principle of law, expressly sanctioned by the Court, but also a principle of good faith, it is particularly appropriate in relation to an instrument of a fiduciary character such as a mandate or a trust in which equitable considerations acting upon the conscience are of compelling application. This, too, is a general principle of law recognized by civilized States. There is therefore no sufficient reason for assuming that if the Permanent Court of International Justice had been called upon to apply its ruling in the Twelfth Advisory Opinion to the question of unanimity in connection with the supervisory function of the Council in the matter of mandates, it would have abandoned the principle there enunciated. It may be strange that ten years after the dissolution of the League this Court should be confronted with the same question, but this is not a valid ground for departing from that principle. There is, it may be added, no reason why the Court should not interpret the Covenant of the League as it existed in 1945. The determination of rights validly acquired under treaties or statutes which have lapsed is a frequent occurrence in judicial practice. There is no occasion for any excess of judicial caution in this respect. Moreover, in the present case the Court interprets primarily the Mandate which, as it repeatedly stated in its Opinion of 1950, continues to exist.

I cannot say that I have arrived without hesitation at my conclusion on this aspect of the question or that I would have been prepared to base my affirmative answer to the question put by the General Assembly solely on this ground. I am impressed by the doubts voiced in this connection by Judge Klaestad in his Separate Opinion. For we ought to attach due weight to the general rule of unanimity in the Covenant and the fact that there is no explicit case on record in which the Council affirmed its right to give a valid decision in face of a formal objection of the interested mandatory State. At the same time, I must attach equal—and, I believe, decisive—weight to the general principle as here outlined and as acted upon by the Court itself in the Twelfth Advisory Opinion; to the preponderant practice of the Council of the League in a sphere not confined to the settlement of disputes; and, above all, to the custom—to what in English practice is referred to as a constitutional convention—according to which the Mandatory States never in fact exercised any right of veto. Also, I have some doubts as to the existence of any vested right of South Africa to an immutable system of voting in face of actual or potential changes in the practice of the League of Nations on the subject of the voting procedure. There is no doubt that, in the course of time and without any formal amendment, the rule of absolute unanimity ceased to be a factor to which there was invariably attached decisive importance. This, in addition to the practice outlined above, is shown by the gradual adoption of such practices as passing the resolutions by way of a "vœu" or recommendation by simple majority; by treating some substantive matters as being questions of procedure; by considering abstention as absence; and by the practice of majority voting in Committees. When in 1937 Members of the League of Nations expressed their view as to whether absolute unanimity of the Council was required for a request for an Advisory Opinion, a large majority of those who formulated their attitude denied the existence of any such requirement. This was so although in this case there were reasons of some cogency for maintaining the rule of absolute unanimity having regard to the principle that States cannot be compelled, directly or indirectly, to bring their disputes before the Court. A proper interpretation of the constitutional instrument must take into account not only the formal letter of the original instrument, but also its operation in actual practice and in the light of the revealed tendencies in the life of the Organization. This being so, although I am not prepared to say that the main contention of South Africa was wholly unfounded, I cannot accept it as being legally correct.

For these reasons, my conclusion is that the proposed Rule F is not inconsistent with a correct interpretation of the Opinion of the Court of 1950 inasmuch as it is based on the view that the opposing vote of the mandatory State could not in all circumstances adversely affect the required unanimity of the Council of the League of Nations.

South Africa refused to participate in the proceedings before the Court on this occasion. After the Opinion had been handed down, South Africa rejected it on the grounds that it was premised on the unacceptable 1950 Opinion.[x]

9. The 1956 Advisory Opinion

In the following year the General Assembly asked for yet another advisory opinion—this time on the legality of granting oral hear-

[x] See the statement to this effect by the South African delegate: *GAOR*, Tenth Session, Fourth Committee, 491st Meeting, §§ 8–9.

ings to petitioners. The Permanent Mandates Commission had not permitted such hearings, but, on the other hand, it had enjoyed the full co-operation of the mandatory. As a result of South Africa's refusal to forward any information to the Committee on South West Africa, the General Assembly considered it necessary to obtain information by other means, including oral hearings. Before it proceeded to grant such hearings, however, it sought an Opinion on the compatibility of this procedure with the 1950 Advisory Opinion. In 1956 the Court handed down its Opinion on the *Admissibility of Hearings of Petitioners by the Committee on South West Africa,* in which it upheld the General Assembly's request for oral hearings: [y]

By a letter of December 19th, 1955, filed in the Registry on December 22nd, the Secretary-General of the United Nations informed the Court that, by a Resolution adopted on December 3rd, 1955, the General Assembly of the United Nations decided to request the Court to give an Advisory Opinion on the following question:

Is it consistent with the advisory opinion of the International Court of Justice of 11 July 1950 for the Committee on South West Africa, established by General Assembly resolution 749 A (VIII) of 28 November 1953, to grant oral hearings to petitioners on matters relating to the Territory of South West Africa?

. . . .

A question arises as to whether the request for the Court's Opinion relates to the authority of the Committee on South West Africa to grant oral hearings in its own right or only under prior authorization of the General Assembly.

. . . .

While the question in terms refers to the grant of oral hearings by the Committee, the Court interprets it as meaning: whether it is legally open to the General Assembly to authorize the Committee to grant oral hearings to petitioners. The Court must therefore deal with the broader question as to whether it would be consistent with its previous Opinion of 11 July 1950 for the General Assembly to authorize the Committee on South West Africa to grant oral hearings to petitioners.

. . . .

The meaning of the question having been thus defined, the Court will proceed to its examination.

In the operative part of the Advisory Opinion of 11 July 1950, the Court stated:

[y] 1956 ICJ Reports 23, 24–32. For a more thorough analysis of this matter, see the separate opinion of Judge Lauterpacht, *ibid.,* pp. 35–59. For academic comments, see J. H. W. Verzijl, *The Jurisprudence of the World Court,* 2:231; Manley O. Hudson, in (1957) 51 *AJIL* 1; J. P. Verloren van Themaat, in (1958) 21 *Tydskrif vir Hedendaagse Romeins-Hollandse Reg* 176.

that South-West Africa is a territory under the international Mandate assumed by the Union of South Africa on December 17th, 1920; that the Union of South Africa continues to have the international obligations stated in Article 22 of the Covenant of the League of Nations and in the Mandate for South-West Africa as well as the obligation to transmit petitions from the inhabitants of that Territory, the supervisory functions to the exercised by the United Nations, to which the annual reports and the petitions are to be submitted, and the reference to the Permanent Court of International Justice to be replaced by a reference to the International Court of Justice, in accordance with Article 7 of the Mandate and Article 37 of the Statute of the Court;

Accordingly, the obligations of the Mandatory continue unimpaired with this difference, that the supervisory functions exercised by the Council of the League of Nations are now to be exercised by the United Nations. The organ of the United Nations exercising these supervisory functions, that is, the General Assembly, is legally qualified to carry out an effective and adequate supervision of the administration of the Mandated Territory, as was the Council of the League.

In determining the question whether in these circumstances it would be consistent with the Opinion of the Court of 11 July 1950 for the Committee on South West Africa to grant oral hearings to petitioners, the Court must have regard to the whole of its previous Opinion and its general purport and meaning.

In that Opinion the Court, having concluded that South West Africa is a territory under the international Mandate and that the Mandatory continues to have the obligations stated in Article 22 of the Covenant of the League of Nations and the Mandate, as well as the obligation to transmit reports and petitions and to submit to the supervision of the General Assembly, made it clear that the obligations of the Mandatory were those which obtained under the Mandates System. These obligations could not be extended beyond those to which the Mandatory had been subject by virtue of the provisions of Article 22 of the Covenant and of the Mandate of South West Africa under the Mandates System. The Court stated, therefore that the degree of supervision to be exercised by the General Assembly should not exceed that which applied under the Mandates System. Following its finding regarding the substitution of the General Assembly of the United Nations for the Council of the League of Nations in the exercise of supervision, the Court stated that the degree of supervision should conform as far as possible to the procedure followed by the Council of the League of Nations in that respect. The Court observed that these considerations were particularly applicable to annual reports and petitions.

At the same time the Court stated that "the effective performance of the sacred trust of civilization by the Mandatory Powers required that the administration of mandated territories should be subject to international supervision" and said: "The necessity for supervision continues to exist despite the disappearance of the supervisory organ under the Mandates System."

In discussing the effect of Article 80 (1) of the Charter, preserving the rights of States and peoples under existing international agreements, the Court observed: "The purpose must have been to provide a real protection for those rights; but no such rights of the peoples could be effectively safeguarded without international supervision and a duty to render reports to a supervisory organ."

The general purport and meaning of the Opinion of the Court of 11 July 1950 is that the paramount purpose underlying the taking over by the General Assembly of the United Nations of the supervisory functions in respect of the Mandate for South West Africa formerly exercised by the Council of the League of Nations was to safeguard the sacred trust of civilization through the maintenance of effective international supervision of the administration of the Mandated Territory.

Accordingly, in interpreting any particular sentences in the Opinion of the Court of 11 July 1950, it is not permissible, in the absence of express words to the contrary, to attribute to them a meaning which would not be in conformity with this paramount purpose or with the operative part of that Opinion.

. . . .

Before proceeding further, it is necessary to refer briefly to the way in which the question of the grant of oral hearings to petitioners was dealt with during the regime of the League of Nations. The Permanent Mandates Commission had under consideration at various meetings the question of the grant of oral hearings to petitioners, both at the request of petitioners and on its own initiative. The Commission felt that in some cases oral hearings would be useful, if not indispensable, in determining whether petitions were well-founded or not. In 1926, the Commission laid the matter before the Council, but refrained from making a definite recommendation on the subject. The Council, in turn, decided that, before taking action, it should consult the Mandatory Powers. After obtaining the views of those Powers, all of whom were opposed to the grant of oral hearings on various grounds, the Council, by Resolution of March 7, 1927, decided that there was no occasion to modify the procedure theretofore followed by the Commission in regard to the question. In his Report to the Council, the Rapporteur stated that, if in any particular case the circumstances should show that it was impossible for all the necessary information to be secured by the usual means, the Council could "decide on such exceptional procedure as might seem appropriate and necessary in the particular circumstances". By its Resolution, the Council directed that copies of the Resolution, of the Report of the Rapporteur and of the replies of the Mandatory Powers, should be transmitted to the Permanent Mandates Commission. It is clear that oral hearings were not granted to petitioners by the Permanent Mandates Commission at any time during the regime of the League of Nations.

The right of petition was introduced into the Mandates System by the Council of the League of January 31st, 1923, and certain rules relating to the matter were prescribed. This was an innnovation designed to render the supervisory function of the Council more effective. The Council having established the right of petition, and regulated the manner of its exercise, was, in the opinion of the Court, competent to authorize the Permanent Mandates Commission to grant oral hearings to petitioners, had it seen fit to do so.

. . . .

It has been contended that the Court, in its Opinion of 11 July 1950, intended to express the view that the Mandates System and the degree of supervision to the exercised by the General Assembly in respect of the Territory of South West Africa must be deemed to have been crystallized, so that, though the General Assembly replaced the Council of the League as the supervisory organ in respect of the Mandate, it could not, in the exercise of its supervisory functions, do anything which the Council had not actually done, even if it had authority to do it. The Court does not consider that its Opinion of 11 July 1950 supports this position.

There is nothing in the Charter of the United Nations, the Covenant of the League, or the Resolution of the Assembly of the League of April 18th, 1946, relied upon by the Court in its Opinion of 1950, that can be construed as in any way restricting the authority of the General Assembly to less than that which was conferred upon the Council by the Covenant and the Mandate; nor does the Court find any justification for assuming that the taking over by the General Assembly of the supervisory authority formerly exercised by the Council of the League had the effect of crystallizing the Mandates System at the point which it had reached in 1946.

The Court having determined that the General Assembly had replaced the Council of the League as the supervisory organ, it was proper for it to point out that the General Assembly could not enlarge its authority but must confine itself to the exercise of such authority as the Mandates System had conferred upon the supervisory organ. The Court was not called upon to determine whether the General Assembly could or could not exercise powers which the Council of the League had possessed but for the exercise of which no occasion had arisen.

The Court held that the obligations of the Mandatory under the Mandate continued unimpaired, and that the supervisory functions in respect of the Mandate were exercisable by the United Nations, the General Assembly replacing in this respect the Council of the League. It followed that the General Assembly in carrying out its supervisory functions had the same authority as the Council. The scope of that authority could not be narrowed by the fact that the Assembly had replaced the Council as the supervisory organ.

Reliance has been placed upon the following sentence in the Court's Opinion of 1950:

The degree of supervision to be exercised by the General Assembly should not therefore exceed that which applied under the Mandates System, and should conform as far as possible to the procedure followed in this respect by the Council of the League of Nations.

It has been suggested that the grant of oral hearings by the Committee on South West Africa to petitioners would involve an excess in the degree of supervision to be exercised by the General Assembly and that the sentence should be interpreted as intended to restrict the activity of the General Assembly to measures which had actually been applied by the League of Nations. On these grounds it has been contended that the grant of oral hearings by the Committee would not be consistent with the Court's Opinion of 1950.

The Court will deal first with the suggestion that the grant of oral hearings to petitioners would, in fact, add to the obligations of the Mandatory and thus lay upon it a heavier burden than it was subject to under the Mandates System. The Court is unable to accept this suggestion. The Committee on South West Africa at present receives petitions from the inhabitants of the Mandated Territory and proceeds to examine them without the benefit of the comments of the Mandatory or of the assistance of its accredited representative during the course of the examination. In many cases, the material available to the Committee from the petitions or from other sources may be sufficient to enable the Committee to form an opinion on the merits of the petitions. In other cases the Committee may not be able to come to a decision on the material available to it. If the Committee cannot have recourse to any further information for the purpose of testing whether a petition is or is not well-founded, it may lead in certain cases to acceptance of statements in the petitions without further test. Oral hearings in such cases might enable the Committee to submit its advice to the General Assembly with greater confidence. If as the result of the grant of oral hearings to petitioners in certain cases the Committee is put in a better position to judge the merits of petitions, this cannot be presumed to add to the burden of the Mandatory. It is in the interest of the Mandatory, as well as of the proper working of the Mandates System, that the exercise of supervision by the General Assembly should be based upon material which has been tested as far as possible, rather than upon material which has not been subjected to proper scrutiny either by or on behalf of the Mandatory, or by the Committee itself.

The Court will deal next with the suggestion that the statement "the degree of supervision to be exercised by the General Assembly should not therefore exceed that which applied under the Mandates System" should be interpreted as intended to restrict the activity of the General Assembly to measures which had actually been applied by the League of Nations. This could not have been the intention of the Court. Neither the Covenant of the League, nor the Mandate for South West Africa, nor the Charter of the United Nations, contains any provision which could justify such a restriction. That it cannot have been the intention of the Court to impose on the General Assembly a rigid limitation on its supervisory function is evidenced by the second part of the same sentence, according to which the degree of supervision "should conform as far as possible to the procedure followed in this respect by the Council of the League of Nations". With regard to this statement, the Court said in its Opinion of 1955:

When the Court stated in its previous Opinion that in exercising its supervisory functions the General Assembly should conform 'as far as possible to the procedure followed in this respect by the Council of the League of Nations', it was indicating that in the nature of things the General Assembly, operating under an instrument different from that which governed the Council of the League of Nations, would not be able to follow precisely the same procedures as were followed by the Council. Consequently, the expression 'as far as possible' was designed to allow for adjustments and modifications necessitated by legal or practical considerations.

. . . .

The Court notes that, under the compulsion of practical considerations arising out of the lack of co-operation by the Mandatory, the Committee on South West Africa provided by Rule XXVI of its Rules of Procedure an alternative procedure for the receipt and treatment of petitions. This Rule became necessary because the Mandatory had refused to transmit to the General Assembly petitions by the inhabitants of the Territory, thus rendering inoperative provisions in the Rules concerning petitions and directly affecting the ability of the General Assembly to exercise an effective supervision. This Rule enabled the Committee on South West Africa to receive and deal with petitions notwithstanding that they had not been transmitted by the Mandatory and involved a departure in this respect from the procedure prescribed by the Council of the League.

The particular question which has been submitted to the Court arose out of a situation in which the Mandatory has maintained its refusal to assist in giving effect to the Opinion of 11 July 1950, and to co-operate with the United Nations by the submission of reports, and by the transmission of petitions in conformity with the procedure of the Mandates System. This sort of situation was provided for by the statement in the Court's Opinion of 1950 that the degree of supervision to be exercised by the General Assembly "should conform as far as possible to the procedure followed in this respect by the Council of the League of Nations".

. . . .

The Court holds that it would not be inconsistent with its Opinion of 11 July 1950 for the General Assembly to authorize a procedure for the grant of oral hearings by the Committee on South West Africa to petitioners who had already submitted written petitions: provided that the General Assembly was satisfied that such a course was necessary for the maintenance of effective international supervision of the administration of the Mandated Territory.

For these reasons,

THE COURT IS OF OPINION,

by eight votes to five,

that the grant of oral hearings to petitioners by the Committee on South West Africa would be consistent with the Advisory Opinion of the Court of 11 July 1950.

10. The Good Offices Committee

The deadlock continued. South Africa persisted in her refusal either to place South West Africa under Trusteeship or to submit reports or transmit petitions to the Committee on South West Africa. The Committee on South West Africa continued to collect information from available sources, including from petitioners such as the Reverend Michael Scott, Mburumba Kerina Getzen, Jariretundu Kozonguizi, Hans Beukes, the Reverend Markus Kooper, Sam Nujoma, Ismail Fortune, and Jacob Kuhangua, from which it concluded that the policies pursued by South Africa were contrary to the provisions of the Mandate.[z] The General Assembly continued to reiterate its pleas that the territory be placed under Trusteeship or that the Court's Opinion of 1950 be implemented. In 1957, in order to break the impasse, a Good Offices Committee was established to discuss with the South African Government "a basis for an agreement which would continue to accord to the Territory of South West Africa an international status."

Resolution 1143(XII):

The General Assembly,

Recalling its previous endeavors to find a settlement with the Union of South Africa regarding the status of South West Africa, particularly under the provisions of resolution 449 A (V) of 13 December 1950 establishing an *ad hoc* committee for the purpose, resolution 570 A (VI) of 19 January 1952 re-establishing the *ad hoc* committee, resolution 749 A (VIII) of 28 November 1953 establishing the Committee on South West Africa, and resolution 1059 (XI) of 26 February 1957 requesting the intervention of the Secretary-General to secure, through negotiation with the Union of South Africa, an agreement concerning the Territory of South West Africa based on the international status accorded to it by Mandate of the League of Nations dated 17 December 1920,

Considering that the Charter of the United Nations makes it incumbent on each Member State to pursue every available means of negotiation and conciliation for the settlement of international problems on the basis of respect for the purposes and principles of the Charter,

Being confident that the Union of South Africa will wish, in the light of its obligations under the Charter, to co-operate in a further endeavour to arrive at a settlement of the question of South West Africa,

1. *Decides* to establish a Good Offices Committee on South West Af-

[z] *GAOR*, Eleventh Session, Suppl. No. 12 (A/3151) (1956); *GAOR*, Twelfth Session, Suppl. No. 12 (A/3626) (1957).

rica, consisting of the United States of America, the United Kingdom of Great Britain and Northern Ireland, and a third member to be nominated by the President of the twelfth session of the General Assembly, to discuss with the Government of the Union of South Africa a basis for an agreement which would continue to accord to the Territory of South West Africa an international status;

2. *Requests* the Committee to submit to the General Assembly, at its thirteenth session, a report on its activities for examination and decision by the Assembly in accordance with the Charter of the United Nations;

3. *Requests* the Secretary-General to provide the Committee with all necessary staff and facilities.

The Good Offices Committee under the Chairmanship of Sir Charles Arden-Clarke met with the South African Government in 1958, but South Africa was prepared to consider only two proposals: an agreement with the remaining Principal Allied and Associated Powers or the partitioning of the territory. This appears from the "Concluding Remarks" of the Good Offices Committee's Report: [a]

52. The Good Offices Committee wishes in conclusion to summarize the results of its activities in the following terms:

(1) The Government of the Union of Soutn Africa is prepared under certain conditions to enter into an agreement concerning the Territory of South West Africa which would specify that the Territory possesses an "international character" deriving from the arrangements made at the Peace Conference at Versailles and that this character could be modified only with the consent of both parties to the agreement; which would contain provisions generally corresponding to those of articles 2–5 of the Mandate, except, in particular, for a modification of the provisions relating to military and security matters; and which would provide for specified kinds of information being made available concerning the administration of, and conditions in, the Territory.

(2) The Good Offices Committee would have felt able to recommend to the General Assembly that arrangements such as those set forth under (1) should be accepted for inclusion in an agreement to which the United Nations would constitute the second party and which would establish arrangements for the supervision of the administration of the Territory within the framework of the United Nations.

(3) The Union Government is not prepared, however, to accept the

[a] *GAOR*, Thirteenth Session, Agenda Item 39, Annexes, pp. 9–10 (A/3900). See, too, the speech by Sir Charles Arden-Clarke, "South West Africa, the Union and the United Nations," reported in (1960) 59 *African Affairs* 26. It is interesting to recall that in 1951 the Anti-Slavery Society had suggested partition as a possible solution to the problem: *GAOR*, Sixth Session, Agenda Item 38, Annexes, pp. 14–15.

United Nations as the second party to such an agreement, nor to undertake any obligations towards the United Nations for its administration of the Territory as a whole; but it is prepared to enter into such an agreement with the Governments of France, the United Kingdom and the United States of America as the three remaining Principal Allied and Associated Powers.

(4) The Good Offices Committee, whose own approach precluded any agency other than the United Nations being the second party to the agreement, does not consider itself in a position to express an opinion on this latter proposal, and submits it to the consideration of the General Assembly.

(5) If the General Assembly should indicate that it would be willing to consider, as a possible alternative basis for an agreement, the partitioning of the Territory, part of it to be placed under trusteeship and the remainder to be annexed to the Union of South Africa, the Union Government is prepared to carry out by its own means an investigation as to the practicability of such a partitioning and, if the Government finds it practicable, to submit thereafter to the United Nations proposals for partition.

(6) The Good Offices Committee is of the opinion that some form of partition under which a part of the Territory would be placed under a trusteeship agreement with the United Nations and the remainder would be annexed to the Union might provide a basis for an agreement, although it is aware that in lending support to such an idea it may be laying itself open to the charge of having exceeded its terms of reference.

(7) The Committee accordingly expresses to the General Assembly (a) the opinion that a form of partition might provide a basis for an agreement concerning the Territory of South West Africa, and (b) the hope that the General Assembly will therefore encourage the Government of the Union of South Africa to carry out an investigation of the practicability of partition, on the understanding that if the investigation proves this approach to be practicable it will be prepared to submit to the United Nations proposals for the partitioning of the Territory.

The General Assembly, which had already rejected the first of these proposals, proceeded to reject the second proposal—that of partition.
Resolution 1243(XIII) of 1958:

The General Assembly,

Having considered, with appreciation of the difficulties of the task, the report of the Good Offices Committee on South West Africa established under General Assembly resolution 1143 (XII) of 25 October 1957,

1. *Decides* not to accept the suggestions contained in the report of the Good Offices Committee on South West Africa that envisage parti-

tion and annexation of any part of the Territory as a basis for the solution of the question of South West Africa;

   2. *Invites* the Committee to renew discussions with the Government
of the Union of South Africa in order to find a basis for an agreement
which would continue to accord to the Mandated Territory of South
West Africa as a whole an international status, and which would be in
conformity with the purposes and principles of the United Nations;

   The debate which preceded the adoption of this Resolution in
the Fourth Committee, and which resulted in the walk-out of the
South African delegate, illustrates the extent to which relations
between South Africa and some members of the United Nations
had deteriorated. The incident is described by Goldblatt: [b]

   The 13th Session of the Fourth Committee began on 25 September,
1958, with the consideration of.—
1. The Report of the Good Offices Committee;
2. The Report of the Committee on South West Africa for 1957;
3. The study of legal action to ensure the fulfilment of the obligations
   of the Mandatory Power under the Mandate of South West Africa.

   Immediately there commenced a game of tactics between two
groups, one led by Ghana which wished items 1, 2, 3, to be discussed
together, and the other led by the Union of South Africa and supported by the United Kingdom and associated nations, which wanted
item 1 to be dealt with separately and first.

   While explaining the reason for his views, the delegate for the
Union of South Africa referred to the circumstances in which the
Good Offices Committee had been established and recalled that at the
12th (i.e., the previous) session, "after years of debate which had served
only to aggravate the problem of South West Africa, many members of
the Fourth Committee had adopted a more conciliatory and constructive attitude".

   He went on to say that "the Government of the Union of South Africa had welcomed that development and had decided not only to
meet with the Members of the Good Offices Committee but to invite
them to visit the Union of South Africa.

   In view of the extremely delicate nature of the issue, the Government had, moreover, taken steps to ensure that no statements on the
subject which were likely to jeopardise the success of the negotiations
should be made either in the South African Parliament or Press.

   It was for the same reason that his delegation now requested that
the report of the Good Offices Committee should be considered separately.

   Some of the suggestions made in the report might make it possible
to reach a permanent solution, and it would be regrettable if that pos-

[b] *The Mandated Territory of South West Africa in Relation to the United
Nations,* pp. 62–64. See, too, Mr. Eric Louw's account of this debate in
House of Assembly Debates, vol. 101, cols. 5563–65 (11 May 1959).

sibility were endangered by the consideration during the same debate of proposed solutions which in the past had merely resulted in a stalemate."

Hereafter the Chairman announced that the Secretariat had received requests for hearings by the Reverend Michael Scott and Mr Mburumba Kerina (Getzen).

The skirmishing in regard to the procedural aspect mentioned, continued and it was noteworthy how cordial were some of the references by various delegations to the return of the Union of South Africa.

.   .   .   .

Mr. Louw again intervened and strongly objected to a general discussion before consideration of sub-items (a), (b) and (c).

In his view a discussion of that nature would "only create unfortunate confusion and greatly compromise the promising results of the Good Offices Committee" (in other words, the suggestion in the report that the Union Government be invited to investigate partition of South West Africa). A compromise solution was suggested by the Chairman and accepted, but it must have been apparent to Mr. Louw, either from the discussions at this early stage or from information gathered before the debate began, that things were not to go the way he wished.

Sir Charles Arden-Clarke, Chairman of the Good Offices Committee, then made his opening statement on the report of the Good Offices Committee. . . .

Then followed Mr. Louw who assured the Fourth Committee that he would try to conform to the spirit of the new approach initiated at the (previous) 12th Session and approved by a very large majority.

He remarked upon the fact that during the procedural debate "some delegations had shown a tendency to speak somewhat disparagingly of the idea of a new approach". He stated that the discussions with the members of the Good Offices Committee had throughout been "conducted in a cordial and friendly spirit and that both sides had been determined to do their utmost to find a way out of the impasse".

He repeated what he said before as to the good intentions of his Government. He mentioned that the Good Offices Committee had initially proposed that "arrangements should be established reproducing as precisely as might be practicable the arrangements existing under the Mandates System, but this was rejected on the grounds stated in previous years". He referred to the proposal by the Union Government in regard to an "agreement with the Three Allied and Associated Powers which he assured the Committee, had met with considerable criticism in the Union of South Africa, when originally proposed in 1951–1952, but which nevertheless his Government had again put forward as proof that it wanted a solution.

This proposal, however, had not been accepted by the Good Offices Committee on the ground that the previous proposal of the same nature had already been rejected by the General Assembly. The Union Government had then enquired whether any other alternatives had been considered by the Good Offices Committee.

Four such alternatives had been mentioned, three of which had proved unacceptable either to the Committee or to his Government, but the fourth alternative mentioned was partition of South West Africa, and his Government's immediate re-action had been that this was the most practical proposal to be made so far, and for that reason it merited serious consideration.

His Government had decided that it was prepared to undertake the investigation if the General Assembly indicated that it was willing to consider it as a basis for an agreement.

He emphasized that the Fourth Committee was not being asked to approve partition but only to invite the Union Government to investigate the practicability of such a scheme.

The investigation would cover, for example, the possibility of moving 4 or 5 reserves in the southern part of the territory to the northern part of the territory which was favoured from the point of view of rainfall and sparsely inhabited.

In addition, the views of all the groups of the population would have to be ascertained.

He could assure the Committee that if his Government were asked to undertake the suggested investigation it would do so as soon as possible and would look into all aspects of the matter."

On the same day, and the same morning, the requests of Reverend Michael Scott and Mr. Kerina Getzen to be heard were introduced for the consideration of the Fourth Committee. Mr Louw immediately arose and said that, as in the past, his delegation strongly objected to the granting of hearings. He questioned Reverend Scott's qualifications to speak on behalf of the Native inhabitants of South West Africa, and particularly the Hereros.

Mr. Louw said that Mr. Scott had spent less than a month in South West Africa and that "his credentials were most questionable. The Union Government had strong reasons for believing that a petition from the Ovambo tribes which Mr. Scott had presented contained certain signatures which were all fictitious, that Chief Kutako, whose communications were always so well drafted, was illiterate, and could sign his name only with difficulty, and lastly that Mr. Scott's past record hardly justified that he should be regarded as a reliable witness".

He also made an attack on Mr. Kerina Getzen, and expressed surprise that the Fourth Committee should have agreed to hear evidence (as it had done on a previous occasion) from "a person having no standing in South West Africa, or in the Herero tribe of which he was a member".

He said that "the granting of the request for hearings would be politically most unwise, having regard particularly to the identity of the two persons concerned". He pointed out that "it was the granting of hearings that had led the Union Government delegation to withdraw from the Fourth Committee in 1949, and from the General Assembly in 1951, and warned the Fourth Committee that a vote in favour of granting hearings would create a very serious situation".

It is likely that these somewhat intemperate remarks were due to a premonition that the whole scheme of partition was doomed to be rejected, but they certainly were not conducive to winning over those who objected to the very idea of partition, and who were not altogether trustful of the way in which it had been hatched.

A number of delegates deplored the personal attacks made against the petitioners.

The Committee decided by 60 votes to 5 with 9 abstentions to grant Reverend Scott and Mr. Getzen hearings.

Mr. Louw then recapitulated his previous warnings, explained the lengths to which the Union Government had gone to co-operate with the Good Offices Committee, and pointed out how seriously his Government must regard any decision to grant the petitioners leave to testify against the Union of South Africa.

He then went on to say that even before the vote, it had been apparent from the procedural debate that a number of delegations had come to the Assembly determined to wreck the work of the Good Offices Committee. That course of events confirmed his Government's contention that the forum of the United Nations was being used for the purpose of waging propaganda and ideological warfare against a member state.

Mr. Louw went on to say that should his Government decide not to proceed with the offer which it had made in a spirit of compromise and co-operation, the blame rested on the large majority which had voted in favour of granting hearings to the Reverend Michael Scott and Mr. Getzen on the report of the Good Offices Committee.

After an adjournment to enable him to ascertain the views of his Government, Mr. Louw on 6 October, 1958, after recapitulating the foregoing events and pointing out that in spite of the very conciliatory attitude of the Union Government, the majority of the members of the Fourth Committee had by its hostile attitude "invalidated the results that had been achieved" announced that the South African delegation would not participate further in the discussion of the Good Offices Committee's report, or of any South West African matters.

So, again, the Union Government withdrew, and the Fourth Committee heard the petitioners, discussed the report of the Good Offices Committee and rejected the partition proposal.

Resolution 1243(XIII) recommended that discussions with the South African Government be renewed in order to find a basis for agreement which would "accord to the Mandated Territory of South West Africa as a whole an international status." As South Africa was not prepared to consider United Nations supervision of South West Africa, and as the United Nations was not prepared to consider partition, there was no basis for an agreement, and the Good Offices Committee reported to that effect in 1959.[c]

While the Good Offices Committee attempted to reach a settlement, the Committee on South West Africa continued to operate

---

[c] *GAOR*, Fourteenth Session, Annexes, Agenda Item 38 (A/4224 § 16).

as before. Its report of 1958, which resembled those of previous years, concluded: [d]

170. No important changes have appeared in the situation previously described by the Committee. The life of the Territory continues to present two distinct and separate aspects. On the one hand, the Committee has been able to report the continued free political activity of the "European" section of the population, the influential role which it plays in the institutions of government, and the further expansion and prosperity of the mining, agricultural and commercial enterprises which it owns or controls or which otherwise provide it with a livelihood. On the other hand, the Committee has shown that the vast majority of the population, classified as "Non-European", continues to be deprived on racial grounds of a voice in the administration of the Territory and of opportunities to rise freely, according to merit, in the economic and social structure of the Territory. The "European" community, which alone enjoys political rights, shares with the Mandatory Power, to the exclusion of the "Non-Europeans", control over the allocation and development of the principal resources of the Territory, reserving for itself a disproportionate interest in those resources. The inferior political, economic and social status of the "Non-Europeans" results from arbitrary and racially discriminatory laws. By means of discriminatory legislative and administrative acts, authority and opportunity are retained as a matter of policy in the hands of the "European" population, while the "Non-European" majority is confined to reserves except to the extent that its manpower is needed in the "European" economy in the form of unskilled labour and under strict regulation.

171. The Committee therefore reaffirms its conclusion that existing conditions in the Territory and the trend of the administration represent a situation not in accord with the Mandates System, the Charter of the United Nations, the Universal Declaration of Human Rights, the advisory opinions of the International Court of Justice and the resolutions of the General Assembly.

The South African Government protested vehemently against the accuracy of the reports of the Committee on South West Africa, but South Africa was herself to blame in this respect, for she had persistently refused to supply the Committee with information. The South West African jurist Goldblatt summed up the position in 1960: [e]

[d] *GAOR*, Thirteenth Session, Suppl. No. 12 (A/3906) pp. 28–29. See, too, the Committee's reports of 1959 (*GAOR*, Fourteenth Session, Suppl. No. 12 [A/4191]) and 1960 (*GAOR* Fifteenth Session, Suppl. No. 12 [A/4464]).
[e] *The Conflict between the United Nations and the Union of South Africa in regard to South West Africa* (1960), pp. 18–22. For criticisms of a similar nature, see the South African scholars R. B. Ballinger, *South West Africa: The Case Against the Union*, pp. 43–44, and J. H. Wellington, *South West Africa and Its Human Issues*, pp. 339–40.

At this stage it is well to pause and see what the results were of the Union's refusal to co-operate with the United Nations.

No representative of the Union Government was sent to the Committee on South West Africa to take part in the examination of the report and to answer questions and give explanations. So the Committee did without the assistance of the Union Government.

In the case of the League of Nations, as already explained, in essence the supervision of the League amounted to no more than the public discussion of the Mandatory's administration based upon its report, and the adoption of resolutions by the members of the League, criticising the Union Government's administration and urging improvements in the way in which it carried out its duties.

The only weapon available to the League, but a most powerful weapon, was the effect of world opinion as reflected in the resolutions of the League.

In the case of the United Nations exactly the same weapons were available.

Just as in the case of the resolutions adopted by the League, the Union Government, could, if it wished, ignore the criticisms and suggestions, so in the case of resolutions of the General Assembly of the United Nations the Union Government could ignore them.

But the United Nations was in fact exercising supervision over South West Africa, no more or less than it could have legally done if the Union Government had acknowledged the right of supervision of the United Nations as laid down by the International Court of Justice.

One great difference in practice, however, showed itself from the proceedings in the days of the League.

Whereas with the co-operation of the Union Government in sending annual reports and sending its own representative to take part in the examination of the report by the Permanent Mandates Commission, a spirit of goodwill existed between the Union Government and the Permanent Mandates Commission and the Assembly of the League, in the case of the United Nations there developed increasingly a feeling of bitterness and hostility, because the Committee on South West Africa, making the best use it could of the materials at its disposal, and without the corrective influence of a Union representative at its deliberations, found cause to condemn the Union Government in many of the aspects of its administration of South West Africa.

This was resented by the Union Government particularly as the report of the Committee on South West Africa and the debates on this report in the Fourth or Trusteeship Committee of the United Nations, were exposed to the full glare of world publicity.

But the attitude of the United Nations was "Well, we have invited you to co-operate, and you have refused to do so, you can only blame yourself if the report on your administration of South West Africa is based upon information which may in some respects be unreliable. Supervision must be exercised by the United Nations and will continue to be so exercised. We would prefer to do it with your assistance, but we will not be prevented from exercising supervision, as best we can, even if you refuse to assist."

This was bad enough for the Union Government but what was far worse was the course adopted by the United Nations in the treatment of petitions from the inhabitants of South West Africa.

It will be recalled that in the days of the League of Nations petitions were transmitted by petitioners to the Mandatory Power which then forwarded the petitions to the League of Nations with its comments. This enabled the Permanent Mandates Commission fairly to assess the value of the petitions.

When the Union Government refused to recognise any supervisory rights by the United Nations it not only declined to send annual reports, but it also refused to transmit any petitions.

The United Nations refused to be baulked, and evolved a system by which petitioners were able to send petitions direct to the United Nations.

As the United Nations wished to act in accordance with the ruling contained in the International Court's advisory opinion of 1950 to wit: 'to exercise its supervisory powers according to procedures which should conform as far as possible to those which were followed by the Council of the League of Nations', it transmitted these petitions to the Union Government for its comment.

The Union Government refused to comment.

The United Nations therefore regarded the petitions as having been properly transmitted by the Union Government to the United Nations and then dealt with the petitions on that basis, without the benefit of comment by the Union Government.

It was futile therefore for the Union Government thereafter to complain that the United Nations was attaching importance to unreliable statements in the petitions, and this was pointedly brought home to the delegates of the Union Government in the United Nations, when they did so protest.

The next serious development occurred when the United Nations through its subsidiary organs like the Committee on South West Africa, was approached by petitioners to be permitted to appear personally and give oral evidence.

. . . .

The International Court in 1956, decided that such evidence was legally permissible, the main reason being that such evidence was in the circumstances necessary to enable the United Nations to perform its supervisory duties effectively.

The United Nations General Assembly accepted this opinion in 1956, and from then on witnesses have appeared personally, in increasing numbers every year, to testify against the way in which the Union Government was administering South West Africa.

Names of witnesses like the Rev. Michael Scott, Messrs. Getzen, and Kozonguizi have become familiar to the people of South West Africa.

The reason for permitting the Rev. Michael Scott to give evidence personally was the fact that the United Nations accepted him as the authorised agent of certain Native Chiefs in South West Africa, whom the Union Government refused, in spite of the request of the United Nations, to permit to attend personally to give evidence.

But more recently others have appeared before the United Nations, like the Rev. Markus Kooper, Messrs. Jacob Kuhangua, Sam Nujoma, and Beukes all of whom had to make their way to the United Nations through devious routes because of the refusal of the Union Government to permit them to attend in the ordinary way, and all of whom were imbued with the one desire, to give the United Nations their account of the way in which the Union Government was administering the Territory.

In addition three United States citizens, Messrs. Lowenstein, Bundy, and Bull, have given evidence.

It stands to reason that the effect of what these witnesses said would be harmful to the prestige of the Union Government, but they could not be prevented by the Union Government from testifying, and the whole world formed its opinion of the position in South West Africa from the report of the Committee on South West Africa, which was based to some extent on this evidence, and the whole world was also able to read this evidence.

It should be remarked that the Committee on South West Africa did not blindly accept everything that these witnesses said. They were all submitted to cross-examination although some members of the Committee were inclined to be sympathetic to the petitioners.

In the absence, however, of corrective assistance by the Union Government the Committee was to a great extent compelled to rely upon the statements of these witnesses.

Although in the earlier period the Union Government adopted the attitude of complete refusal to pay any attention to the views of the United Nations on the Union's administration of South West Africa —seeing that it refused to recognise any supervisory rights claimed by the United Nations—, it became increasingly clear to the Union Government, in later years, that it could not afford to ignore the effect of all this adverse publicity on world opinion.

Consequently for the last two or three years the Union delegate, Mr. Eric Louw, to the United Nations, brought with him one or other gentleman, who was acquainted with the conditions of South West Africa to give the Fourth or Trusteeship Committee an account of the position in South West Africa, but to refuse to answer any questions.

This concession, however, was insufficient to halt the attack upon the Union which was consistently maintained by nations who were strongly opposed to the Union's racial policy, and particularly opposed to the introduction of this policy into South West Africa in the same strong measure as obtained in the Union of South Africa.

There was also a growing impatience at the Union Government's refusal to recognise the rights of the United Nations as determined by the International Court of Justice in 1950.

Goldblatt stated that if the South African Government wished to avoid a conflict situation in South West Africa it would be well advised to submit to international supervision: [f]

What was necessary in order to ease the situation even temporarily, but what the Union Government was determined to resist, was the appearance of the Union Government representatives before the United Nations, not merely to give their version, but to be submitted to questioning by the United Nations through its Committee on South West Africa.

In the days when it was felt that the United Nations was weak it may have been possible to ignore it. Today, however, in spite of surface appearances, the United Nations is not weak, and has become representative of practically the whole world, and it will be impossible for a small power like the Union of South Africa to maintain its present attitude towards the United Nations in regard to South West Africa.

The sooner the Union Government recognises the legal rights of the United Nations to supervision over South West Africa as expressed in the opinion of the International Court of Justice in 1950, the sooner will the tension between the Union Government and the United Nations be resolved, and the better will it be for the inhabitants of South West Africa.

For the absurdity of the whole situation lies in this:

The Union Government refuses to recognise the United Nations' rights of supervision, yet the United Nations does in fact exercise exactly the same supervision as the League of Nations exercised, and the same supervision as it would exercise if the Union Government had recognised the rights of the United Nations.

But the position through non-recognition is worse than if the Union Government had recognised the rights of the United Nations, because now the United Nations through its Committee on South West Africa compiles its own report on South West Africa without the corrective assistance of the Union Government and furthermore the Union Government is now being faced with a steady stream of witnesses, all hostile, from outside and inside South West Africa.

And in this regard it is worth noting, from remarks of delegates in the United Nations, that the appearance of witnesses personally would, in all probability, never have occurred if the Union Government had only co-operated with the United Nations.

. . . .

What should be realised is this:- that the choice for the White man is not between continuing to enjoy his present privileged position and sharing of responsibility with the Africans.

No, the choice is between sharing responsibility through orderly development, and being swept away altogether by hostile and uncon-

[f] The Conflict between the United Nations and the Union of South Africa in regard to South West Africa, pp. 22–23, 29–30. See, too, Goldblatt, *The Mandated Territory of South West Africa in Relation to the United Nations,* pp. 66–67.

trolled African forces, who will be in no mood to extend liberal treatment to those who refuse to extend that treatment to the African.

And it is precisely through the United Nations that the necessary
controlled development can take place.

As members of the United Nations those independent nations which
had made and are making the cause of the African in this Territory
their own, will be subjected to the controls inherent in membership of
the United Nations.

Co-operation between the Union of South Africa and the United
Nations in the form of a Trusteeship Agreement, while it will not suc-
ceed in preventing concerted efforts among the Africans in the United
Nations to speed up the development of the inhabitants of South West
Africa, will at all events avoid the unrestrained and extremely aggres-
sive attitude of these nations which will develop, if the Union of South
Africa were to continue to ignore the United Nations.

The people of South West Africa must realize the seriousness of the
present situation.

On the one hand the way is open through a Trusteeship Agreement
with the United Nations to an orderly development of this Territory,
to a stage when a peaceful transition can take place from Trusteeship
status to self-government or independence, by agreement between all
interested parties, in which property and political rights can be safeguarded.

On the other hand there lies before us the prospect of drastic action
in some form or other by the United Nations, and, outside the United
Nations, mounting hostile action by African independent states, which
all are bound to stir up the Africans within the Territory, and which
may, in the final result, when moods are ugly, and temperatures are
high, sweep away all political and property rights presently enjoyed by
the Whites in the Territory.

This is not a time for party-political bickering on petty points.

There are flood waters gathering which threaten to engulf us. The
days are past when the League of Nations or the United Nations were
concerned to protect only the interests of the African. It is the non-Af-
rican who will require protection.

There is no other agency in the world that can ensure this protection than the United Nations whose supervision of the Territoy embraces all the inhabitants of South West Africa.

The conflict between the Union Government and the United
Nations, which embraces practically the whole world, must be ended,
in so far as South West Africa is concerned, and the only way in which
this can be ended is by the Union Government's recognition of the supervision of the United Nations in the form first of the mandate and
thereafter by transition into the Trusteeship System.

11. New Legal Action is Planned

Towards the end of the 1950s the United Nations considered new
ways of compelling South Africa to submit to her authority. Legal

action was an obvious course. The three advisory opinions requested by the General Assembly were not binding, but it was still open to a member State to arraign South Africa before the International Court of Justice in contentious proceedings which might lead to a binding decision, enforceable by the Security Council under Article 94 of the Charter. In 1957 the General Assembly resolved, in Resolution 1060(XI):

The General Assembly,

Having regard to the provisions of the Mandate for South West Africa, the Covenant of the League of Nations, the Charter of the United Nations and the resolutions of the General Assembly in regard to South West Africa,

Noting that its resolutions endorsing and accepting the advisory opinion of 11 July 1950 of the International Court of Justice and urging the Union of South Africa to place the Territory of South West Africa under trusteeship have been of no avail,

1. *Requests* the Committee on South West Africa to study the following question:

What legal action is open to the organs of the United Nations, or to the Members of the United Nations, or to the former Members of the League of Nations, acting either individually or jointly, to ensure that the Union of South Africa fulfils the obligations assumed by it under the Mandate, pending the placing of the Territory of South West Africa under the International Trusteeship System?;

2. *Further requests* the Committee on South West Africa to submit to the General Assembly at its twelfth session a special report containing conclusions and recommendations on the question.

Later that year the Committee on South West Africa submitted a special report [g] in which it examined the possible legal action open to the organs of the United Nations, to members of the United Nations, and to former members of the League of Nations, which might be used to compel South Africa to fulfil her obligations under the Mandate. The Committee emphasized that organs of the United Nations might request only non-binding advisory opinions, and that it was doubtful whether member States of the United Nations which had not been members of the League of Nations were competent to bring an action in contentious proceedings. The Committee was, however, optimistic about the prospects of legal proceedings brought by former members of the League of Nations which had become members of the United Nations. In this connection it reported: [h]

[g] *GAOR*, Twelfth Session, Suppl. No. A (A/3625).   [h] *Ibid.*, pp. 5–6.

31. The type of action dealt with in the present section is the possibility of the institution of contentious proceedings before the Court under article 7 of the Mandate. The substance of this section is limited to the consideration of the position of former Members of the League of Nations. It should be noted that the remarks in this section depend on the questions raised in the preceding section, for, if article 7 of the Mandate now applies to all Members of the United Nations, the investigation of the position of former Members of the League of Nations becomes irrelevant except in very few cases. Although the question of which States may take advantage of article 7 of the Mandate does not seem to have been specifically dealt with by the Court, it would seem that at least some former Members of the League certainly enjoy that right. Former Members which ceased to be Members prior to the final dissolution of the League apparently lost all rights thereunder, including those in relation to article 7 of the Mandate, at the date of the cessation of their membership. In that event there would not appear to be any reason why those rights should revive after the dissolution of the League.[23] Furthermore, there is an additional category [24] of some doubt, namely, former Members of the League at the date of dissolution of the League which are not now Members of the United Nations or otherwise parties to the Statute of the Court. This category is not dealt with in the 1950 opinion but, in the view of Judge Read,[25] the rights under article 7 of those former Members which did not become parties to the Statute of the present Court lapsed. . . .

32. There would therefore appear to be little doubt that the right to invoke article 7 of the Mandate is enjoyed at any rate by those former Members of the League which were Members at the date of dissolution of the League and which are now Members of the United Nations or are otherwise parties to the Statute of the Court. For the article to apply, there must be a dispute between the Mandatory and such former Members, which cannot be settled by negotiation and which relates to the interpretation or application of the Mandate.

33. The Permanent Court of International Justice defined "dispute" as "a disagreement on a point of law or fact, a conflict of legal views or of interests between two persons". [26] For the purposes of article 7 of the Mandate, such a dispute should be one which cannot be settled by negotiation. Where "a deadlock is reached or . . . one Party definitely declares himself unable, or refuses, to give way . . . there can be no

[23] Separate opinion by Sir Arnold McNair, *ICJ Reports,* 1950, p. 158; see also separate opinion by Judge Read, p. 165.
[24] There may be other categories of some doubt, for example the position of any State which might be regarded as having succeeded to the rights and obligations of any former Member of the League. Such categories raise important and extremely complicated questions of law which the Committee does not feel called upon to decide.
[25] *ICJ Reports,* 1950, p. 169.
[26] *PCIJ, Series A,* 1–8, Judgments, Judgment No. 2, p. 11. The criteria adopted in Judgment No. 2 were specifically retained in Judgment No. 10. See *PCIJ, Series A,* 11.

doubt that the dispute cannot be settled by diplomatic negotiations".[27] Whether the proceedings to date in the United Nations indicate the existence of a dispute between the Union and any State intending proceedings under article 7 is a question for that State to answer and to resolve by any further steps which may be deemed necessary. In this connexion, there would appear to be no legal bar to the General Assembly drawing the attention of such former Members of the League to article 7 of the Mandate or of recommending such action relating thereto as the Assembly deemed appropriate.

34. The dispute may be of any nature. Article 7 does not contain any restrictive words in this connexion, but it must in every case relate to the interpretation or application of the Mandate, that is to say, it must relate to one or more clauses of the Mandate or to the effect of the Mandate as a whole, for example, in relation to the present status of the Territory concerned. From this point of view, the opinion of the Court of 1950 would appear to suggest that a dispute concerning the supervision functions themselves could properly exist, as well as a dispute relating to the administration or the status of the Territory.

35. The Court has given its advisory opinion that it has jurisdiction under article 7 of the Mandate. If contentious proceedings were instituted under this article, the jurisdiction of the Court would depend upon Articles 36, paragraph 1, and 37 of the Statute of the Court.[28] Article 36, paragraph 1, provides that the jurisdiction of the Court comprises all matters specially provided for in treaties or conventions in force. As Sir Arnold McNair indicated [29] "there can be no doubt that the Mandate, which embodies international obligations, belongs to the category of treaty or convention". According to Article 37 of the Statute, a treaty or convention which provides for the reference of a matter to the Permanent Court shall be construed as if it provided for reference to the present Court.

36. In the event of a dispute concerning the Court's jurisdiction over any contentious case brought before it, the Court has under Article 36, paragraph 6, of its Statute the power to settle the issue by its own decision.

37. If a party to a contentious case does not appear or fails to defend its case, the other party may call upon the Court to decide in its favour. If the Court decides to do so it must satisfy itself that it has jurisdiction under Articles 36 and 37 of its Statute and that the claim is well founded in fact and law.[30]

38. If the Court in a contentious case reaches a decision on the substance, the decision is binding as between the parties to the case. Article 59 of the Statute provides that the decision of the Court has no binding force except between the parties and in respect of that particular case.

39. According to Article 60 of the Statute of the Court the judgement

---

[27] *PCIJ, Series A,* 1–8, Judgments, Judgment No. 2, p. 13.
[28] No question of acceptances of the "optional clause" would therefore arise.
[29] *ICJ Reports,* 1950, p. 158.   [30] Article 53 of the Statute of the Court.

is final and without appeal. There may, however, be an application for a revision of a judgement but, according to the provisions of Article 61 of the Statute, such application may be made only when it is based upon the discovery of some fact of such a nature as to be a decisive factor, which fact was, when the judgment was given, unknown to the Court and also to the party claiming revision, provided ignorance was not due to negligence.

40. According to Article 94 of the Charter each Member of the United Nations undertakes to comply with the decision of the International Court in any case to which it is a party. In accordance with paragraph 2 of the same Article, if a party to a case fails to perform the obligations incumbent upon it under the judgement rendered by the Court, the other party may have recourse to the Security Council, which may if it deems necessary make recommendations or decide upon measures to be taken to give effect to the judgement.

41. There is nothing in article 7 of the Mandate or in the Statute of the Court which would prevent former Members of the League acting jointly as well as individually.

42. It also can be pointed out that, according to Article 63 of the Statute, the Registrar is bound to notify all States parties to a Convention the construction of which is in question, and the States notified have a right to intervene. If the right is exercised, the State or States concerned are equally bound by any judgement given.

In Resolution 1142(XII) the General Assembly approved this report and drew the attention of member States

> to the failure of the Union of South Africa to render annual reports to the United Nations, and to the legal action provided for in Article 7 of the Mandate read with Article 37 of the Statute of the International Court of Justice.

In June 1960 at the Second Conference of Independant African States held in Addis Ababa,[i] Ethiopia and Liberia announced that they, as former member States of the League of Nations, intended instituting legal proceedings against South Africa over South West Africa. This decision was unanimously approved by the Conference. In 1960 this proposed course of action received the blessing of the General Assembly in Resolution 1565(XV):

The General Assembly,

Recalling its resolution 1361 (XIV) of 17 November 1959, in which it drew the attention of Member States to the conclusions of the special report of the Committee on South West Africa concerning the legal action open to Member States to submit to the International

---

[i] The States participating in the Conference were Ethiopia, Ghana, Guinea, Libya, Liberia, Morocco, Sudan, Tunisia, and the United Arab Republic. There were also observers from Algeria, Cameroons, Nigeria, and Somalia.

Court of Justice any dispute with the Union of South Africa relating to the interpretation or application of the provisions of the Mandate for the Territory of South West Africa, if such dispute cannot be settled by negotiation,

Noting with grave concern that the administration of the Territory, in recent years, has been conducted in a manner contrary to the Mandate, the Charter of the United Nations, the Universal Declaration of Human Rights and the resolutions of the General Assembly, including resolution 449 A(V) of 13 December 1950, by which the Assembly accepted the advisory opinion of 11 July 1950 of the International Court of Justice on the question of South West Africa,

Noting that all negotiations and efforts on the part of the General Assembly, of its several committees and organs constituted and authorized for this purpose, and of Member States acting through such committees and organs, have failed to bring about compliance on the part of the Government of the Union of South Africa with its obligations under the Mandate, as is evidenced, *inter alia,* by the following reports of the said committees and organs to the Assembly:

(a) Reports of the *Ad Hoc* Committee on South West Africa to the General Assembly at its sixth, seventh and eighth sessions,

(b) Reports of the Committee on South West Africa to the General Assembly at its ninth to fifteenth sessions,

(c) Reports of the Good Offices Committee on South West Africa to the General Assembly at its thirteenth and fourteenth sessions,

Noting the aforesaid reports, and in particular the reports of the Committee on South West Africa concerning the failure of negotiations with the Government of the Union of South Africa and the Committee's conclusions that the Union has at all times declined to co-operate in any way with the Committee in the discharge of its functions,

1. *Notes with approval* the observations of the Committee on South West Africa concerning the administration of the Territory as set out in the Committee's report to the General Assembly at its fifteenth session, and finds that the Government of the Union of South Africa has failed and refused to carry out its obligations under the Mandate for the Territory of South West Africa;

2. *Concludes* that the dispute which has arisen between Ethiopia, Liberia, and other Member States on the one hand, and the Union of South Africa on the other, relating to the interpretation and application of the Mandate has not been and cannot be settled by negotiation;

3. *Notes* that Ethiopia and Liberia, on 4 November 1960, filed concurrent applications in the International Court of Justice instituting contentious proceedings against the Union of South Africa;

4. *Commends* the Governments of Ethiopia and Liberia upon their initiative in submitting such dispute to the International Court of Justice for adjudication and declaration in a contentious proceeding in accordance with article 7 of the Mandate.

7

Political Developments, 1960–1966[a]

The beginning of the 1960s witnessed a series of events which led to a new militancy on the part of the United Nations towards South Africa. First, the Afro-Asian bloc was increased in size by the admission of sixteen newly independent African States, to bring its total number to forty-six out of the ninety-nine member States of the United Nations. Second, the shooting of African demonstrators by the South African Police at Sharpeville in 1960 obliged the Security Council to take cognizance of the racial situation in Southern Africa for the first time.[b] Third, South Africa withdrew from the Commonwealth of Nations in 1961 and thereby lost any claim to the support of members of that "Club" in the United Nations.

1. The Creation of SWAPO and SWANU

On the international scene African nationalism manifested itself in the passing of Resolution 1514(XV), the Declaration on the Granting of Independence to Colonial Countries and Peoples, which clearly extends to South West Africa.[c] In South West Af-

[a] For general studies of this period, see Carroll, *South West Africa and the United Nations,* chap. 7; Imishue, *South West Africa,* chap. 7.
[b] See C.J.R. Dugard, "The Legal Effect of United Nations Resolutions on Apartheid" (1966) 83 *SALJ* 44 at 45.
[c] Paragraph 5 of this historic declaration states that immediate steps shall be taken to grant independence to "Trust and Non-Self-Governing Territories or all other territories which have not yet attained independence." Clearly this formula is wide enough to include South West Africa.

rica it found expression in the creation of two popular nationalist organizations, the South West Africa Peoples' Organization (SWAPO), which was predominantly of Ovambo origin, and the South West Africa National Union (SWANU), which pledged themselves to the ending of racial discrimination and the removal of South African control. These organizations made contact with other African nationalist organizations and thereby came to influence policy-making in the United Nations. The aims of these two organizations were described in the Report of the Commitee on South West Africa in 1961: [d]

93. The basic aims of SWAPO, as enumerated in the programme of the organization, are:

> To establish a free, democratic government in South West Africa founded upon the will and participation of all the people of our country and to cooperate to the fullest extent with all of our brothers and sisters to rid our continent of all forms of foreign domination and to rebuild it according to the desires of our peoples; unification of all people of South West Africa into a cohesive, representative, national political organization, irrespective of their race, ethnic origin, religion or creed; reconstruction of the economic, educational and social foundations which will support and maintain the real African independence which our people desire for themselves.

. . . .

94. The aims and objects of SWANU are:

> To unite and rally the people of South West Africa into one national front, to organize the common people, workers and peasants, of South West Africa and lead them in the struggle for national independence and self-determination; to work with allied movements in Africa for the propagation and promotion of the concept of Pan-Africanism and unity amongst the peoples of Africa.

The formation of these organizations is described by Muriel Horrell of the South African Institute of Race Relations: [e]

ESTABLISHMENT OF S. W. A. N. U.

A few South-West African students who were studying in South Africa at the time of the Defiance Campaign of 1953 and shared the feel-

---

[d] Report of the Committee on South West Africa concerning the Implementation of General Assembly Resolutions 1568(XV) and 1596(XV) *GAOR*, Sixteenth Session, Suppl. No. 12A (A/4926), p. 13.
[e] *South-West Africa* (S.A. Institute of Race Relations, 1967), pp. 81–84. See, too, Goldblatt, *History of South West Africa*, pp. 262–63.

ings of those who participated decided to form a Student Body in the Territory. Leading figures were Jariretundu Kozonguizi, Mburumba Kerina (also known as Erich Getzen), and Zedekia Ngavirue. Soon afterwards, Kerina left to study in the United States.

Kozonguizi was invited to join the Herero Chief's Council, where he put the views of the younger men who were anxious to overcome tribal divisions and foster a broad nationalism. He and Uatja Kautuetu founded a Progressive Association.

Meanwhile, in 1957, Toivo had been busy organizing an Ovamboland People's Organization (O.P.O.); resentment continued among many Ovambo as a result of boundary disputes which led to war against the Portuguese in Angola and a skirmish with a South African military expedition. The boundary, as finally determined, divided the Kuanyama (Ovambo) tribe into two sections. One of the leading chiefs was killed in the fighting, and later, in 1932, another was deposed and exiled. The O.P.O. was founded in Cape Town.

Toivo and Kozonguizi met to discuss the formation of a broader-based organization, and canvassed the idea among the Herero and Nama people. Soon afterwards, however, Kozonguizi left to join the Rev. Michael Scott and Kerina in lobbying at the United Nations.

Finally, in 1959, his idea materialized in the founding of S.W.A.N.U. (the South-West African National Union) which was closely allied to the O.P.O. and the Herero Chief's Council. Besides those mentioned, leading figures were Sam Nujoma and Jacob Kuhangua.

. . . there was a serious disturbance at Windhoek later that year as the result of an objection to an official plan to move Africans to the new township of Katutura where the dwellings were of much improved standard, but the rents and transport costs were higher and no home-ownership was allowed. Thereafter Kuhangua was sent under escort to Angola, Nujoma was repatriated to Ovamboland but escaped in 1961 and left the country, Kautuetu left, too, and Ngavirue was ordered to return to his home in the Epukiro Reserve in the far east of the Territory.

Internal dissensions arose among the members still in South-West Africa. For one thing, the Mbandero group of Herero in the East did not recognize Kutako as chief of all their people, and succeeded in obtaining Government recognition of a chief of their own, Munjuko II. Some people accused certain elements within S.W.A.N.U. of trying to divide the Herero people. As Kutako was a very old man, it was decided that he should be assisted by a deputy chief. Clemens Kapuuo was elected, but a few of the Herero who were members of S.W.A.N.U. resented this, preferring a nominee of their own.

FORMATION OF S.W.A.P.O.

Nujoma and Kozonguizi had been writing letters urging that the O.P.O. and S.W.A.N.U. should merge, while Kerina, on the other hand, recommended that the O.P.O. should become a national organization. His views prevailed, largely because S.W.A.N.U. was encountering opposition from the Herero Chief's Council. It was, thus, decided that the O.P.O. should expand into a South-West African People's Organization (S.W.A.P.O.).

DIFFERENCES IN POLICY

The main difference between these bodies has been that S.W.A.P.O. has relied chiefly on petitioning at the United Nations, whereas S.W.A.N.U. feels that the people of the Territory should themselves work to secure their ambitions.

When giving evidence before the United Nations Committee that visited the Territory during 1962, representatives of both organizations urged that the mandate be terminated immediately, but their views on what should happen thereafter differed. S.W.A.P.O. pressed for a temporary United Nations Commission to arrange for free elections on a basis of one-man-one-vote, followed by the granting of independence. S.W.A.N.U. suggested that a constitutional convention be held under United Nations' auspices to decide on future political arrangements.

NEW POLITICAL ORGANIZATIONS

During 1963 Herero leaders in correspondence with Dr. Kerina and Hermanus Beukes discussed the formation of a new party. Mr. Beukes, from the Rehoboth Gebiet, had escaped from South Africa four years earlier, after his passport had been confiscated when he was on the point of leaving to take up a scholarship offered overseas. He subsequently gave evidence against South Africa before the Trusteeship Committee.

One of those with whom discussions were apparently held was Dr. Kenneth G. Abrahams, originally from Cape Town, who was practising medicine in the Gebiet. In July 1963 the police went to Rehoboth to arrest him on charges including sabotage and an allegation that he and others had formed an organization in Cape Town known as the Yu Chi Chan Club, which was subsequently declared unlawful. (Its membership appears to have been confined to Coloured people in Cape Town.) After vigorous protests from the Baster community the police withdrew, and Dr. Abrahams was informed that the warrant for his arrest would not be exercised as long as he remained in the Gebiet devoting himself to medical work. However he escaped to Bechuanaland, where he was kidnapped by white men and brought back to South-West Africa. The authorities then arrested him; but after Britain had expressed its serious concern over the circumstances leading to the arrest he was returned to Bechuanaland.

In 1964 Dr. Kerina, Chief Kutako, and Clemens Kapuuo formed the National Unity Democratic Organization (N.U.D.O.) with the stated aims, *inter alia,* of achieving equality for persons of all racial groups. They are reported to have had support from the Nama Chief David Witbooi and from Allan Louw, chairman of the Rehoboth Council.

S.W.A.P.O. and S.W.A.N.U. declined to join the N.U.D.O., and formed a South-West African National Liberation Front in which each retained its own identity. The name was changed later to the South-West Africa National United Front (S.W.A.N.U.F.).

Also in 1964 a Caprivi African National Union was established, led by B. K. Simbwaye. It sent a petition to the United Nations asking for help in securing the South African Government's withdrawal from the Caprivi Strip.

2. *South West Africa Before the United Nations,*
1960–1965

Because Ethiopia and Liberia had submitted the dispute over South West Africa to the International Court of Justice, South Africa proposed that the whole dispute be treated as *sub judice* and left untouched pending the decision of the International Court of Justice.[f] This proposal was rejected,[g] and the General Assembly went on to adopt resolution 1565(XV),[h] in which it prejudged the very issue before the Court—whether South Africa had violated her obligations under the Mandate—by finding that South Africa had "failed and refused to carry out its obligations under the Mandate." Subsequent resolutions until 1966, the year in which the Court finally gave its judgment on the dispute, followed this approach.[i] In fact the General Assembly paid little attention to the proceedings before the Court and continued to press for a political settlement (or confrontation). Although these hostile resolutions may have offended the *sub judice* rule, they did achieve an important result: they compelled the United States and the United Kingdom to commit themselves to accept the International Court's decision. According to Anthony A. D'Amato, an American Law Professor who assisted Ethiopia and Liberia in the proceedings before the International Court: [j]

This came about as a result of a possibly inadvertent African strategy at the U.N. Since 1960, the African States have pushed for increasingly sharp resolutions against South Africa, such as breaking off diplomatic relations and trade, and instituting sanctions. These resolutions, which often include South West Africa, risked undercutting the judicial proceedings at The Hague by interfering with an issue that was *sub judice.*

---

[f] See the statement of Mr. B. Fourie, in *GAOR*, Plenary Meetings, 15th Session, 954th Mtg (18 December, 1960), pp. 1385–87.
[g] Ibid., 1386–87.   [h] See above, pp. 214–215.
[i] Resolutions 1596(XV), 1702(XVI), 2674(XX).
[j] "Legal and Political Strategies of the South West Africa Litigation" (1967) 4 *Law in Transition Quarterly* 8 at 20.

They seem to have been actuated by impatience, a desire to achieve direct results, and the need to impress domestic constituents. Nevertheless, the resolutions have had an important strategic result: they have forced the U.S. and U.K. to argue against the resolutions on the primary basis that the legal issues have not been clarified because the Court was considering the South West Africa Case. Thus the African States became the beneficiaries of a commitment—a far more explicit one than the vaunted American commitment to defend South Vietnam—to support the eventual decision of the Court.

These political moves at the United Nations will be examined before attention is directed to other important issues of this period and to the legal proceedings themselves.

In 1961 the General Assembly condemned apartheid, labelled the situation in South West Africa a potential threat to international peace, and requested the Committee on South West Africa to visit South West Africa with or without permission from the South African Government. This resolution illustrates the new militant mood of the General Assembly. Resolution 1596(XV):

The General Assembly,

Bearing in mind the provisions of the General Assembly's Declaration on the granting of independence to colonial countries and peoples, which declares that immediate steps shall be taken to transfer all powers to such peoples, without any conditions or reservations, in accordance with their freely expressed will and desire, without any distinction as to race, creed or colour, in order to enable them to enjoy complete independence and freedom,

Recalling its resolution 1568 (XV) of 18 December 1960 inviting the Committee on South West Africa to go to South West Africa immediately, *inter alia,* to investigate the situation prevailing in the Territory,

Noting with deep regret, from the preliminary report of the Committee on South West Africa called for under the said resolution, that the Government of the Union of South Africa refuses to co-operate with the United Nations by facilitating the mission of the Committee on South West Africa,

Convinced that it is both the right and the duty of the United Nations to discharge fully and effectively its obligations with respect to the proper implementation, under its supervision, of the Mandate for South West Africa conferred upon His Britannic Majesty, to be exercised on his behalf by the Government of the Union of South Africa,

Noting with grave concern the continuing deterioration in the situation in South West Africa resulting from the continued application, in violation of the letter and spirit of the Mandate, of tyrannical policies and practices, such as *apartheid,* of the administration of the Union of South Africa in South West Africa,

Reiterating its concern that this situation constitutes a serious threat to international peace and security,

1. *Recognizes and supports* the passionate yearning of the people of South West Africa for freedom and the exercise of national independence and sovereignty;

2. *Rejects* the position taken by the Government of the Union of South Africa in refusing to co-operate with the United Nations in the implementation of General Assembly resolution 1568 (XV) as well as other resolutions concerning South West Africa;

3. *Deplores* the attempts at the assimilation of the Mandated Territory of South West Africa, culminating in the so-called referendum held on 5 October 1960, as totally unacceptable, having no moral or legal basis and being repugnant to the letter and spirit of the Mandate;

4. *Considers* that the full and effective discharge of the tasks assigned to the Committee on South West Africa in paragraph 4 of General Assembly resolution 1568 (XV) is essential to the protection of the lives and property of the inhabitants of South West Africa, to the amelioration of the prevailing conditions in South West Africa, the continuance of which is likely to endanger international peace and security, and to the exercise of the right of self-determination by the people of South West Africa in complete freedom and of their right of accession to national sovereignty and independence with the least delay;

5. *Requests* the Committee on South West Africa, therefore, immediately to proceed to discharge the special and urgent tasks entrusted to it in resolution 1568 (XV) as fully and expeditiously as possible with the co-operation of the Government of the Union of South Africa if such co-operation is available, and without it if necessary;

6. *Requests* the States Members of the United Nations to extend to the Committee on South West Africa such assistance as it may require in the discharge of these tasks;

7. *Decides* to call the attention of the Security Council to the situation in respect of South West Africa which, if allowed to continue, will in the General Assembly's view endanger international peace and security, and to the present resolution, the full implementation of which is necessary to bring that situation to a speedy end;

8. *Takes note with grave concern* of reports of the terrorization of, and armed action against, the indigenous inhabitants, and calls upon the Government of the Union of South Africa to desist from such acts;

9. *Requests* the Committee on South West Africa to submit to the General Assembly at its sixteenth session a report on the implementation of resolution 1568 (XV) as well as the present resolution.

The South African Government refused the Committee permission to visit the territory and notified the Secretary General that any attempt on its part to enter would be prevented.[k] The Com-

---

[k] Report of the Committee on South West Africa concerning the Implementation of General Assembly Resolutions 1568(XV) and 1596(XV), *GAOR*, Sixteenth Session, Suppl. No. 12A (A/4926), pp. 2 and 25.

mittee was therefore obliged to confine itself to visiting other African territories, where it took evidence from petitioners. The views of petitioners representing SWAPO and SWANU appear from the Committee's report: [1]

128. Representatives of the South West Africa Peoples Organization (SWAPO), and the South West Africa National Union (SWANU), as well as the representatives of all other African organizations appearing before the Committee in Accra, Dar es Salaam and Cairo appealed for immediate intervention by the United Nations to remove the South African Government from South West Africa and to protect the lives of South West Africans, without awaiting the outcome of the case pending before the International Court of Justice.

129. They considered the South African Government the instrument of the suppression and oppression of the indigenous population of the Territory and the principal hindrance to its development. They could foresee no possibility of a change of policy on the part of the South African Government.

130. The removal of the South African Government was therefore an essential prerequisite to the restoration of a climate of peace and security and to the initiation of any measure of self-determination.

.   .   .   .

POSITION OF THE SOUTH WEST AFRICA PEOPLES ORGANIZATION

132. In a statement presented to the Committee in Dar es Salaam, SWAPO requested that action be taken by an emergency special session of the General Assembly to:

(a) Terminate the Mandate for South West Africa immediately, and to entrust the temporary administration of the country to a United Nations Commission composed of African States with a view to arranging for free general elections in the country immediately in order to make possible the conditions necessary for South West Africa to accede:

(1) To self-government now, through the establishment of a democratic African Government based on the principle of one man, one vote, irrespective of tribe, race, religion, education, sex, property, or colour;

(2) To independence not later than 1963.

(b) Establish a United Nations Police Force:

(1) To facilitate the work of the Administrative Commission of African States;

(2) To protect the lives of all inhabitants of the country;

(3) To free all political detainees and imprisoned leaders and members of SWAPO and other groups;

(4) To disarm all South African military and paramilitary personnel and to arrange for their immediate repatriation to South Africa;

(5) To disarm all organized and individual civilian elements;

[1] Ibid., pp. 18–19.

(6) To assist in the restoration of peace and security; and

(7) To maintain law and order.

133. The organization asked that action for the implementation of these objectives commence immediately, and if necessary with the use of force as a last resort.

POSITION OF THE SOUTH WEST AFRICA NATIONAL UNION

134. SWANU took the position that there could never be peace in South West Africa until the "White settlers from the Republic of South Africa who are determined to die fighting against the United Nations or any other administration in South West Africa" had been removed from the Territory. If there was a way which could guarantee that their presence would not constitute a danger to the peace and security of South West Africa they would always be welcome. SWANU emphasized that the departure called for was insofar as the presence of those settlers in South West Africa constituted a danger to peace and security there. In further explanation of the position, the President of SWANU, Mr. Jariretundu Kozonguizi, informed the Committee that the term "settlers" did not include South West Africans, persons born in the Territory, who, in the opinion of his organization, had the same rights as all other South West Africans.

135. Regarding the future of South West Africa, Mr. Kozonguizi indicated that SWANU favoured independence immediately. He considered it impossible to fix the date for independence, however, because that depended on the progress being made to secure independence.

136. Concerning the system of government, Mr. Kozonguizi stated that none of the systems he had observed during his travels in other countries could in his view be applied in South West Africa. He had as yet not come across a system that would solve the special problems of South West Africa. In his view, the Territory had to have its own approach and its own system of government based on the special needs of South West Africa. Mr. Kozonguizi felt that, to that end, South West Africans could profitably consult with the United Nations, which brought together all ideologies, with a view to working out a system of government appropriate to the special needs of the Territory.

137. SWANU held that a clear distinction could be made between political control and administration. The people of South West Africa themselves had to be the ones to decide on the political and other arrangements for their country. In view of the low level of education and the consequent lack of people to carry out the administration, however, assistance would have to be obtained from the United Nations.

138. SWANU submitted the following arrangement for the first stage of self-determination for the people of South West Africa:

(a) Acceptance of the principle that political decisions should be taken by the people of South West Africa themselves.

(b) For this purpose, representatives from various regions of South

West Africa should be selected to participate in a constitutional convention, to be held under the auspices of the United Nations, which would provide advisers on problems of a technical nature.

139. The convention would decide on the following questions:

(1) Political arrangements in the country:

(a) Form of government and its constitution;

(b) Legislative Assembly representation.

(2) Administration:

The United Nations to man the administrative section of the Government, subject to the proviso that all South Africans who were supporters of the South African Government be excluded.

(3) Maintenance of peace and security in the territory:

That United Nations troops police the Territory with troops drawn from African-Asian and other uncommitted countries, the right being reserved to the people of South West Africa to determine which countries they consider uncommitted.

(4) Technical Assistance:

The principles of how the resources of the country could best be exploited; how the desired wealth could best reach all the people; and how the people themselves could best take part in the development of the country.

(5) United Nations and its specialized agencies:

The United Nations might appoint a Committee of African States to advise the Government and administration of the Territory.

On the basis of this investigation the Committee made the following recommendations: [m]

162. The Committee, after a careful appraisal of the extremely delicate and explosive situation in the Territory of South West Africa, came to the conclusion that, in view of the unfitness of the South African Government further to administer the Territory, the best interest of all concerned and of international peace and security demand as a matter of great urgency that the General Assembly should undertake a study of the ways and means by which to terminate South African administration over the Mandated Territory of South West Africa and to have that administration assumed directly or indirectly by the United Nations so as to ensure the institution of the rule of law and such democratic processes, reforms and programmes of assistance as will enable the Mandated Territory to assume the full responsibilities of sovereignty and independence within the shortest possible time. Such a study should contain all consequences of the termination of the South African administration, including all measures necessary to put into effect in the Territory the transfer of Government power to the indigenous people of the Territory who consitute a great majority of the population.

163. The Committee is convinced that, short of compulsive measures within the purview of the Charter, the problem of South West

[m] Ibid., p. 22.

Africa cannot be solved in present circumstances in a manner that will protect the lives of the indigenous inhabitants of the Territory and ensure the maintenance of international peace and security in Africa.

164. The Committee, in accordance with its findings and conclusions, makes the following recommendations:

(a) *With reference to paragraph 4* (a) *of General Assembly resolution 1568* (*XV*)—the conditions for restoring a climate of peace and security:

(1) Urgent consideration by the Security Council and all other organs, sub-organs or Member States of the United Nations of all such measures or courses of action as may be required to ensure the effective implementation of the recommendations made in this report or of any other decisions made by the United Nations on the question of South West Africa;

(2) The immediate institution of a United Nations presence in South West Africa;

(3) Removal of the present Administration from the Territory of South West Africa, with effective and simultaneous transfer of power to the United Nations or to the indigenous inhabitants of the Territory;

(4) United Nations assistance to the indigenous inhabitants, either through the Committee on South West Africa or through a United Nations Special Committee of Assistance to South West Africa;

(5) Training and organization of an indigenous police force by the United Nations, withdrawal of firearms from all Europeans and prohibition of the possession of arms by all civilians, withdrawal of South African military forces, abolition of all discriminatory laws and regulations, and cessation of all organized immigration of Europeans, especially South Africans, to the Mandated Territory.

(6) Attainment of independence by South West Africa through a Constitutional Convention, a popular referendum on the constitution adopted by the Convention, the election of representatives of the people on the basis of universal adult suffrage, the establishment of an independent Government—all with the assistance of the Committee on South West Africa or the suggested United Nations Special Committee of Assistance to South West Africa.

In November 1961 the South African Government condemned this report and offered to invite three past Presidents of the General Assembly to visit the territory to ascertain whether the situation constituted a threat to international peace.[n] The General Assembly, however, opposed this suggestion. Instead it dissolved the Committee on South West Africa [o] and established a Special Committee on South West Africa to prepare the territory for independence, which was now viewed as the desirable goal in lieu

---

[n] *GAOR*, Sixteenth Session, Fourth Committee, I, Nov. 2, 1961, pp. 381–82.
[o] Resolution 1704(XVI).

of a trusteeship agreement. Resolution 1702(XVI) is particularly important, as it illustrates the effect of the new decolonization movement upon United Nations policy towards South West Africa.

Resolution 1702(XVI):

The General Assembly,

Recalling its resolution 1514 (XV) of 14 December 1960 entitled "Declaration on the granting of independence to colonial countries and peoples", and its resolution 1654 (XVI) of 27 November 1961 establishing a Special Committee of seventeen members on the application of the Declaration,

Recalling its resolutions 1568 (XV) of 18 December 1960 and 1596 (XV) of 7 April 1961,

Noting with approval the special report of the Committee on South West Africa,

Bearing in mind the findings, conclusions and recommendations of the special report of the Committee on South West Africa on the measures to be taken to ensure the institution of the rule of law and such democratic processes, reforms and programmes of assistance as will enable the Mandated Territory of South West Africa to assume the full responsibilities of sovereignty and independence within the shortest possible time,

Noting with deep regret that the Government of the Republic of South Africa has prevented the Committee on South West Africa, with threats, from entering the Territory,

Noting with increased disquiet the progressive deterioration of the situation in South West Africa as a result of the ruthless intensification of the policy of *apartheid,* the deep emotional resentments of all African peoples, accompanied by the rapid expansion of South Africa's military forces, and the fact that Europeans, both soldiers and civilians, are being armed and militarily reinforced for the purpose of oppressing the indigenous people, all of which create an increasingly explosive situation which, if allowed to continue, will endanger international peace and security,

Considering that the Government of South Africa has persistently failed in its international obligations in administering the Territory of South West Africa on behalf of the international community,

Reaffirming that it is the right and duty of the United Nations to discharge fully its obligations towards the international Territory of South West Africa,

Convinced that the implementation of resolution 1514 (XV) and the discharge of the responsibility of the United Nations under the Charter towards the international community and the people of South West Africa require the taking of immediate steps by the United Nations,

1. *Solemnly proclaims* the inalienable right of the people of South West Africa to independence and national sovereignty;

2. *Decides* to establish a United Nations Special Committee for South West Africa, consisting of representatives of seven Member States nominated by the President of the General Assembly, whose task will be to achieve, in consultation with the Mandatory Power, the following objectives:

(*a*) A visit to the Territory of South West Africa before 1 May 1962;

(*b*) The evacuation from the Territory of all military forces of the Republic of South Africa;

(*c*) The release of all political prisoners without distinction as to party or race;

(*d*) The repeal of all laws or regulations confining the indigenous inhabitants in reserves and denying them all freedom of movement, expression and association, and of all other laws and regulations which establish and maintain the intolerable system of *apartheid;*

(*e*) Preparations for general elections to the Legislative Assembly, based on universal adult suffrage, to be held as soon as possible under the supervision and control of the United Nations;

(*f*) Advice and assistance to the Government resulting from the general elections, with a view to preparing the Territory for full independence;

(*g*) Co-ordination of the economic and social assistance with which the specialized agencies will provide the people in order to promote their moral and material welfare;

(*h*) The return to the Territory of indigenous inhabitants without risk of imprisonment, detention of punishment of any kind because of their political activities in or outside the Territory;

3. *Requests* the Special Committee to discharge the tasks which were assigned to the Committee on South West Africa by the General Assembly in sub-paragraphs (*a*), (*b*) and (*c*) of paragraph 12 of its resolution 749 A (VIII) of 28 November 1953;

4. *Urges* the Government of South Africa to cooperate fully with the Special Committee and with the United Nations in the execution of the provisions of the present resolution;

5. *Decides* to call the attention of the Security Council to the present resolution, in the light of paragraph 7 of resolution 1596 (XV) in which the General Assembly drew the attention of the Council to the situation in respect of South West Africa, which, if allowed to continue, would in the Assembly's view endanger international peace and security;

6. *Requests* all Member States:

(*a*) To do everything in their power to help the Special Committee to accomplish its task;

(*b*) To refrain, should the occasion arise, from any act likely to delay or prevent the application of the present resolution;

7. *Requests* the Special Committee to keep the Security Council, the Secretary-General and the Special Committee on the application of the Declaration on the granting of independence to colonial countries and

peoples informed of its activities and of any difficulties which it may encounter;

8. *Requests* the Special Committee to study any measures likely to facilitate the execution of the other recommendations of the Committee on South West Africa, and to report to the General Assembly at its seventeenth session;

9. *Decides* to maintain the question of South West Africa on its agenda as a question demanding urgent and constant attention;

10. *Invites* the Secretary-General to facilitate the application of the present resolution.

This new militancy of the United Nations received a setback in 1962 over the confusion caused by the "Carpio affair." Following the adoption of Resolution 1702(XVI), the South African Government invited the Chairman (Mr. Victorio D. Carpio of the Philippines) and the Vice-Chairman (Dr. Salvador Martinez de Alva of Mexico) of the new Special Committee to visit South West Africa. After a brief ten-day tour of the territory they issued a joint communique on 26 May 1962: [p]

1. Discussions between Ambassadors Carpio and Martinez de Alva and the Prime Minister and the Minister of Foreign Affairs were resumed in the same friendly and frank atmosphere that characterised the former meetings. Ambassador Carpio expressed the appreciation of the visitors for all the arrangements made and for the free and uninhibited opportunities given to the Vice-Chairman and himself to meet with all sections of the population of South West Africa desiring to contact them, and hoped that further visits could in the future be arranged.

2. In reply to a proposal that further visits by persons connected with the United Nations could usefully be arranged, particularly one by the whole Special Committee for South West Africa the Prime Minister stated that it would be best to await the issue of the report of the Chairman and Vice-Chairman and its reception by the Committee and the General Assembly before considering this matter further. He added, however, as was indicated in the invitation extended to the Chairman and Vice-Chairman, that South Africa could not be expected to receive a committee with instructions to act contrary to the juridical position of the Republic of South Africa.

3. At the request of the Prime Minister both the Chairman and the Vice-Chairman gave their impressions gained during their ten day visit to the Territory. They stated that in the places visited they had found no evidence and heard no allegations that there was a threat to inter-

[p] See further, *A Survey of Race Relations in South Africa*, 1962, pp. 233–36; *South Africa's Reply to the Secretary General of the United Nations* (Security Council Resolution 269 of 1969), published by the Department of Foreign Affairs (1969), pp. 39–44.

national peace and security within South West Africa; that there were signs of militarisation in the territory; or that the indigenous population was being exterminated.

4. While naturally a detailed investigation as to the question of the detention of political prisoners could not be made, the Chairman and Vice-Chairman noted that no case of detention of political prisoners had been brought to their attention during their visit. They have, however, received allegations that a few persons have been repatriated to Ovamboland or elsewhere because of political activities. The Prime Minister stated that he would have these allegations investigated.

5. The further discussions dealt with suggestions by both Ambassadors to improve relations between South Africa and the United Nations.

Three weeks later, however, Mr. Carpio repudiated this communique on the dubious grounds that he had not been a party to it. The Mexican Government then disowned the statement, too. The final report of Mr. Carpio and Dr. de Alva to the United Nations did not include the joint communique, which was dismissed as an unofficial act.[q] It concluded: [r]

(42) From what they saw and heard during their visit to the Mandated Territory and from their discussions and exchange of views with the authorities of South West Africa, the Chairman and Vice-Chairman of the Special Committee for South West Africa have arrived at the following conclusions:

(a) That the administration of the Mandated Territory by the South African Government has been and continues to be pervaded by the rigorous application of *apartheid* in all aspects of life of the African population, resulting not only in their being racially segregated and discriminated against and in their being deprived of all basic human rights and fundamental freedoms, but also in the complete subordination of their paramount interests to those of a small minority of Europeans.

(b) That the policies and methods, as well as the objectives, followed by the South African Government in its administration of the Mandated Territory has consistently been, and continues to be, in utter contradiction with the principles and purposes of the Mandate, the Charter of the United Nations, the Universal Declaration of Human Rights and the enlightened conscience of mankind.

(c) That the South African Government has revealed no plans to institute reforms or relent from its present policies and methods in its administration of the Territory and is not developing the Territory and its people for self-government or independence.

(d) That because of the foregoing, it is the overwhelming desire of

---

[q] Report of the Special Committee for South West Africa, *GAOR*, Seventeenth Session, Suppl. No. 12 (A/5212), p. 3.

[r] Ibid., p. 7.

the African population that the United Nations assume direct administration of the Territory and thus take all preparatory steps for the granting of freedom to the indigenous population as soon as possible.

(e) That short of the use of force or other compulsive measures within the purview of the Charter, there seems to be no way of implementing General Assembly resolution 1702 (XVI), nor even any hope of finding a solution to this question which would be acceptable to the South African Government other than virtual or outright annexation of the Mandated Territory.

(43) In these circumstances, the Special Committee for South West Africa may wish to draw the attention of the General Assembly to the imperative need for continued firm action on this question by giving the South African Government a short period of time within which to comply with the Assembly resolutions, or, failing that, by considering the feasibility of revoking the Mandate and of simultaneously assuming the administration of the Territory to prepare its people for independence, if need be by imposing sanctions or employing other means to enforce compliance with its decisions or resolutions.

Later that year the General Assembly dissolved the Special Committee for South West Africa [s] and transferred the question of South West Africa to the militant Special Committee on the Situation with regard to the Implementation of the Declaration on the Granting of Independence to Colonial Countries and Peoples (Special Committee of 24).[t] After receiving the first report of this Committee on South West Africa the General Assembly, in Resolution 1899(XVIII), urged

all states which have not yet done so to take, separately or collectively, the following measures with reference to the question of South West Africa:

(a) Refrain forthwith from supplying in any manner or form any arms or military equipment to South Africa;

(b) Refrain also from supplying in any manner or form any petroleum or petroleum products to South Africa;

(c) Refrain from any action which might hamper the implementation of the present resolution and of the previous General Assembly resolutions on South West Africa.

Later, in Resolution 1979(XVIII), the Assembly requested the Security Council to consider the critical situation prevailing in South West Africa.

3. South Africa Becomes a Republic

In 1961 South Africa became a Republic and withdrew from the Commonwealth of Nations. At the time it was suggested that the

[s] Resolution 1806(XVII).   [t] Resolution 1805(XVII).

effect of this act was to deprive South Africa of lawful title to South West Africa on the grounds that the Mandate had been conferred upon the South African Government as an agent of the British Government. This suggestion was discussed and dismissed by Dr. L. J. Blom-Cooper in the *Modern Law Review:* [u]

REPUBLIC AND MANDATE

Considerable credence has been given recently to the view, expressed initially by Mr. Dingle Foot, Q.C., M.P., in a letter to *The Times,*[1] that when South Africa becomes a Republic (within or without the Commonwealth), the Union Government will no longer be entitled in law to administer the Mandated Territory of South-West Africa. Mr. Foot's contentions were that the matter would at least be questionable on the attainment of the status of a Republic and beyond argument if republicanism is accompanied by non-membership of the Commonwealth.

The argument in favour of such a mode of termination of the Mandate rests on the form in which the mandate was granted by the League and accepted by the mandatory Power. Mr. Foot concluded his letter, and the point is endorsed by two subsequent leaders in *The Times,*[2] that it can never have been contemplated that the "duties imposed by the Mandate upon the British Crown should be carried out by a foreign power [which South Africa would automatically become]." The statement is founded upon the fact, if fact it be, that the mandate was granted to and accepted by the "British Crown" and has for practical purposes been administered by the Union Government on behalf of the Crown. Determination of that legal link would mean, so the argument runs, that by a reversion the mandate becomes vested in the Crown.

Reliance is placed—in fact it is the only passage cited by Mr. Foot —upon the second paragraph of the preamble to the mandate. It reads:

Whereas the Principal Allied and Associated Powers [3] agreed that, in accordance with Article 22, Part I (Covenant of the League of Nations) of the said Treaty, a mandate should be *conferred upon His Britannic Majesty to be exercised on his behalf by the Govern-*

---

[u] "Republic and Mandate" (1961) 24 *Mod LR* 256–60. See, too, Ellison Kahn, in *Annual Survey of South African Law*, 1960, p. 54.

[1] May 13, 1960.   [2] September 5 and 14, 1960.

[3] These were Britain, France, United States, Italy and Japan. Since the United States was not a member of the League only four of the Powers were party to the Treaty establishing the Mandate. Normally, the United States Government gave its informal approval to the selection of the mandatory power, but for some inexplicable reason this appears not to have been given in the case of South-West Africa: see pamphlet, "Mandate in Trust," published by Africa 1960 Committee, on September 5, 1960, price 1s. 6d.

ment of the Union of South Africa[4] to administer the Territory. . . .

It is suggested that this is manifestly a conferment of the mandate upon the British Crown. If there were no contrary indications, it might have to be argued contrariwise that only a state and not an individual could administer a mandated territory, a rubric for which the "British Crown" could not qualify. Article 22 of the Covenant refers specifically to "advanced nations" as "mandatories on behalf of the League" and in the case of South-West Africa the Union was selected, as the "advanced nation" which was geographically contiguous to the mandated territory. Moreover, "His Britannic Majesty," namely, King George V, was not himself a member of the League of Nations; the Union of South Africa was a founder member. And Article 22,[5] with its reference to "other members of the League," contemplates that the mandatories must be members of the League. This contention is reinforced by the provision of Article 7 of the Mandate which confers compulsory jurisdiction on the Permanent Court of International Justice in disputes between the "mandatory" and "another member of the League of Nations." It would seem therefore that far from the League's intention being to confer the mandate on the "British Crown" it sought to regulate the system of mandated territories among members only of the League of Nations.

That this is made clear cannot be doubted when the third paragraph of the preamble and Article 1 of the Mandate, to which Mr. Foot made no reference, is read. That part of the preamble states:

Whereas *His Britannic Majesty for an on behalf of the Government of the Union of South Africa*[6] has agreed to accept the Mandate. . . .

and Article 1 echoes this by stating,

the territory over which a Mandate is conferred *upon His Britannic Majesty for and on behalf of the Government of the Union of South Africa.*[6] . . .

There is admittedly a clash between the form of expression of the conferment of the Mandate in the second paragraph of the preamble and these two passages. Even if there were no other external considerations which tended to support either contention, the operative part would be the wording in the Treaty establishing the Mandate. But reliance need not only be placed on a construction of the international agreements. Judicial interpretation of these and identical treaties establishing mandates has been handed down in three Commonwealth countries.

In *R. v. Christian,*[7] the Appellate Division of the Supreme Court of South Africa was concerned with the question whether a citizen of

---

[4] My italics.
[5] See the concluding words of the fifth paragraph.

[6] My italics.
[7] [1924] A.D. 101.

South-West Africa owed allegiance to the Crown so as to make him liable for the charge of treason. In the course of the judgment de Villiers J.A. said [8] :

> . . . the Council of the League, on the 17th December 1920, issued a Mandate in reference to South-West Africa to the terms of which, it is stated in one of the recitals, the Mandatory agreed. The Mandate itself is not very happy in indicating who the mandatory of South-West Africa is. In the second recital it is said that the Principal Allied and Associated Powers agreed that a Mandate should be conferred 'on His Britannic Majesty to be exercised on his behalf by the Government of the Union of South Africa.' Whereas the third recital states that 'His Britannic Majesty for and on behalf of the Union of South Africa' has agreed to accept the Mandate; and according to Article 1 the Mandate was conferred upon 'His Britannic Majesty for and on behalf of the Government of the Union of South Africa.' The latter position is in my opinion the correct one.

The learned appeal judge then cites Article 22 of the Covenant and concludes that the Mandate was not conferred on the "British Empire" but upon the Union Government as an independent sovereign state and a member of the League.

Much the same view was taken by van den Heever J. in *R. v. Offen*,[9] a case in the High Court of South-West Africa. The judge stated [10] :

> The Mandate was conferred on the Union. . . . The language used in the instruments referred to may have been confusing because of the embarrassing situation in which members of the Commonwealth found themselves, but the intention is quite clear. The Covenant was an international document and the parties to it were 'states' or 'nations.'

The learned judge preferred to say that the mode of expression in the different recitals of the preamble made no difference, but that "for the purpose of the allocation of mandates the King acted as head of State of a separate member, the Union." And the learned judge added [11] :

> The signatories to the Covenant were a little concerned about the purely domestic question as to which organs within the Union would exercise the executive and which the legislative function over the Mandated Territory. All that is meant by these expressions is that the mandate is conferred on His Majesty's Government of the Union of South Africa; this is on South Africa as a separate member of the League.

The matter was further restated by Ostler J. in *Tagaloa* v. *Inspector of Police*,[12] a New Zealand case in the Court of Appeal dealing with the mandate of Samoa. The learned judge in this connection said [13] :

---

[8] *Ibid.* at p. 119.
[9] [1934] S.W.A. 73.
[10] *Ibid.*, at p. 84.
[11] *Ibid.*, at p. 85.
[12] [1927] N.Z.L.R. 883.
[13] *Ibid.*, at p. 901.

The mandate for Samoa was conferred by the Council of the League of Nations upon His Majesty the King for and on behalf of the Government of the Dominion of New Zealand. That means it was conferred directly on the Dominion and the Dominion is the sovereign power responsible to the League of Nations. . . . The authority is given by the League of Nations directly to the Dominion as a Member of the League.

And Sim A.C.J. in the earlier judgment of the court [14] said that "it was contended . . . that His Britannic Majesty, and not New Zealand was the mandatory. . . . But this, in our opinion is not so. The Government of the Dominion of New Zealand was intended to be the mandatory. That is clear, we think, from the terms of the Mandate. . . ."

A final judicial pronouncement which establishes the unanimity of the Commonwealth courts on this point comes from the judgment of Evatt J.[15] in *Ffrost* v. *Stevenson*,[16] a case in the High Court of Australia dealing with the mandated territory of New Guinea. That learned judge, with characteristic learning, stated [17]:

> The New Guinea Act correctly assigns the authority of the Commonwealth [18] over the territories to the action of the Principal Allied and Associated Powers in nominating it as mandatory and section 5 of the Act gives statutory authority to the Governor-General not to accept the Mandate from the hands of the King but to accept the Mandate so soon as it is issued to the Commonwealth from the Council of the League of Nations. In other words, the greatest care was taken by the Commonwealth advisers to protect the international status of the Commonwealth as such and to this end the King, acting through his Commonwealth Ministers, accepted the Mandate directly from those who in the eyes of international law had power to grant it. . . . All the documents show that whatever authority was obtained by the Commonwealth in relation to New Guinea was by original grant to itself (the Commonwealth being of course identified with the King in Right of the Commonwealth).

It is not without moment that all the Mandates were granted and accepted before the Resolutions of the Imperial Conferences of 1923, 1926 and 1930. By virtue of these internal Commonwealth declarations the exercise of the treaty-making power of any Dominion cannot now be regarded as a delegation from any central government; it is derived from their own status.[19] The formal recitals in the preamble to the Mandate were therefore merely expressed thus to conform with the procedure then adopted by Commonwealth countries. So far as the in-

[14] *Ibid.*, at p. 894.
[15] Evatt J., after resigning from his High Court judgeship to return to politics, became the Chief Justice of New South Wales last year.
[16] (1937) 58 C.L.R. 528.   [17] *Ibid.*, at pp. 587–588.
[18] References in this extract to "Commonwealth" are to the "Commonwealth of Australia."
[19] Oppenheim, *International Law*, Vol. I, Peace, 8th ed., p. 886.

ternational community was concerned, each dominion country was an independent sovereign state, alone capable of being a mandatory Power under the Covenant of the League of Nations. There could be no question of a divisible mandatory power.

South Africa's impending transition from a dominion of the Crown to a republic within the Commonwealth changes neither its international person nor its personal identity. All the international rights and obligations of the Union Government will remain unaffected. Equally, even if the Union ceases to be a member of the Commonwealth, no international legal change occurs, whatever the political repercussions.

4. *The Odendaal Commission Report* [v]

In 1964, while the legal proceedings at the Hague were still in progress, the South African Government published the controversial Odendaal Commission Report in which the feasibility of extending the Government's policy of separate development to South West Africa was thoroughly examined and finally recommended. This Report, which has formed the blueprint of subsequent constitutional developments in South West Africa, is described by Ellison Kahn [w]:

The Report of the Commission of Enquiry into South West African Affairs, 1962–1963, under the chairmanship of Mr. F. H. Odendaal, Administrator of the Transvaal, was tabled on 27th January, 1964. The document, published as R.P. 12 of 1964, extends to 557 foolscap pages, with 148 tables and 64 maps, plans and graphs. The Commission made detailed proposals for a change of the territory's constitution on the principle of self-determination and self-development of ethnic groups, with a far-reaching plan of economic development. It ruled out one central authority on a one-man-one-vote basis for the diverse population groups, holding that this would be a source of endless friction and clashes that would hamper if not halt the whole development of the territory.

If implemented its recommendation would mean the enlargement of non-White areas from about 26 to nearly 40 per cent of the territory, through accretions partly from adjoining White farms (White areas at

[v] Report of the Commission of Enquiry into South West African Affairs, 1962–63, RP 12/1964.
[w] 1964 *Annual Survey of South African Law*, pp. 41–43. For detailed discussion of this report, see Gordon Lawrie, "New Light on South West Africa" (1964) 23 *African Studies* 105; Philip Mason, "Separate Development and South West Africa" (1964) 5 *Race* 83; Anthony D'Amato, "The Bantustan Proposals for South-West Africa" (1966) 4 *Journal of Modern African Studies* 177–92, and "Apartheid in South West Africa: Five Claims of Equality" (1967) 1 *Portia Law Journal* 1; Mburumba Kerina, "South-West Africa, the United Nations, and the International Court of Justice" (1966–7) 2 *African Forum* 5 at 15–19.

present are 48 per cent of the territory) but mainly from Government land and game reserves.

The total population of 526,004 in 1960 was found to fall into twelve ethnic groups: Whites: 73,464; Coloureds: 12,708, treated separately from the Basters (11,257) despite similarities of language and culture and a common 'Caucasian strain'; Ovambos: 239,363; Hereros: 35,354, treated separately from the Kaokovelders (9,234) despite close relation in 'origin, language and culture'; Okavangos: 27,871; Damaras: 44,353; East Caprivians: 15,840; Tswanas: 9,992; Bushmen: 11,762; Namas: 34,806.

The creation of ten homelands for the non-White groups other than Coloureds is recommended. The government of the remainder of the territory would remain fundamentally as at present, but a 'large range of functions' would be transferred to the South African Government.

The proposed Rehoboth Gebiet of the Basters and Namaland of the Hottentots, both situate in the middle of the southern part of the territory, would be administered by the Department of Coloured Affairs, the other homelands (all situate in the north, except for tiny Tswana-land, on the mid-Eastern border) by the Department of Bantu Administration and Development. 'Diplomatic' links between the homelands and the Republican Government should be through one or perhaps two commissioners-general. (Professor J. P. van S. Bruwer, a member of the Commission, served as one for part of 1964.)

Forms of home rule, varying in details but not in principles, are proposed for Ovamboland, Okavangoland, Kaokoveld, Damaraland, Hereroland, East Caprivi and Namaland. Typical is the plan for Ovamboland. There would be a Legislative Council with limited powers, composed of a majority of *ex officio* chiefs and headmen and a minority of elected members. It would elect an Executive Council. The franchise would be granted to all Ovambos in South West Africa over 18 years of age. 'Citizenship' of Ovamboland, to be created by legislation, would be granted to all Ovambos.

The Tswanas, whose numbers are limited, would initially be placed under a 'community authority' consisting of a headman and two councillors.

The politically innocent Bushmen would be placed 'under the guidance and protection' of a Commissioner as 'there is no conceivable form of self-government' in which they could participate.

The Basters at Rehoboth would be granted a form of self-government 'in terms of a constitution arrived at through consultation between the Baster community and the Government of South Africa'.

The Coloureds would have no territorially distinct homeland, only a Coloured Council on the Republican model.

Where their numbers warranted it, the various non-White groups (Bantu, Coloureds, Basters and Namas) would have their own separate townships in White urban areas, with their own councils.

It has been calculated (see Gordon Lawrie in (1964) 23 *African Studies* 105 at 108) that the creation of the homelands, on 1960 population figures, would involve the movement of 130,000 non-Whites, amounting to nearly 29 per cent of the non-White population and 25 per cent of the total population. They would be mainly Hereros, Damaras, Namas and Bushmen.

The Commission recommended a five-year economic development plan involving an expenditure by the Republican Government of R156 million, followed by a second five-year plan involving such expenditure of some R91 million, during which stage surveys would be made for a suggested third five-year plan.

In a White Paper tabled on 29th April, the Government accepted the report in principle and stated that it would proceed to implement various of its recommendations for the economic and social advancement of the territory, involving an expenditure of at least R110 million over five years. But while it 'also endorses the view that it should be the aim, as far as practicable, to develop for each population group its own homeland, in which it can attain self-determination and self-realization', in view of the possibility that the International Court might be requested to interdict South Africa from proceeding with the constitutions of homelands as self-governing areas and with the reorganization of financial relations and administrative functions envisaged in the report while the case before it on South West Africa was proceeding, and because of the Government's deep respect for the *sub-judice* rule, it would not for the time being give effect to the recommendations on these matters. The Government would, however, advance funds for the purchase of the White-owned farms proposed to be added to the non-White homelands.

The response of the United Nations to the Odendaal Report was sudden and hostile. In 1964 it was condemned by the Special Committee of 24,[x] and in 1965 the General Assembly added its protests.[y] The South African Government announced that although it accepted the proposals in principle it would not implement them pending the decision of the International Court of Justice, as this might have led to a request for an interdict from the International Court to maintain the *status quo* until the Court had given its judgment.[z]

---

[x] *UN Monthly Chronicle,* June 1964, pp. 33 ff.   [y] Resolution 2074(XX).
[z] White Paper tabled on 29 April 1964.

8
Legal Proceedings, 1960–1966

FIRST PHASE: THE PRELIMINARY OBJECTIONS

1. The Nature of the Applications

In their joint application Ethiopia and Liberia made the following submissions to the International Court of Justice: [a]

Wherefore, may it please the Court, to adjudge and declare, whether the Government of the Union of South Africa is present or absent and after such time limitations as the Court may see fit to fix, that:

A. South West Africa is a territory under the Mandate conferred upon His Britannic Majesty by the Principal Allied and Associated Powers, to be exercised on his behalf by the Government of the Union of South Africa, accepted by His Britannic Majesty for and on behalf of the Government of the Union of South Africa, and confirmed by the Council of the League of Nations on December 17, 1920; and that the aforesaid Mandate is a treaty in force, within the meaning of Article 37 of the Statute of the International Court of Justice.

B. The Union of South Africa remains subject to the international obligations set forth in Article 22 of the Covenant of the League of Nations and in the Mandate for South West Africa, and that the General Assembly of the United Nations is legally qualified to exercise the supervisory functions previously exercised by the League of Nations with regard to the administration of the Territory; and that the Union is under an obligation to submit to the supervision and control of the General Assembly with regard to the exercise of the Mandate.

C. The Union of South Africa remains subject to the obligations to

[a] These submissions appear in the *South West Africa Cases, Preliminary Objections*, 1962 ICJ Reports 319 at 322, and *South West Africa, Second Phase*, 1966 ICJ Reports 6 at 10–12.

transmit to the United Nations petitions from the inhabitants of the Territory, as well as to submit an annual report to the satisfaction of the United Nations in accordance with Article 6 of the Mandate.

D. The Union has substantially modified the terms of the Mandate without the consent of the United Nations; that such modification is a violation of Article 7 of the Mandate and Article 22 of the Covenant; and that the consent of the United Nations is a necessary prerequisite and condition to attempts on the part of the Union directly or indirectly to modify the terms of the Mandate.

E. The Union has failed to promote to the utmost the material and moral well-being and social progress of the inhabitants of the Territory: its failure to do so is a violation of Article 2 of the Mandate and Article 22 of the Covenant; and that the Union has the duty forthwith to take all practicable action to fulfil its duties under such Articles.

F. The Union, in administering the Territory, has practised *apartheid,* i.e. has distinguished as to race, color, national or tribal origin in establishing the rights and duties of the inhabitants of the Territory; that such practice is in violation of Article 2 of the Mandate and Article 22 of the Covenant; and that the Union has the duty forthwith to cease the practice of *apartheid* in the Territory.

G. The Union, in administering the Territory, has adopted and applied legislation, regulations, proclamations, and administrative decrees which are by their terms and in their application, arbitrary, unreasonable, unjust and detrimental to human dignity; that the foregoing actions by the Union violate Article 2 of the Mandate and Article 22 of the Covenant; and that the Union has the duty forthwith to repeal and not to apply such legislation, regulations, proclamations, and administrative decrees.

H. The Union has adopted and applied legislation, administrative regulations, and official actions which suppress the rights and liberties of inhabitants of the Territory essential to their orderly evolution toward self-government, the right to which is implicit in the Covenant of the League of Nations, the terms of the Mandate, and currently accepted international standards, as embodied in the Charter of the United Nations and the Declaration of Human Rights; that the foregoing actions by the Union violate Article 2 of the Mandate and Article 22 of the Covenant; and that the Union has the duty forthwith to cease and desist from any action which thwarts the orderly development of self-government in the Territory.

I. The Union has exercised powers of administration and legislation over the Territory inconsistent with the international status of the Territory; that the foregoing action by the Union is in violation of Article 2 of the Mandate and Article 22 of the Covenant; that the Union has the duty to refrain from acts of administration and legislation which are inconsistent with the international status of the Territory.

J. The Union has failed to render to the General Assembly of the United Nations annual reports containing information with regard to the Territory and indicating the measures it has taken to carry out its obligations under the Mandate; that such failure is a violation of Article 6 of the Mandate; and that the Union has the duty forthwith to render such annual reports to the General Assembly.

K. The Union has failed to transmit to the General Assembly of the United Nations petitions from the Territory's inhabitants addressed to the General Assembly; that such failure is a violation of the League of Nations rules; and that the Union has the duty to transmit such petitions to the General Assembly.

The Applicant reserves the right to request the Court to declare and adjudge with respect to such other and further matters as the Applicant may deem appropriate to present to the Court.

May it also please the Court to adjudge and declare whatever else it may deem fit and proper in regard to this Application, and to make all necessary awards and orders, including an award of costs, to effectuate its determinations; . . .

2. The Preliminary Objections

The International Court has no compulsory jurisdiction over States: consent is the basis of the Court's jurisdiction. Ethiopia and Liberia contended that South Africa had consented to the jurisdiction of the Court in Article 7(2) of the Mandate for South West Africa and Article 37 of the Statute of the Court. The former provision states that the "mandatory agrees that, if any dispute whatever should arise between the mandatory and another member of the League of Nations relating to the interpretation or application of the provisions of the Mandate, such dispute, if it cannot be settled by negotiation, shall be submitted to the Permanent Court of International Justice." Article 37 of the Court's Statute reads:

Whenever a treaty or convention in force provides for reference of a matter to . . . the Permanent Court of International Justice, the matter shall, as between parties to the present Statute, be referred to the International Court of Justice.

At the outset South Africa raised several preliminary objections to the jurisdiction of the Court and to the *locus standi* of the applicant States. In terms of the Rules of Court [b] of the International Court of Justice this resulted in the suspension of the hearing on the merits of the case until the Court had given judgment on the preliminary objections. At the hearings of the Court on this phase of the proceedings South Africa made the following submissions: [c]

[b] Article 62(3).
[c] *South West Africa Cases, Preliminary Objections,* 1962 ICJ Reports 319 at 326–27.

For all or any one or more of the reasons set out in its written and oral statements, the Government of the Republic of South Africa submits that the Governments of Ethiopia and Liberia have no *locus standi* in these contentious proceedings, and that the Court has no jurisdiction to hear or adjudicate upon the questions of law and fact raised in the Applications and Memorials, more particularly because:

Firstly, by reason of the dissolution of the League of Nations, the Mandate for South West Africa is no longer a 'treaty or convention in force' within the meaning of Article 37 of the Statute of the Court, this submission being advanced
(a) with respect to the said Mandate Agreement as a whole, including Article 7 thereof, and
(b) in any event, with respect to Article 7 itself;
Secondly, neither the Government of Ethiopia nor the Government of Liberia is 'another Member of the League of Nations', as required for *locus standi* by Article 7 of the Mandate for South West Africa;
Thirdly, the conflict or disagreement alleged by the Governments of Ethiopia and Liberia to exist between them and the Government of the Republic of South Africa, is by reason of its nature and content not a 'dispute' as envisaged in Article 7 of the Mandate for South West Africa, more particularly in that no material interests of the Governments of Ethiopia and/or Liberia or of their nationals are involved therein or affected thereby;
Fourthly, the alleged conflict or disagreement is as regards its state of development not a 'dispute' which 'cannot be settled by negotiation' within the meaning of Article 7 of the Mandate for South West Africa.

3. The Composition of the Court

The International Court [d] consists of fifteen judges, elected by the General Assembly and Security Council, who in terms of the Court's Statute, represent "the main forms of civilization" and "the principal legal system of the world." [e] The Court may, however, sit with less than fifteen judges, as nine judges constitute a quorum. [f] In addition to the permanent judges each party to a dispute before the Court may appoint an *ad hoc* judge to represent its interests on the Court. [g] Where several parties have the same interest they are reckoned as one party for the appointment of *ad hoc* judges. [h]

The proceedings before the Court in 1962 on the preliminary

---

[d] For a comprehensive study of the constitution and operation of the International Court of Justice, see Shabtai Rosenne, *The Law and Practice of the International Court* (1965).
[e] Article 9.   [f] Article 25.   [g] Article 31.   [h] Article 31(5).

objections were heard by thirteen permanent judges and two *ad hoc* judges. The thirteen permanent judges were President Winiarski (Poland), Vice-President Alfaro (Panama), Judges Basdevant (France), Badawi (United Arab Republic), Moreno Quintana (Argentina), Wellington Koo (China), Spiropoulos (Greece), Sir Percy Spender (Australia), Sir Gerald Fitzmaurice (United Kingdom), Koretsky (Soviet Union), Bustamante y Rivero (Peru), Jessup (United States), and Morelli (Italy). The two *ad hoc* judges were Sir Louis Mbanefo of Nigeria, chosen by Ethiopia and Liberia, and Judge Van Wyk of South Africa, chosen by the South African Government.

4. The Judgment of the Court

On 21 December 1962 the Court held by eight votes to seven that it had jurisdiction to adjudicate upon the merits of the dispute. The majority consisted of Vice-President Alfaro, Judges Badawi, Moreno Quintana, Wellington Koo, Koretsky, Bustamante y Rivero, and Jessup, and Judge *ad hoc* Sir Louis Mbanefo.

In its judgment the Court held: [1]

To found the jurisdiction of the Court in the proceedings, the Applicants, having regard to Article 80, paragraph 1, of the Charter of the United Nations, relied on Article 7 of the Mandate of 17 December 1920 for South West Africa, and Article 37 of the Statute of the Court. In response to the Applications and Memorials of Ethiopia and Liberia, the Government of South Africa filed Preliminary Objections to the jurisdiction of the Court. It is these Objections which call for consideration in the present phase of the proceedings.

Before undertaking this task, however, the Court finds it necessary to decide a preliminary question relating to the existence of the dispute which is the subject of the Applications. The view has been advanced that if no dispute within the purview of Article 7 of the Mandate and Articles 36 and 37 of the Statute of the Court exists in fact, a conclusion of incompetence or *fin de non-recevoir* must follow.

It is to be noted that this preliminary question really centres on the point as to the existence of a dispute between the Applicants and the Respondent, irrespective of the nature and subject of the dispute laid before the Court in the present case. In the case of the *Mavrommatis Palestine Concessions* (P.C.I.J., Series A, No. 2, p. 11) the Permanent Court defines a dispute as "a disagreement on a point of law or fact, a conflict of legal views or interests between two persons". The said Judgment, in proceeding to examine the nature of the dispute, enunciates this definition, only after establishing that the conditions for the

[1] *South West Africa Cases, Preliminary Objections,* 1962 ICJ Reports 328–47.

existence of a dispute are fulfilled. In other words it is not sufficient for one party to a contentious case to assert that a dispute exists with the other party. A mere assertion is not sufficient to prove the existence of a dispute any more than a mere denial of the existence of the dispute proves its non-existence. Nor is it adequate to show that the interests of the two parties to such a case are in conflict. It must be shown that the claim of one party is positively opposed by the other. Tested by this criterion there can be no doubt about the existence of a dispute between the Parties before the Court, since it is clearly constituted by their opposing attitudes relating to the performance of the obligations of the Mandate by the Respondent as Mandatory.

. . . .

Inasmuch as the grounds on which the Preliminary Objections rely are generally connected with the interpretation of the Mandate Agreement for South West Africa, it is also necessary at the outset to give a brief account of the origin, nature and characteristics of the Mandates System established by the Covenant of the League of Nations.

Under Article 119 of the Treaty of Versailles of 28 June 1919, Germany renounced in favour of the Principal Allied and Associated Powers all her rights and titles over her overseas possessions. The said Powers, shortly before the signature of the Treaty of Peace, agreed to allocate them as Mandates to certain Allied States which had already occupied them. The terms of all the "C" Mandates were drafted by a Committee of the Supreme Council of the Peace Conference and approved by the representatives of the Principal Allied and Associated Powers in the autumn of 1919, with one reservation which was subsequently withdrawn. All these actions were taken before the Covenant took effect and before the League of Nations was established and started functioning in January 1920. The terms of each Mandate were subsequently defined and confirmed by the Council in conformity with Article 22 of the Covenant.

The essential principles of the Mandates System consist chiefly in the recognition of certain rights of the peoples of the underdeveloped territories; the establishment of a regime of tutelage for each of such peoples to be exercised by an advanced nation as a "Mandatory" "on behalf of the League of Nations"; and the recognition of "a sacred trust of civilisation" laid upon the League as an organized international community and upon its Member States. This system is dedicated to the avowed object of promoting the well-being and development of the peoples concerned and is fortified by setting up safeguards for the protection of their rights.

These features are inherent in the Mandates System as conceived by its authors and as entrusted to the respective organs of the League and the Member States for application. The rights of the Mandatory in relation to the mandated territory and the inhabitants have their foundation in the obligations of the Mandatory and they are, so to speak, mere tools given to enable it to fulfil its obligations. The fact is that each Mandate under the Mandates System constitutes a new international institution, the primary, overriding purpose of which is to pro-

mote "the well-being and development" of the people of the territory
under Mandate.

. . . .

As has already been pointed out, Ethiopia and Liberia indicated in
their Applications the provisions on which they founded the jurisdiction of the Court to hear and determine the dispute which they referred to it; to this the Republic of South Africa replied with a denial
of jurisdiction.

The issue of the jurisdiction of the Court was raised by the Respondent in the form of four Preliminary Objections. Its submissions at the
end of its written and oral statements are substantially the same, except that on the latter occasion the grounds on which the respective
objections are based were summarized under each Objection, and,
with reference to the submissions in the first Preliminary Objection,
the Respondent introduced a modification on 22 October 1962, as a
consequence of its replies to questions put to the Parties by Members
of the Court. The Court will deal first with this modification.

The amended text of the First Objection reads:

> Firstly, the Mandate for South West Africa *has never been, or at any
> rate* is since the dissolution of the League of Nations no longer, a
> 'treaty or convention in force' within the meaning of Article 37 of
> the Statute of the Court, this Submission being advanced
>
> (a) with respect to the Mandate as a whole, including Article 7
> thereof; and
>
> (b) in any event, with respect to Article 7 itself.

The amendment consists in the addition of the italicized words.
Counsel for the Respondent made a statement as a preface to his
amendment of 22 October 1962. From this statement it appears that
originally the Respondent had always considered or assumed that the
Mandate for South West Africa had been a "treaty or convention in itself, that is, an international agreement between the Mandatory on the
one hand, and, on the other, the Council representing the League
and/or its Members"; and that it had stated several times "that that
proposition could be taken to be common cause as related to the period of the lifetime of the League"; but "that the alternative view
might well be taken that in defining the terms of the Mandate, the
Council was taking executive action in pursuance of the Covenant
(which of course was a convention) and was not entering into an
agreement which would itself be a treaty or convention". At the same
time, the statement added: "This view, we put it no higher than a
view that might be taken, would regard the Council's Declaration as
setting forth a resolution of the Council, which would, like any other
valid resolution of the Council, owe its legal force to the fact of having
been duly resolved by the Council in the exercise of powers conferred
upon it by the Covenant."

In the Court's opinion, this modified view is not well-founded for
the following reasons. For its confirmation, the Mandate for South
West Africa took the form of a resolution of the Council of the League

but obviously it was of a different character. It cannot be correctly regarded as embodying only an executive action in pursuance of the Covenant. The Mandate, in fact and in law, is an international agreement having the character of a treaty or convention. The Preamble of the Mandate itself shows this character. The agreement referred to therein was effected by a decision of the Principal Allied and Associated Powers including Great Britain taken on 7 May 1919 to confer a Mandate for the Territory on His Britannic Majesty and by the confirmation of its acceptance on 9 May 1919 by the Union of South Africa. The second and third paragraphs of the Preamble record these facts. It is further stated therein that "His Britannic Majesty, for and on behalf of the Government of the Union of South Africa . . . has undertaken to exercise it on behalf of the League of Nations in accordance with the following provisions". These "provisions" were formulated "in the following terms".

The draft Mandate containing the explicit terms was presented to the Council of the League in December 1920 and, with a few changes, was confirmed on 17 December 1920. The fourth and final paragraph of the Preamble recites the provisions of Article 22, paragraph 8, of the Covenant, and then "confirming the said Mandate, defines its terms as follows: . . .".

Thus it can be seen from what has been stated above that this Mandate, like practically all other similar Mandates, is a special type of instrument composite in nature and instituting a novel international regime. It incorporates a definite agreement consisting in the conferment and acceptance of a Mandate for South West Africa, a provisional or tentative agreement on the terms of this Mandate between the Principal Allied and Associated Powers to be proposed to the Council of the League of Nations and a formal confirmation agreement on the terms therein explicitly defined by the Council and agreed to between the Mandatory and the Council representing the League and its Members. It is an instrument having the character of a treaty or convention and embodying international engagements for the Mandatory as defined by the Council and accepted by the Mandatory.

The fact that the Mandate is described in its last paragraph as a Declaration [exemplaire in the French text] is of no legal significance. The Mandates confirmed by the Council of the League of Nations in the course of 1922 are all called instruments [actes in the French text], such as the French Mandate for Togoland, the British Mandate for the Cameroons, the Belgian Mandate for East Africa (Ruanda-Urundi), etc. Terminology is not a determinant factor as to the character of an international agreement or undertaking. In the practice of States and of international organizations and in the jurisprudence of international courts, there exists a great variety of usage; there are many different types of acts to which the character of treaty stipulations has been attached.

Moreover, the fact that the Mandate confirmed by the Council of the League embodies a provision that it "shall be deposited in the archives of the League of Nations" and that "certified copies shall be forwarded by the Secretary-General of the League of Nations to all Powers Signatories of the Treaty of Peace with Germany", clearly implies that it was intended and understood to be an international treaty or convention embodying international engagements of general interest to the Signatory Powers of the German Peace Treaty.

It has been argued that the Mandate in question was not registered in accordance with Article 18 of the Covenant which provided: "No such treaty or international engagement shall be binding until so registered." If the Mandate was *ab initio* null and void on the ground of non-registration it would follow that the Respondent has not and has never had a legal title for its administration of the territory of South West Africa; it would therefore be impossible for it to maintain that it has had such a title up to the discovery of this ground of nullity. The fact is that Article 18 provided for registration of "Every treaty or international engagement entered into *hereafter* by any Member of the League" and the word "hereafter" meant after 10 January 1920 when the Covenant took effect, whereas the Mandate for South West Africa, as stated in the preamble of the instrument, had actually been conferred on and accepted by the Union of South Africa more than seven months earlier on 7–9 May 1919; and its terms had been provisionally agreed upon between the Principal Allied and Associated Powers and the Mandatory, in August 1919. Moreover, Article 18, designed to secure publicity and avoid secret treaties, could not apply in the same way in respect of treaties to which the League of Nations itself was one of the Parties as in respect of treaties concluded among individual Member States. The Mandate for South West Africa, like all the other Mandates, is an international instrument of an institutional character, to which the League of Nations, represented by the Council, was itself a Party. It is the implementation of an institution in which all the Member States are interested as such. The procedure to give the necessary publicity to the Mandates including the one under consideration was applied in view of their special character, and in any event they were published in the *Official Journal* of the League of Nations.

. . . .

Since the Mandate in question had the character of a treaty or convention at its start, the next relevant question to consider is whether this treaty or convention, with respect to the Mandate as a whole including Article 7 thereof, or with respect to Article 7 itself, is still in force. The Respondent contends that it is not in force, and this contention constitutes the essence of the First Preliminary Objection. It is argued that the rights and obligations under the Mandate in relation to the administration of the territory of South West Africa being of an objective character still exist, while those rights and obligations relating to administrative supervision by the League and submission to the Permanent Court of International Justice, being of a contractual character, have necessarily become extinct on the dissolution of the League of Nations which involved as a consequence the ending of membership of the League, leaving only one party to the contract and resulting in the total extinction of the contractual relationship.

The Respondent further argues that the casualties arising from the demise of the League of Nations are not therefore confined to the provisions relating to supervision by the League over the Mandate but include Article 7 by which the Respondent agreed to submit to the jurisdiction of the Permanent Court of International Justice in any dispute whatever between it as Mandatory and another Member of the League of Nations relating to the interpretation or the application of the provisions of the Mandate. If the object of Article 7 of the Mandate is the submission to the Court of disputes relating to the interpretation or the application of the Mandate, it naturally follows that no Application based on Article 7 could be accepted unless the said Mandate, of which Article 7 is a part, is in force. This proposition, moreover, constitutes the very basis of the Applications to the Court.

Similar contentions were advanced by the Respondent in 1950, and the Court in its Advisory Opinion ruled:

> The authority which the Union Government exercises over the Territory is based on the Mandate. If the Mandate lapsed, as the Union Government contends, the latter's authority would equally have lapsed. To retain the rights derived from the Mandate and to deny the obligations thereunder could not be justified. (*I.C.J. Reports 1950,* page 133.)

After observing that the international obligations assumed by the Union of South Africa were of two kinds, those "directly related to the administration of the Territory" and corresponding "to the sacred trust of civilization referred to in Article 22 of the Covenant" and those "related to the machinery for implementation" and "closely linked to the supervision and control of the League", corresponding to the "'securities for the performance of this trust' referred to in the same article", the Court went on to say with reference to the second group of obligations:

> The obligation incumbent upon a mandatory State to accept international supervision and to submit reports is an important part of the Mandates System. When the authors of the Covenant created this system, they considered that the effective performance of the sacred trust of civilization by the mandatory Powers required that the administration of mandated territories should be subject to international supervision . . . It cannot be admitted that the obligation to submit to supervision has disappeared merely because the supervisory organ has ceased to exist . . . (*Ibid.,* page 136.)

The findings of the Court on the obligation of the Union Government to submit to international supervision are thus crystal clear. Indeed, to exclude the obligations connected with the Mandate would be to exclude the very essence of the Mandate.

That the League of Nations in ending its own existence did not terminate the Mandates but that it definitely intended to continue them by its resolution of 18 April 1946 will be seen later when the Court

states its views as to the true effect of the League's final act of dissolution on the Mandates.

What is relevant to the issue under consideration is the finding of
the Court in the same Advisory Opinion on the effect of the dissolution of the League of Nations on Article 7 of the Mandate. After recalling the provisions of this Article, the Court stated:

> Having regard to Article 37 of the Statute of the International
> Court of Justice, and Article 80, paragraph 1, of the Charter, the
> Court is of opinion that this clause in the Mandate is still in force
> and that, therefore, the Union of South Africa is under an obliga-
> tion to accept the compulsory jurisdiction of the Court according to
> those provisions. (*Ibid.*, page 138.)

It is also to be recalled that while the Court was divided on the
other points involved in the questions put to it for an Advisory Opinion, it was unanimous on the finding that Article 7 of the Mandate relating to the obligation of the Union of South Africa to submit to the
compulsory jurisdiction of this Court is still "in force".

The unanimous holding of the Court in 1950 on the survival and
continuing effect of Article 7 of the Mandate, continues to reflect the
Court's opinion today. Nothing has since occurred which would warrant the Court reconsidering it. All important facts were stated or referred to in the proceedings before the Court in 1950.

The Court finds that, though the League of Nations and the Permanent Court of International Justice have both ceased to exist, the
obligation of the Respondent to submit to the compulsory jurisdiction
of that Court was effectively transferred to this Court before the dissolution of the League of Nations. By its own resolution of 18 April
1946 the League ceased to exist from the following day, i.e. 19 April
1946. The Charter of the United Nations, in accordance with Article
110 thereof, entered into force on 24 October 1945. South Africa,
Ethiopia and Liberia, the three Parties to the present proceedings, deposited their ratifications respectively on 7 November 1945, 2 November 1945 and 13 November 1945, and in accordance with paragraph 4
of the said Article 110 all became original Members of the United Nations from the respective dates. They have since been subjected to the
obligations, and entitled to the rights, under the Charter. One of these
obligations is embodied in Article 37 of the Statute of this Court,
which by Article 92 of the Charter "forms an integral part of the present Charter", and by Article 93 thereof "All Members of the United
Nations are *ipso facto* parties to the Statute of the International Court
of Justice". By the effect of these provisions the Respondent has bound
itself since 7 November 1945, when the League of Nations and the Permanent Court were still in existence and when therefore Article 7 of
the Mandate was also in full force, to accept the compulsory jurisdiction of this Court in lieu of that of the Permanent Court, to which it
had originally agreed to submit under Article 7 of the Mandate.

This transferred obligation was voluntarily assumed by the Respondent when joining the United Nations. There could be no question of

lack of consent on the part of the Respondent as regards this transfer to this Court of the Respondent's obligation under Article 7 of the Mandate to submit to the compulsory jurisdiction of the Permanent Court. The validity of Article 7, in the Court's view, was not affected by the dissolution of the League, just as the Mandate as a whole is still in force for the reasons stated above.

. . . .

The Second Objection of the Respondent consists mainly of an argument which has been advanced in support of the First Objection. It centres on the term "another Member of the League of Nations" in Article 7, of which paragraph 2 reads:

> The Mandatory agrees that, if any dispute whatever should arise between the Mandatory and another Member of the League of Nations relating to the interpretation or the application of the provisions of the Mandate, such dispute, if it cannot be settled by negotiation, shall be submitted to the Permanent Court of International Justice provided for by Article 14 of the Covenant of the League of Nations.

It is contended that since all Member States of the League necessarily lost their membership and its accompanying rights when the League itself ceased to exist on 19 April 1946, there could no longer be "another Member of the League of Nations" today. According to this contention, even assuming that Article 7 of the Mandate is still in force as a treaty or convention within the meaning of Article 37 of the Statute, no State has "locus standi" or is qualified to invoke the jurisdiction of this Court in any dispute with the Respondent as Mandatory.

This contention is claimed to be based upon the natural and ordinary meaning of the words employed in the provision. But this rule of interpretation is not an absolute one. Where such a method of interpretation results in a meaning incompatible with the spirit, purpose and context of the clause or instrument in which the words are contained, no reliance can be validly placed on it.

In the first place, judicial protection of the sacred trust in each Mandate was an essential feature of the Mandates System. The essence of this system, as conceived by its authors and embodied in Article 22 of the Covenant of the League of Nations, consisted, as stated earlier, of two features: a Mandate conferred upon a Power as "a sacred trust of civilisation" and the "securities for the performance of this trust". While the faithful discharge of the trust was assigned to the Mandatory Power alone, the duty and the right of ensuring the performance of this trust were given to the League with its Council, the Assembly, the Permanent Mandates Commission and all its Members within the limits of their respective authority, power and functions, as constituting administrative supervision, and the Permanent Court was to adjudicate and determine any dispute within the meaning of Article 7 of the Mandate. The administrative supervision by the League constituted a normal security to ensure full performance by the Mandatory of the "sacred trust" toward the inhabitants of the mandated territory, but the specially assigned role of the Court was even more essential, since it was to serve as the final bulwark of protection by recourse to the Court against possible abuse or breaches of the Mandate.

The *raison d'être* of this essential provision in the Mandate is obvious. Without this additional security the supervision by the League and its Members could not be effective in the last resort. For example, under Article 6 of the Mandate for South West Africa:

> The Mandatory shall make to the Council of the League of Nations an annual report to the satisfaction of the Council, containing full information with regard to the territory, and indicating the measures taken to carry out the obligations assumed under Articles 2, 3, 4 and 5.

In actual operation the Council when satisfied with the report on the recommendation of the Permanent Mandates Commission would approve the report. If some Member of the Council had doubts on some point or points in the report, explanations would be asked from the representative of the Mandatory present. If the explanations were considered satisfactory, approval of the annual report would follow. In either case the approval meant the unanimous agreement of all the representatives including that of the Mandatory who, under Article 4, paragraph 5, of the Covenant, was entitled to send a representative to such a meeting to take part in the discussion and to vote. But if some measure proposed to the Mandatory on the recommendation of the Permanent Mandates Commission in the interest of the inhabitants of the mandated territory and within the terms of the Mandate and of Article 22 of the Covenant should be opposed by the Mandatory, it could not be adopted by the Council. Or if the Mandatory should adopt some measure in connection with its administration of the Territory notwithstanding the objection of the Permanent Mandates Commission and the Council that it was a violation of the Mandate, and should persist in carrying it out, a conflict would occur. This possibility is not a mere conjecture or hypothesis. As a matter of fact, the Respondent had more than once intimated its desire to incorporate South West Africa into the Union and the Permanent Mandates Commission of the League each time objected to it as being contrary to the Mandate; and the same idea of the Mandatory Power was also conveyed to the United Nations in 1946. If it should have attempted in the days of the League to carry out the idea contrary to paragraph 1 of Article 7, an important dispute would arise between it and the Council of the League.

Under the unanimity rule (Articles 4 and 5 of the Covenant), the Council could not impose its own view on the Mandatory. It could of course ask for an advisory opinion of the Permanent Court but that opinion would not have binding force, and the Mandatory could continue to turn a deaf ear to the Council's admonitions. In such an event the only course left to defend the interests of the inhabitants in order to protect the sacred trust would be to obtain an adjudication by the

Court on the matter connected with the interpretation or the application of the provisions of the Mandate. But neither the Council nor the League was entitled to appear before the Court. The only effective recourse for protection of the sacred trust would be for a Member or Members of the League to invoke Article 7 and bring the dispute as also one between them and the Mandatory to the Permanent Court for adjudication. It was for this all-important purpose that the provision was couched in broad terms embracing "any dispute whatever . . . between the Mandatory and another Member of the League of Nations relating to the interpretation or the application of the provisions of the Mandate . . . if it cannot be settled by negotiation". It is thus seen what an essential part Article 7 was intended to play as one of the securities in the Mandates System for the observance of the obligations by the Mandatory.

In the second place, besides the essentiality of judicial protection for the sacred trust and for the rights of Member States under the Mandates, and the lack of capacity on the part of the League or the Council to invoke such protection, the right to implead the Mandatory Power before the Permanent Court was specially and expressly conferred on the Members of the League, evidently also because it was the most reliable procedure of ensuring protection by the Court, whatever might happen to or arise from the machinery of administrative supervision.

The third reason for concluding that Article 7 with particular reference to the term "another Member of the League of Nations" continues to be applicable is that obviously an agreement was reached among all the Members of the League at the Assembly session in April 1946 to continue the different Mandates as far as it was practically feasible or operable with reference to the obligations of the Mandatory Powers and therefore to maintain the rights of the Members of the League, notwithstanding the dissolution of the League itself. This agreement is evidenced not only by the contents of the dissolution resolution of 18 April 1946 but also by the discussions relating to the question of Mandates in the First Committee of the Assembly and the whole set of surrounding circumstances which preceded, and prevailed at, the session. Moreover, the Court sees no valid ground for departing from the conclusion reached in the Advisory Opinion of 1950 to the effect that the dissolution of the League of Nations has not rendered inoperable Article 7 of the Mandate. Those States who were Members of the League at the time of its dissolution continue to have the right to invoke the compulsory jurisdiction of the Court, as they had the right to do before the dissolution of the League. That right continues to exist for as long as the Respondent holds on to the right to administer the territory under the Mandate.

The Assembly of the League of Nations met in April 1946 specially to arrange for the dissolution of the League. Long before the session important events had taken place which bore a direct influence on its course of action at the indicated session. The Charter of the United Nations with its Chapter XI on non-self-governing territories and

Chapters XII and XIII on the new trusteeship system embodying principles corresponding to those in Article 22 of the Covenant on Mandates and the Mandates System entered into force in October 1945 and the United Nations began to operate in January 1946, and the General Assembly held its first session in the following February. When the Assembly of the League actually met subsequently in April of the same year, it had full knowledge of these events. Therefore before it finally passed the dissolution resolution, it took special steps to provide for the continuation of the Mandates and the Mandate System "until other arrangements have been agreed between the United Nations and the respective mandatory Powers". It was fully realized by all the representatives attending the Assembly session that the operation of the Mandates during the transitional period was bound to be handicapped by legal technicalities and formalities. Accordingly they took special steps to meet them. For example, these special circumstances show that the assembled representatives did not attach importance to the letter of the constitutional procedure. Under the Covenant the role of the Council in the Mandates System was preponderant. But the Council held no meeting to deal with the question of what should be done with the Mandates after the League's dissolution. Instead the Assembly by a resolution of 12 April 1946 attributed to itself the responsibilities of the Council. The resolution reads:

The Assembly, with the concurrence of all the Members of the Council which are represented at its present session: Decides that, so far as required, it will, during the present session, assume the functions falling within the competence of the Council.

On the basis of this resolution, the Assembly also approved the end of the Mandates for Syria, Lebanon and Trans-Jordan.

To provide for the situation certain to arise from the act of dissolution, and to continue the Mandates on the basis of a sacred trust, prolonged discussions were held both in the Assembly and in its First Committee to find ways and means of meeting the difficulties and making up for the imperfections as far as was practicable. It was in these circumstances that all the Mandatory Powers made declarations of their intentions relating to their respective Mandates. Each of the delegates of the Mandatory Powers present solemnly expressed their intention to continue to administer in each case the Territory: for the United Kingdom, "in accordance with the general principles of the existing mandates"; for France, "to pursue the execution of the mission entrusted to it by the League of Nations"; for New Zealand, "in accordance with the terms of the Mandate"; for Belgium, to "remain fully alive to all the obligations devolving on members of the United Nations under Article 80 of the Charter"; for Australia, "in accordance with the provision of the Mandates, for the protection and advancement of the inhabitants". The statement by the delegate of South Africa, at the second plenary meeting of the Assembly on 9 April 1946 is particularly clear. After announcing that

. . . it is the intention of the Union Government, at the forthcoming session of the United Nations General Assembly in New York, to formulate its case for according South West Africa a status under which it would be internationally recognized as an integral part of the Union,

he continues:

In the meantime, the Union will continue to administer the territory scrupulously in accordance with the obligations of the Mandate, for the advancement and promotion of the interests of the inhabitants, as she has done during the past six years when meetings of the Mandates Commission could not be held.

The disappearance of those organs of the League concerned with the supervision of mandates, primarily the Mandates Commission and the League Council, will necessarily preclude complete compliance with the letter of the Mandate. The Union Government will nevertheless regard the dissolution of the League as in no way diminishing its obligations under the Mandate, which it will continue to discharge with the full and proper appreciation of its responsibilities until such time as other arrangements are agreed upon concerning the future status of the territory.

There could be no clearer recognition on the part of the Government of South Africa of the continuance of its obligations under the Mandate for South West Africa, including Article 7, after the dissolution of the League of Nations.

It was on the basis of the declarations of the Mandatory Powers as well as on the views expressed by the other Members that the League Assembly unanimously adopted its final resolution of 18 April 1946, the last two paragraphs of which read:

3. Recognizes that, on the termination of the League's existence, its functions with respect to the mandated territories will come to an end, but notes that Chapters XI, XII and XIII of the Charter of the United Nations embody principles corresponding to those declared in Article 22 of the Covenant of the League;

4. Takes note of the expressed intentions of the Members of the League now administering territories under mandate to continue to administer them for the well-being and development of the peoples concerned in accordance with the obligations contained in the respective Mandates, until other arrangements have been agreed between the United Nations and the respective mandatory Powers.

The Chinese delegate, in introducing the resolution in the Assembly relating to the possible effect of the League's dissolution on the problem of the Mandates from which the two passages are taken, stated:

It was gratifying to the Chinese delegation, as representing a country which had always stood for the principle of trusteeship, that all the Mandatory Powers had announced their intention to administer the territories under their control in accordance with their obligations under the mandates system until other arrangements were agreed upon.

The French delegate in supporting the resolution said that he wished:

to stress once more the fact that all territories under the mandate of his Government would continue to be administered in the spirit of the Covenant and of the Charter.

Professor Bailey of Australia, Rapporteur, speaking as delegate of his country, welcomed:

the initiative of the Chinese delegation in moving the resolution, which he supported. The Australian delegation had made its position clear in the Assembly—namely, that Australia did not regard the dissolution of the League as weakening the obligations of countries administering mandates. They regarded the obligation as still in force and would continue to administer their mandated territories in accordance with the provisions of the mandates for the well-being of the inhabitants.

The delegate of the United Kingdom made it even clearer that there was agreement by all the Mandatory Powers when he "formally seconded the resolution on behalf of his Government":

It had been settled in consultation and agreement by all countries interested in mandates and he thought it could therefore be passed without discussion and with complete unanimity.

It is clear from the foregoing account that there was a unanimous agreement among all the Member States present at the Assembly meeting that the Mandates should be continued to be exercised in accordance with the obligations therein defined although the dissolution of the League, in the words of the representative of South Africa at the meeting, "will necessarily preclude complete compliance with the letter of the Mandate", i.e. notwithstanding the fact that some organs of the League like the Council and the Permanent Mandates Commission would be missing. In other words the common understanding of the Member States in the Assembly—including the Mandatory Powers—in passing the said resolution, was to continue the Mandates, however imperfect the whole system would be after the League's dissolution, and as much as it would be operable, until other arrangements were agreed upon by the Mandatory Powers with the United Nations concerning their respective Mandates. Manifestly, this continuance of obligations under the Mandate could not begin to operate until the day after the dissolution of the League of Nations and hence the literal objections derived from the words "another Member of the League of Nations" are not meaningful, since the resolution of 18 April 1946 was adopted precisely with a view to averting them and continuing the Mandate as a treaty between the Mandatory and the Members of the League of Nations.

In conclusion, any interpretation of Article 7 or more particularly the term therein "another Member of the League of Nations" must take into consideration all of the relevant facts and circumstances relating to the act of dissolution of the League, in order to ascertain the true intent and purpose of the Members of the Assembly in adopting the final resolution of 18 April 1946.

In further support of the finding of an agreement at the time of the dissolution of the League to maintain the *status quo* as far as possible in regard to the Mandates pending other arrangements agreed between the United Nations and the respective Mandatory Powers, it should be stated that the interval was expected to be of short duration and that in due course the different Mandates would be converted by mutual agreement into trusteeship agreements under the Charter of the United Nations. This expectation has been realized and the only exception is the Respondent's Mandate for South West Africa. In the light of this fact the finding of an agreement appears all the more justified.

To deny the existence of the agreement it has been said that Article 7 was not an essential provision of the Mandate instrument for the protection of the sacred trust of civilization. If therefore Article 7 were not an essential tool in the sense indicated, the claim of jurisdiction would fall to the ground. In support of this argument attention has been called to the fact that three of the four "C" Mandates, when brought under the trusteeship provisions of the Charter of the United Nations, did not contain in the respective Trusteeship Agreements any comparable clause and that these three were the Trusteeship Agreements for the territories previously held under Mandate by Japan, Australia and New Zealand. The point is drawn that what was essential the moment before was no longer essential the moment after, and yet the principles under the Mandates system corresponded to those under the Trusteeship system. This argument apparently overlooks one important difference in the structure and working of the two systems and loses its whole point when it is noted that under Article 18 of the Charter of the United Nations, "Decisions of the General Assembly on important questions shall be made by a two-thirds majority of the members present and voting", whereas the unanimity rule prevailed in the Council and the Assembly of the League of Nations under the Covenant. Thus legally valid decisions can be taken by the General Assembly of the United Nations and the Trusteeship Council under Chapter XIII of the Charter without the concurrence of the trustee State, and the necessity for invoking the Permanent Court for judicial protection which prevailed under the Mandates system is dispensed with under the Charter.

For the reasons stated, the First and Second Objections must be dismissed.

. . . .

The Third Preliminary Objection consists essentially of the proposition that the dispute brought before the Court by the Applicants is not a dispute as envisaged in Article 7 of the Mandate—more particu-

larly in that the said conflict or disagreement does not affect any material interests of the Applicant States or their nationals.

In support of this proposition, the Respondent contends that the
word "dispute" must be given its generally accepted meaning in a context of a compulsory jurisdiction clause and that, when so interpreted,
it means a disagreement or conflict between the Mandatory and another Member of the League concerning the legal rights and interests
of such other Member in the matter before the Court; that "the obligations imposed for the benefit of the inhabitants would have been
owed to the League on whose behalf the Mandatory undertook to exercise the Mandate" and that "League Members would then, by virtue
of their membership, be entitled to participate in the League's supervision of the Mandate, but would individually, *vis-à-vis* the Mandatory,
have no legal right or interest in the observance by the Mandatory of
its duties to the inhabitants".

The question which calls for the Court's consideration is whether
the dispute is a "dispute" as envisaged in Article 7 of the Mandate and
within the meaning of Article 36 of the Statute of the Court.

The Respondent's contention runs counter to the natural and ordinary meaning of the provisions of Article 7 of the Mandate, which
mentions "any dispute whatever" arising between the Mandatory and
another Member of the League of Nations "relating to the interpretation or the application of the provisions of the Mandate". The language used is broad, clear and precise: it gives rise to no ambiguity
and it permits of no exception. It refers to any dispute whatever relating not to any one particular provision or provisions, but to "the provisions" of the Mandate, obviously meaning all or any provisions,
whether they relate to substantive obligations of the Mandatory toward the inhabitants of the Territory or toward the other Members of
the League or to its obligation to submit to supervision by the League
under Article 6 or to protection under Article 7 itself. For the manifest
scope and purport of the provisions of this Article indicate that the
Members of the League were understood to have a legal right or interest in the observance by the Mandatory of its obligations both toward
the inhabitants of the Mandated Territory, and toward the League of
Nations and its Members.

Nor can it be said, as argued by the Respondent, that any broad interpretation of the compulsory jurisdiction in question would be incompatible with Article 22 of the Covenant on which all Mandates are
based, especially relating to the provisions of Article 7, because Article
22 did not provide for the Mandatory's submission to the Permanent
Court in regard to its observance of the Mandate. But Article 7, paragraph 2, is clearly in the nature of implementing one of the "securities
for the performance of this trust", mentioned in Article 22, paragraph
1. It was embodied in the draft agreement among the Principal Allied
and Associated Powers and proposed to the Council of the League by
the representative of the United Kingdom as original Mandatory on
behalf of South Africa, the present Mandatory for South West Africa.
The right to take legal action conferred by Article 7 on Member States

of the League of Nations is an essential part of the Mandate itself and inseparable from its exercise. Moreover, Article 7 reads: "The Mandatory agrees that . . .", so that there could be no doubt about the scope and effect of the provision at the time of its stipulation.

While Article 6 of the Mandate under consideration provides for administrative supervision by the League, Article 7 in effect provides, with the express agreement of the Mandatory, for judicial protection by the Permanent Court by vesting the right of invoking the compulsory jurisdiction against the Mandatory for the same purpose in each of the other Members of the League. Protection of the material interests of the Members or their nationals is of course included within its compass, but the well-being and development of the inhabitants of the Mandated territory are not less important.

The foregoing considerations and reasons lead to the conclusion that the present dispute is a dispute as envisaged in Article 7 of the Mandate and that the Third Preliminary Ojection must be dismissed.

. . . .

The Court will now consider the Fourth and last Preliminary Objection raised by the Respondent. In essence it consists of the proposition that if it is a dispute within the meaning of Article 7, it is not one which cannot be settled by negotiation with the Applicants and that there have been no such negotiations with a view to its settlement. The Applicants' reply is to the effect that repeated negotiations have taken place over a period of more than ten years between them and the other Members of the United Nations holding the same views as they, on the one hand, and the Respondent, on the other, in the Assembly and various organs of the United Nations, and that each time the negotiations reached a deadlock, due to the conditions and restrictions the Respondent placed upon them. The question to consider, therefore, is: What are the chances of success of further negotiations between the Parties in the present cases for reaching a settlement?

In considering the question, it is to be noted, first, that the alleged impossibility of settling the dispute obviously could only refer to the time when the Applications were filed. In the second place, it should be pointed out that behind the present dispute there is another and similar disagreement on points of law and fact—a similar conflict of legal views and interests—between the Respondent on the one hand, and the other Members of the United Nations, holding identical views with the Applicants, on the other hand. But though the dispute in the United Nations and the one now before the Court may be regarded as two different disputes, the questions at issue are identical. Even a cursory examination of the views, propositions and arguments consistently maintained by the two opposing sides, shows that an impasse was reached before 4 November 1960 when the Applications in the instant cases were filed, and that the impasse continues to exist. The actual situation appears from a letter of 25 March 1954 from the Permanent Representative of the Union of South Africa to the Chairman of the Committee on South West Africa:

As the terms of reference of your Committee appear to be even more inflexible than those of the *Ad Hoc* Committee the Union Government are doubtful whether there is any hope that new negotiations within the scope of your Committee's terms of reference will lead to any positive results.

This situation remains unchanged as appears clearly from subsequent communications addressed to the Chairman of the Committee on South West Africa on 21 May 1955 and 21 April 1956.

It is immaterial and unnecessary to enquire what the different and opposing views were which brought about the deadlock in the past negotiations in the United Nations, since the present phase calls for determination of only the question of jurisdiction. The fact that a deadlock was reached in the collective negotiations in the past and the further fact that both the written pleadings and oral arguments of the Parties in the present proceedings have clearly confirmed the continuance of this deadlock, compel a conclusion that no reasonable probability exists that further negotiations would lead to a settlement.

In this respect it is relevant to cite a passage from the Judgment of the Permanent Court in the case of the *Mavrommatis Palestine Concessions* (P.C.I.J., Ser. A, No. 2, p. 13) which supports the view stated. The Court said in respect of a similar objection advanced by the Respondent in that case to the compulsory jurisdiction under Article 26 of the Palestine Mandate, which corresponds to Article 7 of the Mandate for South West Africa:

> The true value of this objection will readily be seen if it be remembered that the question of the importance and chances of success of diplomatic negotiations is essentially a relative one. Negotiations do not of necessity always presuppose a more or less lengthy series of notes and despatches; it may suffice that a discussion should have been commenced, and this discussion may have been very short; this will be the case if a deadlock is reached, or if finally a point is reached at which one of the Parties definitely declares himself unable, or refuses, to give way, and there can be therefore no doubt that the dispute cannot be settled by diplomatic negotiation.
>
> But it is equally true that if the diplomatic negotiations between the Governments commence at a point where the previous discussions left off, it may well happen that the nature of the latter was such as to render superfluous renewed discussion of the opposing contentions in which the dispute originated. No general and absolute rule can be laid down in this respect. It is a matter for consideration in each case.

Now in the present cases, it is evident that a deadlock on the issues of the dispute was reached and has remained since, and that no modification of the respective contentions has taken place since the discussions and negotiations in the United Nations. It is equally evident that "there can be no doubt", in the words of the Permanent Court, "that the dispute cannot be settled by diplomatic negotiation", and that it would be "superfluous" to undertake renewed discussions.

It is, however, further contended by the Respondent that the collective negotiations in the United Nations are one thing and direct negotiations between it and the Applicants are another, and that no such direct negotiations have ever been undertaken by them. But in this respect it is not so much the form of negotiation that matters as the attitude and views of the Parties on the substantive issues of the question involved. So long as both sides remain adamant, and this is obvious even from their oral presentations before the Court, there is no reason to think that the dispute can be settled by further negotiations between the Parties.

Moreover, diplomacy by conference or parliamentary diplomacy has come to be recognized in the past four or five decades as one of the established modes of international negotiation. In cases where the disputed questions are of common interest to a group of States on one side or the other in an organized body, parliamentary or conference diplomacy has often been found to be the most practical form of negotiation. The number of parties to one side or the other of a dispute is of no importance; it depends upon the nature of the question at issue. If it is one of mutual interest to many States, whether in an organized body or not, there is no reason why each of them should go through the formality and pretence of direct negotiation with the common adversary State after they have already fully participated in the collective negotiations with the same State in opposition.

For the reasons stated above, the Fourth Objection like the preceding three Objections is not well-founded and should also be dismissed.

. . . .

The Court concludes that Article 7 of the Mandate is a treaty or convention still in force within the meaning of Article 37 of the Statute of the Court and that the dispute is one which is envisaged in the said Article 7 and cannot be settled by negotiation. Consequently the Court is competent to hear the dispute on the merits.

For these reasons,

THE COURT,

by eight votes to seven,

finds that it has jurisdiction to adjudicate upon the merits of the dispute.

5. *The Dissenting Opinions*

Several of the judges comprising the majority, namely, Judges Bustamante y Rivero and Jessup, and Judge *ad hoc* Sir Louis Mbanefo, handed down separate concurring opinions, while President Winiarski, Judges Basdevant, Morelli, Sir Percy Spender, and Sir Gerald Fitzmaurice, and Judge *ad hoc* Van Wyk appended dissenting opinions to the judgment. These separate opinions together run to over three hundred pages and are indispensable to a proper understanding of the issues before the Court. The dissenting judges were generally agreed that the applicant States had no legal right or interest in the subject-matter of the dispute—the well-being of the inhabitants of South West Africa—as their own national interests were not affected.[j] For this reason they held that South Africa should have succeeded in her third objection. The reasoning of the dissenting minority on this matter, which was later to be adopted by the Court in 1966,[k] is well represented by the joint dissenting opinion of Judges Sir Percy Spender and Sir Gerald Fitzmaurice:[1]

The Mandate (and this is still more so in the case of other categories of Mandates) has two main classes of substantive provisions. The first (which might be called the "conduct of the Mandate" class) comprises the provisions inserted for the benefit of the peoples of the territory. The other (which might be called the "State rights and interests" class) comprises those which were inserted for the national benefit of the Members of the League and their nationals (commercial rights, open door, freedom for missionary activities, etc.).

The question is whether Article 7 of the Mandate (this was a common clause in all the Mandate), relates to both these classes of provision, or only to the latter. At first sight, on a literal reading of Article 7, the answer might appear clear: it specifies "any dispute whatever . . . relating to the interpretation or the application of the provisions of the Mandate". Since we believe in the principle of interpreting provisions according to their natural and ordinary meaning in the context in which they occur, and (in the absence of any ambiguities or contradictions) without reference to *travaux préparatoires,* we must state why we feel unable to take the above passage at its face value, and why we consider a reference to the *travaux préparatoires* to be justified in this case, quite apart from the fact that these have in any event been so extensively relied upon in connection with the First and Second Preliminary Objections, that it would hardly be possible to exclude them from consideration of the third, which is definitely related to the others.

The phrase we have just cited from Article 7 does not give the full sense of the relevant passage, and to obtain this a fuller citation is required, as follows: "any dispute whatever . . . between the Mandatory

---

[j] President Winiarski, ibid., 449 ff., Judge Basdevant, ibid., 463–64; Judges Sir Percy Spender and Sir Gerald Fitzmaurice, ibid., 547–60, Judge Morelli, ibid., 564 ff., Judge *ad hoc* Van Wyk, ibid., 658–62.
[k] *South West Africa, Second Phase,* 1966 ICJ Reports 6. Below, pp. 293–325.
[1] 1962 ICJ Reports 549–59.

and another Member of the League of Nations relating to the interpretation or application of the provisions of the Mandate". Having regard to the view we take as to the meaning of a "dispute", and the necessity for a direct dispute between the parties to the proceedings, in
which they have an interest in their own capacity, and not merely as
Members of an international organization, the above passage, in the
context of this case, conceals an ambiguity. The words could be read
as meaning any dispute whatever having the character just mentioned.
In our view the Applicants had not, at the critical date (that of the
Applications), any interest in the matter (*even in the conduct of the
Mandate*) except in their capacity as Members of the United Nations.
On that ground alone we should not regard the case as covered.
. . . .
We find it impossible to reconcile the view that Article 7 relates to dis-
putes about the general conduct of the Mandate, with the supervisory
functions given to the Council of the League under Article 6 of the
Mandate. The conjunction would mean that although the League
Council might have been perfectly satisfied with the Mandatory's conduct of the Mandate, or might even have made suggestions to the
Mandatory about that, which the latter was complying with and carrying out, any Member of the League not satisfied with the Mandatory's
conduct, or not agreeing with the Council's views, could have brought
proceedings before the Permanent Court under Article 7.

There would have been an even more extraordinary possibility. A
Member of the League might, on some point relative to the conduct of
the Mandate, have obtained from the Permanent Court a decision
which was not in fact in the best interests of the peoples of the mandated territory—due, say, to lack of sufficient technical data before the
Court. Yet under Article 59 of the Statute, the Mandatory would have
been bound by the decision, and obliged to apply it vis-à-vis the inhabitants, although the Council of the League might have been
wholly opposed to it and itself not bound by it.

We cannot believe it was ever intended that it should be possible
for such situations to arise, and in estimating this, one must, for reasons we have given earlier in this Opinion, place oneself at the point
in time when these provisions, Articles 6 and 7, were being drafted as
designed portions of a coherent and integrated whole, which the Mandate certainly would not have been if Article 7 had had the meaning
attributed to it by the Court.

The situations we have described as capable of arising if Article 7 is
regarded as relating to disputes about the conduct of the Mandate are
in no way fanciful or hypothetical. One of them has actually arisen in
another case, with reference to a provision substantially the same as
Article 7 in a United Nations trusteeship agreement.

It is in our opinion hardly conceivable that those who created a system according to which the Mandates were to be exercized "on behalf
of the League", and the Mandatory was to be responsible, and solely
responsible, to the Council of the League, should have been willing so
far to dilute the Council's authority (especially when the Council could

itself go to the Permanent Court for an Advisory Opinion), as to give a wholly independent right of recourse to the Court to Members of the League, not merely for the protection of their own individual rights and interests, but in the very field of the general conduct of the Mandate which was peculiarly the Council's.

.   .   .   .

These various considerations lead us to hold that, despite the apparently plain language of Article 7 of the Mandate, on a literal interpretation of the words "any dispute whatever", analysis shows its real meaning and intention to be different, and to exlude disputes about the general conduct of the Mandate. If there is any room for doubt, then this is a case in which reference to the *travaux préparatoires* is justified, in order to see whether they confirm the foregoing interpretation, and to this we shall now proceed.

The learned judges examined the *travaux préparatoires* and concluded:

It seems to us therefore that the record could hardly make it plainer than it does that the drafting of what might for convenience be called the national rights clauses of the Mandates, and the drafting of the adjudication clause, went hand in hand, each reacting on the other, and that the adjudication clause was never discussed in the context of the obligations of the Mandatories relative to the peoples of the mandated territories. To borrow the words of Lord Finlay in one of the *Mavrommatis* cases (P.C.I.J Series A, No. 2, at p. 43) in relation to the Palestine Mandate: "Under these heads [i.e. of the commercial, etc., rights of States and their nationals] there are endless possibilities of dispute between the Mandatory and other Members of the League of Nations, and it was highly necessary that a Tribunal should be provided for the settlement of such disputes". Never at any time during the settlement of the drafts was there the slightest suggestion that the adjudication clause was intended to serve quite a different purpose, namely the policing of the sacred trust.

It is evident that it had no relation to the trust obligations of the Mandatory to the peoples of the territories. It was designed to serve a less lofty purpose. It is quite inconceivable that if Article 7 was of the fundamentally essential character stated by the Court; created as one of the securities for the performance of the Covenant, providing the Court as the final bulwark to secure the performance of the sacred trust, that not one word is to be found in the records which gives support to the Court's view.

To sum up, our study of the record confirms the view which we had antecedently and independently formed, on the basis of the language of Article 7, and in the context of the Mandate as a whole. This view is, *first,* that Article 7 must be understood as referring to a dispute in the traditional sense of the term, as it would have been understood in 1920, namely a dispute between the actual parties before the Court about their own interests, in which they appear as representing themselves and not some other entity or interest; and *secondly,* that Article 7 in the general context and scheme of the Mandate, was intended to enable the Members of the League to protect their own rights and those of their nationals, and not to enable them to intervene in matters affecting solely the conduct of the Mandate in relation to the peoples of the mandated territory.

6. *Academic Comment*

Academic comment[m] on this decision of the Court was fairly favourable and was devoted mainly to a description and analysis of the majority judgment and separate concurring and dissenting opinions. As the issues raised by the third preliminary objection were later to be revived in the 1966 judgment, Elizabeth Landis's analysis of this objection[n] is included:

Article 7 Did Not Apply to Dispute. In their memorials Ethiopia and Liberia stated that they had brought the proceedings on the basis of their "legal interest in seeing to it through judicial process that the sacred trust of civilization created by the Mandate is not violated." [286] The respondent denied that such an interest was sufficient to give the court jurisdiction under Article 7, claiming that the interest must be "personal and direct," arising out of obligations owed individually to the applicant states or to their nationals.[287]

In this connection Judge Morelli raised a point which he claimed was anterior to *any* issue of jurisdiction.[288] He questioned whether

[m] Elizabeth S. Landis, "South West Africa in the International Court: Act II, scene 1" (1964) 49 *Cornell Law Quarterly* 179; R. B. Ballinger, "The International Court of Justice and the South West Africa Cases" (1964) 81 *SALJ* 35; Ernest A. Gross, "The South West African Cases: on the Threshold of Decision" (1964) 3 *Columbia Journal of Transnational Law* 19; Symposium on the South West Africa Cases in (1965) 4 *Columbia Journal of Transnational Law* 47 ff.; L. Favoreu, "L'arrêt du 21 décembre 1962 sur le Sud-Ouest africain et l'évolution du droit des organisations internationales" (1963) 9 *Annuaire français de droit international* 303; J. H. W. Verzijl, "International Court of Justice: South West Africa and Northern Cameroons Cases (Preliminary Objections)" (1964) 11 *Netherlands International Law Review* 1.

[n] "South West Africa in the International Court: Act II, Scene 1" (1964) 49 *Cornell Law Quarterly* at 219–25. (Copyright 1964 by Cornell University.)

[286] Memorials of Ethiopia and Liberia, pp. 62–63, SWA Cases, quoted by Judge Winiarski in SWA Cases 456.

[287] Ibid. (Winiarski, President, dissenting). The court summarized the South African contention on this point, that the "dispute":

[M]ust be given its generally accepted meaning in a context of a compulsory jurisdiction clause and that, when so interpreted, it means a disagreement or conflict between the Mandatory and another Member . . . concerning the legal rights and interests of such other Member in the matter before the Court. . . .

Id. at 343 (opinion of the court).

[288] Id. at 565 (Morelli, J., dissenting).

there was, legally speaking, any "dispute" at all of which the court could take cognizance; if not, he claimed it should dismiss the proceeding before considering the respondent's objections.[289]According to the judge, a "dispute" existed only when there was both (a) a disagreement as to law or fact or a conflict of interests [290] and (b) a "manifestation of the will, at least of one of the parties, consisting in the making of a claim or of a protest." [291] Then, seizing on the same fact which the dissenting Commonwealth judges cited to back up their *jurisdictional* argument as to the "dispute," he argued that Ethiopia and Liberia had continually acted:

> [I]n their capacity as members of a United Nations collegiate organ . . . guided not by their individual interest but by . . . the interest of the Organization. They had in mind . . . an alleged right of the Organization and not . . . a right belonging to them individually . . . .[292]

Hence they failed to demonstrate the second of the two necessary elements of a dispute.

The court, however, quickly dismissed this contention. After noting that the mere assertion of a dispute could not prove its existence any more than a denial could establish its nonexistence, the majority held that, although a mere conflict of interests did not constitute a dispute, proof that the claim of one party was "positively opposed" by the other was sufficient.[293] Tested by this criterion, the "opposing attitudes relating to the performance of the obligations of the Mandate by the . . . Mandatory" clearly did constitute a dispute.[294]

Then, since Article 7 provided for the submission to the court of "any dispute whatever . . . relative to the interpretation or the application . . . of the Mandate," the burden seemed to fall on the respondent to demonstrate what Judge Winiarski stated so flatly: "These words clearly do *not* mean any dispute whatsoever. . . ." [295]

The first argument was based on the general principle that a state

---

[289] Id. at 564–66, 569–70.

[290] Id. at 566–67. But the interest may be either supposed or real:

Each State is the judge of its own interest. If a State, believing itself to have a certain interest, advances a claim . . . or makes a protest . . . that claim or that protest may well constitute one of the elements of a dispute, independently of the real existence of the interest in question.

. . . .

[I]f . . . there had been, on the part of Ethiopia and Liberia, a claim or protest directed against South Africa and relating to an interest regarded by the two former States [sic] as being their interest, the existence of a dispute could not be denied by contesting the existence of that interest. The attitude of Ethiopia and Liberia would in this respect be decisive . . . .

Id. at 570.

[291] Id. at 567. Such manifestation must, of course, precede the commencement of the proceeding. Id. at 568–69.

[292] Id. at 571.   [293] Id. at 328 (opinion of the court).   [294] Ibid.

[295] Id. at 455 (Winiarski, President, dissenting). [Emphasis added.]

may institute proceedings before the court only if it has "a subjective right, a real and existing individual interest which is legally protected." [296] In this case the dissenting Commonwealth judges, employing Judge Morelli's evidence to prove the jurisdictional issue, argued that Ethiopia and Liberia had no personal quarrel with the Republic of South Africa, but merely the same "political conflict of view" as many other U.N. members relating to the conduct of the South West Africa mandate.[297] It was common knowledge that the real dispute was between the General Assembly and the Republic, and the applicants admitted that they had acted "at the instance of the Assembly" to uphold the mandate for the benefit of the inhabitants of the territory, not in their own interest. On that ground alone the judges claimed that there was no dispute between South Africa and the applicants "in their individual capacities." [298]

The relevant documents were alleged to support this view. A comparison of "A," "B," and "C" mandates showed that the "A" mandates contained no "sacred trust of civilization" clause although they did have adjudication clauses similar to Article 7; hence, the dissenting judges contended, the adjudication clauses must have been intended to refer to disputes about interests common to all the mandates, that is, to the direct interests of the League members (and their nationals) in the mandated territories.[299] Along the same line, Judge Winiarski pointed out that the compromissory clause related to disputes which "cannot be settled by negotiation." This phraseology, he claimed, was lifted from traditional arbitration clauses and referred to a dispute in "the classic sense," "a dispute which by its nature lends itself to settlement by negotiation but which in a particular case cannot be so settled." However, a dispute can be so settled only when the parties can deal freely with their rights and interests; since the applicants acted as representatives of the U.N. Assembly, their dispute was *not* one which could be settled by negotiation and hence was not one of which the court could be seized.[300] Furthermore, the judge contended that the requirement of Article 62 of the statute of the court, that a state demonstrate "an interest of a legal nature" to intervene in proceedings,[301] should be applied to proceedings brought under Article 7 of the man-

---

[296] Ibid.
[297] Id. at 549 (Spender and Fitzmaurice, JJ., dissenting).
[F]or all the difference it would have made to the essential character of the present proceedings, these might just as well have been brought by any other States coming within the category of ex-Members of the former League of Nations. The pleadings could have been identical, apart from the name of the plaintiffs.
Ibid.
[298] Id. at 548.   [299] Id. at 559.
[300] Id. at 457 (Winiarski, President, dissenting).
[301] Stat. Int'l Ct. of Just., art. 62, ¶ 1 reads:
Should a state consider that it has an interest of a legal nature which may be affected by the decision in the case, it may submit a request to the Court to be permitted to intervene.

date.[302] And Judge van Wyk, still unconvinced that the League Council was empowered to add the "new" security of Article 7 to the mandate,[303] felt it could be valid only if limited to disputes about the direct interests of the complainant state.[304]

According to the dissenting judges the history of the mandate supported their interpretation of the general law. The only discussion of Article 7 during the drafting of the mandate was in connection with the commercial and other national rights clauses.[305] It was inconceivable that any interpretation of the adjudication clause which would have extended it to cover "conduct of the mandate" cases could have been introduced without "violent debates" or references in the *travaux préparatoires* and, more important, without saying so explicitly.[306]

For, as it was reiterated in connection with almost every objection, the mandatories were reluctant to submit to *any* mandates regime and certainly to one which could have exercised any effective control over the way they ran their mandates.[307]

> It is not reasonable to *assume* that they would have agreed to . . . supervision by every Member and every ex-Member . . . armed with the right to institute legal proceedings . . . whenever it was considered that the Mandate had been breached or abused. [Emphasis by the court.] [308]

The compromissory clause, interpreted as the applicants urged, would have created an *actio popularis,* "a novelty in international relations, going far beyond the novelty of the Mandates system itself in its implications. . . ."[309] Judge Winiarski pointed out that the wording of the clause had been changed by the Council to make the mandatory only subject to the court's compulsory jurisdiction because "Members of the League other than the Mandatory could not be forced against their will to submit their differences to the Permanent Court. . . ."[311] He concluded that if the Powers were so careful not to bind member states without their consent, they would hardly have granted them such a novel right of action under Article 7 without saying so expressly.[312]

The subsequent practice of the League was then cited to confirm the

---

[302] SWA Cases 455–56 (Winiarski, President, dissenting).

[303] Id. at 660–61 (van Wyk, J., dissenting).

[304] SWA Cases 661 (van Wyk, J., dissenting).

[305] Id. at 555–56, 558 (Spender and Fitzmaurice, JJ., dissenting).

[306] Id. at 453 (Winiarski, President, dissenting), 601 (van Wyk, J., dissenting).

[307] Id. at 453 (Winiarski, President, dissenting), 559 (Spender and Fitzmaurice, JJ., dissenting), 600–01 (van Wyk, J., dissenting), 608–09 (van Wyk, J., dissenting).

[308] Id. at 600–01 (van Wyk, J., dissenting).

[309] Id. at 453 (Winiarski, President, dissenting).

[311] SWA Cases 453 (Winiarski, President, dissenting) quoting Viscount Ishii's report on the reason for the change. Viscount Ishii's report is also cited at id. at 397 (separate opinion of Jessup, J.), 597 (van Wyk, J., dissenting).

[312] SWA Cases 453 (Winiarski, President, dissenting).

contention that the court was not intended to exercise judicial control over the mandates—a control which could only have conflicted with that of the Council and "diluted" the latter's authority, the dissenting judges noted.[313] In the first authoritative reports made to the Council of the League in 1920 by the then Belgian representative on the role of the various League organs in relation to the mandates the Permanent Court was not mentioned.[314] The League Council, throughout its twenty-five years of existence, exercised its supervision by essentially political methods, with the assistance of qualified experts, but without once referring to the Permanent Court for an advisory opinion despite the urging of the Permanent Mandates Commission.[315] In the same period only one case was taken to the court under the adjudication clause of any mandate; and that case involved the alleged violation of commercial rights of a Greek national.[316] Finally, leading commentators consistently ignored any possibility of supervision by the Permanent Court, as did an official publication on the mandates system issued by the League itself in 1945.[317]

The majority met the respondent's arguments squarely. First of all, they pointed out, there clearly was a dispute—a truth which U.N. records before the court abundantly documented.[318] Secondly, the dispute concerned the interpretation or application of the mandate.[319] Thirdly, the dispute was within:

> [T]he natural and ordinary meaning . . . of "any dispute whatever". . . . The language used is broad, clear and precise: it gives rise to no ambiguity and it permits of no exception. It refers to any dispute whatever relating . . . to "the provisions" of the Mandate, obviously meaning all or any provisions. / . .
>
> . . . Protection of the material interests of the Members or their nationals is of course included within its compass, but the well-being and development of the inhabitants of the Mandated territory are not less important.[320]

[313] Id. at 553–54 (Spender and Fitzmaurice, JJ., dissenting).

[314] Id. at 451 (Winiarski, President, dissenting). The so-called "Hymans Reports," dated Aug. 5, 1920, and Oct. 26, 1920, are also referred to in the other opinions. Id. at 352–53 (separate opinion of Bustamante, J.), 390–92 (separate opinion of Jessup, J.), 484–85 (Spender and Fitzmaurice, JJ., dissenting).

A Council report to the Assembly, dated Dec. 6, 1920, on League responsibilities under Article 22 (mandates) similarly ignored judicial supervision. SWA Cases 451 (Winiarski, President, dissenting).

[315] Id. at 454.   [316] Ibid. See note 143 supra.

[317] SWA Cases 451–52 (Winiarski, President, dissenting). Judge Winiarski indicated, however, that some jurists did favor general supervision to which any League member could subject a mandatory by bringing it before the Permanent Court. Id. at 451.

[318] Id. at 381 (separate opinion of Bustamante, J.).

[319] Id. at 424 (separate opinion of Jessup, J.), 446 (separate opinion of Mbanefo, J.).

[320] Id. at 343–44 (opinion of the court).

Referring first to the more technical issues of legal construction, the concurring judges argued that the court had no right to investigate the "jurisdictional facts" concerning the merits of the applicants' interest as long as it related to interpretation or application of the mandate.[321] The requirement of an "interest of a legal nature" for intervention found in Article 62 of the court's statute was not applicable to Article 36, which established the general jurisdiction of the court, for its jurisdiction clearly included "all *cases* which the parties refer to it and all *matters* specially provided for in the [U.N.] Charter . . . or in treaties and conventions in force."[322] Moreover, the provisions of both Articles 36 and 38 [323] made it obvious that the scope of the court's jurisdiction, as to facts as well as to law, depends on the will of the parties: "The Court is always competent once the latter [*i.e.*, the parties] have accepted its jurisdiction, since there is no dispute which States entitled to appear before the Court cannot refer to it."[324] Finally, they found the fact that Article 22 of the Covenant did not mention compulsory jurisdiction was no reason to interpret narrowly the adjudication clause: Article 7 clearly implemented the securities of Article 22; it was mutually agreed upon by the victorious Allies and proposed to the Council by the British representative on behalf of the Union; and in the words of Article 7: "The Mandatory agrees . . ."[325]

Judge Jessup then referred to the so-called "Tanganyika clause," unique to the mandate for German East Africa (Tanganyika), which provided that League members might bring actions before the Permanent Court on behalf of their nationals for violation of their rights. This provision followed a compromissory clause substantially identical with that in Article 7(2) of the South West Africa mandate. His conclusion was that the latter must mean "something different from, or more than, what is meant by the Tanganyika clause" or there would have been no reason to include it.[326] (The dissenters considered the Tanganyika clause a sport and suggested that it probably was derived from the original draft proposed by the American representative in 1919, which was somehow not conformed to the accepted final version.[327])

---

[321] Id. at 423–24 (separate opinion of Jessup, J.), 447 (separate opinion of Mbanefo, J.).

[322] Id. at 433 quoting Charter, art. 36, ¶ 1. [Emphasis by the court.] Judge Jessup pointed out that a state is entitled to ask the court for an "abstract interpretation" of a treaty. SWA Cases 433 (separate opinion of Jessup, J.).

[323] Article 38(1) of the statute of the court defines the sources to be applied by the court in deciding disputes in accordance with international law; they include international conventions and custom, general principles recognized by civilized nations, and judicial decisions and teachings of eminent scholars.

[324] SWA Cases 423 (separate opinion of Jessup, J.) quoting Upper Silesia (Minority Schools), P.C.I.J., ser. A, No. 15, at 22.

[325] SWA Cases 343–44 (opinion of the court).

[326] Id. at 431 (separate opinion of Jessup, J.).

[327] Id. at 453–54 (Winiarski, President, dissenting), 559–60 (Spender and Fitzmaurice, JJ., dissenting).

On historical, ethical, and philosophic grounds the majority countered the respondent's emphasis on the mandatories' desire for unfettered control of conquered territory with the professed ideals of the victors after World War I. Returning to his basic theories as to the nature of the mandates, Judge Bustamante argued that since the establishment of Article 22 of the Covenant every League member had borne a trust, not merely "moral" or "humanitarian," but also "undeniably legal," to provide for the well-being and development of former colonial peoples. Hence Article 7 must be interpreted as giving each individual member the power to enforce the trust, more especially since the League could not itself enter into contentious proceedings.[328]

In equally philosophical terms Judge Jessup argued that the mandates were only one of four instances in which postwar statesmen had recognized that every country had an interest in events everywhere in the world. The others included the recognition in Article II of the Covenant that peace was indivisible, the protection of minorities, and the establishment of the International Labor Organization.[329] It followed, therefore, that Article 7 was intended "to recognize and to protect the general interests of Members of the international community in the Mandates System just as somewhat comparable clauses recognize this broad interest in the minority treaties, [etc.] . . . ."[330] In any case, he pointed out, international law recognizes legal interests in issues which do not affect the economic or other tangible interests of a state, such as the suppression of the slave trade, the ending of forced labor, the prevention of genocide, etc.[331] A state might have a recognizable interest in the observance in the territory of another state of general welfare treaty provisions, he asserted, "without alleging any impact upon its own nationals or its direct so-called tangible or material interests. . . ."[332] In view of the broad language of Article 7 and the lack of any intrinsic evidence of a limitation on its literal sense, the interest of Ethiopia and Liberia in the administration of South West Africa sufficed, particularly in view of the regional interest of all African States in events in other parts of the same continent.[333]

Judge Jessup added, citing American cases, that there was no reason why the court could not pass on the sort of abstract questions which might arise if states disputed intangible interests.[334] Nor, on the basis of comparable objections overruled in cases relating to the minorities treaties, would ultimate resort to the judiciary in cases which could not be resolved politically confuse the roles of normal supervisory organs or undermine their authority.[335]

[328] Id. at 380 (separate opinion of Bustamante, J.).
[329] Id. at 429 (separate opinion of Jessup, J.).   [330] Id. at 432.
[331] Id. at 425–28, 432.   [332] Id. at 428.   [333] Id. at 431–32.
[334] Id. at 428–29 citing Engel v. Vitale, 370 U.S. 421 (1962); West Coast Hotel Co. v. Parrish, 300 U.S. 379 (1937); Reynolds v. United States, 98 U.S. 244 (1879).
[335] SWA Cases 432 (separate opinion of Jessup, J.).

When the 1962 judgment of the Court was, in effect, reversed in 1966 the legal philosophy and reasoning of the majority were subjected to severe academic criticism. Lyndel V. Prott anticipated this criticism in his analysis of the traditionalist legal philosophy which inspired the 1962 joint dissent of Judges Sir Percy Spender and Sir Gerald Fitzmaurice.°

One of the main criticisms levelled at the majority judgment [of 1962] is of the method of reasoning, which the dissenting justices characterize thus:

> The general approach adopted by the majority of the Court in the present case can, we think, reasonably, be described as follows— namely that it is desirable and right that a provision for the compulsory adjudication of certain disputes, which figures (or did figure) as part of an institution—the Mandate for South West Africa —which is still in existence as an institution, should not be held to have become inoperative merely on account of a change in circumstances—provided that this change has not affected the *physical* possibility of continued performance. The present Court exists, and is of the same general character and carries out the same kind of functions as the tribunal (the former Permanent Court) which originally had jurisdiction under this provision (i.e. Article 7 of the Mandate for South-West Africa). Since there still exist States (and amongst them the Applicant States) who would have been entitled to invoke Article 7 *before* the changed circumstances came about, this Article must now be interpreted as still giving them this right, notwithstanding anything to the contrary in its actual terms, or resulting from any other relevant factor.
>
> It is evident that once a tribunal has adopted an approach of this nature, its main task will be to discover reasons for rejecting the various objections or contra-indications that may exist, or arise [15].

This criticism faces squarely the problem of judicial reasoning (as one branch of legal reasoning in general). Where legal reasoning is concerned an early theory held that logical operations on given legal materials produced the right solution [16] and some cases occurred where the judge has felt himself (and sometimes reluctantly) compelled to a certain conclusion by logical or legal necessity [17]. Other

---

° "Some Aspects of the Judicial Reasoning in the South West Africa Case of 1962" (1967) 3 *Revue Belge de Droit International* 37 at 40–44.

[15] Joint dissenting opinion of Judges Fitzmaurice and Spender, 1962 ICJ Reports 462–66.

[16] For example, the theory of John AUSTIN (1790–1859). See the assessment and criticism in STONE, J., *Legal Systems and Lawyers' Reasonings*, pp. 64–66.

[17] *Cf.* the regrets of Evershed L.J. in his concurring judgment in *Ball v. London County Council* (1949), 2, *K.B.*, 159.

thinkers would stress rather that there is a range of judicial choice between alternative conclusions, each justifiable [18].

What methods are open to a judge of the *international* court, and of international tribunals in general? This criticism of their Honours Fitzmaurice and Spender is based on the old legal traditions of the Common Law where legal tenets have long been considered the only possible basis of decisions of Her Majesty's judges. Careful study of the Common Law system however reveals the usual English distinction between theory and practice. The origin and principle of the Equity jurisdiction for example was to take into account other factors, and as this branch of law has now ceased to be autonomous and is incorporated into the general body of the Common Law system, traces of this flexibility are inherent in it. Again it is more than clear that the law has taken account of social factors by the very adaptability of the Common Law—it has progressed. Quite apart from legislative tinkering the judges have extended certain legal concepts, once quite limited, to cover whole new areas of social facts unknown in 1066 or for several centuries thereafter [19]. The motivation may be well concealed, even from the author of such a new development, but a serious consideration of the cases will show how these factors have influenced the growth of the law.

Yet in a municipal system of law so highly developed, there is always some legal principle, however vague and however remote, which the judge can invoke as a purely legal argument, however tenuous connection such argument may have with the case in hand. The situation is quite different in International Law where there are very few established principles and where even the most general principles, for example *pacta sunt servanda,* are likely to be the object of controversy as to scope and exceptions and even existence. It is not surprizing, therefore, that Common Law judges move most uneasily where corresponding developments or precisations are called for in International Law.

Civil law judges may act more confidently in this area because the "extra-legal" bases of their judicial reasonings are less hidden from them [20]. The necessary developments of the Code systems, which in some cases have had a merely mythical relationship to the text, allow one to see more clearly that judicial reasoning sometimes requires a clear derogation from the principle of sufficiency of the law. This judicial liberty is now admitted tacitly if not conferred explicitly [21] in

[18] STONE, J., *op. cit. supra* n. 16, pp. 274 ff.

[19] The adaptation of the action on the case is but too well-known. Developments which have deduced legal principles to deal with motor accident injury and the modern insurance system have required a good deal of judicial originality; as did the first cases on the development of the limited company (Salomon's Case, 1897, *A.C.,* 22).

[20] On the general question of justification in law see TAMMELO, I. & PROTT, L., Legal and Extra-Legal Justification, *Journal of Legal Education,* vol. 17, 1965, No. 4, p. 412.

[21] Tacitly in France for example, explicitly in the Swiss Code, Article 4.

modern Civil Law systems, and Civil Law judges therefore feel more at home with the additional authority granted by the incompleteness of the international order.

A reply to the criticisms of the dissenting Justices might in the first place take issue with their description of the Court's method of work as put a little strongly: it is not so much an object "to discover reasons for rejecting the various objections or contra-indications that may exist" as to use this approach as a means for choosing between them. Where the Court considers that the indications are ranged in fairly equal order on either side of the question, is it not entitled to consider the *desirable* end as the one that was in fact desired? The difference of opinion may therefore not be as simple as characterised; there is a difference of opinion as to the relative weight of the legal factors and indications themselves—the majority considered that they created an ambiguity or dilemma of interpretation, whereas the dissenting justices felt that this discrepancy was already sufficiently clear to settle the legal question. It is rather, therefore, not a case of taking a decision "notwithstanding anything to the contrary" in the document, but of considering the incidences and essential features of the institution as the more important factor in the interpretation of it.

There are some cases where domestic law interprets in the spirit and purpose of a document rather than the strict letter—the construction of testamentary instruments is an example found in every jurisdiction. More closely analogous to the case in hand is the supervision of the administration of trusts [22]—the trust will not be allowed to fail for want of a trustee; and the charitable trust receives in several respects the advantage of a beneficial interpretation (it will not fail for want of a beneficiary either). It would certainly be justifiable for the court to consider this form of legal reasoning more appropriate to the novel institution of the mandate than that more commonly employed of strict interpretation. This latitude is expressed in and confined by rules of interpretation proper to these instruments; there is room for the enunciation of similar rules in international law.

With the suggested method of their Honours all lawyers would surely agree that the "only method of procedure is to begin by the examination of the legal elements, with especial reference, where questions of interpretation are concerned, to the actual language employed, and then, on the basis of this examination, to consider what are the correct conclusions which as a matter of law, should be drawn from them" [23].

The difficulty is to apply this general statement to the realities of litigation. What exactly are "legal elements"? Certainly a legally valid

---

[22] This analogy, though with a warning against too facile a transposition from domestic to international law, was extensively used by McNair, J., in his Separate Opinion, *Advisory Opinion on the International Status of South-West Africa, I.C.J. Reports,* 1950, pp. 146 ff.

[23] Joint dissenting opinion of Judges Fitzmaurice and Spender, *I.C.J. Reports,* 1962, p. 466.

document is. But are "surrounding circumstances", not binding documents and expressions of opinion? They are taken account of in their Honours' Opinion [24]. The element of intention is often the vital one in the problem of interpretation—but is this strictly a legal element? The obligation is binding whatever the intention—in this sense it is not a legal element; but when recourse is had to intention to determine the *extent* of such an obligation, it would seem that it is. Their Honours also speak of drawing the correct conclusions, which as a matter of law, should be drawn from them. What conclusion, as a *matter of law*, is drawn from a consideration of the elements? The very terms "law" and "legal" are in themselves so hedged around with uncertainty, and more especially in the international field. Is a conclusion of law one which is logically dictated? dictated by factors internal to the legal system (such as the force of a precedent that is absolutely binding—and can such a compulsion exist in the infant international legal system?)? To most problems of law it would seem that, unlike arithmetic, there can be more than one right answer.

In agreeing with their Honours Fitzmaurice and Spender that the Court was not obliged to take the approach it did, one can surely argue that it was a reasonable and *justifiable* [25] mode of argument. Very few are the cases where logic would dictate the result (and if it could why would the parties come to court? since they could themselves foretell the result). The importance of a submission to a legal body dwells in the fact that it deals in something more than that logic—rights and duties, of "ought" (or "ought not") rather than "is"—for which a perfect system of logic has not up to now been conspicuous in any province, morals, theology, or philosophy itself. Indeed a good deal of the advantage of law has subsisted in the fact that it can, and when required, does, reject an expected result by the use of some distinction or reliance on some factor hitherto considered not relevant.

"Looking at the matter as a whole and in the light of its history since the dissolution of the League, it seems to us quite clear that the applicants (and we think the Court also) are seeking to apply a sort of 'hindsight' . . . and some doctrine of 'subsequent necessity' quite unknown in international law" [26]. In considering whether a decision is "desirable" or not the majority of the International Court of Justice is exercising hindsight and foresight in a way perfectly common to municipal judges. Cases which have reversed a long line of precedents [27] have justifiably paid regard to the "desirability" of a result; and so have those which have considered the possible effect of one such deci-

---

[24] Cf. *ibid.*, 483–486 on the framing of the mandate agreement, and 543–545 on the events of 1946 concerning the survival of Mandate obligations.

[25] On justification as a legal method, see article cited n. 20.

[26] Joint dissenting opinion of Judges Fitzmaurice and Spender, *I.C.J. Reports*, 1962, pp. 521 ff.

[27] *Cf.* the hypothetical examples suggested by the Lord Chancellor in *Smith v. Charles Baker & Sons*, 1891, *A.C.*, 325, which restricted the extent of one wider doctrine of common employment.

sion on cases not yet come to pass for which the instant case would be authority [28]. Considering the long-term effects of a decision is surely as much a consideration of desirability (in advance or in retrospect) as the majority of the Court indulged in the South-West Africa case on the jurisdiction question. An analogy could be drawn from domestic cases such as *Donoghue v. Stephenson* [29] where Lord Atkin justifies the addition of a general negligence category to the English law of tort.

7. South African Response to the Judgment

Shortly after the Court delivered its judgment the Prime Minister of South Africa, Dr. H. F. Verwoerd, announced that his Government had decided to contest the merits of the dispute: [p]

The International Court has, by the closest margin in the history of that Court—indeed by the narrowest margin possible—decided that it is competent to entertain the complaints of Liberia and Ethiopia on the South West African issue.

In view of the narrow majority of one vote in a Court of 15 judges, and having regard to the fact that some of the seven distinguished judges, who delivered dissenting judgments, not only denied the jurisdiction of the Court, but also disagreed with the 1950 Advisory Opinion on the same question, the Government of the Republic has to decide whether in these circumstances, South Africa should participate in the second phase of the proceedings, by filing counter-memorials in reply to the allegations of the applicants, viz. that the Republic is not administering the territory in accordance with the provisions of the mandate originally granted by the defunct League of Nations.

South Africa's representatives to the United Nations have, since the first Assembly in 1946, denied these allegations, and have regularly given to the Fourth Committee the true facts regarding certain of the more serious allegations. Furthermore, the South African Government has repeatedly given proof of its *bona fides,* by inviting representatives of the United Nations to visit the territory including three distinguished past-Presidents of the organization—invitations which were unfortunately not accepted.

The most recent was the invitation extended to the Chairman and the Vice-Chairman of the Special United Nations Committee of Seven. This invitation was accepted, and the two United Nations emissaries duly visited South West Africa, where they were given every facility to go wherever they pleased, and to meet any person, or the representatives of organizations that had expressed a desire to see them.

[p] *House of Assembly Debates,* vol. 5, cols. 14–15 (21 January 1963).
[28] *Cf. Haseldine v. Daw* (1941), 2, *K.B.,* 343 (assimilating responsibility for lifts to that of the common carrier rather than to the lesser standards of occupier's liability); and *Donoghue v. Stephenson,* 1932, *A.C.,* 562, on the general duty of care necessarily owed by modern manufacturers to the customer.
[29] Cited n. 28, esp. pp. 580, 582–593.

Subsequent events are familiar to all. In spite of the South African Government's readiness to co-operate in providing facilities for an objective assessment of its administration of South West Africa, it became only too clear that all that was desired and expected of the United Nations emissaries was that they should produce a series of findings and judgments in keeping with the predetermined policies and prejudices of the majority of the United Nations membership.

In the circumstances set out above, particularly the very narrow majority in the matter of the Court's jurisdiction, the Government of the Republic would be fully justified in not filing counter-memorials in reply to the allegations contained in the memorials of the two complainants.

The position is, however, that the decision of the majority of the Court entitles the complainants to proceed with the merits of the case, and unless South Africa files counter-memorials, its case will go by default. The South African Government, being satisfied that the Republic is administering South West Africa in the spirit of and in keeping with the intentions of the original mandate, has decided to enter into the second phase of the case and to file counter-memorials in reply to the allegations of the complainants.

The Government's decision should, however, not be construed as implying a change in the attitude which it has consistently held in regard to the South West Africa issue, namely that the International Court has no jurisdiction—a matter on which the present members of the Court are themselves so sharply divided.

Although the Statute of the International Court of Justice does not provide for an appeal against a decision of the Court, Article 61 does permit the revision of a judgment where some new fact has come to light which materially affects its validity. In 1964 Mr. Justice George Wynne of the South African Supreme Court claimed to have discovered a new fact which would justify an application for such a revision of the Court's judgment,[q] a claim which was disputed by Mr. R. B. Ballinger[r] and the present writer[s] in the *South African Law Journal*. The South African Government did not raise the matter before the Court, however, and instead submitted to the jurisdiction of the Court for the Second Phase of the proceedings.

[q] "Grounds for Revision of the Judgment of the International Court of Justice of 21st December, 1962, that it had Jurisdiction to Adjudicate upon the South West Africa Case: *Ad Hoc* Judge Improperly Chosen as Liberia had no *Locus Standi*" (1964) 81 *SALJ* 449.

[r] "Grounds for Revision Revised" (1965) 82 *SALJ* 26.

[s] "Objections to the Revision of the 1962 Judgment of the International Court of Justice in the South West Africa Case" (1965) 82 *SALJ* 178.

SECOND PHASE: THE MERITS

1. The Political Aims of the Legal Action

The main purpose of the litigation over South West Africa, as far as the applicants were concerned, was to obtain an enforceable judgment against South Africa. In terms of Article 94 of the Charter of the United Nations each member State agrees to comply with the decision of the International Court "in any case to which it is a party," and "if any party to a case fails to perform the obligations incumbent upon it under a judgment rendered by the Court, the other party may have recourse to the Security Council, which may, if it deems necessary, make recommendations or decide upon measures to be taken to give effect to the judgment." The motives of the applicant States were clearly spelt out by their chief counsel, Mr. Ernest A. Gross, in *Foreign Affairs*.[t]

Early in 1960, the Asian-African group at the United Nations discussed the feasibility of judicial recourse and explored availability of legal counsel. Subsequently, the Liberian Government requested the author to prepare a Memorandum of Law for circulation to governments in advance of the Second Conference of Independent African States, scheduled to convene at Addis Ababa in June 1960. After full discussion, in which the author was privileged to participate, the conference concluded "that the international obligations of the Union of South Africa concerning the Territory of South West Africa should be submitted to the International Court of Justice for adjudication in a contentious proceeding." Note was taken in the resolution of the Report of the Special Committee concerning legal action open to former League members.

The decision was a combined product of frustration and of a sense of responsibility. The objective was not to resolve doubt concerning the jurisprudence of the Mandate, which had its firm foundation in the Advisory Opinion of 1950, but to transform a dishonored, though authoritative, Opinion into an enforceable Judgment. The Court would, moreover, be given an opportunity to adjudicate upon the compatibility of an official policy of extreme racial discrimination with the international obligation "to promote to the utmost the material and moral well-being and the social progress of the inhabitants of the Territory." (Mandate, Article 2.)

t "The South West Africa Case: What Happened?" (1966–7) 45 *Foreign Affairs* 36 at 40–42. (Excerpted by permission from *Foreign Affairs* October 1966. Copyright by Council on Foreign Relations, Inc. New York.)

There was, if possible, even less room for doubt that an official policy of extreme racial discrimination is legally, no less than morally, repugnant to such an obligation than there was that the Mandate subsisted and that South Africa owed a duty of international accountability for the conduct of its administration of the Territory.

Denunciations of apartheid, voiced by all responsible governments, and recorded in countless United Nations resolutions and international declarations, furnish a thesaurus of terms of opprobrium and revulsion: "a cancer on the body politic" (Japan); "a venomous and contagious disease" (Poland); a "bitter toxic" (United States); "morally abominable, intellectually grotesque and spiritually indefensible" (United Kingdom).

It was known—and confirmed out of the mouths of South Africa's own witnesses at the lengthy Court hearings on the merits—that, in the more than forty years of the conduct of this trust, not one "native" ever has been qualified in law, medicine, engineering, dentistry or registered nursing; none may form or join a labor organization with rights of collective bargaining; none may be employed in a skilled occupation; none may move from place to place without official permission; none may reside (except for purposes of labor) in areas designated as "White"; and none has a voice in government or in the administration of "Native" affairs.

If any realistic prospect had existed that members of the United Nations would repress, rather than merely condemn, South Africa's violations of its clear and present duties under the Mandate, the hazards, burdens and, above all, the time involved in litigation no doubt would have been avoided.

The difficulties with which enforcement of the Mandate would confront members—particularly South Africa's principal trading partners, the United States and the United Kingdom—are matters of public knowledge. More than one-third of South Africa's total trade is with these two countries. Britain's investments in South Africa total about one billion pounds sterling. Britain is South Africa's largest customer; South Africa is one of her principal markets. The economic stake of the United States in South Africa is large (of the order of $500,-000,000) and growing. Both the United States and the United Kingdom, more particularly the latter, are vulnerable to South African economic and financial retaliation.

The new ingredient which would be introduced by a favorable judgment in a contentious proceeding—and this was the heart of the matter—would be the potential application of Article 94 of the United Nations Charter. The explicit grant of power to the Security Council to compel compliance with a Court Judgment (as distinguished from an Advisory Opinion) expressly vests in the Council what may be called an "executive" function, analogous to that in normal municipal systems. There was never any secret about the significance of Article 94 in the decision to seek judicial recourse.

It was the hope and expectation of the Applicant States, as well as of most other members of the international community, that a Judgment would impel the United Nations—in particular, South Africa's principal trading partners—to take effective action in support of the rule of law, embodied and reflected in the judicial process.

While the applicants' reasons for instituting the proceedings were clear, South Africa's decision to contest the merits of the dispute, rather than boycott these proceedings, rested on more complex grounds. Some of the possible reasons for this decision are discussed by Anthony A. D'Amato,[u] who assisted the applicants in the preparation of their brief:

First, not showing up in Court would probably mean an adverse default judgment which would be just as legally binding as a contested decision, although there would be ways, as suggested previously, to minimize it politically. Second, South Africa was rocked in 1960 by the Sharpeville episode, a stock market crash, and the attempted assassination of the Prime Minister. The "winds of change" were sweeping Africa; racial matters seemed to be peaking in the Rhodesias; and South Africa was feeling the initial pangs of separation from the Commonwealth, which was finally effected on May 31, 1961. Thus the prospect of a protracted World Court case seemed to be a good way of buying time. Third, there was a good prospect of actually winning the decision. The World Court, because of its decision in 1950 on trusteeships, must have appeared to be an oasis of rationality in the bleak Sahara of United Nations hostility. Also, the Cape Town lawyers had become masters of the legal intricacies of the Mandate history since they argued these issues at the Hague in 1950, 1955 and 1956. The feeling of victory was almost vindicated, and of course foreshadowed, in 1962 when the Court came within one vote of throwing the case out of Court for want of jurisdiction. When it was announced in the South African House of Assembly that the Court upheld jurisdiction by a vote of 8 to 7, a loud cheer went up! Fourth, the marvelous institution of the *ad hoc* judge in international law must be mentioned. The applicant and respondent States are each entitled to have a judge of their own nationality on the bench; if one is not already there, they may select an *ad hoc* judge. This guarantees that the State's point of view will be argued in the Court's secret deliberations. It also ensures that the final vote will not be unanimous and that a strong dissent will be given for the losing State, both of which help to save face. These factors in turn help slightly to induce a government to be sued. Fifth, the Applicants' case was grounded on the premise that South Africa was the rightful administering authority over South West Africa, and the Court was asked to enforce the Mandate, not terminate it. South Africa may have decided to argue the case on a shrewd forecast in 1960 that in a few years African opinion would shift radically in favor of independence for South West Africa, and thus the pending litigation

[u] "Legal and Political Strategies of the South West Africa Litigation" (1967) 4 *Law in Transition Quarterly* 8 at 21–22.

would forestall more radical steps. Finally, one should not underesti-
mate the sincere and widespread feeling in South Africa that if only
the rest of the world knew the *facts* they would surely understand the
necessity for apartheid. This desire to be heard, understood, and for-
given had been repeatedly frustrated in the United Nations when delegates would walk out of the room if any South African official attempted to defend apartheid. But a Court case would be different. (To
the extent that this factor is operative, the African delegates in the
U.N. had adopted an inadvertent strategy.) In Court South Africa
could paint a picture of "African reality" and the other side would
have to listen. Here South african counsel could demolish the biased
reports of "professional petitioners" who had spread gross lies about
conditions in Southern Africa. And it would not be possible for the
Applicants to make false accusations without supporting evidence in
the World Court. This last motive was translated into a strategy which
scored unbelievable gains for the South Africans in Court and yet
made no appreciable dent on world public opinion.

2. The Applicants' Change in Legal Strategy

Basically the applicants sought two orders from the International
Court: first, an order that South Africa was accountable to the
United Nations for her administration of South West Africa and,
second, a finding that apartheid violates Article 2 of the Mandate,
which imposes a duty on the mandatory to "promote to the utmost the material and moral well-being and the social progress of
the inhabitants of the territory." The latter finding was undoubtedly the prime aim of the applicants. Initially they claimed that
apartheid was oppressive, but later they varied their tactics by accepting South Africa's version of the facts and arguing that even
on these facts there was a violation of the Mandate. This tactical
change,[v] designed *inter alia* to shorten proceedings before the
Court, was seized upon by the South African legal team as a
major victory and exploited to the full, both during the proceedings and afterwards.[w] The way in which this change in emphasis

---

[v] For an explanation of the reasons for this move, see Richard A. Falk (one
of the applicants' counsel), "The South West Africa Cases: The Limits of
Adjudication," in *Ethiopia and Liberia vs South Africa: The South West Africa Cases* (Occasional Paper no. 5, 1968: African Studies Center, University
of California, Los Angeles), p. 31.
[w] See D. P. De Villiers, S.C., the leader of the South African legal defence,
"The South West Africa Cases: The Moment of Truth," ibid., n. v, 13;
D. P. De Villiers and E. M. Grosskopf (also a member of the South African
legal defence) in (1967) 1 *International Lawyer* 457. *South West Africa Survey* 1967, pp. 142–52. Sed contra, see Ernest A. Gross, "The South West Africa Case," in (1967) 1 *International Lawyer* 256.

in the applicants case came about is well described by Anthony A. D'Amato: [x]

Prior to July 1966 the Applicants would not have been content with a victory only on the issue of the existence of the Mandate. Nor would they have been happy if three other submissions were affirmed and the rest denied, the three being that South Africa has a duty to submit annual reports on the territory to the U.N., to transmit petitions, and not to modify unilaterally the terms of the Mandate. These submissions could be derived from the 1950 advisory opinion. Yet one point in the 1950 opinion would have been very important if reaffirmed by the Court in the contentious case: the duty of South Africa to submit to the supervision of the General Assembly with respect to the Mandate.

Yet from the Applicants' point of view, the most important submissions in the Case concerned apartheid, which was not at issue in the 1950 opinion. In their initial brief the Applicants argued that apartheid or its effects constituted a violation of one of the provisions in the Mandate instrument, namely, the duty to "promote to the utmost the material and moral well-being and the social progress of the inhabitants of the territory." The following is typical of the strong language used in the initial brief:

> Deliberately, systematically and consistently, the Mandatory has discriminated against the "Native" population of South West Africa, which constitutes overwhelmingly the larger part of the population of the Territory. In so doing, the Mandatory has not only failed to promote *to the utmost* the material and moral well-being, the social progress and the development of the people of South West Africa, but it has failed to promote such well-being and social progress in any significant degree whatever. To the contrary, the Mandatory has thwarted the well-being, the social progress and the development of the people of South West Africa throughout varied aspects of their lives: in agriculture; in industry, industrial employment and labor relations; in government, whether territorial, local or tribal; in respect of security of the person, rights of residence and freedom of movement; and in education.[18]

One other submission rounds out the picture. The Applicants charged that, in violation of another specific provision of the Mandate instrument, South Africa had established military bases within South West Africa. They asked the Court to declare that South Africa has the duty to remove such bases.

The Applicants' Memorials bear the ear-marks of hurriedly drafted documents with considerable legal vagueness couched in highly con-

---

[x] Above, n. u, at 24–29, 32–39. See, too, Elizabeth S. Landis, "The South West Africa Cases: Remand to the United Nations" (1967) 52 *Cornell Law Quarterly* 627 at 640–52.

[18] South West Africa Cases, Memorials, at p. 133.

tentious language. Yet this proved to be of vital inadvertent strategic importance. First, the legal vagueness may have helped lure South Africa into showing up in Court to argue the case. Second, it helped to throw South Africa somewhat off base in answering the charges. Third, it provided a convenient umbrella for the sharp turns that the case later took by allowing the Applicants to argue that their seemingly new positions could be found somewhere or other in the Memorials if they were properly construed.

In any event, South Africa had a field day with the Memorials. The Respondent submitted ten volumes of Counter-Memorials which dealt with in precise detail every single charge contained in the Memorials. The Counter-Memorials produced an incredible amount of hitherto unavailable information about South West Africa and presented as well a complete explanation of the policy of apartheid. Apartheid is grounded, the Respondent argued, in sheer political necessity; without it there would be a repetition, with greater bloodshed and chaos, of the "Congo" and the "Mau Mau" in South West Africa. For "African reality" demands that the "white" bearers of civilization" treat the "Natives" as their wards, protect them against exploitation by not allowing them to own their own land, and give them the benefits of modern government without the burden, which might be abused, of direct political representation. Moreover, the Respondent contended, there is an object lesson in the racial problems that other countries are experiencing (such as the United States) where the Negroes constitute only a small fraction of the population rather than the overwhelming majority. More tellingly, the Respondent pointed out the benefits to the "Natives" of the system of apartheid: the standard of living of the "Natives" of South West Africa is high compared to "Blacks" in other African countries, including Ethiopia and Liberia. This is true in education, income, hospitals, and other indicia of well-being and social progress.

But the Counter-Memorials were not simply a collection of assertions and refutations. They were boldly attuned to a single theme, repeated at every turn, that gave them great power and unity. This single theme was that the Applicants' case boiled down to a charge of "bad faith" on the part of South Africa as administrator of the Mandate. The Applicants' charges of "deliberate, systematic, and consistent" discrimination could only amount to a charge of *mala fides*. By thus reducing the Applicants' case to this one charge, South Africa could then demolish the case in two ways. First, the Respondent argued that it did not act and had not acted in bad faith, specifying not only the improvement in the living conditions of the "Natives" since 1920, but also arguing that all the appurtenances of apartheid—pass laws, influx control legislation, wage contracts, detention laws, curfew regulations, etc.—evidenced a sincere desire on the part of the administering authority to prevent social friction. Without these laws, many of the "Whites" (whom any impartial observer would agree are far more "right-wing" on this issue than the Verwoerd government) might misbehave toward the "Natives." Thus the laws operated to protect the

"Natives" as well as possible in a difficult situation, and therefore the government officials could not be considered to have acted in bad faith. Moreover, the "good faith" of the Respondent is shown by its lengthy argument in this very Court, by its willingness to spread all the facts out for the world to see, by its submission to the rule of law in the teeth of its own conviction that the Mandate has lapsed and that Ethiopia and Liberia have no standing to sue. Second, by characterizing the Applicants' case as resting on "bad faith," the Respondent could and did argue that a Court cannot judicially determine such a vague problem as good or bad faith anyway, and thus the case should be dismissed as not justiciable.

Surprised by the detail, cogency, and boldness of the Counter-Memorials, the Applicants responded with a Reply Brief 2.2 times as long as their initial Memorials and far more precise and legally sophisticated. They contended that the "bad faith" characterization was completely erroneous and in any event irrelevant since it would not give a Court any legal basis upon which to judge with sufficient clarity whether South Africa violated the Mandate (and thus on this point there was complete agreement with the Respondent). In addition, Mr. Gross argued eloquently in the oral proceedings that "without any purpose or intimation of comparison . . . history teaches that the greatest excesses of policy, and the most reprehensible doctrines, frequently are propounded and executed with professions of good faith and lofty purpose. . . . When sincerity of purpose is carried to unreasonable lengths, or improper ends, it is often difficult to distinguish from obsession." [19]

The Applicants also argued that it was irrelevant to compare the conditions in South West Africa with those in independent, nonmandated countries such as Ethiopia, Liberia, and the United States; what was relevant was the living standard of the "Natives" of South West Africa compared with the extremely higher living standard of the "Whites." This latter argument of irrelevancy of comparison won out over the other tack that the applicants could have taken, of actually contrasting conditions in South West Africa with the rest of the world and showing the slow but steady progress of desegregation elsewhere. For such a strategy would have led to interminable argument about conditions in 110 other countries and might have led to mixed evidence which could divert the Court from its main concern and also stretch out the proceedings.

But it was not enough for the Applicants to charge that the Respondent had misread the Memorials. For, what exactly was the legal basis of the Applicants' case? Two bases emerged in the Reply Brief. The first and most radical was that it was contrary to international law for a government to allot status, rights, duties, privileges or burdens upon the basis of membership in a group, class or race, rather than on the basis of individual merit, capacity or potential. This argument was not pressed heavily in the Reply Brief, probably out of conviction that the

[19] Verbatim Record, C.R. 65/6, at p. 20.

legally conservative judges would not accept it. For it is difficult to find an explicit rule of customary international law grounded in the practice of States that prohibits such differentiation. Indeed South Africa might have argued (but apparently never thought of it) that international law itself allots rights and duties on the basis of membership in groups—called "States"—and thus the Applicants' suggested norm of non-separation, pressed to the limit of its logic, would result in international law being in violation of international law. South Africa did not fail to argue, however, that the Mandate instrument which gave the Court its jurisdiction contained clauses that differentiated according to groups. For instance, the Mandate prohibits the "supply of intoxicating spirits and beverages to the natives" (article 3) and the "military training of the natives" (article 4). Yet the Applicants' argument may have been worth making because a victory on this point would be enormous for them: it would mean that the South African government could not justify in law or by any recitations of fact the system of apartheid. Nor could the government get out from under an adverse decision by relocating the "Natives" in "homelands" or "Bantustans" (which shall be discussed below). Furthermore, an international norm against differentiation according to groups would apply as much to South Africa as to South West Africa.

The second basis for the Applicants' legal position was much more conservative. Rather than invoking international law as a whole, it focused on article 2 of the Mandate. The argument was that the effects of apartheid, and not group differentiation per se, resulted factually in below-standard treatment for the "Natives" in violation of article 2. A difficulty was that article 2 ("well-being and social progress") was extremely vague, and it was not helpful to look to its application by the Permanent Mandates Commission under the League of Nations since the P.M.C. did not strenuously complain about the treatment of the "Natives." Rather it was necessary to argue that given the Court's finding in the jurisdiction aspect of the case in 1962 that the Mandate is still in force, and given the fact that but for its demise with the League of Nations the P.M.C. would still be supervising the territory, we are compelled to find present-day standards which would be used by the P.M.C. if it were in existence today. Fortunately there are organs of the United Nations set up under Charter provisions very close in wording to the Mandate provisions in the League Covenant. The Trusteeship Council is one such organ; it is more strict from South Africa's point of view than the P.M.C. The Committee on Information (subsequently the Committee of Seventeen and then the Committee of Twenty-Four) is another; it balances the picture by being less strict. In addition, the General Assembly exercises supervision over both these organs. Thus if we could find general rules or standards that were applied by both the Trusteeship Council and the Committee on Information, and moreover were accepted by the General Assembly, then these rules would clearly represent the boundaries for standards that the P.M.C. would be applying today if it were in existence. An examination of Trusteeship Council and Committee on Information reports and General Assembly resolutions approving these reports revealed a large number of specific standards on the treatment of indigenous populations by administering authorities. Then by a factual examination of the fields of education, economic development, civil freedoms, government, and citizenship, it was argued that South Africa's treatment of the "Natives" and "Coloured persons" of South West Africa violated these standards of administration.

This second basis was more conservative than the norm of non-separation because it did not condemn apartheid per se and thus would not put the Court in the position of issuing a judgment that would not be obeyed by South Africa. Yet if the Court accepted this argument, it would still mean that South Africa could only comply by undertaking a crash program of betterment for the "Natives"—to train them in school subjects relevant to the management of a complex industrial society and not just in handicrafts, to teach them English and Afrikaans and not their tribal languages which are unsuited to the comprehension of abstract ideas, to educate them politically as other administering authorities have done with the people under their tutelage, to start a program of political enfranchisement, to repeal the "pass" and "curfew" laws, to allow "Natives" to own land, to provide them with low-cost loans to set up business enterprises, and so forth. These reforms could be undertaken on a "group" basis; indeed, they call for preferential treatment for the "Native" and "Coloured" groups for a time until all the groups are brought to the same level of social and economic status. Thus the current-standards-of-administration basis was clearly separate from the norm of non-separation.

. . . .

THE SAFARI GAMBIT

At a pretrial conference on March 12, 1965 at the Hague, some unexpected moves were made which resulted in radical changes in the Case. The first was a seemingly innocuous ruling by the President of the Court that the case would be divided into two phases, arguments first on law and then on facts. Second, on obvious orders from Pretoria, the Respondent's counsel proposed that the judges of the Court undertake a personal inspection visit to South West Africa to see firsthand "African reality." The Respondent asked Mr. Gross, who would have the floor for his opening argument, to yield the floor briefly for the purposes of this proposal.

It was then the Respondent's turn to be surprised. The Applicants objected vigorously to the "safari" and declined to yield the floor. The latter was in itself sensible since the Court would be packed on opening day with representatives of the world's press and it would be foolish to allow the South African counsel to make a grandiloquent speech on the order of "we have nothing to hide; let the Court come and see for itself whether the charges levelled against us all these years are true." But it is less understandable strategically why the Applicants opposed the safari gambit in the pretrial conference and again when it

was finally introduced in open session. Of course they were concerned
with delay of the Case; Ethiopia and Liberia were chafing at the unexpected expenses involved. Moreover the judges were old and not active; the trip might result in serious illness for some of them and thus
delay the case even more. Yet these reasons do not seem compelling
nor adequate to explain the apparent conflict on the safari proposal
between Applicants and Respondent. In the first place, a visit by the
judges would enhance the stature of the Case and its public importance, and thus increase the chances that the U.S. and U.K. would not
be able to veto implementing the final decision in the Security Council. Moreover, in retrospect, it is possible that a thorough safari might
have convinced at least one of the seven judges who wrote the final
opinion that it was far too late to throw the Case out on a jurisdictional issue. In addition, unless the Court accepted the invitation
South Africa could always claim that the Court did not really understand the facts, that the Applicants were afraid lest the Court see the
true facts, and that South Africa was not given a full fair chance to
prove that its policies over the years had been beneficial to the people.
Finally, a careful examination of the terms of South Africa's invitation
demonstrated that South Africa was proposing a mere inspection trip
where the judges could see anything they desired but could not question the inhabitants or take oral evidence. When Mr. Gross pointed
out the exclusion of oral evidence from the proposal, the South African lawyers became very defensive and stated that there was no need
to take such evidence. This reaction could have signalled an effective
counter-gambit. The Applicants could have agreed to the safari on
condition that the judges take oral evidence. Then the burden would
have shifted to the Respondent to explain why, if it had nothing to
hide, the judges could not question dissatisfied "Native" leaders, political prisoners, shanty-town laborers, subsistence-level farmers, and so
forth. But this counter-gambit was never made, and the oral-evidence
exclusion was merely cited as a reason why the inspection proposal was
incomplete and thus would be a relative waste of time for the Court to
undertake.

Naturally the mere reason that the safari would delay the Case was
not enough to convince the Court not to undertake it, since the Court
has always done its utmost to please both sovereign parties to an international dispute. Yet the Applicants felt so strongly that the safari proposal should be defeated that their entire case underwent a tremen-
dous radicalization in order to convince the Court not to go on the
safari.

The sequence of events was as follows: Mr. Gross gave his opening
arguments on the "law" of the case, stating that he would consider certain matters of "fact" later in the factual half of the proceedings. Then
Mr. de Villiers for the Respondent took the floor, invited the Court to
go on an inspection trip, and proceeded to give his rebuttal on the
"law". After that Mr. Gross replied both to the "law" points and to the
safari proposal. It was at this stage that the safari gambit acted as the
impetus for a great change in the Applicants' position. Mr. Gross
argued that the safari was superfluous since there *were no facts sub-*

stantially in dispute in this case; the Applicants should prevail on the *admitted* fact of apartheid alone. All that was at issue was the legality of the Respondent's policy of allotting rights and duties on the basis of group membership and not on individual qualities. Whether this allocation was reasonable, sincere, or even beneficial is irrelevant; all that matters is that some "Natives" of unusual ability or talent are forced, because of group affiliation, to accept a lower standard of living and fewer political rights than they would have merited on the basis of their ability.

The Respondent's lawyers were shocked by this turn in the argument. At first they could not believe that they had actually been conceded all the facts in the case. For this meant that previous charges in the United Nations that South Africa was engaged in deliberate oppression, including genocide and police terrorization, were now conceded to be untrue. Moreover, the Applicants' own charge of militarization of the territory contrary to article 4 of the Mandate was presumably abandoned since the Respondent's alleged facts on this point showed no militarization. In short, the Applicants' concession to South Africa appeared to be the complete vindication of South Africa's side of the story that the U.N. had refused to listen to, and South Africa of course made full use of this fact in later public relations releases. Second and more importantly, the South African lawyers now had the chance to press their arguments on the "law" to the hilt, for contradictions might show up in the Applicants' case given their acceptance of South Africa's version of the facts.

Still there was an issue as to the meaning of "facts"—did it include implications to be drawn from the facts? Mr. Gross argued that he was not admitting to South Africa's own interpretations from their facts, but that he was free to draw his own implications. But what was he trying to imply? questioned the judges and the opposing counsel. Was he interested in whether apartheid was good or bad? Was he concerned with the issue of whether apartheid in fact promoted to the utmost the moral and material well-being of the inhabitants? Pressed to reply to these questions, Mr. Gross began to take the extreme position that although he did not "concede" either the facts or their implications, facts were *superfluous*. There was no need to inquire as to the facts of apartheid; nothing South Africa could prove on this point was relevant. The safari was superfluous, and so were the "witnesses" that South Africa indicated it would call to testify in the case. Nor was there any need to have oral argument on the facts as originally planned by the Court and agreed to by Mr. Gross in his opening argument. All that mattered was that apartheid was contrary to an international norm and/or standard of non-discrimination or non-separation. The Applicants rested their case.

With the entire cumbersome case resting like an inverted pyramid on this narrow point of the illegality of apartheid, the safari proposal surely had become irrelevant. Eight out of fourteen judges agreed. However, South Africa was allowed to call fourteen out of their contemplated thirty-eight witnesses.

A more important consequence of the Applicants' decision to rest the case on the legal issue was the abandonment of the second more "conservative" basis for the case—the current standards of administration of dependent territories. The earlier term "standards of administration" now metamorphosed into a "standard of non-discrimination" having exactly the same content as the international norm of non-discrimination (the reason for this will appear below). Indeed the original second basis for the case may have been discarded permanently, for when Mr. Gross was asked by a judge whether there was any difference now between his submissions 3 and 4 which originally had distinguished between the fact of apartheid and the effects of apartheid, he replied that they were one and the same.

What were the reasons for the Applicants' new position? The most important has been suggested: defeating the safari proposal. Coupled with this may have been a fear of getting too enmeshed in a "factual" dispute with South Africa who had the upper hand because of access to the facts. Also, pressures from the African States to get a quick decision played a part. Fourth, the norm of non-separation would, if the Court accepted it, preclude the Bantustan proposal even after the decision was handed down. Fifth, a straight anti-apartheid position would put the case on its most solid moral foundation. Sixth, it was probably felt that focusing solely on apartheid would force even the most conservative judge to acquiesce in a general condemnation. Seventh, a norm of law against apartheid would apply equally to South Africa, though it would still be difficult to bring that matter before a court. Finally, the Verwoerd government certainly would not be able to comply with an anti-apartheid decision, and thus sanctions might be voted by the Security Council against South Africa itself. The only trouble was that the Court, knowing South Africa would not comply, might look for a way to avoid deciding the Case on this issue so that the Court's own authority might not be compromised.

THE FINAL LEGAL-ARGUMENTATIVE STRATEGIES

The focal point of the entire case now became the Applicants' alleged norm and/or standard of non-discrimination or non-separation. Difficult conceptual issues were involved, the most important being that of "discrimination." South Africa boldly agreed that discrimination would be a violation of the Mandate, but argued that apartheid did not involve discrimination but was merely a policy of separate development of the races. If apartheid was more than a mere separate development, then a factual inquiry would be necessary to see if apartheid involved unfair, unequal, undesirable or discriminatory treatment.

But the Applicants had now based their case on an avoidance of a factual inquiry. Were they arguing then that any policy of differentiation according to race violated the alleged norm of non-discrimination? Although South Africa tried to characterize the norm as being a norm of non-differentiation, the Applicants objected violently to this. Their reason for objecting is clear: the Mandate itself differentiates according to racial groups, and the many "minorities provisions" in treaties concluded after World War I were explicitly designed to protect the existence of population minorities as separate groups. It would be virtually impossible to prove that non-differentiation per se was illegal under international law.

Yet how could a distinction be articulated between differentiation and discrimination? At one point the Applicants suggested that the difference was that differentiation in the Mandate was protective, whereas apartheid is coercive. Mr. de Villiers countered by arguing that protection and coercion are two sides of a coin; *e.g.*, if the clause in the Mandate prohibiting the sale of intoxicating spirits to the "Natives" operates to protect them, it must also be coercively enforced against any "White" person who would privately try to engage in the sale of liquor. At another point Mr. Gross argued that the difference is that allotment of rights on a group basis is differentiation without being discrimination if it concerns a group which an individual is normally free to quit. Mr. de Villiers rejoined that laws in most countries give different rights to minors as opposed to adults, men as opposed to women, or in some countries to people of certain religions. Yet people are not normally free to quit these groups or, in the case of religion, it would be onerous to require someone to give up his faith in order to be dissociated from the group. Thus Mr. de Villiers concluded by admitting that South Africa differentiates, but argued that the Applicants were really trying to use the *term* "discrimination" to mean "differentiation" so that it would apply automatically to South West Africa without the need for factual inquiries. Indeed, he stressed, the Applicants had argued that even if apartheid were a benefit to the inhabitants it would be illegal, a position which seemed to the Respondent to come a long way from the factual allegations in the Memorials of "deliberate, systematic and consistent" discrimination to the detriment of the moral and material well-being of the inhabitants.

The Applicants countered by resort to international law. Resolutions of the General Assembly had made it clear, they argued, that apartheid itself was illegal and discriminatory. And the Court must follow what the U.N. has resolved. Nevertheless, there are difficulties with this position. The Applicants had to concede that resolutions of the U.N. are not binding upon member states. They may express a near-universal sentiment, but customary international law that is binding on everyone must be grounded in actual state practice and acquiescence; it is not enough for most States to say that a dissenting State should change its own practice, a position which Mr. de Villiers termed a "collectivist approach." On the general question, the Applicants conceded that their contention on the norm issue perhaps rested on a law-creating process "which has not heretofore been considered or passed upon by this honourable Court." [21]

The Applicants then tried arguing that even if the Court were to find no generally binding norm of international law, nevertheless

[21] Verbatim Record, C.R. 65/23 at p. 43.

South Africa was bound by a "standard" of precisely the same (anti-apartheid) content of the norm solely because of South Africa's duties as a Mandatory. But the Respondent soon pointed out that this reliance on a standard to bolster the norm argument really meant the abandonment of the norm and thus the abandonment of the effort of trying to get the Court to declare that apartheid itself was illegal. This point was clarified by a question from the bench: Judge Fitzmaurice elicited from Mr. Gross a concession that there was no attempt to prove in the present case that apartheid was illegal in general, but merely that it was illegal for South West Africa. Thus it may have been a strategic error to argue on the basis of the norm, even though a motive may have been a desire to create a salutary rule of international law, for such an argument created a risk that a loss in Court on the norm might carry with it a loss on the companion argument of standards.

The Applicants' case on the standard seemed more solid than the case on the norm, although it still created for the Court the problem of condemning apartheid outright. The Respondent's best counter-arguments were that since apartheid did not exist in other dependent territories it was hard to find an anti-apartheid standard (South Africa being perfectly willing to concede an anti-discrimination standard), and that the U.N. resolutions based on apartheid were grounded on distorted and untrue facts alleged by professional petitioners and publicity-seekers. The present Case would have been the proper place to look at the true facts, but the Applicants avoided a factual inquiry and indeed accepted the Respondent's version of the facts!

South Africa concluded by showing its distress at the use of the norm and/or standard borrowed from condemnatory U.N. resolutions. It characterized the Applicants as assigning to the Court "a most unworthy role," that of a "revolutionary tribunal to aid and abet, and to rubber-stamp, the usurpation by the political majorities in international organizations of legislative powers which have not been granted to them in the constitutive instruments." [22] The Court's only function would be to "blindly adopt standards laid down by others," letting the organized international society become legislator, witness, judge, jury and executioner.[23] The use of this language as a capstone to extremely protracted argumentation may have had great effect upon the Court.

3. The Proceedings and the Court's Composition

Public hearings in this phase of the proceedings lasted from 15 March to 29 November 1965. South Africa called fourteen expert witnesses to testify on the merits of the case, but the Court declined an invitation extended by South Africa to carry out an inspection *in loco* in South West Africa as well as the request that

[22] Verbatim Record, C.R. 65/48 at pp. 9–10.
[23] Verbatim Record, C.R. 65/20 at p. 57.

it should visit South Africa, Ethiopia, and Liberia and one or two African countries south of the Sahara of the Court's own choosing.[y]

Between 1962 and 1965 the composition of the International Court underwent several changes as a result of the triennial election of five judges in 1964.[z] The Court, as constituted at the start of the proceedings, consisted of the same two *ad hoc* judges who sat in 1962—namely, Judges *ad hoc* Van Wyk and Sir Louis Mbanefo—and the following fifteen permanent judges: President Sir Percy Spender (Australia), Vice-President Wellington Koo (China), Judges Winiarski (Poland), Spiropoulos (Greece), Sir Gerald Fitzmaurice (United Kingdom), Koretsky (Soviet Union), Tanaka (Japan), Jessup (United States), Morelli (Italy), Padilla Nervo (Mexico), Forster (Senegal), Gros (France), Bustamante Y Rivero (Peru), Badawi (United Arab Republic), Sir Mohammad Zafrulla Khan (Pakistan). These fifteen judges were, however, reduced to twelve as a result of recusal, death, and illness.

On the first day of the hearings the President of the Court, Sir Percy Spender, announced that Judge Sir Muhammad Zafrulla Khan "will not participate in the decision in this case." [a] No reason was given, but after the Court had delivered its judgment Judge Khan confirmed a report that he had not voluntarily recused himself but that the President had informed him that it would be improper for him to sit, as he had previously been nominated as an *ad hoc* judge by Ethiopia and Liberia before his election to the Court.[b] There is no public record of a meeting of the Court to decide on the disqualification of Judge Khan, as required by Article 24 of the Statute of the Court, where there is a disagreement over recusal between the President and the member concerned. Doubts have therefore been raised as to whether the correct procedure was followed in this case as well as whether the

[y] *South West Africa, Second Phase,* 1966 ICJ Reports 6 at 9. The invitation to visit South West Africa and South Africa was rejected by 8 votes to 6 and the request that the Court visit the other African countries by 9 votes to 5. For a full description of the proceedings before the Court, see *Ethiopia and Liberia versus South Africa* (published by the Department of Information, Pretoria), and C. A. W. Manning, "The South West Africa Cases: A Personal Analysis" (1966) 3 *International Relations* 98.

[z] Five judges are elected every three years for a nine-year period of office: Article 13 of the Statute of the Court.

[a] ICJ, Year 1965, Public Sitting, Verbatim Record C. R. 65/1 (uncorrected), p. 10.

[b] UN Document A/6388 (17 August 1966).

reason given for Judge Khan's disqualification was a valid one.[c]

South Africa attempted to reduce the size of the court still further by applying for the recusal of Judge Nervo of Mexico on the ground that, prior to his election to the Court, he had revealed his opposition to the South African administration of South West Africa in debates in the United Nations.[d] This application was rejected, and it has been pointed out that, if it had been upheld, the applicants might have succeeded in obtaining the recusal of Sir Percy Spender on the ground that he had spoken in favour of South Africa while a delegate to the United Nations.[e]

Judge Bustamante Y Rivero, who had voted against South Africa in 1962, was ill when the hearings began and did not recover in time to participate in the oral hearings and hence the decision. During the course of the hearings, on 4 August 1966, Judge Badawi, who had also found against South Africa in 1962, died, and although his place on the Court was filled by Judge Ammoun of Lebanon, it was too late for him to take part in the proceedings.

Consequently, by the end of the proceedings the Court had been reduced to twelve judges and two *ad hoc* judges. In terms of Article 55 of the Court's Statute all questions are to be decided "by a majority of the judges present" and "in the event of an equality of votes, the President . . . shall have a casting vote."

4. The Judgment of the Court [f]

On 18 July 1966 the Court delivered the most controversial judgment in its history. Although the entire proceedings in the *South West Africa Cases* had been directed at the merits of the dispute —whether South Africa was accountable to the United Nations for her administration of South West Africa and whether apartheid violated the provisions of the Mandate—the Court declined

---

[c] William M. Reisman, "Revision of the South West Africa Cases" (1966) 7 *Virginia Journal of International Law* 1 at 55–58; Bin Cheng, "The 1966 South-West Africa Judgment of the World Court" 1967 *Current Legal Problems* 181 at 196–99; Rosalyn Higgins, "The International Court and South West Africa: The Implications of the Judgment" (1966) 42 *International Affairs* 573 at 587–88; Landis, above, n. x, 653.

[d] Cheng, above, n. c, 196; Landis, above, n. x, 653.

[e] Landis, above, n. x, 653; Mburumba Kerina, "South-West Africa, the United Nations, and the International Court of Justice" (1966–7) 2 *African Forum* no. 2, 1 at 20–21.

[f] Academic writings on this decision are far too numerous to include in one footnote. A full list of the literature on this significant decision appears in the bibliography.

to pronounce on these issues, and instead returned to a matter which it was generally believed had been finally disposed of in 1962—the legal standing of the applicant States. By the casting vote of the President, Sir Percy Spender, the Court held that it could not make any of the orders sought by the applicants, because they had failed to establish "any legal right or interest appertaining to them in the subject-matter" of their claims. In effect, this decision constituted a reversal of the finding of the Court in 1962 on the third preliminary objection and was the consequence of changes in the composition of the Court which had resulted in the minority of 1962 becoming the majority. The majority consisted of President Sir Percy Spender (two votes), Judges Winiarski, Spiropoulos, Sir Gerald Fitzmaurice, Morelli, and Gros, and Judge *ad hoc* Van Wyk. Of these only Judge Gros of France, who had replaced his compatriot Judge Basdevant in 1964, had not formed part of the minority of 1962. The seven dissenting judges on this occasion were Judges Koo, Koretsky, Tanaka, Jessup, Nervo, and Forster, and Judge *ad hoc* Sir Louis Mbanefo. The judgment of the Court reads as follows:[g]

1. In the present proceedings the two applicant States, the Empire of Ethiopia and the Republic of Liberia (whose cases are identical and will for present purposes be treated as one case), acting in the capacity of States which were members of the former League of Nations, put forward various allegations of contraventions of the League of Nations Mandate for South West Africa, said to have been committed by the respondent State, the Republic of South Africa, as the administering authority.

2. In an earlier phase of the case, which took place before the Court in 1962, four preliminary objections were advanced, based on Article 37, of the Court's Statute and the jurisdictional clause (Article 7, paragraph 2) of the Mandate for South West Africa, which were all of them argued by the Respondent and treated by the Court as objections to its jurisdiction. The Court, by its Judgment of 21 December 1962, rejected each of these objections, and thereupon found that it had "jurisdiction to adjudicate upon the merits of the dispute".

3. In the course of the proceedings on the merits, comprising the exchange of written pleadings, the oral arguments of the Parties and the hearing of a considerable number of witnesses, the Parties put forward various contentions on such matters as whether the Mandate for South West Africa was still in force,—and if so, whether the Mandatory's obligation under Article 6 of the Mandate to furnish annual reports to the Council of the former League of Nations concerning its administration of the mandated territory had become transformed by one

[g] 1966 ICJ Reports 6 at 17–51.

means or another into an obligation to furnish such reports to the General Assembly of the United Nations, or had, on the other hand, lapsed entirely;—whether there had been any contravention by the Respondent of the second paragraph of Article 2 of the Mandate which required the Mandatory to "promote to the utmost the material and moral well-being and the social progress of the inhabitants of the territory",—whether there had been any contravention of Article 4 of the Mandate, prohibiting (except for police and local defence purposes) the "military training of the natives", and forbidding the establishment of military or naval bases, or the erection of fortifications in the territory. The Applicants also alleged that the Respondent had contravened paragraph 1 of Article 7 of the Mandate (which provides that the Mandate can only be modified with the consent of the Council of the League of Nations) by attempting to modify the Mandate without the consent of the General Assembly of the United Nations which, so it was contended, had replaced the Council of the League for this and other purposes. There were other allegations also, which it is not necessary to set out here.

4. On all these matters, the Court has studied the written pleadings and oral arguments of the Parties, and has also given consideration to the question of the order in which the various issues would fall to be dealt with. In this connection, there was one matter that appertained to the merits of the case but which had an antecedent character, namely the question of the Applicants' standing in the present phase of the proceedings,—not, that is to say, of their standing before the Court itself, which was the subject of the Court's decision in 1962, but the question, as a matter of the merits of the case, of their legal right or interest regarding the subject-matter of their claim, as set out in their final submissions.

5. Despite the antecedent character of this question, the Court was unable to go into it until the Parties had presented their arguments on the other questions of merits involved. The same instruments are relevant to the existence and character of the Respondent's obligations concerning the Mandate as are also relevant to the existence and character of the Applicants' legal right or interest in that regard. Certain humanitarian principles alleged to affect the nature of the Mandatory's obligations in respect of the inhabitants of the mandated territory were also pleaded as a foundation for the right of the Applicants to claim in their own individual capacities the performance of those same obligations. The implications of Article 7, paragraph 1, of the Mandate, referred to above, require to be considered not only in connection with paragraph (9) and certain aspects of paragraph (2) of the Applicants' final submissions, but also, as will be seen in due course, in connection with that of the Applicants' standing relative to the merits of the case. The question of the position following upon the dissolution of the League of Nations in 1946 has the same kind of double aspect, and so do other matters.

6. The Parties having dealt with all the elements involved, it became the Court's duty to begin by considering those questions which

had such a character that a decision respecting any of them might render unnecessary an enquiry into other aspects of the matter. There are two questions in the present case which have this character. One is whether the Mandate still subsists at all, as the Applicants maintain that it does in paragraph (1) of their final submissions; for if it does not, then clearly the various allegations of contraventions of the Mandate by the Respondent fall automatically to the ground. But this contention, namely as to the continued subsistence of the Mandate, is itself part of the Applicants' whole claim as put forward in their final submissions, being so put forward solely in connection with the remaining parts of the claim, and as the necessary foundation for these. For this reason the other question, which (as already mentioned) is that of the Applicants' legal right or interest in the subject-matter of their claim, is even more fundamental.

. . . .

7. It is accordingly to this last question that the Court must now turn. Before doing so however, it should be made clear that when, in the present Judgment, the Court considers what provisions of the Mandate for South West Africa involve a legal right or interest for the Applicants, and what not, it does so without pronouncing upon, and wholly without prejudice to, the question of whether that Mandate is still in force. The Court moreover thinks it necessary to state that its 1962 decision on the question of competence was equally given without prejudice to that of the survival of the Mandate, which is a question appertaining to the merits of the case. It was not in issue in 1962, except in the sense that survival had to be assumed for the purpose of determining the purely jurisdictional issue which was all that was then before the Court. It was made clear in the course of the 1962 proceedings that it was upon this assumption that the Respondent was arguing the jurisdictional issue; and the same view is reflected in the Applicants' final submissions (1) and (2) in the present proceedings, the effect of which is to ask the Court to declare (*inter alia*) that the Mandate still subsists, and that the Respondent is still subject to the obligations it provides for. It is, correspondingly, a principal part of the Respondent's case on the merits that since (as it contends) the Mandate no longer exists, the Respondent has no obligations under it, and therefore cannot be in breach of the Mandate. This is a matter which, for reasons to be given later in another connection, but equally applicable here, could not have been the subject of any final determination by a decision on a purely preliminary point of jurisdiction.

8. The Respondent's final submissions in the present proceedings ask simply for a rejection of those of the Applicants, both generally and in detail. But quite apart from the recognized right of the Court, implicit in paragraph 2 of Article 53 of its Statute, to select *proprio motu* the basis of its decision, the Respondent did in the present phase of the case, particularly in its written pleadings, deny that the Applicants had any legal right or interest in the subject-matter of their claim,—a denial which, at this stage of the case, clearly cannot have been intended merely as an argument against the applicability of the

jurisdictional clause of the Mandate. In its final submissions the Respondent asks the Court, upon the basis, *inter alia,* of "the statements of fact and law as set forth in [its] pleadings and the oral proceedings", to make no declaration as claimed by the Applicants in their final submissions.

. . . .

9. The Court now comes to the basis of its decision in the present proceedings. In order to lead up to this, something must first be said about the structure characterizing the Mandate for South West Africa, in common with the other various mandates; and here it is necessary to stress that no true appreciation of the legal situation regarding any particular mandate, such as that for South West Africa, can be arrived at unless it is borne in mind that this Mandate was only one amongst a number of mandates, the Respondent only one amongst a number of mandatories, and that the salient features of the mandates system as a whole were, with exceptions to be noted where material, applicable indifferently to all the mandates. The Mandate for South West Africa was not a special case.

10. The mandates system, as is well known, was formally instituted by Article 22 of the Covenant of the League of Nations. As there indicated, there were to be three categories of mandates, designated as 'A', 'B' and 'C' mandates respectively, the Mandate for South West Africa being one of the 'C' category. The differences between these categories lay in the nature and geographical situation of the territories concerned, the state of development of their peoples, and the powers accordingly to be vested in the administering authority, or mandatory, for each territory placed under mandate. But although it was by Article 22 of the League Covenant that the system as such was established, the precise terms of each mandate, covering the rights and obligations of the mandatory, of the League and its organs, and of the individual members of the League, in relation to each mandated territory, were set out in separate instruments of mandate which, with one exception to be noted later, took the form of resolutions of the Council of the League.

11. These instruments, whatever the differences between certain of their terms, had various features in common as regards their structure. For present purposes, their substantive provisions may be regarded as falling into two main categories. On the one hand, and of course as the principal element of each instrument, there were the articles defining the mandatory's powers, and its obligations in respect of the inhabitants of the territory and towards the League and its organs. These provisions, relating to the carrying out of the mandates as mandates, will hereinafter be referred to as "conduct of the mandate", or simply "conduct" provisions. On the other hand, there were articles conferring in different degrees, according to the particular mandate or category of mandate, certain rights relative to the mandated territory, directly upon the members of the League as individual States, or in favour of their nationals. Many of these rights were of the same kind as

are to be found in certain provisions of ordinary treaties of commerce, establishment and navigation concluded between States. Rights of this kind will hereinafter be referred to as "special interests" rights, embodied in the "special interests" provisions of the mandates. As regards the 'A' and 'B' mandates (particularly the latter) these rights were numerous and figured prominently—a fact which, as will be seen later, is significant for the case of the 'C' mandates also, even though, in the latter case, they were confined to provisions for freedom for missionaries ("nationals of any State Member of the League of Nations") to "enter into, travel and reside in the territory for the purpose of prosecuting their calling"—(Mandate for South West Africa, Article 5). In the present case, the dispute between the Parties relates exclusively to the former of these two categories of provisions, and not to the latter.

12. The broad distinction just noticed was a genuine, indeed an obvious one. Even if it may be the case that certain provisions of some of the mandates (such as for instance the "open door" provisions of the 'A' and 'B' mandates) can be regarded as having a double aspect, this does not affect the validity or relevance of the distinction. Such provisions would, in their "conduct of the mandate" aspect, fall under that head; and in their aspect of affording commercial opportunities for members of the League and their nationals, they would come under the head of "special interests" clauses. It is natural that commercial provisions of this kind could redound to the benefit of a mandated territory and its inhabitants in so far as the use made of them by States members of the League had the effect of promoting the economic or industrial development of the territory. In that sense and to that extent these provisions could no doubt contribute to furthering the aims of the mandate; and their due implementation by the mandatories was in consequence a matter of concern to the League and its appropriate organs dealing with mandates questions. But this was incidental, and was never their primary object. Their primary object was to benefit the individual members of the League and their nationals. Any action or intervention on the part of member States in this regard would be for that purpose—not in furtherance of the mandate as such.

13. In addition to the classes of provisions so far noticed, every instrument of mandate contained a jurisdictional clause which, with a single exception to be noticed in due course, was in identical terms for each mandate, whether belonging to the 'A', 'B' or 'C' category. The language and effect of this clause will be considered later; but it provided for a reference of disputes to the Permanent Court of International Justice and, so the Court found in the first phase of the case, as already mentioned, this reference was now, by virtue of Article 37 of the Court's Statute, to be construed as a reference to the present Court. Another feature of the mandates generally, was a provision according to which their terms could not be modified without the consent of the Council of the League. A further element, though peculiar to the 'C' mandates, may be noted: it was provided both by Article 22 of the Covenant of the League and by a provision of the instruments of 'C'

mandates that, subject to certain conditions not here material, a 'C' mandatory was to administer the mandated territory "as an integral portion of its own territory".

14. Having regard to the situation thus outlined, and in particular to the distinction to be drawn between the "conduct" and the "special interests" provisions of the various instruments of mandate, the question which now arises for decision by the Court is whether any legal right or interest exists for the Applicants relative to the Mandate, apart from such as they may have in respect of the latter category of provisions;—a matter on which the Court expresses no opinion, since this category is not in issue in the present case. In respect of the former category—the "conduct" provisions—the question which has to be decided is whether, according to the scheme of the mandates and of the mandates system as a whole, any legal right or interest (which is a different thing from a political interest) was vested in the members of the League of Nations, including the present Applicants, individually and each in its own separate right to call for the carrying out of the mandates as regards their "conduct" clauses;—or whether this function must, rather, be regarded as having appertained exclusively to the League itself, and not to each and every member State, separately and independently. In other words, the question is whether the various mandatories had any direct obligation towards the other members of the League individually, as regards the carrying out of the "conduct" provisions of the mandates.

15. If the answer to be given to this question should have the effect that the Applicants cannot be regarded as possessing the legal right or interest claimed, it would follow that even if the various allegations of contraventions of the Mandate for South West Africa on the part of the Respondent were established, the Applicants would still not be entitled to the pronouncements and declarations which, in their final submissions, they ask the Court to make. This is no less true in respect of their final submissions (1) and (2) than of the others. In these two submissions, the Applicants in substance affirm, and ask the Court to declare, the continued existence of the Mandate and of the Respondent's obligations thereunder. In the present proceedings however, the Court is concerned with the final submissions of the Applicants solely in the context of the "conduct" provisions of the Mandate. It has not to pronounce upon any of the Applicants' final submissions as these might relate to any question of "special interests" if a claim in respect of these had been made. The object of the Applicants' submissions (1) and (2) is to provide the basis for the remaining submissions, which are made exclusively in the context of a claim about provisions concerning which the question immediately arises whether they are provisions in respect of which the Applicants have any legal right or interest. If the Court finds that the Applicants do have such a right or interest, it would then be called upon to pronounce upon the first of the Applicants' final submissions—(continued existence of the Mandate), since if that one should be rejected, the rest would automatically fall to the ground. If on the other hand the Court should find that

such a right or interest does not exist, it would obviously be inappropriate and misplaced to make any pronouncement on this first submission of the Applicants, or on the second, since in the context of the present case the question of the continued existence of the Mandate, and of the Respondent's obligations thereunder, would arise solely in connection with provisions concerning which the Court had found that the Applicants lacked any legal right or interest.

. . . .

16. It is in their capacity as former members of the League of Nations that the Applicants appear before the Court; and the rights they claim are those that the members of the League are said to have been invested with in the time of the League. Accordingly, in order to determine what the rights and obligations of the Parties relative to the Mandate were and are (supposing it still to be in force, but without prejudice to that question); and in particular whether (as regards the Applicants) these include any right individually to call for the due execution of the "conduct" provisions, and (for the Respondent) an obligation to be answerable to the Applicants in respect of its administration of the Mandate, the Court must place itself at the point in time when the mandates system was being instituted, and when the instruments of mandate were being framed. The Court must have regard to the situation as it was at that time, which was the critical one, and to the intentions of those concerned as they appear to have existed, or are reasonably to be inferred, in the light of that situation. Intentions that might have been formed if the Mandate had been framed at a much later date, and in the knowledge of circumstances, such as the eventual dissolution of the League and its aftermath, that could never originally have been foreseen, are not relevant. Only on this basis can a correct appreciation of the legal rights of the Parties be arrived at. This view is supported by a previous finding of the Court (*Rights of United States Nationals in Morocco, I.C.J. Reports 1952,* at p. 189), the effect of which is that the meaning of a juridical notion in a historical context, must be sought by reference to the way in which that notion was understood in that context.

17. It follows that any enquiry into the rights and obligations of the Parties in the present case must proceed principally on the basis of considering, in the setting of their period, the texts of the instuments and particular provisions intended to give juridical expression to the notion of the "sacred trust of civilization" by instituting a mandates system.

18. The enquiry must pay no less attention to the juridical character and structure of the institution, the League of Nations, within the framework of which the mandates system was organized, and which inevitably determined how this system was to operate,—by what methods, —through what channels,—and by means of what recourses. One fundamental element of this juridical character and structure, which in a sense governed everything else, was that Article 2 of the Covenant provided that the "action of the League under this Covenant shall be effected through the instrumentality of an Assembly and of a Council,

with a permanent Secretariat". If the action of the League as a whole was thus governed, it followed naturally that the individual member States could not themselves act differently relative to League matters, unless it was otherwise specially so provided by some article of the Covenant.

19. As is well known, the mandates system originated in the decision taken at the Peace Conference following upon the world war of 1914–1918, that the colonial territories over which, by Article 119 of the Treaty of Versailles, Germany renounced "all her rights and titles" in favour of the then Principal Allied and Associated Powers, should not be annexed by those Powers or by any country affiliated to them, but should be placed under an international régime, in the application to the peoples of those territories, deemed "not yet able to stand by themselves", of the principle, declared by Article 22 of the League Covenant, that their "well-being and development" should form "a sacred trust of civilization".

20. The type of régime specified by Article 22 of the Covenant as constituting the "best method of giving practical effect to this principle" was that "the tutelage of such peoples should be entrusted to advanced nations . . . who are willing to accept it",—and here it was specifically added that it was to be "on behalf of the League" that "this tutelage should be exercised by those nations as Mandatories". It was not provided that the mandates should, either additionally or in the alternative, be exercised on behalf of the members of the League in their individual capacities. The mandatories were to be the agents of, or trustees for the League,—and not of, or for, each and every member of it individually.

21. The same basic idea was expressed again in the third paragraph of the preamble to the instrument of mandate for South West Africa, where it was recited that the Mandatory, in agreeing to accept the Mandate, had undertaken "to exercise it on behalf of the League of Nations". No other behalf was specified in which the Mandatory had undertaken, either actually or potentially, to exercise the Mandate. The effect of this recital, as the Court sees it, was to register an implied recognition (a) on the part of the Mandatory of the right of the League, acting as an entity through its appropriate organs, to require the due execution of the Mandate in respect of its "conduct" provisions; and (b) on the part of both the Mandatory and the Council of the League, of the character of the Mandate as a juridical régime set within the framework of the League as an institution. There was no similar recognition of any right as being additionally and independently vested in any other entity, such as a State, or as existing outside or independently of the League as an institution; nor was any undertaking at all given by the Mandatory in that regard.

22. It was provided by paragraph 1 of Article 22 of the Covenant that "securities for the performance" of the sacred trust were to be "embodied in this Covenant". This important reference to the "performance" of the trust contemplated, as it said, securities to be afforded by the Covenant itself. By paragraphs 7 and 9 respectively of Article

22, every mandatory was to "render to the Council [of the League—not to any other entity] an annual report in reference to the territory committed to its charge"; and a permanent commission, which came to be known as the Permanent Mandates Commission, was to be constituted "to receive and examine" these annual reports and "to advise the Council on all matters relating to the observance of the mandates". The Permanent Mandates Commission alone had this advisory role, just as the Council alone had the supervisory function. The Commission consisted of independent experts in their own right, appointed in their personal capacity as such, not as representing any individual member of the League or the member States generally.

23. The obligation to furnish annual reports was reproduced in the instruments of mandate themselves, where it was stated that they were to be rendered "to the satisfaction of the Council". Neither by the Covenant nor by the instruments of mandate, was any role reserved to individual League members in respect of these reports, furnishable to the Council, and referred by it to the Permanent Mandates Commission. It was the Council that had to be satisfied, not the individual League members. The part played by the latter, other than such as were members of the Council, was exclusively through their participation in the work of the Assembly of the League when, acting under Article 3 of the Covenant, that organ exercised in respect of mandates questions its power to deal with "any matter within the sphere of action of the League". It was as being within the sphere of the League as an institution that mandates questions were dealt with by its Assembly.

24. These then were the methods, and the only methods, contemplated by the Covenant as "securities" for the performance of the sacred trust, and it was in the Covenant that they were to be embodied. No security taking the form of a right for every member of the League separately and individually to require from the mandatories the due performance of their mandates, or creating a liability for each mandatory to be answerable to them individually,—still less conferring a right of recourse to the Court in these regards,—was provided by the Covenant.

25. This result is precisely what was to be expected from the fact that the mandates system was an activity of the League of Nations, that is to say of an entity functioning as an institution. In such a setting, rights cannot be derived from the mere fact of membership of the organization in itself: the rights that member States can legitimately claim must be derived from and depend on the particular terms of the instrument constitutive of the organization, and of the other instruments relevant in the context. This principle is necessarily applicable as regards the question of what rights member States can claim in respect of a régime such as results from the mandates system, functioning within the framework of the organization. For this reason, and in this setting, there could, as regards the carrying out of the "conduct" provisions of the various mandates, be no question of any legal tie between the mandatories and other individual members. The sphere of authority assigned to the mandatories by decisions of the organization could

give rise to legal ties only between them severally, as mandatories, and the organization itself. The individual member States of the organization could take part in the administrative process only through their participation in the activities of the organs by means of which the League was entitled to function. Such participation did not give rise to any right of direct intervention relative to the mandatories: this was, and remained, the prerogative of the League organs.

26. On the other hand, this did not mean that the member States were mere helpless or impotent spectators of what went on, or that they lacked all means of recourse. On the contrary, as members of the League Assembly, or as members of the League Council, or both, as the case might be, they could raise any question relating to mandates generally, or to some one mandate in particular, for consideration by those organs, and could, by their participation, influence the outcome. The records both of the Assembly and of other League organs show that the members of the League in fact made considerable use of this faculty. But again, its exercise—always through the League—did not confer on them any separate right of direct intervention. Rather did it bear witness to the absence of it.

27. Such is the background against which must be viewed the provisions by which the authority of the various mandatories was defined, and which the Court will now proceed to consider.

28. By paragraph 8 of Article 22 of the Covenant, it was provided that the "degree of authority, control or administration" which the various mandatories were to exercise, was to be "explicitly defined in each case by the Council", if these matters had not been "previously agreed upon by the Members of the League". The language of this paragraph was reproduced, in effect textually, in the fourth paragraph of the preamble to the Mandate for South West Africa, which the League Council itself inserted, thus stating the basis on which it was acting in adopting the resolution of 17 December 1920, in which the terms of mandate were set out. Taken by itself this necessarily implied that these terms had not been "previously agreed upon by the Members of the League". There is however some evidence in the record to indicate that in the context of the mandates, the allusion to agreement on the part of "the Members of the League" was regarded at the time as referring only to the five Principal Allied and Associated Powers engaged in the drafting; but this of course could only lend emphasis to the view that the members of the League generally were not considered as having any direct concern with the setting up of the various mandates; and the record indicates that they were given virtually no information on the subject until a very late stage.

29. There is also evidence that the delays were due to difficulties over certain of the commercial aspects of the mandates, but that the Principal Powers had already decided that the mandates should in any event be issued by the Council of the League, thereby giving them a definitely institutional basis. Preliminary and private negotiations and consideration of drafts by member States, or certain of them, is a nor-

mal way of leading up to the resolutions adopted by an international organ, and in no way affects their character as eventually adopted. Accordingly the League Council proceeded to issue the Mandate which, being in the form of a resolution, did not admit of those processes of separate signature and ratification generally utilized at the time in all cases where participation on a "party" basis was intended. This method was common to all the mandates, except the 'A' mandate for Iraq which, significantly, was embodied in a series of treaties between the United Kingdom, as Mandatory, and Iraq. No other member of the League was a party to these treaties. It was to the League Council alone that the United Kingdom Government reported concerning the conclusion of these treaties, and to which it gave assurances that the general pattern of their contents would be the same as for the other mandates.

30. Nor did even the Principal Allied and Associated Powers as a group have the last word on the drafting of the Mandate. This was the Council's. In addition to the insertion as already mentioned, of the fourth paragraph of the preamble, the Council made a number of alterations in the draft before finally adopting it. One of these is significant in the present context. Unlike the final version of the jurisdictional clause of the Mandate as issued by the Council and adopted for all the mandates, by which the Mandatory alone undertook to submit to adjudication in the event of a dispute with another member of the League, the original version would have extended the competence of the Court equally to disputes referred to it by the Mandatory as plaintiff, as well as to disputes arising between other members of the League *inter se*. The reason for the change effected by the Council is directly relevant to what was regarded as being the status of the individual members of the League in relation to the Mandate. This reason was that, as was soon perceived, an obligation to submit to adjudication could not be imposed upon them without their consent. But of course, had they been regarded as "parties" to the instrument of Mandate, as if to a treaty, they would thereby have been held to have given consent to all that it contained, including the jurisdictional clause. Clearly they were not so regarded.

31. Another circumstance calling for notice is that, as mentioned earlier, the Mandate contained a clause—paragraph 1 of Article 7 (and similarly in the other mandates)—providing that the consent of the Council of the League was required for any modification of the terms of the Mandate; but it was not stated that the consent of individual members of the League was additionally required. There is no need to enquire whether, in particular cases—for instance for the modification of any of their "special interests" under the mandate—the consent of the member States would have been necessary, since what is now in question is the "conduct" provisions. As to these, the special position given to the Council of the League by paragraph 1 of Article 7 confirms the view that individual member States were not regarded as having a separate legal right or interest of their own respecting the

administration of the Mandate. It is certainly inconsistent with the view that they were considered as separate parties to the instrument of mandate.

32. The real position of the individual members of the League relative to the various instruments of mandate was a different one. They were not parties to them; but they were, to a limited extent, and in certain respects only, in the position of deriving rights from these instruments. Not being parties to the instruments of mandate, they could draw from them only such rights as these unequivocally conferred, directly or by a clearly necessary implication. The existence of such rights could not be presumed or merely inferred or postulated. But in Article 22 of the League Covenant, only the mandatories are mentioned in connection with the carrying out of the mandates in respect of the inhabitants of the mandated territories and as regards the League organs. Except in the procedural provisions of paragraph 8 (the "if not previously agreed upon" clause) the only mention of the members of the League in Article 22 is in quite another context, namely at the end of paragraph 5, where it is provided that the mandatories shall "also secure equal opportunities for the trade and commerce of other Members of the League". It is the same in the instruments of mandate. Apart from the jurisdictional clause, which will be considered later, mention of the members of the League is made only in the "special interests" provisions of these instruments. It is in respect of these interests alone that any direct link is established between the mandatories and the members of the League individually. In the case of the "conduct" provisions, mention is made only of the mandatory and, where required, of the appropriate organ of the League. The link in respect of these provisions is with the League or League organs alone.

.   .   .   .

33. Accordingly, viewing the matter in the light of the relevant texts and instruments, and having regard to the structure of the League, within the framework of which the mandates system functioned, the Court considers that even in the time of the League, even as members of the League when that organization still existed, the Applicants did not, in their individual capacity as States, possess any separate self-contained right which they could assert, independently of, or additionally to, the right of the League, in the pursuit of its collective, institutional activity, to require the due performance of the Mandate in discharge of the "sacred trust". This right was vested exclusively in the League, and was exercised through its competent organs. Each member of the League could share in its collective, institutional exercise by the League, through their participation in the work of its organs, and to the extent that these organs themselves were empowered under the mandates system to act. By their right to activate these organs (of which they made full use), they could procure consideration of mandates questions as of other matters within the sphere of action of the League. But no right was reserved to them, individually as States, and independently of their participation in the institutional activities of

the League, as component parts of it, to claim in their own name,—still less as agents authorized to represent the League,—the right to invigilate the sacred trust,—to set themselves up as separate custodians of the various mandates. This was the role of the League organs.

34. To put this conclusion in another way, the position was that under the mandates system, and within the general framework of the League system, the various mandatories were responsible for their conduct of the mandates solely to the League—in particular to its Council—and were not additionally and separately responsible to each and every individual State member of the League. If the latter had been given a legal right or interest on an individual "State" basis, this would have meant that each member of the League, independently of the Council or other competent League organ, could have addressed itself directly to every mandatory, for the purpose of calling for explanations or justifications of its administration, and generally to exact from the mandatory the due performance of its mandate, according to the view which that State might individually take as to what was required for the purpose.

35. Clearly no such right existed under the mandates system as contemplated by any of the relevant instruments. It would have involved a position of accountability by the mandatories to each and every member of the League separately, for otherwise there would have been nothing additional to the normal faculty of participating in the collective work of the League respecting mandates. The existence of such an additional right could not however be reconciled with the way in which the obligation of the mandatories, both under Article 22 of the League Covenant, and (in the case of South West Africa) Article 6 of the instrument of Mandate, was limited to reporting to the League Council, and to its satisfaction alone. Such a situation would have been particularly unimaginable in relation to a system which, within certain limits, allowed the mandatories to determine for themselves by what means they would carry out their mandates: and *a fortiori* would this have been so in the case of a 'C' mandate, having regard to the special power of administration as "an integral portion of its own territory" which, as already noted, was conferred upon the mandatory respecting this category of mandate.

36. The foregoing conclusions hold good whether the League is regarded as having possessed the kind of corporate juridical personality that the Court, in its Advisory Opinion in the case of *Reparation for Injuries Suffered in the Service of the United Nations (I.C.J. Reports 1949*, p. 174), found the United Nations to be invested with,—or whether the League is regarded as a collectivity of States functioning on an institutional basis, whose collective rights in respect of League matters were, as Article 2 of the Covenant implied, exercisable only through the appropriate League organs, and not independently of these.

37. In order to test the conclusions thus reached, it is legitimate to have regard to the probable consequences of the view contended for by the Applicants,—or at any rate to the possibilities that would have

been opened up if each member of the League had individually possessed the standing and rights now claimed. One question which arises is that of how far the individual members of the League would have been in a position to play the role ascribed to them. The Applicants, as part of their argument in favour of deeming the functions previously discharged by the Council of the League to have passed now to the General Assembly of the United Nations, insisted on the need for "informed" dealings with the Mandatory: only a body sufficiently endowed with the necessary knowledge, experience and expertise could, it was said, adequately discharge the supervisory role. Yet at the same time it was contended that individual members of the League,—not directly advised by the Permanent Mandates Commission,—not (unless members of the Council) in touch with the mandates questions except through their participation in the work of the League Assembly,—nevertheless possessed a right independently to confront the various mandatories over their administration of the mandates, and a faculty to call upon them to alter their policies and adjust their courses accordingly. The two contentions are inconsistent, and the second affronts all the probabilities.

38. No less difficult than the position of a mandatory caught between a number of possible different expressions of view, would have been that of the League Council whose authority must have been undermined, and its action often frustrated, by the existence of some 40 or 50 independent centres of invigilatory rights.

39. Equally inconsistent would the position claimed for individual League members have been with that of the mandatory as a member of the Council on mandates questions. As such, the mandatory, on the basis of the normal League voting rule, and by virtue of Article 4, paragraphs 5 and 6, and Article 5, paragraph 1, of the Covenant, possessed a vote necessary to the taking of any formal Council decision on a question of substance relative to its mandate (at least in the sense that, if cast, it must not be adversely cast); so that, in the last resort, the assent, or non-dissent, of the mandatory had to be negotiated.

40. In the opinion of the Court, those who intended the one system cannot simultaneously have intended the other: and if in the time of the League,—if as members of the League,—the Applicants did not possess the rights contended for,—evidently they do not possess them now. There is no principle of law which, following upon the dissolution of the League, would operate to invest the Applicants with rights they did not have even when the League was still in being.

. . . .

41. The Court will now turn to the various contentions that have been or might be advanced in opposition to the view it takes; and will first deal with a number of points which have a certain general affinity.

42. Firstly, it may be represented that the consequences described above as being rendered possible if individual members of the League had had the rights now contended for by the Applicants, are unreal, —because the true position under the mandates system was that, even

if in all normal circumstances the mandatories were responsible to the Council of the League alone, nevertheless the individual members of the League possessed a right of last resort to activate the Court under the jurisdictional clause if any mandate was being contravened. The Court will consider the effect of the jurisdictional clause later; but quite apart from that, the argument is misconceived. It is evident that any such right would have availed nothing unless the members of the League had individually possessed substantive rights regarding the carrying out of the mandates which they could make good before the Court, if and when they did activate it. If, however, they possessed such rights then, as already noted, irrespective of whether they went to the Court or not, they were entitled at all times, outside League channels, to confront the mandatories over the administration of their mandates, just as much as in respect of their "special interests" under the mandate. The theory that the members of the League possessed such rights, but were precluded from exercising them unless by means of recourse to adjudication, constitutes an essentially improbable supposition for which the relevant texts afford no warrant. These texts did not need to impose any such limitation, for the simple reason that they did not create the alleged rights.

43. Again, it has been pointed out that there is nothing unprecedented in a situation in which the supervision of a certain matter is, on the political plane, entrusted to a given body or organ, but where certain individual States—not all of them necessarily actual parties to the instruments concerned—have parallel legal rights in regard to the same matter, which they can assert in specified ways. This is true but irrelevant, since for the present purposes the question is not whether such rights could be, but whether they were in fact conferred. In various instances cited by way of example, not only was the intention to confer the right and its special purpose quite clear,—it was also restricted to a small group of States, members, either permanent or elected, of the supervisory organ concerned. In such a case, the right granted was, in effect, part of the institutional or conventional machinery of control, and its existence could occasion no difficulty or confusion. This type of case, which will be further discussed later, in connection with the jurisdictional clause of the mandates, is not the same as the present one.

44. Next, it may be said that a legal right or interest need not necessarily relate to anything material or "tangible", and can be infringed even though no prejudice of a material kind has been suffered. In this connection, the provisions of certain treaties and other international instruments of a humanitarian character, and the terms of various arbitral and judicial decisions, are cited as indicating that, for instance, States may be entitled to uphold some general principle even though the particular contravention of it alleged has not affected their own material interests;—that again, States may have a legal interest in vindicating a principle of international law, even though they have, in the given case, suffered no material prejudice, or ask only for token damages. Without attempting to discuss how far, and in what particu-

lar circumstances, these things might be true, it suffices to point out that, in holding that the Applicants in the present case could only have had a legal right or interest in the "special interests" provisions of the Mandate, the Court does not in any way do so merely because these relate to a material or tangible object. Nor, in holding that no legal right or interest exists for the Applicants, individually as States, in respect of the "conduct" provisions, does the Court do so because any such right or interest would not have a material or tangible object. The Court simply holds that such rights or interests, in order to exist, must be clearly vested in those who claim them, by some text or instrument, or rule of law;—and that in the present case, none were ever vested in individual members of the League under any of the relevant instruments, or as a constituent part of the mandates system as a whole, or otherwise.

45. Various miscellaneous propositions are also advanced: the Mandate is more deserving of protection than the "special interests" of any particular State;—there would be nothing extraordinary in a State having a legal right to vindicate a purely altruistic interest;—and so forth. But these are not really legal propositions: they do not eliminate the need to find the particular provisions or rules of law the existence of which they assume, but do not of themselves demonstrate.

46. It is also asked whether, even supposing that the Applicants only had an interest on the political level respecting the conduct of the Mandate, this would not have sufficed to enable them to seek a declaration from the Court as to what the legal position was under the Mandate, so that, for instance, they could know whether they would be on good ground in bringing before the appropriate political organs, acts of the mandatory thought to involve a threat to peace or good international relations.

47. The Court is concerned in the present proceedings only with the rights which the Applicants had as former members of the League of Nations—for it is in that capacity alone that they are now appearing. If the contention above described is intended to mean that because, for example, the Applicants would, under paragraph 2 of Article 11 of the League Covenant, have had "the friendly right . . . to bring to the attention of the Assembly or of the Council any circumstance . . . which threatens to disturb international peace or the good understanding . . . upon which peace depends", they would therefore also—and on that account—have had the right to obtain a declaration from the Court as to what the mandatory's obligations were, and whether a violation of these had occurred;—if this is the contention, the Court can only reply to it in the negative. A provision such as Article 11 of the Covenant could at most furnish a motive why the Applicants (or other members of the League) might wish to know what the legal position was. It could not of itself give them any right to procure this knowledge from the Court which they would not otherwise have had under the Mandate itself.

48. On the other hand, an appropriate organ of the League such as the Council could of course have sought an advisory opinion from the

Court on any such matter. It is in this connection that the chief objection to the theory under discussion arises. Under the Court's Statute as it is at present framed, States cannot obtain mere "opinions" from the Court. This faculty is reserved to certain international organs empowered to exercise it by way of the process of requesting the Court for an advisory opinion. It was open to the Council of the League to make use of this process in case of any doubt as to the rights of the League or its members relative to mandates. But in their individual capacity, States can appear before the Court only as litigants in a dispute with another State, even if their object in so doing is only to obtain a declaratory judgment. The moment they so appear however, it is necessary for them, even for that limited purpose, to establish, in relation to the defendant party in the case, the existence of a legal right or interest in the subject-matter of their claim, such as to entitle them to the declarations or pronouncements they seek: or in other words that they are parties to whom the defendant State is answerable under the relevant instrument or rule of law.

. . . .

49. The Court must now turn to certain questions of a wider character. Throughout this case it has been suggested, directly or indirectly, that humanitarian considerations are sufficient in themselves to generate legal rights and obligations, and that the Court can and should proceed accordingly. The Court does not think so. It is a court of law, and can take account of moral principles only in so far as these are given a sufficient expression in legal form. Law exists, it is said, to serve a social need; but precisely for that reason it can do so only through and within the limits of its own discipline. Otherwise, it is not a legal service that would be rendered.

50. Humanitarian considerations may constitute the inspirational basis for rules of law, just as, for instance, the preambular parts of the United Nations Charter constitute the moral and political basis for the specific legal provisions thereafter set out. Such considerations do not, however, in themselves amount to rules of law. All States are interested—have an interest—in such matters. But the existence of an "interest" does not of itself entail that this interest is specifically juridical in character.

51. It is in the light of these considerations that the Court must examine what is perhaps the most important contention of a general character that has been advanced in connection with this aspect of the case, namely the contention by which it is sought to derive a legal right or interest in the conduct of the mandate from the simple existence, or principle, of the "sacred trust". The sacred trust, it is said, is a "sacred trust of civilization". Hence all civilized nations have an interest in seeing that it is carried out. An interest, no doubt;—but in order that this interest may take on a specifically legal character, the sacred trust itself must be or become something more than a moral or humanitarian ideal. In order to generate legal rights and obligations, it must be given juridical expression and be clothed in legal form. One such form might be the United Nations trusteeship system,—

another, as contained in Chapter XI of the Charter concerning non-self-governing territories, which makes express reference to "a sacred trust". In each case the legal rights and obligations are those, and only those, provided for by the relevant texts, whatever these may be.

52. In the present case, the principle of the sacred trust has as its sole juridical expression the mandates system. As such, it constitutes a moral ideal given form as a juridical régime in the shape of that system. But it is necessary not to confuse the moral ideal with the legal rules intended to give it effect. For the purpose of realizing the aims of the trust in the particular form of any given mandate, its legal rights and obligations were those, and those alone, which resulted from the relevant instruments creating the system, and the mandate itself, within the framework of the League of Nations.

53. Thus it is that paragraph 2 of Article 22 of the Covenant, in the same breath that it postulates the principle of the sacred trust, specifies in terms that, in order to give "effect to this principle", the tutelage of the peoples of the mandated territories should be entrusted to certain nations, "and that this tutelage should be exercised by them" as mandatories "on behalf of the League". It was from this that flowed all the legal consequences already noticed.

54. To sum up, the principle of the sacred trust has no residual juridical content which could, so far as any particular mandate is concerned, operate *per se* to give rise to legal rights and obligations outside the system as a whole; and, within the system equally, such rights and obligations exist only in so far as there is actual provision for them. Once the expression to be given to an idea has been accepted in the form of a particular régime or system, its legal incidents are those of the régime or system. It is not permissible to import new ones by a process of appeal to the originating idea—a process that would, *ex hypothesi,* have no natural limit. Hence, although, as has constantly been reiterated, the members of the League had an interest in seeing that the obligations entailed by the mandates system were respected, this was an interest which, according to the very nature of the system itself, they could exercise only through the appropriate League organs, and not individually.

55. Next, it may be suggested that even if the legal position of the Applicants and of other individual members of the League of Nations was as the Court holds it to be, this was so only during the lifetime of the League, and that when the latter was dissolved, the rights previously resident in the League itself, or in its competent organs, devolved, so to speak, upon the individual States which were members of it at the date of its dissolution. There is, however, no principle of law which would warrant such a conclusion. Although the Court held in the earlier 1962 phase of the present case that the members of a dissolved international organization can be deemed, though no longer members of it, to retain rights which, as members, they individually possessed when the organization was in being, this could not extend to ascribing to them, upon and by reason of the dissolution, rights which, even previously as members, they never did individually possess. Nor

of course could anything that occurred subsequent to the dissolution of the League operate to invest its members with rights they did not, in that capacity, previously have,—and it is the rights which they had as members of the League that are now in question.

56. The Court can equally not read the unilateral declarations, or statements of intention as they have been called, which were made by the various mandatories on the occasion of the dissolution of the League, expressing their willingness to continue to be guided by the mandates in their administration of the territories concerned, as conferring on the members of the League individually any new legal rights or interests of a kind they did not previously possess.

57. Another argument which requires consideration is that in so far as the Court's view leads to the conclusion that there is now no entity entitled to claim the due performance of the Mandate, it must be unacceptable. Without attempting in any way to pronounce on the various implications involved in this argument, the Court thinks the inference sought to be drawn from it is inadmissible. If, on a correct legal reading of a given situation, certain alleged rights are found to be non-existent, the consequences of this must be accepted. The Court cannot properly postulate the existence of such rights in order to avert those consequences. This would be to engage in an essentially legislative task, in the service of political ends the promotion of which, however desirable in itself, lies outside the function of a court-of-law.

. . . .

58. The Court comes now to a more specific category of contention arising out of the existence and terms of the jurisdictional clause of the Mandate, and of the effect of the Court's Judgment of 21 December 1962 in that regard. The Court's present Judgment is founded on the relevant provisions of the Covenant of the League of Nations, the character of the League as an organization, and the substantive provisions of the instrument of Mandate for South West Africa. The question now to be considered is whether there is anything arising out of its previous Judgment, or the terms of the jurisdictional clause of the Mandate, which should lead the Court to modify the conclusions arrived at on those foundations.

59. In the first place, it is contended that the question of the Applicants' legal right or interest was settled by that Judgment and cannot now be reopened. As regards the issue of preclusion, the Court finds it unnecessary to pronounce on various issues which have been raised in this connection, such as whether a decision on a preliminary objection constitutes a *res judicata* in the proper sense of that term,—whether it ranks as a "decision" for the purposes of Article 59 of the Court's Statute, or as "final" within the meaning of Article 60. The essential point is that a decision on a preliminary objection can never be preclusive of a matter appertaining to the merits, whether or not it has in fact been dealt with in connection with the preliminary objection. When preliminary objections are entered by the defendant party in a case, the proceedings on the merits are, by virtue of Article 62, paragraph 3, of the Court's Rules, suspended. Thereafter, and until the proceedings on

the merits are resumed, the preliminary objections having been rejected, there can be no decision finally determining or pre-judging any issue of merits. It may occur that a judgment on a preliminary objection touches on a point of merits, but this it can do only in a provisional way, to the extent necessary for deciding the question raised by the preliminary objection. Any finding on the point of merits therefore, ranks simply as part of the motivation of the decision on the preliminary objection, and not as the object of that decision. It cannot rank as a final decision on the point of merits involved.

60. It is however contended that, even if the Judgment of 1962 was, for the above-mentioned reasons, not preclusive of the issue of the Applicants' legal right or interest, it did in essence determine that issue because it decided that the Applicants were entitled to invoke the jurisdictional clause of the Mandate, and that if they had a sufficient interest to do that, they must also have a sufficient interest in the subject-matter of their claim. This view is not well-founded. The faculty of invoking a jurisdictional clause depends upon what tests or conditions of the right to do so are laid down by the clause itself. To hold that the parties in any given case belong to the category of State specified in the clause,—that the dispute has the specified character,—and that the forum is the one specified,—is not the same thing as finding the existence of a legal right or interest relative to the merits of the claim. The jurisdictional clause of the Mandate for South West Africa (Article 7, paragraph 2), which appeared in all the mandates, reads as follows:

> The Mandatory agrees that, if any dispute whatever should arise between the Mandatory and another Member of the League of Nations relating to the interpretation or the application of the provisions of the Mandate, such dispute, if it cannot be settled by negotiation, shall be submitted to the Permanent Court of International Justice provided for by Article 14 of the Covenant of the League of Nations.

Looking at this provision; assuming the existence of a dispute; assuming that negotiations had taken place; that these had not settled the dispute; and that the Court was, by the operation of Article 37 of its Statute, duly substituted for the Permanent Court as the competent forum (all of which assumptions would be in accordance with the Court's Judgment of 1962);—then all that the Applicants had to do in order to bring themselves under this clause and establish their capacity to invoke it, was to show (a) *ratione personae,* that they were members of the League, constructively if not actually, or must be deemed still so to be for the purposes of this provision, notwithstanding the dissolution of the League; and (b) *ratione materiae,* that the dispute did relate to the interpretation or application of one or more provisions of the Mandate. If the Court considered that these requirements were satisfied, it could assume jurisdiction to hear and determine the merits without going into the question of the Applicants' legal right or interest relative to the subject-matter of their claim; for the jurisdictional clause did not, according to its terms, require them to establish the existence of such a right or interest for the purpose of founding the competence of the Court.

61. Hence, whatever observations the Court may have made on that matter, it remained for the Applicants, on the merits, to establish that they had this right or interest in the carrying out of the provisions which they invoked, such as to entitle them to the pronouncements and declarations they were seeking from the Court. Since decisions of an interlocutory character cannot pre-judge questions of merits, there can be no contradiction between a decision allowing that the Applicants had the capacity to invoke the jurisdictional clause—this being the only question which, so far as this point goes, the Court was then called upon to decide, or could decide,—and a decision that the Applicants have not established the legal basis of their claim on the merits.

62. It is next contended that this particular jurisdictional clause has an effect which is more extensive than if it is considered as a simple jurisdictional clause: that it is a clause conferring a substantive right,—that the substantive right it confers is precisely the right to claim from the Mandatory the carrying out of the "conduct of the Mandate" provisions of the instrument of mandate,—and that in consequence, even if the right is derivable from no other source, it is derivable from and implicit in this clause.

63. Let it be observed first of all that it would be remarkable if this were the case,—that is to say if so important a right, having such potentially far-reaching consequences,—intended, so the Applicants contend, to play such an essential role in the scheme of the Mandate—of all the mandates, and of the system generally—had been created indirectly, and in so casual and almost incidental a fashion, by an ordinary jurisdictional clause, lacking as will shortly be seen in any of the special features that might give it the effect claimed,—and which would certainly be requisite in order to achieve that effect. The Court considers it highly unlikely that, given the far-reaching consequences involved and, according to the Applicants, intended, the framers of the mandates system, had they had any such intention, would have chosen this particular type of jurisdictional clause as the method of carrying it out.

64. In truth however, there is nothing about this particular jurisdictional clause to differentiate it from many others, or to make it an exception to the rule that, in principle, jurisdictional clauses are adjectival not substantive in their nature and effect. It is of course possible to introduce into such a clause extra paragraphs or phrases specifically conveying substantive rights or imposing substantive obligations; but the particular section of any clause which provides for recourse to an indicated forum, on the part of a specified category of litigant, in relation to a certain kind of dispute—or those words in it which provide this—cannot simultaneously and *per se* invest the parties with the substantive rights the existence of which is exactly what they will have to demonstrate in the forum concerned, and which it is the whole ob-

ject of the latter to determine. It is a universal and necessary, but yet almost elementary principle of procedural law that a distinction has to be made between, on the one hand, the right to activate a court and the right of the court to examine the merits of the claim,—and, on the other, the plaintiff party's legal right in respect of the subject-matter of that which it claims, which would have to be established to the satisfaction of the Court.

65. In the present case, that subject-matter includes the question whether the Applicants possess any legal right to require the performance of the "conduct" provisions of the Mandate. This is something which cannot be predetermined by the language of a common-form jurisdictional clause such as Article 7, paragraph 2, of the Mandate for South West Africa. This provision, with slight differences of wording and emphasis, is in the same form as that of many other jurisdictional clauses. The Court can see nothing in it that would take the clause outside the normal rule that, in a dispute causing the activation of a jurisdictional clause, the substantive rights themselves which the dispute is about, must be sought for elsewhere than in this clause, or in some element apart from it,—and must therefore be established *aliunde vel aliter*. Jurisdictional clauses do not determine whether parties have substantive rights, but only whether, if they have them, they can vindicate them by recourse to a tribunal.

66. Such rights may be derived from participation in an international instrument by a State which has signed and ratified, or has acceded, or has in some other manner become a party to it; and which in consequence, and subject to any exceptions expressly indicated, is entitled to enjoy rights under all the provisions of the instrument concerned. Since the Applicants cannot bring themselves under this head, they must show that the "conduct" provisions of the mandates conferred rights in terms on members of the League as individual States, in the same way that the "special interests" provisions did. It is however contended that there is a third possibility, and that on the basis of the jurisdictional clause alone, the Applicants, as members of the League, were part of the institutional machinery of control relative to the mandates, and that in this capacity they had a right of action of the same kind as, for instance, members of the League Council had under the jurisdictional clauses of the minorities treaties of that period, for the protection of minority rights. On this footing the essence of the contention is that the Applicants do not need to show the existence of any substantive rights outside the jurisdictional clause, and that they had—that all members of the League had—what was in effect a policing function under the mandates and by virtue of the jurisdictional clause.

67. The Court has examined this contention, but does not think that the two cases are in any way comparable. When States intend to create a right of action of this kind they adopt a different method. Such a right has, in special circumstances, been conferred on States belonging to a body of compact size such as the Council of the League of Nations, invested with special supervisory functions and even a power

of intervention in the matter, as provided by the jurisdictional clause of the minorities treaties—see for instance Article 12 of the minorities treaty with Poland, signed at Versailles on 28 June 1919, which was typical. Even so the right, as exercisable by members of the League Council, in effect as part of the Council's work, with which they would *ex hypothesi* have been fully familiar, was characterized at the time by an eminent Judge and former President of the Permanent Court as being "in every respect very particular in character" and as going "beyond the province of general international law". The intention to confer it must be quite clear; and the Court holds that for the reasons which have already been given, and for others to be considered later, there was never any intention to confer an invigilatory function of this kind on each and every member of the League.

68. It has to be asked why, if anything of the sort was thought necessary in the case of the mandates, it was not done in the same way as under the minorities clauses (which, in general, were drafted contemporaneously by the same authors)—namely by conferring a right of action on members of the League Council as such, seeing that it was the Council which had the supervisory function under the mandates? This would have been the obvious, and indeed the only workable method of procedure. Alternatively, it must be asked why, if it was indeed thought necessary in the case of mandates to invest all the members of the League with this function, for the protection of the mandates, it was apparently considered sufficient in the minorities case to bring in only the members of the League Council?

69. The Court finds itself unable to reconcile the two types of case except upon the assumption, strongly supported by every other factor involved, that, as regards the mandates, the jurisdictional clause was intended to serve a different purpose, namely to give the individual members of the League the means, which might not otherwise be available to them through League channels, of protecting their "special interests" relative to the mandated territories. In the minorities case, the right of action of the members of the Council under the jurisdictional clause was only intended for the protection of minority populations. No other purpose in conferring a right of action on members of the League Council would have been possible in that case. This was not so in regard to the mandates, the provisions of which afforded another and perfectly natural explanation of the jurisdictional clause and of its purpose; whereas, if a policing function had been intended, it is obviously to the members of the Council that it would have been given, and in the same sort of terms as in the minorities case.

70. In this last connection it is of capital importance that the right as conferred in the minorities case was subjected to certain characterizations which were wholly absent in the case of the jurisdictional clause of the mandates. Any "difference of opinion" was characterized in advance as being justiciable, because it was to be "held to be a dispute of an international character" within the meaning of Article 14 of the Covenant (this was the well-known "deeming" clause), so that no question of any lack of legal right or interest could arise. The deci-

sions of the Court were moreover, to be final and, by means of a reference to Article 13 of the Covenant, were given an effect *erga omnes* as a general judicial settlement binding on all concerned. The jurisdictional clause of the mandates on the other hand, was essentially an ordinary jurisdictional clause, having none of the special characteristics or effects of those of the minorities treaties.

71. That the League Council had functions in respect of mandates, just as it did in respect of minorities, can only serve to underline the fact that in the former case no right of recourse to the Court was conferred on the members of the Council in their capacity as such, although the mandates were drafted in full knowledge of what the minorities treaties contained. The true significance of the minorities case is that it shows that those who framed the mandates were perfectly capable of doing what the Applicants claim was done, when they intended to. The conclusion must be that in the case of the mandates they did not intend to.

72. Since the course adopted in the minorities case does not constitute any parallel to that of the mandates, the Applicants' contention is seen to depend in the last analysis almost entirely on what has been called the broad and unambiguous language of the jurisdictional clause—or in other words its literal meaning taken in isolation and without reference to any other consideration. The combination of certain phrases in this clause, namely the reference to "any dispute whatever", coupled with the further words "between the Mandatory and another Member of the League of Nations" and the phrase "relating . . . to the provisions of the Mandate", is said to permit of a reference to the Court of a dispute about any provision of the Mandate, and thus to imply, reflect or bear witness to the existence of a legal right or interest for every member of the League in the due execution of every such provision. The Court does not however consider that the word "whatever" in Article 7, paragraph 2, does anything more than lend emphasis to a phrase that would have meant exactly the same without it; or that the phrase "any dispute" (whatever) means anything intrinsically different from "a dispute"; or that the reference to the "provisions" of the Mandate, in the plural, has any different effect from what would have resulted from saying "a provision". Thus reduced to its basic meaning, it can be seen that the clause is not capable of carrying the load the Applicants seek to put upon it, and which would result in giving such clauses an effect that States accepting the Court's jurisdiction by reason of them, could never suppose them to have.

73. In this connection the Court thinks it desirable to draw attention to the fact that a considerable proportion of the acceptances of its compulsory jurisdiction which have been given under paragraph 2 of Article 36 of the Statute of the Court, are couched in language similarly broad and unambiguous and even wider, covering all disputes between the accepting State and any other State (and thus "any dispute whatever")—subject only to the one condition of reciprocity or, in some cases, to certain additional conditions such as that the dispute must have arisen after a specified date. It could never be supposed

however that on the basis of this wide language the accepting State, by invoking this clause, was absolved from establishing a legal right or interest in the subject-matter of its claim. Otherwise, the conclusion would have to be that by accepting the compulsory jurisdiction of the Court in the widest terms possible, States could additionally create a legal right or interest for themselves in the subject-matter of any claim they chose to bring, and a corresponding answerability on the part of the other accepting State concerned. The underlying proposition that by conferring competence on the Court, a jurisdictional clause can thereby and of itself confer a substantive right, is one which the Court must decline to entertain.

. . . .

74. The Court must now, though only as a digression, glance at another aspect of the matter. The present Judgment is based on the view that the question of what rights, as separate members of the League, the Applicants had in relation to the performance of the Mandate, is a question appertaining to the merits of their claim. It has however been suggested that the question is really one of the admissibility of the claim, and that as such it was disposed of by the Court's 1962 Judgment.

75. In the "dispositif" of the 1962 Judgment, however, the Court, after considering the four preliminary objections advanced—which were objections to the competence of the Court—simply found that it had "jurisdiction to adjudicate upon the merits". It thus appears that the Court in 1962 did not think that any question of the admissibility of the claim, as distinct from that of its own jurisdiction arose, or that the Respondent had put forward any plea of inadmissibility as such: nor had it,—for in arguing that the dispute was not of the kind contemplated by the jurisdictional clause of the Mandate, the purpose of the Respondent was to show that the case was not covered by that clause, and that it did not in consequence fall within the scope of the competence conferred on the Court by that provision.

76. If therefore any question of admissibility were involved, it would fall to be decided now, as occurred in the merits phase of the *Nottebohm* case (*I.C.J. Reports 1955,* p. 4); and all that the Court need say is that if this were so, it would determine the question in exactly the same way, and for the same reasons, as in the present Judgment. In other words, looking at the matter from the point of view of the capacity of the Applicants to advance their present claim, the Court would hold that they had not got such capacity, and hence that the claim was inadmissible.

. . . .

77. Resuming the main thread of its reasoning, the Court will now refer to a supplementary element that furnishes indications in opposition to the interpretation of the jurisdictional clause advanced by the Applicants. This contra-indication is afforded by the genesis of the jurisdictional clause appearing in all the instruments of mandate. The original drafts contained no jurisdictional clause. Such a clause was first introduced in connection with the 'B' mandates by one of the

States participating in the drafting, and concurrently with proposals made by that same State for a number of detailed provisions about commercial and other "special interests" rights (including missionary rights) for member States of the League. It was little discussed but, so far as it is possible to judge from what is only a summary record, what discussion there was centred mainly on the commercial aspects of the mandates and the possibility of disputes arising in that regard over the interests of nationals of members of the League. This appears very clearly from the statements summarized on pages 348, 349 and 350 of Part VI A of the *Recueil des Actes* of the Paris Peace Conference, 1919–1920, if these statements are read as a whole. No corresponding clear connection emerges between the clause and possible disputes between mandatories and individual members of the League over the conduct of the mandates as mandates. That such disputes could arise does not seem to have been envisaged. In the same way, the original drafts of the 'C' mandates which, in a different form, contained broadly all that now appears in the first four articles of the Mandate for South West Africa, had no jurisdictional clause and no "missionary clause" either. The one appeared when the other did.

78. The inference to be drawn from this drafting history is confirmed by the very fact that the question of a right of recourse to the Court arose only at the stage of the drafting of the instruments of mandate, and that as already mentioned, no such right figured among the "securities" for the performance of the sacred trust embodied in the League Covenant.

79. After going through various stages, the jurisdictional clause finally appeared in the same form in all the mandates, except that in the case of the Mandate for Tanganyika (as it then was) a drafting caprice caused the retention of an additional paragraph which did not appear, or had been dropped in all the other cases. Once the principle of a jurisdictional clause had been accepted, the clause was then introduced as a matter of course into all the mandates. This furnishes the answer to the contention that, in the case of the 'C' mandates, it must have been intended to relate to something more than the single "missionary clause" (Article 5 in the Mandate for South West Africa). Also, it must not be forgotten that it was simultaneously with the missionary clause that the jurisdictional clause was introduced; and that at the time much importance was attached to missionary rights. In any event, whatever the purpose of the jurisdictional clause, it was the same for all the mandates, and for the three categories of mandate. It is in the light of the mandates system generally that this purpose must be assessed,—and, so considered, the purpose is clear.

. . . .

80. The Court will now consider a final contention which has been advanced in support of the Applicants' claim of right, namely the so-called "necessity" argument.

81. In order to do this, and at the risk of some unavoidable repetition, it is necessary to review a little more closely the functioning of the mandates system. This system, within the larger setting of the

League, was an entirely logical one. The various mandatories did not deal with the individual members of the League over the "conduct" provisions of their mandates, but with the appropriate League organs. If any difficulty should arise over the interpretation of any mandate, or the character of the mandatory's obligations, which could not be cleared up by discussion or reference to an *ad hoc* committee of jurists —a frequent practice in the League—the Council could in the last resort request the Permanent Court for an advisory opinion. Such an opinion would not of course be binding on the mandatory—it was not intended that it should be—but it would assist the work of the Council.

82. In the Council, which the mandatory was entitled to attend as a member for the purposes of any mandate entrusted to it, if not otherwise a member—(Article 4, paragraph 5, of the Covenant), the vote of the mandatory, if present at the meeting, was necessary for any actual "decision" of the Council, since unanimity of those attending was the basic voting rule on matters of substance in the main League organs —(Article 5, paragraph 1, of the Covenant). Thus there could never be any formal clash between the mandatory and the Council as such. In practice, the unanimity rule was frequently not insisted upon, or its impact was mitigated by a process of give-and-take, and by various procedural devices to which both the Council and the mandatories lent themselves. So far as the Court's information goes, there never occurred any case in which a mandatory "vetoed" what would otherwise have been a Council decision. Equally, however, much trouble was taken to avoid situations in which the mandatory would have been forced to acquiesce in the views of the rest of the Council short of casting an adverse vote. The occasional deliberate absence of the mandatory from a meeting, enabled decisions to be taken that the mandatory might have felt obliged to vote against if it had been present. This was part of the above-mentioned process for arriving at generally acceptable conclusions.

83. Such were the methods, broadly speaking, adopted in the relations between the various mandatories and the League over the conduct of the mandates, and it can be seen how out of place in the context would have been the existence of substantive rights for individual members of the League in the conduct of the mandates (particularly if backed up by a right of recourse to the Court) exercisable independently of the Council at the will of the member State. On the other hand—and here again the concept was entirely logical—by the combined effect of the "special interests" provisions and the jurisdictional clause—(the latter alone could not have sufficed)—a right of recourse was given to the individual League members in respect of such interests, since the League Council could not be expected to act in defence of a purely national, not "League", interest.

84. Under this system, viewed as a whole, the possibility of any serious complication was remote; nor did any arise. That possibility would have been introduced only if the individual members of the League had been held to have the rights the Applicants now contend

for. In actual fact, in the 27 years of the League, all questions were, by one means or another, resolved in the Council; no request was made to the Court for an advisory opinion; so far as is known, no member of the League attempted to settle direct with the mandatory any question that did not affect its own interests as a State or those of its nationals, and no cases were referred to the Permanent Court under the adjudication clause except the various phases of one single case (that of the *Mavrommatis Concessions*) coming under the head of "special interests". These facts may not be conclusive in themselves; but they have a significance which the Court cannot overlook, as suggesting that any divergences of view concerning the conduct of a mandate were regarded as being matters that had their place in the political field, the settlement of which lay between the mandatory and the competent organs of the League,—not between the mandatory and individual members of the League.

85. Such then is the background against which the "necessity" argument has to be viewed. The gist of the argument is that since the Council had no means of imposing its views on the mandatory, and since no advisory opinion it might obtain from the Court would be binding on the latter, the mandate could have been flouted at will. Hence, so the contention goes, it was essential, as an ultimate safeguard or security for the performance of the sacred trust, that each member of the League should be deemed to have a legal right or interest in that matter and, in the last resort, be able to take direct action relative to it.

86. It is evident on the face of it how misconceived such an argument must be in the context of a system which was expressly designed to include all those elements which, according to the "necessity" argument, it was essential to guard or provide securities against. The Court will leave on one side the obvious improbability that had the framers of the mandates system really intended that it should be possible in the last resort to impose a given course or policy on a mandatory, in the performance of the sacred trust, they would have left this to the haphazard and uncertain action of the individual members of the League, when other much more immediate and effective methods were to hand—for instance, by providing that mandatories should not be members of the Council for mandates purposes, though entitled to attend, or should not be entitled to exercise a vote on mandates questions; or again by investing members of the Council itself with a right of action before the Court, as in the minorities case. The plain fact is that, in relation to the "conduct" provisions of the mandates, it was never the intention that the Council should be able to impose its views on the various mandatories—the system adopted was one which deliberately rendered this impossible. It was never intended that the views of the Court should be ascertained in a manner binding on mandatories, or that mandatories should be answerable to individual League members as such in respect of the "conduct" provisions of the mandates. It is scarcely likely that a system which, of set purpose, created a position such that, if a mandatory made use of its veto, it would

thereby block what would otherwise be a decision of the Council, should simultaneously invest individual members of the League with, in effect, a legal right of complaint if this veto, to which the mandatory was entitled, was made use of. In this situation there was nothing at all unusual. In the international field, the existence of obligations that cannot in the last resort be enforced by any legal process, has always been the rule rather than the exception,—and this was even more the case in 1920 than today.

87. As regards the possibility that a mandatory might be acting contrary not only to the views of the rest of the Council but to the mandate itself, the risk of this was evidently taken with open eyes; and that the risk was remote, the event proved. Acceptance of the Applicants' contention on the other hand, would involve acceptance of the proposition that even if the Council of the League should be perfectly satisfied with the way in which a mandatory was carrying out its mandate, any individual member of the League could independently invoke the jurisdiction of the Court in order to have the same conduct declared illegal, although, as mentioned earlier, no provision for recourse to the Court was included amongst the "securities" provided for by the Covenant itself. Here again the difference is evident between this case and that of the minorities, where it was the members of the Council itself who had that right. The potential existence of such a situation as would have arisen from investing all the members of the League with the right in question is not reconcilable with the processes described above for the supervision of the mandates. According to the methods and procedures of the League as applied to the operation of the mandates system, it was by argument, discussion, negotiation and co-operative effort that matters were to be, and were, carried forward.

88. For these reasons the Court, bearing in mind that the rights of the Applicants must be determined by reference to the character of the system said to give rise to them, considers that the "necessity" argument falls to the ground for lack of verisimilitude in the context of the economy and philosophy of that system. Looked at in another way moreover, the argument amounts to a plea that the Court should allow the equivalent of an *"actio popularis"*, or right resident in any member of a community to take legal action in vindication of a public interest. But although a right of this kind may be known to certain municipal systems of law, it is not known to international law as it stands at present: nor is the Court able to regard it as imported by the "general principles of law" referred to in Article 38, paragraph 1 (*c*), of its Statute.

.   .   .   .

89. The Court feels obliged in conclusion to point out that the whole "necessity" argument appears, in the final analysis, to be based on considerations of an extra-legal character, the product of a process of after-knowledge. Such a theory was never officially advanced during the period of the League, and probably never would have been but for the dissolution of that organization and the fact that it was then con-

sidered preferable to rely on the anticipation that mandated territories would be brought within the United Nations trusteeship system. It is these subsequent events alone, not anything inherent in the mandates system as it was originally conceived, and is correctly to be interpreted, that give rise to the alleged "necessity". But that necessity, if it exists, lies in the political field. It does not constitute necessity in the eyes of the law. If the Court, in order to parry the consequences of these events, were now to read into the mandates system, by way of, so to speak, remedial action, an element wholly foreign to its real character and structure as originally contemplated when the system was instituted, it would be engaging in an *ex post facto* process, exceeding its functions as a court of law. As is implied by the opening phrase of Article 38, paragraph 1, of its Statute, the Court is not a legislative body. Its duty is to apply the law as it finds it, not to make it.

90. It is always open to parties to a dispute, if they wish the Court to give a decision on a basis of *ex aequo et bono,* and are so agreed, to invoke the power which, in those circumstances, paragraph 2 of this same Article 38 confers on the Court to give a decision on that basis, notwithstanding the provisions of paragraph 1. Failing that, the duty of the Court is plain.

91. It may be urged that the Court is entitled to engage in a process of "filling in the gaps", in the application of a teleological principle of interpretation, according to which instruments must be given their maximum effect in order to ensure the achievement of their underlying purposes. The Court need not here enquire into the scope of a principle the exact bearing of which is highly controversial, for it is clear that it can have no application in circumstances in which the Court would have to go beyond what can reasonably be regarded as being a process of interpretation, and would have to engage in a process of rectification or revision. Rights cannot be presumed to exist merely because it might seem desirable that they should. On a previous occasion, which had certain affinities with the present one, the Court declined to find that an intended three-member commission could properly be constituted with two members only, despite the (as the Court had held) illegal refusal of one of the parties to the jurisdictional clause to appoint its arbitrator—and although the whole purpose of the jurisdictional clause was thereby frustrated. In so doing, the Court (*I.C.J. Reports 1950,* p. 229) said that it was its duty "to interpret the Treaties, not to revise them". It continued:

> The principle of interpretation expressed in the maxim: *Ut res magis valeat quam pereat,* often referred to as the rule of effectiveness, cannot justify the Court in attributing to the provisions for the settlement of disputes in the Peace Treaties a meaning which, as stated above, would be contrary to their letter and spirit.

In other words, the Court cannot remedy a deficiency if, in order to do so, it has to exceed the bounds of normal judicial action.

92. It may also be urged that the Court would be entitled to make good an omission resulting from the failure of those concerned to fore-

see what might happen, and to have regard to what it may be presumed the framers of the Mandate would have wished, or would even have made express provision for, had they had advance knowledge of what was to occur. The Court cannot however presume what the wishes and intentions of those concerned would have been in anticipation of events that were neither foreseen nor foreseeable; and even if it could, it would certainly not be possible to make the assumptions in effect contended for by the Applicants as to what those intentions were.

93. In this last connection, it so happens that there is in fact one test that can be applied, namely by enquiring what the States who were members of the League when the mandates system was instituted did when, as Members of the United Nations, they joined in setting up the trusteeship system that was to replace the mandates system. In effect, as regards structure, they did exactly the same as had been done before, with only one though significant difference. There were of course marked divergences, as regards for instance composition, powers, and voting rules, between the organs of the United Nations and those of the League. Subject to that however, the Trusteeship Council was to play the same sort of role as the Permanent Mandates Commission had done, and the General Assembly (or Security Council in the case of strategic trusteeships) was to play the role of the League Council; and it was to these bodies that the various administering authorities became answerable. No right of supervision or of calling the administering authority to account was given to individual Members of the United Nations, whose sphere of action, as in the case of the League members, is to be found in their participation in the work of the competent organs.

94. The significant difference referred to lies in the distribution of the jurisdictional clause amongst the various trusteeship agreements. The clause itself is almost identical in its terms with that which figured in the mandates, and was clearly taken straight from these ("any dispute whatever", "between the Administering Authority and another Member of the United Nations", "relating to . . . the provisions of this Agreement"). But whereas the jurisdictional clause appeared in all the mandates, each of which contained "special interests" provisions, it figures only in those trusteeship agreements which contain provisions of this type, and not in agreements whose provisions are confined entirely to the performance of the trust in accordance with the basic objectives of the system as set out in Article 76 of the Charter.

95. If therefore, the contention put forward by the Applicants in the present case were correct in principle (and this contention is in a major degree founded on the existence and wording of the jurisdictional clause, and also involves the erroneous assumption that it can *per se* confer substantive rights), it would follow that, in the case of some of the trusteeships, individual members of the United Nations would be held to have a legal right or interest in the conduct and administration of the trust, but in relation to others they would not, although these were no less trusteeships,—no less an expression of the

"sacred trust of civilization". The implications become even more striking when it is realized that the trusteeships to which no jurisdictional clause attaches are three previous Pacific 'C' mandates—that is to say the class of territory inhabited by precisely the most undeveloped categories of peoples, the least "able to stand by themselves".

96. It has been sought to explain this apparent anomaly by reference to the strong negotiating position in which the various mandatories found themselves, inasmuch as they were not legally obliged to place their mandated territories under trusteeship at all, and could therefore, within limits, make their own terms. But this would in no way explain why they seem to have been willing to accept a jurisdictional clause in the case of trusteeships that contained "special interests" provisions, including one Pacific 'C' mandate of this kind, but were not willing to do so in the case of trusteeships whose terms provided only for the performance of the trust in accordance with the basic objectives of the system.

97. No doubt, as has been pointed out, even where no jurisdictional clause figures in a trusteeship agreement, it would be possible, in those cases where the administering authority had made an appropriately worded declaration in acceptance of the Court's compulsory jurisdiction under the optional clause provision of Article 36 of the Court's Statute, for another member of the United Nations having made a similar and interlocking declaration, to seise the Court of a dispute regarding the performance of the trust. The number of cases in which this could occur has, however, always been very limited, and the process is rendered precarious and uncertain, not only by the conditions contained in, and the nature of the disputes covered by certain of these declarations, but also by their liability to amendment, withdrawal, or non-renewal. The optional clause system could therefore in no way have afforded a substitute for a general obligation to adjudicate, if such an obligation had really been regarded as essential;— moreover, even in those cases where an optional clause declaration could be invoked, it would still be necessary for the invoking State—as here—to establish the existence of a legal right or interest in the subject-matter of its claim.

98. It has also been sought to explain why certain trusteeship agreements do not contain the jurisdictional clause by a further appeal to the "necessity" argument. This clause was no longer necessary, so it was contended, because the United Nations voting rule was different. In the League Council, decisions could not be arrived at without the concurrence of the mandatory, whereas in the United Nations the majority voting rule ensured that a resolution could not be blocked by any single vote. This contention would not in any event explain why the clause was accepted for some trusteeships and not for others. But the whole argument is misconceived. If decisions of the League Council could not be arrived at without the concurrence, express or tacit, of the mandatory, they were, when arrived at, binding: and if resolutions of the United Nations General Assembly (which on this hypothesis would be the relevant organ) can be arrived at without the concur-

rence of the administering authority, yet when so arrived at—and subject to certain exceptions not here material—they are not binding, but only recommendatory in character. The persuasive force of Assembly resolutions can indeed be very considerable,—but this is a different thing. It operates on the political not the legal level: it does not make these resolutions binding in law. If the "necessity" argument were valid therefore, it would be applicable as much to trusteeships as it is said to be to mandates, because in neither case could the administering authority be coerced by means of the ordinary procedures of the organization. The conclusion to be drawn is obvious.

. . . .

99. In the light of these various considerations, the Court finds that the Applicants cannot be considered to have established any legal right or interest appertaining to them in the subject-matter of the present claims, and that, accordingly, the Court must decline to give effect to them.

100. For these reasons,

THE COURT,

by the President's casting vote—the votes being equally divided,

decides to reject the claims of the Empire of Ethiopia and the Republic of Liberia.

5. *The Separate and Dissenting Opinions*

Article 57 of the Court's Statute provides that "if the judgment does not represent in whole or in part the unanimous opinion of the judges, any judge shall be entitled to deliver a separate opinion." According to the President of the International Court in 1966, Sir Percy Spender, in a declaration attached to the Court's judgment,[h] such opinions, whether concurring or dissenting, should be limited to matters considered by the Court in its judgment. In the present case it was impermissible, he said, for a judge in giving a separate opinion to express his views on the merits of the dispute, as the judgment had turned on a preliminary matter not relevant to the ultimate merits.[i]

These remarks by the President, with which the present author disagrees,[j] did not deter concurring and dissenting judges from dealing at considerable length with the merits of the dispute. Altogether these separate opinions run to 447 pages compared with the majority judgment's mere 51 pages. Of the two concurring judges who delivered separate opinions, one, Judge Morelli,[k] con-

[h] 1966 ICJ Reports 51.   [i] Ibid., 56–57.
[j] "The South West Africa Cases, Second Phase" (1966) 83 *SALJ* 429 at 452.
[k] 1966 ICJ Reports 59.

fined himself to the preliminary issue raised by the majority, but the other, Judge *ad hoc* Van Wyk,[1] canvassed the full merits of the case and found in favour of South Africa on all issues. All seven dissenting judges delivered separate opinions of which six (Judge Koretsky's opinion excluded) dealt with the merits of the case. Six judges held that the Mandate was still in force and that South Africa was obliged to submit to United Nations supervision in respect to South West Africa,[m] while five judges found that apartheid violated the injunction in the Mandate to "promote to the utmost" the well-being of the inhabitants of the territory.[n] The gist of the dissenting opinions are briefly summarized by Elizabeth S. Landis: [o]

All seven "minority" judges filed dissenting opinions. These opinions made it clear that the judges did not merely disagree with the rejection of the applicants' claim on the narrow ground of their lack of legal interest, but that they also felt that a favorable judgment should have been given on the accountability issue and also on the apartheid issue, in large part at least.[188] Substantially all cited the 1950 Advisory Opinion and the 1962 judgment with approval, both as to the points decided therein and also as to the spirit in which the mandate was construed.[189] Although each dissenter advanced separate reasons for his position, certain common ideas ran through most of the opinions.

The dismay which Judge Jessup expressed in one short paragraph was explicit or implicit in the opinion of all the dissenters:

The Court now in effect sweeps away this record of 16 years and, *on a theory not advanced by the Respondent in its final submissions of 5 November 1965,* decides that the claim must be rejected on the ground that the Applicants have no legal right or interest.[190]

---

1 Ibid., 67.

m Ibid., at 236–38 (Judge Koo), 278 (Judge Tanaka), 388 (Judge Jessup), 460–61 (Judge Nervo), 483 (Judge Forster), and 489–90 (Judge *ad hoc* Mbanefo).

n Ibid., at 235 (Judge Koo), 315 (Judge Tanaka), 464 (Judge Nervo), 483 (Judge Forster), 490 (Judge *ad hoc* Mbanefo).

o "The South West Africa Cases. Remand to the United Nations" (1967) 52 *Cornell Law Quarterly* at 657–59. (Copyright 1967 by Cornell University.)

188 SWA Cases 1966, at 238 (Koo, Vice Pres., dissenting); 286–324 (Tanaka, J., dissenting); 418–42 (Jessup, J., dissenting); 457, 460–61, 464–70 (Nervo, J., dissenting); 480–83 (Forster, J., dissenting); 489–90 (Mbanefo, J. ad hoc, dissenting). Only Judge Koretsky limited his opinion strictly to the issue as framed by the majority. As to the propriety of going beyond that issue, see the declaration of President Spender, id. 51–57. His position was either repudiated or ignored by most of the dissenting judges and particularly by ad hoc Judge van Wyk in his separate opinion.

189 See passages cited in note 188 supra.

190 SWA Cases 1966, at 328 (Jessup, J., dissenting).

The seven were virtually unanimous in scouting the distinction made by the Court between the point decided in 1962 on the third preliminary objection and that decided in 1966 as the basis for rejecting the applicants' claim.[191] Again and again they referred to the 1966 judgment as a reversal not made in accordance with required procedure.[192]

Their dissents indicated that they thought the 1962 judgment neither "provisional" nor "hypothetical." [193] Thus Judge Koretsky stated:

> The reason of the 1962 Judgment relating to "a legal right or interest" of the Applicants served as a ground for the Court's decision to dismiss the third preliminary objection. . . . [W]hat was then decided with the reasons "on which it is based" is finally not provisionally decided. . . . [T]hese reasons cannot be reversed in the way chosen by the Court.[194]

And Judge Jessup insisted: *"something* must have been finally decided by the 1962 Judgment." [195] Elaborating, he applied this argument to each preliminary objection made by respondent and decided by the Court in 1962. As to the third he found that:

> The Court . . . expressly decided that the objection must be dismissed because there was a dispute within the meaning of Article 7. This decision that the dispute could concern "the well-being and development of the inhabitants" and need not include material interests of the Applicants, is *res judicata*.[196]

Each dissenter had, in addition, more or less individual grounds for finding that the applicants had a legal right or interest in the subject matter of their claim. Several judges emphasized that the compromissory clause related to "provisions" of the mandate, whereas it would have read "provision" had only the special interest clause been involved.[197] Judge Tanaka analogized the proceeding brought by the applicants (in their capacity as League members) and their interest to the position and interest of stockholders in a representative action to protect a corporation's rights.[198] Judges Koretsky,[199] Jessup,[200] and Mbanefo [201] emphasized that the applicants had sought, in effect, a declaratory judgment (an interpretation of the mandatory's obliga-

---

[191] Id. at 239, 248 (Koretsky); 329, 425–29 (Jessup); 450, 452–53 (Nervo); 482 (Forster); 490, 496 (Mbanefo).

[192] Id. at 239 (Koretsky); 250 (Tanaka); 330–38 (Jessup); 450, 452–53 (Nervo). Ad hoc Judge van Wyk also viewed the 1966 judgment as a reversal of the 1962 decision: 67.

[193] "I am at a loss to understand how the Court can say that the Court's disposal of these first submissions in its 1962 Judgment was merely basing itself upon an hypothesis or some sort of provisional basis. No such thought is expressed in the Court's 1962 Judgment." SWA Cases 1966, at 336 (Jessup, J., dissenting).

[194] Id. at 241.   [195] Id. at 333.   [196] Id. at 336.

[197] See, e.g., id. at 219–20 (Koo, Vice President, dissenting).

[198] Id. at 254 (Tanaka, J., dissenting).   [200] Id. at 328.

[199] Id at 248.   [201] Id. at 493.

tions), not an award for themselves. Under these circumstances, all argued, no legal interest in the subject-matter could possibly be required beyond that which gave the Court jurisdiction to hear the case.

By far the longest dissents were written by Judges Jessup and Tanaka. Both make extremely interesting reading for lawyers.

Judge Jessup analyzed and replied to the Court's opinion point by point, though not necessarily in the same order (the Court's opinion did not, in fact, seem entirely logically ordered). He had studied carefully the documents relating to the inception and development of the mandates system, and his presentation of the historical case opposing the Court's reading (and much that the respondent had argued) was persuasive. He accepted the applicants' argument that South African administration of its mandate was to be measured against current international standards of non-discrimination; [202] but he conservatively denied the existence of the governing international legal norm which the applicants had postulated.[203]

Judge Tanaka, by contrast, in a long argument of great interest, supported the concept of the international legal norm.[204] Having posited the norm, he thereupon proceeded to evaluate the applicants' last seven submissions against that norm and to indicate how he would decide as to each one on the basis of the evidence submitted by the parties.[205] For creativeness, subtlety, and careful reasoning this opinion will probably long be cited as a master exemplar.

Considerations of space make it impossible to include more than one extract from the dissenting opinions. The passages included below are selected from Judge Tanaka's opinion, in which he held that apartheid violates Article 2 of the Mandate, which requires the mandatory to "promote to the utmost" the well-being of the inhabitants of South West Africa: [p]

. . . the alleged norm of non-discrimination and non-separation, being based on the United Nations Charter, particularly Articles 55 (c), 56, and on numerous resolutions and declarations of the General Assembly and other organs of the United Nations, and owing to its nature as a general principle, can be regarded as a source of international law according to the provisions of Article 38, paragraph 1 (a)–(c). In this case three kinds of sources are cumulatively functioning to defend the above-mentioned norm: (1) international convention, (2) international custom and (3) the general principles of law.

Practically the justification of any one of these is enough, but theoretically there may be a difference in the degree of importance among the three. From a positivistic, voluntaristic viewpoint, first the convention, and the next the custom, is considered important, and general principles occupy merely a supplementary position. On the contrary, if we

[p] 1966 ICJ Reports at 300–1, 313–15.
[202] Id. at 433, 441 (Jessup, J., dissenting).   [203] Id. at 432–33, 441.
[204] Id. at 280–300 (Tanaka, J., dissenting).   [205] Id. at 286–324.

take the supra-national objective viewpoint, the general principles would come first and the two others would follow them. If we accept the fact that convention and custom are generally the manifestation and concretization of already existing general principles, we are inclined to attribute to this third source of international law the primary position vis-à-vis the other two.

To sum up, the principle of the protection of human rights has received recognition as a legal norm under three main sources of international law, namely (1) international conventions, (2) international custom and (3) the general principles of law. Now, the principle of equality before the law or equal protection by the law presents itself as a kind of human rights norm. Therefore, what has been said on human rights in general can be applied to the principle of equality. (Cf. Wilfred Jenks, *The Common Law of Mankind,* 1958, p. 121. The author recognizes the principle of respect for human rights including equality before the law as a general principle of law.)

Here we must consider the principle of equality in relationship to the Mandate. The contention of the Applicants is based on this principle as condemning the practice of apartheid. The Applicants contend not only that this practice is in violation of the obligations of the Respondent imposed upon it by Article 2 of the Mandate and Article 22 of the Covenant (Submission No. 3), but that the Respondent, by virtue of economic, political, social and educational policies has, in the light of applicable international standards or international legal norms, or both, failed to promote to the utmost the material and moral well-being and social progress of the inhabitants of the Territory. What the Applicants seek to establish seems to be that the Respondent's practice of apartheid constitutes a violation of international standards and/or an international legal norm, namely the principle of equality and, as a result, a violation of the obligations to promote to the utmost, etc. If the violation of this principle exists, this will be necessarily followed by failure to promote the well-being, etc. The question is whether the principle of equality is applicable to the relationships of the Mandate or not. The Respondent denies that the Mandate includes in its content the principle of equality as to race, colour, etc.

. . . .

We consider that the principle of equality, although it is not expressly mentioned in the mandate instrument constitutes, by its nature, an integral part of the mandates system and therefore is embodied in the Mandate. From the natural-law character of this principle its inclusion in the Mandate must be justified.

. . . .

Next, we shall consider the content of the principle of equality which must be applied to the question of apartheid.

. . . .

1. The principle of equality before the law requires that what are equal are to be treated equally and what are different are to be treated differently. The question arises: what is equal and what is different.

2. All human beings, notwithstanding the differences in their appearance and other minor points, are equal in their dignity as persons. Accordingly, from the point of view of human rights and fundamental freedoms, they must be treated equally.

3. The principle of equality does not mean absolute equality, but recognizes relative equality, namely different treatment proportionate to concrete individual circumstances. Different treatment must not be given arbitrarily; it requires reasonableness, or must be in conformity with justice, as in the treatment of minorities, different treatment of the sexes regarding public conveniences, etc. In these cases, the differentiation is aimed at the protection of those concerned, and it is not detrimental and therefore not against their will.

4. Discrimination according to the criterion of "race, colour, national or tribal origin" in establishing the rights and duties of the inhabitants of the territory is not considered reasonable and just. Race, colour, etc., do not constitute in themselves factors which can influence the rights and duties of the inhabitants as in the case of sex, age, language, religion, etc. If differentiation be required, it would be derived from the difference of language, religion, custom, etc., not from the racial difference itself. In the policy of apartheid the necessary logical and material link between difference itself and different treatment, which can justify such treatment in the case of sex, minorities, etc., does not exist.

We cannot imagine in what case the distinction between Natives and Whites, namely racial distinction apart from linguistic, cultural or other differences, may necessarily have an influence on the establishment of the rights and duties of the inhabitants of the territory.

5. Consequently, the practice of apartheid is fundamentally unreasonable and unjust. The unreasonableness and injustice do not depend upon the intention or motive of the Mandatory, namely its *mala fides*. Distinction on a racial basis is in itself contrary to the principle of equality which is of the character of natural law, and accordingly illegal.

The above-mentioned contention of the Respondent that the policy of apartheid has a neutral character, as a tool to attain a particular end, is not right. If the policy of apartheid is a means, the axiom that the end cannot justify the means can be applied to this policy.

6. As to the alleged violation by the Respondent of the obligations incumbent upon it under Article 2, paragraph 2, of the Mandate, the policy of apartheid, including in itself elements not consistent with the principle of equality before the law, constitutes a violation of the said Article, because the observance of the principle of equality before the law must be considered as a necessary condition of the promotion of the material and moral well-being and the social progress of the inhabitants of the territory.

7. As indicated above, so far as the interpretation of Article 2, paragraph 2, of the Mandate is concerned, only questions of a legal nature belong to the matter upon which the Court is competent. Diverse ac-

tivities which the Respondent as Mandatory carries out as a matter of discretion, to achieve the promotion of the material and moral well-being and the social progress of the inhabitants, fall outside the scope of judicial examination as matters of a political and administrative nature.

Accordingly, questions of whether the ultimate goal of the mandates system should be independence or annexation, and in the first alternative whether a unitary or federal system in regard to the local administration is preferable, whether or in what degree the principle of indirect rule or respect for tribal custom may or must be introduced —such questions, which have been very extensively argued in the written proceedings as well as in the oral proceedings, have, despite their substantial connection with the policy of apartheid, no relevance to a decision on the question of apartheid, from the legal viewpoint.

These questions are of a purely political or administrative character, the study and examination of which might have belonged or may belong to competent organs of the League or the United Nations.

8. The Court cannot examine and pronounce the legality or illegality of the policy of apartheid as a whole; it can decide that there exist some elements in the apartheid policy which are not in conformity with the principle of equality before the law or international standard or international norm of non-discrimination and non-separation. The Court can declare if it is requested to examine the laws, proclamations, ordinances and other governmental measures enacted to implement the policy of apartheid in the light of the principle of equality. For the purpose of the present cases, the foregoing consideration of a few points as illustrations may be sufficient to establish the Respondent's violation of the principle of equality, and accordingly its obligations incumbent upon it by Article 2, paragraph 2, of the Mandate and Article 22 of the Covenant.

9. Measures complained of by the Applicants appear in themselves to be violations of some of the human rights and fundamental freedoms such as rights concerning the security of the person, rights of residence, freedom of movement, etc., but such measures, being applied to the "Natives" only and the "Whites" being excluded therefrom, these violations, if they exist, may constitute, at the same time, violations of the principle of equality and non-discrimination also.

In short, we interpret the Applicants' Submissions Nos. 3 and 4 in such a way that their complaints include the violation by the Respondent of two kinds of human rights, namely individual human rights and rights to equal protection of the law. There is no doubt that the Respondent as Mandatory is obliged to protect all human rights and fundamental freedoms including rights to equal protection of the law as a necessary prerequisite of the material and moral well-being and the social progress of the inhabitants of the Territory. By this reason, what has been explained above about the principle of equality in connection with Article 38, paragraph 1 (c), is applicable to human rights and fundamental freedoms in general.

6. Academic Reaction to the Judgment

In one of the first comments on this decision, the present writer predicted that studies on this case would "soon proliferate like mushrooms in the legal journals of the world." [q] This prediction has been abundantly fulfilled, as the decision has provoked academic criticism unparalleled in the history of the International Court. Broadly, academic criticism has been levelled at three aspects of the Court's finding: first, at the reversal of the 1962 decision; second, at the distinction drawn between "conduct" and "special interests" provisions in the Mandate; and third, at the majority's approach to the judicial function. Although little attempt was made by scholars to suggest any immediate legal remedy, Professor William M. Reisman, of the Yale Law School, contended that the judgment was so studded with substantive and procedural irregularities—notably the disqualification of Judge Sir Muhammad Zafrulla Khan—that the applicant States should apply for a revision of the Court's judgment under Article 61 of the Court's Statute. [r]

The Reversal of the 1962 Judgment.—Four studies are included on this aspect of the Court's reasoning, two of a critical nature [s] and two in defence of the Court's judgment. The first two are by the present writer and by Dr. Rosalyn Higgins, Research Specialist in International Law at the Royal Institute of International Affairs. The latter two are by Professor Marinus Wiechers, of the University of South Africa, and Professor D. H. N. Johnson of the University of London.
John Dugard: [t]

[q] Above, n. j at 429.   [r] Above, n. c, especially at 83.
[s] For further criticisms along these lines, see "The South West Africa Cases: *Ut Res Magis Pereat Quam Valeat*," (1967) 115 *University of Pennsylvania Law Review* 1170 at 1176–82; Milton Katz, *The Relevance of International Adjudication* (1968) 87–99; Robert W. Scrivner, "The South-West Africa Case: 1962 Revisited" (1966–7) *African Forum*, no. 2, 33 at 36 ff.; Landis, above, n. o, at 664–65; Ernest A. Gross, "The South West Africa Cases: An Essay on Judicial Outlook," in *Ethiopia and Liberia vs South Africa: The South West Africa Cases,* (Occasional Paper No. 5, African Studies Center, University of California, Los Angeles), pp. 4–5; L. C. Green, "South West Africa and the World Court," (1966–7) 22 *International Journal* 39; Bin Cheng, above, n. c, at 206–12; Reisman, above, n. c, at 65–71; J. H. W. Verzijl, "The South West Africa Cases (Second Phase)" (1966) 3 *International Relations* 87 at 95–96; Richard A. Falk, "The South West Africa Cases: An Appraisal" (1967) 21 *International Organization* 1 at 11–13.
[t] "South West Africa Cases, Second Phase 1966" (1966) 83 *SALJ* 429 at 438–47.

THE COURT'S JUDGMENT AND THE 1962 DECISION
IN THE SOUTH WEST AFRICA CASES
(PRELIMINARY OBJECTIONS)

It will be recalled that in 1961 South Africa raised four preliminary objections to the *locus standi* of the applicants and the jurisdiction of the Court, as a result of which the proceedings on the merits were suspended. The third of these objections was that

> the conflict or disagreement alleged by the Governments of Ethiopia and Liberia to exist between them and the Government of the Republic of South Africa, is by reason of its nature and content not a "dispute" as envisaged by Article 7 of the Mandate for South West Africa, more particularly in that no material interests of the Governments of Ethiopia and/or Liberia or of their nationals are involved therein or affected thereby.[42]

In December, 1962, the Court dismissed the four preliminary objections and found that it had 'jurisdiction to adjudicate upon the merits of the dispute'.[43] In rejecting the third objection the Court declared that

> [t]he manifest scope and purport of the provisions of [Article 7] indicate that the Members of the League were understood *to have a legal right or interest in the observance by the Mandatory of its obligations both toward the inhabitants of the Mandated Territory*, and toward the League of Nations and its Members.[44]

In its judgment of 1966 the Court in effect reversed this finding, for it held that it could not entertain the claims of the applicants as they 'cannot be considered to have established any legal right or interest appertaining to them in the subject-matter of the present claims',[45] i.e. 'in the observance by the Mandatory of its obligations . . . toward the inhabitants of the Mandated Territory'. It is this aspect of the Court's judgment which is perhaps its most controversial feature and which calls for closer consideration.

In reply to the contention that the question of the applicants' 'legal right or interest' in the due performance of the Mandate had been finally settled in 1962 and could not be reopened, the Court declared that the matter related to the *merits* of the dispute and could not, therefore, have been finally disposed of in 1962. This meant that it was unnecessary to decide whether the 1962 judgment was *res judicata*, for a 'decision on a preliminary objection can never be preclusive of *a matter appertaining to the merits*, whether or not it has in fact been dealt with in connection with the preliminary objection',[46] as the hear-

---

42 *South West Africa Cases, Preliminary Objections*, 1962 ICJ Reports 319 at 327.
43 Ibid., at p. 347.
44 Ibid., p. 343. Italics added.
45 *South West Africa, Second Phase*, at p. 51.
46 Ibid., at p. 37. Italics added.

ing on the merits is suspended for the course of the inquiry into the preliminary objections. Any finding by the Court in 1962 which touched on the merits could only have been 'provisional' and have formed 'part of the motivation of the decision on the preliminary objection'.[47] It could not have constituted a final decision on the point of the merits involved. Whatever the Court may have said in 1962 on the question of the applicants' right or interest in the subject-matter of their claim, it still remained for the applicants—on the merits—to establish such a right.

That the Court appeared to be uncertain of its classification of the question of the applicants' interest as one appertaining to the merits of the case, is suggested by its subsequent admission that even if it was of a preliminary character relating to the admissibility of the claim, it would have determined the matter 'in exactly the same way',[48] for questions of admissibility might be decided at the merits phase as in the *Nottebohm Case (Second Phase)*.[49] The Court, however, denied that the matter had been disposed of as a question of the admissibility of the claim in the preliminary hearing in 1962. Evidence of this was that the Court in 1962 had found that it had *'jurisdiction* to adjudicate upon the merits',[50] which indicated 'that the Court in 1962 did not think that any question of the admissibility of the claim, as distinct from that of its own jurisdiction, arose'.[51]

In brief the Court held that in 1962 it had been faced solely with a question of jurisdiction and that it had not been called upon to decide whether the applicants had an interest in the due performance by South Africa of her obligations under the Mandate (even if it had in fact done so in a 'provisional' way). This was a question for determination at the merits stage, irrespective of whether it was classified as a question relating to the merits but of an 'antecedent character' or as a question relating to the admissibility of the claim.

The Court's finding that the question of the applicants' interest belongs to the merits is reiterated by Judges Morelli and Van Wyk in their concurring separate opinions.[52] Judge Van Wyk, however, frankly admits that the Court in 1966 overruled the 1962 finding, for he states that 'it is true that a great deal of the reasoning of the present Judgment is in conflict with the reasoning of the 1962 Judgment. . . . The Court is not bound to perpetuate faulty reasoning.'[53]

Judge Van Wyk's words pinpoint the problem. The Court did in 1962 find that the applicants had the necessary interest in the subject-matter of their claim. But did it do so in a 'provisional' way because

[47] Ibid., at p. 37.
[48] Ibid., at p. 43. Judge Mbanefo in his dissenting opinion contends that the Court in 1966, in dealing with the applicants' interest, had adopted 'an approach which relates more to admissibility than to the merits': ibid., at p. 491.
[49] I.C.J. Reports, 1955, p. 4.
[50] *South West Africa Cases, Preliminary Objections,* at p. 347. Italics added.
[51] *South West Africa, Second Phase,* at pp. 42–3. See, too, at p. 17.
[52] Ibid., at pp. 59–66 and 67–72 respectively.   [53] Ibid., at p. 67.

the matter related to the merits and could not therefore be decided in 1962, or did it make a final determination of the matter as a preliminary objection which fell to be decided at the preliminary stage? And, if the latter was the case, did the Court's finding become a final decision which the Court in 1966 was bound to 'perpetuate' however 'faulty' the reasoning? This entails two questions, which call for examination:

(a) Is the question of the applicants' interest of a preliminary nature and was it treated as such in 1962?

(b) If the answer to (a) is in the affirmative, did the matter become *res judicata* for the Court of 1966?

(a) *The Preliminary Nature of the Objection*

Article 62(3) of the Court's Rules provides that proceedings on the merits of a dispute shall be suspended on the filing of a 'preliminary objection'. An objection is of a preliminary character 'if its object . . . is to prevent proceedings on the merits until (and unless) it is over-ruled, or if . . . the effect of the objection will be, if upheld, to interrupt further proceedings, so that it would be appropriate for the Court to deal with it before enquiring into the merits'.[54] Preliminary objections are traditionally divided into two groups:

(a) objections to jurisdiction in which it is pleaded 'that the tribunal itself is incompetent to give any ruling at all whether as to the merits or as to the admissibility of the claim'; [55]

(b) objections to the admissibility of the claim in which the tribunal is requested to 'rule the claim to be inadmissible on some ground other than its ultimate merits'.[56]

Objections of the latter nature may be closely related to the merits and are not infrequently joined to the merits of the dispute.[57] The distinction between pleas to jurisdiction and admissibility is 'apt . . . to get blurred' [58] and international courts have refrained from rigidly classifying the component parts of preliminary objections: they have even

---

[54] Rosenne, op. cit., I, p. 443; and *Panevezys-Saldutiskis Railway Case,* Permanent Court of International Justice, 1939, Series A/B, No. 76 at p. 16. See, too, Sir Gerald Fitzmaurice (now Judge), 'The Law and Procedure of the International Court of Justice, 1951–4: Questions of Jurisdiction, Competence and Procedure' (1958) 34 *British Year Book of International Law* (below: *B.Y.I.L.*) 1 at 12.

[55] Fitzmaurice, op. cit., at 12–13.

[56] Loc. cit. Rosenne, op. cit., I, p. 442, points out that recent practice indicates the possibility of a third type of preliminary objection termed 'receivability'. As this type of objection is not relevant to the present enquiry, the traditional dichotomy of pleas to jurisdiction and pleas to admissibility will be maintained.

[57] As, for example, in the recent decision in the *Barcelona Traction Case,* I.C.J. Reports, 1964, p. 6 at p. 47.

[58] Per Judge Fitzmaurice, separate opinion, *Case Concerning the Northern Cameroons,* I.C.J. reports, 1963, p. 15 at p. 102.

declared such distinctions to be of secondary importance.[59] Consequently the Court sometimes simply refers to objections to jurisdiction and to admissibility of the claim as 'preliminary objections', while on other occasions they are both described as relating to 'jurisdiction', for the word jurisdiction is often loosely used in a broad sense wide enough to embrace both types of plea.[60]

South Africa's third preliminary objection denying the existence of a dispute as a result of the absence of a legally recognizable interest on the part of the applicants was definitely of a preliminary character in that it sought to prevent proceedings on the merits of the dispute over South West Africa. But was it in the nature of a plea to jurisdiction or of a plea to admissibility? The Court of 1962 itself gives no guidance and, according to Rosenne, 'seems deliberately not to have classified the different objections, a matter concerning which opinions in the Court were divided'.[61] This division of opinion is clear from the separate opinions, both concurring and dissenting, given in 1962. Judge Bustamante, in his separate concurring opinion, classifies the first two South African preliminary objections as 'denying the jurisdiction of the Court' and the latter two as 'maintaining that the Applications are inadmissible owing to lack of fulfilment of certain conditions'.[62] Judge Morelli, in his dissenting opinion, in 1962 found that, irrespective of article 7 of the Mandate, the applicants in terms of the Statute and Rules of the Court had to prove the existence of a dispute between themselves and South Africa (as distinct from a dispute between the General Assembly and South Africa) and that, having failed in this respect, their claims 'should be held to be inadmissible'.[63] This classification would appear to extend to the third objection in the form in which it was raised by South Africa, i.e. in the context of article 7, for in his 1966 concurring separate opinion Judge Morelli suggests that the 1962 preliminary objections related both to jurisdiction and to the admissibility of the claim.[64] Other judges in 1962 referred simply to the third objection as a question of 'jurisdiction' without explaining whether they meant jurisdiction in the wide sense as including pleas

---

[59] Fitzmaurice in (1958) 34 *B.Y.I.L.* at 13; *Rosenne, op. cit., I, pp. 442–3 and 448; Case Concerning the Northern Cameroons, supra,* at p. 27; *Mavrommatis Case,* Permanent Court of International Justice, Series A, No. 2, at p. 10; *Polish Upper Silesia Case,* Permanent Court of International Justice, Series A, No. 6, at p. 19.

[60] Rosenne, op. cit., I, pp. 442–3.

[61] Rosenne, op. cit., I, p. 444. Cf. the *Barcelona Traction Case, supra,* at p. 16, in which the Court classified the preliminary objections before it as relating either to jurisdiction or to the admissibility of the claim.

[62] *South West Africa Cases, Preliminary Objections,* at p. 349. See, too, at p. 379 and p. 386.

[63] Ibid., at p. 573.

[64] *South West Africa, Second Phase,* at p. 59. In his dissenting opinion, Judge Jessup states that in 1962 Judge Morelli emphasized that the preliminary objections related to admissibility as well as jurisdiction: ibid., at p. 336.

both to jurisdiction and to admissibility or whether they used the term in the narrow sense to exclude the element of admissibility.[65] Neither the Court's decision for the views of individual judges, with the exception of that of Judge Bustamante, are clear on this point, and it is difficult to accept Judge Jessup's statement in his 1966 dissenting opinion that the four preliminary objections included objections to the admissibility of the claim 'as explained in the 1962 judgment'.[66]

Although the Court in 1962 did not consider it necessary to classify the preliminary objections before it, it is essential to examine the question in greater detail in order to decide whether the third objection in 1962 was purely a plea to jurisdiction (as stated by the Court in 1966), and was therefore capable of being re-examined at the merits stage, or whether it contained elements of admissibility as well and had therefore been finally disposed of in its entirety in 1962.

Whether a dispute exists between parties as a result of a conflict of legal interests is essentially a question concerning the admissibility of the claim, for it does not relate to the competence of the tribunal to hear the claim but rather to the claim itself. This is particularly so when one party denies the existence of a dispute on account of the absence of a legal interest in the subject-matter of the dispute in the other party. In principle there is no distinction between a plea that State A has no legal interest in how a mandatory treats the inhabitants of the mandated territory which are not nationals of State A (as in the *South West Africa Cases*) and a plea that State A has no legal interest in how another State treats persons which are not nationals of State A (as in the *Nottebohm Case*)[67] and it is accepted that the latter type of plea constitutes a plea to admissibility.[68]

But the question of the existence of a dispute between the parties in the *South West Africa Cases* is not so easily classified, as the requirement of a 'dispute' is also to be found in the clause on which the applicants alleged the jurisdiction of the Court to be based, viz. article

[65] In their joint dissenting opinion in the *South West Africa Cases, Preliminary Objections,* Judges Spender and Fitzmaurice described the 1962 proceedings as 'purely jurisdictional' (at p. 472), but, as this phrase was used to distinguish those proceedings from the 1950 Advisory Opinion findings, it is not clear whether they intended to convey that no questions relating to the admissibility of the claim were involved.

[66] *South West Africa, Second Phase,* at p. 336. (See, too, Judge Mbanefo at p. 494 and Judge Nervo at p. 447.) Equally untenable is the statement by the majority that the Court in 1962 treated all the objections as relating to jurisdiction alone: ibid., at p. 17.

[67] *Second Phase,* I.C.J. Reports, 1955, p. 4.

[68] Ibid., at p. 26. In the dissenting opinions of Judges Winiarski and Morelli in the *South West Africa Cases, Preliminary Objections,* at p. 449 and pp. 565, 573, respectively, as well as in Judge Fitzmaurice's separate opinion in the *Case Concerning the Northern Cameroons, supra,* at pp. 105 and 109, it is shown that in principle the question of the existence of a dispute—viz. when not found in a jurisdictional clause—is matter relating to the admissibility of the claim.

7(2) of the Mandate. Does this result in a plea which would otherwise relate to the admissibility of the claim being transformed into a pure plea to jurisdiction? In his separate opinion in the *Case Concerning the Northern Cameroons,* Judge Fitzmaurice states:

> A given preliminary objection may on occasion be partly one of jurisdiction and partly of receivability,[69] but the real distinction and test would seem to be whether or not the objection is based on, or arises from, the jurisdictional clause or clauses under which the jurisdiction of the tribunal is said to exist. If so, the objection is *basically* one of jurisdiction. If it is founded on considerations lying outside the ambit of any jurisdictional clause, and not involving the interpretation or application of such a provision then it will normally be an objection to the receivability of the claim.[70]

The third objection in the 1962 *South West Africa Cases* was 'basically one of jurisdiction' in that it was founded on the jurisdictional clause. But in so far as it demanded an examination of the substantive provisions of the Mandate (notably articles 5 and 6) and the mandates system as a whole, i.e. 'considerations lying outside the ambit of the jurisdictional clause', it retained strong elements of a plea to the admissibility of the claim. The third objection of 1962 therefore was a forensic hybrid: looked at from the point of view of the claim, it related to admissibility, but, looked at from the point of view of the competence of the Court, it was a question of jurisdiction.

The third preliminary objection of 1962 therefore appears to have contained elements of both a plea to jurisdiction and a plea to the admissibility of the claim. It was for the Court in 1962 to determine whether the elements of admissibility predominated and called for the matter to be joined to the merits in terms of article 62(5) of the Rules of Court.[71] The Court has recently stated that an objection should be joined to the merits when it 'is so related to the merits or to questions of fact or law touching the merits, that it cannot be considered separately without going into the merits (which the Court cannot do while proceedings on the merits stand suspended under article 62)'.[72] This was a decision to be taken in 1962—and not with retrospective effect in 1966. The Court in 1962 determined the objection to be a purely preliminary one which could be disposed of without going into the merits, and gave a final decision on the matter to the effect that the applicants did have a 'legal right or interest in the observance by the

---

[69] In this passage 'receivability' must be equated with admissibility.

[70] *Supra,* at pp. 102–3. Italics added. This formulation is supported by D. H. N. Johnson, 'The Case Concerning the Northern Cameroons' (1964) 13 *International and Comparative Law Quarterly* 1143 at 1186.

[71] This provides that after the Court has heard the parties' submissions on a preliminary objection it 'shall give its decision on the objection or shall join the objection to the merits'.

[72] *Barcelona Traction Case, supra,* at p. 43. See, too, Rosenne, op. cit., I, pp. 464–6.

Mandatory of its obligations . . . toward the inhabitants of the Mandated Territory'. Nowhere did it expressly indicate that this determination was 'provisional'.

The view that the third objection of 1962 was of an inherently preliminary character, which called for determination before an inquiry into the merits, is supported by the fact that the dissenting judges of 1962 generally treated it as such and did not indicate that the matter might have been more appropriately joined to the merits.[73] Significantly, when the same question arose before the Court in 1963 in the *Case Concerning the Northern Cameroons,* in which the Court was confronted with a jurisdictional clause in the Trust Agreement for the former British Cameroons which closely resembled that of article 7(2) in the Mandate for South West Africa, the matter was again raised as a preliminary objection by the respondent State (United Kingdom) and viewed as such by Judges Spender and Fitzmaurice in their separate opinions in that case.[74]

That the third objection was of a preliminary nature not requiring an examination of the merits is further substantiated by the fact that the reasons advanced by the Court in 1966 for holding that the applicants had no 'legal right or interest' in the administration of South West Africa are essentially the same as those advanced by Judges Spender and Fitzmaurice in their joint dissenting opinion of 1962.[75] Indeed, Judge Nervo, in his dissenting opinion of 1966, complained that 'the majority of the Court is reproducing on the present occasion the arguments adduced in dissenting opinions against the Judgment of 1962'.[76] A matter should only be joined to the merits if it cannot be examined without going into those facts which appertain to the merits. But the facts on which the 1966 judgment on a matter of an 'antecedent character' are based are facts which from the report appear to have been before the Court in 1962. Judge Koretsky declared in his dissenting opinion of 1966 that the Court decided the question of the applicants' interest in 1962 and 'did not consider it necessary to join it to the merits . . . [as] both parties dealt with the question in a sufficiently complete manner. . . . To join the question of the applicants' "interest" in their claims to the merits would not "reveal" anything new as became evident at this stage of the cases.'[77]

---

[73] In his dissenting opinion, *South West Africa Cases, Preliminary Objections,* at p. 464, Judge Basdevant did, however, suggest that the whole question of jurisdiction might have been postponed until the third objection had been examined in the light of the merits. Judge Morelli also indicated that certain aspects of the question of the applicants' interest appertained to the merits. Ibid., at pp. 569 and 574.

[74] *Supra,* at pp. 65 and 111 respectively. See, too, Johnson, op. cit., at 1168–9, where he points out that at no stage was joinder to the merits considered in this case.

[75] *South West Africa Cases, Preliminary Objections,* at pp. 547–60.

[76] *South West Africa, Second Phase,* at p. 447. See, too, Judge Jessup's statement: ibid., at p. 352, footnote 1.

[77] Ibid., at p. 240. Cf. the majority opinion, at p. 18.

(b) *The Finality of the Court's Decision in* 1962 *on the Applicants' Interest*

The argument might be advanced that the finding of the Court in 1962 that it had 'jurisdiction to adjudicate upon the merits of the dispute' should not have been construed by the Court in 1966 as meaning that no questions of admissibility were then decided.[78] It has already been shown that elements of admissibility as well as jurisdiction were inherent in the third objection. It has also been shown that the word 'jurisdiction' is often loosely used to include both matters of jurisdiction and admissibility.[79] It might therefore be argued that the Court in 1962 found that it had jurisdiction to hear the merits of the dispute and, in so far as the applicants' interest related to admissibility, that the claim was admissible. The question would then arise whether this finding became *res judicata*—even if based on what Judge Van Wyk has termed 'faulty reasoning'.

The Court itself in 1966 left open the question whether the judgment of the Court at the preliminary stage became *res judicata*.[80] The matter was, however, dealt with exhaustively by Judges Jessup and Koretsky in their dissenting opinions, in which they held that not only the Court's *dispositif*, but also its essential reasons for dismissing each preliminary objection, including the finding that the applicants had a 'legal right or interest' in the observance of the Mandate in respect of the Territory's indigenous inhabitants, became *res judicata* and thus binding not only on the parties before the Court, but on the Court itself.[81] This view they substantiate as follows: article 60 of the Statute of the Court provides that a 'judgment is final and without appeal'; the 'judgment' in this provision includes the Court's decision on preliminary objections as well as on the merits; the result is that such a judgment becomes *res judicata* and 'being final it is . . . final for the Court itself'.[82] This finality does not extend only to the operative part of the judgment (or *dispositif*) but to the reasons on which it was based, for, in the words of Judge Koretsky:

> The two parts of a judgment—the operative part and the reasons—do not "stand apart" one from another. Each of them is a constituent part of the judgment in its entirety.[83]

In the absence of a pronouncement by the Court on this matter it seems difficult to refute these arguments, particularly as they are sup-

---

[78] Ibid., at pp. 42–3.   [79] Footnote 60.
[80] *South West Africa, Second Phase*, at p. 36.
[81] Ibid., at pp. 331–7 (Judge Jessup) and 239–42 (Judge Koretsky). See, too, at pp. 490–1 and 494–7 (Judge Mbanefo). Judge Nervo also mentions, without discussion, that he considered the 1962 decision to be *res judicata* (at p. 460). Cf. the view expressed by Judge Tanaka to the effect that he did 'not deny the power of the Court to re-examine jurisdictional and other preliminary matters at any stage of proceedings' but that he did not believe that there were 'sufficient reasons' to overrule the 1962 judgment (at p. 250).
[82] Ibid., at p. 240.
[83] Ibid., at p. 241. Cf. the separate opinion of Judge Morelli, ibid., at p. 59.

ported by Rosenne, the leading commentator on the law of the Court, in his magisterial work *The Law and Practice of the International Court,* in which he submits that

> the word "decision" (*décision*) appearing in Article 59 of the Statute is identical in meaning with the word "judgment" (*arrêt*) appearing in Article 60, and refers not merely to the operative clause of the judgment, but to its reasons as well.[84]

The view that the question of the applicants' interest was finally decided in 1962 appears to have been shared by South Africa, for the issue was not *expressly* raised in her final submissions in 1965.[85] In this respect the two phases of the *South West Africa Cases* are, it is submitted, distinguishable from the two phases of the *Nottebohm Case* [86]—a precedent which is recalled by the Court in its 1966 judgment.[87] In the first phase of the *Nottebohm Case* the respondent, Guatamala, raised one objection to the Court's jurisdiction but at the same time reserved the right to raise further preliminary objections.[88] In the second phase Guatamala *expressly* raised several pleas to the admissibility of the claim of Lichtenstein, which were treated by the Court as preliminary objections (one of them being upheld).[89] But none of these new preliminary objections had been raised at all in the first phase of the proceedings. In the *South West Africa Cases,* on the other hand, South Africa did not reserve her right to raise further preliminary objections at the merits stage and she did not attempt to do so. The Court appears to have upheld a preliminary objection (or a point of an 'antecedent character' in the words of the Court) which, it seems, had been canvassed and dismissed in 1962.

The conclusion seems to be that the Court, in reversing the 1962 finding on the applicants' interest—*even if this finding was based on 'faulty reasoning'*—offended the rule of *res judicata,* which, as a general

---

[84] At pp. 627–8. See, too, at pp. 125, 438–9, 445, 463, 466, 602, and 623–8.

[85] While South Africa did not *expressly* raise this objection in her final submissions, the Court held that she had denied the existence on the part of the applicants of an interest in the subject-matter of their claim—'a denial which, at this stage of the case, clearly cannot have been intended merely as an argument against the applicability of the jurisdictional clause of the Mandate'. Furthermore South Africa had asked the Court to make no declaration on the applicants' submissions. The Court indicated that apart from this it had the right, 'implicit in article 53(2) of its Statute, to select *proprio motu* the basis of its decision'. *South West Africa, Second Phase, supra,* at p. 19. See, too, to the same effect, Judge Van Wyk, separate opinion, at pp. 68–9. Cf., however, the statements by Judges Jessup (at pp. 328 and 337), Koretsky (at p. 240) and Mbanefo (at pp. 493–4) to the effect that the question of the applicants' interest in the Second Phase of the proceedings was raised *proprio motu* by the Court.

[86] I.C.J. Reports, 1953, p. 111 (*Preliminary Objection*) and I.C.J. Reports, 1955, p. 4 (*Second Phase*).

[87] *South West Africa, Second Phase,* at p. 43.

[88] I.C.J. Reports, 1953, p. 111 at p. 124. See, too, Rosenne, op. cit., I, p. 455.

[89] I.C.J. Reports, 1955, p. 4 at pp. 9–12. See, too, Rosenne, op. cit., I, pp. 455–6.

principle of law 'recognised by civilized nations' (within the meaning of article 38 (1) (c) of the Court's Statute), forms part of the law binding on the Court. Furthermore, there is room for the argument that the 1966 decision has introduced an element of uncertainty into the Court's practice. In this request Judge Koretsky remarks that

> the principle of immutability, of the consistency of final judicial decisions, which is so important for national courts, is still more important for international courts.[90]

Rosalyn Higgins:[u]

A. How does it come about at this stage that the Court can decide—after a judgment in 1962 on the preliminary issues, and after four years' litigation on the substantive merits of the dispute—that it must decline to pronounce at all on the Applicants' claims?

There are several closely related points here. The first is to ask whether, in a case on the merits of the dispute, the Court can base its Judgment on the Applicants' legal standing, rather than on the rights and wrongs of their legal arguments. In the present stage of international law, the competence of the International Court is only a limited one, and a reluctant litigant—that is to say, a Respondent to a legal claim which the Applicant wishes to place before the Court for adjudication—may seek to show that the Court's competence is inadequate in this particular regard. The Court will then hear arguments from both the parties on this matter, and will then pronounce on these preliminary objections raised by the Respondent. This is, of course, exactly what happened in the 1962 Judgment of the Court in which it found, by eight votes to seven, that it had jurisdiction to proceed to an adjudication of the merits of this dispute over South West Africa.

It must be explained, however, that it is not legally necessary for there to be a rigid separation in time between consideration of the jurisdiction of the Court and consideration of the merits of the arguments. The Court may, after a hearing on a preliminary point, either accept the Respondent's arguments (in which case the Applicant's case will be dismissed, and he will not be entitled to proceed to the next phase of the litigation, to argue the merits of the dispute); or reject the Respondent's arguments (in which case the Applicant will be entitled so to proceed). But a third alternative is available to the Court, whereby it may decide (under Article 62 (5) of the Rules of Court) to attach all of the preliminary objections, or such preliminary objections as it so chooses, to the subsequent case on the merits of the dispute. The major reason for this is, quite simply, because the arguments on a particular preliminary jurisdictional point may be very similar to those which would be raised on the merits of the case; and thus it is convenient and economical for the Court to look at them together.

---

[u] "The International Court and South West Africa: the Implications of the Judgment" (1966) 42 *International Affairs* 573 at 577–82.
[90] *South West Africa, Second Phase*, at pp. 240–1.

The Court has availed itself on many occasions of this right to join preliminary objections to its examination of the merits.[7]

The logical outcome of this is that it is possible, after extended litigation on the merits of a dispute, for the Court to decide the case against the Applicant on the grounds of what originally appeared as a preliminary objection. The instinctive reaction of many laymen is to assume that this is a scandalous waste of time and resources, and yet another example of the law as an ass. Yet it has to be remembered that the attachment of a preliminary objection to the merits of the case may in fact have prevented a wasteful repetition of the arguments in both phases of the case. Thus, in so far as criticism of the Judgment of July 1962 rests simply on the fact that the Court's grounds for this decision, after long litigation on matters of substance, appeared to rest on preliminary or jurisdictional matters, the criticism rather misses the point.

The really relevant point, in the view of this writer, is the Court's reliance on such points, at the end of a long case on the merits, when it had *given no indication at all* to the parties at the end of the preliminary case that it proposed to carry certain points forward to be attached to the merits. Not only is there no precedent for this, but the failure to give notice that certain preliminary points will be attached to the subsequent case on the merits effectively removes from the Applicant the option to withdraw at that stage if he believes that the risks are too great to proceed to the merits. In the case of poor nations, facing the cost of protracted litigation, this is an option which should certainly be safeguarded. Moreover, a failure to indicate that certain preliminary points remain to be examined at the same time as the merits, makes it exceedingly difficult for counsel to direct their pleadings to all the relevant points.

Ethiopia and Liberia had every reason to believe that all questions relating to their right to obtain a Judgment had already been settled in 1962. The Court has now classified the grounds on which it declined to pronounce on the merits of the case as a question 'that appertained to the merits of this case but which had an antecedent character'. It further said that 'despite the antecedent character of the question, the Court was unable to go into it until the parties had presented their arguments on the other questions of merits involved'.[8] The question remains, however—why were the parties given no warning in 1962 that an 'antecedent question' remained to be answered, and why did the Court proceed to assume, without full argument, the propriety of its action in raising the point at this juncture? There is nothing in the Judgment which, to this writer, provides a satisfactory answer.

B. *Has the Court really reversed its own decision of 1962? That is to*

---

[7] See, for example, the *Barcelona Traction Case* (preliminary objections) 1964, p. 43; *Rights of Passage Case* (preliminary objections) 1957, pp. 150–152.

[8] [South West Africa, Second Phase, 1966 ICJ Reports 6 at 18.]

*say, how compatible is its present Judgment with its Judgment in 1962
that it had jurisdiction to proceed to the merits?*

In fact the Court never addressed itself to the line of argument laid
out in the preceding paragraph, because it indicated that the right or
otherwise of Ethiopia and Liberia to obtain an answer from it, though
of an 'antecedent character' was *not* a 'preliminary question'. Now, the
question is not whether such an exceedingly fine distinction is known
to the law (conceptually, it is, under the established distinction between jurisdiction and admissibility) but whether it was appropriate
or valid to this particular case. It is extremely difficult to see that the
question of Ethiopia's and Liberia's legal right in the subject-matter of
their claims (which was the point at issue) was not a preliminary matter to be disposed of in the first phase of proceedings culminating in
1962, and that it had indeed been so disposed of.

It will be recalled that in 1962 the Court had been asked by South
Africa to declare that Ethiopia and Liberia could not institute proceedings under the enabling clause of Article 7(2) of the Mandate.
Among the arguments she had advanced was that no 'dispute' (as required in Article 7(2)) existed as between herself and Ethiopia and
Liberia, because they had no special, national interest in the Mandate
over South West Africa. The Court had rejected this argument. But
now, in 1966, the Court sought to explain this effective reversal by saying: 'To hold that the parties in any given case belong to the category
of State specified in the Clause—that the dispute has the specified
character—and that the forum is the one specified—is not the same
thing as finding the existence of a legal right or interest relative to the
merits of the claim.' [9] But it *must* be the same thing—for the categories of states specified in the clause are presumably those who *do*
have a legal interest in the carrying out of the Mandate. Moreover, the
Court in 1962 classified the Applicants as falling within that category,
not as an abstract proposition but in relation to an already existing
and formulated set of claims.

If the Court is really saying that Ethiopia and Liberia can be adjudicated in 1962 to have legal standing to bring a case but not to be entitled to get an answer in 1966 because of lack of legal interest in the
subject-matter, then one is entitled to ask the Court: 'What claim
could Ethiopia and Liberia present after they had been deemed entitled to proceed in 1962, in order to get an answer from the Court?' To
reply, as the Court does by implication, that a claim which rested on a
'special interest' would have got an answer, is hardly satisfactory. For
the Court knew in 1962 that Ethiopia and Liberia were claiming no
'special' or 'national' interest in the Mandate, but only that legal interest inherent in all former members of the League. Moreover, in 1962
the Court had heard much argument on the point of whether a dispute sufficient to institute proceedings existed between the Applicants
and the Respondent, and it had addressed itself to the question of this
relying in turn upon Ethiopia and Liberia showing a special, particu-

[9] [Ibid 37.]

lar interest in the implementation of the Mandate. The Court explicitly stated that

> . . . the Members of the League were understood to have a legal right or interest in the observance by the Mandatory of its obligations both towards the inhabitants of the Mandated Territory, and towards the League of Nations and its Members.[10]

It thus remains baffling for the Court to assert that it was now dealing with a new point, which had not been covered in 1962. It seems impossible to disagree with the view expressed by the distinguished United States member of the Court, Judge Jessup, that the Court had in effect reversed its judgment of 1962.[11] (This is a point separate from, though related to, the question of *res judicata*—namely, the finality of a judicial decision, and whether a decision on jurisdiction can so be classified, thus not allowing of reversal subsequently. The various judges did address themselves at some length to this question, but the Court did not regard it as directly relevant, simply because it declared that the finding that the Court had jurisdiction in 1962 was different from a finding that the Applicants did not have legal standing in the next phase of the case.)

Two other points require mention in this context. The first is that the grounds upon which the Court gave its Judgment—namely, a lack of legal interest by the Applicants in the subject-matter of the claim—was not even advanced in the final submissions by the Respondent.[12] The Court, however, while conceding that South Africa's final submissions 'ask simply for a rejection of those of the Applicants, both generally and in detail' (that is, on the substantive issues), point out that the final submissions did at least ask the Court to base its findings on 'statements of fact and law as set forth in (its) pleadings . . .', and that South Africa had, in the course of its pleadings, denied that the Applicants had any legal standing in the subject-matter of their claim. The Court then continued to suggest that, given the 1962 Judgment, 'it clearly cannot have been intended merely as an argument against the applicability of the jurisdictional clause of the Mandate'. Thus the Court points to a legal argument made by South Africa at one remove, supposes that it relates to the merits and not to jurisdiction (though several of South Africa's arguments on the merits were in effect a mere repetition of its previous objections to the Court's jurisdiction, presumably entered for the record) and then relies on that argument rather than addressing itself to the clear and unambiguous, albeit voluminously large, argument on the substance of the dispute.

This leads us to the second point. The Court then also indicated in its latest Judgment, undoubtedly correctly, that it is entitled to select *proprio motu* the basis of its decision. That is to say, under Article 53 of its Statute, it is not required to rely on arguments advanced by the litigants but can rely on what it finds the most telling and relevant

---

[10] *ICJ Reports 1962*, p. 343.   [11] [1966 ICJ Reports 330.]
[12] As pointed out by Judge Jessup, at p. [326]

legal grounds. This is a well-established legal principle, but, with all due deference, its invocation does not really seem to answer all the points we have raised. As with any other legal principle, its nature and scope are subject to certain limitations: and it remains relevant to ask whether, when there has already been a judicial decision on preliminary questions, and when the Court has failed to avail itself of its right to declare that certain outstanding preliminary points shall be attached to the subsequent case on the merits, is it really open to the Court to rely, after four years of litigation, upon the *proprio motu* principle to discover an outstanding 'antecedent question pertaining to the merits'? Reliance on the *proprio motu* argument in the particular circumstances of this case seems to this writer to run counter to another well-established principle of international law—'*interest rei publicae res judicata non rescindi*'. The *proprio motu* principle is not a licence to ignore established legal concepts, nor to avoid issues upon which one has legal jurisdiction to pronounce; it is a principle designed to affirm the Court's superior understanding of the law to that of the parties before it.

Marinus Wiechers: [v]

The main criticism directed against the Court's decision that Ethiopia and Liberia had no legal right or interest in the performance of the Mandate is that it violated the rule of *res judicata,* because the Court had expressly decided in its judgment in 1962 that "the manifest scope and purport of the provisions of [Article 7(2) of the Mandate] indicate that the Members of the League were understood to have a legal right or interest in the observance by the Mandatory of its obligations both toward the inhabitants of the Mandated Territory, and toward the League of Nations and its Members".[7] All the dissenting judges in the 1966 case took up the point of *res judicata,* and almost all of the writers who protested against the outcome of the case did the same.

The critics speak in such tones of common condemnation as make it seem incredible that an international court could have erred so grossly. It is therefore necessary to analyze the questions of legal rights and interests and of *res judicata* to establish whether this is really such a highly contestable issue that it leaves no room for the view adopted by the Court.

The whole matter must be divided into three separate questions: (1) whether the applicants had a legal right or interest in the subject-matter of their claim; (2) whether the Court, in the preliminary stage, in

---

v "South West Africa: The Decision of 18 July 1966 and its Aftermath" (1968) 1 *Comparative and International Law Journal of Southern Africa* 408 at 410–15. See, too, by the same writer, "The Judgment of 18 July 1966" *Codicillus,* Special Edition 1966, p. 6, and "Die Suidwes-Afrika Saak" (1966) 29 *Tydskrif vir Hedendaagse Romeins-Hollandse Reg* 297.

[7] *South West Africa Cases (Ethiopia v. South Africa; Liberia v. South Africa), Preliminary Objections,* ICJ Rep. (1962) 343.

1962, had given a decision on this point; and (3) whether, if the Court had given such a decision, it was binding on any subsequent decision on the merits of the case.

The Court, in its 1966 decision, tried to give definite answers to these questions. First, it denied the applicants any legal right or interest in the subject-matter of the claim. Second, it dismissed the submission that this issue had been finally decided in 1962. And third, it rejected the contention that the 1962 decision had any binding effect on a subsequent finding on such rights and interests.

It is true that the Court's reasoning is very dogmatic. Indeed, it can safely be said that the whole judgment of 1966 is a careful elaboration of the warning sounded by Judge Basdevant in his 1962 dissenting opinion: "It is possible that the third objection would be upheld or overruled and hence a decision taken on the *jurisdiction of the Court* only after discussion of the merits of the dispute referred to the Court." [13] What the French judge foresaw, in 1962, actually happened. The Court, after hearing all the evidence and arguments on the merits, decided to revert to the third objection of the respondent *in limine:* namely, that the conflict or disagreement between the applicants and South Africa was not a dispute as envisaged by Article 7 of the Mandate, the more particularly so since no material interests of the Governments of Ethiopia and Liberia or their nationals were involved therein or affected thereby.

The Court thus chose to revert to a technical ground for its decision. But in doing so it had to distinguish the *ratio* of its own decision from that of the 1962 decision on the preliminary objections, and also show that the question of the legal rights and interests of the applicants had not been decided in 1962. The way in which the Court drew this distinction and explained the differences between the issues decided in 1962 and the grounds for its decision in 1966 is surely not far-fetched nor without any legal basis; though it is conceded that the Court employed some very imprecise notions and definitions of procedure—more particularly as regards preliminary objections—to support its judgment that the question of rights and interests had not been dealt with in 1962.[14]

[13] ICJ Rep. (1962) 464 (own emphasis).

[14] The Court expressed the view that all four preliminary objections related to the Court's jurisdiction to hear and to determine the merits of the case, and that by dismissing these objections in 1962 the Court had established the capacity of the applicants to invoke the jurisdiction of the Court *ratione personae* (*i.e.* that they were members of the League) and *ratione materiae* (*i.e.* that the dispute did relate to the interpretation or application of the Mandate) ICJ Rep. (1966) 38. The Court then went on to say that the question of the legal right and interest was related to the admissibility of the claim ("recevabilité de la demande") and that the decision of 1962 (as evidenced in its "dispositif") declared expressly that it (the Court) had jurisdiction to adjudicate upon the merits without expressing itself on the admissibility of the claim (*ibid.,* 42), thus leaving that part of the question (*i.e.* of admissibility) to the merits stage.

The whole problem, in short, is whether the Court in 1962 decided solely

The problem of *res judicata,* however, is quite different. It is one thing to admit that there may have been some overlapping between the two decisions (which can be ascribed to the imprecise nature and scope of the preliminary objections), but quite another to assert that

---

on its subject-matter jurisdiction, or whether it had also expressed itself on the admissibility of the claim. Stated more concretely, the final question is whether the third preliminary objection advanced by the respondents was only aimed at the jurisdictional incapacity of the Court, or whether it was also aimed at the inadmissibility of the claim.

It is quite impossible to give a precise and final answer to this question for the following reasons:

First, because the third preliminary objection was in its nature not clearly defined. "The third objection of 1962 . . . was a forensic hybrid: looked at from the point of view of the claim, it related to admissibility, but looked at from the point of view of the competence of the Court, it was a question of jurisdiction"—Dugard, "The South West Africa Cases, Second Phase, 1966' 83 *SALJ* (1966) 429 at 444. The only judge who gave a definite opinion on this matter was Judge Bustamante who called the third objection an objection pertaining to the admissibility of the application—ICJ Rep. (1962) 349. See also Mohieddine Mabrouk, *Les Exceptions de Procédure devant les Juridictions Internationales* (1966) 29 note 9, and 269, who concludes that aside from Judge Bustamante (who treated the third objection as pertaining to the admissibility of the claim) and Judge Winiarski, all the other judges treated the third objection as pertaining to the competence (jurisdiction) of the Court. Judge Winiarski, in his dissenting opinion, denied the applicants the capacity to take legal action ("qualité pour agir en justice")—ICJ Rep. (1962) 456. But it is not clear from his opinion whether he regarded this lack of capacity as flowing from a jurisdictional defect or from the inadmissibility of the applicant's claim.

Second, because the Court, in rejecting the third objection, did not qualify or describe the consequences which would flow from the dismissal. In other words it did not state whether it thereby simply accepted subject-matter jurisdiction, or whether it also held the applicants' claim to be admissible. Judge Morelli was of the opinion that the Court in 1962 had only held that the applicants had the "right to institute proceedings" and not that they had a substantive right of their own—ICJ Rep. (1966) 62. Some writers, however, are of the opinion that "in 1962, the Court viewed the substantive rights of the Mandate as coextensive with the subject-matter jurisdiction of Article 7 (of the Mandate)".—See "The South West Africa Cases: Ut Res Magis Pereat quam Valeat", 115 *U Pa L Rev* (1967) 1180; Favoreu, "Affairs du Sud-Ouest Africain", *Ann Fr de Dr Int* (1966) 129. Ch. de Visscher, *Aspects récents du droit procédural de la Cour Internationale de Justice* (1966) 22, criticizes the 1962 decision for confusing the issues by coupling the question of a right of action ("droit d'action") to the question of the existence of a justiciable dispute and the admissibility of the claim ("existence d'un différend et recevabilité").

Third, and this is perhaps the most important reasons—the classification of preliminary objections into jurisdiction objections ("exceptions d'incompétence") and admissibility objections ("exceptions d'irrecevabilité") is in itself vague and overlapping. Mabrouk, *op. cit.,* 76 and 78, describes, for example, a lack of quality ("défaut de qualité") and a lack of capacity ("défaut de capacité") as instances which will be contested by an admissibil-

the Court violated the rule against overruling a previous binding and final decision. The main reason why the *res judicata* rule could not have been applied to the question of the legal rights and interests of the applicants is the fact that this question, although presented in the form of a preliminary objection, could not have been fully evaluated

---

ity objection, without explaining how these defects vary from defects *ratione personae* (which he admits would be contested by a jurisdiction objection— see at 51). On the other hand, De Visscher, *op. cit.*, 20 and 75, describes the quality to act as "le pouvoir en vertu duquel un Etat est admis à figurer à une instance. C'est le jus standi in judicio"—thereby clearly grouping it under the jurisdictional elements of a litigious proceeding. For a discussion of these procedural niceties in terms of German legal science, see Knitel, "Das Mandat über Sudwestafrika", 89 *Juristische Blätter* (1967) 8, 12.

It is also not clear whether these two categories of objections had to be dealt with in any particular order. Judging from the 1966 decision, it would seem that a court has first to deal with objections relating to its jurisdiction and then to deal with the objections relating to the admissibility of the claim. But in the 1962 decision (ICJ Rep. (1962) 574) Judge Morelli, who is really the only judge who based his opinions solely on procedural aspects, stated that there is an objection which in fact precedes the question of jurisdiction ("précéde l'examen de la juridiction"), namely, that of the validity of the application ("la validité de la requête.) This objection relating to the validity of the application must fall within the ambit of admissibility objections. It seems therefore that Judge Morelli did, in 1962, express himself on the admissibility of the claim. In 1966 he chose to qualify the Court's decision to dismiss the application as a "rejet fondé sur le défaut de qualité des demandeurs"—ICJ Rep. (1966) 65. But, as has been explained above, a lack of capacity ("défaut de qualité") may relate to a jurisdictional defect (*ratione personae*) as well as to an admissibility defect. See also page 64 of the Report where Judge Morelli expressed the view that the Court should have found that it had no jurisdiction, instead of rejecting the claim on the merits.

The Court in its 1966 judgment stated that should the legal rights and interests of the applicants be treated as preliminary matters (and the Court did not think that they should), it would hold that the applicants had not the capacity ("aptitude") to advance their claim, and that therefore the claim was inadmissible—ICJ Rep. (1966) 43. Again, this statement is ambiguous. One would have thought that a lack of capacity would result in the absence of a *locus standi*, which is a jurisdictional defect, and not affect the admissibility of the claim as such.

Perhaps the simple truth is that defects relating to jurisdiction and defects relating to admissibility are completely interrelated, and that the so-called distinction between them is, ultimately, merely a question of semantics. It would, for example, be inadmissible for a court to hear a claim if that court has no jurisdiction in the particular case; *vis-a-vis* the court, the claim itself then becomes inadmissible. Also, if a court hears an inadmissible claim, it would overstep the limits of its own jurisdiction, since it does not fall within the court's jurisdiction to hear inadmissible claims. *Cf.* Etienne Grisel, *Les exceptions d'incompétence et d'irrecevabilité dans la procédure de la Cour Internationale de Justice* (1968) 65 and 71, who gives an excellent analysis of the various categories of preliminary objections, although he admits (on 75 and 225) that the distinction is sometimes difficult to draw in practice.

without an enquiry into the merits of the case. It is therefore not surprising that strong indications that the question as to the legal rights
and interests of the applicants might crop up again at the merits stage
were already to be found in some of the 1962 majority opinions.[15]
In its 1962 decision on the preliminary objections the Court, in arriving at its conclusion that the applicants had a legal right and interest
in the performance of the Mandate, looked at the "manifest scope
and purport" of Article 7(2) of the Mandate.[16] But this does not mean
that the Court had thereby come to a final and binding decision on
this point, particularly if a hearing on the merits would have exposed
the applicants' lack of a legal right or interest in the subject-matter
of the claim.[17] It is even suggested by one writer that the Court, "relying on the declaratory nature of its pronouncement on jurisdiction,
can, in the future, reverse a decision affirming its competence to deal
with the case if it later finds beyond doubt that its prior decision was
erroneous, and provided that a decision on the merits was not yet
pronounced".[18] The Court is not bound by its own previous judg-

---

[15] Judge Jessup, although he discussed the problem *in extenso* and was prepared to accept the general interest of the applicants in the operation of the
Mandate as a legal interest (ICJ Rep. (1962) 433), nonetheless expressed the
warning: "It may be possible to imagine a case where the allegation of a
legal right was so obviously absurd and frivolous that the Court would dismiss the application on a plea to the jurisdiction, but such a situation would
be rare. In any event it is not the situation in the instant cases." *Ibid.*, 424.

Sir Mbanefo, in his 1966 dissenting opinion, stated: "In my separate opinion on the preliminary objections I said that a good deal of argument on the
first three preliminary objections in the judgment went to the merits of the
case"—ICJ Rep. (1966) 495–6. See in this respect, and particularly in regard
to the third objection, his separate 1962 opinion—ICJ Rep. (1962) 447–8.

[16] ICJ Rep. (1962) 343.

[17] Grisel, *supra* note 14, 87: "Aussi la troisième exception exigeait-elle un examen approfondi des dispositions matérielles du Mandat . . . Peut-être même
eût-il été plus opportun de la déclarer irrecevable en tant qu'exception
préliminaire parce que le moyen tiré du défaut d'intérêt appartenait en
réalité au fond."

Judge Morelli, in his separate opinion, expressed the opinion that a judgment on preliminary questions is final and binding in the further proceedings, but that its binding effect is confined to the questions decided—ICJ
Rep. (1966) 59. Mabrouk, *supra* note 14, 304, maintains that a decision on a
preliminary objection is only final and irreversible if that decision is "auton-
ome" and "exclusif"; if the decision on the preliminary objection is reached
after an "examen sommaire et provisoire du fond", the Court is entitled to
reverse its previous judgment. See also the *Mavrommatis Case*, PCIJ Ser. A,
No. 2 (1924) 16.

[18] Shihata. *The Power of the International Court to Determine its Own Jurisdiction* (1965) 79. In 1966, the *ad hoc* Judge for the respondent said: "It
follows that if in 1962 this Court, *per incuriam* or for any other reason, dealt
with the Applicants' alleged substantive rights or interests, its statements
with regard thereto cannot now prejudice its decision at this—the merits-
stage."—ICJ Rep. (1966) 68. And at 67 of the Report: "The Court is not
bound to perpetuate faulty reasoning." This dictum of Judge van Wyk has

ment.[19] And it would be an extremely rigid view to hold that the Court is in all instances bound by its judgments on *preliminary matters;* the more so in cases where decision on preliminary issues may be influenced profoundly by a subsequent hearing on the merits.

D.H.N. Johnson: [w]

. . . the Applicants must have been aware in 1960 that, despite the encouragement given in the special report of the Committee on South-West Africa, they were embarking upon a very hazardous operation. . . . As regards technicalities they would know that the Court had developed a rather complicated jurisprudence involving distinctions between jurisdiction, admissibility and merits, although they would not know then that Professor Verzijl was later to describe this jurisprudence, with considerable justification, as "an ambiance of complete juridical chaos".[14]

As regards this jurisprudence the Applicants would know:

(i) that under Article 62 of the Rules of Court the Respondent could file a preliminary objection, and that, if he did so, the proceedings on the merits would be suspended;

(ii) that in the *Case concerning Certain German Interests in Polish Upper Silesia* [15] the Court had been confronted with a plea to the jurisdiction which could not be adjudicated upon without touching upon the merits. The Court had upheld its jurisdiction but had said: "The Court cannot . . . in any way prejudge its future decision on the merits" and again "nothing which the Court says in the present judgment can be regarded as restricting its entire freedom to estimate the value of any arguments advanced by either side on the same subjects during the proceedings on the merits";

(iii) that in the *Panevezys-Saldutiskis Railway* case [16] the Court had treated an objection based on the alleged lack of standing of the Applicants as not preliminary but as part of the merits;

(iv) that in the *Nottebohm* case, after finding that it had jurisdiction, the Court had rejected the claim of the Applicant as inadmissible for a reason which had also to do with the Applicant's lack of standing. Moreover, to quote Professor Verzijl, "the Court has seen no objection to deciding the *Nottebohm* case on the strength of a princi-

---

been used by some critics to prove that the Court in 1966 overruled its 1962 decision: *cf., inter alia,* Green, "The United Nations, South West Africa, and the World Court", 7 *Indian J of Int Law* (1967) 491; Dugard, *supra,* 440. Apart from the fact that this was only the individual opinion of one judge, it is hardly understandable how the *ad hoc* Judge's remarks could be taken so amiss.

[19] Article 59 of the Statute of the Court.

[w] "The South-West Africa Cases (Second Phase)" (1967) 3 *International Relations* 157 at 166–72.

[14] *The Jurisprudence of the World Court.* Vol. II. The International Court of Justice (1947–1965), Leyden, A. W. Sijthoff, 1966, p. 530.

[15] (1925) Series A, No. 6, pp. 15–16.   [16] (1939) Series A/B, Nos. 75 and 76.

ple which has never been professed during the proceedings either by the claimant or by the defendant State and on which it had felt no necessity to hear their opinion".[17] Or, as another learned commentator, referring to the *Ndoteboh m* case, puts it: "Here the Court, after describing the relevant facts and the submissions of the parties, reformulated the issue to be decided, adding that it would reach its decision 'on the basis of such reasons as it may itself consider relevant and proper'. The issue, as thus reformulated, had not been argued between the parties although they could have done so had they foreseen the possibility that the Court would have acted in that way".[18]

In the light of the above it is reasonable to assume that the Applicants would know that, even if all the Respondent's preliminary objections were to fail, the Court would not give final judgment in their favour unless it was entirely satisfied both as to its own jurisdiction and that "the claim is well founded in fact and in law"; and moreover that, in the second phase of the case just as much as in the first, the Court would feel itself free to reach its own decisions for reasons which it might itself "consider relevant and proper" irrespective of whether or not the Parties had argued the points in question in the first phase or indeed not at all.

. . . .

The Applicants must . . . have emerged from the 1962 proceedings reasonably satisfied in that they had so far established the jurisdiction of the Court. They would know that it was not impossible that the Court would come back even on that finding, although it would be uncharacteristic, to say the least, of the Court thus badly to reverse itself. However, only one of the four preliminary objections rejected in 1962 related to a purely jurisdictional issue. I refer of course to the fourth preliminary objection and in particular to the Court's finding that, notwithstanding the lack of direct talks between the Applicants and the Respondent, it had been demonstrated that there was a dispute which "cannot be settled by negotiation".

. . . [T]he other three preliminary objections all had bearings upon the merits as well as upon the question of jurisdiction. The first objection, concerned with the question whether the Mandate was still in force as a treaty, was at the very centre of the merits, seeing that the continuing existence of the Mandate was the indispensable basis of the Applicants' claims. The second objection, concerned as it was with the effect of the demise of the League of Nations, raised no less central an issue of the merits. As for the third objection, the Applicants could not hope to succeed on the merits unless they could establish that they had a legal interest in the subject matter of their claims. All three objections should therefore, in my view, have been joined to the merits.

It is true that in 1962 these three objections were not joined to the

[17] *Op. cit.*, p. 212.
[18] S. Rosenne, *The International Court of Justice*, Leyden, A. W. Sijthoff, 1957, p. 381. The reference is to p. 16 of the *Nottebohm* case (second phase), *I.C.J. Reports* 1955, p. 4. The decision in the first phase is reported at *I.C.J. Reports* 1953, p. 111.

merits by the Court but were rejected. This does not, however, detract from the fact that they were rejected only qua preliminary objections. It will be remembered that the proceedings on the merits had been suspended and that at the preliminary stage "the Court cannot in any way prejudge its future decision on the merits". It therefore remained open to the Respondent to bring the same points up again in relation to the merits, just as it remained not merely open to, but compelling upon, the Court to satisfy itself on these points before rendering a decision on the "ultimate merits". In the light of the jurisprudence of the Court analysed all too briefly above, it can hardly be supposed that the Applicants were not aware of this.

I have already expressed the view that the Court should have made use of its power under Article 62(5) of the Rules expressly to join at least some of the preliminary objections to the merits. In fact, there now seems to be some regret among the majority in 1962 (the minority in 1966) that this was not done.[25] It is also significant that in the *Barcelona Traction* case, which came before the Court in 1964, a preliminary objection involving the Applicant's lack of standing was joined to the merits.[26]

It is an extremely delicate question for the Court to decide whether a preliminary objection should be upheld, rejected or joined to the merits. If an objection is upheld, the whole case falls to the ground. Clearly this should not be done at what after all is only a preliminary hearing unless there is some fundamental bar which makes it quite hopeless for the Applicant to go on. On the other hand, it is understandable that the Court should wish to deal at the preliminary stage with as many preliminary points as possible so as to obviate a situation in which both Parties are involved in extensive and costly proceedings which eventually result in the Applicant failing on an apparently preliminary point. The difficulty lies, in this case as well as in some of the other cases that have been discussed, in determining (i) precisely what is a preliminary point, and (ii) what weight should be given to a preliminary decision on a preliminary point.

Looking over the jurisprudence of the Court during the last forty years the present writer is inclined to the view that there has been a tendency on the part of the Court to decide too much at the preliminary stage.[27] This is undesirable for a number of reasons, not the least

[25] *I.C.J. Reports* 1966, p. 261 (Separate Opinion of Judge Tanaka).
[26] *I.C.J. Reports* 1964, p. 6.
[27] To take another example, the Court in the *Anglo-Iranian Oil Co.* case accepted as a preliminary objection the view that the Company's concession convention of 1933 with the Imperial Government of Iran did not also have, as the British Government contended for certain special reasons, the character of a convention between the two Governments. There would seem to have been good reasons why this objection should have been joined to the merits. (*I.C.J. Reports* 1952, p. 93). It should be remembered that what I have called "the preliminary stage" is not expressly provided for in the Statute. It is an invention of the Court itself through Article 62 of the Rules, although of course Article 30 of the Statute entitles the Court to frame its own Rules.

of which is that it seems to place the Applicant at a disadvantage. The Respondent can put forward preliminary objections which touch both on jurisdiction and on merits. If he succeeds at the preliminary stage, well and good. If he fails, he can put forward the same points again on the merits. Even if he does not put them forward again, the Court can consider them *proprio motu*. If the Court is evenly divided, as in this case, the Applicant stands a chance of losing at either stage. But the Applicant (who will of course have considered this danger before instituting proceedings) can guard against it to some extent by refraining from asking that objections which touch on merits as well as jurisdiction be rejected at the preliminary stage and by requesting instead that they be joined to the merits. This is what France wisely did in the *Norwegian Loans* case.[28] In the present case, however, the Applicants did not take this course, but requested that all four preliminary objections be dismissed. It is submitted that, if it became generally known that the Court would join to the merits all preliminary objections that were *prima facie* not unrelated thereto, the result would on the whole be salutary. Certainly it would mean that some cases might be argued more fully than was strictly necessary. But there would probably be a falling off in the number of preliminary objections made, and above all the risk of double proceedings with apparently contradictory decisions at the two stages, such as occurred in this case, would be largely eliminated.

The Distinction between "Conduct" and "Special Interests" Provisions in the Mandate.—The assertion that the Mandate permitted judicial protection in the case of the "special interests" of States only and not in the interests of the inhabitants of the mandated territory is thoroughly examined and convincingly refuted by Judge Jessup in his dissenting opinion in 1966.[x] Scholars have generally given support to Judge Jessup's interpretation of the preparatory works of the mandates systems which the Court relied on in reaching its interpretation.[y] For example, Rosalyn Higgins asks: [z]

C. *Was the Court in any event correct in its assertion that the Applicants had to show a 'special' legal interest in the Mandate before they could require the Court to give a declaratory Judgment on litigation relating to it?*

---

[x] 1966 ICJ Reports at 352 ff.

[y] See, in particular, the scholarly study by Charles H. Alexandrowicz, "The Juridical Expression of the Sacred Trust of Civilization" (1971) 65 *AJIL* 149. See further, Verzijl, above, n. s at 94–95; Reisman, n. c (above, p. 292), at 77–83; Bin Cheng, n. c (above, p. 292), at 208–11; sed contra, Johnson, above, n. w at 174–75.

[z] Above, n. u at 582–85.

[28] *I.C.J. Reports* 1957, p. 9.

Quite apart from the question of the compatibility of the Court's insistence that such a 'special' interest be shown with its own Judgment of 1962, is this alleged requirement really valid at law? This problem is argued out very fully in the Judgment itself, and one can do no more here than to provide a brief and compressed version of the different views.

On this question, the Court rested its case on the view that the substantive provisions of the Mandate fell into two broad categories— those provisions which conferred certain rights relative to the mandated territory upon members of the League as individual States, and those provisions which defined the Mandatory's powers and obligations. This latter category the Court termed 'conduct' provisions, and they include the system of international accountability by the Mandatory for the proper carrying out of its obligations. An example which the Court gave of the former 'particular' category was the guarantee in Article 5 of the South West Africa Mandate that missionaries of the nationality of any League Member should be able to enter South West Africa. As we have seen, Article 7 of the Mandate provides that 'if any dispute whatever should arise between the Mandatory and another Member of the League of Nations relating to the interpretation or the application of the provisions of the Mandate, such dispute . . . shall be submitted to the Permanent Court of International Justice . . .'

The Court, basing itself upon the distinction it had drawn between the two categories of provisions in the Mandate, said in the 1966 Judgment that the right of access to the Court provided for in Article 7 *was only available to individual States in relation to alleged breaches of particular rights which they had been granted in respect of the mandated territory* (such as the right of entry for missionaries of their own nationality). The Court thus *rejected the notion that individual States could submit to it a dispute about the 'conduct' provisions,* that is, about the proper carrying out of the Mandate by the Mandatory. The Court found that it was for the League Council to go to the Court about such aspects of the Mandate.

Several things need to be said about this. The first is that the distinction which the Court is seeking to draw between 'particular' provisions and 'conduct' provisions—and especially the corollary that different legal interests exist for the implementation of these two categories —is a concept hitherto unpropounded in international law. There is nothing in the wording of Article 7 of the Mandate which supports it: while it is ambiguous as to whether the League Council or individual members (or both) may take a dispute to the Court, it does not indicate that individual Members may go to the Court about disputes over 'particular rights' provisions, while only the League Council itself may go to the Court over 'conduct' provisions.

The implications of what the Court has here said are exceedingly important, not only in respect of this particular litigation, but because it clearly implies that only the United Nations may go to the Court for legal determination of disputed matters relating to the 'conduct' provisions. Yet—and this is a point the repercussions of which the Court completely sidesteps in its Judgment—the United Nations (like the League Council) is only entitled at law to ask for an Advisory Opinion. An Advisory Opinion is not legally binding, and South Africa has already shown, by her response to the three earlier Advisory Opinions on South West Africa, that she does not feel obliged to comply with these judicial Opinions. Only states may seek from the Court a Judgment, which *is* legally binding. Thus the effect of the Court's Judgment is to rule that in spite of the recourse to judicial procedure provided for in Article 7 of the Mandate, no Mandatory in breach of its obligations under the Mandate will be faced by a binding judgment thereon. There is removed from the Mandatory the sanction of being publicly seen to not to comply with a binding Judgment of the International Court. And of course, the possibility of enforcing compliance with such a Judgment, under the terms of Article 94 of the Charter, is also removed. By its judgment then, the Court is, in principle, protecting a Mandatory who may be in breach of a Mandate, both from the full legal force of a binding adjudication and from ensuing political action (should it be deemed necessary) to secure compliance with that adjudication. This can hardly be what was envisaged by those who framed the Mandate provisons, given their intention to promote a system of effective international accountability. The Court's pronouncement on this point militates against any effective supervision of the 'conduct' provisions of the Mandate—provisions which lie at the heart of a Mandate. This point, it must be emphasised, is a general one: it does not entail any assumptions as to whether South Africa is, or is not, in breach of her obligations under the Mandate for South West Africa.

As early as 1950, in the Advisory Opinion (though this particular point was not then directly in issue) the then British member of the International Court, Sir Arnold McNair (as he then was), stated:

> every State which was a Member of the League at the time of its dissolution still has a legal interest in the proper exercise of the Mandate . . .[16]

And Judge Read—who, like Sir Arnold McNair formed part of the majority of the Court on this occasion, and attached a separate opinion—also firmly declared:

> the first, and the most important [of the international obligations of the Mandatory] were obligations designed to secure and protect the well-being of the inhabitants. They did not enure to the benefit of the Members of the League, although each and every Member had a legal right to insist upon their discharge . . . and a legal right to assert its interest against the Union by invoking the compulsory jurisdiction of the Permanent Court (Article 7 of the Mandate Agreement).[18]

[16] Advisory Opinion on the International Status of South West Africa, *ICJ Reports 1950*, at p. 158.
[18] *Ibid.*, pp. 164, 165.

In 1962 the Court (the majority of which did not, of course, comprise those members forming the majority in 1966) itself declared:

> The only effective recourse for protection of the sacred trust would be for a member or members of the League to . . . bring the dispute . . . to the Court for adjudication

Indeed

> without this additional security the supervision by the League and its members could not be effective in the last resort.[19]

It only remains to add that a considerable body of evidence supporting this viewpoint was pressed by Judge Jessup and the other dissenting Judges in the 1966 Judgment.

The Majority's Judicial Philosophy.—The disagreement between the majority of 1962 and that of 1966 is best viewed as a conflict of judicial philosophies.[a] As Judge Tanaka pointed out in 1966, the difference was essentially one "between two methods of interpretation, teleological or sociological and conceptual or formalistic." [b] This is emphasized by Professor Wolfgang Friedmann of the Columbia Law School, Professor Richard A. Falk, Milbank Professor of International Law at Princeton University and counsel to the applicant States, the present writer, and Professor William M. Reisman of the Yale Law School.

Wolfgang Friedmann:[c]

> The way in which the Court was divided is . . . politically and psychologically even more important than such divisions are in national jurisdictions. The International Court of Justice, like its predecessor, represents an important but as yet weak attempt to detach international legal issues from national prejudices and passions. Although there are some notable instances of judges having rendered opinions contrary to the views and interests of the state of their own nationality, such cases form the exceptions. In the present case, it is not so much

---

[a] For views in favour of the majority's judicial philosophy, see: J. T. Van Wyk (South African *ad hoc* Judge), "The International Court of Justice at the Cross-Roads" 1967 *Acta Juridica* 201, and "The United Nations, South West Africa and the Law" (1969) 2 *Comparative and International Law Journal of Southern Africa* 48; A. C. Cilliers, "Die Suidwes-Afrika-saak en die Volkereg" (1971) 34 *Tydskrif vir Hedendaagse Romeins-Hollandse Reg* 25. For opposing views, see Dugard, n. t (above, p. 332), at 447–51; Bin Cheng, n. c (above, p. 292), at 184–87; Gross, n. s (above, p. 332), at 5–8; Landis, n. o (above, p. 326), at 662; Scrivner, n. s (above, p. 332), at 41–43; "The South West Africa Cases: *Ut Res Magis Pereat Quam Valeat*" (1967) 115 *University of Pennsylvania Law Review* 1170 at 1190–94.

[b] 1966 ICJ Reports at 278.

[c] "The Jurisprudential Implications of the South West Africa Case" (1967) 6 *Columbia Journal of Transnational Law* 1 at 2–10, 16.

[19] *ICJ Reports 1962*, p. 336.

the division according to nationality as it is the division of representatives between the older and the newer countries, or, in a different perspective, between the "developed" and the "less-developed" countries that inevitably will be analyzed and remembered. In geographical terms, the United States judge was the only judge of a Western nation on the side of dissenters. One may add, as a representative of an industrially developed, though not in the geographical sense, "Western" state, the dissenting opinion of Judge Tanaka (Japan). If the political analysis is pursued further, it is not surprising that the Soviet judge, like the Mexican and the two African judges, is found on the side of the dissenters. The Australian President, and the British, French and Italian judges formed part of the majority.

Any analysis of the Judgment according to national or other political criteria would no doubt be indignantly rejected by the judges who voted with the majority, and by many others. The present writer does not in fact believe that national or other superficially political considerations were determining factors. Far more significant, in his opinion, is the stark division of jurisprudential approaches between the majority judgments, and most of the minority opinions, of which those of Judge Tanaka and Judge Jessup are the most important. Indeed, more significant than nationality may be the fact that Judges Spender, Fitzmaurice and Gros, came to the Court from long careers of legal and diplomatic service for their respective governments rather than from a judicial or professorial background.

The many detailed arguments on the "interest" or "right" of member states of the League not directly affected by the administration of the Mandate, or on the relation of the United Nations to the League of Nations, or on the general interpretation of international documents of a humanitarian character, and many other issues discussed in the individual opinions have been ably analyzed and will continue to be analyzed in many learned contributions. The present writer will therefore confine himself to a few observations on the crucial issue of the jurisprudential approach to international problems that, like almost all vital issues, have a mixed legal and political character, and particularly on the validity of the contrast between an "analytical" as against a "teleological" or "humanitarian" approach.

The legal philosophy of the majority is clearly expressed in the following passage:

> It may be urged that the Court is entitled to engage in a process of "filling in the gaps," in the application of a teleological principle of interpretation, according to which instruments must be given their maximum effect in order to ensure the achievement of their underlying purposes. The Court need not here enquire into the scope of a principle the exact bearing of which is highly controversial, for it is clear that it can have no application in circumstances in which the Court would have to go beyond what can reasonably be regarded as being a process of interpretation, and would have to engage in a process of rectification or revision. Rights cannot be pre-

sumed to exist merely because it might seem desirable that they should. On a previous occasion, which had certain affinities with the present one, the Court declined to find that an intended three-member commission could properly be constituted with two members only, despite the (as the Court had held) illegal refusal of one of the parties to the jurisdictional clause to appoint its arbitrator—and although the whole purpose of the jurisdictional clause was thereby frustrated. In so doing, the Court (*I.C.J. Reports 1950*, p. 229) said that it was its duty "to interpret the Treaties, not to revise them." It continued: "The principle of interpretation expressed in the maxim: *Ut res magis valeat quam pereat*, often referred to as the rule of effectiveness, cannot justify the Court in attributing to the provisions for the settlement of disputes in the Peace Treaties a meaning which as stated above, would be contrary to their letter and spirit."

In other words, the Court cannot remedy a deficiency if, in order to do so, it has to exceed the bounds of normal judicial action.

It may also be urged that the Court would be entitled to make good an omission resulting from the failure of those concerned to foresee what might happen, and to have·regard to what it may be presumed the framers of the Mandate would have wished, or would even have made express provision for, had they had advance knowledge of what was to occur. The Court cannot, however, presume what the wishes and intentions of those concerned would have been in anticipation of events that were neither foreseen nor foreseeable; and even if it could, it would certainly not be possible to make the assumptions in effect contended for by the Applicants as to what those intentions were.[6]

The implication is clearly that the Court's approach is a truly juridical one because it is directed to the "interpretation" as distinct from the "rectification or revision" of the relevant provisions and documents. Any student of jurisprudence is familiar with this approach, the heritage of the age of analytical positivism, as represented in the common law world by Austin and his successors, and on the Continent by the Nineteenth Century exponents of a strict division between "is" and "ought" in Germany, France and other countries. It is difficult to think of any contemporary jurisprudential treatise, many of them the work of eminent judges, and particularly of any modern study of the judicial process which has not rejected this approach as untenable in logic and disproved by experience.[7] Contemporary analytical jurists have analyzed the ambiguity of the meaning of statutory words, and

---

[6] Final Judgment at 48–49.

[7] *See* CARDOZO, THE NATURE OF THE JUDICIAL PROCESS (1921); STONE, HUMAN LAW AND HUMAN JUSTICE (1965); *see also* FRIEDMANN, LEGAL THEORY, ch. 32 (4th ed. 1960), referring to the work of Francois Gèny, Roscoe Pound, Karl Lewellyn, and many other contemporary writers. *See also* LEGAL INSTITUTIONS TODAY AND TOMORROW; THE CENTENNIAL CONFERENCE VOLUME OF THE COLUMBIA LAW SCHOOL 1–66 (PAULSEN ed. 1959) and in particular the observations by Judges Traynor and Breitel.

the openness of their interpretation.[8] The almost limitless possibilities of overcoming the binding nature of stare decisis have been analyzed by virtually every contemporary writer on the problems of judicial law-making.

In view of the assertion that the British tradition "demands a more literal interpretation,"[9] a view held strongly by Judges Spender and Fitzmaurice, it is apposite to quote two contemporary British Judges, Lord Wright and Lord Jowitt:

> The sub-section must, I think, be construed with due regard to its apparent object, and to the character of the legislation to which it belongs. The provision was to reduce the evils of bad housing accommodation and to protect working people by a compulsory provision. . . . It is a measure aimed at social amelioration, no doubt in a small and limited way. It must be construed so as to give proper effect to that object.[10]

> It appears to their Lordships that it is not consistent with the political conception which is embodied in the British Commonwealth of Nations that one member of that Commonwealth should be precluded from setting up, if it so desires, a Supreme Court of Appeal having a jurisdiction both ultimate and exclusive of any other member. . . . [I]t is, as their Lordships think, irrelevant that the question is one that might have seemed unreal at the date of the British North America Act. To such an organic statute the flexible interpretation must be given that changing circumstances require, and it would be alien to the spirit with which the preamble to the Statute of Westminister is instinct, to concede anything less than the widest amplitude of power to the Dominion legislature under s. 101 of the [British North America] Act.[11]

Even if in municipal law, where the spheres of the legislature, executive and judiciary are relatively clearly marked off, the judge can justify his reluctance to adopt a wider rather than a narrow interpretation of a given statute or precedent by reference to the function of the legislature; such an argument fails utterly in the sphere of international law. Even at this day, international law, while aspiring to be a comprehensive system governing the conduct of nations in international relations, is a loose collection of customs, treaties, and some judicial decisions, supplemented, in the language of the Statute of the International Court, by "general principles of law recognized by civilized nations," most of them still inarticulate. It can only survive by

[8] For some representative analyses *see* Radin, *Statutory Interpretations,* 43 HARV. L. REV. 863 (1930); Willis, *Statute Interpretation in a Nutshell,* 16 CAN. BAR REV. 1 (1938); C. ALLEN, LAW IN THE MAKING (6th ed. 1958) ch. 6; Hart, *Definition and Theory in Jurisprudence,* 70 L. Q. REV. 37 (1954).

[9] BRIERLY, THE LAW OF NATIONS 325 (6th ed., Waldock 1963) as quoted by Judge Jessup, *infra* note 15.

[10] Lord Wright in Summers v. Salford Corp., [1943] A.C. 283, 293.

[11] Lord Jowitt in Att.-Gen. for Ontario v. Att.-Gen. for Canada, [1947] A.C. 127, 153–54 (P. C.).

constantly expanding to meet new conditions, by a continuous inter-action of law-finding and law-making, for which there is no neat division between legislative, executive and judicial organs. The Nuremberg Judgments are a conspicuous example of the making of new international law in the form of judicial fiat. Over a century ago Sir Henry Maine compared international law to ancient jurisprudence insofar as it was "filling nothing, as it were, excepting the interstices between the great groups which are the atoms of society." [12] Nowadays such a conception of international law, in an international society which, for better or worse, is linked by enormously stronger bonds of interdependence in all spheres of life, such an atomistic and stationary conception of international law is impossible. An international legal system that does not develop through the interplay of the traditional sources of international law with imaginative judicial interpretation, taking into account new principles of "international public policy" [13] as expressed in international conventions, U.N. resolutions, and the newer forms of international transactions in the economic, social and other domains, will decline into an increasingly insignificant collection of rules of diplomatic intercourse.

In denying standing to the Applicants, and thereby cutting off any means of legal supervision over the administration of the former Mandate of South West Africa by the Union of South Africa, the Court leaves a void. It cannot accept the implication that South Africa now is free to deal with South West Africa as she likes, as part of her own territory. But the Court's opinion indicates no alternative.

An approach close to that briefly outlined here, and diametrically opposed to that of the Court's Judgment, is expressed strongly in two dissenting opinions. One represents the civilian (especially Germanic) legal tradition of Japan (Judge Tanaka):

> Undoubtedly a court of law declares what is the law, but does not legislate. In reality, however, where the borderline can be drawn is a very delicate and difficult matter. Of course, judges declare the law, but they do not function automatically. We cannot deny the possibility of some degree of creative element in their judicial activities. What is not permitted to judges, is to establish law independently of an existing legal system, institution or norm. What is permitted to them is to declare what can be logically inferred from the *raison d'etre* of a legal system. . . . In the latter case the lacuna in the intent of legislation or parties can be filled.
>
> So far as the continuance of international supervision is concerned, the above-mentioned conclusion cannot be criticized as exceeding the function of the Court to interpret law. The Court's opinion of 1950 on this question is not creating law simply for the reason of necessity or desirability without being founded in law and fact. . . . The importance of international supervision in the man-

---

[12] MAINE, ANCIENT LAW 98 (Everyman's library ed. 1917).
[13] On "international public policy" *see* JENKS, THE PROSPECTS OF INTERNATIONAL ADJUDICATION 428 ff. (1964).

dates system, the appearance of the United Nations which, as the organized international community, it characterized [sic] by political and social homogeneity with the defunct League of Nations, particularly in respect of the "sacred trust" for peoples who have not yet attained a full measure of self-government, and the establishment of the international trusteeship system, the Respondent's membership in the United Nations, and finally, the refusal by the Respondent to conclude a trusteeship agreement as expected by the Charter: these factors, individually and as a whole, are enough to establish the continuation of international supervision by the United Nations.

Consideration of the necessity that the paralysis of mandate without supervision must be avoided, can by no means be denied. But we are not going to deduce the above-mentioned conclusion from mere necessity or desirability but from the *raison d'etre* and the theoretical construction of the mandates system as a whole.

We, therefore, must recognize that social and individual necessity constitutes one of the guiding factors for the development of law by the way of interpretation as well as legislation. The principle of effectiveness often referred to, may be applied to explain the viewpoint of the "necessity" argument of the 1950 Advisory Opinion recognizing the continued existence of the Mandate as well as international supervision. . . .

In this case, we cannot deny that the necessity created the law independently of the will of the parties and those concerned. The explanation by the reasonably assumed intention of the parties (Oppenheim-Lauterpacht, *International Law*, Vol.I, 8th ed., p. 168) seems a compromise with voluntarism. "The reasonably assumed intention" is not identical with the psychological intention which very probably did not exist. The former shall be assumed by the Court taking into consideration all legal and extralegal factors, from which the "necessity" is not excluded. These kinds of activities of judges are not very far from those of legislators.

.   .   .   .

Such attitude of interpretation has been known as a method of "*libre recherche scientifique*" or "*Freirecht*", mainly in civil-law countries for three-quarters of a century as emancipating judges from the rigid interpretation of written laws and emphasizing the creative role in their judicial activities. There is no reason to believe that the same method should be denied in the field of international law except the opposing tendency of strong voluntarism derived from the concept of sovereignty and not being in conformity with the concept of law which attributes to law an objective and independent existence from the will and intention of those to whom law is addressed[14]

Judge Jessup arrives at substantially the same conclusion from a common law background:

[14] Dissenting opinion by Judge Tanaka, Final Judgment at 277–78.

The task of interpretation in this case requires the Court to ascertain what meaning must be given to certain important provisions of the Covenant of the League of Nations, and of the Mandate for South West Africa.

At the outset:

> . . . one must bear in mind that in the interpretation of a great international constitutional instrument, like the United Nations Charter, the individualistic concepts which are generally adequate in the interpretation of ordinary treaties do not suffice. (Separate opinion of Judge de Visscher, *Status of South West Africa, I.C.J. Reports 1950,* p. 189.)

In particular it is true that one cannot understand or analyse the proceedings of a great international conference like those at Paris or San Francisco if one regards it as essentially the same as a meeting between John Doe and Richard Roe for the purpose of signing a contract for the sale of bricks.

> But lawyers who are trained in the methods of interpretation applied by an English court should bear in mind that English draftsmanship tends to be more detailed than continental, and it receives, and perhaps demands a more literal interpretation. Similarly, diplomatic documents, including treaties, do not as a rule invite the very strict methods of interpretation that an English court applies, for example, to an Act of Parliament. (*The Law of Nations* by J. L. Brierly, 6th ed., 1963, by Sir Humphrey Waldock, p. 325.)

It may be agreed that there are dangers in dealing with multipartite treaties as "international legislation," but if municipal law precedents are invoked in the interpretive process, those precedents dealing with constitutional or statutory construction are more likely to be in point than ones dealing with the interpretation of contracts. . . .

I adopt with emphatic approval what Judge Lauterpacht said in his separate opinion in 1955 on South West Africa about the so-called "clear meaning" rule which to my mind is often a cloak for a conclusion reached in other ways and not a guide to correct conclusion. Judge Lauterpacht said:

> This diversity of construction provides some illustration of the unreliability of reliance on the supposed ordinary and natural meaning of words.
>
> Neither having regard to the integrity of the function of interpretation, is it desirable that countenance be given to *a method* which by way of construction may result in a summary treatment or disregard of the principal issue before the court. (*I.C.J. Reports 1955,* p. 93)[15]

[15] Dissenting opinion by Judge Jessup, Final Judgement at 352, 355 (emphasis by Judge Jessup; footnotes in the opinion have been omitted).

Judge Tanaka describes the difference of opinions as one "between two methods of interpretaion, teleological or sociological and conceptual or formalistic." [16] The Legal Adviser to the British Foreign Office, Sir Francis Vallat, in a recent address supporting the Judgment of the Court, would seem to adopt a similar distinction in saying that "in five or six years time, it will be realized that this . . . was a great turning point because [the Court] did not give way to political pressure." [17] To put it more crudely, the Court's Judgment is justified as being "non-political," *i.e.* "objective" and based on strictly juristic interpretation, whereas the opposite approach is "political" which means directed by a desire to reach a certain conclusion.

Of all the illusions of the so-called analytical approach to jurisprudence, as it is represented in the above quoted passage from the majority judgment, and in Sir Francis Vallat's observation, this is perhaps the greatest. If we judge the merits of the South West Africa decision in terms of the strength of the desire to reach a certain conclusion as compared with "detached" legal analysis, the judgment of the majority is probably the most "political" ever rendered by the International Court or its predecessor. After the Judgment of December, 1962, nobody, including the Respondent, South Africa, which devoted a prodigious amount of effort to the substantive analysis of the case, expected, in the decision of July 1966, anything but a decision on the merits. Nor had the Court, at any time during the lengthy proceedings and voluminous discussion on the merits of the issue, given any indication that it regarded the discussion of the merits as irrelevant and proposed to deal with the case as purely one of an "antecedent character."

. . . .

It is to be feared that the Judgment of the International Court in the South West Africa case has dealt a devastating blow to the hope that the International Court might be able to deal with explosive and delicate international issues.[29] The valuable and penetrating discus-

---

[16] Final Judgment at 278.

[17] Address to the Association for World Government as reported in The Times (London), Oct. 31, 1966, at 9, col. 1.

[29] Need it be said that the distinction between "political" and "legal" issues, which appears to underlie some of the Court's reasoning, has no juridical validity? The distinction between political and legal disputes as a legal test was demolished by Sir Hersch Lauterpacht, more than a generation ago in his classic treatise, THE FUNCTION OF LAW IN THE INTERNATIONAL COMMUNITY (1930). Every international dispute has political and legal aspects, although the political element is more pronounced in some than in others. The difference is not one of principle but of approach. Any issue, whether it is the status of Berlin, the right of foreign fishing fleets to fish off the coast of Iceland, or the fixing of boundaries between Italy and Yugoslavia, can be handled as a "political" or as a "legal" matter.

For a more extensive analysis of this question see Higgins, *Some Reflections on the Concept of "Political Disputes" Before the International Court of Justice* (not yet published). The gist of Dr. Higgins' analysis is that there

sion of these matters in some of the dissenting judgments cannot miti-
gate the fact that the Court, for whatever reasons, failed to meet the
challenge. This doubt that the Court will function as a judicial arbiter
in some of the major international issues of our time is likely to be a
far graver consequence of the Court's verdict than the political disappointment of some of the states, and of many groups and individuals,
that the Court failed to condemn the apartheid policies of South Africa.

Richard A. Falk [d]

THE 1966 JUDGMENT AS THE TRIUMPH
OF JUDICIAL CONSERVATISM

The fundamental policy issue dividing the ICJ cuts far deeper than
a technical disagreement about the scope of legal interests possessed by
League Members in the enforcement of the Mandate or about the extent to which the findings in 1962 were *res judicata* in 1966. The basic
disagreement dividing the ICJ is concerned with the character of international law and the implications of this character for international
adjudication. The majority in 1966 is positivistic in its orientation and
takes very seriously the role of sovereign discretion in the formation of
legal obligations. As such, this conservative perspective is antagonistic
to any attempt to compel a sovereign state to alter conduct performed
within its national domain. The mandate concept must be, in this
view, reconciled with the notions of sovereign discretion prevailing at
the time of its creation. In this regard it would have been unthinkable
for South Africa to be compelled to justify its basic social system before an international tribunal, a social system that it was expected to
extend to South West Africa by the very terms of the Mandate and
Covenant.[35]

According to this view General Assembly initiatives against South
Africa's policies are expressions of moral and political disapproval that
conflict with this voluntaristic conception of international society. The
ICJ should not implement these initiatives as its role is to apply "the
law" regardless of its moral or political effects.

In contrast, the 1962 majority deplores these attitudes. International
law develops under pressure from the will of the international community. The General Assembly is a forum within which evolving norma-
tive standards can be accurately identified. Especially in the context of

---

is no substantive distinction between "political" and "legal" disputes. The
term "a legal dispute" describes a dispute "to which is applied the process of
legal decision-making. The term is not descriptive of the nature of the dispute but rather of the process employed for its resolution."
[d] "South West Africa Cases: An Appraisal" (1967) 21 *International Organization* 1 at 13–16.
[35] See especially Article 22 (6) of the Covenant and Article 2 (1) of the Mandate.

a trust relationship, as established by the mandate notion, the evolving will of the international community is legally relevant. The discretion of a sovereign state must be reconciled with, and even subordinated to, the need of the international community to find legally effective means to discharge its responsibilities to safeguard the welfare of mandated territories.[36] The ICJ, as the judicial arm of the organized international community, should facilitate the discharge of this overriding responsibility. Thus, the majority in 1966 can be associated with the precepts of legal positivism whereas the minority may be associated with functional jurisprudence, sometimes called sociological jurisprudence.[37]

To understand this distinction somewhat more concretely it may be helpful to examine the controversy about the justiciability of the contention that apartheid violates the duty to promote well-being in Article 2(2). Judges Fitzmaurice and Spender in their joint dissent in 1962 write that they are

> not unmindful of, nor . . . insensible to, the various considerations of a nonjuridical character, social, humanitarian and other, which underlie this case. . . . [38]

The next phrase in their opinion exposes the underlying controversy among the factions of the ICJ about the nature of law and the function of courts: *"But these [humanitarian, social and other considerations] are matters for the political rather than the legal arena."* [39] The jurisprudential gravamen appears to be that the sort of question presented to the Court for adjudication by the contention that the policies of the Mandatory are violating the legal duty to promote the well-being of the inhabitants is essentially nonjusticiable. That is, there exist no legal criteria available for adjudication that are sufficiently objective to be applied by a court of law.[40] The 1966 majority considers that Ethiopia and Liberia came to the World Court with a *political* dispute between the United Nations and South Africa that is not convertible into a *legal* dispute susceptible to adjudication. There is no very satisfying approach to this basic question of distinguishing political disputes from legal disputes. I find the distinction a misleading way to raise the key problem of identifying a category of disputes for which a court is unable to render a judgment that will be accepted by the overall community as authoritative. In this regard I think that

---

[36] It is realistic to conceive of "this dispute" as one between the organized international community and South Africa. Ethiopia and Liberia are in the role of agents of the organized international community, especially as manifest in the General Assembly. Article 34 of the Statute of the Court allows only states to initiate contentious proceedings.

[37] For a discussion of these issues of jurisprudential orientation see R. A. Falk, "New Approaches to the Study of International Law," in *New Approaches to International Relations,* ed. Morton A. Kaplan (1968) by St. Martin's Press in New York.

[38] *South West Africa Cases, Preliminary Objections,* p. 466.

[39] *Ibid.* (Emphasis added.)   [40] See *ibid.,* pp. 466–467.

a court must be able to rely in its legal reasoning either upon legal rules that have been laid down by the traditional law-creating procedures set forth in Article 38 of the Statute or upon a consensus in the international community as to the values that should animate the evolution of legal standards. If such a consensus as to values is present, then the ICJ is in a position to evolve by its own reasoning legal criteria that govern the controversy and render a decision that will be accepted as authoritative by the overwhelming majority of states in the world community. In this respect the *South West Africa* setting is one in which the issue of justiciability seems far less severe than in the setting of the advisory opinion in *Certain Expenses of the United Nations*.[41] In the latter controversy, especially in retrospect, it is now quite plausible to contend that the Court should have refused to pronounce upon the questions presented for legal assessment because the answers were neither provided by clearly relevant preexisting legal criteria nor was there a sufficient consensus on the underlying values at stake to anticipate the acceptability of newly evolved legal criteria. In effect, I am arguing that under these circumstances of value divergence it is predictable that the decision of the Court will be received as nonauthoritative or arbitrary by an important segment of the legal community and that this reception will diminish the prestige of the Court as well as make it difficult to mount a campaign, if such is necessary, to coerce respect with its decision.

This interpretation of the division on the Court throughout the *South West Africa* controversy as one of antagonistic jurisprudential outlooks becomes more persuasive if it can be shown that the judgment in 1966 was not intended as a covert decision in favor of South Africa on the real merits. One superficial reaction to the judgment has been that the artificial rationale based on a denial of legal interests was advanced to cover up a disposition to decide the substantive questions in South Africa's favor. As might be expected, South African officials hailed the judgment of the World Court as "a complete justification of South Africa's sustained denial of any right to interference by other states in the Republic's administration of South West Africa." "Any further attempt at interference by other means would spring from a spirit of persecution and should find no support from any respectable state or organization of states."[42] Such statements deliberately, and quite understandably, blur the distinction between a *jurisdictional dismissal* and a finding for South Africa on the *real merits*. It is important to emphasize that the Court refused to inquire whether South Africa was or was not acting in conformity with the provisions of the Mandate. The decision in 1966 determined only that it was impossible for a League Member to test compliance in a judicial forum.

---

[41] *Certain Expenses of the United Nations (Article 17, paragraph 2, of the Charter), Advisory Opinion of July 20, 1962: I.C.J. Reports, 1962,* p. 151.
[42] E.g., Charles Swart, State President of South Africa, in a speech opening the new session of Parliament, Release of Information Service of South Africa, June 1966.

Such a bar on inquiry does not, in any formal respect, impair the capacity of Ethiopia or Liberia to allege and establish noncompliance in some other forum—for instance, in the General Assembly. It is possible for South Africa or other states to argue that a determination in a nonjudicial forum is nonauthoritative and is, therefore, not binding upon South Africa.

John Dugard: [e]

The main task of a tribunal in construing a treaty is to give effect to the 'expressed intention of the parties, that is, their intention *as expressed in the words used by them in the light of the surrounding circumstances*'.[91] In its search for this intention the tribunal will be guided by various rules of treaty interpretation, but these, in the words of Sir Hersch Lauterpacht, 'are not the determining cause of judicial decision, but the form in which the judge cloaks a result arrived at by *other means*'.[92] Among the 'other means' used in this process of interpretation must be included the views of the individual judge on the nature of the judicial function and the precepts of the particular school of interpretation to which he belongs. Basically there are two opposing philosophies in treaty interpretation: the restrictive school which seeks to impose the minimum limitations on the sovereignty of the State and which inclines towards literalism; and the teleological school which aims to give effect to the purpose of the treaty and whose main weapon is the rule of effectiveness expressed in the maxim *ut res magis valeat quam pereat*.[93] This difference in outlook is apparent in the present judgment: the majority favours the restrictive approach while the minority adheres to the teleological school.

In 1962 the Court found no difficulty in interpreting the phrase 'any dispute whatever' in article 7(2) of the Mandate. It rejected the interpretation advanced by South Africa which sought to restrict it to disagreements over the material interests of the parties, as it

> runs counter to the natural and ordinary meaning of the provisions of Article 7 of the Mandate, which mentions "any dispute whatever" arising between the Mandatory and another Member of the League of Nations "relating to the interpretation or the application of the provisions of the Mandate". The language used is broad, clear and precise: it gives rise to no ambiguity and it permits of no exception. It refers to any dispute whatever relating not only to any one partic-

---

[e] "South West Africa Cases, Second Phase, 1966" (1966) 83 *SALJ* 429 at 447–451.

[91] Lord McNair, *The Law of Treaties* (1961), p. 365.

[92] 'Restrictive Interpretation and the Principle of Effectiveness in the Interpretation of Treaties' (1949) 26 *B.Y.I.L.* 48 at 53. Italics added.

[93] Ibid., and Sir Hersch Lauterpacht, *The Development of International Law by the International Court* (below: *Development of International Law*) (1958), p. 297. See, too, Edward Gordon, 'The World Court and the Interpretation of Constitutive Treaties' (1965) 59 *American Journal of International Law* (below: *A.J.I.L.*) 794 at 796.

ular provision or provisions, but to the "provisions" of the Mandate, obviously meaning all or any provisions, whether they relate to substantive obligations of the Mandatory toward the inhabitants of the Territory or toward the other Members of the League. . . .[94]

In 1966 the Court professed itself to be concerned with an 'antecedent' matter on the *merits* and not with the jurisdictional clause which had been disposed of in 1962. Nevertheless, in holding that the applicants had no 'legal right or interest' in the well-being of the local inhabitants which they could vindicate before the Court, it reversed the above finding of 1962 and placed a restrictive interpretation on the phrase 'any dispute *whatever*', limiting it to any dispute concerning the applicants' material interests. The reason given by the Court for this restriction was that a jurisdictional clause could not confer a substantive right and that the word 'whatever' did not do 'anything more than lend emphasis to a phrase that would have meant exactly the same without it'.[95] In reaching this conclusion the Court was accused by the dissenting judges of ignoring the cardinal rule that words are to be given their 'natural and ordinary' meaning. Judge Koretsky states that article 7(2)'s wording 'is quite clear to anyone who is not seeking to read into it what it does not contain'.[96]

The Court rejected the contention that the provision should be read 'in isolation and without reference to any other consideration'. Instead it nailed its colours to the mast of another rule—that the preparatory works (*travaux préparatoires*) may be examined to establish the intention of the parties.[97] At first sight this approach appears to offend the earlier ruling of the Court to the effect that 'the first duty of a tribunal which is called upon to interpret and apply the provisions of a treaty, is to endeavour to give effect to them in their natural and ordinary meaning in the context in which they occur' [98] and that 'there is no occasion to resort to preparatory work if the text of a convention is sufficiently clear in itself'.[99] Despite these dicta it is submitted that the

[94] *South West Africa Cases, Preliminary Objections, supra,* at p. 343. See, too, the separate opinions of Judges Bustamante (at p. 381) and Mbanefo (at pp. 446–8).

[95] *South West Africa, Second Phase, supra,* at p. 42.

[96] Ibid., at p. 248. See to the same effect the dissenting opinions of Judges Koo (at pp. 219 and 222), Tanaka (at p. 259) and Mbanefo (at pp. 449–500).

[97] Ibid., at pp. 43–4.

[98] *Competence of the General Assembly for the Admission of a State to the United Nations,* I.C.J. Reports, 1950, p. 4 at p. 8. See, too, Sir Gerald Fitzmaurice, 'The Law and Procedure of the International Court of Justice' (1957) 33 *B.Y.I.L.* 203 at 211; and the dissenting opinion of Judge Van Wyk, *South West Africa Cases, Preliminary Objections, supra,* at p. 580.

[99] *Conditions of Admission of a State to Membership in the United Nations,* I.C.J. Reports, 1948, p. 57 at p. 63. See, too, *Ambatielos Case, Jurisdiction,* I.C.J. Reports, 1952, p. 28 at p. 45. The conflict between the Court's ready recourse to the *travaux préparatoires* in 1966 and its previous pronouncements was emphasized by Judge Mbanefo in his dissenting opinion, *South West Africa, Second Phase, supra,* at pp. 499–501.

Court's approach accords with the practice in more recent years to resort to the *travaux préparatoires* 'except where the meaning of the disputed term or provision is so abundantly clear as to render resort to *travaux préparatoires* patently redundant or abusive'.[1]

The recourse of the Court to preparatory works is to be welcomed, as refusal to do so usually leads to literalism. *In casu*, it is interesting to note that the Court imposed a more restrictive interpretation as a result of examining the *travaux préparatoires* than it would have if it had accepted the 'natural and ordinary' meaning.

The Court adopted a cautious approach towards teleological methods of interpretation and the rule of effectiveness. In reply to the argument that it was 'entitled to engage in a process of "filling in the gaps", in the application of a teleological principle of interpretation, according to which instruments must be given their maximum effect in order to ensure the achievement of their underlying purposes', the Court stated that it was unnecessary to 'enquire into the scope of a principle the exact bearing of which is highly controversial', for it was clear that it could not be applied if the Court 'would have to go beyond what can reasonably be regarded as being a process of interpretation, and would have to engage in a process of rectification or revision'.[2] The Court indicated that it was aware of the fact that a restrictive interpretation would reduce the effectiveness of the Mandate by depriving it of enforcement machinery, but stressed that it could not 'fill in the gaps; for this 'would be to engage in an essentially legislative task'.[3] Given the composition of the Court in 1966 this approach was inevitable as it had already been approved by Judges Spender and Fitzmaurice in their joint dissenting opinion in 1962,[4] and support for this approach is implicit in many of Judge Fitzmaurice's writings.[5]

[1] Lauterpacht, *Development of International Law*, pp. 126–7; and Gordon, op. cit., 823. Perhaps the best example of the Court's recourse to extra-treaty sources where the text was clear was in the *South West Africa Cases, Preliminary Objections, supra;* at p. 336, where the Court rejected the 'natural and ordinary' meaning of the phrase 'member of the League of Nations' and interpreted it to mean 'ex-member of the League of Nations'.

[2] *South West Africa, Second Phase*, at p. 48. In support of this view the Court cited the dictum of the Court in the *Peace Treaties*, I.C.J. Reports, 1950, p. 221 at p. 229: 'The principle of interpretation expressed in the maxim: *Ut res magis valeat quam pereat*, often referred to as the rule of effectiveness, cannot justify the Court in attributing to the provisions for the settlements of disputes in the Peace Treaties a meaning which . . . would be contrary to their letter and spirit.' In his concurring separate opinion, at p. 128, Judge Van Wyk further criticizes the adoption of a teleological approach to the merits of the dispute.

[3] Ibid., at p. 36. At p. 48, the Court repeated that it was 'its duty to apply the law as it finds it, not to make it'. The same sentiment is reiterated by Judge Van Wyk in respect of the merits (at p. 91). Cf. Lauterpacht, *Development of International Law*, pp. 227–8.

[4] *South West Africa Cases, Preliminary Objections, supra*, at pp. 468 and 511–13. See, too, Judge Van Wyk, ibid., at pp. 584 and 591.

[5] (1951) 28 *B.Y.I.L.* 1 at 7–8; (1957) 33 *B.Y.I.L.* 203 at 208, 223; (1963) 39 *B.Y.I.L.* 133 at 140.

This support for the restrictive philosophy of interpretation should be contrasted with the favour shown to teleological methods by the dissenting judges. Taking the 'sacred trust of civilization' as the ultimate purpose of the mandates system, they interpret article 7(2) so that it is given maximum effect, permitting individual ex-member States of the League to invoke the protection of the Court on behalf of the indigenous inhabitants of the Mandated Territory. The Vice-President of the Court, Judge Koo, states that

> while it may be true that acceptance of the concept of a sacred trust of civilization in and of itself does not necessarily imply more than a moral or humanitarian obligation to respect it, once this concept is made the "corner-stone" of the mandates system and implemented in the legal instruments based upon it such as Article 22 of the Covenant and Article 7(2) of the Mandate Agreement for South West Africa, full account must be taken of this fact in interpreting the legal relations, the rights and obligations of the parties to these instruments. Such a course does not mean, nor could be said to imply, judicial legislation. It is only a legitimate application of the recognised canons of interpretation, in order to give a full effect, as regards the Mandate, to "its policy, its object and its spirit".[6]

This view is echoed by Judge Tanaka:

> it is quite natural that we should seek the just criterion of interpretation *in* the principle of the Mandate, that the well-being and development of peoples not yet able to stand by themselves form a sacred trust of civilization.[7]

It is arguable that the Court ought to have adopted the teleological approach in interpreting article 7(2) as it coincided with the 'natural and ordinary' meaning of the text. If the preparatory works had revealed the clear intention of the parties this might have warranted a rejection of the 'natural and ordinary' meaning and the result arrived at by an application of the doctrine of effectiveness. But that the preparatory works themselves presented no clear answer is shown by the fact that Judge Jessup, after a thorough analysis of the same works analysed by the Court, was able to reach a completely different conclusion.[8]

In this connection it should be mentioned that the teleological method of interpretation and its handservant, the rule of effectiveness, have been accepted by international courts and publicists as an essential feature in the dynamic development of international law.[9] Restric-

---

[6] *South West Africa, Second Phase, supra,* at p. 228.

[7] Ibid., at pp. 258–9. Judge Jessup also expresses favour for a method of interpretation which gives effect to the 'spirit of the Mandate' and cites in support of such an approach the South African decisions of *R.* v. *Offen*, 1934 S.W.A. 73 at 84, and *R.* v. *Christian*, 1924 A.D. 101 at 121: ibid., at pp. 354–5.

[8] Ibid., at pp. 356–73, and *infra*, pp. 453–5.

[9] Lauterpacht in (1949) 26 *B.Y.I.L.* at 67–8, 73 and 83; Lauterpacht, *Development of International Law*, pp. 227–8 and 279; C. Wilfred Jenks, 'Hersch

tive interpretation is generally out of favour.[10] Although the Court's own approach has vacillated, in recent years it appears to have shown a preference for effective methods of interpretation.[11] It might therefore be contended that in the *South West Africa Cases, Second Phase,* the Court departed from its own more recent practice. The reason given by the Court for its refusal to apply the teleological method in this case was that this would have amounted to judicial legislation. But on this point the words of Sir Hersch Lauterpacht might be recalled:

> The judicial function is not that of an automaton which registers a gap, an obscurity, an absurdity, a frustrated purpose, without an attempt to fill the lacuna by reference to the intentions of the parties in the wider context of the agreement as a whole and the circumstances accompanying its adoption, to the needs of the community and to the requirement of good faith. In particular, in cases of doubt it may not be improper to rely on the rule of effectiveness so as to promote the operation of general principles of law and of the rule of law in international society.[12]

William M. Reisman: ᶠ

The July 18th Judgment brings out, with stunning clarity, that the theories *about* law held by judges are a highly significant, if not decisive, determinant of judicial outcomes. The method by which facts

---

Lauterpacht—The Scholar as Prophet' (1960) 36 *B.Y.I.L.* 1 at 91–2; Gordon, op. cit., at 815; Judge Lauterpacht, separate opinion, *Admissibility of Hearings of Petitioners,* I.C.J. Reports, 1956, p. 23 at p. 56; Judge Spender, separate opinion, *Certain Expenses of the United Nations,* I.C.J. Reports, 1962, p. 151 at p. 185.

[10] Lauterpacht in (1949) 26 *B.Y.I.L.* at 60, 65, 66–7, 73, 83 and 84; Lauterpacht, *Development of International Law,* pp. 297–9.

[11] *International Status of South West Africa,* I.C.J. Reports, 1950, p. 128 at pp. 136–7; *South West Africa Cases, Preliminary Objections, supra,* at p. 336; and Gordon, op. cit., at 816–20 for a general survey of the practice of the Court in this respect.

[12] (1949) 26 *B.Y.I.L.* at 74. See, too, the remarks on the nature of the judicial function by Judge Tanaka in his dissenting opinion, *South West Africa, Second Phase, supra,* at p. 277: 'Undoubtedly a court of law declares what is the law, but does not legislate. In reality, however, where the borderline can be drawn is a very delicate and difficult matter. Of course, judges declare the law, but they do not function automatically. We cannot deny the possibility of some degree of creative element in their judicial activities. What is not permitted to judges, is to establish law independently of an existing legal system, institution or norm. What is permitted to them is to declare what can be logically inferred from the *raison d'être* of a legal system, legal institution or norm. In the latter case the lacuna in the intent of legislation or parties can be filled.'

ᶠ "Revision of the South West Africa Cases" (1966) 7 *Virginia Journal of International Law* 1 at 87–88.

and rules are approached is as important as the facts and rules themselves. The World Court and the world community require a theory about law of broad contextuality. A jurisprudence which fabricates a distinction between law and policy and proceeds to apply the desiccated results of the distinction without judicial cognizance of the most intense expectations and demands of the vast majority of the peoples of the world is a retreat into mysticism. A jurisprudence which has so little confidence in the vigor of law that it must concern itself first with the purity of its own "discipline" rather than the functional and instrumental character of law in social process can hardly serve the needs of a rapidly changing world community. A jurisprudence that can, in the name of law, reach a conclusion which is against the moral and humanitarian principles that it itself concedes, is disquieting. A jurisprudence, which cannot grasp the inevitable, subjective, policy-choice element in legal decision but shuttles through the corridors of Aristotelean logic in order to be "forced" to a conclusion which is not consonant with community policy, lacks the spleen which the modern world may properly demand of theories about law.

If the International Court is to make its full contribution to world legal order, it must be staffed by individuals who appreciate the dynamic quality of legal process, who understand its techniques for reacting to change and responding to new social needs as they arise, who respect the past but are not shackled to it to the point where they must deny the present. It would be salutary if in the future the requirements of Article 2 of the Statute were construed broadly enough to include an examination of the nominee's theory about law and its relation to the social process. It is one of the ironies of our age that the knowledge which the behavioral sciences have put at our disposal about the impacts of personality on decision is applied only at the clerk-typist level of our bureaucracies.

. . . .

An adequate contemporary jurisprudence must be capable of distinguishing the elements of authority and control in authoritative decision. This matter is of direct relevance to the question of enforcement of a possible decision regarding the conduct of the Mandate for South West Africa. Both the Permanent Court and the International Court have stated that their function is to declare the law and to presume that the parties to the judgment will comply.[277] Yet, the decisions of the Courts indicate what Dr. Jenks has termed a judicial "preoccupation with enforceability".[278] Some *obiter* comments in the dissenting opinions as well as reports of participants in the litigation intimate that the possible problem of enforcement weighed heavily on the Court's mind.[279] In certain circumstances, there may be sound reasons

[277] *E.g.*, Case of the S.S. "Wimbledon," P.C.I.J., ser. A, No. 1, at 32 (1923); Case of the Readaptation of the Mavrommatis Jerusalem Concessions, P.C.I.J., ser. A, No. 10, at 4 (1927).
[278] JENKS, THE PROSPECTS OF INTERNATIONAL ADJUDICATIONS 667 (1964).
[279] South West Africa Cases, 1966, at 329–30 (dissenting opinion of Judge Jessup).

for sidestepping a decision; a judicial institution may be quite validly concerned with the continuation of its own authority and may consider the effects a repudiated judgment may have on it. Yet such considerations stretch to the limit the realm of judicial discretion. The decision to "duck" a case may be taken in only the most exigent of circumstances and should not defeat its own purposes. An image of temerity is hardly distinguishable from an image of political impotence.

7. Political Reaction to the Judgment

While scholarly reaction to the Court's judgment was often couched in strong language, it did not exceed the bounds of permissible literary criticism. Politicians, free from the restraints of academic discipline, reacted more sharply. The judgment was variously described as "scandalous," "a distortion of law," "an insult to the international conscience of mankind," "perverse," "scandalous and wicked," and "grotesque." Doubts were cast on the integrity of the judges and pleas made for a reconstitution of the International Court.[g] This unwarranted abuse directed at the International Court was in many instances made by the representatives of States which do not accept the compulsory jurisdiction of the International Court and which had previously rejected the Court as a means of settling international disputes. As Dr. Rosalyn Higgins has pointed out:

If the nations of the world *really* want an International Court which will decide questions which may have highly political repercussions, then they must act accordingly and accept in advance, and on the broadest possible basis, the Court's right to settle disputes.[h]

Several thoughtful scholars have suggested that while the Court's judgment might be untenable on legal grounds it was based on solid political considerations. Some have contended that the Court was haunted by the recent failure of the United Nations to enforce the Court's 1962 advisory opinion on expenses incurred by United Nations forces in the Congo and the Middle East [i] and that it was reluctant to render an unenforceable decision. Consequently, it preferred to find a technical escape-route which would not weaken the authority of the Court.[j] Others

[g] For a survey of these views, see R. P. Anand, *Studies in International Adjudication* (1969), pp. 144–45, and the Statement submitted by the Government of South Africa to the International Court in its advisory proceedings of 1971, vol. 1, chap. IV, Part B II and Annex A.
[h] Note u (above, p. 342), at 589.
[i] *Certain Expenses of the United Nations* 1962 ICJ Reports 151.
[j] For a discussion of this point of view, see Falk, above, n. d, at 20; Higgins, n. u (above, p. 342), at 589; and Anand, above, n. g, at 143.

have suggested that the dispute was too "political" for the Court to handle and that the Court had acted wisely in refusing to become embroiled in a highly charged political issue which would have undermined its forensic "aloofness." Sir Francis Vallat, Legal Advisor to the British Foreign Office, forecast that "in five or six years time it will be realized that this case was a great turning point because it (i. e. the Court) did not give way to political pressure." [k] This optimistic prediction has not been realized by the passage of time. The 1966 decision of the International Court is still viewed as an unfortunate blemish on its jurisprudence, as a failure to promote the international settlement of disputes, however contentious, by judicial means.

[k] *The Times* 31 October 1966. See, too, the series of articles in *The Australian* by Julius Stone (26–28 September 1966).

9

The Revocation of the Mandate and Its Aftermath, 1966–1970

1. Prelude to the Revocation

The 1966 decision of the International Court of Justice shattered the United Nations' program for change in South West Africa, which, since 1960, had been constructed on the assumption that the Court would hand down a judgment adverse to South Africa and enforceable under Article 94 of the Charter. South Africa, South West African political organizations, and the United Nations were all obliged to revise their political strategies.

The South African Government seized the initiative and in hailing the decision as a "victory" subtly suggested that the Court had found on the merits for South Africa. The Prime Minister, Dr. H. F. Verwoerd, for instance, announced that "the Court decided that *all the claims* of the applicant States, Ethiopia and Liberia, *be rejected*. The basis of this decision was that South Africa has as regards the Mandate provisions in favour of the inhabitants of South-West Africa no legal obligations towards the applicant States or any individual States" (italics added). This statement was followed by a skilful propaganda campaign,[a] which on one occasion became so misleading as to what the Court had actually decided that Judge Sir Gerald Fitzmaurice felt obliged to publicly correct the "misleading" impressions caused by South Afri-

[a] See Vernon McKay, "South African Propaganda on the International Court's Decision" (1966–7) 2 *African Forum*, no. 2, 51.

can advertisements in the British press.[b] The American Department of State also attempted to curb the excesses of this campaign by a timely reminder that the 1966 judgment in no way affected the validity of the three advisory opinions on South West Africa.[c]

South West African black political leaders, who had pinned their faith on the International Court, now turned their attention to revolutionary means of change. Shortly after the judgment had been delivered Jariretundu Kozonguizi, former president of the South West Africa National Union, declared: [d]

In fact, the decision of the International Court of Justice has had one positive result: It has underlined, for the people of South-West Africa, that a direct confrontation with the government of South Africa may be inevitable. Unless the South-West Africans are prepared to work from within, to rely primarily upon themselves, to mobilize their own physical and moral resources, it is difficult to see how, in the foreseeable future, South Africa can be uprooted from its entrenched position within the Territory. Since experience has taught Africans that external intervention in a struggle for liberation has never proved decisive against an organized internal force like that of South Africa, final victory in South-West Africa can be guaranteed only by a disciplined resistance movement, above-or underground, within the country itself.

If this is the case, then the choices before the people of South-West Africa, whether political or military, are only four. In the political realm, the choices seem to be three: (1) capitulation—by which I mean that South-West Africa may bow to fate by accepting the South African settlers as their rulers and abiding by the dictates of the Pretoria government; (2) negotiation—in the hope that the South African government may modify its position—which would amount to capitulation; (3) indifference—in the hope that other countries, other powers, may take up their struggle and attain freedom for them. None of these, especially the first, seems very likely.

The fourth is armed struggle—which is always easier to discuss than to plan, easier to organize than to carry out, for it must be pursued with a ruthless determination to win and it must be reinforced by a principled dedication to the cause. From their public pronouncements, it seems clear that the leaders of South-West Africa are moving in the direction of armed struggle. For example, in a telegram to the Secretary-General of the United Nations, released to the press, the South-West African Peoples Organization (SWAPO) charged that the "judgment of the International Court grossly betrayed the South-West African people. . . . SWAPO determined [to] continue struggle for

---

[b] Letter to the *Spectator,* 24 February 1967, p. 222.

[c] (1966) 55 *Department of State Bulletin* 231.

[d] "South West African Nationalism and the International Court of Justice" (1966–7) 2 *African Forum,* no. 2, 23 at 27–29.

liberation of our country with arms in hand." At The Hague, the President of SWAPO, Sam Nujoma, declared that SWAPO was preparing for an armed struggle; in Windhoek, John Muundjua, of the National Executive Committee of the South-West Africa National Union (SWANU), said that the patience of the South-West Africans was now exhausted and that the way was open for planning a direct confrontation with the South African government. In Dar-es-Salaam, the SWANU representative said: "Now the international community must bear the consequences of what may follow. We have repeatedly warned that South-West Africa could be turned into another Congo."

Yet the first question these leaders and representatives must ask themselves is whether or not the people are in a position to embark on such a venture. Only the people themselves can answer that question —not by indulging in sporadic sabotage activities or ineffectual invasion attempts, but by inculcating within themselves the desire and determination to fight. Even an army of a thousand men, trained and sent as invaders from abroad, can do little without the help of a population prepared to rise in disciplined force against the South African government; no matter how technically proficient such an army may be, its technical skills can be useful only to the extent that they are placed at the disposal of organized resistance movements within the country itself. There are instances, it is true, in which leaders-in-exile have successfully, from their bases abroad, organized revolutions in their own countries; but modern defense strategies and the requirements of military logistics decrease the likelihood of success today. A mission abroad, then, however well organized, can do little to direct an internal struggle; at best, it can but disseminate propaganda and organize external aid. But such aid is useless if there is not an organized resistance within the country itself. Hence—and I am trying merely to analyze the situation rather than to tell the people of South-West Africa what to do—the leaders of South-West Africa must, it seems to me, plan to organize the homefront as carefully as possible in order to make external aid effective. For demonstrations abroad, useful as they may be for propaganda purposes, will not of themselves bring freedom to South-West Africa.

The political organs of the United Nations were clearly caught off balance and resorted to hasty, unconsidered [e] action. The immediate enemy, the International Court of Justice, was punished when the Fifth Committee of the Assembly refused to approve an additional budgetary appropriation for the Court.[f] Later, when triennial elections to the Court were held, the Assembly made sure that no white Commonwealth judge was elected.[g] Judges

[e] Milton Katz, *The Relevance of International Adjudication* (1968), pp. 103–27.
[f] *UN Monthly Chronicle*, 1966, November, p. 62.
[g] Sir Kenneth Bailey of Australia was a strong contender for Sir Percy Spender's place on the Court, but African delegates made it clear that, following the 1966 decision of the Court, he was no longer acceptable.

Bengzon (Philippines), Lachs (Poland), Onyeama (Nigeria), and Petrén (Sweden) were elected to fill the vacancies caused by the retirement of Judges Sir Percy Spender, Spiropoulos, Winiarski, and Bustamante. Judge Ammoun, elected in 1965 to fill the vacancy caused by the death of Judge Badawi, was re-elected for a second term.

2. The Revocation of the Mandate

The most drastic action of the General Assembly was directed at South Africa when, on 27 October 1966, by 114 votes to 2 (Portugal and South Africa), with 3 abstentions (France, Malawi, and the United Kingdom), it adopted Resolution 2145(XXI) terminating the Mandate for South West Africa.
Resolution 2145(XXI):

> *The General Assembly,*
> *Reaffirming* the inalienable right of the people of South West Africa to freedom and independence in accordance with the Charter of the United Nations, General Assembly resolution 1514(XV) of 14 December 1960 and earlier Assembly resolutions concerning the Mandated Territory of South West Africa,
> *Recalling* the advisory opinion of the International Court of Justice of 11 July 1950, accepted by the General Assembly in its resolution 449 A (V) of 13 December 1950, and the advisory opinions of 7 June 1955 and 1 June 1956 as well as the judgement of 21 December 1962, which have established the fact that South Africa continues to have obligations under the Mandate which was entrusted to it on 17 December 1920 and that the United Nations as the successor to the League of Nations has supervisory powers in respect of South West Africa,
> *Gravely concerned* at the situation in the Mandated Territory, which has seriously deteriorated following the judgement of the International Court of Justice of 18 July 1966,
> *Having studied* the reports of the various committees which had been established to exercise the supervisory functions of the United Nations over the administration of the Mandated Territory of South West Africa,
> *Convinced* that the administration of the Mandated Territory by South Africa has been conducted in a manner contrary to the Mandate, the Charter of the United Nations and the Universal Declaration of Human Rights,
> *Reaffirming* its resolution 2074 (XX) of 17 December 1965, in particular paragraph 4 thereof which condemned the policies of apartheid and racial discrimination practised by the Government of South Africa in South West Africa as constituting a crime against humanity,
> *Emphasizing* that the problem of South West Africa is an issue falling within the terms of General Assembly resolution 1514 (XV),

Considering that all the efforts of the United Nations to induce the Government of South Africa to fulfil its obligations in respect of the administration of the Mandated Territory and to ensure the well-being and security of the indigenous inhabitants have been of no avail,

Mindful of the obligations of the United Nations towards the people of South West Africa,.

Noting with deep concern the explosive situation which exists in the southern region of Africa,

Affirming its right to take appropriate action in the matter, including the right to revert to itself the administration of the Mandated Territory,

1. *Reaffirms* that the provisions of General Assembly resolution 1514 (XV) are fully applicable to the people of the Mandated Territory of South West Africa and that, therefore, the people of South West Africa have the inalienable right to self-determination, freedom and independence in accordance with the Charter of the United Nations;

2. *Reaffirms further* that South West Africa is a territory having international status and that it shall maintain this status until it achieves independence;

3. *Declares* that South Africa has failed to fulfil its obligations in respect of the administration of the Mandated Territory and to ensure the moral and material well-being and security of the indigenous inhabitants of South West Africa and has, in fact, disavowed the Mandate;

4. *Decides* that the Mandate conferred upon His Britannic Majesty to be exercised on his behalf by the Government of the Union of South Africa is therefore terminated, that South Africa has no other right to administer the Territory and that henceforth South West Africa comes under the direct responsibility of the United Nations;

5. *Resolves* that in these circumstances the United Nations must discharge those responsibilities with respect to South West Africa;

6. *Establishes* an *Ad Hoc* Committee for South West Africa—composed of fourteen Member States to be designated by the President of the General Assembly—to recommend practical means by which South West Africa should be administered, so as to enable the people of the Territory to exercise the right of self-determination and to achieve independence, and to report to the General Assembly at a special session as soon as possible and in any event not later than April 1967;

7. *Calls upon* the Government of South Africa forthwith to refrain and desist from any action, constitutional, administrative, political or otherwise, which will in any manner whatsoever alter or tend to alter the present international status of South West Africa;

8. *Calls the attention* of the Security Council to the present resolution;

9. *Requests* all States to extend their whole-hearted co-operation and to render assistance in the implementation of the present resolution;

10. *Requests* the Secretary-General to provide all the assistance necessary to implement the present resolution and to enable the *Ad Hoc* Committee for South West Africa to perform its duties.

During the debate which preceded the adoption" of this resolution serious doubts were expressed about its legality by the representatives of France, the United Kingdom, and Portugal,[h] doubts which have not been cured by the passage of time. The South African Government, too, has consistently maintained that Resolution 2145(XXI) is illegal on the ground that the General Assembly has no authority to deprive South Africa of the Mandate unilaterally.[i] In 1968 the present writer examined the three main legal problems presented by this resolution, namely, whether the General Assembly had the right to make a determination of the compatibility of apartheid with the provisions of the Mandate without prior recourse to the International Court; whether the League of Nations had the right to terminate the Mandate unilaterally; and, if so, whether the United Nations has succeeded to this right.[j]

I. THE RIGHT OF THE GENERAL ASSEMBLY TO DETERMINE THE COMPATIBILITY OF APARTHEID WITH THE PROVISIONS OF THE MANDATE AS A PRELUDE TO REVOCATION

In the days of the League of Nations it appears to have been generally accepted that a prerequisite for the revocation of a Mandate by the Council of the League was a decision by the Permanent Court of International Justice that the Mandatory's conduct violated its obligations under the Mandate. In a report to the Permanent Mandates Commission on the subject of revocation of a mandate, Lord Lugard wrote:

> Wherever the power of revocation (in consequence of breach of contract by maladministration) may exist, there can be no doubt that in this almost inconceivable contingency the international court of justice would be the agency employed. . . .[6]

[h] *UN Monthly Chronicle,* 1966, November, pp. 21, 25, and 26 respectively.

[i] See Prime Minister B. J. Vorster's statement to this effect, made shortly after the adoption of the resolution, in *The Star,* Johannesburg, 2 November 1966.

[j] "The Revocation of the Mandate for South West Africa" (1968) 62 *AJIL* 78 at 79–97.

[6] Permanent Mandates Commission, Minutes, 5th Sess., 1924, p. 177. Mme. Bugge-Wicksell, on the other hand, appears to have taken the attitude that both the Court and the Council of the League were capable of making a determination on whether a Mandatory complied with its obligations under a mandate. In a report to the Commission she stated that revocation "could

Writers on the mandates system inclined to the same view. Quincy Wright stated that revocation would have to be preceded by a "decision" of the Permanent Court, and "if the Court decided that the Mandatory had violated the Mandate, and its decision were not observed, then the final paragraph of Article 13 of the Covenant would become applicable." [7] This latter provision specified that, in the event of failure to carry out a decision of the Court, "the Council [of the League] shall propose what steps should be taken to give effect thereto." James C. Hales was of a similar opinion:

> It would seem clear that only a signal breach of trust on the part of the Mandatory could cause the revocation: it would then be proper for a Member of the League to invoke the clause in the various Mandate Statutes referring unsettled disputes to the Permanent Court. If the latter gave a decision vindicating the Member State, then it would be open to the Council to admonish the Mandatory Power, and to invite it to conform. In the event of a refusal, the Council, which allocated the Mandates, could revoke the trust in question and the Mandatory would then cease to have a legal title to exercise its trust.[8]

The view that a decision of the Permanent Court was a prerequisite for the revocation of a mandate was clearly based on the assumption that the Court had jurisdiction over a dispute between a Mandatory Power and a Member of the League relating to the policy pursued by the Mandatory towards the indigenous inhabitants of the mandated territory, and that it consequently had the power to render a legally binding judgment in respect of such a dispute.[9] Hence the fact that

---

only occur if the Mandatory Power had misused its administrative rights over the territory, to the detriment of the native population or of other members of the League of Nations, to such an extent that one of the latter felt bound to petition the Council *or* the Permanent Court of International Justice for the transfer of the Mandate to another country" (italics added). *Ibid.*, 6th Sess., 1925, p. 154.

[7] Mandates under the League of Nations 521 (1930).

[8] "Some Legal Aspects of the Mandate System: Sovereignty-Nationality-Termination and Transfer," 23 Grotius Society Transactions 85 at 122 (1938). See also *idem*, "The Creation and Application of the Mandate System," 25 *ibid*. 185 at 211 (1940).

[9] Wright, *op. cit.* 475–476; Hales, *loc. cit* (1940) 256. Opposed to this view is that of Nathan Feinberg, who insisted that Member States of the League were permitted to invoke the jurisdiction of the Permanent Court in respect of their own interests alone and not in respect of the welfare of the inhabitants of a mandated territory (La Juridiction de la Cour Permanente de Justice Internationale dans le Système des Mandats 205 (1930)). He contended that, before the Council revoked a mandate, it should request the Court to give an advisory opinion on the question of whether the Mandatory had failed to comply with its obligations contained in the mandate agreement (at p. 201). To Feinberg the effect of such an opinion differed little from that of a judgment of the Court in contentious proceedings, for *"il est certain que cet avis serait, dans tous les cas, observé par la puissance mandataire en*

Quincy Wright referred to Article 13 (4) of the Covenant, which dealt with binding decisions in disputes between states and not with mere advisory opinions sought by one of the organs of the League of Nations.[10]

It was due to the above commonly held belief that Ethiopia and Liberia brought an application before the International Court of Justice in 1960 in which they asked the Court to adjudge and declare, *inter alia,* that South Africa

> has failed to promote to the utmost the material and moral well-being and social progress of the inhabitants of the Territory; its failure to do so is a violation of Article 2 of the Mandate and Article 22 of the Covenant; and that [South Africa] has the duty forthwith to take all practicable action to fulfil its duties under such Articles.[11]

It was confidently expected that the Court would find that it had the power to pronounce on the compatibility of *apartheid* with the provisions of the Mandate [12] and that, if it found against South Africa on this issue, the judgment would be enforceable at the instance of the Security Council in accordance with Article 94 of the Charter of the United Nations, the counterpart of Article 13 (4) of the Covenant. No doubt the belief was entertained that if all other means to induce South Africa to comply with an adverse judgment failed, the Mandate itself might be revoked by the United Nations as successor to the League of Nations, in accordance with the procedure suggested by Quincy Wright and James C. Hales.

These expectations were destroyed by the judgment of the International Court of Justice in the Second Phase of the *South West Africa Cases.* In this judgment the Court held that it was unable to entertain a dispute between an ex-member state of the League of Nations and a Mandatory Power over the latter's treatment of the indigenous inhabi-

---

cause" (at p. 196). (Of course subsequent events, viz. South Africa's refusal to accept three advisory opinions of the International Court of Justice, have disproved Feinberg's belief.) It should, however, be stressed that Feinberg did not contend that such an advisory opinion was *obligatory,* for he was well aware of the reluctance of the Council to hand over a dispute to the Permanent Court for a legal opinion, and of its preference for a political decision (at pp. 197–200).

[10] See 2 Rosenne, The Law and Practice of the International Court 651 (1965) on the non-binding nature of an advisory opinion under the Covenant.

[11] South West Africa, Second Phase, [1966] I.C.J. Rep. 6 at 10–11.

[12] By holding that it had jurisdiction in a dispute between a "member of the League of Nations" and a Mandatory Power over "the observance by the mandatory of its obligations . . . toward the inhabitants of the Mandated Territory" in 1962 (South West Africa Cases, Preliminary Objections, [1962] I.C.J. Rep. 319 at 343), the Court implicitly recognized that it *did* have the power to determine whether or not South Africa had fulfilled her obligations towards the indigenous inhabitants of South West Africa. This finding of 1962 was, however, reversed in 1966 by the International Court . . .

tants of the mandated territory, because member states of the League had enjoyed "no legal right or interest" in such a matter.[14] The Court indicated that the political organs of the League had been the appropriate agencies for investigating a Mandatory's administration of her "sacred trust" under the mandates system, not the Court itself. It stated that

> the Applicants did not, in their individual capacity as States, possess any separate self-contained right which they could assert, independently of, or additionally to, the right of the League, in pursuit of its collective institutional activity, to require the due performance of the Mandate in discharge of the "sacred trust." This right was vested exclusively in the League and was exercised through its competent organs. . . .[15]

Probably the Court was influenced by the view expressed in 1962 by Judges Spender and Fitzmaurice in their joint dissenting opinion in the *South West Africa Cases, Preliminary Objections,* in respect of Article 2 of the Mandate for South West Africa, which provides for the obligation to "promote to the utmost" the well-being of the indigenous inhabitants, that

> The proper forum for the appreciation and application of a provision of this kind is unquestionably a technical or political one, such as (formerly) the Permanent Mandates Commission, or the Council of the League of Nations—or today (as regards Trusteeships), the Trusteeship Council and the Assembly of the United Nations. . . .[16]

The result of the Court's decision, whether intended or not, was that the South West African dispute was handed over to the political organs of the United Nations for determination. For while the Court held that only the political organs of the League had been empowered to decide on the compatibility of a policy pursued in a mandated territory with the provisions of the Mandate in the days of the League of Nations, it failed to disturb its own previous finding of 1950 to the effect that the United Nations had succeeded to the supervisory functions of the League.[17] The combined effect of the International Court's two most important pronouncements on South West Africa,

---

[14] South West Africa, Second Phase, *loc. cit.* note 11 above, 51.
[15] *Ibid.* 29; see also 24, 26 and 44.   [16] *Loc. cit.* note 12 above, 467.
[17] In 1966 the Court stated that it made no finding on any of the issues before it, which included the question of the United Nations' succession to the supervisory functions of the League of Nations (South West Africa, Second Phase, *loc. cit.* at 18–19 and 22–23). Thus the decision left unblemished the Court's previous finding in the International Status of South West Africa, [1950] I.C.J. Rep. 128 at 143, that such succession had occurred. This obvious truth was emphasized by the Department of State in a statement issued shortly after the 1966 judgment, 55 Department of State Bulletin 231 (1966); 61 A.J.I.L. 597 (1967).

viz. those of 1950 and 1966, can only be that it is for the General Assembly, as successor to the Council of the League, to decide whether or not *apartheid* violates the provisions of the Mandate.

Of course the General Assembly was free to ask the International Court for an advisory opinion to assist it in its task of deciding upon the lawfulness of *apartheid* under the Mandate but, like the Council of the League,[18] it was not legally obliged to do so. Although recourse to the Court for such an opinion was regarded as desirable by the Committee on South West Africa in its Report of 1957, the hazards of such an action were even then clearly foreseen, for the Committee warned that the Court might decline to give an opinion [19] in accordance with the rule laid down in the *Eastern Carelia Case* [20] that the advisory machinery of the Court should not be used for obtaining a decision in an actual dispute between states. Mere suspicion that the Court might refuse to give an opinion was transformed into an expectation by the "technical" decision of the Court in 1966, so it is hardly surprising that the General Assembly was reluctant to send the dispute back to the Court for an advisory opinion. Furthermore, advisory opinions are not binding and, as South Africa has already ignored three on strictly legal points,[21] there no doubt appeared to be little likelihood, in the opinion of the Assembly, that she would accept one of a politico-legal nature which found that the policy of *apartheid* failed to "promote to the utmost" the welfare of the inhabitants of South West Africa.[22]

Another factor militating against an advisory opinion on the question of South Africa's compliance with the provisions of the Mandate

[18] In 1966 the Court stated of the mandates system under the League of Nations: "If any difficulty should arise over the interpretation of any mandate, or the character of the mandatory's obligations, which could be cleared up by discussion or reference to an *ad hoc* committee of jurists—a frequent practice in the League—the Council *could* in the last resort request the Permanent Court for an advisory opinion. Such an opinion would not of course be binding on the mandatory . . . but it would *assist* the work of the Council." (South West Africa, Second Phase, *loc. cit.* at 44; italics added.) This passage clearly indicates that an advisory opinion was not compulsory in such circumstances.

[19] General Assembly, 12th Sess., Official Records, Supp. 12A (A/3625), p. 3.

[20] P.C.I.J. (1923), Series B, No. 5.

[21] South Africa has declined to accept all three advisory opinions of the Court rendered in respect of South West Africa, namely, those on the International Status of South West Africa, note 17 above; the Voting Procedure on Questions Relating to Reports and Petitions Concerning the Territory of South West Africa, [1955] I.C.J. Rep. 67; and the Admissibility of Hearings of Petitioners by the Committee on South West Africa, [1956] I.C.J. Rep. 23.

[22] As a result of these refusals to accept the advisory opinions of the Court, the General Assembly can hardly be accused of ignoring Nathan Feinberg's suggestion that the revocation of a mandate should be preceded by an advisory opinion of the Court, for that suggestion was based on the view that an advisory opinion would always be accepted (see note 9 above).

was that such an opinion could only have served to provide the Assembly with *additional* judicial assistance, for that body already had considerable judicial opinion to guide it in the form of the separate opinions of those judges who did direct their attention to the ultimate merits of the South West African dispute in 1966.[23] Six of the fourteen judges examined the compatibility of *apartheid* with South Africa's obligation to "promote to the utmost" the welfare of the inhabitants, and only the South African, Judge *ad hoc* Van Wyk, found in favor of South Africa.[24] Judges Wellington Koo,[25] Tanaka,[26] Padilla Nervo [27] and Forster,[28] and Judge *ad hoc* Mbanefo [29] all found against South Africa on this vital issue.

In the light of the above considerations it can hardly be contended that the General Assembly acted improperly in determining that "South Africa has failed to fulfil its obligations in respect of the administration of the Mandated Territory," as a prelude to revocation, without first obtaining an opinion from the Court on this matter. Provided that the Assembly made this decision in good faith, it falls within the supervisory functions of the Assembly over the administration of the Territory.[31]

II. THE RIGHT OF THE LEAGUE OF NATIONS TO TERMINATE THE MANDATE UNILATERALLY

The Principle of Revocation

The two chief proponents of the mandates system, General Smuts and President Wilson, both envisaged that the League of Nations would have the authority to terminate the rights of a mandatory state which abused its "sacred trust." In his monograph, *The League of Nations, A Practical Suggestion,* General Smuts wrote:

> The mandatory State should look upon its position as a great trust and honor, not as an office of profit or a position of private advantage for its nationals. And in case of any flagrant and prolonged abuse of this trust the population concerned should be able to appeal for redress to the League, who should in a proper case assert its authority to the full, even to the extent of removing the mandate, and entrusting it to some other State if necessary.[32]

[23] In a declaration attached to the judgment of the Court, the President, Judge Spender, criticized the discussion of the merits of the dispute in the separate opinions. (See South West Africa, Second Phase, *loc. cit.* note 11 above, at 51–57.) *Sed contra,* see the views of Judges Tanaka (at 262–263) and Jessup (at 325–326).

[24] *Ibid.* at 140–193.   [26] *Ibid.* at 315.   [28] *Ibid.* at 483.
[25] *Ibid.* at 235.   [27] *Ibid.* at 464.   [29] *Ibid.* at 490.

[31] See the statement by Judge Lauterpacht in his separate opinion in the Voting Procedure Case, note 21 above, that the supervisory organ may pronounce "a verdict upon the conformity of the action of the administering State with its international obligations" (at 99).

[32] *Op. cit.* 21–22.

Similarly, in his Second Paris Draft, President Wilson suggested that the proposed mandates system should provide "for the redress or correction of any breach of the mandate by the mandatory State or agency or for the substitution of some other State or agency, as mandatory." [33]

In the light of these views it is surprising that neither Article 22 of the Covenant nor the individual mandate agreements contained any reference to the right of the League to revoke a mandate. The main reason for this omission appears to have been the fact that prospective mandatory states had indicated their unwillingness to commit themselves financially in territories of which they might later be deprived. The French Minister for the Colonies, M. Simon, in the course of the Paris Peace Conference, pointed out that his government favored annexation in preference to the mandates scheme, for the reason that

> Every mandate was revocable, and there would therefore be no guarantee for its continuance. There would thus be little inducement for the investment of capital and for colonization in a country whose future was unknown.[34]

A similar view was expressed by Mr. Massey, the Prime Minister of New Zealand, who, in pleading for annexation, stated that

> [t]he difference between the mandatory principle and that instituted by New Zealand [viz. annexation] was that between leasehold and freehold tenure. No individual would put the same energy into a leasehold as into a freehold. It would be the same with governments.[35]

Probably express mention of the right of revocation was therefore omitted to make the mandates system more attractive to those states which still had doubts about it.

Despite this omission, the right of revocation must be regarded as an implied part of the mandates system, as the obligation of accountability by a Mandatory to the League for the administration of its "sacred trust" (contained in both Article 22 of the Covenant and the individ-

---

[33] David Hunter Miller, The Drafting of the Covenant, Doc. 9, p. 104 (1928).

[34] U. S. Foreign Relations: Paris Peace Conference, 1919, Vol. 3, p. 761. From this statement R. N. Chowdhuri concludes that the power of termination was deliberately excluded to suit M. Simon and others who were of a like mind on this subject [International Mandates and Trusteeship Systems 62 (1955)]. It is submitted that this is incorrect. M. Simon and the Prime Minister of New Zealand, Mr. Massey (see note 35 below) opposed the mandates system as a whole and favored outright annexation instead. They recognized that revocation was a necessary part of the mandates system, even if it was only implied, and therefore were opposed to the system itself. M. Simon's statement should therefore be seen as a recognition of the fact that revocation was implied, rather than as a rejection of the right of revocation.

[35] U. S. Foreign Relations, cited above, p. 752.

ual mandates) [36] must surely be seen as including the sanction of revocation as the ultimate deterrent against abuse of the trust.

That the right of revocation was to be implied is clear from statements made by members of the Permanent Mandates Commission. Fear of frightening investors in the mandated territories compelled members of this body to describe revocation as "inconceivable," but at the same time they were obliged to concede, albeit reluctantly, that such a right existed. The matter was first raised by the Commission in 1923, when it drew the attention of the League Council to the fact that the investment of private capital in the mandated territories was being hindered by the view that a Mandate was revocable.[37] As a result of this, Lord Lugard presented a memorandum to the Commission in 1924 in which he declared that

> revocation of a mandate may for practical purposes be regarded as inconceivable. It could only take place in the event of gross violation of the Mandate. . . .[38]

In the discussion which ensued M. Van Rees went further in stating that the possibility of unilateral revocation "did not really exist either in law or in fact." [39] In support of this thesis he cited the view of Henri Rolin that there could be "no question of revocation." [40] That M. Van Rees really meant that revocation was inconceivable rather than impossible, however, is shown by the fact that in the very statement of Rolin cited by him there appears the assertion that a mandate agreement might be revoked "in the event of so grave a failure to comply with the conditions under which it was granted that this failure could be taken as proof of the fundamental unsuitability of the mandatory to administer the territory in conformity with the Covenant." [41] Indeed this possibility was conceded by M. Van Rees [42] after M. Rappard had asked him whether it would

> not be dangerous to exclude, even in theory, the hypothesis of revocability in case of serious abuse—an hypothesis that appeared to be entirely in conformity with the character of any mandate, and with all general legal principles.[43]

The ultimate sanction of revocation was reluctantly admitted in subsequent sessions of the Commission: by Mme. Bugge-Wicksell in 1925 [44] and by Count de Penha Garcia in 1930.[45] An over-all examination of the matter before the Permanent Mandates Commission there-

[36] Accountability to the League is provided for in Art. 6 of the Mandate for South West Africa.
[37] Permanent Mandates Commission, 3rd Sess., 1923, pp. 311–312.
[38] Ibid., 5th Sess., 1924, pp. 177–178.   [39] Ibid., p. 155.
[40] "Le Système des Mandats Coloniaux," 3–4 Revue du Droit International et de Législation Comparée 351 (1920).
[41] Ibid.   [42] Permanent Mandates Commission, 5th Sess., 1924, p. 156.
[43] Ibid.   [44] Ibid., 6th Sess., 1925, p. 154, and note 6 above.
[45] Ibid., 19th Sess., 1930, p. 175.

fore reveals an optimistic expectation that circumstances warranting revocation would never occur,[46] coupled with a refusal to deny the League this right as a final sanction.

The approach of commentators on the mandates system to revocation resembled that of the Permanent Mandates Commission. Wright,[47] Stoyanovsky,[48] Bentwich,[49] Wessels,[50] Feinberg[51] and Hales,[52] all of whose works appeared some time after the inception of the system, accepted the possibility of revocation. More significant perhaps is the opinion expressed by Goudy in 1919, viz. before the Mandate for South West Africa was conferred on South Africa, that "Undoubtedly, on legal principle, failure by the mandatory State to carry out its instructions will warrant revocation."[53]

The presence of an implied right of revocation in the mandates system is endorsed by an examination of the private law institutions upon which the system is based, viz. mandate, trust and tutelage. Clearly all the detailed characteristics of these institutions were not absorbed by the mandates system for, as Lord McNair declared in his separate opinion in the *International Status of South West Africa* case, international law does not borrow from municipal law institutions by means of importing them "'lock stock and barrel', ready-made and fully equipped with a set of rules."[54] Nevertheless the learned Judge stressed that regard should be had to "any features or terminology which are reminiscent of the rules and institutions of private law as an indication of policy and principles. . . ."[55]

[46] See, for example, the statement by Mme. Bugge-Wicksell, *ibid.*, 6th Sess., 1925, p. 154.

[47] *Op. cit.* 519–522.

[48] La Théorie Général des Mandats Internationaux 115–116 (1925). Cited and criticized by A. Berriedale Keith in "The Mandatory System," 7 Journal of Comparative Legislation and International Law (3rd Series) 280 (1925).

[49] The Mandates System 16 (1930).

[50] Die Mandaat vir Suidwes-Afrika 131 (1938).

[51] *Op. cit.* note 9 above, 200–201.

[52] 23 Grotius Society Transactions 122 (1938), and 25 *ibid.* 204 (1940).

[53] "On Mandatory Government in the Law of Nations," 1 Journal of Comparative Legislation and International Law (3rd Series) 175 at 180 (1919). Baty, writing at about the same time, was skeptical about the powers of control retained by the League, but was prepared to concede that it did possess control (including presumably the right to revoke a mandate) where the Mandatory's conduct was "patently revolting" ("Protectorates and Mandates," 2 Brit. Yr. Bk. of Int. Law 109 at 116 (1921–1922)). *Sed contra*, see the view of Berriedale Keith in "Mandates," 4 Journal of Comparative Legislation and International Law (3rd Series) 71 (1922).

[54] Note 17 above, at 148.

[55] *Loc. cit.* It is submitted that the Court went too far in this case in stating that it was "not possible to draw any conclusion by analogy from the notions of mandate in national law" (at 132), for, taken literally, this statement is at variance with Art. 38 (1) (c) of the I.C.J. Statute, which directs the Court to apply "the general principles of law recognized by civilized nations." It is probable that the Court only intended to warn against taking the analogy too far.

Article 22 of the Covenant, in providing that the welfare of the inhabitants of the mandated territories should "form a sacred *trust* of civilization" and that "the *tutelage* of such peoples should be *entrusted* to advanced nations . . . and that this *tutelage* should be exercised by them as *mandatories* on behalf of the League," makes reference to three private law institutions, viz. trust, *tutela* and *mandatum*. Differing views have been expressed as to which concept governs the mandates system,[56] but for the present purpose it is not necessary to take sides, for a characteristic of all three institutions is that revocation or termination attends upon failure to promote the interests of the ward. In Roman law a mandate might be revoked [57] and a tutor might be removed from office on grounds of misconduct.[58] Similarly, the law of trusts, as applied in England,[59] America [60] and South Africa,[61] recognizes that the rights of a trustee are terminable in the event of an abuse of the trust.[62]

Taking the above private law institutions into account "as an indication of policy and principles," it is difficult to reject the presence of an implied right of revocation in the mandates system. Significantly, when the nature of the mandates system was discussed by the South African Appeal Court in *R. v. Christian*,[63] two judges raised the issue of the right of revocation and neither denied its existence.[64]

---

[56] For a discussion of the mandates system and its municipal law analogies, see Lord McNair, separate opinion, International Status of South West Africa, note 17 above, at 148–153; J. L. Brierly "Trusts and Mandates," 10 Brit. Yr. Bk. of Int. Law 217 (1929); Quincy Wright, *op. cit.* 375–390; de Villiers, J. A., in R. *v.* Christian, 1924 A.D. (South Africa) 101 at 121.

[57] W. W. Buckland states that the right of revocation "resulted from the confidential aspect of mandate. So long as nothing had been done, the *mandator* could revoke with impunity, but if he did so when the mandatory had incurred expenses or liabilities he must take these over" (A Text Book of Roman Law 517 (3rd ed.)). See also, Digest 17.15; Gaius 3.159; and Institutes 3.26.9. It is submitted that Quincy Wright is incorrect in saying that the *mandans* "may not revoke after execution has begun" (*op. cit.* 379), for, as Buckland points out, this was possible, provided that the mandatory was compensated for any losses incurred.

[58] Buckland, *op. cit.* 160; and Institutes 1.26.

[59] 38 Halsbury's Laws of England 942 (3rd ed.).

[60] American Law Institute, Second Restatement of the Law. Trusts 2d., Vol. 1 (1959), par. 107.

[61] A. M. Honoré, The South African Law of Trusts 156–159 (1966); L. I. Coertze, Die Trust in die Romeins-Hollandse Reg 95 (1948).

[62] It should be noted that in the case of a trust the trustee's rights are terminated. The trust itself is not revoked. This is analogous to the position of South West Africa for the international trust remains (*i.e.,* the territory is still viewed by the General Assembly as having an international status); it is only South Africa's rights as trustee which have been "terminated."

[63] 1924 A.D. 101.

[64] *Ibid*. Innes, C. J. (at 112–113), and de Villiers, J. A. (at 121), left this question undecided. In In re Tamasese, 1933–1934 Annual Digest and Re-

A final factor which supports the presence of an implied right of revocation appertaining to the League is that the law of treaties permits the innocent party to renounce a treaty in the event of a fundamental breach.[65] And, as the International Court found in 1962,[66] the Mandate for South West Africa was a treaty between the League, represented by the Council, and South Africa. Hence it would appear that the League of Nations enjoyed the right to renounce the Mandate agreement in the event of a violation of the obligations therein contained. It was for this reason that Quincy Wright [67] and L. H. Wessels [68] recognized a right of revocation.

The Procedure for Revocation

It has been contended that, while the Council of the League may have had the right to revoke a mandate *in principle*, it could not have exercised such a right *in practice*, for the procedure of the Council was to invite each Mandatory not represented on the Council to attend and vote at those of its meetings which concerned the affairs of the mandated territory entrusted to its care.[69] The Mandatory would therefore have been able to "veto" any resolution aimed at revocation, as Article 5 of the Covenant required unanimity for the passing of a resolution. It was this procedural rule that led M. Van Rees of the

---

ports of Public International Law Cases, Case No. 16, the Supreme Court of New Zealand accepted the competence of the League of Nations to revoke New Zealand's Mandate for Samoa and appoint another Mandatory "if New Zealand were to fail in its obligations to the Samoan people."

[65] Lord McNair, The Law of Treaties 553 (1961). The I.L.C. Draft Articles on the Law of Treaties confirm this fundamental principle. Art. 57 (1) provides that: "A material breach of a bilateral treaty by one of the parties entitles the other to invoke the breach as a ground for terminating the treaty or suspending its operation in whole or in part." Art. 57 (3)(b) defines a material breach as "the violation of a provision essential to the accomplishment of the object or purpose of the treaty." See 61 A.J.I.L. 421–422 (1967).

[66] South West Africa Cases, Preliminary Objections, note 12 above, at 330–332. In their joint dissenting opinion of 1962, Judges Spender and Fitzmaurice denied that the Mandate was a treaty and asserted that it was simply "a Declaration promulgated by a resolution of the Council of the League" in the nature of a quasi-legislative act (*ibid.* at 490). The Court of 1966 carefully avoided referring to the Mandate as a treaty and instead referred to it as a "resolution" of the Council of the League (South West Africa, Second Phase, *loc. cit.,* at 20, 26 and 27). Nevertheless, as the matter was clearly *res judicata,* the Court of 1966 did not attempt to disturb the finding of 1962 on this point.

[67] *Op. cit.* note 7 above, at 520.   [68] *Op. cit.* note 50 above, at 132.

[69] Quincy Wright, *op. cit.* 129. This practice accorded with Art. 4 (5) of the Covenant, which stipulated that "Any Member of the League not represented on the Council shall be invited to send a Representative to sit as a member at any meeting of the Council during the consideration of matters specially affecting the interests of that Member of the League."

Permanent Mandates Commission [70] and L. H. Wessels [71] to doubt the possibility of revocation as a practical measure.

The presence of a "veto" power appertaining to South Africa in the days of the League of Nations was assumed, without examination, by the International Court of Justice in both phases of the *South West Africa Cases*.[72] Such a view, however, fails to take into account the Advisory Opinion of the Permanent Court in the *Mosul Case*,[73] in which it was held that the unanimity procedure was subject to the "well-known rule that no one can be judge in his own suit." [74] On the basis of this decision, Judge Lauterpacht, in his separate opinion in the *Voting Procedure Case*,[75] declared that South Africa would have been prevented from voting in the Council on a dispute over South West Africa.[76] As far as legal principle was concerned, the learned Judge stated that the above "well-known rule"

> must be held to apply to the case in which an international organ, even when acting otherwise under the rule of unanimity, judges in a supervisory capacity the legal propriety of the conduct of a State administering an international mandate or trust.[77]

And again:

> In so far as the principle *nemo judex in re sua* is not only a general principle of law, expressly sanctioned by the Court, but also a principle of good faith, it is particularly appropriate in relation to an instrument of a fiduciary character such as a mandate or trust in which equitable considerations acting upon the conscience are of compelling application. This, too, is a general principle of law recognized by civilized States. There is therefore no sufficient reason for assuming that if the Permanent Court of International Justice had been called upon to apply its ruling in the Twelfth Advisory Opinion [the *Mosul Case*] to the question of unanimity in connection with the supervisory function of the Council in the matter of mandates, it would have abandoned the principle there enunciated.[78]

---

[70] Permanent Mandates Commission, 5th Sess., 1924, p. 156. It should, however, be noted that this statement by M. Van Rees on the unanimity rule was made prior to the decision of the Permanent Court in the Mosul Case (Interpretation of Article 3 of the Treaty of Lausanne, P.C.I.J. (1925), Series B, No. 12).

[71] *Op. cit.* note 50 above, at 132.

[72] South West Africa Cases, Preliminary Objections, note 12 above, at 336–337; Second Phase, note 11 above, at 31, 44–45, 46 and 50. See also the separate opinions of Judge Wellington Koo and Judge *ad hoc* Van Wyk to the same effect in the Second Phase (at 218–219 and 135 respectively).

[73] Interpretation of Article 3 of the Treaty of Lausanne, P.C.I.J. (1925), Series B, No. 12.

[74] *Ibid.* 32.   [75] Note 21 above.

[76] *Ibid.* 98–106. *Sed contra,* see the separate opinion of Judge Klaestad, *ibid.* 85–86.

[77] *Ibid.* 99.   [78] *Ibid.* 105.

Furthermore Judge Lauterpacht declared that the retention of a "veto" right by South Africa was unsupported by League practice:

> The fact which . . . emerges with some clarity from a survey of the practice of the Council of the League of Nations on the subject is that it supplies no conclusive or convincing evidence in support of the view that as a matter of practice the rule of unanimity operated and was interpreted in a manner substantiating any right of veto on the part of the mandatory Power. It would probably be more accurate to say that, assuming that it existed during the initial period of the functioning of the League, that right fell into desuetude and lapsed as the result.[79]

That the practice of the League Council in this respect was not unequivocal was in fact recognized by the majority in the 1966 decision in the *South West Africa Cases*. While accepting that South Africa enjoyed a right of "veto" in principle, it stated that

> In practice, the unanimity rule was frequently not insisted upon, or its impact was mitigated by a process of give-and-take, and by various procedural devices to which both the Council and the mandatories lent themselves. So far as the Court's information goes, there never occurred any case in which a mandatory "vetoed" what would otherwise have been a Council decision.[80]

The relaxation of the rigors of the unanimity rule led writers on the mandates system to cast doubts on the validity of the argument that a Mandatory would be able to block a resolution of revocation by means of a negative vote.[81] These doubts are not dispelled by the fact that the International Court in the two phases of the *South West Africa Cases* accepted the principle of a "veto" power appertaining to South Africa. For in neither of these phases was the scope of the unanimity rule itself before the Court for a decision, nor was it thoroughly examined in either case. On both occasions it was simply assumed: on the first, to substantiate the argument that there was a need for a method of recourse to the Court, as the Council could not impose its will on a

---

[79] *Ibid.* 103. See also Judge Jessup, separate opinion, South West Africa, Second Phase, note 11 above, at 402–406. Wellington Koo, Jr., in Voting Procedures in International Political Organizations (1947), concludes, after an examination of the practice of the League, that "whenever the Council deemed itself to be acting in a judicial capacity, it was willing to apply the legal principle that a person shall not be judge and party in his own cause," but "where the function was primarily political, the Council was reluctant to adopt a resolution in the face of an adverse vote of one of the parties" (at p. 107). In determining whether a Mandatory's conduct was compatible with its obligations under the mandate and, if not, what measures were to be taken in consequence, it is submitted that the Council would be exercising a quasi-judicial function and not a strictly political function.

[80] Note 11 above, at 44–45.

[81] Quincy Wright, *op. cit.* 522; Hales, 23 Grotius Society Transactions 121 (1938).

delinquent Mandatory;[82] and on the second, to illustrate the view that the mandates system did not envisage the dictation of terms to a Mandatory but rather the negotiation of such terms.[83] The only occasion on which the Court was called upon to pronounce on the full implications of the unanimity rule to the South West African dispute was in 1955 in the *Voting Procedure Case,* when the Court held that, in the light of its findings, it was unnecessary "to examine the extent and scope of the operation of the rule of unanimity under the Covenant of the League of Nations."[84] This leaves Judge Lauterpacht's separate opinion in that case as the only exhaustive judicial examination of the question and, in the light of that judge's high standing, it is submitted that his views should be accepted.[85]

In addition to the above view, there is yet a more telling reason why the Council of the League could not have been denied the right of revocation of a mandate by reason of the Mandatory's "veto." In terms of Article 16 of the Covenant, the Mandatory could have been expelled from the League "by a vote of the Council concurred in by the representatives of all the *other* Members of the League represented thereon." A Mandatory which had violated its trust could therefore have been expelled from the Organization itself by the *"other* Members" of the Council, after which its mandate could have been revoked in its absence from the Council, for its invitation to participate in the debates of the Council was dependent upon its membership of the League.[86]

III. THE SUCCESSION OF THE UNITED NATIONS TO
THE SUPERVISORY FUNCTIONS OF THE LEAGUE OF
NATIONS (INCLUDING THE RIGHT OF REVOCATION)

In its decision in the Second Phase of the *South West Africa Cases* the International Court did not pronounce on the question whether the United Nations has succeeded to the supervisory powers of the League of Nations over the administration of the mandated territory of South West Africa.[87] Indeed, in finding that the applicants had no

[82] Preliminary Objections, note 12 above, at 336–337.
[83] Second Phase, note 11 above, at 46.   [84] Note 21 above, at 74.
[85] According to Shabtai Rosenne, "opinions are sometimes encountered flatly contradicting both the underlying principles and their application by the majority, and here, dependent upon the author's general reputation and the cogency of the reasoning, the individual opinion may in the course of time come to be seen by enlightened and informed opinion as expressive of better law." 2 The Law and Practice of the International Court 597 (1965).
[86] Hales, 23 Grotius Society Transactions 121 (1938); Quincy Wright, *op. cit.* 522. Stoyanovsky went further and suggested that the expulsion of a mandatory state from the League would automatically result in the loss of its mandate (La Théorie Générale des Mandats Internationaux 55 (1925); cited in Quincy Wright, *op. cit.* 440).
[87] The writer considers it necessary to emphasize this obvious point in the light of the attempts of the South African Government to attribute more than is permissible to the judgment of the Court. (See, for example, Ethiopia

legal right or interest in the subject matter of their claims, the Court
stated that it did so "without pronouncing upon, and wholly without
prejudice to, the question of whether the Mandate is still in force." [88]
Consequently, it is necessary to turn to the previous findings of the
Court in its Advisory Opinions on South West Africa for legal guidance, as the authority of these Opinions has in no way been diminished by the recent proceedings.[89]

In its Advisory Opinion of 1950 on the *International Status of
South-West Africa* the International Court held that "the General Assembly of the United Nations is legally qualified to exercise the supervisory functions previously exercised by the League of Nations with regard to the administration of the Territory." [90] By this was meant that
the General Assembly was empowered to exercise all the supervisory
functions which the League might have exercised—including the right
of revocation—and not only those which had in fact been exercised by
the League prior to its dissolution.[91] The Court did, however, stress
that

> The degree of supervision to be exercised by the General Assembly
> should not . . . exceed that which applied under the Mandates Sys-

---

and Liberia versus South Africa, published by the Department of Information, Pretoria, South Africa, pp. 80 and 282). Indeed certain advertisements
inserted in foreign publications by the South African Government, describing the findings of the Court, are so misleading that Judge Fitzmaurice felt
obliged to correct the "misleading" impressions caused by them in a letter to
the Spectator (Feb. 24, 1967, p. 222); see also the letter of Mr. Ernest A.
Gross (Spectator, March 24, 1967, p. 353).

[88] South West Africa, Second Phase, *loc. cit.* 19. See also at 18 and 22–23.

[89] This fact was stressed by Judge Jessup in his dissenting opinion of 1966:
"The Court has *not* rendered a decision contrary to the fundamental legal
conclusions embodied in its Advisory Opinion of 1950 supplemented by its
Advisory Opinions of 1955 and 1956 and substantially reaffirmed in its Judg-
ment of 1962" (South West Africa, Second Phase, *loc. cit.* 331). See also 55
Department of State Bulletin 231 (1966); . . .

[90] Note 17 above, at 137. This finding was reaffirmed by several of the dissenting judges in the Second Phase of the South West Africa Cases, viz.
Judges Wellington Koo (p. 236), Tanaka (p. 278), Jessup (p. 388) and Padilla Nervo (p. 461); and Judge *ad hoc* Mbanefo (p. 490). *Sed contra,* the separate opinion of Judge *ad hoc* Van Wyk, *ibid.* 125; and the joint dissenting
opinion of Judges Spender and Fitzmaurice, South West Africa Cases, Preliminary Objections, note 12 above, at 532, note 2.

[91] This point was clarified by the International Court in the Admissibility of
Hearings of Petitioners Case, [1956] I.C.J. Rep. 23. In reply to the argument that the effect of the 1950 Opinion was only to allow the General Assembly to do anything which the League Council *had done* in the exercise of
its supervisory functions and not to allow it to do something which the
Council had had the authority to do but had *not done,* the Court stated that
it did not find "any justification for assuming that the taking over by the
General Assembly of the supervisory authority formerly exercised by the
Council of the League had the effect of crystallizing the Mandates System at
the point which it had reached in 1946" (at 29).

tem, and should conform as far as possible to the procedure followed in this respect by the Council of the League of Nations.[92]

This Opinion was confirmed by the Court in its subsequent Opinions of 1955 and 1956. Of particular importance is the finding of the
Court in the *Voting Procedure Case* of 1955 that the fact that resolutions on South West Africa were passed by a two-thirds' majority vote
in the General Assembly in accordance with the provisions of the
Charter of the United Nations instead of unanimously, as in the case
of the League of Nations, could not be "considered as instituting a
greater degree of supervision than that which was envisaged by the
previous Opinion of the Court." [93]

Consequently, on the assumption that the supervisory powers of the
Council of the League included the right to resolve to terminate the
Mandate, it would appear that the General Assembly succeeded to this
right, which it was entitled to exercise by a resolution passed by a two-
thirds' majority vote in accordance with the provisions of Article
18 of its own Charter.

Against this view it must be pointed out that the Court in 1950 held
that

> South Africa acting alone has not the competence to modify the in-
> ternational status of the Territory of South-West Africa, and that
> the competence to determine and modify the international status of
> the Territory rests with the Union of South Africa acting with the
> consent of the United Nations.[94]

This passage has led to the suggestion that the Court intended the
converse to apply too; that is, that the United Nations, acting alone,
likewise has no capacity to modify the status of the Territory and that
any modification would require the consent of South Africa. This
would seem to be attributing a meaning to the finding of the Court
which could not possibly have been intended, for the Court was simply reaffirming the continued existence of Article 7(1) of the Mandate
for South West Africa, which provides that "the consent of the Council
of the League of Nations is required for any modifications of the terms
of the present Mandate," and substituting the United Nations for the
League.[95] The question of the right of the United Nations, acting
alone, to revoke the Mandate was not in any way before the Court and
was not considered by it. The only reference to revocation of the Mandate in this Advisory Opinion is to be found in the dissenting opinion
of Judge Alvarez, who declared that

> It may happen that a mandatory State does not perform the obliga-
> tions resulting from its Mandate. In that case the United Nations

[92] International Status of South West Africa, note 17 above, at 138.
[93] Note 21 above, at 73. See also the separate opinion of Judge Tanaka,
South West Africa, Second Phase, *loc. cit.* 275.
[94] International Status of South West Africa, note 17 above, at 144.
[95] *Ibid.* 141.

Assembly may make admonitions, and if necessary, revoke the Mandate. It has this right under Article 10 of the Charter.[96]

IV. THE LEGAL EFFECT OF THE GENERAL ASSEMBLY'S RESOLUTION TO TERMINATE THE MANDATE

An examination of the mandates system, supplemented by the Advisory Opinions of the International Court on South West Africa, leads to the conclusion that the General Assembly inherited the right *to resolve* to terminate the Mandate and to take such a resolution by a two-thirds' majority vote. It is therefore not possible to fault the October, 1966, resolution on constitutional grounds: it falls within the purview of the powers conferred upon the Assembly by Article 10 of the United Nations Charter.[97]

The argument that the resolution terminating the Mandate is "illegal" or "unconstitutional" fails to grasp the real difficulty presented by the resolution, namely, the question of its legal effect. It is trite law that resolutions of the General Assembly not concerned with its own internal management [98] are not legally binding upon states. This fact was emphasized by Judges Klaestad and Lauterpacht in their separate opinions in the *Voting Procedure Case* [99] and has more recently been confirmed by the International Court in the Second Phase of the *South West Africa Cases*.[100] Such resolutions are only recommendatory in their effect and, at the most, impose an obligation upon the states to which they are directed to consider them in good faith to see whether they are able to accept and implement them.[101] Decisions of

---

[96] *Ibid*. 182. See also the observations by Judge Alvarez to the same effect at 180 and 183.

[97] International Status of South West Africa, note 17 above, at 137.

[98] Resolutions dealing with internal matters such as budgetary assessments (Art. 17), the establishment of subsidiary organs (Art. 22), requests for advisory opinions from the International Court of Justice (Art. 96), the suspension of rights and privileges of membership (Art. 5) and the expulsion of Members from the Organization (Art. 6) have full binding force. See Certain Expenses of the United Nations, [1962] I.C. J. Rep. 151 at 163.

[99] Note 21 above, at 87–88 and 114–122, respectively.

[100] Note 11 above, at 50–51.

[101] Judge Lauterpacht, separate opinion, Voting Procedure Case, note 21 above, at 118–119; Judge Klaestad, separate opinion, *ibid*. 88; and the statement by Mr. Lawrence, South Africa's representative at the United Nations in 1947, reported in General Assembly, 2nd Sess. (1947), Official Records, 105th Meeting, p. 637. See generally on this topic, F. Blaine Sloan, "The Binding Force of a 'Recommendation' of the General Assembly of the United Nations," 25 Brit. Yr. Bk. of Int. Law 1 (1948); D. H. N. Johnson, "The Effect of Resolutions of the General Assembly of the United Nations," 32 *ibid*. 121 (1955–1956); Sir Gerald Fitzmaurice, "Hersch Lauterpacht—the Scholar as Judge," 38 *ibid*. 2–12 (1962); and the present writer, "The Legal Effect of United Nations Resolutions on Apartheid," 83 South African Law Journal 44 (1966).

the Council of the League of Nations, on the other hand, were legally binding.[102] Herein lies the real anomaly of the resolution of October, 1966. Although it is constitutionally sound, it does not achieve its desired legal object of putting an end to South Africa's rights as Mandatory in the same way as a unanimous decision (excluding South Africa's vote) of the Council of the League would have done. The resolution only obliges South Africa to consider its terms in good faith. Presumably this necessitates consideration of the possibility of accepting the General Assembly's recommendation that South Africa cease to administer the Territory, or, failing this, a willingness on the part of South Africa to enter into discussions with the United Nations over the future administration of the Territory. However imprecise this legal obligation [103] to consider the resolution in good faith may be, one thing is clear: South Africa has no right simply to ignore the resolution.[104]

The conclusion that General Assembly Resolution 2145 (XXI), purporting to terminate the Mandate for South West Africa, does not have the desired effect may, at first, appear to be ridiculous. But it is a conclusion which flows logically from an examination of the powers conferred upon the General Assembly by its own Charter and, as the International Court stressed in the *Voting Procedure Case,*

> the authority of the General Assembly to exercise supervision over the administration of South-West Africa as a mandated Territory is based on the provisions of the Charter. While, in exercising that supervision, the General Assembly should not deviate from the Mandate, its authority to take decisions in order to effect such supervision is derived from its own constitution.[105]

The above conclusion does not mean that the United Nations lacks the competence to terminate South Africa's Mandate with full legal effect. It only means that the General Assembly must enlist the co-operation of the Security Council which, in terms of the Charter of the United Nations, is empowered to take legally binding decisions.

The Security Council might take such a decision under Article 41,

[102] South West Africa, Second Phase, note 11 above, at 50; and Judge Klaestad, Voting Procedure Case, note 21 above, at 87. Judge Lauterpacht prefers to state that resolutions of the General Assembly "do not possess a degree of legal authority equal to that of the decisions of the Council of the League of Nations" (*ibid.* 123).
[103] In the Norwegian Loans Case, [1957] I.C.J. Rep. at 53, Judge Lauterpacht stated: "Unquestionably, the obligation to act in accordance with good faith, being a general principle of law, is also part of international law." Commenting on this statement Sir Gerald Fitzmaurice declared that "action in good faith is an international law obligation . . . and accordingly action not in good faith must be considered as a breach of international law, even if one difficult to establish, and the consequences of which may be uncertain." 38 Brit. Yr. Bk. of Int. Law 9 (1962).
[104] Judge Lauterpacht, separate opinion, Voting Procedure Case, *loc. cit.* 118.
[105] Note 21 above, at 76.

after determining South Africa's continued presence in South West Africa to constitute a "threat to the peace" in terms of Article 39. Article 41 provides that the Security Council may decide on "measures not involving the use of armed force" to restore international peace, and suggests the economic and diplomatic measures which "may" be used to effect this object. The "measures" listed in Article 41 are not intended to be exclusive,[106] and it would not be straining the letter of the provision unduly to regard termination of the Mandate as a "measure" necessary to restore peace. Such a decision would clearly be legally binding by virtue of Article 25 of the Charter, under which Member States of the United Nations "agree to accept and carry out the decisions of the Security Council."

The objections to such a course are twofold: first, it is not certain that the situation in South West Africa warrants the drastic measures of Chapter VII; [107] secondly, as the 1950 Advisory Opinion on South West Africa indicates that it is the General Assembly and not the Security Council which is to exercise the rights of supervision,[108] revocation of the Mandate (a sanction arising out of the supervisory function) should be agreed to by the General Assembly as well as by the Security Council. It is therefore suggested that a preferable procedure, which would, in terms of the Charter, have legal effect, would be one analogous to that described in Article 6 of the Charter dealing with the expulsion of a Member of the United Nations, viz. a resolution of termination by the General Assembly on the recommendation of the Security Council. The advantage of this course is that it would not constitute the introduction of a system of voting foreign to the United Nations and, at the same time, it would approximate more closely to the procedure of the Council of the League which required the consent of the principal Powers for revocation of the Mandate.[109] This

[106] L. M. Goodrich and E. Hambro, Charter of the United Nations 277 (2nd ed., 1949).

[107] The question whether the continued presence of South Africa in the Territory of South West Africa constitutes a "threat to the peace" warranting sanctions under Ch. VII is, of course, a political decision which must be left to the Security Council. See Dr. Rosalyn Higgins' discussion of the finding that the Rhodesian situation constitutes a "threat to the peace" in 23 The World Today 99–103 (1967). In this respect the suggestion should be rejected that, because three judges found in 1966 that there was no evidence of militarization within South West Africa (South West Africa, Second Phase, cited note 11 above, at 320–322 (Judge Tanaka), 330 (Judge Jessup) and 205–213 (Judge ad hoc Van Wyk), South Africa's continued administration of the Territory cannot constitute a "threat to the peace." (This suggestion is made in an advertisement of the Government of South Africa in the Spectator of Feb. 24, 1967, p. 218.) Such an approach ignores the repercussions caused by the application of apartheid in South West Africa upon other African states.

[108] International Status of South West Africa, note 17 above, at 137.

[109] In terms of the Covenant of the League, no decision could have been taken by the Council to revoke the Mandate for South West Africa without the concurring votes of the representatives of the Principal Allied and Associated Powers (Arts. 4 (1) and 5 (1)). The suggested procedure for revocation

would entail using the procedure of Article 6 for a purpose not fore-seen by the Founding Fathers but, as has been pointed out by Judge Tanaka,

> The replacement of the League as a supervisory organ by the United Nations is not normal; it is an exceptional phenomenon of the transitional period which was produced by the non-conclusion of a trusteeship agreement by [South Africa].[110]

Such a decision, it is submitted, would be legally binding on South Africa in the same way as a decision of expulsion from the United Nations.[111] More important, perhaps, would be the political ef-fect of such a decision. The Permanent Members of the Security Coun-cil, upon whom enforcement of such a resolution would be dependent, would be given the opportunity of allowing or disallowing the passage of such a resolution by reason of their "veto" power.[112] Support for the termination of the Mandate for South West Africa by the Security Council would therefore indicate a willingness on the part of the major Powers to enforce such a decision and might serve to bring a much delayed end to the dispute over the future of that Territory.

Academic opinion was divided in its response to Resolution 2145(XXI). While several writers supported the resolution[k] oth-ers expressed reservations about its legality,[1] and it was con-demned outright as illegal by Professor Marinus Wiechers, of the University of South Africa:[m]

---

by the United Nations would ensure that the consent of the Permanent Mem-bers of the Security Council was obtained in the same way and would, it is submitted, thereby approximate more closely to the procedure of the League. See, further, on this point, Judge Lauterpacht, in Voting Proce-dure Case, note 21 above, at 95.

[110] South West Africa, Second Phase, note 11 above, at 275. Judge Lauter-pacht indicated that the exceptional circumstances of the case may demand a procedure of supervision not specifically provided for in the Charter and that the resort to such a course should be permissible (Voting Procedure Case, *loc. cit.* 106–114).

[111] Certain Expenses of the United Nations, [1962] I.C.J. Rep. 151 at 163.

[112] Hans Kelsen, The Law of the United Nations 711 (1951); Goodrich and Hambro, *op. cit.* 142.

[k] John F. Crawford, "South West Africa: Mandate Termination in Historical Perspective" (1967) 6 *Columbia Journal of Transnational Law* 91 at 136; R. P. Anand, *Studies in International Adjudication* (1969), pp. 145–49; Charles H. Alexandrowicz, "The Juridical Expression of the Sacred Trust of Civiliza-tion" (1971) 65 *AJIL* 149 at 158. On the competence of the General Assem-bly to terminate a trusteeship, see Geoffrey Marston, "Termination of Trus-teeship" (1969) 18 *International and Comparative Law Quarterly* 11.

[1] Rosalyn Higgins, "The International Court and South West Africa: The Implications of the Judgment" (1967) 8 *Journal of the International Com-mission of Jurists* 3 at 27–35; Katz, above, n. e, at 123–24.

[m] "South West Africa: The Decision of 16 July 1966 and its Aftermath" (1968) 1 *Comparative and International Law Journal of Southern Africa* 408

THE REVOCATION OF THE MANDATE
OVER SOUTH WEST AFRICA

During the League of Nations period, the evolution of the mandates system from its inception made it sufficiently clear that no specific provision had been made for the *revocation* of any particular mandate. There were, however, a variety of views on the *termination* of mandates in general as well as one clear example of such termination.

The most definite example of mandate termination is afforded by the termination of the British "A" Mandate over Iraq. The termination of the Iraq Mandate flowed from the treaty between Iraq and Great Britian, of 13 January 1926, in terms of which Great Britain stated that it proposed to recommend Iraq for admission to the League of Nations in 1932. Britain duly informed the League of its intention to recommend the termination of its Mandate over Iraq and the admission of Iraq as a member. This resulted in the appointment of a special commission to report on mandate termination in general;[79] the commission's report was adopted by the Permanent Mandates Commission and finally (on 28 January 1932) approved by the Council; and Iraq was admitted by the Assembly as a member of the League on 3 October 1932.

Although the termination of the Iraq Mandate provides some insight into the workings and attitudes of members of the Permanent Mandates Commission, it does not provide any guiding principles for the termination of mandates in general. Iraq, it must be remembered, was an international law subject under an "A" Mandate, and it acceded to its status of full independence partly on the ground of the accord between itself and Great Britain. Even as a mandated state, then, Iraq had already possessed such a degree of independence that it qualified for international law subjectivity. It was only necessary for the Mandates Commission, and later the Council, to decide on its *degree* of independence so that they could give their approval to terminate the Mandate.[80] The termination of the Iraq Mandate affords no authority, and very little precedent, for the termination of "C" Mandates.

Turning to the writers, it will be noted they advance various theories on the termination of mandates during the lifetime of the League of Nations. It is said[81] that "most writers took the position that the

---

at 433-42. See, too, W. M. van der Westhuizen, "Die Bevoegdheid van die Verenigde Volke om die Mandaat vir Suidwes-Afrika te Beëindig" (1968) 31 *Tydskrif vir Hedendaagse Romeins-Hollandse Reg* 330.

[79] The well-known Van Rees Commission. *Cf.* Evans, "The General Principles Governing the Termination of a Mandate", 26 *AJIL* (1932) 735 where he gives an accurate account of the events leading to the termination of the Iraq Mandate.

[80] Although a decision by the Council to terminate the Mandate could be taken only at the request of the Mandatory; *cf.* Evans, *supra* note 79, 743.

[81] *Cf.* Crawford, "South West Africa: Mandate Termination in Historical Perspective", 6 *Col J of Transn Law* (1967) 91, 106.

mandatory, acting with the consent of the Council, could legally terminate the mandate, thus rendering the mandated territory completely
independent". Others were of the opinion that termination could be
effected *de facto* if the Council accepted the independence of the mandate territory by permitting that territory to be admitted as a member
of the League.[82] And some authors, in later articles, postulated the
possibility of a unilateral revocation of the mandate by the Council in
the case of non-performance of its obligations by the mandatory.[83]
This latter possibility was rarely entertained by writers during the
League period, nor by members of the League or of the Permanent
Mandates Commission. The only possible conclusion that can be
drawn from the law and practice during this period is that the mandatory could not terminate the mandate on its own, and that a mandate
could be terminated by the mandatory and the Council, acting together.[84]

From 1945 on, the position regarding the termination of mandates
has become even more obscure. It is possible that some practice and
rules might have crystallized had the League still been in existence.
But since its demise in 1945, the position has remained cloaked in ob-

---

[82] *Ibid.*, 107.

[83] See, for example, Crawford, *supra* note 81, 114; Verzijl, "Territorial con-
troversies before the International Court of Justice", I *Tijdschrift voor Int
Recht* (1953/4) 234, 238: ". . . [I]t was reasonable to hold that the League
should have the power to revoke the Mandate should the Mandatory fail to
discharge its duties or should act against the fundamental principles of the
League." This opinion, for which no authority is quoted, was adopted by
Roskam, "Het Mandaat Zuid-West-Afrika–'A sacred Trust' ", *Volkenrechte-
lijke Opstellen* (1962) 111, 113.

Perhaps the most farreaching statement in this regard comes from Dugard,
"The Revocation of the Mandate for South West Africa", 62 *AJIL* (1968) 78,
85: "Despite this omission (*i.e.* express mention of the right of revocation),
the right of revocation must be regarded as an implied part of the mandates
system, as the obligation of accountability by a Mandatory to the League for
the administration of its 'sacred trust' (contained in both Article 22 of the
Covenant and the individual mandates) must surely be seen as including
the sanction of revocation as the ultimate deterrent against abuse of the
trust." But the justification of this view according to private law principles
which regulate the institutions of tutela, mandatum and trust (*cf.* Dugard,
on 87) is not convincing since it ignores the basic international character of
the mandates system—*cf.* Verzijl, *supra*, 244. Dugard then goes on to state
that the General Assembly of the United Nations assumed all the powers in
regard to the mandates, including the power of unilateral revocation (see
this article at 92). His views in this respect are an accurate reflection of the
opinions voiced in the many debates of the General Assembly on the South
West Africa issues, but lack solid legal argument. The simple fact is that the
United Nations is not the successor to the League of Nations.

[84] It has been suggested by H. M. J. van Rensburg, *Die Internasionale Status
van Suidwes-Afrika* (1956) 135, that the Mandate could be terminated by
South Africa acting alone by recognizing the independence of the Territory.
It is, however, doubtful whether this opinion is sound, especially in the light
of the termination of the Iraq Mandate.

scurities. In this respect, the well-known *dictum* of H. D. Hall,[85] namely: ". . . in the case of the mandates, the League died without a testament", has become even more applicable. The so-called "winding-up" resolution of the League, of 18 April 1946, in so far as it related to the mandate system, is essentially a statement which recognized the *status quo* for the transitional period. The fact that the League Assembly, by means of this resolution, expressly recognized the continued administration of the mandated territories "for the well-being and development of the peoples concerned in accordance with the obligations contained in the respective Mandates, until other arrangements have been agreed between the United Nations and the respective Mandatory Powers", makes it very clear that the fate of the administration of mandated territories was a matter for reciprocal agreement.

Even an enquiry into the United Nations trusteeship system provides no answer which may be used by way of analogy, because the United Nations Charter and existing trusteeship agreements also contain no indication as to their termination.

In the absence of authority on mandate termination and, more especially, mandate revocation, it is necessary to scrutinize the opinions and judgments of the International Court on the South West Africa issue to see if there are any *dicta* on this subject. It must, of course, be remembered that any *dictum* by the Court or by its individual members on mandate *revocation* can only be *obiter,* since this particular issue has never been referred to the Court.

The important 1950 opinion [87] did not seek to define the powers of the General Assembly of the United Nations over South West Africa, but limited itself to the question put before it, *i.e.* the degree of supervision to be exercised by the General Assembly.[88] The Court based its opinion as to the continuation of supervisory powers on Article 80(1) of the Charter. It did not try to define the scope of the powers of the United Nations; nor did it assume that the United Nations, whilst acting under Article 80(1), was the successor to the League of Nations.[89] The crux of the 1950

---

[85] *Mandates, Dependencies and Trusteeship* (1948) 273.

[87] *The International Status of South West Africa, Advisory Opinion* of 11 July 1950—hereinafter quoted as the 1950 opinion.

[88] 1950 opinion, 136 and 138: "The degree of supervision to be exercised by the General Assembly should not therefore exceed that which applied under the Mandates System, and should conform as far as possible to the procedure followed in this respect by the Council of the League of Nations."

[89] This was explained very well in the joint dissenting opinion of Judges Badawi, Basdevant, Hsu Mo, Armand-Ugon and Moreno Quintana in the *Advisory Opinion of the Admissibility of hearings of petitioners by the Committee on South West Africa* of 1 June 1956, ICJ Rep. (1956) 230 note 64: "It [the Court in 1950] sought to ascertain whether, after the disappearance of the League of Nations, there still existed an international authority qualified for this function of supervision." See also page 66 of the Opinion, and Judge Winiarski's opinion at page 33, where it is repeated that the 1950 opinion was not based on the idea that the United Nations is the successor to the League of Nations.

opinion was, in the words of Professor Ch. Rousseau,[90] the continuance of a "système juridiquement abstrait, privé de tout support institutionnel et de toute l'armature qui caractérisait le régime des mandats (Conseil de la S.D.N., Commission permanente des mandats) et dont il serait téméraire de prétendre que l'Organisation Unies est aujourd'hui la continuatrice". To read into the 1950 opinion of the Court something extra, relating to the power of the United Nations to terminate existing League of Nations mandates, is not simply to misread the opinion of the Court, but shows a disregard for the provisions of the Charter, on which that opinion was based.

On the other hand, the Court in its 1950 opinion did express itself on the question who is competent to *determine* and *modify* the status of the Territory. The answer of the Court, in terms of Article 7(1) of the Mandate, that "competence to determine and modify the international status of South West Africa rests with the Union of South Africa acting with the consent of the United Nations",[91] speaks for itself. It is clear that the power to determine and modify the international status of South West Africa rests, in the first place, with the Mandatory. Some authors took exception to this statement of the Court. Verzijl, for example,[92] states that "the Court should . . . have resolutely declared that such authority—to modify the Status of the Territory—resides exclusively in the paramount powers of the World Organisation (*i.e.* the General Assembly),[93] after previous consultation with the Mandatory". But he leaves open the question whether in fact the United Nations is competent, under the prevailing provisions of the Charter, to determine and modify, unilaterally, the international status of the Territory. The answer to this question must be in the negative. As was stated by Judge Tanaka in his 1966 opinion: "The prohibition of unilateral modification exists not only in regard to the Mandatory but in regard to the League of Nations also . . . So long as the Mandate survives on an institutional basis after the dissolution of the League, the necessity for the future amendment of the Mandate by consent of both parties (*i.e.* South Africa and the General Assembly) subsists. In this sense the contractual element is recognized as remaining together with the institutional elements." [94]

The position is that none of the opinions of the Court, nor its judgments of 1962 and 1966, give a clear answer to the question of termination of the South West Africa Mandate, let alone to the question of United Nations power to terminate or revoke the Mandate. As mentioned above, even the very existence of the Mandate has been left undecided since the July 1966 decision.

In only two separate opinions of members of the Court does one find definite remarks on mandate revocation. The first, and by far the most outspoken opinion, is that of Judge Alvarez in his 1950 separate

---

[90] "Chronique des faits internationaux", *Rev Gén de Droit Int Pub* (1967) 382, 383.

[91] 1950 opinion, 143.

[92] *Supra* note 83, 247–8.

[93] *Ibid.,* 249.

[94] ICJ Rep. (1966) 323.

opinion, in which he stated that the General Assembly may, in terms of Article 10 of the Charter, revoke the Mandate if South Africa does not fulfil its obligations thereunder.[95] The other opinion, that of Judge Lauterpacht, joined to the 1955 opinion of the Court, has more nuances, and may even be called vague. In discussing the legal force of General Assembly resolutions *vis-à-vis* the Mandatory, he says: [96] "An administering State may not be acting illegally by declining to act upon a recommendation or series of recommendations on the same subject. But in doing so it acts at its peril when a point is reached when the cumulative effect of the persistent disregard of the articulate opinion of the Organization is such as to foster the conviction that the State in question has become guilty of disloyalty to the Principles and Purposes of the Charter. Thus an Administering State which consistently sets itself above the solemnly and repeatedly expressed judgment of the Organization, in particular in proportion as that judgment approximates to unanimity, may find that it has overstepped the imperceptible line between impropriety and illegality, between discretion and arbitrariness, between the excercise of the legal right to disregard the recommendation and the abuse of that right, and that it has exposed itself to consequences legitimately following as a legal sanction."

Although these two opinions have become the basis of the General Assembly Resolution of 27 October 1966, their legal soundness is, with respect, questionable. A writer has remarked on the first opinion: "[I]t is difficult to see how, even under the dispensation of the new international law, Article 10, the 'discussion clause' of the Charter, can be construed to give this extensive power" (*i.e.* to revoke the Mandate).[97] More cannot be said. Judge Lauterpacht's *dictum,* on the other hand, has all the elegance and persuasion of an attractive argument, but it raises the following serious questions: How can a state, by not acting on a recommendation of the General Assembly, become "guilty of disloyalty to the Principles and Purposes of the Charter" if, according to the Principles of that same Charter, he is not bound by such recommendations? How can the exercise of a legal right to disregard these recommendations at any stage become the "abuse" of that very legal right? What are the "consequences legitimately following as a legal sanction"?

It is evident that the legal problems in connection with mandate termination have by no means been resolved. The writers who have so far commented on the October 1966 Resolution "revoking" the Mandate have either criticized its legal validity,[98] or tried to justify it

---

[95] 1950 opinion, 182.

[96] *South West Africa—Voting Procedure, Advisory Opinion* of 7 June 1955, ICJ Rep. (1955) 67, 120.

[97] Ellison Kahn, in (1951) 4 *International Law Quarterly* 78 at 97.

[98] *Cf.* Rousseau, *supra* note 90, 384: "On n'a ici, est-il besoin de le dire? aucune sympathie pour la politique raciste du gouvernement du Pretoria et particulièrement pour la manière dont celui-ci a usé—et abusé—du mandat qui lui avait été attribué en 1920 sur le Sud-Ouest africain. Mais on ne peut avoir davantage d'indulgence pour les abus de pouvoir multipliés depuis des

in rather ambiguous terms. One writer expressed herself as follows: "As to *authority* to revoke, I indicated that I saw certain legal obstacles; as to *power,* I was merely noting that the Assembly would have the votes . . . Nor, may I note, did I contend that the Assembly had power to make its resolution *effective,* which is a different matter again." [99] By acknowledging a power without authority one is taken back in the history to the time when international law was nothing more nor less than self-help. Another writer claimed that the revocation of the South West Africa Mandate by the General Assembly was legal, but that it lacks legal effect.[100] But, surely, a legal act without legal effect is a nullity? It may lack legal or executory *force,* but it must have a legal effect, *i.e.* a meaning within a legal system, in order to be a legal act. Yet other writers simply claimed, without explaining its legality, that the October Resolution marked an important new era of decolonialization.

The present position is that although the October 1966 Resolution is widely accepted, no solid legal arguments can be advanced to justify this General Assembly action. The difficulties and frustrations already experienced by the United Nations Council for South West Africa, and in the General Assembly itself, may well be ascribed to this fact. Once again, it seems as though the majority of the members of the General Assembly have embarked on a perilous course beyond the boundaries of the law.

So far, nothing direct has been said about the Mandatory's position. Before proceeding to do so, the writer wishes to make it quite clear that the ensuing discussion is not meant to justify South Africa's actions or to decry United Nations actions. As stated in the introduction to this article, a certain sense of reality can be preserved only by presenting a full picture of the problems involved.

The writer's point of view can be summed up in one sentence. It is that South Africa, although it might have acted constantly against the wishes of the majority of the General Assembly, did not necessarily act against rules of international law.

By refusing to accept the supervisory powers of the United Nations, South Africa did not adhere to the advisory opinion of 1950. But this does not mean that South Africa acted contrary to any principle of international law—certainly not traditional international law. It is trite law that an advisory opinion of the Court has no binding force. It is true, and it has repeatedly been stressed by judges and writers, that advisory opinions carry much persuasive weight, and that they may al-

---

années par l'Assemblée générale des Nations Unies, sous la pression démagogique de certains de ses membres extra-européens. Toutes les institutions meurent tôt ou tard de leurs excès—et pas seulement dans l'ordre interne." See also "The South West Africa Cases", *Wash Univ L Q* (1967) 159, 196; and W. M. van der Westhuizen, "Die Bevoegdheid van die VV om die Mandaat vir SWA te beëindig", XXXI *THRHR* (1968) 330.

[99] Dr Rosalyn Higgins in a letter to Professor C. A. W. Manning, 43 *International Affairs* (1967) 215.

[100] Dugard, *supra* note 83, 94–5.

most be regarded as binding judicial findings by the Court. If this is so, then the same principle must apply to individual opinions of judges, especially if those opinions are joined to an advisory opinion and not to a judgment. This is only logical, since an individual opinion joined to a judgment is necessarily diminished in the light of the judgment's legal force,[102] whereas an individual opinion, joined to an advisory opinion, may have the same persuasive force as the opinion of the Court since both of them are on the same non-binding persuasive level. Now, South Africa, by refusing to acknowledge the supervision of the General Assembly, has acted on the advice of two eminent former members of the Court, namely, Judge Read and Sir Arnold McNair. Both these judges concluded, in their 1950 separate opinions, that in the absence of an express agreement the "continuing international obligations of the Union of South Africa for South West Africa do not include the obligation to accept the administrative supervision of the United Nations and to render annual reports to that Organization".[103] It cannot therefore be said that South Africa, in denying the United Nation's supervisory powers, has acted without any advice from the International Court.

To this moment there is no judicial finding in existence, to the effect that the South African administration of the Territory violates the provisions of the Mandate. The argument is often advanced that the numerous resolutions of the General Assembly on the mandated Territory must be considered as authoritative findings. No matter how anxious one may be to read more into the Court's opinions and judgments,[104] the truth is that nothing can be found anywhere to support the suppostion that the General Assembly has the power to judge (and condemn) the Mandatory's administration of the Territory. Even if one accepts the General Assembly's power to discuss the Mandate and to make recommendations in terms of Article 10 of the Charter, such power does not permit the General Assembly to pass binding decisions on the matter. It would also be wrong, as was indicated above, to consider that the General Assembly's resolutions on South West Africa have acquired legislative force of a supranational kind. The "declaration" of 27 October 1966 that South Africa "has failed to fulfil its obligations in respect of the administration of the Mandated Territory" is based on very doubtful—if on any—authority.

South Africa, in its constant refusal to accept United Nations supervision for the Territory, has at least made it clear that it in no way en-

---

[102] See in this connection the declaration of the President of the Court in regard to individual opinions by virtue of Article 57 of the Court's Statute, ICJ Rep. (1966) 45 *et seq.* It is submitted that dissenting opinions sometimes undermine the authority of a judgment.

[103] 1950 opinion, 162 and 173 respectively.

[104] See, for example, Dugard, *supra* note 83, 82: "The combined effect of the International Court's two most important pronouncement on South West Africa, *viz.*, those of 1950 and 1966, can only be that it is for the General Assembly, as successor to the Council of the League (sic), to decide whether or not *apartheid* violates the provisions of the Mandate."

dorses the General Assembly's action on this matter. This express attitude was necessary in order to make it sufficiently clear that South
Africa did not want to conclude any agreement with the United Nations on the subject, lest it should be said that some agreement—albeit a
tacit one—had been reached in terms of Articles 79 and 80 of the
Charter.[106] In opposing the October 1966 Resolution South Africa opposed the "revocation" of the Mandate. This refusal by South Africa to
conform to the wishes of the General Assembly renders the Resolution
ineffective, because according to the law and practice of the Council of
the League, effective resolutions on mandate questions could have
been taken only by a vote of unanimity, including that of the mandatory.[107] It is impossible to see how, and in accordance with what legal
principles, the Mandate for South West Africa—which was an international onus voluntarily accepted by the Mandatory—could be taken
away without the concurrence of South Africa. It would have been
wrong (nor was it done) to advance principles, based on the *exceptio
non adimpleti contractus* or the principle of *rebus sic stantibus*, to account for the General Assembly's action, since the Mandate was not a
treaty in the ordinary sense of the word and was never concluded between the United Nations and South Africa.[108]

---

[106] The idea that the Mandate and the rights and obligations thereunder are
based on a continued contractual relationship, is found mainly in the opinions of Judge Jessup. In his 1962 opinion he said: "The Mandate is a contractual arrangement between the Mandatory and the four Principal Allied
Powers. The contractual arrangement between the Mandatory and four Principal Powers was not terminated by the dissolution of the League . . ." (ICJ
Rep. (1962) 416). In his opinions, Judge Jessup ascribed the utmost importance to even the minutest sign of agreement by a member of the South African delegation or South African Government which might show acceptance
by South Africa of the United Nations' supervisory powers and functions—
cf. ICJ Rep. (1966) 388 *et seq.*

[107] This is contested by Dugard, *supra* note 83, 89, who relies on Judge
Lauterpacht's opinion of 1955 (ICJ Rep. (1955) 67, 99 *et seq.*) and the *Mosul*
case (PCIJ (1925), Ser. B, No. 12). The *Mosul* case, however, dealt with the
Council's powers to settle a dispute in terms of Article 15 of the Covenant
by virtue of Article 3(2) of the Treaty of Lausanne, and not with the Council's functions as regards the mandates. In any event, had this author studied
the 1956 opinion of Judge Lauterpacht, he would have found the following:
"They (*i.e.* the powers of the League Council) were powers of a body acting
under the rule of unanimity scrupulously observed"—ICJ Rep. (1956) 23, 41.
In 1962 the Court found: "Under the unanimity rule (Articles 4 and 5 of the
Covenant), the Council could not impose its own view on the Mandatory."
—ICJ Rep. (1962) 319, 337. This was repeated in the 1966 judgment—ICJ
Rep. (1966) 31 and 44. *Cf,* too, Nisot "La question du Sud-Ouest Africain devant la Cour Internationale de Justice", *Rev Belge de Dr Int* (1967) 24, 31.

[108] *Cf.* Ch. Rousseau, *supra* note 90, 384.

3. The Creation
of the United Nations Council
for South West Africa

In order to implement Resolution 2145 an *Ad Hoc* Committee for South West Africa was established consisting of fourteen member States, which was charged with the task of recommending "practical means by which South West Africa should be administered, so as to enable the people of the territory to exercise the right of self-determination and to achieve independence." [n] The representatives of the following States were elected to the Committee: Canada, Chile, Czechoslovakia, Ethiopia, Finland, Italy, Japan, Mexico, Nigeria, Pakistan, Senegal, the Soviet Union, the United Arab Republic, and the United States. This Committee met in 1967, under the chairmanship of Mr. Max Jakobson of Finland, and considered several proposals. Ethiopia, Nigeria, Senegal, and the United Arab Republic proposed the establishment of a United Nations Council for South West Africa to assume responsibility for the administration of South West Africa until the territory became independent. A deadline for independence should be set at June 1968, and, in the event of non-cooperation on the part of South Africa, the scheme should be enforced by the Security Council in terms of Chapter VII of the Charter of the United Nations. This proposal was supported by Pakistan. A similar suggestion, which made no provision for a deadline for independence or for recourse to enforcement action by the Security Council, was put forward by Chile and Mexico, and later endorsed by Japan. A third proposal, by the United States, Canada, and Italy, recommended the appointment of a Special Representative for South West Africa, whose task it would be to study the situation in the territory and to "consult with all representative elements in order that, with their accord, a nucleus of self government may be established in South West Africa as soon as possible." The Committee was unable to reach unanimity on any of these proposals, with the result that they were all put forward in the Committee's report for consideration by the General Assembly. [o]

These proposals were considered by the General Assembly at its

[n] Resolution 2145(XXI), § 6.
[o] *UN Monthly Chronicle,* 1967, February, pp. 3–7, March, pp. 6–10, April, pp. 11–16.

fifth Special Session, which commenced on 24 April 1967. South Africa did not take part in the debate, because it did not wish to create the impression that it was bound by what Mr. Vorster described as "the manifestly unlawful decision of the General Assembly on 27th October, 1966," namely, Resolution 2145(XXI).[P] On May 19 the Assembly adopted, by 85 votes to 2 (Portugal and South Africa), with 30 abstentions, a resolution (2248[S-V]) establishing an eleven-member United Nations Council for South West Africa to administer the Territory until independence.

2248 (S-V).

The General Assembly,

Having considered the report of the *Ad Hoc* Committee for South West Africa,

Reaffirming its resolution 1514 (XV) of 14 December 1960 containing the Declaration on the Granting of Independence to Colonial Countries and Peoples,

Reaffirming its resolution 2145 (XXI) of 27 October 1966, by which it terminated the Mandate conferred upon his Britannic Majesty to be exercised on his behalf by the Government of the Union of South Africa and decided that South Africa had no other right to administer the Territory of South West Africa,

Having assumed direct responsibility for the Territory of South West Africa in accordance with resolution 2145 (XXI),

Recognizing that it has thereupon become incumbent upon the United Nations to give effect to its obligations by taking practical steps to transfer power to the people of South West Africa,

I

Reaffirms the territorial integrity of South West Africa and the inalienable right of its people to freedom and independence, in accordance with the Charter of the United Nations, General Assembly resolution 1514 (XV) and all other resolutions concerning South West Africa;

II

1. *Decides* to establish a United Nations Council for South West Africa (hereinafter referred to as the Council) comprising eleven Member States to be elected during the present session and to entrust to it the following powers and functions, to be discharged in the Territory:

(*a*) To administer South West Africa until independence, with the maximum possible participation of the people of the Territory;

(*b*) To promulgate such laws, decrees and administrative regulations as are necessary for the administration of the Territory until a

[P] *House of Assembly Debates,* vol. 20, col. 5221 (2 May 1967).

legislative assembly is established following elections conducted on the basis of universal adult suffrage;

(c) To take as an immediate task all the necessary measures, in consultation with the people of the Territory, for the establishment of a constituent assembly to draw up a constitution on the basis of which elections will be held for the establishment of a legislative assembly and a responsible government;

(d) To take all the necessary measures for the maintenance of law and order in the Territory;

(e) To transfer all powers to the people of the Territory upon the declaration of independence;

2. *Decides* that in the exercise of its powers and in the discharge of its functions the Council shall be responsible to the General Assembly;

3. *Decides* that the Council shall entrust such executive and administrative tasks as it deems necessary to a United Nations Commissioner for South West Africa (hereinafter referred to as the Commissioner), who shall be appointed during the present session by the General Assembly on the nomination of the Secretary-General;

4. *Decides* that in the performance of his tasks the Commissioner shall be responsible to the Council;

III

1. *Decides* that:

(a) The administration of South West Africa under the United Nations shall be financed from the revenues collected in the Territory;

(b) Expenses directly related to the operation of the Council and the Office of the Commissioner—the travel and subsistence expenses of members of the Council, the remuneration of the Commissioner and his staff and the cost of ancillary facilities—shall be met from the regular budget of the United Nations;

2. *Requests* the specialized agencies and the appropriate organs of the United Nations to render to South West Africa technical and financial assistance through a co-ordinated emergency programme to meet the exigencies of the situation;

IV

1. *Decides* that the Council shall be based in South West Africa;

2. *Requests* the Council to enter immediately into contact with the authorities of South Africa in order to lay down procedures, in accordance with General Assembly resolution 2145 (XXI) and the present resolution, for the transfer of the administration of the Territory with the least possible upheaval;

3. *Further requests* the Council to proceed to South West Africa with a view to:

(a) Taking over the administration of the Territory;

(b) Ensuring the withdrawal of South African police and military forces;

(c) Ensuring the withdrawal of South African personnel and their replacement by personnel operating under the authority of the Council;

(*d*) Ensuring that in the utilization and recruitment of personnel preference be given to the indigenous people;

4. *Calls upon* the Government of South Africa to comply without delay with the terms of resolution 2145 (XXI) and the present resolution and to facilitate the transfer of the administration of the Territory of South West Africa to the Council;

5. *Requests* the Security Council to take all appropriate measures to enable the United Nations Council for South West Africa to discharge the functions and responsibilities entrusted to it by the General Assembly;

6. *Requests* all States to extend their whole-hearted co-operation and to render assistance to the Council in the implementation of its task;

V

Requests the Council to report to the General Assembly at intervals not exceeding three months on its administration of the Territory, and to submit a special report to the Assembly at its twenty-second session concerning the implementation of the present resolution;

VI

Decides that South West Africa shall become independent on a date to be fixed in accordance with the wishes of the people and that the Council shall do all in its power to enable independence to be attained by June 1968.

On 13 June the General Assembly elected the following eleven States as members of the Council for South West Africa: Chile, Colombia, Guyana, India, Indonesia, Nigeria, Pakistan, Turkey, the United Arab Republic, Yugoslavia, and Zambia. Mr. Constantin A. Stavropoulos, Legal Counsel of the United Nations, was appointed as Acting Commissioner for South West Africa.[q] The Council met in August and approved a letter to the Government of South Africa asking it to "kindly indicate" the measures that it proposed to facilitate the transfer of the administration of the Territory to the Council,[r] to which the South African Minister of Foreign Affairs replied that South Africa regarded the resolution establishing the Council as invalid.[s] At a later meeting the Council considered the possibility of issuing United Nations passports to South West Africans after Mr. Stavropoulos had indicated that

[q] *UN Monthly Chronicle*, 1967, July, p. 87.
[r] Ibid., 1967, August–September, pp. 39–40.   [s] Ibid., 1967, November, p. 28.

there had been requests for such documents. Mr. Stavropoulos stated that there was a precedent for such action, namely, during the United Nations' administration of West Irian. It was also suggested that South West African representatives should be appointed to the United Nations Economic Commission for Africa.[t]

When the General Assembly again took up the question of South West Africa in December, it had before it a report from the Council for South West Africa in which it was conceded that the Council had been unable to discharge any of its functions in the light of South Africa's continued "illegal" presence in South West Africa. On 16 December the Assembly, by 93 votes to 2, with 18 abstentions, in Resolution 2325(XXII) condemned South Africa's refusal to comply with Resolutions 2145(XXI) and 2248 (S-V), declared that the continued presence of South Africa in the territory "is a flagrant violation of its territorial integrity and international status as determined by General Assembly Resolution 2145(XXI)," called upon South Africa to withdraw from the territory, and requested the Council for South West Africa "to fulfil by every available means the mandate entrusted to it." At the same time the Assembly renewed the appointment of Mr. Stavropoulos as Acting Commissioner for South West Africa.[u]

4. The "Terrorism Trial" (State v Tuhadeleni and others)

South Africa's position on the international plane in the wake of the revocation of the Mandate was extremely delicate and vulnerable. Nevertheless, the Government appeared deliberately to court new danger with its handling of the "terrorism trial" of 1967. The trial is described below by the present writer:[v]

RÉSUMÉ OF THE TRIAL

In 1966, after the decision of the International Court of Justice in the Second Phase of the *South West Africa Cases,* outbreaks of violence occurred in the northern part of South West Africa (Ovamboland), as a result of which several arrests were made by the South Afri-

[t] Ibid., 1967, November, pp. 28–30.   [u] Ibid., 1968, January, pp. 62–67.
[v] "South West Africa and the 'Terrorist Trial'" (1970) 64 *AJIL* 19 at 21–24. See further on this trial, Richard A. Falk, "Observers Report: The State v Tuhadeleni and Others," in *Erosion of the Rule of Law in South Africa* (International Commission of Jurists, August 1968); *South Africa and the Rule of Law* (Department of Foreign Affairs, South Africa, 1968); and the South African Government's report on the trial to the Secretary-General in Doc. S/8357/Add. 9.

can authorities. Those arrested included South West Africans who had received military training outside South West Africa, inhabitants of Ovamboland who had received forms of military training locally, and the political leaders of the South West African Peoples Organization (S.W.A.P.O.). These persons were detained [14] without trial for over a year in some cases, until the passing of the Terrorism Act, No. 83 of 1967, which was made retroactive to June 27, 1962.

Although there were several common law crimes, ranging from treason to attempted murder, with which the accused might have been charged, the South African Parliament saw fit to pass the Terrorism Act under which the accused were later indicted. The Draconian nature of this statute evoked almost as much protest as the subsequent trial of the accused.[15] Section 2 of the Act provides that any person who, with intent to endanger the maintenance of law and order in South Africa and South West Africa, performs an act or aids or incites others to perform acts likely to have any one of a number of possible results is guilty of the offense of participation in terroristic activities and liable on conviction to the penalties for treason, which include the death penalty. Not only is the offense broadly defined but, unlike common law treason and other offenses, the burden of proof is upon the accused to establish his own innocence, once the prosecution has proved the commission of some overt act likely to have certain results. In other words, the burden is upon the accused to show beyond a reasonable doubt that he did not intend to endanger the maintenance of law and order—a difficult task, as he will have to show, *inter alia,* that his act was not intended to cause or encourage feelings of hostility between whites and other inhabitants of South and South West Africa, to hamper any person in maintaining law and order, or "to embarrass the administration of the affairs of the State." Section 6 of the Act per-

[14] The legal authority for this detention was not expressly revealed, but it could have been either Sec. 22 of the General Law Amendment Act, No. 62 of 1966, which permits detention of persons suspected of certain offenses for periods of fourteen days (which may be renewed by a judge in chambers), or Sec. 215 *bis* of the Criminal Procedure Act, No. 56 of 1955, which allows potential state witnesses to be detained without trial for up to six months, though this period of detention is often renewed in practice. Although expressly designed to detain witnesses, it has in practice also been used for potential accused persons.

[15] The Act was described as "arbitrary" by the Security Council (Res. 245) and as offending "basic concepts of justice, due process and the rule of law accepted by civilized nations" by the Association of the Bar of the City of New York (Res. of Dec. 20, 1967, cited in Erosion of the Rule of Law in South Africa, Appendix 2, p. 61). It has also been criticized by writers both within and outside the Republic. See Arthur Suzman, "South Africa and the Rule of Law," 85 South African Law Journal 261 (1968); Jean Davids and the present writer in Annual Survey of South African Law, 1967, pp. 327, 377; Mary Jean Pew, "South Africa and Terrorism," 11 World View 7 (February, 1968). The Act has, however, been vigorously defended by the South African Government in South Africa and the Rule of Law (published by the Department of Foreign Affairs, 1968), p. 43, and in Doc. S/8357/Add. 9.

mits the arrest without warrant at the instance of a senior police officer of any person he has reason to suspect is a "terrorist" or has information relating to "terrorists," and the detention for an unlimited period of such a person for the purpose of interrogation. No court of law is entitled to pronounce upon the validity of any action taken under this section. Section 5 deprives the accused of the right to bail, of the right to be tried by a jury, of the benefit of a preparatory examination, and of the plea of *autrefois acquit* to any charge arising out of the same acts as those alleged in the charge of "participation in terroristic activities." Why the South African Government, presumably aware of its vulnerability in respect of South West Africa, decided to indict the accused under this newly created statute which departs so radically from accepted standards of criminal justice, rather than under the existing common law, is a mystery.

The accused were charged in Pretoria before the Transvaal Provincial Division of the Supreme Court of South Africa with having participated in a conspiracy to overthrow the existing government of South West Africa and to replace it with a government constituted by S.W.A.P.O. members. In furtherance of this conspiracy the accused were alleged to have received guerrilla training both inside and outside South West Africa and to have taken part in isolated incidents of violence committed in Northern Ovamboland. In the alternative, the accused were charged with having committed offenses under the Suppression of Communism Act, No. 44 of 1950.

At the start of the trial on September 11, 1967, defense counsel raised a special plea to the jurisdiction of the Court on the ground that

> the Terrorism Act, No. 83 of 1967, in so far as it purports to apply to the Territory of South West Africa, is invalid and of no effect, in that the Legislature of the Republic of South Africa was not competent to enact the said Act, by reason of the fact that:
> (a) Its competence to legislate for the Territory of South West Africa was derived from a Mandate issued by the Council of the League of Nations and given effect to by the Government of the Union of South Africa in terms of the Treaty of Peace and South West Africa Mandate Act, No. 49 of 1919, the Treaties of Peace Act, No. 32 of 1921, and the South West Africa Constitution Act, No. 42 of 1925, as amended.
> (b) The said Mandate was on 27th October, 1966 (and before the said Terrorism Act was enacted) terminated by the General Assembly of the United Nations, the successor to the said Council of the League of Nations.

In reply to this special plea the Attorney General raised the argument *in limine* that the court had no jurisdiction to inquire into the validity of the Terrorism Act by virtue of Section 59 (2) of the Republic of South Africa Constitution Act No. 32 of 1961, which provides that, with certain limited exceptions, "no court of law shall be competent to enquire into or to pronounce upon the validity of any Act passed by Parliament." Defense counsel argued that, while Section 59 (2) clearly precluded the power of judicial review in respect of legislation for South Africa, it did not and could not deprive the court of the power to test legislation extending to South West Africa against the provisions of the Mandate. Consequently, if it had power to test the Terrorism Act against the Mandate, it had the competence to inquire whether the Mandate still existed at all. The court, however, rejected this argument and upheld the Attorney General's point *in limine*.

The trial then proceeded and on January 26, 1968, the court found thirty of the accused guilty of offenses under the Terrorism Act and three guilty on alternative charges of contravening the Suppression of Communism Act. Of the remaining four accused, one died, one was too ill to attend court [16] and the other two were discharged. Nineteen of those convicted under the Terrorism Act were sentenced to life imprisonment, nine to twenty years' imprisonment and two to five years' imprisonment. The three convicted under the Suppression of Communism Act were sentenced to five years' imprisonment, of which four years and eleven months were suspended on certain conditions.

On September 25, 1968, an appeal was heard by a full court of the Appellate Division [17] against the finding of the trial court that it had no right to test the validity of the Terrorism Act, and against the sentences imposed on several of the accused. On November 22, 1968, the Appellate Division unanimously upheld the decision of the trial court on the testing right, but by eight to three reduced the sentences of life imprisonment imposed on five of the accused to twenty years' imprisonment.[18]

After the accused in this trial had been convicted, one of the SWAPO leaders, Toivo Herman Ja Toivo, made the following statement to the Court before he was sentenced to twenty years' imprisonment.[w]

My Lord,

We find ourselves here in a foreign country, convicted under laws made by people whom we have always considered as foreigners. We find ourselves tried by a Judge who is not our countryman and who has not shared our background.

When this case started, Counsel tried to show that this Court had no jurisdiction to try us. What they had to say was of a technical and

---

[w] The text of this speech appears in *Erosion of the Rule of Law in South Africa*, above, n. v, pp. 55–60.

[16] He was later convicted and sentenced to life imprisonment.

[17] A full Appeal Court of eleven judges sits only when the validity of an Act of Parliament is challenged. The previous occasion on which such a full court sat was in 1956 in Collins *v.* Minister of the Interior, 1957 (1) South African Law Reports 552 (A.D.), in which the validity of the statute removing Colored voters from the common roll was questioned.

[18] State *v.* Tuhadeleni, 1969 (1) South African Law Reports 153 (A.D.).

legal nature. The reasons may mean little to some of us, but it is the deep feeling of all of us that we should not be tried here in Pretoria.

You, my Lord, decided that you had the right to try us, because your Parliament gave you that right. That ruling has not and could not have changed our feelings. We are Namibians and not South Africans. We do not now, and will not in the future recognise your right to govern us; to make laws for us in which we had no say; to treat our country as if it were your property and use us as if you were our masters. We have always regarded South Africa as an intruder in our country. This is how we have always felt and this is how we feel now, and it is on this basis that we have faced this trial.

I speak of "we" because I am trying to speak not only for myself, but for others as well, and especially for those of my fellow accused who have not had the benefit of any education. I think also that when I say "we", the overwhelming majority of non-White people in South West Africa would like to be included.

We are far away from our homes; not a single member of our families has come to visit us, never mind be present at our trial. The Pretoria Gaol, the Police Headquarters at Compol, where we were interrogated and where statements were extracted from us, and this Court is all we have seen of Pretoria. We have been cut off from our people and the world. We all wondered whether the headmen would have repeated some of their lies if our people had been present in Court to hear them.

The South African Government has again shown its strength by detaining us for as long as it pleased; keeping some of us in solitary confinement for 300 to 400 days and bringing us to its Capital to try us. It has shown its strength by passing an Act especially for us and having it made retrospective. It has even chosen an ugly name to call us by. One's own are called patriots; or at least rebels; your opponents are called Terrorists.

A Court can only do justice in political cases if it understands the position of those that it has in front of it. The State has not only wanted to convict us, but also to justify the policy of the South African Government. We will not even try to present the other side of the picture, because we know that a Court that has not suffered in the same way as we have, can not understand us. This is perhaps why it is said that one should be tried by one's equals. We have felt from the very time of our arrest that we were not being tried by our equals but by our masters, and those who have brought us to trial very often do not even do us the courtesy of calling us by our surnames. Had we been tried by our equals, it would not have been necessary to have any discussion about our grievances. They would have been known to those set to judge us.

It suits the Government of South Africa to say that it is ruling South West Africa with the consent of its people. This is not true. Our organisation, S.W.A.P.O., is the largest political organisation in South West Africa. We considered ourselves a political party. We know that Whites do not think of Blacks as politicians—only as agitators. Many of our people, through no fault of their own, have had no education at all. This does not mean that they do not know what they want. A man does not have to be formally educated to know that he wants to live with his family where he wants to live, and not where an official chooses to tell him to live; to move about freely and not require a pass; to earn a decent wage; to be free to work for the person of his choice for as long as he wants; and finally, to be ruled by the people that he wants to be ruled by, and not those who rule him because they have more guns than he has.

Our grievances are called "so-called" grievances. We do not believe South Africa is in South West Africa in order to provide facilities and work for non-Whites. It is there for its own selfish reasons. For the first forty years it did practically nothing to fulfil its "sacred trust". It only concerned itself with the welfare of the Whites.

Since 1962 because of the pressure from inside by the non-Whites and especially my organisation, and because of the limelight placed on our country by the world, South Africa has been trying to do a bit more. It rushed the Bantustan Report so that it would at least have something to say at the World Court.

Only one who is not White and has suffered the way we have can say whether our grievances are real or "so-called."

Those of us who have some education, together with our uneducated brethren, have always struggled to get freedom. The idea of our freedom is not liked by South Africa. It has tried in this Court to prove through the mouths of a couple of its paid Chiefs and a paid official that S.W.A.P.O. does not represent the people of South West Africa. If the Government of South Africa were sure that S.W.A.P.O. did not represent the innermost feelings of the people in South West Africa, it would not have taken the trouble to make it impossible for S.W.A.P.O. to advocate its peaceful policy.

South African officials want to believe that S.W.A.P.O. is an irresponsible organisation and that it is an organisation that resorts to the level of telling people not to get vaccinated. As much as White South Africans may want to believe this, this is not S.W.A.P.O. We sometimes feel that it is what the Government would like S.W.A.P.O. to be. It may be true that some member or even members of S.W.A.P.O. somewhere refused to do this. The reason for such refusal is that some people in our part of the world have lost confidence in the governors of our country and they are not prepared to accept even the good that they are trying to do.

Your Government, my Lord, undertook a very special responsibility when it was awarded the mandate over us after the First World War. It assumed a sacred trust to guide us towards independence and to prepare us to take our place among the nations of the world. We believe that South Africa has abused that trust because of its belief in racial supremacy (that White people have been chosen by God to rule the world) and apartheid. We believe that for fifty years South Africa has failed to promote the development of our people. Where are our trained men? The wealth of our country has been used to train your people for leadership and the sacred duty of preparing the indigenous people to take their place among the nations of the world has been ignored.

I know of no case in the last twenty years of a parent who did not want his child to go to school if the facilities were available, but even if, as it was said, a small percentage of parents wanted their children to look after cattle, I am sure that South Africa was strong enough to impose its will on this, as it has done in so many other respects. To us it has always seemed that our rulers wanted to keep us backward for their benefit.

1963 for us was to be the year of our freedom. From 1960 it looked as if South Africa could not oppose the world for ever. The world is important to us. In the same way as all laughed in Court when they heard that an old man tried to bring down a helicopter with a bow and arrow, we laughed when South Africa said that it would oppose the world. We knew that the world was divided, but as time went on it at least agreed that South Africa had no right to rule us.

I do not claim that it is easy for men of different races to live at peace with one another. I myself had no experience of this in my youth, and at first it surprised me that men of different races could live together in peace. But now I know it to be true and to be something for which we must strive. The South African Government creates hostility by separating people and emphasising their differences. We believe that by living together, people will learn to lose their fear of each other. We also believe that this fear which some of the Whites have of Africans is based on their desire to be superior and privileged and that when Whites see themselves as part of South West Africa, sharing with us all its hopes and troubles, then that fear will disappear. Separation is said to be a natural process. But why, then, is it imposed by force, and why then is it that Whites have the superiority?

Headmen are used to oppress us. This is not the first time that foreigners have tried to rule indirectly—we know that only those who are prepared to do what their masters tell them become headmen. Most of those who had some feeling for their people and who wanted independence have been intimidated into accepting the policy from above. Their guns and sticks are used to make people say they support them.

I have come to know that our people cannot expect progress as a gift from anyone, be it the United Nations or South Africa. Progress is something we shall have to struggle and work for. And I believe that the only way in which we shall be able and fit to secure that progress is to learn from our own experience and mistakes.

Your Lordship emphasised in your Judgment the fact that our arms came from communist countries, and also that words commonly used by communists were to be found in our documents. But, my Lord, in the documents produced by the State there is another type of language. It appears even more often than the former. Many documents finish up with an appeal to the Almighty to guide us in our struggle for freedom. It is the wish of the South African Government that we should be discredited in the Western world. That is why it calls our struggle a communist plot; but this will not be believed by the world. The world knows that we are not interested in ideologies. We feel that the world as a whole has a special responsibility towards us. This is because the land of our fathers was handed over to South Africa by a world body. It is a divided world, but it is a matter of hope for us that it at least agrees about one thing—that we are entitled to freedom and justice.

Other mandated territories have received their freedom. The judgment of the World Court was a bitter disappointment to us. We felt betrayed and we believed that South Africa would never fulfil its trust. Some felt that we would secure our freedom only by fighting for it. We knew that the power of South Africa is overwhelming, but we also knew that our case is a just one and our situation intolerable—why should we not also receive our freedom?

We are sure that the world's efforts to help us in our plight will continue, whatever South Africans may call us.

We do not expect that independence will end our troubles, but we do believe that our people are entitled—as are all peoples—to rule themselves. It is not really a question of whether South Africa treats us well or badly, but that South West Africa is our country and we wish to be our own masters.

There are some who will say that they are sympathetic with our aims, but that they condemn violence. I would answer that I am not by nature a man of violence and I believe that violence is a sin against God and my fellow men. S.W.A.P.O. itself was a non-violent organisation, but the South African Government is not truly interested in whether opposition is violent or non-violent. It does not wish to hear any opposition to apartheid. Since 1963, S.W.A.P.O. meetings have been banned. It is true that it is the Tribal Authorities who have done so, but they work with the South African Government, which has never lifted a finger in favour of political freedom. We have found ourselves voteless in our own country and deprived of the right to meet and state our own political opinions.

Is it surprising that in such times my countrymen have taken up arms? Violence is truly fearsome, but who would not defend his property and himself against a robber? And we believe that South Africa has robbed us of our country.

I have spent my life working in S.W.A.P.O., which is an ordinary political party like any other. Suddenly we in S.W.A.P.O. found that a war situation had risen and that our colleagues and South Africa were facing each other on the field of battle. Although I had not been responsible for organising my people militarily and although I believed we were unwise to fight the might of South Africa while we were so weak, I could not refuse to help them when the time came.

My Lord, you found it necessary to brand me a coward. During the Second World War, when it became evident that both my country and your country were threatened by the dark clouds of Nazism, I risked my life to defend both of them, wearing a uniform with orange bands on it.

But some of your countrymen when called to battle to defend civilisation resorted to sabotage against their own fatherland. I volunteered to face German bullets, and as a guard of military installations, both in South West Africa and the Republic, was prepared to be the victim of their sabotage. Today they are our masters and are considered the heroes, and I am called the coward.

When I consider my country, I am proud that my countrymen have taken up arms for their people and I believe that anyone who calls himself a man would not despise them.

In 1964 the A.N.C. and P.A.C. in South Africa were suppressed. This convinced me that we were too weak to face South Africa's force by waging battle. When some of my country's soldiers came back I foresaw the trouble there would be for S.W.A.P.O., my people and me personally. I tried to do what I could to prevent my people from going into the bush. In my attempts I became unpopular with some of my people, but this, too, I was prepared to endure. Decisions of this kind are not easy to make. My loyalty is to my country. My organisation could not work properly—it could not even hold meetings. I had no answer to the question "Where has your non-violence got us?" Whilst the World Court judgment was pending I at least had that to fall back on. When we failed, after years of waiting, I had no answer to give to my people.

Even though I did not agree that people should go into the bush, I could not refuse to help them when I knew that they were hungry. I even passed on the request for dynamite. It was not an easy decision. Another man might have been able to say "I will have nothing to do with that sort of thing." I was not, and I could not remain a spectator in the struggle of my people for their freedom.

I am a loyal Namibian and I could not betray my people to their enemies. I admit that I decided to assist those who had taken up arms. I know that the struggle will be long and bitter. I also know that my people will wage that struggle, whatever the cost.

Only when we are granted our independence will the struggle stop. Only when our human dignity is restored to us, as equals of the Whites, will there be peace between us.

We believe that South Africa has a choice—either to live at peace with us or to subdue us by force. If you choose to crush us and impose your will on us then you not only betray your trust, but you will live in security for only so long as your power is greater than ours. No South African will live at peace in South West Africa, for each will know that his security is based on force and that without force he will face rejection by the people of South West Africa.

My co-accused and I have suffered. We are not looking forward to our imprisonment. We do not, however, feel that our efforts and sacrifice have been wasted. We believe that human suffering has its effect even on those who impose it. We hope that what has happened will persuade the Whites of South Africa that we and the world may be right and they may be wrong. Only when White South Africans realise this and act on it, will it be possible for us to stop our struggle for freedom and justice in the land of our birth.

International response to this trial was swift. During the course of the proceedings the General Assembly, on 16 December 1967, adopted Resolution 2324 (XXII) by 110 votes to 2 (Portugal and South Africa), with 1 abstention (Malawi), in which it

condemns the illegal arrest, deportation and trial in Pretoria of the thirty-seven South West Africans as a flagrant violation by the Government of South Africa of their rights, of the international status of the Territory and of General Assembly Resolution 2145 (XXI); [and] *calls upon* the Government of South Africa to discontinue forthwith this illegal trial and to release and repatriate the South West Africans concerned.

On the eve of the judgment in the trial on 25 January 1968, the Security Council, which became seised of the question of South West Africa for the first time in the twenty-year-old dispute, reiterated this call. In a unanimous resolution (No. 245) it "took note" of General Assembly Resolutions 2145 (XXI) and 2324(XXII) and of the "trial . . . being held under arbitrary laws whose application has been *illegally* extended to the Territory of South West Africa in defiance of General Assembly resolutions," and called upon the Government of South Africa "to discontinue forthwith this *illegal* trial and to release and repatriate the South West Africans concerned."

On 14 March the Security Council, in another unanimous resolution (No. 246), censured South Africa for defying its resolution of 25 January and demanded that she release the convicted prisoners "forthwith." The Secretary-General was asked to report not later than 31 March on South Africa's decision. If South Africa failed to comply with the resolution, the Council agreed to take further "effective steps or measures."

Commenting on the international repercussions of this trial, the present writer declared: [x]

Undoubtedly the most important result of the trial, on the international plane, was the elevation of the twenty-year-old dispute over South West Africa to the Security Council and the tacit approval given by that body to General Assembly Resolution 2145 (XXI), because the trial could only be regarded as "illegal" if the Mandate was terminated.[5] The legal effect of this endorsement is interesting to con-

---

[x] Above, n. v, at 19–20.

[5] Both the United Kingdom and France, which had not voted for Res. 2145 (XXI), reserved their positions on the termination of the Mandate in the explanations of their votes for Resolutions 245 and 246: U.N. Monthly Chronicle, February, 1968, p. 14; April, 1968, pp. 34–35.

template. If, as has been suggested by the present writer,[6] Resolution 2145 (XXI) could not be described as legally binding because of its origin, could the *subsequent* ratification by the Security Council render it legally binding in the same way that a resolution of the Assembly *preceded* by a recommendation of the Council under Article 4, 5 or 6 of the Charter, dealing with admission to, suspension of rights in, and expulsion from the Organization, is binding? Whether this is the legal effect of the Security Council's intervention in the dispute is problematical, but it seems that its intervention has strengthened the view *outside* South Africa that South Africa's right to administer the Territory has been terminated.

Paradoxically, while the "terrorism trial" weakened South Africa's position vis-à-vis South West Africa internationally, it strengthened it domestically, as it placed beyond all doubt the unlimited supremacy of the South African Parliament over South West Africa. In *State* v *Tuhadeleni and others*[y] the Appellate Division held that it was no more competent to exercise powers of judicial review over legislation of the South African Parliament extending to South West Africa than it was over such legislation extending to the Republic of South Africa. In reaching this finding the Court put an end to the speculation raised during the time of the League over whether the domestic courts of a mandatory power had the authority to strike down legislation of the mandatory in conflict with the guarantees enshrined in the mandate agreement.[z] This matter is analysed by the present writer:[a]

SOUTH WEST AFRICA AND JUDICIAL REVIEW

Before the passing of the Statute of Westminster in 1931 South Africa, like the other British Dominions, was not competent to legislate extraterritorially. Section 59 of the 1909 South Africa Act empowered the South African Parliament to "make laws for the peace, order and good government *of the Union*" only. Despite this apparent limitation on the legislative power of the Union, it accepted the Mandate for South West Africa and proceeded to legislate extraterritorially in respect of that territory. No Order in Council authorizing such legislation was issued, as is the case of New Zealand in respect of Western Samoa; nor was there any authority in the South Africa Act itself, as in Sections 51 (XXIX) and 122 of the Constitution Act of the Commonwealth of Australia. This defect did not pass unnoticed and one emi-

[y] 1969 (1) *South African Law Reports* 153 (AD).
[z] For a discussion of this contention, see Dugard, above, n. v, at 24–31.
[a] Note v (p. 413 above), at 31–38.
[6] "The Revocation of the Mandate for South West Africa," 62 A.J.I.L. 78 (1968). See, too, Doc. S/8357/Add. 9.

nent South African constitutional lawyer, Walter Pollak, went so far as to declare that all South African legislation extending to South West Africa prior to the Statute of Westminster was invalid! [75] Before 1931 the South African courts paid little attention to this difficulty. In *Rex v. Christian* [76] the Appellate Division found the source of legislative power in respect of the mandated territory in the fact of the conferment of the Mandate upon South Africa as a fully sovereign person. [77] This was not an entirely satisfactory answer for, as Pollak pointed out, "neither the League of Nations nor the Principal Allied and Associated Powers can, in as far as *constitutional law* is concerned, increase the legislative power possessed by the Union Parliament." [78] Whether Britain's acquiescence is this seizure of legislative authority could confer the necessary power is also doubtful. The only solution, which is not altogether satisfactory, is that before 1931 South Africa possessed legislative competence because of Section 59 of the South Africa Act: either because the administration of South West Africa, due to its geographical proximity and strategic importance, was indispensable to the "peace, order and good government of the Union," [80] or because the "discharge of the Union's international obligations" fell within this purpose.[81]

In 1919, before the actual confirmation of the Mandate, the South African Parliament passed the Treaty of Peace and South West Africa Mandate Act,[82] which provided for the acceptance of the Mandate and vested wide powers of legislation in the Governor General. Unlike the

---

[75] "The Legislative Competence of the Union Parliament," 48 South African Law Journal 269 at 273–275 (1931).

[76] 1924 A.D. 101.

[77] Per Innes, C.J., at 114, and De Villiers, J. A., at 119–120. See, too, L. J. Blom-Cooper, "Republic and Mandate," 24 Modern Law Review 256 (1961).

[78] *Loc. cit.* 274. My italics.

[80] When the Treaty of Peace and South West Africa Mandate Bill of 1919 was first read in the House of Assembly of the South African Parliament, Mr. Tielman Roos, who later became a judge of appeal, objected to the Bill on the ground that South Africa lacked the necessary competence to legislate extraterritorially. In overruling this objection the Speaker of the House held that the administration of South West Africa fell within the "peace, order and good government of the Union," and warned that refusal to accept the Mandate might result in the territory passing into hostile foreign hands. This he considered would constitute a failure to carry out "the spirit, if not the letter, of the South Africa Act where the obligation is imposed upon this Parliament to pass laws for the peace, order and good government of the Union" (Cape Times, Sept. 11, 1919). *Cf.* Van den Heever, J., in Rex *v.* Offen, 1934 S.W.A. 73 at 79–80.

[81] Van den Heever, J., in Rex *v.* Offen, *loc. cit.* 87. L. H. Wessels, however, considered the argument that Sec. 59 was the source of legislative competence to be of somewhat doubtful validity. Die Mandaat vir Suidwes-Afrika 103–104 (1938).

[82] No. 49 of 1919. This Act was intended as a temporary measure only, but its operation was extended by Sec. 2 of the Treaties of Peace Act, No. 32 of 1921.

1920 New Guinea Act of the Commonwealth of Australia, no mention was made of the guarantees (such as freedom from slavery, freedom of worship, etc.) contained in the Mandate. In 1925 the South West Africa Constitution Act [83] established a form of representative government for the whites in South West Africa with a Legislative Assembly which had power to legislate on any subject except those specially withheld.[84] Prohibited topics included "native affairs or any matters specially affecting natives" and "the establishment or control of any military organization in the territory." [85] This in effect meant that any ordinance of the Legislative Assembly in conflict with the provisions of the Mandate would be *ultra vires* that body, as the guarantees in the Mandate related largely to the interests of the native population and the demilitarization of the territory. No express mention of these guarantees was made in the Act, however, and the Mandate itself is referred to only once in the Act.[86] The Preamble to the Act, on the other hand, recites the history of the Mandate: its conferment on South Africa, its acceptance in 1919, and the fact that it gave "full power of administration and legislation over the territory of South West Africa . . . as an integral portion of the Union *but subject to the terms of the said Mandate.*" Finally it declared that it was desirable for the white inhabitants of the territory to be represented in a local legislative body "to make laws therefor, *subject always to the provisions of the said Mandate* and to the provisions, exceptions, reservations and restrictions contained in this Act." [87] Although no enactment of the South African Parliament *expressly* spelt out the guarantees contained in the Mandate, the Mandate itself was published for general information in the *Official Gazette* of South West Africa in 1921.[88]

Despite the absence of any direct statutory incorporation of the provisions of the Mandate in South African law, in *Rex* v. *Christian* Innes, C.J., referred to them as "limitations interwoven with the constitution of the mandated territory," [89] and judicial cognizance of these limitations and of their content was taken on numerous occasions by

[83] No. 42 of 1925. This Act was substantially amended by Act No. 23 of 1949, and in 1968 it was replaced by a consolidating measure, the South West Africa Constitution Act, No. 39 of 1968.
[84] Sec. 25.   [85] Sec. 26 (a) and (g).
[86] Sec. 44 (1), which states: "Nothing in this Act contained shall be construed as in any way abolishing, diminishing or derogating from those full powers of administration and legislation over the territory as an integral portion of the Union which are conferred by the mandate. . . ."
[87] Italics added. The Preamble also recognizes that "the Government of the Union is, under the said Mandate, to promote to the utmost the material and moral well-being and the social progress of the inhabitants of the territory."
[88] June 17, 1921. Government Notice No. 72.
[89] Note 76 above, at 111. In the same judgment Innes, C. J., referred to the restrictions contained in the Mandate as being "incorporated in the Constitution of the new territory" (at 112).

the South African courts.[90] An attempt was made in *Winter* v. *Minister of Defence* (1939) [91] to set aside wartime emergency regulations (providing for detention without trial) in a proclamation issued by the Governor General, on the ground that these regulations could not be reconciled with the Mandatory's obligation to "promote to the utmost the material and moral well-being and the social progress of the inhabitants of the territory" contained in Article 2 of the Mandate. The court, however, held that, as the purpose of the Proclamation was to safeguard the welfare of the inhabitants and to protect the security of the state in time of war, it could not be held to be in conflict with the obligation contained in Article 2. As a result the court left undecided "the question whether the courts in South West Africa would have jurisdiction to declare *ultra vires* any legislation in conflict with the provisions of the Mandate." [92] Not only did the court in this case fail to reject the possibility of judicial review, but, by examining the question of compatibility, it gave encouragement to this notion.[93]

In 1967 the question whether South West African (and South African) [94] courts might test legislation emanating from the Mandatory was directly and pertinently raised in *State* v. *Tuhadeleni*. In this case the defense asked the court to find that General Assembly Resolution 2145 (XXI) of October 27, 1966, had terminated South Africa's legislative authority in respect of South West Africa prior to the passing of the Terrorism Act in 1967, and that the Act, and hence the trial held under its authority, was null and void. But before this inquiry could be embarked on it was necessary to establish the competence of the court to pronounce on the validity of an Act of the South African Parliament extending to South West Africa. If it could be shown that the court was permitted to test legislation against the Mandate, then, it was argued, the court was free to inquire whether the Mandate still existed at all.

The obstacle in the way of such an inquiry was Section 59 of the Republic of South Africa Constitution Act of 1961 which provides:

---

[90] Rex *v.* Christian, note 76 above, at 120, 122, 128, 132; Verein für Schutzgebietsanleihen E.V. *v.* Conradie N.O., 1937 A.D. 113 at 133, 144, 150; Winter *v.* Minister of Defence, 1940 A.D. 194 at 196–197; Faul *v.* S.A. Railways and Harbours, 1949 (1) South African Law Reports 630 (S.W.A.) at 632.

[91] 1940 A.D. 194.   [92] *Ibid.* at 198.

[93] J. F. Hewat in his chapter on South West Africa in H. J. May's The South African Constitution (1955), stated (at 403) that, as a result of this decision "it may be argued that legislation by the Union Parliament over the Territory is invalid to the extent to which it contravenes the provisions of the Mandate and the same argument applies to enactments by the Legislative Assembly of the Territory."

[94] In normal circumstances this trial would have been held in South West Africa, where the offenses were alleged to have been committed, but the trial was held in Pretoria before the Transvaal Provincial Division of the Supreme Court of South Africa by virtue of Sec. 4 of the Terrorism Act, which gives the Minister of Justice *carte blanche* to decide where the trial is to be held.

(1) Parliament shall be the sovereign legislative authority in and over the Republic, and shall have full power to make laws for the peace, order and good government of the Republic.

(2) No court of law shall be competent to enquire into or to pronounce upon the validity of any Act passed by Parliament, other than an Act which repeals or amends or purports to repeal or amend the provisions of sections 108 or 118.[95]

Defense counsel conceded that this section barred any inquiry into the validity of the Terrorism Act insofar as it applied to South Africa, but denied its applicability to legislation extending to South West Africa. In brief, it was contended that the Mandate Agreement formed part of the fundamental law of the Territory together with those statutes accepting it into South African law;[96] that this gave the Territory a rigid constitution as it could not be varied save with the leave of the Council of the League of Nations (and now the General Assembly of the United Nations); that the guarantees enshrined in the Mandate were to be viewed as a Bill of Rights; and that these rights were to be protected by the local courts by means of the sanction of invalidity in the same way that the Supreme Court of the United States insures legislative compliance with the rights enshrined in the American Constitution. In the first place, the court was asked to find that, as a matter of interpretation, Section 59 does not apply to South African legislation extending to South West Africa—a point on which both Section 59 in particular and the South African Constitution in general are silent; and, secondly, if it did purport to do so, that it was itself invalid insofar as it sought to deprive the inhabitants of South West Africa of their remedy against invasions of their rights contained in a rigid constitution.[97]

The trial court, in rejecting the above argument and holding that Section 59 applied to legislation extending to South West Africa, accepted that the Mandate had been incorporated into South African law, but held that it had not acquired the status of fundamental law. Consequently it did not fetter the South African Parliament in the exercise of its will.[98]

On appeal the defense fared little better: the court held that Section 59 of the South African Constitution applied to legislation of the South African Parliament extending to South West Africa as well as to the Republic, and that the court therefore had no right to pronounce

---

[95] Secs. 108 and 118 entrench the equality of English and Afrikaans as official languages by providing for a special procedure for their repeal.

[96] This notion of a composite *grundnorm* or fundamental law was propounded by the Rhodesian Appeal Court in its decision on the legality of the Smith regime, Madzimbamuto v. Lardner-Burke N.O., 1968 (2) South African Law Reports 284 (R.A.D.) at 334, 416.

[97] Support for this last proposition was sought in Minister of the Interior v. Harris, 1952 (4) South African Law Reports 769 (A.D.) . . .

[98] State v. Tuhadeleni and others, 1967 (4) South African Law Reports 511 (T).

upon the validity of the Terrorism Act. The Appellate Division expressed doubt as to whether the Mandate [99] had been incorporated into municipal law, as required by South African law,[100] but in any event it held that it had not been made part of the fundamental law of the Territory with entrenched rights which required judicial protection. Chief Justice Steyn, delivering the judgment of the full court, stated that

> had a . . . curb been contemplated in the form of an absolute restraint . . . upon the legislative powers of Parliament, the Mandatory would have been bound to introduce such a curb into its constitution in order to bring it into operation. Even if it had been explicitly provided for in the Mandate, that would not have made it part of the law of the land enforceable by our Courts. . . . I would have the greatest difficulty in accepting that such an obligation could ever have been undertaken with any confident prospect of performance. If there was any way in which such a restraint could have been effectively self-imposed in our Constitution, I am unaware of it. There has certainly never been any attempt to achieve such a result.[101]

The court therefore held that there were no limitations in *municipal law* on the legislative powers of the Mandatory, and indicated that "it would rather seem that the parties concerned were content to leave enforcement of the obligations under the Mandate to procedures and restraints available in the international field. It was presumably to that intent that provision was made in Article 6 for annual reports by the mandatory to the satisfaction of the Council of the League. . . ." [102] The court conceded that some of the language used in *Rex* v. *Christian* might be ambiguous, but held that on the whole the comments of the judges in that case "seem to proceed from the concept of treaty obligations rather than from limitations upon sovereignty arising from an internal constitutional restraint upon the powers of Parliament." [103] The court also declined to accept *Winter's* case as authority for the defense contentions because the court had there been concerned with a Proclamation issued by the Governor General and not with a statute emanating from the sovereign legislature of South Africa.

The judgment of the Appeal Court shows a firm devotion to the

---

[99] For the purpose of the judgment the court assumed, without deciding, that the Mandate was still in force. State v. Tuhadeleni, 1969 (1) *ibid.* 153 (A.D.) at 171.

[100] South African law, like English law, does not accept treaties as part of municipal law unless they are incorporated by an Act of Parliament. Pan American World Airways Incorporated v. S.A. Fire and Accident Insurance Co. Ltd., 1965 (3) *ibid.* 150 (A.D.) at 161.

[101] State v. Tuhadeleni, 1969 (1) *ibid.* 153 (A.D.) at 173–174. The court also declared that it was unlikely that the Mandate would have omitted to provide expressly for a municipal limitation if it had been intended.

[102] *Ibid.* at 173.   [103] *Ibid.* at 176.

Diceyan concept [104] of the supremacy of Parliament which the National Party Government promoted so vigorously in the course of the struggle between Parliament and the courts over the Colored voters' rights during the 1950's.[105] This is reflected in the Chief Justice's comment that

> I would further add that I cannot conceive of any British Court declaring any Act of the British Parliament invalid on the ground that it violates an obligation under a Mandate. Under our Constitution our Courts have no greater authority.[106]

It is not inconceivable that a court unshackled by the English concept of the absolute supremacy of Parliament might have reached a different conclusion. Indeed, it is interesting to speculate what the decision of a court accustomed to the exercise of a testing right in its own municipal law might have been. Quincy Wright no doubt adopted a more sanguine approach to judicial review under the mandates system because of his familiarity with the *Marbury* v. *Madison* tradition of the United States Supreme Court.[107]

In reaching its conclusion the court indicated that the testing of legislation against the provisions of the Mandate in general and Article 2 in particular could not be reconciled with the judicial function. Commenting on Article 2 which obliges the Mandatory to "promote to the utmost the material and moral well-being and the social progress of the inhabitants of the territory," the court declared:

> That obligation is described in terms covering a very wide area of political action and could not be carried out without decisions of policy, legislative and administrative. If the Courts are to be the guardians of its legislative observance, they would have to be arbiters of the policies pursued. That is not the function of our Courts. Where the subject matter is within the competence of the lawgiver, our Courts will not sit in judgment on matters of policy.[108]

[104] "The principle of Parliamentary sovereignty means neither more nor less than this, namely, that Parliament . . . has, under the English constitution, the right to make or unmake any law whatever; and further that no person or body is recognized by the law of England as having a right to override or set aside the legislation of Parliament." A. V. Dicey, Introduction to the Study of the Law of the Constitution 39–40 (10th ed., 1959).

[105] For an account of this struggle see Denis V. Cowen, "Legislature and Judiciary," 15 Modern Law Review 282 (1952), and 16 *ibid.* 273 (1953); B. Beinart, "Parliament and the Courts," Butterworth's South African Law Review 135 (1954); H. R. Hahlo and Ellison Kahn, South Africa: The Development of its Laws and Constitution 151–163 (1960).

[106] *Loc. cit.* note 101, at 177.

[107] *Op. cit.* 534; and "Some Recent Cases on the Status of Mandated Areas," 20 A.J.I.L. 768 at 769 (1926).

[108] *Loc. cit.* note 101, at 172.

The other obligations under the Mandate presented similar problems but of lesser degree.[109] This cautious approach to the judicial function brings to mind the comment of Judges Spender and Fitzmaurice in their joint dissenting opinion in the 1962 *South West Africa Cases (Preliminary Objections)*, that "The proper forum for the appreciation and application of a provision of this kind [Article 2] is unquestionably a technical or political one," [110] an approach which motivated the later majority decision in the Second Phase of the *South West Africa Cases*.[111]

This approach is not altogether convincing either in respect of international tribunals or municipal tribunals. Judge Jessup, in his dissenting opinion in the 1966 *South West Africa Cases,* showed that both international and municipal courts have had experience in passing judgment on obligations described in terms "covering a very wide area of political action":

> One can trace in many legal fields the judicial applications of tests for the interpretation of constitutions or laws—tests such as *due* process of law, *unreasonable* restraint of trade, *unfair* competition, *equal* protection of the laws, *unreasonable* searches and seizures, *good moral* character, etc.[112]

Although many of these phrases may be more meaningful to the American constitutional lawyer than to his English (or South African) counterpart, they cannot be viewed as entirely foreign to the latter. For have not English and South African courts for many years set aside the enactments of subordinate legislative bodies on grounds of unreasonableness if, in the words of Lord Russell in *Kruse* v. *Johnson,*[113] "they were found to be partial and unequal in their operation as between different classes" or "manifestly unjust"? As Quincy Wright pointed out, "the mandates were intended to be documents susceptible of judicial interpretation" on both the international and the national level.[114] The courts of Palestine certainly did not decline to test local

---

[109] In respect of the other provisions of the Mandate, *viz.,* those relating to prohibition of the slave trade, of forced labor, of the supply of liquor to natives, of the establishment of military bases and to freedom of worship, the court stated its difficulties as follows: "In relation to these articles, legislation allowing what is to be prohibited or prohibiting what is to be allowed, could, if they should have the testing power, be declared invalid by the Courts. But if Parliament should refrain from passing legislation necessary to allow what is to be allowed, or to effect what is to be effected, or if it should pass inadequate legislation, the Courts would be powerless to order Parliament to legislate or to legislate to better purpose. At best the authority which Courts would be able to exercise would be imperfect and could not ensure full or even substantial legislative compliance with these obligations by Parliament" (*loc. cit.* note 101, at 173).

[110] [1962] I.C.J. Rep. 319 at 467.

[111] [1966] I.C.J. Rep. 6 at 24, 26, 29 and 44; 61 A.J.I.L. 116 (1967). See, too, Dugard, 62 A.J.I.L. 81–82 (1968).

[112] [1966] I.C.J. Rep. 6 at 435· 61 A.J.I.L. at 202–203 (1967).

[113] [1898] 2 Q.B. 91 at 99.   [114] *Op. cit.* 412.

legislation on the grounds advanced by the court in *Tuhadeleni*. In *Murrah* v. *District Governor of Jerusalem* Haycroft, C. J., declared:

> The Mandate is a political and not a legal document and likely to contain expressions of good intention which are more easy to write than to read. We are, however, bound to read them and give them a practical value.[115]

Ironically, a similar approach was adopted by the South African Appeal Court in *Winter's* case in which the wartime emergency regulations issued by the Governor General were held to be compatible with Article 2 of the Mandate.[116] In testing legislation emanating from the supreme legislative body of the Mandatory no greater hardship would be experienced in this respect. Admittedly the legal and political *implications* of a judgment setting aside such legislation would be greater, but the legal tests would be the same as those applied to subordinate legislation.

5. The Implementation of Separate Development in South West Africa

Since 1968 the South African Government has accelerated the implementation of its separate development policy in South West Africa by a series of enactments designed to give effect to the recommendations of the Odendaal Commission.[b] First, the South African Parliament passed the Development of Self-Government for Native Nations in South West Africa Act.[c] The background and purpose of the Act was explained by the Government in an accompanying memorandum: [d]

---

[b] Above, p. 236.   [c] 54 of 1968.

[d] Memorandum explaining the Background and Objects of the Development of Self-Government for Native Nations in South West Africa Bill, 1968. W.P. 3 of 1968, pp. 2, 4–5.

[115] Cited in Wright, *op. cit.* 411. On appeal, the Privy Council confirmed the principle of the testing right, but indicated that it "cannot be the duty of the Court to examine . . . the legislative and administrative acts of the Administration, and to consider in every case whether they are in accordance with the view held by the Court as to the requirements of natural justice." (Jerusalem-Jaffa District Governor *v.* Suleiman Murra, 1926 A.C. 321 at 328.) See, further, Wright, *op. cit.* 412. The decision of the Supreme Court of Israel in Yosipof *v.* Attorney-General, 1951 Int. Law Rep., No. 58, affords a good example of the way in which legislation was tested against the provisions of the Mandate.

[116] In Tuhadeleni the court expressed no opinion on the question whether the courts of South West Africa are competent to test subordinate legislation against the provisions of the Mandate. This is hardly surprising, as South Africa's official attitude is that the Mandate lapsed on the dissolution of the League of Nations and the court could hardly have been expected to pronounce on so delicate a subject in an *obiter dictum*.

Although it is the contention of the Government of the Republic of South Africa that the Mandate for South-West Africa has lapsed, it had continued to administer the Territory in the spirit of the Mandate and has ever been mindful of *inter alia* the obligation to "promote to the utmost the material and moral well-being and the social progress of the inhabitants", which is interpreted as including political development on the basis of the inalienable right of every nation in South-West Africa to govern itself in its area in accordance with that system of government best suited to its needs, having due regard to the rights and obligations of the individual and the welfare of the community.

In recent years it became increasingly evident that conditions in South-West Africa were developing to a stage where accelerated and co-ordinated application of the constructive aspects of a suitably adapted concept of development was becoming possible and highly desirable, and consequently a Commission (referred to as the Odendaal Commission) was appointed during September, 1962, to investigate the conditions of the inhabitants of South-West Africa and more particularly the non-White inhabitants and to make recommendations in respect of their further advancement.

The Odendaal Commission's Report was Tabled in Parliament on the 27th January, 1964, and on the 29th April, 1964, the Government Tabled a Memorandum stating its attitude towards the Commission's recommendations.

For various reasons, the Government refrained from taking any decisions at that time in respect of the comprehensive recommendations concerning the constitution of self-governing areas for the different Native groups, the demarcation of their boundaries and changes in their forms of government. However, as a result of subsequent developments, the Government is now able to state that it accepts those recommendations in principle, subject to what follows, and to re-affirm its general attitude as stated in paragraph 21 of the aforementioned Memorandum, namely—

> . . . that the objective of self-determination for the various population groups will, in the circumstances prevailing in the Territory, not be promoted by the establishment of a single multiracial central authority in which the whole population could potentially be represented, but in which some groups would in fact dominate others . . . The Government also endorses the view that it should be the aim, as far as practicable, to develop for each population group its own Homeland, in which it can attain self-determination and self-realization . . . The Government moreover accepts that for this purpose considerable additional portions of the Territory, including areas now owned by White persons, should be made available to certain non-White groups. And it shares the view that there should be no unnecessary delay in taking the next steps in regard to this important aspect of the development of the population groups concerned . . .
>
> .   .   .   .

The Bill is designed to enable the different groups in South-West Africa to exist in every respect as nations proper, each with its own area and its own political system, and by presenting the Bill the Government is taking an irrevocable first step in the direction of conferring self-government on such nations.

The development envisaged in the Bill will be determined on the one hand by the inherent vigour of the different nations and on the other hand by responsible guidance by the Government, in its role as guardian, which means that the Government must meet its obligations on the basis of creative self-withdrawal.

Accordingly provision is made in the Bill for—

(a) confirmation that certain areas are areas for the different nations;

(b) the fundamental principles of self-government for each nation through a system of central government, consisting of a legislative council and an executive council, and a system of local government through subordinate authorities, the details of which are to be determined by Proclamation in respect of each nation, after consultation with the nation concerned;

(c) the vesting in the central government of each nation, of legislative powers and general powers over subordinate authorities;

(d) the linking of the members of a nation working outside their home area with the central government by empowering an executive council to nominate, in consultation with the Minister, representatives in urban areas and other centres where there are large numbers of such members;

(e) the central government to assume a leading role in connection with matters affecting the material, spiritual, moral and social welfare of the nation in question.

The Act itself is briefly summarized by Ellison Kahn: [e]

The preamble reads: 'Whereas it is desirable that the native nations in the territory of South-West Africa should in the realization of their right of self-determination develop in an orderly manner to self-governing nations and independence.' Six areas are named and defined for 'the different native nations'—Damaraland, Hereroland, Kaokoland, Okavangoland,* Eastern Caprivi and Ovamboland.* Further areas may by proclamation be reserved and set apart for the exclusive use of and occupation by any native nation.

After consultation with the native nation concerned, the State President may establish a legislative council for an area in the manner he determines. Such a council is empowered to make enactments for its area on a scheduled matter, and, with the approval of the State President, provide for the enforcement of any such enactment in respect of members of the native nation outside the area but within South West Africa—the application of the personality principle to laws. An enact-

---

[e] *Annual Survey of South African Law*, 1968, pp. 44–45.
* Renamed Kavango and Owambo, respectively, in 1972 by Act 23 of 1972.

ment requires approval of the State President and publication in the *Gazette* before it is of force or effect.

Only the principal scheduled matters can be outlined here: education; welfare services; control of business and trading undertakings of members of the native nation; carrying on of business projects and undertakings for the economic progress of the native nation; construction and maintenance of roads, bridges and works for sanitation, water supply and combating soil erosion; farming; afforestation; markets and pounds; the administration of justice; labour bureaux; registration of members of the native nation; a direct tax on or on the income of such members, including those outside the area but within South West Africa; any matter assigned by resolution of the Senate and the House of Assembly.

Executive government is vested in an executive council constituted from among the members of the legislative council as determined in the State President's proclamation. It may with the State President's approval establish departments. The Minister of Bantu Administration and Development may second officers and employees of the public service to assist the executive council.

The State President is also empowered to establish tribal, community and regional authorities and determine their functions, duties and powers in relation to a scheduled matter, which, with regional authorities, may include the power to make enactments.

.   .   .   .

Provision is made whereby an executive council may be permitted to nominate representatives in urban local authorities. Such a representative acts for the executive council with members of the native nation away from the homeland.

Later in 1968 legislative and executive councils were established for the Ovambos, the largest population group in South West Africa. On 2 October 1968,[f] the State President granted recognition to the seven tribal authorities of Ovamboland, stating that they should continue to function according to tribal law and custom. Then, on the same day,[g] a Legislative Council was established to consist of not more than six members designated by each of these seven tribal authorities. The Legislative Council elects from among its members by majority vote a Chairman and Deputy-Chairman. In other proceedings, such as the passing of motions and draft enactments, voting is by delegations, that is, the tribal representatives vote as a unit, each delegation having one vote. The Executive Council consists of seven councillors, each nominated by one of the tribal authorities. From these councillors a Chief Councillor is elected by members of the Legislative

[f] Proclamation No. 290, *GGE* No. 2177 (Reg. Gaz. No. 1025).
[g] Ovamboland Legislative Council Proclamation, No. R291, *GGE* No. 2177 (*Reg. Gaz.* No. 1025).

Council. It will thus be seen that the Legislative and Executive Councils operate on a federal non-elective basis, founded on the seven tribal authorities.[h] The first session of the Ovamboland Legislative Council was opened on 17 October 1968.

In 1970 and 1972 legislative and executive councils were created for the Kavango and "the Native Nation of Eastern Caprivi"[i] respectively, which are based substantially on the Ovambo model.

While the political power of the African peoples in South West Africa has been increased, there has been a corresponding reduction in legislative power of the white Legislative Assembly of South West Africa. In 1968 the old South-West Africa Constitution Act of 1925[j] was replaced by a new consolidating measure,[k] and in 1969 the South-West Africa Affairs Act[l] was introduced, which transfers certain matters that had previously fallen within the competence of the South West African local administration and the Legislative Assembly to the central Republican Government.[m] This has resulted in the extension of a considerable number of Republican statutes to the territory.[n]

These new measures, designed to integrate South West Africa more closely with the Republic from an administrative point of view and to develop separate homelands for the different ethnic groups, were vigorously condemned by the United Nations. In December 1968 the General Assembly complained that the Development of Self-government for Native Nations in South West Africa Act was designed to "destroy the national unity and territorial integrity of Namibia,"[o] while in 1969 the Security Council described this Act as "contrary to the provisions of the United Nation Charter" and the South-West Africa Affairs Act as "a violation of the relevant resolutions of the General Assembly."[p]

[h] For further details about Ovamboland's political development, see the following two publications of the Department of Foreign Affairs: *South West Africa: South Africa's Reply to the Secretary General of the United Nations* (Security Council Resolution 269), pp. 29–34; and *Owambo* (1971), pp. 9–12.

[i] Kavango Legislative Council Proclamation R196 *GG* 2770 of 14 August 1970 (*Reg. Gaz.* 1313); Eastern Caprivi Legislative Council Proclamation R6 *GG* 3373 of 2 February 1972 (*Reg. Gaz.* 1566).

[j] Act 42 of 1925.

[k] South West Africa Constitution Act 39 of 1968.   [l] Act 25 of 1969.

[m] For a summary of this statute and the changes it brings about, see Ellison Kahn in *Annual Survey of South African Law*, 1969, pp. 43–45.

[n] For details of this new trend, see *Annual Survey of South African Law*, 1970, pp. 65–66, 79–80.

[o] Resolution 2403(XXIII) of 16 December 1968.

[p] Resolution 264 (1969). Below, p. 439.

6. *The Activities of the United Nations Council for Namibia*

In April 1968 the United Nations Council for South West Africa attempted to enter South West Africa in pursuance of its mandate "to proceed to South West Africa with a view to . . . taking over the administration of the territory."[q] Not surprisingly, this body was refused landing rights by the South African Government and, to add insult to injury, it was unable to charter an aeroplane in Zambia to fly to South West Africa in defiance of the Government's order. It therefore returned to New York with its task unaccomplished.[r] South Africa's refusal to allow the Council to enter South West Africa was condemned by the General Assembly on 12 June 1968 in Resolution 2372(XXII) adopted by 96 votes to 2, with 18 abstentions. This resolution also proclaimed that from henceforth South West Africa would be known as Namibia. Resolution 2372(XXII):

The General Assembly,

. . . .

1. *Proclaims* that, in accordance with the desires of its people, South West Africa shall henceforth be known as "Namibia";

2. *Takes note* of the report of the United Nations Council for South West Africa and expresses its appreciation for the Council's efforts to discharge the responsibilities and functions entrusted to it;

3. *Decides* that the United Nations Council for South West Africa shall be called "United Nations Council for Namibia" and that the United Nations Commissioner for South West Africa shall be called "United Nations Commissioner for Namibia";

4. *Decides* that, taking into account the provisions of General Assembly resolution 2248 (S-V), the United Nations Council for Namibia shall perform, as a matter of priority, the following functions:

(*a*) In consultation and co-operation with the specialized agencies and other appropriate organs of the United Nations, which under section III, paragraph 2, of resolution 2248 (S-V) were requested to render technical and financial assistance to Namibia, the Council shall assume responsibility for establishing a co-ordinated emergency programme for rendering such assistance, in order to meet the exigencies of the present situation;

(*b*) The Council shall organize a training programme for Namibians, in consultation with those Governments which indicate their interest and concern, so that a cadre of civil servants and of technical and professional personnel may be developed who would be in a position to undertake the public administration and the social, political and economic development of the State;

[q] Resolution 2248 (S-V). Above, p. 410.
[r] *UN Monthly Chronicle*, 1968, May, p. 50.

(c) The Council shall continue with a sense of urgency its consultations on the question of issuing to Namibians travel documents enabling them to travel abroad;

5. *Reaffirms* the inalienable right of the Namibian people to freedom and independence and the legitimacy of their struggle against foreign occupation;

6. *Condemns* the Government of South Africa for its persistent refusal to comply with the resolutions of the General Assembly and the Security Council, its refusal to withdraw from Namibia and its obstruction of the efforts of the United Nations Council for Namibia to proceed to Namibia;

7. *Condemns* the action of the Government of South Africa designed to consolidate its illegal control over Namibia and to destroy the unity of the people and the territorial integrity of Namibia;

8. *Condemns* the actions of those States which by their continued political, military and economic collaboration with the Government of South Africa have encouraged that Government to defy the authority of the United Nations and to obstruct the attainment of independence by Namibia;

9. *Calls upon* all States to desist from those dealings with the Government of South Africa which would have the effect of perpetuating South Africa's illegal occupation of Namibia and to take effective economic and other measures with a view to securing the immediate withdrawal of the South African administration from Namibia;

10. *Further calls upon* all States to provide the necessary moral and material assistance to the Namibian people in their legitimate struggle for independence and to assist the United Nations Council for Namibia in the discharge of its mandate;

11. *Considers* that the continued foreign occupation of Namibia by South Africa in defiance of the relevant United Nations resolutions and of the Territory's established international status constitutes a grave threat to international peace and security;

12. *Reiterates* its demand that the Government of South Africa withdraw from Namibia, immediately and unconditionally, all its military and police forces and its administration;

13. *Recommends* the Security Council urgently to take all appropriate steps to secure the implementation of the present resolution and to take effective measures in accordance with the provisions of the Charter of the United Nations to ensure the immediate removal of the South African presence from Namibia and to secure for Namibia its independence in accordance with General Assembly resolution 2145(XXI);

. . . .

The United Nations Council for Namibia continued to study methods of wresting South West Africa from the control of the Republic, and in its fourth report covering the period from 13 November 1968 to 24 October 1969 it recommended resort to mandatory sanctions to induce withdrawal. Other points raised in its report to the General Assembly were that States should ensure that their nationals "at present operating concessions or commercial or industrial undertakings in Namibia pay such royalties to the Council [for Namibia]"; that States should "extend necessary assistance to the Council with regard to the issuance of travel documents to Namibians"; and that South Africa should "respect the Geneva Convention of 12th August, 1949, relative to the Treatment of Prisoners of War with regard to the Namibian freedom fighters." [s] On 1 December 1969 Agha Abdul Hamid, Assistant Secretary-General for Public Information, was appointed as Acting Commissioner for Namibia in the place of Mr. Constantin A. Stavropoulos, Legal Counsel of the United Nations.

In 1970 the United Nations Council for Namibia persevered in its attempts to obtain travel documents for South West African refugees. In July the Council concluded agreements with Zambia and Uganda for the issue of United Nations travel and identity documents to South West Africans residing in those countries. Negotiations were also held with the Governments of Kenya, Tanzania, and Ethiopia in this connection. [t]

7. The Dispute Goes to the Security Council

The Security Council first assumed jurisdiction over the South West African dispute at the time of the "terrorism trial." On that occasion the Security Council gave implicit support to Resolution 2145 (XXI) by holding that the trial was "illegal." [u] On 20 March 1969 the Security Council gave its express imprimatur [v] to the revocation of the Mandate in Resolution 264, adopted by thirteen votes to none with two abstentions (France and the United Kingdom).

Resolution 264 (1969):

---

[s] *UN Monthly Chronicle*, 1969, November, pp. 44–45.

[t] *UN Monthly Chronicle*, 1970, August–September, pp. 37–39. For a thorough study of the legal implication of granting travel documents to Namibians, see J. F. Engers, "The United Nations Travel and Identity Document for Namibians" (1971) 65 *AJIL* 571.

[u] Above, p. 422.

[v] That this was the most significant feature of Resolution 264 was stressed by the representatives of Nepal and Finland. France and the United Kingdom, which had abstained from voting on Resolution 2145(XXI) on account of its doubtful legal basis, announced that they were abstaining because of the approval given to this resolution by Resolution 264: *UN Monthly Chronicle*, 1969, April, pp. 7–10.

The Security Council,

Taking note of General Assembly resolutions 2248 (S-V) of 19 May 1967; 2324 (XXII) and 2325 (XXII) of 16 December 1967; 2372 (XXII) of 12 June 1968 and 2403 (XXIII) of 16 December 1968,

Taking into account General Assembly resolution 2145 (XXI) of 27 October 1966 by which the General Assembly of the United Nations terminated the Mandate of South West Africa and assumed direct responsibility for the territory until its independence,

Recalling its resolution 245 (1968) of 25 January 1968 and 246 (1968) of 14 March 1968,

Reaffirming the inalienable right of the people of Namibia to freedom and independence in accordance with the provisions of General Assembly resolution 1514 (XV) of 14 December 1960,

Mindful of the grave consequences of South Africa's continued occupation of Namibia,

Reaffirming its special responsibility towards the people and the territory of Namibia,

1. *Recognizes* that the United Nations General Assembly terminated the mandate of South Africa over Namibia and assumed direct responsibility for the territory until its independence;

2. *Considers* that the continued presence of South Africa in Namibia is illegal and contrary to the principles of the Charter and the previous decisions of the United Nations and is detrimental to the interests of the population of the territory and those of the international community;

3. *Calls upon* the Government of South Africa to immediately withdraw its administration from the territory;

4. *Declares* that the actions of the Government of South Africa designed to destroy the national unity and territorial integrity of Namibia through the establishment of Bantustans are contrary to the provisions of the United Nations Charter;

5. *Declares* that the Government of South Africa has no right to enact the "South West Africa Affairs Bill", as such an enactment would be a violation of the relevant resolutions of the General Assembly;

6. *Condemns* the refusal of South Africa to comply with General Assembly resolutions 2145 (XXI); 2248 (S-V); 2324 (XXII); 2325 (XXII); 2372 (XXII); and 2403 (XXIII) and Security Council resolutions 245 and 246 of 1968;

7. *Invites* all States to exert their influence in order to obtain compliance by the Government of South Africa with the provisions of the present resolution;

8. *Decides* that in the event of failure on the part of the Government of South Africa to comply with the provisions of the present resolution, the Security Council will meet immediately to determine upon necessary steps or measures in accordance with the relevant provisions of the Charter of the United Nations;

9. *Requests* the Secretary-General to follow closely the implementation of the present resolution and to report to the Security Council as soon as possible;

10. *Decides* to remain actively seized of the matter.

In its reply of April 30, the South African Government rejected the resolution on the ground that "there is no legal basis for the activities of the so-called Council for South West Africa or for Security Council intervention." [w]

Following this rebuff, the Security Council in Resolution 269 (1969) of 12 August, passed by eleven votes to none, with four abstentions (Finland, France, United Kingdom, and United States), condemned South Africa for its refusal to comply with Resolution 264 (1969), decided that South Africa's continued presence in Namibia "constitutes an aggressive encroachment on the authority of the United Nations," and called upon South Africa "to withdraw its administration from the territory immediately and in any case before 4th October, 1969."

Resolution 269:

The Security Council,

Recalling its resolution 264 (1969) of 20 March 1969,

Taking note of the report of the Secretary-General contained in document S/9204,

Mindful of its responsibility to take necessary action to secure strict compliance with the obligations entered into by States Members of the United Nations under the provisions of Article 25 of the Charter of the United Nations,

Mindful also of its responsibilities under Article 6 of the Charter of the United Nations,

1. *Reaffirms* its resolution 264 (1969);

2. *Condemns* the Government of South Africa for its refusal to comply with resolution 264 (1969) and for its persistent defiance of the authority of the United Nations;

3. *Decides* that the continued occupation of the territory of Namibia by the South African authorities constitutes an aggressive encroachment on the authority of the United Nations, a violation of the territorial integrity and a denial of the political sovereignty of the people of Namibia;

4. *Recognizes* the legitimacy of the struggle of the people of Namibia against the illegal presence of the South African authorities in the territory;

5. *Calls upon* the Government of South Africa to withdraw its ad-

---

[w] *UN Monthly Chronicle,* 1969, June, p. 31. See further, the statement by the Minister of Foreign Affairs in the Senate on 20 March (*Senate Debates,* 20 March, 1969, cols. 1053 ff.)

ministration from the territory immediately and in any case before 4 October 1969;

6. *Decides* that in the event of failure on the part of the South African Government to comply with the provisions of the preceding paragraph of the present resolution, the Security Council will meet immediately to determine upon effective measures in accordance with the appropriate provisions of the relevant chapters of the United Nations Charter;

7. *Calls upon* all States to refrain from all dealings with the Government of South Africa purporting to act on behalf of the territory of Namibia;

8. *Requests* all States to increase their moral and material assistance to the people of Namibia in their struggle against foreign occupation;

9. *Requests* the Secretary-General to follow closely the implementation of the present resolution and to report to the Security Council as soon as possible;

10. *Decides* to remain actively seized of the matter.

South Africa's reply to Resolution 269 (1969) took the form of a 115-page document published by the Department of Foreign Affairs.[x] In this publication, which includes an analysis of the legal basis of United Nations resolutions on the termination of the Mandate, of the substantive parts of Resolution 269 (1969), and of the administration of South West Africa, the South African Government announced that it would not comply with the resolution for a number of reasons. The legal reasons advanced for non-compliance related both to the juridical basis of Resolution 2145(XXI) and to the procedure followed by the Security Council in adopting Resolution 269 (1969). It was contended that Resolution 2145(XXI) was invalid on the ground that the United Nations did not succeed to the supervisory powers of the League of Nations and that, even if it did, this did not include the right to terminate unilaterally South Africa's administration of South West Africa. It was also contended that, as several of the Permanent Members of the Security Council abstained from voting on Resolution 269 (1969), the resolution was not properly passed.

South Africa's refusal to withdraw from Namibia by 4 October 1969 compelled the Security Council to resort to more cautious and realistic action. On 30 January 1970 it adopted Resolution 276 by thirteen votes to none, with two abstentions (France and the United Kingdom), in which it called upon States to take certain measures against South Africa to compel her to withdraw

---

[x] *South Africa's Reply to the Secretary-General of the United Nations (Security Council Resolution 269 of 1969).* (S/9463.)

from Namibia and established an *ad hoc* sub-committee consisting of all members of the Security Council to study ways and means by which the decisions of the Security Council could be effectively implemented.

Resolution 276 (1970):

The Security Council,

Reaffirming the inalienable right of the people of Namibia to freedom and independence recognized in General Assembly resolution 1514 (XV) of 14 December 1960,

Reaffirming General Assembly resolution 2145 (XXI) of 27 October 1966, by which the United Nations decided that the mandate of South West Africa was terminated and assumed direct responsibility for the Territory until its independence.

Reaffirming Security Council resolution 264 (1969) which recognized the termination of the Mandate and called upon the Government of South Africa immediately to withdraw its administration from the Territory,

Reaffirming that the extension and enforcement of South African laws in the Territory together with the continued detentions, trials and subsequent sentencing of Namibians by the Government of South Africa constitute illegal acts and flagrant violations of the rights of the Namibians concerned, the Universal Declaration of Human Rights and of the international status of the Territory, now under direct United Nations responsibility,

Recalling Security Council resolution 269 (1969),

1. *Strongly condemns* the refusal of the Government of South Africa to comply with General Assembly and Security Council resolutions pertaining to Namibia;

2. *Declares* that the continued presence of the South African authorities in Namibia is illegal and that consequently all acts taken by the Government of South Africa on behalf of or concerning Namibia after the termination of the Mandate are illegal and invalid;

3. *Declares further* that the defiant attitude of the Government of South Africa towards the Council's decisions undermines the authority of the United Nations.

4. *Considers* that the continued occupation of Namibia by the Government of South Africa in defiance of the relevant United Nations resolutions and of the United Nations Charter has grave consequences for the rights and interests of the people of Namibia;

5. *Calls upon* all States, particularly those which have economic and other interests in Namibia, to refrain from any dealings with the Government of South Africa which are inconsistent with operative paragraph 2 of this resolution;

6. *Decides* to establish in accordance with rule 28 of the provisional rules of procedure an *ad hoc* sub-committee of the Council to study, in consultation with the Secretary-General, ways and means by which the relevant resolutions of the Council, including the present resolution,

THE REVOCATION OF THE MANDATE, 1966-1970   443

can be effectively implemented in accordance with the appropriate provisions of the Charter, in the light of the flagrant refusal of South Africa to withdraw from Namibia, and to submit its recommendations by 30 April 1970;

7. *Requests* all States as well as the specialized agencies and other relevant United Nations organs to give the sub-committee all the information and other assistance that it may require in pursuance of this resolution;

8. *Further requests* the Secretary-General to give every assistance to the sub-committee in the performance of its task;

9. *Decides* to resume consideration of the question of Namibia as soon as the recommendations of the sub-committee have been made available.

In its report the sub-committee of the Security Council recommended a variety of political, economic, legal, and military actions which might be pursued by the United Nations in order to compel South Africa to vacate Namibia.[y] *Inter alia,* it suggested that an advisory opinion be obtained from the International Court of Justice.

When the Security Council next considered the question of Namibia, it adopted two resolutions. In the first, Resolution 283 of 29 July 1970, it requested all States to refrain from "any relations —diplomatic, consular or otherwise—with South Africa implying recognition of the authority of the South African Government over the territory of Namibia." The voting on this resolution was thirteen in favour with none against, and two abstentions (France and the United Kingdom).

In the second resolution—284—passed by twelve votes to none, with Poland, the Soviet Union, and the United Kingdom abstaining, the Security Council sent the dispute back to the International Court of Justice.

Resolution 283 (1970):

The Security Council

Reaffirming once more the inalienable right of the people of Namibia to freedom and independence recognized in General Assembly resolution 1514 (XV) of 14 December 1960,

Reaffirming its resolution 264 (1969) and 276 (1970) by which the Security Council recognized the decision of the General Assembly to terminate the Mandate of South West Africa and assume direct responsibility for the territory until its independence and in which the continued presence of the South African authority in Namibia as well as

[y] For a summary of these recommendations, see *UN Monthly Chronicle,* 1970, August–September, pp. 28–29.

all acts taken by that Government on behalf of or concerning Namibia after the termination of the Mandate were declared illegal and invalid,

Recalling its resolution 269 (1969),

Noting with great concern the continued flagrant refusal of the Government of South Africa to comply with the decisions of the Security Council demanding the immediate withdrawal of South Africa from the territory,

Deeply concerned that the enforcement of South African laws and juridical procedures in the territory have continued in violation of the international status of the territory,

Reaffirming its resolution 282 (1970) on the arms embargo against the Government of South Africa and the significance of that resolution with regard to the territory and people of Namibia,

Recalling the decisions taken by the Security Council on 30 January 1970 to establish, in accordance with rule 28 of the provisional rules of procedure, an *Ad Hoc* Sub-Committee of the Security Council to study, in consultation with the Secretary-General, ways and means by which the relevant resolutions of the Council, including resolution 276 (1970), could be effectively implemented in accordance with the appropriate provisions of the Charter in the light of the flagrant refusal of South Africa to withdraw from Namibia, and to submit its recommendations to the Council,

Having examined the report submitted by the *Ad Hoc* Sub-Committee (S/9863) and the recommendations contained in that report,

Bearing in mind the special responsibility of the United Nations with regard to the territory of Namibia and its people,

1. *Requests* all States to refrain from any relations—diplomatic, consular or otherwise—with South Africa implying recognition of the authority of the South African Government over the territory of Namibia;

2. *Calls upon* all States maintaining diplomatic or consular relations with South Africa to issue a formal declaration to the Government of South Africa to the effect that they do not recognize any authority of South Africa with regard to Namibia and that they consider South Africa's continued presence in Namibia illegal;

3. *Calls upon* all States maintaining such relations to terminate existing diplomatic and consular representation as far as they extend to Namibia and to withdraw any diplomatic or consular mission or representative residing in the territory;

4. *Calls upon* all States to ensure that companies and other commercial and industrial enterprises owned by, or under direct control of the State, cease all dealings with respect to commercial or industrial enterprises or concessions in Namibia;

5. *Calls upon* all States to withhold from their nationals or companies of their nationality not under direct government control, government loans, credit guarantees and other forms of financial support that would be used to facilitate trade or commerce with Namibia;

6. *Calls upon* all States to ensure that companies and other commercial enterprises owned by the State or under direct control of the State cease all further investment activities including concessions in Namibia;

7. *Calls upon* all States to discourage their nationals or companies of their nationality not under direct governmental control from investing or obtaining concessions in Namibia, and to this end withhold protection of such investment against claims of a future lawful government of Namibia;

8. *Requests* all States to undertake without delay a detailed study and review of all bilateral treaties between themselves and South Africa in so far as these treaties contain provisions by which they apply to the territory of Namibia;

9. *Requests* the Secretary-General of the United Nations to undertake without delay a detailed study and review of all multilateral treaties to which South Africa is a party, and which either by direct reference or on the basis of relevant provisions of international law might be considered to apply to the territory of Namibia;

10. *Requests* the United Nations Council for Namibia to make available to the Security Council the results of its study and proposals with regard to the issuance of passports and visas for Namibians and to undertake a study and make proposals with regard to special passport and visa regulations to be adopted by States concerning travel of their citizens to Namibia;

11. *Calls upon* all States to discourage the promotion of tourism and emigration to Namibia;

12. *Requests* the General Assembly at its twenty-fifth session to set up a United Nations Fund for Namibia to provide assistance to Namibians who have suffered from persecution and to finance a comprehensive education and training programme for Namibians with particular regard to their future administrative responsibilities of the territory;

13. *Requests* all States to report to the Secretary-General on measures they have taken in order to give effect to the provisions set forth in the present resolution;

14. *Decides* to re-establish, in accordance with rule 28 of the provisional rules of procedure, the *Ad Hoc* Sub-Committee on Namibia and request the *Ad Hoc* Sub-Committee to study further effective recommendations on ways and means by which the relevant resolutions of the Council can be effectively implemented in accordance with the appropriate provisions of the Charter, in the light of the flagrant refusal of South Africa to withdraw from Namibia;

15. *Requests* the *Ad Hoc* Sub-Committee to study the replies submitted by Governments to the Secretary-General in pursuance of operative paragraph 13 of the present resolution and to report to the Council as appropriate;

16. *Requests* the Secretary-General to give every assistance to the *Ad Hoc* Sub-Committee in the performance of its tasks;

17. *Decides* to remain actively seized of this matter.

Resolution 284:

The Security Council

Reaffirming the special responsibility of the United Nations with regard to the territory and the people of Namibia,

Recalling Security Council resolution 276 (1970) on the question of Namibia,

Taking note of the report and recommendations submitted by the *Ad Hoc* Sub-Committee established in pursuance of Security Council resolution 276 (1970),

Taking further note of the recommendation of the *Ad Hoc* Sub-Committee on the possibility of requesting an advisory opinion from the International Court of Justice,

Considering that an advisory opinion from the International Court of Justice would be useful for the Security Council in its further consideration of the question of Namibia and in furtherance of the objectives the Council is seeking,

1. *Decides* to submit in accordance with Article 96(1) of the Charter, the following question to the International Court of Justice with the request for an advisory opinion which shall be transmitted to the Security Council at an early date:

What are the legal consequences for States of the continued presence of South Africa in Namibia, notwithstanding Security Council resolution 276 (1970)?

2. *Requests* the Secretary-General to transmit the present resolution to the International Court of Justice, in accordance with Article 65 of the Statute of the Court, accompanied by all documents likely to throw light upon the question.

10

The Court's Opinion of 1971[a]
and the Future

1. Proceedings before the International Court of Justice

Between 1966 and 1971 the composition of the International Court of Justice underwent important changes as a result of the two triennial elections to the Court held in 1966 and 1969. Of the 1966 majority only two remained, namely, Judges Sir Gerald Fitzmaurice and Gros, while African representation on the Court had increased from one in 1966 to three in 1971. In 1971 the Court was composed of the following judges: President Sir Muhammad Zafrulla Khan (Pakistan), Vice-President Ammoun (Lebanon), Judges Sir Gerald Fitzmaurice (United Kingdom), Padilla Nervo (Mexico), Forster (Senegal), Gros (France), Bengzon (Philippines), Petrén (Sweden), Lachs (Poland), Onyeama (Nigeria), Dillard (United States), Ignacio-Pinto (Dahomey), De Castro (Spain), Morozov (Soviet Union), and Jiménez de Aréchaga (Uruguay). The last five judges were elected in 1969.

Despite the fact that the South African Government could not have expected a repetition of the 1966 judgment from this newly constituted Court, it nevertheless elected to make written submissions and appear before the Court as it had done in 1950.[b] As in

---

[a] *Legal Consequences for States of the Continued Presence of South Africa in Namibia (South West Africa) notwithstanding Security Council Resolution 276 (1970),* 1971 ICJ Reports 16.
[b] See the announcement to this effect by the Minister of Foreign Affairs, *House of Assembly Debates,* vol. 30, col. 3125 (1 September 1970).

1962 and 1965, the South African Government was represented by a strong legal "team" under the co-leadership of D. P. De Villiers, S.C., and E. Grosskopf, S.C.[c] Doubtless the Government hoped that, as in the contentious proceedings of 1960–1966, it would be able to obtain more favourable publicity for its policies and legal arguments before this forum than before the political organs of the United Nations. Moreover, there was the factor of judicial unpredictability to reckon with.

The South African legal "team" exploited the advisory proceedings to the full. In addition to disputing the legal validity of Resolution 2145(XXI) and subsequent United Nations action based upon it, it contested the correctness of the procedures used by the Security Council for bringing the question before the Court and attacked the impartiality of several of the judges. These "preliminary objections" and the Court's reply are briefly described by the present writer: [d]

THE PRELIMINARY OBJECTIONS

South Africa raised a host of preliminary objections at the outset of the proceedings, some directed at the composition of the court, others at the validity of resolution 284, and a third group at the propriety of the court's giving an opinion at all.

The preliminary points relating to the composition of the court comprised applications for the recusal of three of its members, namely Judges Khan (Pakistan), Nervo (Mexico) and Morozov (Soviet Union),[11] and for the appointment of a South African *ad hoc* judge. The recusals were sought on the ground that the three judges in question had revealed their antagonism towards South Africa's policies in South-West Africa while representing their respective States in the United Nations prior to their election to the International Court. One of these judges, Judge Morozov, had in addition participated in the formulation of the Security Council resolution condemning the 'terrorist trial', which was one of the resolutions which required consideration in the proceedings before the court. The court rejected the applications for recusal on the ground that article 17(2) of the court's Statute does not oblige judges to recuse themselves in such circumstances.[12] The case for the recusal of Judge Morozov was, however,

---

[c] The other legal advisors were Messrs J. D. Viall, R. F. Botha, M.P., Dr. H. J. O. van Heerden, and Professor M. Wiechers.

[d] "The Opinion on South-West Africa ('Namibia'): The Teleologists Triumph" (1971) 88 *SALJ* 460 at 461–63. For further discussions of these preliminary issues, see J. T. Van Wyk (*ad hoc* Judge 1962–1966), "The Request for an Advisory Opinion on South West Africa" *Acta Juridica,* 1970, p. 219 at pp. 226–29.

[11] South Africa's written submissions, 1971, vol 1, 121–6.

[12] 1971 ICJ Reports 18–9.

particularly strong, as is shown by the fact that four judges dissented on this issue.[13] The application for the appointment of a South African *ad hoc* judge also caused a division and five judges dissented from the majority on this issue,[14] three finding that article 83 of the rules of court obliged the court to make such an appointment [15] and two that the court should have exercised its discretion in favour of such an appointment under article 68 of the court's Statute, which empowers the court in the exercise of its advisory functions to be guided by the provisions of the Statute which apply in contentious cases.[16]

South Africa's major objection to the validity of resolution 284 was that two of the permanent members of the Security Council had abstained from voting on its adoption and that an abstention could not be described as a 'concurring' vote as required by article 27(3) of the Charter of the United Nations. This argument, however, runs counter to the consistent practice of the Security Council since 1946. The court accordingly rejected it on the ground that States in the Security Council, particularly the permanent members, have 'consistently and uniformly interpreted the practice of voluntary abstention by a permanent member as not constituting a bar to the adoption of resolutions' and this procedure 'has been generally accepted by Members of the United Nations and evidences a general practice of that Organization'.[17]

The other objections raised to the validity of resolution 284 were less substantial. The court (and particularly Judge Morozov) was no doubt embarrassed by the argument that China was not properly represented in the Security Council [18] and this probably accounts for the failure of the court to reply to the argument. But, as Judge Nervo of Mexico points out in his separate opinion,[19] the right of representation between the two rival Chinese Governments must be decided upon by the General Assembly, which, like the South African Government, had recognized the Government of Nationalist China. South Africa's other arguments, first, that she should have been invited to the debate in the Security Council which preceded the adoption of resolution 284, and, secondly, that certain States should have abstained from voting on that resolution in terms of the proviso to article 27(3), are points which could quite validly have been taken at the time of the debate but, as the court holds, were now made before the wrong forum at the wrong time.[20]

South Africa's objections to the propriety of the court's giving an opinion were twofold. First, it was suggested that the court should re-

[13] Judges Petrén (Sweden) ibid 130, Onyeama (Nigeria) ibid 138–9, Fitzmaurice (United Kingdom) ibid 309, 317 and Gros (France) ibid 323–4.

[14] Ibid 19, 24–7.

[15] Judges Petrén ibid 128–30, Fitzmaurice ibid 308–17 and Gros ibid 323–31.

[16] Judges Onyeama ibid 139–41 and Dillard (United States) ibid 152–3.

[17] Ibid 22.   [18] Written submissions, 1971, vol 1, 49–55.

[19] 1971 ICJ Reports 117.   [20] Ibid 22–3. See too Judge Dillard ibid 154–6.

frain from giving an opinion on account of the political pressure to which it had been or might be subjected. To this the court replied that it would not be proper for it to entertain these observations because it 'acts only on the basis of the law, independently of all outside influence or interventions whatsoever, in the exercise of the judicial function'.[21] Secondly, it was argued, in accordance with the decision of the Permanent Court in the *Eastern Carelia* case,[22] that the court should decline to exercise its advisory functions on a legal question relating to an existing dispute between South Africa and other States. The court first sought to distinguish this precedent on the facts by pointing out that in that case, which involved a legal dispute between Russia and Finland, Russia, a non-member of the League of Nations, had refused to appear before the court, while in the present proceedings South Africa, a member State of the United Nations, had made written and oral submissions to the court. In any event, the court concluded, the Security Council had not requested the opinion in order to settle a dispute between States but to guide it in respect of its own actions.[23]

Undoubtedly the most spectacular feature of the proceedings was South Africa's suggestion that a plebiscite be held in South West Africa in order to determine whether the local inhabitants wished to be governed by South Africa or the United Nations. South Africa contended that Resolution 2145(XXI) was illegal, *inter alia,* because it rested on an incorrect factual basis, namely, that apartheid was repressive. In order to disprove this allegation the South African Government requested that it be permitted to place factual evidence about Namibia before the Court and that a plebiscite be held under the joint supervision of the Court and the Government of South Africa to test the wishes of the inhabitants. South Africa's request for a plebiscite was set out in a letter addressed to the International Court of Justice on 5 February 1971.[e]

In view of the fundamental nature of the proposal for a plebiscite and of the far-reaching influence it may have on the future course of these proceedings, I am instructed by my Government to make it now by letter. . . . I accordingly hereby apply formally that the Court take all necessary steps to put the following proposal into effect:-

[e] For a discussion of the merits of a plebiscite, see Clifford J. Hynning, "The Future of South West Africa: A Plebiscite?" *Proceedings of the American Society of International Law,* 1971, p. 144. Cf., see Ernest A. Gross, ibid., pp. 150, 164.
[21] 1971 ICJ Reports 23. See too Judges Nervo ibid 103, De Castro (Spain) ibid 170–1 and Fitzmaurice ibid 304–8.
[22] 1923 PCIJ, Series B No 5, 29.
[23] 1971 ICJ Reports 23–4. See too Judges Dillard ibid 156 and De Castro ibid 171–7.

(a) That a plebiscite of the inhabitants of South West Africa be held to determine whether it is their wish that the Territory should continue to be administered by the South African Government or should henceforth be administered by the United Nations.

(b) That the plebiscite be jointly supervised by the International Court of Justice and the South African Government. It is suggested that the Court could appropriately act in this respect through a committee of independent experts appointed in accordance with the Statute.

(c) That the detailed arrangements for the plebiscite, including the membership and terms of reference of any committee appointed by the Court, be agreed upon by the South African Government.

These proposals are, it is submitted, self-explanatory and require little elaboration. Unfortunately experience has shown that many people who profess concern for the inhabitants of South West Africa are in fact motivated by political considerations entirely unrelated to the wellbeing of the Territory or the wishes of its inhabitants. One can therefore expect that the proposal contained herein will be misrepresented in certain quarters, and that certain people will examine it with great care in an attempt to find excuses for opposing it or for minimizing its significance. Indeed, a number of such reactions have already been noted in the press and elsewhere. In order to avoid all possibility of misrepresentation or misunderstanding I would accordingly add the following explanatory comment:-

1. The immediate object of the proposal is to place relevant evidence before the Court. Acceptance of the proposal by the Court, or support for it by any state, person or organization, will be entirely without prejudice to the legal positions adopted by them, or to any contentions or findings which might later be advanced or made. Thus, for example, support for the proposal by the Secretary-General of the United Nations or by any State will not and cannot be interpreted as implying his or its recognition of the legality of South Africa's presence in the Territory, just as the making of this proposal in no way implies recognition of international accountability in respect of the Territory by South Africa.

2. The detailed procedures are to be a matter for discussion and agreement between the Court and the South African Government. I must emphasize that these matters are still entirely open as far as the South African Government is concerned. It is not opposed in principle to any method which could be fairly and practically employed to ascertain the wishes of the inhabitants of the Territory. In particular, the South African Government is definitely not committed, as has been suggested in certain quarters, to any procedure which would, as regards the indigenous inhabitants, be limited to consultations with chiefs of tribes.

3. The power of the Court to obtain information in the manner proposed in this application seems beyond doubt, but will be elaborated if necessary.

4. The relevance of the information to be obtained by means of the

proposed plebiscite also seems beyond question. There are numerous allegations in the written statements before the Court of the effect that the indigenous inhabitants in South West Africa are being oppressed, ill-treated, etc. (*vide* e.g., Hungary, p. 9, Czechoslovakia, p. 10, Pakistan, p. 14, Finland, p. 28, U.S.A., pp. 63 *et seq.*, Nigeria, p. 99, Secretary-General, paras. 63, 78, 80, 108 and 109). Moreover, the Secretary-General and others have placed great stress on the alleged denial by the South African Government of self-determination to the inhabitants of South West Africa. (See e.g. the written statements of the Secretary-General, particularly paras. 52 to 65, Netherlands, pp. 2, 3–4; Poland, p. 5; Hungary, pp. 7–9). The expressed wishes of the inhabitants of the Territory would clearly be relevant to both classes of allegations and could indeed be of decisive significance. This aspect also can be elaborated later if required.

. . . .

In my letter of 14th January, 1971 which was circulated that afternoon to representatives of participating states, I referred to the wide ambit and lack of definition of the allegations of fact in the written statements. Voluminous documentation, mainly in United Nations proceedings, is referred to in support of broad allegations of violation by South Africa of her obligations, particularly in the statements by the Secretary-General and the United States, as cited in my earlier letter. When referring to the documents, one finds that their ambit is not only vast, but that they are riddled with inherent contradictions and inconsistencies. Charges very popular at one stage, are apparently abandoned later—at any rate by most States, if not by all (e.g. militarization, genocide, etc.). This point could be considerably elaborated. Moreover, particular charges fail to indicate the ground of complaint, e.g. whether one of deliberate oppression; or failure in fact to promote well being and progress; or violation of an alleged international obligation solely by reason of distinguishing between people on an ethnic basis.

Unless some particularity is introduced into the statements to the Court, indicating both the areas of fact and the nature of the complaint relied upon, a proper traversal of the detailed factual field would be an almost impossible task, not only for South Africa but also for the Court. I therefore have to draw attention to this matter very specifically, particularly since the Court has, as indicated above, not acceded to my Government's request to cause these issues to be defined in some way.

In my Government's contention, however, the plebiscite proposal made herein could have an important and possibly decisive influence on this problem. The outcome of the plebiscite might well rule out the need for traversing the factual field in much further detail at all.

It would, accordingly, be of great assistance to my Government and, I am sure, to the Court, if participants in the oral proceedings were to indicate clearly not only exactly what their factual allegations are, but also to what extent these allegations would or could be affected by the outcome of the proposed plebiscite. To put it more concretely, what would their attitude be if the plebiscite, held under conditions approved by the Court or its committee, showed that the overwhelming wish of the inhabitants was to remain under South African guidance in the exercise of their rights of self-determination? A clear and unambiguous answer to this question would be of great assistance to all concerned in these proceedings.

It would be appreciated if this letter were circulated as soon as possible to all participants in the oral proceedings so as to enable them to bear its contents in mind when making their presentations.

On 17 March the President of the Court announced that the Court had decided to defer a decision on whether to admit factual evidence on the situation in Namibia and on whether to hold a plebiscite until certain legal questions had been resolved. Later, on 14 May 1971 the President declared that the Court had refused both these requests.[f]

Written submissions on the issues before the Court were made by the Secretary-General of the United Nations and the following States: Czechoslovakia, Finland, France, Hungary, India, the Netherlands, Nigeria, Pakistan, Poland, South Africa, the United States of America, and Yugoslavia.[g] Oral submissions to the Court were made on behalf of the Secretary-General, the Organization of African Unity, and the following States: Finland, the Netherlands, Nigeria, Pakistan, South Africa, the Republic of Vietnam, and the United States of America.

2. The Court's Advisory Opinion

On 21 June 1971 the International Court handed down its Opinion on Namibia in which it held that the Mandate for South West Africa had been lawfully terminated. It then spelt out in some detail the consequences of this termination for States. The Court's Opinion reads as follows: [h]

42. Having established that it is properly seised of a request for an advisory opinion, the Court will now proceed to an analysis of the question placed before it: "What are the legal consequences for States of the continued presence of South Africa in Namibia, notwithstanding Security Council resolution 276 (1970)?"

43. The Government of South Africa in both its written and oral statements has covered a wide field of history, going back to the origin

[f] 1971 ICJ Reports 21.
[g] For extracts from these submissions, see (1971) 10 *International Legal Materials* (March) 295.
[h] 1971 ICJ Reports 27–58.

and functioning of the Mandate. The same and similar problems were dealt with by other governments, the Secretary-General of the United Nations and the Organization of African Unity in their written and oral statements.

44. A series of important issues is involved: the nature of the Mandate, its working under the League of Nations, the consequences of the demise of the League and of the establishment of the United Nations and the impact of further developments within the new organization. While the Court is aware that this is the sixth time it has had to deal with the issues involved in the Mandate for South West Africa, it has nonetheless reached the conclusion that it is necessary for it to consider and summarize some of the issues underlying the question addressed to it. In particular, the Court will examine the substance and scope of Article 22 of the League Covenant and the nature of "C" mandates.

45. The Government of South Africa, in its written statement, presented a detailed analysis of the intentions of some of the participants in the Paris Peace Conference, who approved a resolution which, with some alterations and additions, eventually became Article 22 of the Covenant. At the conclusion and in the light of this analysis it suggested that it was quite natural for commentators to refer to " 'C' mandates as being in their practical effect not far removed from annexation". This view, which the Government of South Africa appears to have adopted, would be tantamount to admitting that the relevant provisions of the Covenant were of a purely nominal character and that the rights they enshrined were of their very nature imperfect and unenforceable. It puts too much emphasis on the intentions of some of the parties and too little on the instrument which emerged from those negotiations. It is thus necessary to refer to the actual text of Article 22 of the Covenant, paragraph 1 of which declares:

> 1. To those colonies and territories which as a consequence of the late war have ceased to be under the sovereignty of the States which formerly governed them and which are inhabited by peoples not yet able to stand by themselves under the strenuous conditions of the modern world, there should be applied the principle that the well-being and development of such peoples form a sacred trust of civilisation and that securities for the performance of this trust should be embodied in this Covenant.

As the Court recalled in its 1950 Advisory Opinion on the *International Status of South-West Africa,* in the setting-up of the mandates system "two principles were considered to be of paramount importance: the principle of non-annexation and the principle that the well-being and development of such peoples form 'a sacred trust of civilization' " (*I.C.J. Reports 1950,* p. 131).

46. It is self-evident that the "trust" had to be exercised for the benefit of the peoples concerned, who were admitted to have interests of their own and to possess a potentiality for independent existence on the attainment of a certain stage of development: the mandates system

was designed to provide peoples "not yet" able to manage their own affairs with the help and guidance necessary to enable them to arrive at the stage where they would be "able to stand by themselves". The requisite means of assistance to that end is dealt with in paragraph 2 of Article 22:

> 2. The best method of giving practical effect to this principle is that the tutelage of such peoples should be entrusted to advanced nations who by reason of their resources, their experience or their geographical position can best undertake this responsibility, and who are willing to accept it, and that this tutelage should be exercised by them as Mandatories on behalf of the League.

This made it clear that those Powers which were to undertake the task envisaged would be acting exclusively as mandatories on behalf of the League. As to the position of the League, the Court found in its 1950 Advisory Opinion that: "The League was not, as alleged by [the South African] Government, a 'mandator' in the sense in which this term is used in the national law of certain States." The Court pointed out that: "The Mandate was created, in the interest of the inhabitants of the territory, and of humanity in general, as an international institution with an international object—a sacred trust of civilisation." Therefore, the Court found, the League "had only assumed an international function of supervision and control" (*I.C.J. Reports 1950*, p. 132).

47. The acceptance of a mandate on these terms connoted the assumption of obligations not only of a moral but also of a binding legal character; and, as a corollary of the trust, "securities for [its] performance" were instituted (para. 7 of Art. 22) in the form of legal accountability for its discharge and fulfilment:

> 7. In every case of mandate, the Mandatory shall render to the Council an annual report in reference to the territory committed to its charge.

48. A further security for the performance of the trust was embodied in paragraph 9 of Article 22:

> 9. A permanent Commission shall be constituted to receive and examine the annual reports of the Mandatories and to advise the Council on all matters relating to the observance of the mandates.

Thus the reply to the essential question, *quis custodiet ipsos custodes?*, was given in terms of the mandatory's accountability to international organs. An additional measure of supervision was introduced by a resolution of the Council of the League of Nations, adopted on 31 January 1923. Under this resolution the mandatory Governments were to transmit to the League petitions from communities or sections of the populations of mandated territories.

49. Paragraph 8 of Article 22 of the Covenant gave the following directive:

8. The degree of authority, control or administration to be exercised by the Mandatory shall, if not previously agreed upon by the Members of the League, be explicitly defined in each case by the Council.

In pursuance of this directive, a Mandate for German South West Africa was drawn up which defined the terms of the Mandatory's administration in seven articles. Of these, Article 6 made explicit the obligation of the Mandatory under paragraph 7 of Article 22 of the Covenant by providing that "The Mandatory shall make to the Council of the League of Nations an annual report to the satisfaction of the Council, containing full information with regard to the territory, and indicating the measures taken to carry out the obligations assumed under Articles 2, 3, 4 and 5" of the Mandate. As the Court said in 1950: "the Mandatory was to observe a number of obligations, and the Council of the League was to supervise the administration and see to it that these obligations were fulfilled" (*I.C.J. Reports 1950*, p. 132). In sum the relevant provisions of the Covenant and those of the Mandate itself preclude any doubt as to the establishment of definite legal obligations designed for the attainment of the object and purpose of the Mandate.

50. As indicated in paragraph 45 above, the Government of South Africa has dwelt at some length on the negotiations which preceded the adoption of the final version of Article 22 of the League Covenant, and has suggested that they lead to a different reading of its provisions. It is true that as that Government points out, there had been a strong tendency to annex former enemy colonial territories. Be that as it may, the final outcome of the negotiations, however difficult of achievement, was a rejection of the notion of annexation. It cannot tenably be argued that the clear meaning of the mandate institution could be ignored by placing upon the explicit provisions embodying its principles a construction at variance with its object and purpose.

51. Events subsequent to the adoption of the instruments in question should also be considered. The Allied and Associated Powers, in their Reply to Observations of the German Delegation, referred in 1919 to "the mandatory Powers, which in so far as they may be appointed trustees by the League of Nations will derive no benefit from such trusteeship". As to the Mandate for South West Africa, its preamble recited that "His Britannic Majesty, for and on behalf of the Government of the Union of South Africa, has agreed to accept the Mandate in respect of the said territory and has undertaken to exercise it on behalf of the League of Nations".

52. Furthermore, the subsequent development of international law in regard to non-self-governing territories, as enshrined in the Charter of the United Nations, made the principle of self-determination applicable to all of them. The concept of the sacred trust was confirmed and expanded to all "territories whose peoples have not yet attained a full measure of self-government" (Art. 73). Thus it clearly embraced

territories under a colonial régime. Obviously the sacred trust continued to apply to League of Nations mandated territories on which an
international status had been conferred earlier. A further important
stage in this development was the Declaration on the Granting of Independence to Colonial Countries and Peoples (General Assembly resolution 1514 (XV) of 14 December 1960), which embraces all peoples
and territories which "have not yet attained independence". Nor is it
possible to leave out of account the political history of mandated territories in general. All those which did not acquire independence, excluding Namibia, were placed under trusteeship. Today, only two out
of fifteen, excluding Namibia, remain under United Nations tutelage.
This is but a manifestation of the general development which has led
to the birth of so many new States.

53. All these considerations are germane to the Court's evaluation of
the present case. Mindful as it is of the primary necessity of interpreting an instrument in accordance with the intentions of the parties at
the time of its conclusion, the Court is bound to take into account the
fact that the concepts embodied in Article 22 of the Covenant—"the
strenuous conditions of the modern world" and "the well-being and
development" of the peoples concerned—were not static, but were by
definition evolutionary, as also, therefore, was the concept of the "sacred trust". The parties to the Covenant must consequently be deemed
to have accepted them as such. That is why, viewing the institutions of
1919, the Court must take into consideration the changes which have
occurred in the supervening half-century, and its interpretation cannot
remain unaffected by the subsequent development of law, through the
Charter of the United Nations and by way of customary law. Moreover, an international instrument has to be interpreted and applied
within the framework of the entire legal system prevailing at the time
of the interpretation. In the domain to which the present proceedings
relate, the last fifty years, as indicated above, have brought important
developments. These developments leave little doubt that the ultimate
objective of the sacred trust was the self-determination and independence of the peoples concerned. In this domain, as elsewhere, the *cor-
pus iuris gentium* has been considerably enriched, and this the Court,
if it is faithfully to discharge its functions, may not ignore.

54. In the light of the foregoing, the Court is unable to accept any
construction which would attach to "C" mandates an object and purpose different from those of "A" or "B" mandates. The only differences
were those appearing from the language of Article 22 of the Covenant,
and from the particular mandate instruments, but the objective and
safeguards remained the same, with no exceptions such as considerations of geographical contiguity. To hold otherwise would mean that
territories under "C" mandate belonged to the family of mandates
only in name, being in fact the objects of disguised cessions, as if the
affirmation that they could "be best administered under the laws of
the Mandatory as integral portions of its territory" (Art. 22, para. 6)
conferred upon the administering Power a special title not vested in

States entrusted with "A" or "B" mandates. The Court would recall in this respect what was stated in the 1962 Judgment in the *South West Africa* cases as applying to all categories of mandate:

> The rights of the Mandatory in relation to the mandated territory and the inhabitants have their foundation in the obligations of the Mandatory and they are, so to speak, mere tools given to enable it to fulfil its obligations. (*I.C.J. Reports 1962*, p. 329.)

. . . .

55. The Court will now turn to the situation which arose on the demise of the League and with the birth of the United Nations. As already recalled, the League of Nations was the international organization entrusted with the exercise of the supervisory functions of the Mandate. Those functions were an indispensable element of the Mandate. But that does not mean that the mandates institution was to collapse with the disappearance of the original supervisory machinery. To the question whether the continuance of a mandate was inseparably linked with the existence of the League, the answer must be that an institution established for the fulfilment of a sacred trust cannot be presumed to lapse before the achievement of its purpose. The responsibilities of both mandatory and supervisor resulting from the mandates institution were complementary, and the disappearance of one or the other could not affect the survival of the institution. That is why, in 1950, the Court remarked, in connection with the obligations corresponding to the sacred trust:

> Their *raison d'être* and original object remain. Since their fulfilment did not depend on the existence of the League of Nations, they could not be brought to an end merely because this supervisory organ ceased to exist. Nor could the right of the population to have the Territory administered in accordance with these rules depend thereon. (*I.C.J. Reports 1950*, p. 133.)

In the particular case, specific provisions were made and decisions taken for the transfer of functions from the organization which was to be wound up to that which came into being.

56. Within the framework of the United Nations an international trusteeship system was established and it was clearly contemplated that mandated territories considered as not yet ready for independence would be converted into trust territories under the United Nations international trusteeship system. This system established a wider and more effective international supervision than had been the case under the mandates of the League of Nations.

57. It would have been contrary to the overriding purpose of the mandates system to assume that difficulties in the way of the replacement of one régime by another designed to improve international supervision should have been permitted to bring about, on the dissolution of the League, a complete disappearance of international supervision. To accept the contention of the Government of South Africa on this point would have entailed the reversion of mandated terri-

tories to colonial status, and the virtual replacement of the mandates régime by annexation, so determinedly excluded in 1920.

58. These compelling considerations brought about the insertion in the Charter of the United Nations of the safeguarding clause contained in Article 80, paragraph 1, of the Charter, which reads as follows:

> 1. Except as may be agreed upon in individual trusteeship agreements, made under Articles 77, 79 and 81, placing each territory under the trusteeship system, and until such agreements have been concluded, nothing in this Chapter shall be construed in or of itself to alter in any manner the rights whatsoever of any States or any peoples or the terms of existing international instruments to which Members of the United Nations may respectively be parties.

59. A striking feature of this provision is the stipulation in favour of the preservation of the rights of "any peoples", thus clearly including the inhabitants of the mandated territories and, in particular, their indigenous populations. These rights were thus confirmed to have an existence independent of that of the League of Nations. The Court, in the 1950 Advisory Opinion on the *International Status of South-West Africa,* relied on this provision to reach the conclusion that "no such rights of the peoples could be effectively safeguarded without international supervision and a duty to render reports to a supervisory organ" (*I.C.J. Reports 1950,* p. 137). In 1956 the Court confirmed the conclusion that "the effect of Article 80 (1) of the Charter" was that of "preserving the rights of States and peoples" (*I.C.J. Reports 1956,* p. 27).

60. Article 80, paragraph 1, of the Charter was thus interpreted by the Court as providing that the system of replacement of mandates by trusteeship agreements, resulting from Chapter XII of the Charter, shall not "be construed in or of itself to alter in any manner the rights whatsoever of any States or any peoples".

61. The exception made in the initial words of the provision, "Except as may be agreed upon in individual trusteeship agreements, made under Articles 77, 79 and 81, placing each territory under the trusteeship system, and until such agreements have been concluded", established a particular method for changing the status quo of a mandate régime. This could be achieved only by means of a trusteeship agreement, unless the "sacred trust" had come to an end by the implementation of its objective, that is, the attainment of independent existence. In this way, by the use of the expression "until such agreements have been concluded", a legal hiatus between the two systems was obviated.

62. The final words of Article 80, paragraph 1, refer to "the terms of existing international instruments to which Members of the United Nations may respectively be parties". The records of the San Francisco Conference show that these words were inserted in replacement of the words "any mandate" in an earlier draft in order to preserve "any rights set forth in paragraph 4 of Article 22 of the Covenant of the League of Nations".

63. In approving this amendment and inserting these words in the report of Committee II/4, the States participating at the San Francisco Conference obviously took into account the fact that the adoption of the Charter of the United Nations would render the disappearance of the League of Nations inevitable. This shows the common understanding and intention at San Francisco that Article 80, paragraph 1, of the Charter had the purpose and effect of keeping in force all rights whatsoever, including those contained in the Covenant itself, against any claim as to their possible lapse with the dissolution of the League.

64. The demise of the League could thus not be considered as an unexpected supervening event entailing a possible termination of those rights, entirely alien to Chapter XII of the Charter and not foreseen by the safeguarding provisions of Article 80, paragraph 1. The Members of the League, upon effecting the dissolution of that organization, did not declare, or accept even by implication, that the mandates would be cancelled or lapse with the dissolution of the League. On the contrary, paragraph 4 of the resolution on mandates of 18 April 1946 clearly assumed their continuation.

65. The Government of South Africa, in asking the Court to reappraise the 1950 Advisory Opinion, has argued that Article 80, paragraph 1, must be interpreted as a mere saving clause having a purely negative effect.

66. If Article 80, paragraph 1, were to be understood as a mere interpretative provision preventing the operation of Chapter XII from affecting any rights, then it would be deprived of all practical effect. There is nothing in Chapter XII—which, as interpreted by the Court in 1950, constitutes a framework for future agreements—susceptible of affecting existing rights of States or of peoples under the mandates system. Likewise, if paragraph 1 of Article 80 were to be understood as a mere saving clause, paragraph 2 of the same Article would have no purpose. This paragraph provides as follows:

> 2. Paragraph 1 of this Article shall not be interpreted as giving grounds for delay or postponement of the negotiation and conclusion of agreements for placing mandated and other territories under the trusteeship system as provided for in Article 77.

This provision was obviously intended to prevent a mandatory Power from invoking the preservation of its rights resulting from paragraph 1 as a ground for delaying or postponing what the Court described as "the normal course indicated by the Charter, namely, conclude Trusteeship Agreements" (*I.C.J. Reports 1950*, p. 140). No method of interpretation would warrant the conclusion that Article 80 as a whole is meaningless.

67. In considering whether negative effects only may be attributed to Article 80, paragraph 1, as contended by South Africa, account must be taken of the words at the end of Article 76 (*d*) of the Charter, which, as one of the basic objectives of the trusteeship system, ensures equal treatment in commercial matters for all Members of the United Nations and their nationals. The proviso "subject to the provisions of

Article 80" was included at the San Francisco Conference in order to preserve the existing right of preference of the mandatory Powers in "C" mandates. The delegate of the Union of South Africa at the Conference had pointed out earlier that "the 'open door' had not previously applied to the 'C' mandates", adding that "his Government could not contemplate its application to their mandated territory". If Article 80, paragraph 1, had no conservatory and positive effects, and if the rights therein preserved could have been extinguished with the disappearance of the League of Nations, then the proviso in Article 76 (d) *in fine* would be deprived of any practical meaning.

68. The Government of South Africa has invoked as "new facts" not fully before the Court in 1950 a proposal introduced by the Chinese delegation at the final Assembly of the League of Nations and another submitted by the Executive Committee to the United Nations Preparatory Commission, both providing in explicit terms for the transfer of supervisory functions over mandates from the League of Nations to United Nations organs. It is argued that, since neither of these two proposals was adopted, no such transfer was envisaged.

69. The Court is unable to accept the argument advanced. The fact that a particular proposal is not adopted by an international organ does not necessarily carry with it the inference that a collective pronouncement is made in a sense opposite to that proposed. There can be many reasons determining rejection or non-approval. For instance, the Chinese proposal, which was never considered but was ruled out of order, would have subjected mandated territories to a form of supervision which went beyond the scope of the existing supervisory authority in respect of mandates, and could have raised difficulties with respect to Article 82 of the Charter. As to the establishment of a Temporary Trusteeship Committee, it was opposed because it was felt that the setting up of such an organ might delay the negotiation and conclusion of trusteeship agreements. Consequently two United States proposals, intended to authorize this Committee to undertake the functions previously performed by the Mandates Commission, could not be acted upon. The non-establishment of a temporary subsidiary body empowered to assist the General Assembly in the exercise of its supervisory functions over mandates cannot be interpreted as implying that the General Assembly lacked competence or could not itself exercise its functions in that field. On the contrary, the general assumption appeared to be that the supervisory functions over mandates previously performed by the League were to be exercised by the United Nations. Thus, in the discussions concerning the proposed setting-up of the Temporary Trusteeship Committee, no observation was made to the effect that the League's supervisory functions had not been transferred to the United Nations. Indeed, the South African representative at the United Nations Preparatory Commission declared on 29 November 1945 that "it seemed reasonable to create an interim body as the Mandates Commission was now in abeyance and countries holding mandates should have a body to which they could report".

70. The Government of South Africa has further contended that the

provision in Article 80, paragraph 1, that the terms of "existing inter-national instruments" shall not be construed as altered by anything in Chapter XII of the Charter, cannot justify the conclusion that the duty to report under the Mandate was transferred from the Council of the League to the United Nations.

71. This objection fails to take into consideration Article 10 in Chapter IV of the Charter, a provision which was relied upon in the 1950 Opinion to justify the transference of supervisory powers from the League Council to the General Assembly of the United Nations. The Court then said:

> The competence of the General Assembly of the United Nations to exercise such supervision and to receive and examine reports is de-rived from the provisions of Article 10 of the Charter, which author-izes the General Assembly to discuss any questions or any matters within the scope of the Charter and to make recommendations on these questions or matters to the Members of the United Nations. *(I.C.J. Reports 1950,* p. 137.)

72. Since a provision of the Charter—Article 80, paragraph 1—had maintained the obligations of the Mandatory, the United Nations had become the appropriate forum for supervising the fulfilment of those obligations. Thus, by virtue of Article 10 of the Charter, South Africa agreed to submit its administration of South West Africa to the scru-tiny of the General Assembly, on the basis of the information fur-nished by the Mandatory or obtained from other sources. The transfer of the obligation to report, from the League Council to the General Assembly, was merely a corollary of the powers granted to the General Assembly. These powers were in fact exercised by it, as found by the Court in the 1950 Advisory Opinion. The Court rightly concluded in 1950 that—

> . . . the General Assembly of the United Nations is legally qualified to exercise the supervisory functions previously exercised by the League of Nations with regard to the administration of the Terri-tory, and that the Union of South Africa is under an obligation to submit to supervision and control of the General Assembly and to render annual reports to it. *(I.C.J. Reports 1950,* p. 137.)

In its 1955 Advisory Opinion on *Voting Procedure on Questions relat-ing to Reports and Petitions concerning the Territory of South-West Africa,* after recalling some passages from 1950 Advisory Opinion, the Court stated:

> Thus, the authority of the General Assembly to exercise supervision over the administration of South-West Africa as a mandated Terri-tory is based on the provisions of the Charter. *(I.C.J. Reports 1955,* p. 76.)

In the 1956 Advisory Opinion on *Admissibility of Hearings of Peti-tioners by the Committee on South West Africa,* again after referring to certain passages from the 1950 Advisory Opinion, the Court stated:

Accordingly, the obligations of the Mandatory continue unimpaired with this difference, that the supervisory functions exercised by the Council of the League of Nations are now to be exercised by the United Nations. (*I.C.J. Reports 1956,* p. 27.)

In the same Opinion the Court further stated:

. . . the paramount purpose underlying the taking over by the General Assembly of the United Nations of the supervisory functions in respect of the Mandate for South West Africa formerly exercised by the Council of the League of Nations was to safeguard the sacred trust of civilization through the maintenance of effective international supervision of the administration of the Mandated Territory (*ibid.,* p. 28).

. . . .

73. With regard to the intention of the League, it is essential to recall that, at its last session, the Assembly of the League, by a resolution adopted on 12 April 1946, attributed to itself the responsibilities of the Council in the following terms:

The Assembly, with the concurrence of all the Members of the Council which are represented at its present session: Decides that, so far as required, it will, during the present session, assume the functions falling within the competence of the Council.

Thereupon, before finally dissolving the League, the Assembly on 18 April 1946, adopted a resolution providing as follows for the continuation of the mandates and the mandates system:

The Assembly . . .

. . . .

3. Recognises that, on the termination of the League's existence, its functions with respect to the mandated territories will come to an end, but notes that Chapters XI, XII and XIII of the Charter of the United Nations embody principles corresponding to those declared in Article 22 of the Covenant of the League;

4. Takes note of the expressed intentions of the Members of the League now administering territories under mandate to continue to administer them for the well-being and development of the peoples concerned in accordance with the obligations contained in the respective Mandates, until other arrangements have been agreed between the United Nations and the respective mandatory Powers.

As stated in the Court's 1962 Judgment:

. . . the League of Nations in ending its own existence did not terminate the Mandates but . . . definitely intended to continue them by its resolution of 18 April 1946 (*I.C.J. Reports 1962,* p. 334).

74. That the Mandate had not lapsed was also admitted by the Government of South Africa on several occasions during the early period of transition, when the United Nations was being formed and the

League dissolved. In particular, on 9 April 1946, the representative of South Africa, after announcing his Government's intention to transform South West Africa into an integral part of the Union, declared before the Assembly of the League:

> In the meantime, the Union will continue to administer the territory scrupulously in accordance with the obligations of the Mandate, for the advancement and promotion of the interests of the inhabitants, as she has done during the past six years when meetings of the Mandates Commission could not be held.
>
> The disappearance of those organs of the League concerned with the supervision of mandates, primarily the Mandates Commission and the League Council, will necessarily preclude complete compliance with the letter of the Mandate. The Union Government will nevertheless regard the dissolution of the League as in no way diminishing its obligations under the Mandate, which it will continue to discharge with the full and proper appreciation of its responsibilities until such time as other arrangements are agreed upon concerning the future status of the territory.

The Court referred to this statement in its Judgment of 1962, finding that "there could be no clearer recognition on the part of the Government of South Africa of the continuance of its obligations under the Mandate after the dissolution of the League of Nations" (*I.C.J. Reports 1962*, p. 340).

75. Similar assurances were given on behalf of South Africa in a memorandum transmitted on 17 October 1946 to the Secretary-General of the United Nations, and in statements to the Fourth Committee of the General Assembly on 4 November and 13 November 1946. Referring to some of these and other assurances the Court stated in 1950: "These declarations constitute recognition by the Union Government of the continuance of its obligations under the Mandate and not a mere indication of the future conduct of that Government." (*I.C.J. Reports 1950*, p. 135.)

76. Even before the dissolution of the League, on 22 January 1946, the Government of the Union of South Africa had announced to the General Assembly of the United Nations its intention to ascertain the views of the population of South West Africa, stating that "when that had been done, the decision of the Union would be submitted to the General Assembly for judgment". Thereafter, the representative of the Union of South Africa submitted a proposal to the Second Part of the First Session of the General Assembly in 1946, requesting the approval of the incorporation of South West Africa into the Union. On 14 December 1946 the General Assembly adopted resolution 65 (I) noting—

> . . . *with satisfaction* that the Union of South Africa, by presenting this matter to the United Nations, recognizes the interest and concern of the United Nations in the matter of the future status of territories now held under mandate

and declared that it was—

. . . *unable to accede* to the incorporation of the territory of South West Africa in the Union of South Africa.

The General Assembly, the resolution went on,

> *Recommends* that the mandated territory of South West Africa be placed under the international trusteeship system and invites the Government of the Union of South Africa to propose for the consideration of the General Assembly a trusteeship agreement for the aforesaid Territory.

A year later the General Assembly, by resolution 141 (II) of 1 November 1947, took note of the South African Government's decision not to proceed with its plan for the incorporation of the Territory. As the Court stated in 1950:

> By thus submitting the question of the future international status of the Territory to the 'judgment' of the General Assembly as the 'competent international organ', the Union Government recognized the competence of the General Assembly in the matter. (*I.C.J. Reports 1950*, p. 142.)

77. In the course of the following years South Africa's acts and declarations made in the United Nations in regard to South West Africa were characterized by contradictions. Some of these acts and declarations confirmed the recognition of the supervisory authority of the United Nations and South Africa's obligations towards it, while others clearly signified an intention to withdraw such recognition. It was only on 11 July 1949 that the South African Government addressed to the Secretary-General a letter in which it stated that it could "no longer see that any real benefit is to be derived from the submission of special reports on South West Africa to the United Nations and [had] regretfully come to the conclusion that in the interests of efficient administration no further reports should be forwarded".

78. In the light of the foregoing review, there can be no doubt that, as consistently recognized by this Court, the Mandate survived the demise of the League, and that South Africa admitted as much for a number of years. Thus the supervisory element, an integral part of the Mandate, was bound to survive, and the Mandatory continued to be accountable for the performance of the sacred trust. To restrict the responsibility of the Mandatory to the sphere of conscience or of moral obligation would amount to conferring upon that Power rights to which it was not entitled, and at the same time to depriving the peoples of the Territory of rights which they had been guaranteed. It would mean that the Mandatory would be unilaterally entitled to decide the destiny of the people of South West Africa at its discretion. As the Court, referring to its Advisory Opinion of 1950, stated in 1962:

> The findings of the Court on the obligation of the Union Government to submit to international supervision are thus crystal clear. Indeed, to exclude the obligations connected with the Mandate

would be to exclude the very essence of the Mandate. (*I.C.J. Reports 1962*, p. 334.)

79. The cogency of this finding is well illustrated by the views presented on behalf of South Africa, which, in its final submissions in the *South West Africa* cases, presented as an alternative submission, "in the event of it being held that the Mandate as such continued in existence despite the dissolution of the League of Nations",

> . . . that the Respondent's former obligations under the Mandate to report and account to, and to submit to the supervision, of the Council of the League of Nations, lapsed upon the dissolution of the League, and have not been replaced by any similar obligations relative to supervision by any organ of the United Nations or any other organization or body (*I.C.J. Reports 1966*, p. 16).

The principal submission, however, had been:

> That the whole Mandate for South West Africa lapsed on the dissolution of the League of Nations and that Respondent is, in consequence thereof, no longer subject to any legal obligations thereunder. (*Ibid.*)

80. In the present proceedings, at the public sitting of 15 March 1971, the representative of South Africa summed up his Government's position in the following terms:

> Our contentions concerning the falling away of supervisory and accountability provisions are, accordingly, absolute and unqualified. On the other hand, our contentions concerning the possible lapse of the Mandate as a whole are secondary and consequential and depend on our primary contention that the supervision and the accountability provisions fell away on the dissolution of the League.
> In the present proceedings we accordingly make the formal submission that the Mandate has lapsed as a whole by reason of the falling away of supervision by the League, but for the rest we assume that the Mandate still continued . . .
> . . . on either hypothesis we contend that after dissolution of the League there no longer was any obligation to report and account under the Mandate.

He thus placed the emphasis on the "falling-away" of the "supervisory and accountability provisions" and treated "the possible lapse of the Mandate as a whole" as a "secondary and consequential" consideration.

81. Thus, by South Africa's own admission, "supervision and accountability" were of the essence of the Mandate, as the Court had consistently maintained. The theory of the lapse of the Mandate on the demise of the League of Nations is in fact inseparable from the claim that there is no obligation to submit to the supervision of the United Nations, and vice versa. Consequently, both or either of the claims advanced, namely that the Mandate has lapsed and/or that

there is no obligation to submit to international supervision by the United Nations, are destructive of the very institution upon which the presence of South Africa in Namibia rests, for:

> The authority which the Union Government exercises over the Territory is based on the Mandate. If the Mandate lapsed, as the Union Government contends, the latter's authority would equally have lapsed. To retain the rights derived from the Mandate and to deny the obligations thereunder could not be justified. (*I.C.J. Reports 1950*, p. 133; cited in *I.C.J. Reports 1962*, p. 333.)

82. Of this South Africa would appear to be aware, as is evidenced by its assertion at various times of other titles to justify its continued presence in Namibia, for example before the General Assembly on 5 October 1966:

> South Africa has for a long time contended that the Mandate is no longer legally in force, and that South Africa's right to administer the Territory is not derived from the Mandate but from military conquest, together with South Africa's openly declared and consistent practice of continuing to administer the Territory as a sacred trust towards the inhabitants.

In the present proceedings the representative of South Africa maintained on 15 March 1971:

> . . . if it is accepted that the Mandate has lapsed, the South African Government would have the right to administer the Territory by reason of a combination of factors, being (*a*) its original conquest; (*b*) its long occupation; (*c*) the continuation of the sacred trust basis agreed upon in 1920; and, finally (*d*) because its administration is to the benefit of the inhabitants of the Territory and is desired by them. In these circumstances the South African Government cannot accept that any State or organization can have a better title to the Territory.

83. These claims of title, which apart from other considerations are inadmissible in regard to a mandated territory, lead by South Africa's own admission to a situation which vitiates the object and purpose of the Mandate. Their significance in the context of the sacred trust has best been revealed by a statement made by the representative of South Africa in the present proceedings on 15 March 1971: "it is the view of the South African Government that no legal provision prevents its annexing South West Africa." As the Court pointed out in its Advisory Opinion on the *International Status of South-West Africa*, "the principle of non-annexation" was "considered to be of paramount importance" when the future of South West Africa and other territories was the subject of decision after the First World War (*I.C.J. Reports 1950*, p. 131). What was in consequence excluded by Article 22 of the League Covenant is even less acceptable today.

. . . .

84. Where the United Nations is concerned, the records show that, throughout a period of twenty years, the General Assembly, by virtue of the powers vested in it by the Charter, called upon the South African Government to perform its obligations arising out of the Mandate. On 9 February 1946 the General Assembly, by resolution 9 (I), invited all States administering territories held under mandate to submit trusteeship agreements. All, with the exception of South Africa, responded by placing the respective territories under the trusteeship system or offering them independence. The General Assembly further made a special recommendation to this effect in resolution 65 (I) of 14 December 1946; on 1 November 1947, in resolution 141 (II), it "urged" the Government of the Union of South Africa to propose a trusteeship agreement; by resolution 227 (III) of 26 November 1948 it maintained its earlier recommendations. A year later, in resolution 337 (IV) of 6 December 1949, it expressed "regret that the Government of the Union of South Africa has withdrawn its previous undertaking to submit reports on its administration of the Territory of South West Africa for the information of the United Nations", reiterated its previous resolutions and invited South Africa "to resume the submission of such reports to the General Assembly". At the same time, in resolution 338 (IV), it addressed specific questions concerning the international status of South West Africa to this Court. In 1950, by resolution 449 (V) of 13 December, it accepted the resultant Advisory Opinion and urged the Government of the Union of South Africa "to take the necessary steps to give effect to the Opinion of the International Court of Justice". By the same resolution, it established a committee "to confer with the Union of South Africa concerning the procedural measures necessary for implementing the Advisory Opinion. . .". In the course of the ensuing negotiations South Africa continued to maintain that neither the United Nations nor any other international organization had succeeded to the supervisory functions of the League. The Committee, for its part, presented a proposal closely following the terms of the Mandate and providing for implementation "through the United Nations by a procedure as nearly as possible analogous to that which existed under the League of Nations, thus providing terms no more extensive or onerous than those which existed before". This procedure would have involved the submission by South Africa of reports to a General Assembly committee, which would further set up a special commission to take over the functions of the Permanent Mandates Commission. Thus the United Nations, which undoubtedly conducted the negotiations in good faith, did not insist on the conclusion of a trusteeship agreement; it suggested a system of supervision which "should not exceed that which applied under the Mandates System. . .". These proposals were rejected by South Africa, which refused to accept the principle of the supervision of its administration of the Territory by the United Nations.

85. Further fruitless negotiations were held from 1952 to 1959. In total, negotiations extended over a period of thirteen years, from 1946 to 1959. In practice the actual length of negotiations is no test of

whether the possibilities of agreement have been exhausted; it may be sufficient to show that an early deadlock was reached and that one side adamantly refused compromise. In the case of Namibia (South West Africa) this stage had patently been reached long before the United Nations finally abandoned its efforts to reach agreement. Even so, for so long as South Africa was the mandatory Power the way was still open for it to seek an arrangement. But that chapter came to an end with the termination of the Mandate.

86. To complete this brief summary of the events preceding the present request for advisory opinion, it must be recalled that in 1955 and 1956 the Court gave at the request of the General Assembly two further advisory opinions on matters concerning the Territory. Eventually the General Assembly adopted resolution 2145 (XXI) on the termination of the Mandate for South West Africa. Subsequently the Security Council adopted resolution 276 (1970), which declared the continued presence of South Africa in Namibia to be illegal and called upon States to act accordingly.

. . . .

87. The Government of France in its written statement and the Government of South Africa throughout the present proceedings have raised the objection that the General Assembly, in adopting resolution 2145 (XXI), acted *ultra vires*.

88. Before considering this objection, it is necessary for the Court to examine the observations made and the contentions advanced as to whether the Court should go into this question. It was suggested that though the request was not directed to the question of the validity of the General Assembly resolution and of the related Security Council resolutions, this did not preclude the Court from making such an enquiry. On the other hand it was contended that the Court was not authorized by the terms of the request, in the light of the discussions preceding it, to go into the validity of these resolutions. It was argued that the Court should not assume powers of judicial review of the action taken by the other principal organs of the United Nations without specific request to that effect, nor act as a court of appeal from their decisions.

89. Undoubtedly, the Court does not possess powers of judicial review or appeal in respect of the decisions taken by the United Nations organs concerned. The question of the validity or conformity with the Charter of General Assembly resolution 2145 (XXI) or of related Security Council resolutions does not form the subject of the request for advisory opinion. However, in the exercise of its judicial function and since objections have been advanced the Court, in the course of its reasoning, will consider these objections before determining any legal consequences arising from those resolutions.

90. As indicated earlier, with the entry into force of the Charter of the United Nations a relationship was established between all Members of the United Nations on the one side, and each mandatory Power on the other. The mandatory Powers while retaining their mandates assumed, under Article 80 of the Charter, vis-à-vis all United Na-

tions Members, the obligation to keep intact and preserve, until trusteeship agreements were executed, the rights of other States and of the peoples of mandated territories, which resulted from the existing mandate agreements and related instruments, such as Article 22 of the Covenant and the League Council's resolution of 31 January 1923 concerning petitions. The mandatory Powers also bound themselves to exercise their functions of administration in conformity with the relevant obligations emanating from the United Nations Charter, which member States have undertaken to fulfil in good faith in all their international relations.

91. One of the fundamental principles governing the international relationship thus established is that a party which disowns or does not fulfil its own obligations cannot be recognized as retaining the rights which it claims to derive from the relationship.

92. The terms of the preamble and operative part of resolution 2145 (XXI) leave no doubt as to the character of the resolution. In the preamble the General Assembly declares itself "*Convinced* that the administration of the Mandated Territory by South Africa has been conducted in a manner contrary" to the two basic international instruments directly imposing obligations upon South Africa, the Mandate and the Charter of the United Nations, as well as to the Universal Declaration of Human Rights. In another paragraph of the preamble the conclusion is reached that, after having insisted with no avail upon performance for more than twenty years, the moment has arrived for the General Assembly to exercise the right to treat such violation as a ground for termination.

93. In paragraph 3 of the operative part of the resolution the General Assembly "*Declares* that South Africa has failed to fulfil its obligations in respect of the administration of the Mandated Territory and to ensure the moral and material well-being and security of the indigenous inhabitants of South West Africa and has, in fact, disavowed the Mandate". In paragraph 4 the decision is reached, as a consequence of the previous declaration "that the Mandate conferred upon His Britannic Majesty to be exercised on his behalf by the Government of the Union of South Africa is *therefore* terminated . . .". (Emphasis added.) It is this part of the resolution which is relevant in the present proceedings.

94. In examining this action of the General Assembly it is appropriate to have regard to the general principles of international law regulating termination of a treaty relationship on account of breach. For even if the mandate is viewed as having the character of an institution, as is maintained, it depends on those international agreements which created the system and regulated its application. As the Court indicated in 1962 "this Mandate, like practically all other similar Mandates" was "a special type of instrument composite in nature and instituting a novel international régime. It incorporates a definite agreement . . ." (*I.C.J. Reports 1962*, p. 331). The Court stated conclusively in that Judgment that the Mandate ". . . in fact and in law, is an international agreement having the character of a treaty or con-

vention" (*I.C.J. Reports 1962*, p. 330). The rules laid down by the Vienna Convention on the Law of Treaties concerning termination of a treaty relationship on account of breach (adopted without a dissenting vote) may in many respects be considered as a codification of existing customary law on the subject. In the light of these rules, only a material breach of a treaty justifies termination, such breach being defined as:

(*a*) a repudiation of the treaty not sanctioned by the present Convention; or

(*b*) the violation of a provision essential to the accomplishment of the object or purpose of the treaty (Art. 60, para. 3).

95. General Assembly resolution 2145 (XXI) determines that both forms of material breach had occurred in this case. By stressing that South Africa "has, in fact, disavowed the Mandate", the General Assembly declared in fact that it had repudiated it. The resolution in question is therefore to be viewed as the exercise of the right to terminate a relationship in case of a deliberate and presistent violation of obligations which destroys the very object and purpose of that relationship.

. . . .

96. It has been contended that the Covenant of the League of Nations did not confer on the Council of the League power to terminate a mandate for misconduct of the mandatory and that no such power could therefore be exercised by the United Nations, since it could not derive from the League greater powers than the latter itself had. For this objection to prevail it would be necessary to show that the mandates system, as established under the League, excluded the application of the general principle of law that a right of termination on account of breach must be presumed to exist in respect of all treaties, except as regards provisions relating to the protection of the human person contained in treaties of a humanitarian character (as indicated in Art. 60, par. 5, of the Vienna Convention). The silence of a treaty as to the existence of such a right cannot be interpreted as implying the exclusion of a right which has its source outside of the treaty, in general international law, and is dependent on the occurrence of circumstances which are not normally envisaged when a treaty is concluded.

97. The Government of South Africa has contended that it was the intention of the drafters of the mandates that they should not be revocable even in cases of serious breach of obligation or gross misconduct on the part of the mandatory. This contention seeks to draw support from the fact that at the Paris Peace Conference a resolution was adopted in which the proposal contained in President Wilson's draft of the Covenant regarding the right of appeal for the substitution of the mandatory was not included. It should be recalled that the discussions at the Paris Peace Conference relied upon by South Africa were not directly addressed to an examination of President Wilson's proposals concerning the regulation of the mandates system in the League

Covenant, and the participants were not contesting these particular proposals. What took place was a general exchange of views, on a political plane, regarding the questions of the disposal of the former German colonies and whether the principle of annexation or the mandatory principle should apply to them.

98. President Wilson's proposed draft did not include a specific provision for revocation, on the assumption that mandates were revocable. What was proposed was a special procedure reserving "to the people of any such territory or governmental unit the right to appeal to the League for the redress of correction of any breach of the mandate by the mandatory State or agency or for the substitution of some other State or agency, as mandatory". That this special right of appeal was not inserted in the Covenant cannot be interpreted as excluding the application of the general principle of law according to which a power of termination on account of breach, even if unexpressed, must be presumed to exist as inherent in any mandate, as indeed in any agreement.

99. As indicated earlier, at the Paris Peace Conference there was opposition to the institution of the mandates since a mandate would be inherently revocable, so that there would be no guarantee of long-term continuance of administration by the mandatory Power. The difficulties thus arising were eventually resolved by the assurance that the Council of the League would not interfere with the day-to-day administration of the territories and that the Council would intervene only in case of a fundamental breach of its obligations by the mandatory Power.

100. The revocability of a mandate was envisaged by the first proposal which was made concerning a mandates system:

> In case of any flagrant and prolonged abuse of this trust the population concerned should be able to appeal for redress to the League, who should in a proper case assert its authority to the full, even to the extent of removing the mandate and entrusting it to some other State if necessary. (J. C. Smuts, *The League of Nations: A Practical Suggestion,* 1918, pp. 21–22.)

Although this proposal referred to different territories, the principle remains the same. The possibility of revocation in the event of gross violation of the mandate was subsequently confirmed by authorities on international law and members of the Permanent Mandates Commission who interpreted and applied the mandates system under the League of Nations.

101. It has been suggested that, even if the Council of the League had possessed the power of revocation of the Mandate in an extreme case, it could not have been exercised unilaterally but only in co-operation with the mandatory Power. However, revocation could only result from a situation in which the Mandatory had committed a serious breach of the obligations it had undertaken. To contend, on the basis of the principle of unanimity which applied in the League of Nations, that in this case revocation could only take place with the concurrence

of the Mandatory, would not only run contrary to the general principle of law governing termination on account of breach, but also postulate an impossibility. For obvious reasons, the consent of the wrongdoer to such a form of termination cannot be required.

102. In a further objection to General Assembly resolution 2145 (XXI) it is contended that it made pronouncements which the Assembly, not being a judicial organ, and not having previously referred the matter to any such organ, was not competent to make. Without dwelling on the conclusions reached in the 1966 Judgment in the *South West Africa* contentious cases, it is worth recalling that in those cases the applicant States, which complained of material breaches of substantive provisions of the Mandate, were held not to "possess any separate self-contained right which they could assert . . . to require the due performance of the Mandate in discharge of the 'sacred trust' " (*I.C.J. Reports 1966*, pp. 29 and 51). On the other hand, the Court declared that: ". . . any divergences of view concerning the conduct of a mandate were regarded as being matters that had their place in the political field, the settlement of which lay between the mandatory and the competent organs of the League" (*ibid.*, p. 45). To deny to a political organ of the United Nations which is a successor of the League in this respect the right to act, on the argument that it lacks competence to render what is described as a judicial decision, would not only be inconsistent but would amount to a complete denial of the remedies available against fundamental breaches of an international undertaking.

103. The Court is unable to appreciate the view that the General Assembly acted unilaterally as party and judge in its own cause. In the 1966 Judgment in the *South West Africa* cases, referred to above, it was found that the function to call for the due execution of the relevant provisions of the mandate instruments appertained to the League acting as an entity through its appropriate organs. The right of the League "in the pursuit of its collective, institutional activity, to require the due performance of the Mandate in discharge of the 'sacred trust' ", was specifically recognized (*ibid.*, p. 29). Having regard to this finding, the United Nations as a successor to the League, acting through its competent organs, must be seen above all as the supervisory institution, competent to pronounce, in that capacity, on the conduct of the mandatory with respect to its international obligations, and competent to act accordingly.

. . . .

104. It is argued on behalf of South Africa that the consideration set forth in paragraph 3 of resolution 2145 (XXI) of the General Assembly, relating to the failure of South Africa to fulfil its obligations in respect of the administration of the mandated territory, called for a detailed factual investigation before the General Assembly could adopt resolution 2145 (XXI) or the Court pronounce upon its validity. The failure of South Africa to comply with the obligation to submit to supervison and to render reports, an essential part of the Mandate, cannot be disputed in the light of determinations made by this Court on

more occasions than one. In relying on these, as on other findings of the Court in previous proceedings concerning South West Africa, the Court adheres to its own jurisprudence.

.   .   .   .

105. General Assembly resolution 2145 (XXI), after declaring the termination of the Mandate, added in operative paragraph 4 "that South Africa has no other right to administer the Territory". This part of the resolution has been objected to as deciding a transfer of territory. That in fact is not so. The pronouncement made by the General Assembly is based on a conclusion, referred to earlier, reached by the Court in 1950:

> The authority which the Union Government exercises over the Territory is based on the Mandate. If the Mandate lapsed, as the Union Government contends, the latter's authority would equally have lapsed. (*I.C.J. Reports 1950*, p. 133.)

This was confirmed by the Court in its Judgment of 21 December 1962 in the *South West Africa* cases (Ethiopia v. South Africa; Liberia v. South Africa) (*I.C.J. Reports 1962*, p. 333). Relying on these decisions of the Court, the General Assembly declared that the Mandate having been terminated "South Africa has no other right to administer the Territory". This is not a finding on facts, but the formulation of a legal situation. For it would not be correct to assume that, because the General Assembly is in principle vested with recommendatory powers, it is debarred from adopting, in specific cases within the framework of its competence, resolutions which make determinations or have operative design.

.   .   .   .

106. By resolution 2145 (XXI) the General Assembly terminated the Mandate. However, lacking the necessary powers to ensure the withdrawal of South Africa from the Territory, it enlisted the co-operation of the Security Council by calling the latter's attention to the resolution, thus acting in accordance with Article 11, paragraph 2, of the Charter.

107. The Security Council responded to the call of the General Assembly. It "took note" of General Assembly resolution 2145 (XXI) in the preamble of its resolution 245 (1968); it took it "into account" in resolution 246 (1968); in resolutions 264 (1969) and 269 (1969) it adopted certain measures directed towards the implementation of General Assembly resolution 2145 (XXI) and, finally, in resolution 276 (1970), it reaffirmed resolution 264 (1969) and recalled resolution 269 (1969).

108. Resolution 276 (1970) of the Security Council, specifically mentioned in the text of the request, is the one essential for the purposes of the present advisory opinion. Before analysing it, however, it is necessary to refer briefly to resolutions 264 (1969) and 269 (1969), since these two resolutions have, together with resolution 276 (1970), a combined and a cumulative effect. Resolution 264 (1969), in paragraph 3 of its operative part, calls upon South Africa to withdraw its adminis-

tration from Namibia immediately. Resolution 269 (1969), in view of South Africa's lack of compliance, after recalling the obligations of Members under Article 25 of the Charter, calls upon the Government of South Africa, in paragraph 5 of its operative part, "to withdraw its administration from the territory immediately and in any case before 4 October 1969". The preamble of resolution 276 (1970) reaffirms General Assembly resolution 2145 (XXI) and espouses it, by referring to the decision, not merely of the General Assembly, but of the United Nations "that the Mandate of South-West Africa was terminated". In the operative part, after condemning the non-compliance by South Africa with General Assembly and Security Council resolutions pertaining to Namibia, the Security Council declares, in paragraph 2, that "the continued presence of the South African authorities in Namibia is illegal" and that consequently all acts taken by the Government of South Africa "on behalf of or concerning Namibia after the termination of the Mandate are illegal and invalid". In paragraph 5 the Security Council "*Calls upon* all States, particularly those which have economic and other interests in Namibia, to refrain from any dealings with the Government of South Africa which are inconsistent with operative paragraph 2 of this resolution".

109. It emerges from the communications bringing the matter to the Security Council's attention, from the discussions held and particularly from the text of the resolutions themselves, that the Security Council, when it adopted these resolutions, was acting in the exercise of what it deemed to be its primary responsibility, the maintenance of peace and security, which, under the Charter, embraces situations which might lead to a breach of the peace (Art. 1, para. 1). In the preamble of resolution 264 (1969) the Security Council was "*Mindful* of the grave consequences of South Africa's continued occupation of Namibia" and in paragraph 4 of that resolution it declared "that the actions of the Government of South Africa designed to destroy the national unity and territorial integrity of Namibia through the establishment of Bantustans are contrary to the provisions of the United Nations Charter". In operative paragraph 3 of resolution 269 (1969) the Security Council decided "that the continued occupation of the territory of Namibia by the South African authorities constitutes an aggressive encroachment on the authority of the United Nations, . . .". In operative paragraph 3 of resolution 276 (1970) the Security Council declared further "that the defiant attitude of the Government of South Africa towards the Council's decisions undermines the authority of the United Nations".

110. As to the legal basis of the resolution, Article 24 of the Charter vests in the Security Council the necessary authority to take action such as that taken in the present case. The reference in paragraph 2 of this Article to specific powers of the Security Council under certain chapters of the Charter does not exclude the existence of general powers to discharge the responsibilities conferred in paragraph 1. Reference may be made in this respect to the Secretary-General's Statement, presented to the Security Council on 10 January 1947, to the effect that "the powers of the Council under Article 24 are not restricted to

the specific grants of authority contained in Chapters VI, VII, VIII and XII . . . the Members of the United Nations have conferred upon the Security Council powers commensurate with its responsibility for the maintenance of peace and security. The only limitations are the fundamental principles and purposes found in Chapter I of the Charter."

111. As to the effect to be attributed to the declaration contained in paragraph 2 of resolution 276 (1970), the Court considers that the qualification of a situation as illegal does not by itself put an end to it. It can only be the first, necessary step in an endeavour to bring the illegal situation to an end.

112. It would be an untenable interpretation to maintain that, once such a declaration had been made by the Security Council under Article 24 of the Charter, on behalf of all member States, those Members would be free to act in disregard of such illegality or even to recognize violations of law resulting from it. When confronted with such an internationally unlawful situation, Members of the United Nations would be expected to act in consequence of the declaration made on their behalf. The question therefore arises as to the effect of this decision of the Security Council for States Members of the United Nations in accordance with Article 25 of the Charter.

113. It has been contended that Article 25 of the Charter applies only to enforcement measures adopted under Chapter VII of the Charter. It is not possible to find in the Charter any support for this view. Article 25 is not confined to decisions in regard to enforcement action but applies to "the decisions of the Security Council" adopted in accordance with the Charter. Moreover, that Article is placed, not in Chapter VII, but immediately after Article 24 in that part of the Charter which deals with the functions and powers of the Security Council. If Article 25 had reference solely to decisions of the Security Council concerning enforcement action under Articles 41 and 42 of the Charter, that is to say, if it were only such decisions which had binding effect, then Article 25 would be superfluous, since this effect is secured by Articles 48 and 49 of the Charter.

114. It has also been contended that the relevant Security Council resolutions are couched in exhortatory rather than mandatory language and that, therefore, they do not purport to impose any legal duty on any State nor to affect legally any right of any State. The language of a resolution of the Security Council should be carefully analysed before a conclusion can be made as to its binding effect. In view of the nature of the powers under Article 25, the question whether they have been in fact exercised is to be determined in each case, having regard to the terms of the resolution to be interpreted, the discussions leading to it, the Charter provisions invoked and, in general, all circumstances that might assist in determining the legal consequences of the resolution of the Security Council.

115. Applying these tests, the Court recalls that in the preamble of resolution 269 (1969), the Security Council was "*Mindful* of its responsibility to take necessary action to secure strict compliance with the ob-

ligations entered into by States Members of the United Nations under the provisions of Article 25 of the Charter of the United Nations". The Court has therefore reached the conclusion that the decisions made by the Security Council in paragraphs 2 and 5 of resolution 276 (1970), as related to paragraph 3 of resolution 264 (1969) and paragraph 5 of resolution 269 (1969), were adopted in conformity with the purposes and principles of the Charter and in accordance with its Articles 24 and 25. The decisions are consequently binding on all States Members of the United Nations, which are thus under obligation to accept and carry them out.

116. In pronouncing upon the binding nature of the Security Council decisions in question, the Court would recall the following passage in its Advisory Opinion of 11 April 1949 on *Reparation for Injuries Suffered in the Service of the United Nations:*

> The Charter has not been content to make the Organization created by it merely a centre 'for harmonizing the actions of nations in the attainment of these common ends' (Article 1, para. 4). It has equipped that centre with organs, and has given it special tasks. It has defined the position of the Members in relation to the Organization by requiring them to give it every assistance in any action undertaken by it (Article 2, para. 5), and to accept and carry out the decisions of the Security Council. (*I.C.J. Reports 1949*, p. 178.)

Thus when the Security Council adopts a decision under Article 25 in accordance with the Charter, it is for member States to comply with that decision, including those members of the Security Council which voted against it and those Members of the United Nations who are not members of the Council. To hold otherwise would be to deprive this principal organ of its essential functions and powers under the Charter.

. . . .

117. Having reached these conclusions, the Court will now address itself to the legal consequences arising for States from the continued presence of South Africa in Namibia, notwithstanding Security Council resolution 276 (1970). A binding determination made by a competent organ of the United Nations to the effect that a situation is illegal cannot remain without consequence. Once the Court is faced with such a situation, it would be failing in the discharge of its judicial functions if it did not declare that there is an obligation, especially upon Members of the United Nations, to bring that situation to an end. As this Court has held referring to one of its decisions declaring a situation as contrary to a rule of international law: "This decision entails a legal consequence, namely that of putting an end to an illegal situation" (*I.C.J. Reports 1951*, p. 82).

118. South Africa, being responsible for having created and maintained a situation which the Court has found to have been validly declared illegal, has the obligation to put an end to it. It is therefore under obligation to withdraw its administration from the Territory of Namibia. By maintaining the present illegal situation, and occupying

the Territory without title, South Africa incurs international responsibilities arising from a continuing violation of an international obligation. It also remains accountable for any violations of its international obligations; or of the rights of the people of Namibia. The fact that South Africa no longer has any title to administer the Territory does not release it from its obligations and responsibilities under international law towards other States in respect of the exercise of its powers in relation to this Territory. Physical control of a territory, and not sovereignty or legitimacy of title, is the basis of State liability for acts affecting other States.

119. The member States of the United Nations are, for the reasons given in paragraph 115 above, under obligation to recognize the illegality and invalidity of South Africa's continued presence in Namibia. They are also under obligation to refrain from lending any support or any form of assistance to South Africa with reference to its occupation of Namibia, subject to paragraph 125 below.

120. The precise determination of the acts permitted or allowed— what measures are available and practicable, which of them should be selected, what scope they should be given and by whom they should be applied—is a matter which lies within the competence of the appropriate political organs of the United Nations acting within their authority under the Charter. Thus it is for the Security Council to determine any further measures consequent upon the decisions already taken by it on the question of Namibia. In this context the Court notes that at the same meeting of the Security Council in which the request for advisory opinion was made, the Security Council also adopted resolution 283 (1970) which defined some of the steps to be taken. The Court has not been called upon to advise on the legal effects of that resolution.

121. The Court will in consequence confine itself to giving advice on those dealings with the Government of South Africa which, under the Charter of the United Nations and general international law, should be considered as inconsistent with the declaration of illegality and invalidity made in paragraph 2 of resolution 276 (1970), because they may imply a recognition that South Africa's presence in Namibia is legal.

122. For the reasons given above, and subject to the observations contained in paragraph 125 below, member States are under obligation to abstain from entering into treaty relations with South Africa in all cases in which the Government of South Africa purports to act on behalf of or concerning Namibia. With respect to existing bilateral treaties, member States must abstain from invoking or applying those treaties or provisions of treaties concluded by South Africa on behalf of or concerning Namibia which involve active intergovernmental cooperation. With respect to multilateral treaties, however, the same rule cannot be applied to certain general conventions such as those of a humanitarian character, the non-performance of which may adversely affect the people of Namibia. It will be for the competent international organs to take specific measures in this respect.

123. Member States, in compliance with the duty of non-recognition imposed by paragraphs 2 and 5 of resolution 276 (1970), are under obligation to abstain from sending diplomatic or special missions to South Africa including in their jurisdiction the Territory of Namibia, to abstain from sending consular agents to Namibia, and to withdraw any such agents already there. They should also make it clear to the South African authorities that the maintenance of diplomatic or consular relations with South Africa does not imply any recognition of its authority with regard to Namibia.

124. The restraints which are implicit in the non-recognition of South Africa's presence in Namibia and the explicit provisions of paragraph 5 of resolution 276 (1970) impose upon member States the obligation to abstain from entering into economic and other forms of relationship or dealings with South Africa on behalf of or concerning Namibia which may entrench its authority over the Territory.

125. In general, the non-recognition of South Africa's administration of the Territory should not result in depriving the people of Namibia of any advantages derived from international co-operation. In particular, while official acts performed by the Government of South Africa on behalf of or concerning Namibia after the termination of the Mandate are illegal and invalid, this invalidity cannot be extended to those acts, such as, for instance, the registration of births, deaths and marriages, the effects of which can be ignored only to the detriment of the inhabitants of the Territory.

126. As to non-member States, although not bound by Articles 24 and 25 of the Charter, they have been called upon in paragraphs 2 and 5 of resolution 276 (1970) to give assistance in the action which has been taken by the United Nations with regard to Namibia. In the view of the Court, the termination of the Mandate and the declaration of the illegality of South Africa's presence in Namibia are opposable to all States in the sense of barring *erga omnes* the legality of a situation which is maintained in violation of international law: in particular, no State which enters into relations with South Africa concerning Namibia may expect the United Nations or its Members to recognize the validity or effects of such relationship, or of the consequences thereof. The Mandate having been terminated by decision of the international organization in which the supervisory authority over its administration was vested, and South Africa's continued presence in Namibia having been declared illegal, it is for non-member States to act in accordance with those decisions.

127. As to the general consequences resulting from the illegal presence of South Africa in Namibia, all States should bear in mind that the injured entity is a people which must look to the international community for assistance in its progress towards the goals for which the sacred trust was instituted.

. . . .

128. In its oral statement and in written communications to the Court, the Government of South Africa expressed the desire to supply the Court with further factual information concerning the purposes

and objectives of South Africa's policy of separate development or *apartheid,* contending that to establish a breach of South Africa's substantive international obligations under the Mandate it would be necessary to prove that a particular exercise of South Africa's legislative or administrative powers was not directed in good faith towards the purpose of promoting to the utmost the well-being and progress of the inhabitants. It is claimed by the Government of South Africa that no act or omission on its part would constitute a violation of its international obligations unless it is shown that such act or omission was actuated by a motive, or directed towards a purpose other than one to promote the interests of the inhabitants of the Territory.

129. The Government of South Africa having made this request, the Court finds that no factual evidence is needed for the purpose of determining whether the policy of *apartheid* as applied by South Africa in Namibia is in conformity with the international obligations assumed by South Africa under the Charter of the United Nations. In order to determine whether the laws and decrees applied by South Africa in Namibia, which are a matter of public record, constitute a violation of the purposes and principles of the Charter of the United Nations, the question of intent or governmental discretion is not relevant; nor is it necessary to investigate or determine the effects of those measures upon the welfare of the inhabitants.

130. It is undisputed, and is amply supported by documents annexed to South Africa's written statement in these proceedings, that the official governmental policy pursued by South Africa in Namibia is to achieve a complete physical separation of races and ethnic groups in separate areas within the Territory. The application of this policy has required, as has been conceded by South Africa, restrictive measures of control officially adopted and enforced in the Territory by the coercive power of the former Mandatory. These measures establish limitations, exclusions or restrictions for the members of the indigenous population groups in respect of their participation in certain types of activities, fields of study or of training, labour or employment and also submit them to restrictions or exclusions of residence and movement in large parts of the Territory.

131. Under the Charter of the United Nations, the former Mandatory had pledged itself to observe and respect, in a territory having an international status, human rights and fundamental freedoms for all without distinction as to race. To establish instead, and to enforce, distinctions, exclusions, restrictions and limitations exclusively based on grounds of race, colour, descent or national or ethnic origin which constitute a denial of fundamental human rights is a flagrant violation of the purposes and principles of the Charter.

. . . .

132. The Government of South Africa also submitted a request that a plebiscite should be held in the Territory of Namibia under the joint supervision of the Court and the Government of South Africa (para. 16 above). This proposal was presented in connection with the request to submit additional factual evidence and as a means of bring-

ing evidence before the Court. The Court having concluded that no further evidence was required, that the Mandate was validly terminated and that in consequence South Africa's presence in Namibia is illegal and its acts on behalf of or concerning Namibia are illegal and invalid, it follows that it cannot entertain this proposal.

133. For these reasons,

THE COURT IS OF OPINION,

in reply to the question:

"What are the legal consequences for States of the continued presence of South Africa in Namibia, notwithstanding Security Council resolution 276 (1970)?"

by 13 votes to 2,

(1) that, the continued presence of South Africa in Namibia being illegal, South Africa is under obligation to withdraw its administration from Namibia immediately and thus put an end to its occupation of the Territory;

by 11 votes to 4,

(2) that States Members of the United Nations are under obligation to recognize the illegality of South Africa's presence in Namibia and the invalidity of its acts on behalf of or concerning Namibia, and to refrain from any acts and in particular any dealings with the Government of South Africa implying recognition of the legality of, or lending support or assistance to, such presence and administration;
(3) that it is incumbent upon States which are not Members of the United Nations to give assistance, within the scope of subparagraph (2) above, in the action which has been taken by the United Nations with regard to Namibia.

A declaration was appended to the Court's Opinion by the President, Sir Muhammad Zafrulla Khan, while separate opinions were delivered by Vice-President Ammoun, and Judges Padilla Nervo, Petrén, Onyeama, Dillard, and De Castro. Strong dissenting opinions were given by Judges Sir Gerald Fitzmaurice and Gros. The tenor of Sir Gerald's 100-page dissent is illustrated by his introductory remarks: [i]

1. Although I respect the humanitarian sentiments and the avowed concern for the welfare of the peoples of S.W. Africa which so clearly underlie the Opinion of the Court in this case, I cannot as a jurist accept the reasoning on which it is based. Moreover, the Opinion seems to me insufficiently directed to those aspects of the matter which really require to be established in order to warrant the conclusion that South Africa's mandate in respect of SW. Africa stands validly revoked.

i 1971 ICJ Reports 220–23.

Much of the substance of the Opinion (i.e., that part of it which does not deal with formal, preliminary or incidental matters) is taken up with demonstrating that League of Nations mandates, as an international institution, survived the dissolution of the League—whereas what is really in issue in this case is not the survival of the Mandate for SW. Africa but its purported revocation. Whether or not South Africa still disputes the survival of the Mandate, it certainly disputes its survival in the form of an obligation *owed to the United Nations* (this is the basic issue in the case); and denies that the organs of the United Nations have any competence or power to revoke it.

2. As regards the Court's conclusion that the Mandate has been validly revoked, this can be seen to rest almost exclusively on two assumptions—or rather, in the final analysis, on one only. I speak of assumptions advisedly,—and indeed, concerning the second and more far-reaching of the two (which in one form or another really underlies and entirely motivates the whole Opinion of the Court), there is an open admission that nothing more is needed—the matter being "self-evident". These two assumptions are *first* that there was, or there must have been, an inherent right, vested in the United Nations, unilaterally to revoke the Mandate in the event of fundamental breaches of it (unilaterally determined to exist),—and *secondly,* that there have in fact been such breaches. Since it is clear that the supposed inherent right of revocation, even if it exists, could never be invoked *except* on a basis of fundamental breaches (several passages in the Opinion specifically recognize that only a material breach could justify revocation), it follows that the whole Opinion, or at least its central conclusion, depends on the existence of such breaches. How then does the Opinion deal with this essential matter?—essential because, if there is insufficient justification *in law* for the assumption, the whole Opinion must fall to the ground, as also (though not only for that reason) must the General Assembly's Resolution 2145 of 1966 purporting to revoke, or declare the termination of the Mandate, which was predicated on a similar assumption.

3. The charges of breaches of the Mandate are of two main kinds. The first relates to the failure to carry out, *in relation to the United Nations* an obligation which, in the relevant provision of the Mandate itself (Article 6), is described as an obligation to make an annual report "to the Council of the League of Nations". At the critical date however, at which the legal situation has to be assessed, namely in October 1966 when the Assembly's resolution 2145 purporting to revoke the Mandate, or declare its termination, was adopted, the view that the failure to report to the Assembly of the United Nations constituted a breach of it—let alone a fundamental one—rested basically (not on a judgment but) on an Advisory Opinion given by this Court in 1950 which, being advisory only, and rendered to the United Nations, not South Africa, *was not binding on the latter* and, as regards this particular matter, was highly controversial in character, attracted important dissents, and was the subject of much subsequent serious professional criticism. This could not be considered an adequate basis in law for the exercise of a power of unilateral revocation, even if such a power

existed. There cannot be a fundamental breach of something that has never—*in a manner binding upon the entity supposed to be subject to it*—been established as being an obligation at all,—which has indeed always been, as it still is, the subject of genuine legal contestation. That South Africa denied the existence of the obligation is of course quite a different matter, and in no way a sufficient ground for predicating a breach of it.

4. The second category of charges relates to conduct, said to be detrimental to "the material and moral well-being and the social progress" of the inhabitants of the mandated territory, and thus contrary to Article 2 of the Mandate. *These charges had never, at the critical date of the adoption of Assembly resolution 2145, been the subject of any judicial determination at all,*—and in the present proceedings the Court has specifically refused to investigate them, having rejected the South African application to be allowed to present further factual evidence and connected argument on the matter. The justification for this rejection is said to be that practices of "apartheid", or separate development, are self-evidently detrimental to the welfare of the inhabitants of the mandated territory, and that since these practices are evidenced by laws and decrees of the Mandatory which are matters of public record there is no need for any proof of them. This is an easy line to take, and clearly saves much trouble. But is it becoming to a court of law?—for the ellipsis in the reasoning is manifest. Certainly the authenticity of the laws and decrees themselves does not need to be established, and can be regarded as a matter of which, to use the common law phrase, "judicial notice" would be taken without specific proof. But the *deductions* to be drawn from such laws and decrees, as to the effect they would produce in the particular local circumstances, must obviously be at least *open* to argument,—and there are few, if any, mature systems of private law, the courts of which, whatever conclusions they might ultimately come to, would refuse to hear it. Yet it was on the very question of the alleged self-evidently detrimental effect of its policies of apartheid *in SW. Africa,* that the Mandatory wanted to adduce further factual evidence. Thus the Court, while availing itself of principles of contractual law when it is a question of seeking to establish a right of unilateral revocation for fundamental breaches, fails to apply those corresponding safeguards which private law itself institutes, directed to ensuring that there have indeed *been* such breaches. It is not by postulations that this can be done.

5. In consequence, since the whole Opinion of the Court turns, in the final analysis, on the view that fundamental breaches of the Mandate have occurred, it must (regrettably) be concluded that, in the circumstances above described, this finding has been reached on a basis that must endanger its authority on account of failure to conduct any adequate investigation into the ultimate foundation on which it professes to rest.

. . . .

6. What, in truth, the present proceedings are or should properly speaking, and primarily, be concerned with, is not any of this, but issues of competence and powers,—for unless the necessary competence

and power to revoke South Africa's mandate duly resided in the organs of the United Nations,—unless the Mandatory, upon the dissolution of the League of Nations, became accountable to such an organ, —no infringements of the Mandate, however serious, could operate in law to validate an act of revocation by the United Nations, or impart to it any legal effect. Here the fallacy, based on yet another unsubstantiated assumption underlying the whole Opinion of the Court, namely that the survival of the Mandate *necessarily* entailed the supervisory role of the United Nations, becomes prominent.

7. As to unilateral revocability itself, the Opinion proceeds according to a conception of the position of the various League of Nations mandatories, in relation to their mandates, which would have been considered unrecognizable in the time of the League, and unacceptable if recognized. My reading of the situation is based—in orthodox fashion—on what appears to have been the intentions of those concerned at the time. The Court's view, the outcome of a different, and to me alien philosophy, is based on what has become the intentions of new and different entities and organs fifty years later. This is not a legally valid criterion, and those thinking of having recourse to the international judicial process at the present time must pay close attention to the elaborate explanation of its attitude on this kind of matter which the Court itself gives in its Opinion.

3. Academic Comment on the Opinion

Shortly after the Opinion was delivered the present writer analysed the majority Opinion and the separate and dissenting opinions: [j]

THE REVOCATION OF THE MANDATE

The reasoning of the court on the revocation of the mandate is broadly as follows: the United Nations succeeded to the supervisory powers of the League of Nations on the demise of the League, which meant that it could exercise any supervisory power which the League could have exercised over South-West Africa; the League of Nations was competent to terminate the mandate unilaterally in the event of a material breach of its obligations; *ergo* the United Nations was competent to terminate the mandate. This part of the court's opinion is backed by thirteen of the fifteen judges, the two dissenters being Judges Fitzmaurice of the United Kingdom and Gros of France.

The court devotes more than half of its discussion of this aspect of the opinion to the succession of the United Nations to the supervisory powers of the League,[24] with the result that too little attention is paid

[j] "The Opinion on South West Africa ('Namibia'): The Teleologists Triumph" (1971) 88 *SALJ* 463–68. See, too, Marinus Wiechers, "South West Africa and the International Court of Justice" (1971) 2 *Codicillus*, no. 2, p. 46.

[24] 1971 ICJ Reports 32–43.

to the subject of revocation itself.[25] This is surprising, because the question of the survival of the mandate and of the United Nations' succession to the League's powers had already been dealt with by the court in its 1950 advisory opinion on the *International Status of South West Africa* [26] and its 1962 judgment on the preliminary objections in the *South West Africa Cases*,[27] and the present opinion does little more than confirm these findings. The way in which the court constantly reaffirms its previous findings suggests that it was determined to emphasize the continuity of the court's jurisprudence on this subject.

As in 1950, article 80(1) of the United Nations Charter is construed as preserving the rights of peoples in mandated territories to continued international supervision pending the placing of the mandated territory under trusteeship,[28] and the General Assembly of the United Nations is found to be the appropriate body for exercising this supervision by the combined operation of articles 80 and 10 of the Charter.[29] South Africa's official statements before the League of Nations and the United Nations in 1946 are seen as an acceptance of this state of affairs.[30] Although there may be weaknesses in this reasoning the court could hardly have been expected to go back in time and erase its jurisprudence of 1950, 1955,[31] 1956 [32] and 1962 on this subject. Indeed, even Judge Gros was not prepared to advocate such a course and he concurs with the majority on the correctness of the 1950 advisory opinion.[33] Judge Fitzmaurice alone makes the anarchic suggestion that the court overthrow all its previous decisions on South-West Africa.[34]

The court then turns to resolution 2145 (XXI). It holds that the mandate was an agreement in the nature of a treaty,[35] which rendered it liable to termination in the event of a fundamental breach. The principle that treaties may be terminated in this way is a customary rule of international law (now codified in article 60(3) of the Vienna Convention on the Law of Treaties) which was to be considered as impliedly included in the mandates system.[36] 'The silence of a treaty as to the existence of such a right', said the court, 'cannot be interpreted as implying the exclusion of a right which has its source outside of the treaty, in general international law.' [37] Support for such an implied

---

[25] See the comment to this effect by Judge Fitzmaurice ibid 220.

[26] 1950 ICJ Reports 128.   [28] 1971 ICJ Reports 33–5.

[27] 1962 ICJ Reports 318 at 332–42.   [29] Ibid 36–8.

[30] Ibid 39–40.

[31] *South-West Africa, Voting Procedure* 1955 ICJ Reports 67.

[32] *Admissibility of Hearings of Petitioners by Committee on South-West Africa* 1956 ICJ Reports 22.

[33] 1971 ICJ Reports 335.   [34] Ibid 227–63.

[35] In this respect it relies on the finding of the court in the 1962 South-West Africa proceedings: 1962 ICJ Reports 330.

[36] 1971 ICJ Reports 46–8.

[37] Ibid 47. See too Judge De Castro ibid 216. *Sed contra*, Judge Fitzmaurice ibid 266–8.

right of revocation is found in the *travaux préparatoires,* and in the views of members of the Permanent Mandates Commission and commentators on the mandates system.[38]

South Africa's contention that even if an implied right of revocation existed in principle it could not have been applied in practice because she would have been able to veto any resolution of revocation under the unanimity rule applicable to proceedings of the Council of the League is rejected as it 'would not only run contrary to the general principle of law governing termination on account of breach, but also postulate an impossibility'.[39] This terse rejection of the unanimity rule, with no attempt to distinguish the previous affirmations of this rule in 1962 and 1966,[40] is unsatisfactory. This weakness is, however, remedied to some extent by the excellent separate opinion of Judge De Castro of Spain,[41] who shows that the unanimity rule in the League Council was designed to safeguard the sovereignty of States, a consideration which did not apply to the mandates system, where the concept of sovereignty was inapplicable. Mandatory States were therefore denied the right of veto in matters affecting their mandated territories. Supported by Judge Khan,[42] he claims that this is borne out by League practice, which indicated that the veto was never used in matters affecting mandated territories.

The court finds that the General Assembly, as political successor to the Council of the League, was the appropriate body to decide whether South Africa had violated her obligations under the mandate.[43] This conclusion follows logically from the 1966 decision of the court to the effect that it was for a political and not a legal body to decide whether the mandate had been violated.[44] Although it would have been preferable for an advisory opinion to have been sought on this matter prior to the revocation,[45] it is difficult to understand how Judge Fitzmaurice can find this to be obligatory,[46] in the light of the 1966 majority finding and of his own statement in 1962 that the 'proper forum for the appreciation and application of a provision of

---

[38] Ibid 48–9. For a more detailed account of such support, see Judge De Castro ibid 211–13 and John Dugard 'The Revocation of the Mandate for South-West Africa' (1968) 62 *American Journal of International Law* 78 at 84–8.

[39] 1971 ICJ Reports 49.

[40] The present writer has submitted that neither of these decisions is conclusive on this matter: op cit n. 38 at 90–1.

[41] 1971 ICJ Reports 199–207. *Sed contra,* Judge Fitzmaurice ibid 272–7.

[42] Ibid 60–1.   [43] Ibid 49.

[44] *South West Africa, Second Phase* 1966 ICJ Reports 6, 29. Clearly the court in 1966 did not envisage its decision's being used in this way, but, as the present writer pointed out in 1968, this conclusion is a logical consequence of its decision: op cit n. 38 at 82.

[45] See Judge Petrén's comment to this effect: 1971 ICJ Reports 132–3.

[46] Ibid 299–301. See too at 221–3 and 266 (note 43).

this kind [article 2 of the mandate] is unquestionably a technical or political one'.[47]

Having decided that resolution 2145 (XXI) was valid, the court then turns to its legal effect. Resolutions of the General Assembly are recommendatory and not legally binding, except in certain exceptional cases. Did resolution 2145 (XXI) fall within one of these exceptions or was it à recommendation which acquired full legal effect only on receiving the endorsement of the Security Council? Here the court's decision is extremely ambiguous. First, it suggests that resolution 2145 (XXI) was binding per se by declaring that the General Assembly's normal recommendatory powers do not debar it 'in specific cases' from adopting 'resolutions which make determinations or have operative design'[48] and that '[b]y resolution 2145 (XXI) the General Assembly terminated the Mandate'.[49] Later, however, it states that, 'lacking the necessary powers to ensure the withdrawal of South Africa from the Territory', the General Assembly 'enlisted the co-operation of the Security Council',[50] which implies that resolution 2145 (XXI) obtained its full effect from the combined operation of the resolutions of both political bodies. In his separate opinion Judge Dillard of the United States indicates that, although the majority were divided on this issue,[51] the reasoning of the court is 'mainly based' on the view that subsequent Security Council resolutions 'served to convert a recommendation [resolution 2145 (XXI)] into a binding decision operative as against non-consenting States'.[52] This latter view is preferable, as such a procedure is analogous to that described in article 6 of the Charter dealing with the expulsion of a member from the United Nations and does not constitute a procedure foreign to the United Nations. At the same time it approximates to the procedure of the Council of the League, which required the consent of the principal powers for the revocation of the mandate.[53]

LEGAL CONSEQUENCES FOR STATES OF THE REVOCATION

The court finally directs its attention to resolution 276 and holds that, although it does not fall under chapter VII of the Charter dealing with enforcement measures, it is nevertheless legally binding under

[47] Joint dissenting opinion with Sir Percy Spender, 1962 ICJ Reports at 467. A similar view was expressed by the South African Appellate Division in *S v Tuhadeleni* 1969 (I) SA 153 (AI) at 172.
[48] 1971 ICJ Reports 50.   [49] Ibid 51.   [50] loc cit.
[51] The following judges favour the view that the General Assembly alone was competent to terminate the mandate with full legal effect: Khan ibid 61, Petrén ibid 131–2, Onyeama ibid 146–7, Dillard ibid 163–5. Those in favour of the 'combined effect' view were Nervo ibid 113–14 and De Castro ibid 189 and 218.
[52] Ibid 164.
[53] See Dugard op cit n. 38 at 96. This view is rejected by Judge Fitzmaurice: 1971 ICJ Reports 283.

article 25 of the Charter.[54] South Africa is therefore under a legal obligation to withdraw its administration from South-West Africa and member States of the United Nations are obliged to recognize the illegality of South Africa's presence in the territory and to refrain from acts which might imply recognition of South Africa's illegal presence. This means that States are under a legal obligation to abstain from:

(i) entering into treaty relations with South Africa in all cases where she purports to act on behalf of South-West Africa;

(ii) applying existing bilateral treaties concluded by South Africa on behalf of South-West Africa;

(iii) maintaining diplomatic and consular relations in so far as they extend to South-West Africa;

(iv) entering into economic relations with South Africa where it acts on behalf of South-West Africa 'which may entrench its authority over the Territory'.[55]

Although the sanction of invalidity is to be extended to South African acts in respect of South-West Africa, the court adds that 'this invalidity cannot be extended to those acts, such as, for instance, the registration of births, deaths and marriages, the effects of which can be ignored only to the detriment of the inhabitants of the Territory'.[56] (Consequently the court's decision is not as far-reaching as that of the Privy Council in respect of Rhodesia,[57] which extends the sanction of illegality to all acts of the Smith Government.) The court concludes that although States which are not members of the United Nations are not legally obliged to comply with resolution 276 'it is incumbent' upon them to give their assistance to the United Nations action with regard to Namibia.[58]

This final part of the court's opinion is backed by eleven of the fifteen judges. Judge Petrén of Sweden and Onyeama of Nigeria join Judges Fitzmaurice and Gros in dissent. Although he does not formally dissent, Judge Dillard too shows his dissatisfaction with the court's reasoning by restricting the finding to the issue of South-West Africa alone.[59]

This is undoubtedly the most revolutionary feature of the court's opinion, as hitherto it had been assumed that article 25, conferring binding force on resolutions, applied only to resolutions adopted under chapter VII.[60] The court, however, finds that the Security

---

[54] Ibid 51–4.   [55] Ibid 54–6.   [56] Ibid 56.

[57] *Madzimbamuto* v *Lardner-Burke and George* [1969] 1 AC 645 (PC). See too *Adams* v *Adams* [1970] 3 WLR 934.

[58] 1971 ICJ Reports 58. See too at 56.

[59] Ibid 150. See too 165–7. Judge De Castro also seeks to limit the implied powers under article 24 to matters affecting the mandate: ibid 186–8.

[60] See the separate opinions of Judges Fitzmaurice ibid 293, 297–8 and Petrén 133–7. See too L M Goodrich, E Hambro and A P Simons *Charter of the United Nations* 3 ed (1969) 207–11 and Amos Shapira 'The Security Council Resolution of November 22, 1967—its Legal Nature and Implications' (1969) 4 *Israel LR* 229 at 230–3. *Sed contra,*

Council adopted resolution 276 in the exercise of its primary responsibility, the maintenance of international peace and security, under general implied powers flowing from article 24(1) which are limited only by the fundamental purposes and principles of the Charter. Moreover, it was clear from the wording of resolution 276 and the circumstances in which it was adopted that it was intended to be binding upon States under article 25, which 'is not confined to decisions in regard to enforcement action but applies to "the decisions of the Security Council" adopted in accordance with the Charter'.[61]

This reasoning of the court is difficult to accept. It is submitted that the better view is that put forward by Judges Petrén [62] and Onyeama.[63] Articles 24 and 25 cannot be used to evade the conditions laid down by chapter VII [64] as a prerequisite for coercive measures of the kind included in resolution 276, and in the absence of a finding that the situation in Namibia threatens international peace the resolution is only recommendatory; South Africa's legal obligation to withdraw from South-West Africa arises from resolution 2145 (XXI) [65] and States are only obliged to apply the customary rules of non-recognition to South Africa's administration of South-West Africa; resolution 276 may, however, authorize States to '[take] up a position in their legal relationships with South Africa which would otherwise have been in conflict with rights possessed by that country'.[66]

TWO MISCELLANEOUS MATTERS OF MAGNITUDE

Two final comments of the court, delivered almost as postscripts, are of vital importance, despite the brief treatment they receive. First, the court rejects South Africa's request that she be permitted to lead factual evidence to show that apartheid does not violate her obligations under the mandate on the ground that the policy patently contravenes South Africa's obligation to respect human rights and fundamental freedoms under the Charter.[67] This pronouncement was quite unnecessary as the court had already decided that the General Assembly was the competent body to make such a determination. In any event it is unfortunate—to put it mildly—that the court should have pronounced on so complex a matter without hearing and examining any

---

Jorge Castañeda *Legal Effects of United Nations Resolutions* (1969) 71–5.

[61] 1971 ICJ Reports 53.   [62] Ibid 133–7.   [63] Ibid 147–8.

[64] Article 39 makes chapter VII enforcement action dependent on a finding that there is a threat to the peace, a breach of the peace or an act of aggression.

[65] The writer prefers the view that this obligation arises from the combined effect of resolution 2145 (XXI) and the subsequent Security Council resolutions.

[66] Per Judge Petrén, 1971 ICJ Reports 137. See further on this subject CJR Dugard 'The Legal Effect of United Nations Resolutions on Apartheid' (1966) 83 *SALJ* 44 at 59.

[67] Ibid 57.

evidence. Secondly, the court refuses South Africa's proposal that a plebiscite be held in South-West Africa to ascertain the views of the local inhabitants, on the ground that South Africa is in illegal occupation of the territory 'and its acts on behalf of or concerning Namibia are illegal and invalid'.[69]

4. The South African Government's Response to the Opinion

The South African Government was quick to reject the Court's Opinion. On the same day on which the Court handed down its Opinion the Prime Minister, Mr. B. J. Vorster, declared: [k]

I do not intend to embark this evening on a complete juridical analysis of the advisory opinion on South West Africa of the International Court of Justice. That would require more time. It is, however, already quite clear that the argument of the court will not stand up to the test of juridical analysis, and that too familiar double standards are evident in the latest opinion.

Thus, it is rather ironic that considerable emphasis is placed in the reasoning on the right of peoples to self-determination, while South Africa's proposal to let the peoples of South West Africa have the opportunity of expressing their opinions is dismissed in a sentence or two. The court rejected its own reasoning when it came to the exercise thereof by the peoples of South West Africa.

The pronouncement of the majority opinion in The Hague was the culmination of a systematic process of erosion of the authority and prestige of the International Court. The majority opinion is not only entirely untenable, but is clearly and demonstrably the result of political maneuvering instead of objective jurisprudence.

This erosion began as far back as 1966, soon after the court delivered a verdict which was favourable to South Africa in respect of the earlier South West Africa case. Frustration reigned among the leaders of the anti-apartheid campaign and feelings ran high.

. . . .

South Africa's enemies indicated in the United Nations that the court would in future have to be packed with persons who would see to it that a verdict favourable to South Africa would not again be forthcoming from that quarter. And they, in fact, took great pains to see to it that this happened in the election of judges in 1966 and 1969.

A characteristic of today's opinion is that the 1966 verdict was dismissed with contempt, or was ignored—and with it the basic principles on which it rested. Principles that had been built up through the long years of jurisprudence of the International Court and its predecessor, the Permanent Court.

I believe that no one in the world can be so naive as to think that this result was achieved by pure coincidence or by objective jurispru-

[k] *Rand Daily Mail,* 22 June 1971.
[69] 1971 ICJ Reports 57–8.

dence. I am waiting with interest to see how many states will in future have the necessary confidence to submit their disputes voluntarily for adjudication to the court.

.   .   .   .

Throughout, it was not South Africa but its opponents who were on the defensive and on the retreat in regard to the merits of the case. From the time that the South African legal team arrived in The Hague in January for the preliminary aspects of the oral proceedings, it was however clear that the majority of the court had a steamroller approach which is foreign to a court of justice.

In the same way, the participation in the proceedings of judges who had previously attacked South Africa in the United Nations in the most unrestrained language, particularly with regard to policy and activity in South West Africa, is unknown in civilised legal systems.

The court even continued to hear the case although the political pressure which the United Nations was putting on it obviously made it impossible to give an objective opinion.

Although South Africa's request for the appointment of an ad hoc judge was refused, the OAU was on the other hand allowed to take part in the proceedings, in spite of the fact that three judges of its member states served on the Bench.

Against the background I have just sketched, it is not surprising that the opinions of the majority were clearly politically motivated, however they tried to clothe them in legal language.

.   .   .   .

The untenability of the majority opinions was underlined by the minority judges, Sir Gerald Fitzmaurice of Britain, and Judge Gros of France.

In the light of their analyses and findings, it is clear that legal considerations were not a deciding factor for the majority. They even say so pertinently, and have recorded their protest.

Judge Fitzmaurice even warned states to study the reasoning of the majority carefully before they risked making use of the court's jurisdiction in present circumstances.

Indeed, the minority opinion shows not only disagreement, but also the strong protest against the violation of law, contained in the majority opinion.

It will be clear from what I have already said that the Government has no hesitation in rejecting the majority opinion. An advisory opinion, by its very nature, is of no binding force and in the present case is totally unconvincing.

It is our duty to administer South West Africa so as to promote the well-being and progress of its inhabitants. We will carry out this duty with a view to self-determination for all population groups.

We have guided and administered the peoples of South West Africa for more than half a century in a manner which has earned their whole-hearted confidence. We have set them on the way of peace, prosperity and self-determination and we do not intend to fail that trust. We shall, therefore, proceed with our task and shall not neglect our responsibility towards South West Africa and its peoples.

Further abuse was heaped upon the International Court by Mr. Justice J. T. Van Wyk, the South African *ad hoc* judge in the 1962–66 contentious proceedings. He stated:

My accusation against the 1971 Court is that it arrived at its cardinal conclusion without advancing any principled reasons in support thereof. An analysis leads irresistibly to a finding that the majority judges first decided what their conclusion should be and then set out to find reasons for rejecting any contentions inconsistent therewith. Where no reasons, however weak, could be found, none were advanced. I accuse those judges of substituting mere mumbo jumbo for sound legal reasoning. Their meaningless legal jargon may impress the uninformed, but cannot bear even superficial analysis.[1]

The two main charges levelled at the Court by Mr. Vorster and Mr. Justice Van Wyk, namely, that the Court was "packed" for the proceedings and that it adopted "untenable" legal reasoning, are examined by the present writer: [m]

WAS THE COURT 'PACKED' FOR THE PROCEEDINGS?

It is unfortunate that Mr. Vorster has seen fit to describe the court as having been 'packed' for the 1971 advisory opinion. On the very day on which the opinion was handed down he contended that after the 1966 decision in the *South-West Africa Cases* 'South Africa's enemies' declared that 'the court would in future have to be packed with persons who would see to it that a verdict favourable to South Africa would not again be forthcoming from that quarter and they, in fact, took great pains to see that this happened in the election of judges in 1966 and 1969'. This 'packed' court, he continued, had then adopted 'a steamroller approach' to the proceedings.[70]

Undoubtedly the 1966 decision had some influence on the subsequent elections to the court,[71] but this should not be exaggerated. It is possible to identify two jurists who probably were unsuccessful in the November 1966 elections to the court because of the July decision in the *South-West Africa Cases,* namely Sir Kenneth Bailey of Australia and Antonio de Luna of Spain. The former suffered for the part played by his compatriot in that case,[72] while the latter's apparent offence was that he was a national of a colonial power.[73] Apart from

---

[1] Address to students at the University of Cape Town on 17 August 1971 (unpublished).

[m] Above, n. j, 468–77.

[70] *Rand Daily Mail* 22 June 1971.

[71] Elections to the court are held every three years in respect of five vacancies: see article 13 of the court's Statute.

[72] L C Green 'South West Africa and the World Court' (1966) 22 *International Journal* 39 at 66.

[73] Elizabeth Landis 'South West Africa Cases: Remand to the United Nations' (1967) 52 *Cornell LQ* 627 at 668.

these two, however, it is difficult to point to any judges who were omitted by reason of their views on southern Africa or who were expressly elected for that reason.

It is true that the African judges on the court have increased from one in 1966 [74] to three in 1971,[75] but so has African representation in other international bodies.[76] One of these judges, Charles Onyeama of Nigeria, however, represents the conservative English common-law tradition and should be more acceptable to South Africa than Latin-American teleologists, particularly since he sided with South Africa on several of the issues in 1971.

Allegations that the court was deliberately packed for the 1971 opinion fail to take into account the fact that after the 1966 decision the Afro-Asian States totally rejected the court as an instrument of change in South-West Africa and resisted attempts to have the matter referred back to the court.[77] Even in 1970 the Afro-Asian States were unenthusiastic about the Finnish proposal that an advisory opinion be sought and expressed misgivings about the court.[78]

While there is no evidence to support the accusations of court 'packing' there was much substance in at least one of South Africa's applications for recusal (namely in respect of Judge Morozov) and in its request for the appointment of an *ad hoc* judge. One suspects that an extra-legal factor may have influenced some of the judges among the majority on this subject. Doubtlessly some recalled that the recusal of Judge Khan in 1966 had drastically affected the outcome of those proceedings and did not wish to see history repeat itself. However unfortunate this aspect of the court's opinion may be, one can safely say, with the knowledge of hindsight, that even if South Africa had succeeded in her request for three recusals and the appointment of an *ad hoc* judge, the opinion of the court on the merits of the case would not have been materially different.

The unpalatable truth is that the present court is substantially the same as its predecessors. As required by its Statute, it still comprises 'jurisconsults of recognized competence' and represents the 'main forms of civilization and . . . the principal legal systems of the world'.[80] Like pre-1966 judges, the present judges show a preference for a functional and teleological approach to the interpretation of humanitarian and constitutive treaties, but, as will be shown, this is nothing new.

The accusation of court 'packing' is as unfortunate as it is ill-

[74] Judge Forster of Senegal.
[75] Judges Forster, Onyeama (Nigeria) and Ignacio-Pinto (Dahomey).
[76] Leo Gross 'The International Court of Justice: Consideration of Requirements for Enhancing its Rôle in the International Legal Order' (1971) 65 *American Journal of International Law* 253 at 282.
[77] Landis op cit 669. See too the statements cited in South Africa's written submissions of 1971: vol 1, 129–30.
[78] See the statements referred to in Judge Onyeama's separate opinion: 1971 ICJ Reports 141–2. See too the statements reported in *UN Monthly Chronicle* August–September 1970, 33 ff.
[80] Articles 2 and 9.

founded. Politically it is an unwise line of attack for the Government to pursue as its own record in this field is not above criticism. After all, the National Party Government did not merely replace retiring judges with judges at least some of whom no doubt it hoped would more fully reflect its legal values and philosophy after its setbacks in the two *Harris* cases [81] of the early 1950s. It enlarged the size of the Appellate Division from five to eleven in constitutional matters [82] and in making appointments to fill the new posts overlooked several eminent and more senior judges.[83]

CONFLICTING APPROACHES TO INTERNATIONAL
LAW AND TO THE INTERNATIONAL
JUDICIAL PROCESS

The latest opinion of the court is not a model of perfection and much of its reasoning suffers from the brevity and ellipsis which has characterized past decisions of the court.[84] This is, however, one of the hazards of a large tribunal with judges drawn from different legal cultures who 'can more easily reach an agreement on the disposition of the dispute than on the grounds for the disposition'.[85] Although the present majority opinion represents the lowest common denominator of thirteen judges,[86] it is nevertheless remarkable for the doctrinal unity it displays in its firm commitment to the teleological method of interpretation.

The history of the dispute before the International Court over South-West Africa has been marked by a conflict between teleological (or sociological) and formalistic (or positivistic) methods of interpretation.[87] In 1966 the formalists triumphed. In 1971 they did not. This is the root cause of South Africa's *legal* antagonism towards the court and explains the extravagant outbursts of Mr. Vorster and Mr. Justice Van Wyk against the court.

The 'formalists' are not a homogeneous group in their approach to treaty interpretation. Some favour a 'textual approach, which places emphasis on the text of the treaty, while others favour an 'intentions approach', according to which the prime goal of treaty interpretation is to ascertain the intentions of the signatories by reference to both the

[81] *Harris* v *Minister of the Interior* 1952 (2) SA 428 (AD) and *Minister of the Interior* v *Harris* 1952 (4) SA 769 (AD).

[82] Appellate Division Quorum Act 27 of 1955. See further B Beinart 'The South African Appeal Court and Judicial Review' (1958) 21 *Mod LR* 587.

[83] H J May *The South African Constitution* 3 ed (1955) 73.

[84] Shabtai Rosenne *The Law and Practice of the International Court* (1965) II 617.

[85] Leo Gross 'Treaty Interpretation: the Proper Rôle of an International Tribunal' 1969 *Proceedings of the American Society of International Law* 108 at 110.

[86] Rosenne op cit 618.

[87] See the comment by Judge Tanaka to this effect in his dissenting opinion in the 1966 *South West Africa Cases:* 1966 ICJ Reports 278.

text and to the *travaux préparatoires*.[89] Jurisprudentially they belong to the school of legal positivism, which sees international law as a body of rules to which States have consented and which emphasizes State sovereignty as the corner-stone of the international legal order.[90] Consequently they incline to the view that ambiguities and 'gaps' in treaties should be resolved in favour of State sovereignty and no distinction is drawn in this regard between ordinary treaties and treaties of a constitutive or humanitarian nature. In true positivist fashion this school insists on rigid adherence to the distinction between law and morals (or law and politics) and discounts humanitarian and sociological considerations as part of the legal process. Another feature of legal formalism is its devotion to the principle of contemporaneity, according to which treaty terms are to be interpreted in accordance with the meaning they possessed at the time the treaty was entered into.[91] Finally, this school condemns judicial innovation and at times appears to believe that the judge's task is limited to *declaring* the law.

The teleological school emphasizes the role of the objects and purposes of a treaty in the interpretative process. Ambiguities in a treaty are to be resolved by choosing that interpretation which gives the maximum effect to the main purpose and object of the treaty in accordance with the maxim *ut res magis valeat quam pereat*.[92] Although this method is assigned a subordinate role in the interpretation of ordinary treaties, it assumes first place among the rules of interpretation to be employed in the elucidation of constitutive treaties, such as the Charter of the United Nations, and humanitarian treaties, such as the mandate for South-West Africa. Treaties of this kind are viewed as 'living law' and not static instruments, with the result that they are to be interpreted in accordance with contemporary standards and expectations, if necessary at the expense of the principle of contemporaneity.[93] Jurisprudentially teleologists share a common antipathy towards positivism, with its subservience to State sovereignty and insistence on the separation of law and morality, and show a preference for sociological or natural-law theories of international law. They adopt a functionalist approach to the judicial process and maintain that judges do not merely declare the law. The judge's function is to choose between alternative rules in the case of 'gaps' in the law, and in making this choice he must be guided by the humanitarian, social and moral purposes of the law.[94]

[89] I M Sinclair 'Vienna Conference on the Law of Treaties' (1970) 19 *ICLQ* 47 at 61.
[90] J L Brierly *The Basis of Obligation in International Law* (1958) 9–18.
[91] Sir Gerald Fitzmaurice 'The Law and Procedure of the International Court of Justice 1951–4: Treaty Interpretation and Other Treaty Points' (1957) 33 *British Year Book of International Law* 203 at 225.
[92] Ibid 211.
[93] Edward Gordon 'The World Court and the Interpretation of Constitutive Treaties' (1965) 59 *American Journal of International Law* 794 at 827–32.
[94] Rosalyn Higgins 'Policy Considerations and the International Judicial Process' (1968) 17 *ICLQ* 58 at 62.

This teleological philosophy is a thread which runs through the court's opinion. Only on two occasions does the court err on the side of literalism, namely in its unfortunate interpretation of the provisions dealing with recusals and the appointment of an *ad hoc* judge.

The first task of the teleologist is to identify the objects and purposes of the instruments before him. This the court does at the outset of its opinion, after dismissing South Africa's preliminary objections. It finds that the mandates system was founded on the principle of non-annexation and that its prime object was the 'well-being and development' of the peoples of mandated territories, which was to form a 'sacred trust of civilization'.[96] It rejects the South African contention that the 'C' mandates were 'in their practical effect not far removed from annexation', as such a construction of the mandate institution would be 'at variance with its object and purpose'.[97] The concepts of 'well-being and development' and 'sacred trust', says the court, were not 'static, but were by definition evolutionary' and parties to the Covenant of the League 'must consequently be deemed to have accepted them as such'.[98] Consequently, although it was '[m]indful . . . of the primary necessity of interpreting an instrument in accordance with the intentions of the parties at the time of its conclusion', the court was obliged to take into account the subsequent development of the law in the areas of self-determination and decolonization.[99] Developments during the last fifty years, said the court, left 'little doubt that the ultimate objective of the sacred trust was the self-determination and independence of the peoples concerned'.[1] Similar interpretative methods are enunciated in several of the separate opinions.[2]

Like the court of 1950,[3] the court relies heavily on the principle of effectiveness in reaching its finding that the United Nations succeeded to the supervisory powers of the League. Fundamental to the court's reasoning on this point is the presumption against the lapse of 'an institution established for the fulfilment of a sacred trust . . . before the achievement of its *purpose*'[4] and the philosophy that '[i]t would have been contrary to the *overriding purpose* of the mandates system to assume that difficulties in the way of the replacement of one régime by another designed to improve international supervision should have been permitted to bring about, on the dissolution of the League, a complete disappearance of international supervision'.[5] Implicit in the finding that the mandates system contained an implied right of revocation is the acknowledgment of the ultimate purpose of the system, the

[96] 1971 ICJ Reports 28. In this respect the court endorses its 1950 finding: 1950 ICJ Reports 131.
[97] Ibid 28, 30.   [98] Ibid 31.   [99] loc cit.   [1] loc cit.
[2] See in particular the separate opinions of Judges Ammoun ibid 72, Nervo ibid 112, De Castro ibid 183–4 and Dillard ibid 157. *Sed contra*, the positivist approach of Judge Fitzmaurice ibid 220–4.
[3] *International Status of South-West Africa* 1950 ICJ Reports 128 at 136–7. See too Sir Hersch Lauterpacht *The Development of International Law by the International Court* (1958) 280.
[4] 1971 ICJ Reports 32. Italics added.   [5] Ibid 33. Italics added.

well-being and development of the peoples under international supervision and their right to self-determination and independence. The President of the Court, Sir Muhammad Zafrulla Khan, makes this clear in his declaration appended to the court's opinion, in which he rejects the applicability of the unanimity rule on the ground that this would have defeated 'the declared purpose of the mandates system'.[6] In passing, one may add that the court's finding that there was an implied right of termination in accordance with the customary rules relating to breach of a treaty is not foreign to municipal systems of law. It is simply an adoption of the rule of statutory interpretation that the legislature is presumed not to intend to alter the existing law—a rule well known to our own law.[7]

The court's finding that resolution 276 is legally binding is premised on a teleological endeavour to give the maximum effect to the Charter at the expense of State sovereignty.[8] Although it is believed that this ruling oversteps the imperceptible line between permissible and impermissible judicial innovation,[9] it must be borne in mind that the court's finding that the Security Council has implied general powers to take binding decisions in the fulfilment of its primary object, the maintenance of international peace, is no more revolutionary than the decision of the court in 1949 in the *Reparations for Injuries Case,*[10] when it found that international personality of the United Nations and the right of the United Nations to sue for injury to an official were implied in the Charter.[11]

Finally, the hand of the teleological interpreter is discernible in the court's rejection of South Africa's main preliminary objection, that an abstention in the Security Council is tantamount to a veto. Here the court relies on the subsequent practice of States in the Security Council as a guide to the interpretation of article 27(3).[13] But this practice is invoked not to prove the *original* intention of the signatories, which the formalists insist is the only purpose for which subsequent practice can be used,[14] but to show the *contemporary* expectation of parties,[15] the use to which it is put by teleologists.[16]

---

[6] Ibid 60–1. See too Judge De Castro ibid 202–3, 206.

[7] L C Steyn *Die Uitleg van Wette* 3 ed (1963) 96; H R Hahlo and Ellison Kahn *The South African Legal System and its Background* (1968) 202.

[8] Cf the statement of Judge Gros that this interpretation constitutes a modification of the principles of the Charter which could convert the Security Council into a world government: 1971 ICJ Reports 340–1.

[9] See on this subject the helpful comment by Judge Tanaka in the 1966 *South West Africa Cases:* 1966 ICJ Reports 277.

[10] 1949 ICJ Reports 174.   [11] Ibid 179, 182.

[13] 1971 ICJ Reports 22. The court also sees this practice as evidence of a new customary rule modifying the Charter.

[14] Separate opinion of Sir Percy Spender in *Certain Expenses of the United Nations* 1962 ICJ Reports 151 at 189–92. Gordon op cit 826–7.

[15] This is clear from the separate opinion of Judge Dillard, 1971 ICJ Reports 153–4.

[16] Gordon op cit 827–32.

South African lawyers not only find the court's approach deplorable; they find it impermissible and perhaps even 'illegal'.[17] The reason for this, it is suggested, is the devotion of the South African legal profession to positivist formalism. The writer has already shown the extent to which positivism permeates the domestic legal scene.[18] It is believed that the South African attitude towards international law and to the International Court is simply a reflection of this domestic attitude. International law is seen as a static [19] body of rules between States to which they have consented.[20] The principle of non-intervention remains the immutable corner-stone of the international legal order and overrides the whole Charter.[21] And, as in domestic law, the rigid distinction between law and morals, and law and politics, must be maintained. This approach manifests itself in the opposition to the creation of new rules of customary law by general consensus rather than consent in the political organs of the United Nations [22] and in the refusal to accept the human rights provisions in the Charter as legally binding.[23] Moreover, the International Court of Justice is required to adopt the same narrow approach to the judicial function as that taken by South African and British courts.[24] The court is expected to interpret all treaties (including the Charter) restrictively in the interests of State sovereignty, to refrain from applying teleological methods of interpretation to all treaties (including those of a constitutive and humanitarian nature), to apply the principle of contemporaneity, and to invoke the subsequent practice of parties to a treaty as a guide to the original common intent of the signatories only.[26] Consequently it is small wonder that Sir Gerald Fitzmaurice's dissenting opinion of 1971 is hailed as the only correct statement of the law [27] and his more

[17] See for example A C Cilliers 'Die Suidwes-Afrika-saak en die Volkereg' (1971) 34 THR-HR 25 at 42–3 and *Whither the International Court?* (University of Port Elizabeth, inaugural address D1) 4, 8, 18.

[18] 'The Judicial Process, Positivism and Civil Liberty' (1971) 88 *SALJ* 181.

[19] See Wolfgang Friedmann's description of the positivists' attitude in this respect: *The Changing Structure of International Law* (1964) 76–7.

[20] This approach is evident in South Africa's arguments before the court in 1966: ICJ Pleadings, South-West Africa, vol. 9, 629–36, 653–4.

[21] See the statement to this effect by Mr B Fourie in the Security Council: SCOR, 15th Year (1960) 851st Mtg § 46.

[22] 1966 ICJ Pleadings, South West Africa, vol 9, 653–4, vol 10, 40, and the separate opinion of Mr Justice Van Wyk in the 1966 *South West Africa Cases* 1966 ICJ Reports 169–70.

[23] See the doubts expressed in this respect in 1966 ICJ Pleadings, South West Africa, vol 10, 60–6.

[24] Ibid, vol 9, 634–5. Mr Justice J T van Wyk 'The International Court of Justice at the Cross-Roads' 1967 *Acta Juridica* 201 at 204. For a discussion of the British attitude, see Higgins op cit.

[26] For an exposition of South Africa's approach to treaty interpretation, see South Africa's written submission to the court in 1971 (vol 1, 10–43) and the oral submission made by Mr D P de Villiers SC in 1962 (ICJ Pleadings, South West Africa, vol 7, 37–64).

[27] See the statements by Mr Vorster (*Rand Daily Mail* 22 June 1971) and Mr Justice Van Wyk (address to students at the University of Cape Town on 17 August 1971).

extravagant condemnations of the court [28] accepted as gospel truth.
However much the South African Government and South African
lawyers may dislike teleological and sociological methods of reasoning,
they are as much part of the jurisprudential fabric of the international
legal order as are the tenets of positivism. The teleological method has
been employed by the International Court in all its previous decisions
on South-West Africa [29] except the one of 1966.[30] The circumstances of
that decision were, however, exceptional and the positivist majority of
that year was not the product of a swing towards legal formalism, but
the result of the death (Judge Badawi), illness (Judge Bustamante) and
recusal (Judge Khan) of three teleologists. The dynamic, teleological
approach has been a regular feature of the court's advisory opinions
interpreting the United Nations Charter,[31] particularly the *Reparations for Injuries Case* [32] and the *Certain Expenses of the United Nations Case,*[33] and has been invoked frequently by judges with differing
legal and political backgrounds, including the British judge on the
court from 1955 to 1959, Sir Hersch Lauterpacht.[34] Indeed, it has even
been approved in its more moderate form by those two high-priests of
positivism, Sir Gerald Fitzmaurice [35] and Sir Percy Spender.[36] As Edward Gordon comments in his 1965 study of the court's methods of interpreting constitutive treaties,

> [t]eleological consistency may be expected as a norm for judges
> whose fondness for social justice exceeds their fondness for legal

[28] 1971 ICJ Reports 220, 223, 251–2, 257, 263.

[29] *International Status of South-West Africa* 1950 ICJ Reports 128 at 136–7.
(See further on the role played by the principle of effectiveness in this opin-
ion, Sir Hersch Lauterpacht *The Development of International Law by the
International Court* 280.) *South-West Africa, Voting Procedure* 1955 ICJ Re-
ports 67 at 99, 104–5 (separate opinion of Sir Hersch Lauterpacht). *Admissi-
bility of Hearings of Petitioners by Committee on South-West Africa* 1956
ICJ Reports 22, 28, 32 (majority), 44–6, 50, 55–6 (separate opinion of Sir
Hersch Lauterpacht). *South West Africa Cases, Preliminary Objections* 1962
ICJ Reports 318 at 329 and 336.

[30] *South West Africa Cases, Second Phase* 1966 ICJ Reports 6 at 48. For
detailed comments on the methods of interpretation employed in 1966, see
C J R Dugard 'The South-West Africa Cases, Second Phase, 1966'
(1966) 83 *SALJ* 429 at 447; Richard A Falk 'The South West Africa Cases:
An Appraisal' (1967) 21 *International Organization* 1 at 14; Wolfgang G Friedmann 'The Jurisprudential Implications of the South-West Africa Case'
(1967) 6 *Columbia Journal of Transnational Law* 1.

[31] Leo Gross 'The International Court of Justice and the United Nations'
(1967) 120 *Recueil des Cours* 312 at 370 and 385.

[32] 1949 ICJ Reports 174 at 179, 182. Gross op cit 392.

[33] 1962 ICJ Reports 151 at 168. Gross op cit 396–400.

[34] Sir Gerald Fitzmaurice 'Hersch Lauterpacht—The Scholar as Judge'
(1963) 39 *British Year Book of International Law* 133 at 158–64.

[35] In 1963 Sir Gerald wrote that '[i]n the case of general multilateral conventions of a sociological, welfare or humanitarian . . . character, there is
some room . . . for the application of certain specifically teleological criteria
of interpretation': ibid at 139.

[36] Separate opinion, *Certain Expenses of the United Nations* 1962 ICJ Reports 151 at 186.

neatness, but what may be surprising is that end-oriented interpretation has been accepted by all but a handful of judges.[37]

The legitimacy of teleological methods of interpretation has not been affected by the 1969 Vienna Convention on the Law of Treaties.[38] Article 31 of that convention expressly provides that 'a treaty shall be interpreted in good faith in accordance with the ordinary meaning to be given to the terms of the treaty in their context and *in the light of its object and purpose*'. Although the International Law Commission, in compiling the draft of this treaty, expressed itself strongly against *extreme* methods of teleological interpretation,[39] it is clear from its endorsement of purpose-oriented interpretation in article 31 that it was not opposed to more moderate forms of teleological interpretation.[40] In any event, it is doubtful whether the Vienna Convention is intended to cover constitutive and humanitarian treaties, where special rules of interpretation apply designed to adapt the letter of the treaty to circumstances of the time and contemporary expectations.[41] It would be a sad day for international adjudication if the International Court were to model itself on the Privy Council [42] and the present South African Appellate Division, and treat great conventions on the future of which mankind depends as if they were ordinary treaties. The interpretative method employed by the United States Supreme Court is the better domestic model in this rapidly changing world.[43]

Finally on this subject, it must be recalled that rules of interpretation designed to give the maximum effect to the object and purpose of a statute are well known to our own law,[44] while the teleological philosophy appears to have motivated the Appellate Division in the two

---

[37] op cit at 815.

[38] Cf the argument to this effect in South Africa's written submissions, vol 1, 17.

[39] See the commentary of the International Law Commission on articles 27 and 28 of the Draft Articles on the Law of Treaties in (1967) 61 *American Journal of International Law* 350. See too Shabtai Rosenne 'Interpretation of Treaties in the Restatement and the International Law Commission's Draft Articles: A Comparison' (1966) 5 *Columbia Journal of Transnational Law* 205 at 221.

[40] See the commentary of the International Law Commission in (1967) 61 *American Journal of International Law* 351–2.

[41] See the comments of Judge De Castro 1971 ICJ Reports 184. Sir Gerald Fitzmaurice also recognizes the need for a different approach to constitutive treaties: 'Judicial Innovation—Its Uses and its Perils' in *Cambridge Essays in International Law* (1965) 24.

[42] The Privy Council has frequently been criticized for applying the same rules of statutory interpretation to Constitutions as it does to ordinary statutes: see for example E McWhinney *Judicial Review in the English-Speaking World* (1956) 16, 28–30; Louis L Jaffe *English and American Judges as Lawmakers* (1969) 25–7.

[43] C Wilfred Jenks *The Prospects of International Adjudication* (1964) 461.

[44] L C Steyn *Uitleg van Wette* 3 ed (1963) 115–20; H R Hahlo and Ellison Kahn *The South African Legal System and its Background* (1968) 210–11.

historic *Harris* cases [45] and Mr. Justice Schreiner in his laudable dissent in the *Collins* case.[46]

5. *The Security Council Accepts the Opinion*

On 27 September the Security Council met to consider "the Situation in Namibia" in the wake of the Court's Opinion. The debate was opened by the President of the Organization of African Unity, Moktar Ould Daddah of Mauritania, who called upon the Great Powers to support mandatory sanctions against South Africa under Chapter VII of the United Nations Charter to compel South Africa to withdraw its administration from Namibia. South Africa, invited to attend the session of the Council by special leave, was represented by its Minister of Foreign Affairs, Hilgard Muller, who in condemning the 1971 Advisory Opinion told the Council that [n]

the fundamental issue was whether there was any provision of the Charter under which the General Assembly could have terminated South Africa's right of administration. Article 10 of the Charter said: "The General Assembly may discuss any questions or any matters within the scope of the present Charter . . . and . . . may make recommendations . . . on any such question or matters."

When the question of the Assembly's powers was asked of the International Court, however, the Court did not even attempt to answer. It evaded the issue and said: ". . . It would not be correct to assume that, because the General Assembly is in principle vested with recommendatory powers, it is debarred from adopting, in specific cases within the framework of its competence, resolutions which make determinations or have operative design."

That was pure question-begging; for the question the Court was called upon to answer was precisely whether the Assembly's purported revocation of South Africa's Mandate was within the framework of its competence. If a provision of the Charter did confer the power claimed by the Assembly, then why had the International Court not indicated what that provision was?

If the Court's findings were unreasoned and unconvincing in regard to action taken by the General Assembly, they were even more so in regard to that taken by the Security Council. The Court accepted the interpretation that when the Council adopted its relevant resolutions, it was acting for the maintenance of international peace and security. The evidence, however, was crystal clear that the Council had not acted for that purpose but for a completely different one: namely, to

---

[n] *UN Monthly Chronicle,* 1971, October, pp. 35–36.

[45] *Harris* v *Minister of the Interior* 1952 (2) SA 428 (AD) and *Minister of the Interior* v *Harris* 1952 (4) SA 769 (AD).

[46] *Collins* v *Minister of the Interior* 1957 (1) SA 552 (AD) at 571–81.

secure as an end in itself the removal of South Africa from South West Africa so that the United Nations could take over the Territory and bring about its almost immediate independence as a single political entity—regardless of the consequences.

The implications, which flowed from the Court's attempt to attribute to the General Assembly and the Security Council implied powers which they were never intended to have under the Charter, were enormous in their scope. It would follow from the Court Opinion that, "within the framework of its competence", whatever that may mean, the Assembly would not be able to abrogate or alter territorial rights. The power of the Security Council would, according to the Court's interpretation, be still more drastic. No longer would it be restricted to acting in situations which constituted "a threat to the peace" or which were "likely to endanger" the peace—it would be sufficient that in the Council's view a situation might lead to a breach of the peace.

Another disturbing feature of the Court's Opinion was its treatment of its previous Opinions and Judgments. It relied heavily on those of its previous pronouncements adverse to South Africa's contentions while it simply ignored or brushed aside those which substantiated them. However, the most extraordinary aspect was that the Court, having decided not to go into the factual issues, nevertheless made findings thereon. It went out of its way to censure South Africa's policies in the Territory. To crown it all, it did that after refusing to hear detailed evidence, or to co-operate with South Africa in the holding of a plebiscite, which South Africa had offered. The purpose of the Court's censure was clearly political rather than legal, and emphasized the basically political nature of the Opinion.

After several adjournments on 20 October 1971, the Security Council, by thirteen votes to none with two abstentions, adopted Resolution 301 in which it accepted the Court's Advisory Opinion.

The Security Council,

Reaffirming the inalienable right of the people of Namibia to freedom and independence as recognized in General Assembly resolution 1514 (XV) of 14 December 1960,

Recognizing that the United Nations has direct responsibility for Namibia following the adoption of General Assembly resolution 2145 (XXI), and that States should conduct any relations with or involving Namibia in a, manner consistent with that responsibility,

Reaffirming its resolutions 264 (1969) of 20 March 1969, 276 (1970) of 30 January 1970 and 283 (1970) of 29 July 1970,

Recalling its resolution 284 (1970) of 29 July 1970 requesting the International Court of Justice for an advisory opinion on the question: "What are the legal consequences for States of the continuing presence of South Africa in Namibia notwithstanding Security Council resolution 276 (1970)?",

Gravely concerned at the refusal of the Government of South Africa to comply with the resolutions of the Security Council pertaining to Namibia,

Recalling its resolution 282 (1970) of 23 July 1970 on the arms embargo against the Government of South Africa and stressing the significance of that resolution with regard to the Territory of Namibia,

Recognizing the legitimacy of the movement of the people of Namibia against the illegal occupation of their Territory by the South African authorities and their right to self-determination and independence,

Taking note of the statements by the delegation of the Organization of African Unity led by the President of Mauritania, in his capacity as current Chairman of the OAU Assembly of Heads of State and Government,

Noting further the statement by the President of the United Nations Council for Namibia,

Having heard the statements by the delegation of the Government of South Africa,

Having considered the report of the *Ad Hoc* Sub-Committee on Namibia (S/10330),

1. *Reaffirms* that the Territory of Namibia is the direct responsibility of the United Nations and that this responsibility includes the obligation to support and promote the rights of the people of Namibia in accordance with General Assembly resolution 1514 (XV);

2. *Reaffirms* the national unity and territorial integrity of Namibia;

3. *Condemns* all moves by the Government of South Africa designed to destroy that unity and territorial integrity, such as the establishment of Bantustans;

4. *Declares* that South Africa's continued illegal presence in Namibia constitutes an internationally wrongful act and a breach of international obligations and that South Africa remains accountable to the international community for any violations of its international obligations or the rights of the people of the Territory of Namibia;

5. *Takes note* with appreciation of the advisory opinion of the International Court of Justice of 21 June 1971;

6. *Agrees with* the Court's opinion expressed in paragraph 133 of the advisory opinion:

(1) that, the continued presence of South Africa in Namibia being illegal, South Africa is under obligation to withdraw its administration from Namibia immediately and thus put an end to its occupation of the Territory;

(2) that States Members of the United Nations are under obligation to recognize the illegality of South Africa's presence in Namibia and the invalidity of its acts on behalf of or concerning Namibia, and to refrain from any acts and in particular any dealing with the Government of South Africa implying recognition of the legality of, or lending support or assistance to, such presence and administration;

(3) that it is incumbent upon States which are not Members of the United Nations to give assistance, within the scope of subparagraph (2) above, in the action which has been taken by the United Nations with regard to Namibia.

7. *Declares* that all matters affecting the rights of the people of Namibia are of immediate concern to all Members of the United Nations and as a result the latter should take this into account in their dealings with the Government of South Africa, in particular in any dealings implying recognition of the legality of or lending support or assistance to such illegal presence and administration;

8. *Calls once again* on South Africa to withdraw from the Territory of Namibia;

9. *Declares* that any further refusal of the South African Government to withdraw from Namibia could create conditions detrimental to the maintenance of peace and security in the region;

10. *Reaffirms* the provisions of resolution 283 (1970), in particular paragraphs 1 to 8 and 11;

11. *Calls upon* all States in discharge of their responsibilities towards the people of Namibia and subject to the exceptions set forth in paragraphs 122 and 125 of the advisory opinion of 21 June 1971:

(a) To abstain from entering into treaty relations with South Africa in all cases in which the Government of South Africa purports to act on behalf of or concerning Namibia;

(b) To abstain from invoking or applying those treaties or provisions of treaties concluded by South Africa on behalf of or concerning Namibia which involve active intergovernmental co-operation;

(c) To review their bilateral treaties with South Africa in order to ensure that they are not inconsistent with paragraphs 5 and 6 above;

(d) To abstain from sending diplomatic or special missions to South Africa that includes the Territory of Namibia in their jurisdiction;

(e) To abstain from sending consular agents to Namibia and withdraw any such agents already there;

(f) To abstain from entering into economic and other forms of relationship or dealings with South Africa on behalf of or concerning Namibia which may entrench its authority over the Territory;

12. *Declares* that franchises, rights, titles or contracts relating to Namibia granted to individuals or companies by South Africa after the adoption of General Assembly resolution 2145 (XXI) are not subject to protection or espousal by their States against claims of a future lawful Government of Namibia;

13. *Requests* the *Ad Hoc* Sub-Committee on Namibia to continue to carry out the tasks entrusted to it by paragraphs 14 and 15 of resolution 283 (1970) and, in particular, taking into account the need to provide for the effective protection of Namibian interests at the international level, to study appropriate measures for the fulfilment of the responsibility of the United Nations towards Namibia;

14. *Requests* the *Ad Hoc* Sub-Committee on Namibia to review all treaties and agreements which are contrary to the provisions of the present resolution in order to ascertain whether States have entered

into agreements which recognize South Africa's authority over Namibia, and to report periodically thereon;

15. *Calls upon* all States to support and promote the rights of the people of Namibia and to this end to implement fully the provisions of the present resolution;

16. *Requests* the Secretary-General to report periodically on the implementation of the provisions of the present resolution.

The United Kingdom and France, doubtlessly encouraged by the dissents of their national judges in the 1971 proceedings, were the two abstainers.[o] Resort to the Court for legal backing of its action on Namibia therefore failed to change the attitude of these two States towards the legality of the revocation of the Mandate.

6. British Objections to the Court's Opinion Examined

One of the British Government's main objections to the Court's Opinion was that it conferred wide powers on the Security Council which, it was contended, had no basis in the Charter. In the debate in the Security Council preceding the adoption of Resolution 301 the British delegate, Sir Colin Crowe, criticized the finding of the Court that the Security Council resolutions on Namibia were "decisions" binding upon all member States of the United Nations under Article 25 of the Charter. He declared that the Security Council was only competent to take binding decisions when it had found the situation to constitute a threat to international peace within the meaning of Article 39—which had not been done in the case of the resolutions on Namibia.[p] The correctness of this argument is disputed by the British jurist, Dr. Rosalyn Higgins.[q]

WHAT SECURITY COUNCIL RESOLUTIONS ARE BINDING UNDER ARTICLE 25 OF THE CHARTER?

Article 25 stipulates that "Members of the United Nations agree to accept and carry out the decisions of the Security Council in accordance

[o] Although he rejected the Court's Advisory Opinion, the French delegate argued that South Africa was under an obligation to negotiate in good faith with the United Nations for the establishment of an international regime: *UN Monthly Chronicle,* November, 1971, p. 14. The British delegate explained that his Government would abstain on the grounds that it was unable to accept the Court's Opinion and the validity of Resolution 2145(XXI): ibid., p. 19.
[p] S/PV 1589, p. 26.
[q] "The Advisory Opinion on Namibia: Which United Nations Resolutions Are Binding under Article 25 of the Charter?" (1972) 21 *International and Comparative Law Quarterly* 270 at 275–86.

with the present Charter." Article 25 comes within Chapter V broadly entitled "The Security Council," which deals with the composition, functions and powers, voting and procedural requirements of that organ. Chapter VI, which follows, is entitled "Pacific settlement of Disputes"; and Chapter VII is entitled "Action with respect to threats to the peace, breaches of the peace, and acts of aggression." On the face of it, the Security Council could take "decisions" within each of these Chapters which would be binding on UN members under the terms of Article 25. Is this in fact a correct reading of Article 25?—or is the term "decisions" there meant to mean only decisions under Chapter VII pursuant to a finding under Article 39 that there has been a threat to the peace, breach of the peace, or act of aggression?

The issue arose in the context of the *Namibia Case* because, though the Chapter under which the relevant Security Council resolutions fell was not clearly designated, there is reason to suppose that they were not Chapter VII decisions. Yet the International Court found that:

> the decisions made by the Security Council in paragraphs 2 and 5 of resolution 276 (1970), as related to paragraph 3 of resolution 264 (1969) and paragraph 5 of resolution 269 (1969), were adopted in conformity with the purposes and principles of the Charter and in accordance with its Articles 24 and 25. The decisions are consequently binding on all States Members of the United Nations which are thus under obligation to accept and carry them out.[17]

There seems to have been considerable confusion in the minds of UN delegations as to under which Charter provisions these resolutions were passed. Mr. Castrén, making the oral presentation on behalf of the Finnish Government agreed that the Security Council had not intended to act within the framework of Chapter VII of the Charter. There was as yet no "threat to the peace or act of aggression"—even though in certain speeches views to the contrary had been expressed. However, Mr. Castrén found the wording of Articles 33 and 34 clearly applicable, that is to say, it was a situation the prolongation of which was "likely to endanger the maintenance of international peace and security." He therefore believed that: "the legal foundation for Security Council resolution 276 may be sought in the powers conferred upon the Council in paragraph 1 of Article 36." [18] But Article 36 (1), it may be noted, allows the Security Council to *recommend* appropriate procedures or methods of adjustment in respect of a situation or dispute,[19] the continuance of which was likely to endanger international peace and security. Mr. Castrén nonetheless stated that Article 25 of the

---

[17] [1971] I.C.J.Rep. 53. Of these resolutions, SC resolution 269 (1969) had specifically invoked Art. 25 of the Charter.

[18] I.C.J. *Namibia Case*, C.R. 71/2 (translation from French) p. 20.

[19] South Africa had contended that this was indeed a "dispute" to which she was a party, and that the Court should have declined to give an Opinion thereon. Castrén supported the Secretary General's view, which was later confirmed by the Court, that this was a "situation."

Charter applied (though he also relied on the proposition—to which we shall later return—that the Security Council resolutions found an additional basis under Article 24 of the Charter).

Only two oral statements appeared to suggest that the relevant resolutions did in fact fall within Chapter VII. The representative of Pakistan somewhat unconvincingly contended that the designation in resolution 264 of South Africa's presence in Namibia as "an aggressive encroachment on the authority of the United Nations" was tantamount to a finding of an act of aggression. Therefore, he suggested, Articles 39, 40 and 42 came into play.[21] Mr. C. A. Stavropoulos, appearing on behalf of the Secretary General, relied primarily on Article 24 as the legal basis for the resolutions, but cast his net wide in asserting that "The action which the Security Council took finds full constitutional justification in Chapters VI and VII and also in Chapter V." [22] But there is no real internal evidence that the resolutions were regarded as falling within Chapter VII: they all stopped short of a finding of a threat to the peace, breach of the peace or act of aggression under Article 39. Certain governments took the view that the language of the resolutions indicated not only that they were not Chapter VII resolutions, but that in any event they were intended to be mere recommendations. This point was particularly made by the Government of France in its written statement,[23] where the Chapter VII language of the Rhodesia resolutions was contrasted with the recommendatory language of the Namibia resolutions. The Secretary General, *per contra,* while conceding that the verb "to decide" had only been used once in the resolutions on an operative matter, claimed that a series of equivalent terms had been used. Resolutions 276 (1970) and 283 (1970) had referred to *decisions* taken by the Security Council. The Finnish representative advanced the view that the resolutions contained provisions of different kinds, some intended to be recommendatory, and some intended to be decisions.[24]

If the resolutions were not in fact taken under Chapter VII, could they still be "decisions" binding upon the members under Article 25? In a statement that has important implications considerably beyond the confines of the *Namibia Case,* the representative of the United Kingdom said:

[21] Oral Statements [1971] I.C.J.Rep. C.R. 5 at 47.

[22] Oral Statements [1971] I.C.J.Rep. C.R. 71/1 at 54.

[23] Written Statements [1971] I.C.J.Rep. I 16–21.

[24] Mr. Stavropoulos, on behalf of the Secretary General, gave an extraordinary reply to this. Noting that Southern Rhodesia was in law a dependency of the United Kingdom, he commented that a determination of a threat to the peace, breach of the peace, or act of aggression was necessary in order to take action "in regard to a territory which is under the sovereignty of a State Member of the United Nations without the consent of that State" (C.R. 71/1, p. 55). But no action has been taken in Rhodesia without the consent of the United Kingdom, because, of course, the United Kingdom has had the veto. The United Nations has taken only that action to which United Kingdom consent could be secured.

My Government considers that the Security Council can take decisions generally binding on Member States only when the Security Council has made a determination under Article 39. . . . Only in these circumstances are the decisions binding under Article 25.[25]

Is this in fact a correct reading of the Charter? Leaving aside for the moment the position of Article 24 in relation to Article 25, can decisions be taken under Chapter VI which bind UN members?

The Provisions of the Charter

On the face of it, a reading of the Charter itself does not necessarily lead to the conclusion of the United Kingdom. There is nothing in the titles of Chapters VI and VII which leads one to believe that they should be read, respectively, as "Recommendations for the settlement of disputes" and "Decisions with respect to a breakdown of peace." Article 25 stands separately from both Chapter VI and Chapter VII. Its provision that UN members are bound by decisions of the Security Council flows from Article 24(1) by which members confer on the Security Council primary responsibility for the maintenance of international peace and security. In paragraph 2 of Article 24 it is stated that the specific powers granted to the Security Council for the discharge of these duties are laid down in Chapters VI, VII, VIII and XII. If Article 25 applied only to Chapter VII, one might perhaps have expected to see it located in that chapter. Moreover, there is some strength to the view that Articles 48 and 49 achieve a binding effect for Chapter VII decisions; and that if Article 25 refers to Chapter VII alone, then it is superfluous.

On the other hand, it is less easy to see in the wording of Chapter VI any opportunities for "decision." Article 33(2) provides that the Security Council may "call upon" parties to settle their dispute by certain peaceful means listed in Article 33 (1). This phrase is stronger than the phrase "recommend" used in Articles 36 or 37. However, the Council is in effect requiring the parties to note an obligation which they have already accepted under Article 33(1).[26] Possibly Articles 34 and 36 may allow of decisions. These possibilities are referred to above. A further argument merits consideration: why, it may be asked, if decisions are possible under Chapter VI do UN members not attempt always to pass substantive resolutions on disputes within Chapter VI, so that a party to the dispute will be obliged to abstain from voting?[28] Would not this interpretation, the argument runs, counter-

[25] Per Sir Colin Crowe, S/PV. 1589, p. 26.
[26] Goodrich, Hambro and Simons, Charter of the United Nations, 3rd rev. ed., p. 209. Art. 33 (1) requires parties to any dispute, the continuance of which is likely to endanger the maintenance of international peace and security, shall, first of all, seek a solution by negotiation, enquiry, mediation, conciliation, arbitration, judicial settlement, resort to regional agencies or arrangements, or other peaceful means of their own choice."
[28] Art. 27 (3) provides that "in decisions under Chapter VI, and under paragraph 3 of Article 52, a party to dispute shall abstain from voting."

act the veto? The reply would seem to lie in the fact that it is in reality comparatively rare for UN members to identify themselves as parties to a dispute, and voluntarily to abstain from voting.[29] The protection of Article 27(3) in relation to Chapter VI is more apparent than real.

The Travaux Préparatoires

These are surprisingly opaque on the point at issue, providing no direct guidance on whether Article 25 was intended to apply to Chapter VI as well as Chapter VII. When the Co-ordination Committee prepared the final draft of Article 25, it changed the wording "so as to make it clear that members would only be obliged to carry out those Council decisions that are legally mandatory," [30]—a clarification that is more circular than helpful. The main controversy, however, concerned whether the obligation to carry out decisions of the Security Council *was limited to decisions taken under Chapters VI, VII and VIII.* A Belgian proposal to limit thus the application of Article 25 was defeated.[31] By implication, therefore, the *travaux* provide some evidence that Article 25 was not intended to be limited to Chapter VII, or inapplicable to Chapter VI.

Subsequent Practice

Practice bearing directly and clearly upon this point is scant. Again, much of the controversy has revolved around whether the Security Council could adopt binding decisions *solely* within the framework of Chapters VI, VII and VIII. The question has also arisen as to whether only enforcement measures for maintaining or restoring peace can be decisions under Article 25, or whether directions for the substantive settlement of a dispute may also be binding. Between 1949 and 1958 the Council took at least two clear decisions bearing on the application of Article 25 to the provisions of Chapter VI.[32] In the course of consideration of the Corfu Channel incidents in 1947, the United Kingdom submitted a draft resolution recommending that the dispute be referred to the International Court of Justice. Both before and after the adoption of this resolution the question arose as to whether Article 25 applied to a recommendation under Article 36.[33] The United King-

[29] See Higgins, "The Place of International Law in the Settlement of Disputes by the UN Security Council" (1970) 64 A.J.I.L. 2–3.
[30] Russell and Muther, *A History of the United Nations Charter,* p. 665.
[31] UNCIO Docs., Committee 111/11, May 25, 1945, Vol. XI, p. 393.
[32] On these questions, see J. Casteñeda, *Legal Effects of United Nations Resolutions,* Chap. 3.
[33] Art. 36 (1) provides "The Security Council may, at any stage of a dispute of the nature referred to in Art. 33 or of a situation of like nature, recommend appropriate procedures or methods of adjustment." Art. 36 (3) provides "In making recommendations under this Article the Security Council should also take into consideration that legal disputes should as a general rule be referred by the parties to the International Court of Justice. . . ."

dom (taking a position not apparently on all fours with that pronounced by Sir Colin Crowe in respect of Namibia) contended that the Court had jurisdiction in the case under Article 36(1) of its Statute which referred to "all matters . . . provided for in the Charter." The United Kingdom claimed that its dispute with Albania was such a matter since the Security Council resolution adopted under Article 36 of the Charter was binding upon the parties by virtue of Albania's acceptance of all the obligations of a Member State and in conformity with Article 25. The degree to which the United Kingdom statement on Namibia represents a change in its views on the scope of Article 25 is worth emphasising. In his statement to the Court in the *Corfu Channel Case* Sir Hartley Shawcross had asserted that recommendations "under Chapter VI of the Charter, relating to *methods* of settling disputes which endanger peace, are binding." As for the view that Article 25 applies only to Chapter VII of the Charter:

> that position, in my submission, is completely untenable. [Even] if one were to disregard . . . the preparatory work and the commentaries, one could not find in the Charter itself a shred of support for the view that Article 25 is limited in its application to Chapter VII of the Charter.[34]

Albania insisted, *per contra,* that Article 25 could only apply to decisions of the Council taken under Chapter VII; and that therefore the Security Council resolution could not provide for an indirect form of compulsory jurisdiction. Nevertheless, Albania then stated that it accepted "the jurisdiction of the Court for this case." In its judgment of March 25, 1948, the Court established its jurisdiction on the basis of Albania's voluntary acceptance. Although there was thus no need to pronounce on the United Kingdom arguments, seven judges in a separate opinion stated that they could not accept that a recommendation under Article 36(3) of the Charter could involve the compulsory jurisdiction of the Court.[35]

During 1947 the Security Council was also concerned with the Greek frontier incidents question. The United States proposed the establishment of a commission of investigation and good offices. Albania, Bulgaria and Yugoslavia, who were parties involved in the dispute, objected, stating that Chapter VI could not give rise to actions which were binding upon members. The United States, however, drew a distinction between conciliation and investigation. While conciliation might imply voluntary will on the part of those who oppose each other, Article 34 must be understood to give the Security Council the right to investigate a dispute, regardless of whether or not

[34] *Corfu Channel Case,* Prelim. Objections, Pleadings Vol. III, [1949] I.C.J.Rep. 72, 76–77.
[35] *Repertory of practice of United Nations Organs,* Vol. II, pp. 42–43; *Corfu Channel Case,* preliminary objections [1948] I.C.J.Rep. 15–32. For a distinction between this case and other examples of *forum prorogatum,* see Rosenne, *The Law and Practice of the International Court,* Vol. I, pp. 352–356.

the State being investigated approves. If the power to decide on an investigation under Article 34 were not a binding decision within Article 25, the peaceful settlement tasks of the United Nations would be frustrated.[36] The outcome was inconclusive, the United States draft vote failing to be adopted because of a Soviet veto.[37]

The binding or non-binding quality of decisions under Chaper VI had also arisen in the context of the Kashmir dispute when it was discussed in 1957. A Security Council resolution of March 30, 1951 (S/2017/rev.1) calling for, among other things, a plebiscite,[38] was rejected by India on the grounds that it was a mere recommendation under Chapter VI. Other Security Council members merely asserted that Security Council resolutions, validly concluded, were binding decisions upon the membership. The matter was never clearly resolved. India also complained that a draft resolution of February 15, 1957, urging demilitarisation failed to appreciate that resolutions under Chapter VI had no binding effect. No opposition was specifically voiced to India's view, and a resolution was adopted calling for a plebiscite and demilitarisation.[39]

This emerging consensus—if such it was—represents a change from early views of the relationship between Chapter VI and Article 25. Not only do the *travaux préparatoires* indicate that the uncertainty was solely as to whether the applicability of Article 25 was limited to Chapters VI, VII and VIII, but this perspective continued throughout the discussion of the *Trieste* case, to which we shall refer below. The representative of France, speaking in 1947, thought that if the Trieste question:

> has been brought before us under Chapter VI and, particularly, Chapter VII, we should be invested with extremely wide powers extending even to, these are the very words of Article 42, demonstrations and the use of force.[40]

Both the *travaux préparatoires* and the wording of the Charter lead one in the direction that the application of Article 25 is not limited to Chapter VII resolutions, excluding Chapter VI resolutions. The practice of the UN, in the early years at least, has been ambiguous on this point. It is difficult to discern from the discussions in the Council any clear consensus as to what amounts to a "decision" within the terms of Article 25. An argument can certainly be advanced that the applicability of Article 25 depends, quite simply, upon a contextual reading of whether a decision or a recommendation was intended. Clearly, some resolutions passed under Chapter VII are never intended to be binding. They are meant as mere recommendations—even if there has

---

[36] *Per* the representative of the U.S.A., SCOR 2nd yr. No. 51, 166th meeting, pp. 1525.
[37] SCOR 2nd year No. 66, 170 meeting, p. 1612.
[38] See Higgins, *United Nations Peacekeeping*, Vol. II Asia, pp. 376–377.
[39] S/3922, SCOR 12th yr. Suppl. Oct.–Dec., p. 21.
[40] SCOR (1947), 91st meeting, pp. 58–59.

been a finding of a threat to the peace, breach of the peace, or act of aggression under Article 39. Again, one has seen in UN practice examples of resolutions which carefully avoid using the phraseology of Article 39, but which call upon States to take measures of the kind that are enumerated in Article 41. The resolutions on the embargo of arms to South Africa are cases in point.[41] The binding or non-binding nature of those resolutions turns not upon whether they are to be regarded as "Chapter VI" or "Chapter VII" resolutions (they are in some ways a curious hybrid) but upon whether the parties intended them to be "decisions" or "recommendations." In that particular case, certain States made it clear that they did not regard the resolutions as binding, and other States did not protest at this interpretation. One is left with the view that in certain limited, and perhaps rare, cases a binding decision may be taken under Chapter VI (just as non-binding resolutions may be passed under Chapter VII). "Decisions" to investigate could perhaps have this operative effect, though "recommendations" under Articles 36 or 37 would not.

The United Kingdom, in reaching the conclusion that the Security Council can only bind members when it has made a determination under Article 39, did not in its public statement deal with these considerations. Sir Colin Crowe made his statement in a political body— the Security Council—and avoided legal technicalities. At the same time, the United Kingdom Government had decided not to avail itself of the right, under Article 66 of the Court's Statute, to submit a written or oral presentation in the *Namibia Case*. It is therefore fair to say that there exists no published, closely reasoned analysis of the legal conclusions which it has reached on this case. But the British representative did indicate that his Government particularly had in mind another aspect of what we may term subsequent practice. Having stated, correctly, that the issue affects the whole working of the Security Council, he observed:

> I think it is fair to say that some of the arguments of the Court on the question of the force of Security Council decisions came as a surprise not only to my delegation, but to Members of the United Nations generally. Members of the Council have in the past formed their positions on draft resolutions on the clear understanding that the Council could take decisions binding on Member States generally only if there had been a determination under Article 39. If this is no longer accepted, the working basis which results from a clear understanding of the legal effects of what the Council does may be seriously prejudiced. As a practical matter therefore, it is surely in the interest of all of us that we should continue to operate on the understanding, well founded in the Charter, to which I have referred. Otherwise, yet a new source of uncertainty and potential disagreement will complicate the already difficult tasks which the Council faces.[42]

---

[41] Security Council resolutions 181 (1962), 182 (1963) and 191 (1964).
[42] S/PV 1589, pp. 26–27.

To this writer, the extent to which the "understanding" is "well founded in the Charter" is more open to debate than this statement allows.[43] But there is no doubt that Sir Colin is right to point to this practical understanding which in recent years has come to replace the early uncertain debates within the Security Council on this matter. This operational understanding is not of a character that finds its way into the *UN Repertories of Practice* (though it will be interesting to see if it finds mention when the latest supplements are published). It nonetheless exists. The United Kingdom, interestingly, is essentially adopting a teleological posture here, placing the main weight of its argument not on the letter of the Charter, or the *travaux*, but rather on the operational understanding which best allows the Security Council to carry out its business. A practice that perhaps had been regarded by some international lawyers as of rough and ready convenience— namely, that in the drafting of resolutions, Chapter VII resolutions are to be regarded as capable of binding, while Chapter VI resolutions are not—is now said to be endowed with the status of law. If one accepts the high importance of subsequent practice as a guide to interpreting international constitutions, then there is considerable strength in the United Kingdom assertion. If one looks to the major purposes of the United Nations Charter, an argument can be made that their achievement is enhanced by the common understanding that Article 25 operates in respect of Chapter VII but not Chapter VI. But much the same ends could be achieved by looking to see whether a resolution was intended as a recommendation or decision, and avoiding the somewhat artificial designation of resolutions which recommend Article 41 type measures as Chapter VI resolutions.

We therefore regard as preferable the fully contextual approach suggested by the Court. The Court said:

> It has been contended that Article 25 of the Charter applies only to enforcement measures adopted under Chapter VII of the Charter. It is not possible to find in the Charter any support for this view. Article 25 is not confined to decisions in regard to enforcement action but applies to "the decisions of the Security Council" adopted in accordance with the Charter. Moreover, that Article is placed, not in Chapter VII, but immediately after Article 24 in that part of the Charter which deals with the functions and powers of the Security Council . . . The language of a resolution of the Security Council should be carefully analysed before a conclusion can be made as to its binding effect. In view of the nature of the powers of Article 25,

---

[43] Goodrich, Hambro and Simons, *Charter of the United Nations. Commentary and Documents,* 3rd rev. ed., seem to support this view. They state "There is certainly room for argument whether there are any decisions the Security Council may take in the field of pacific settlement that are binding upon members," p. 209. *Cf.* Dugard, "The Opinion on South West Africa ('Namibia'): the teleologists triumph" (1971) 88 *South African Law Journal* 460 at 467, who believes the Court's view is "revolutionary" in so far as it asserts the application of Art. 25 outside of Chap. VII.

the question is to be determined in each case, having regard to the terms of the resolution to be interpreted, the discussions leading to it, the Charter provision invoked and, in general, all circumstances that might assist in determining the legal consequences of the resolution of the Security Council.[44]

This approach seems not unduly to endanger that operational agreement so greatly valued by the United Kingdom.

ARTICLE 24 AND THE OPERATION OF ARTICLE 25

The International Court of Justice found that the legal basis of Security Council resolution 276 (1970) was Article 24 of the Charter. The United Kingdom statement does not indicate whether it thought Article 24 applicable, nor in so many terms does it state that a decision under Article 24 could not be binding under Article 25. However, its broad pronouncement that the Council can only bind members when acting under Chapter VII after a finding under Article 39, must be taken to mean that neither Article 24 nor Chapter VI can be the basis of a binding resolution.

The great majority of the oral and written statements presented to the Court did not try to specify the legal basis of the resolutions (though that was, one would have thought, essential in order to establish the legal consequences for Member States). South Africa, however, examined this question in very considerable detail. South Africa asserted both that Article 25 did not apply to Chapter VI, and that, in any event, the resolutions had not been validly taken under Chapter VI. There had been, argued South Africa, no objective investigation that the situation was one the continuance of which was likely to endanger international peace and security. South Africa regarded an investigation under Article 34 a condition precedent to the operation of Chapter VI, in much the same way as it believed that a formal finding under Article 39 was a condition precedent to the operation of Chapter VII. The South African Government advanced detailed arguments to suggest that Article 24 of the Charter could not be an alternative basis. Article 24 provides:

> 1. In order to ensure prompt and effective action by the United Nations, its Members confer on the Security Council primary responsibility for the maintenance of international peace and security, and

---

[44] [1971] I.C.J.Rep. 52–53. *Cf.* the view of Judge Sir Gerald Fitzmaurice. He had asked the United States if UN members were obliged by customary international law to apply sanctions against a tortfeasor. The United States replied that there was no obligation under customary international law, but that it might be obliged to act if a finding under Art. 39 was followed by a directive under Arts. 41 or 42. Judge Fitzmaurice did not, in an otherwise immensely detailed dissenting opinion, address himself to the series of arguments concerning Art. 25 and Chap. VI. He contented himself with agreeing with the United States response in so far as it was intended to indicate that only decisions taken under Art. 39 could give rise to a legal duty to take specific measures. *Ibid. Dissenting Opinion,* pp. 297–298.

agree that in carrying out its duties under this responsibility the Security Council acts on their behalf.

2. In discharging these duties the Security Council shall act in accordance with the Purposes and Principles of the United Nations. The specific powers granted to the Security Council for the discharge of these duties are laid down in Chapters VI, VII, VIII and XII.

South Africa contended that Article 24 cannot be read to give the Security Council authority to act in situations which are not covered by the more detailed provisions of the other Chapters. The purpose of the Article was to emphasise the paramount importance of the "peace-keeping" function of the Security Council. It did not involve a hidden reserve of powers. The reference to the ensuing Chapters was by way of limitation upon the ways in which its duties were to be carried out —the Council can only act within the means of execution provided in Chapters VI, VII, VIII and XII.[45] The South African statement suggested that it was the achievement of political objectives not provided for in the Charter which had led nations to support the proposition that Article 24 provided a separate basis for action by the Security Council.[46]

This is not the place or occasion to recall all the arguments concerning the scope of Article 24 of the Charter. The issue arose sharply in the case of Trieste, and the arguments, and the case history, have been analysed elsewhere.[47] Under the Peace Treaty with Italy, various responsibilities were assigned to the Security Council with regard to the Free Territory of Trieste, and as a result, the Council of Foreign Ministers requested the Security Council to adopt the three instruments relating to the administration of the Free Territory and to accept the responsibilities devolving upon it under the same instruments. The Australian representative had queried whether the Security Council had the authority to accept these responsibilities. The Secretary General had provided a legal opinion which pointed to Article 24 of the Charter, and asserted that the powers of the Council thereunder are not restricted to the specific grants of authority contained in Chapters VI, VII, VIII and XII.[48] The *travaux préparatoires* also supported this view: all the delegations, speaking for and against the proposition that Members were only obliged to accept decisions made under the specific powers of Chapters VI, VII, VIII and XII, agreed in recognising that the authority of the Council was not restricted to such specific powers.[49]

The Court in the *Namibia Case* cited with approval the Secretary General's statement, made to the Council in respect of Trieste, that

---

[45] Written Statements, Vol. III, pp. 339–350.

[46] *Ibid.*, pp. 348–349. See also Oral Statement, C.R. 71/10.

[47] See particularly Schachter, "The Development of International Law through the Legal Opinions of the United Nations Secretariat" (1948) 25 B.Y.I.L. 91 at 96 *et seq.*

[48] SCOR 2nd yr., 91st meeting, Jan. 10, 1947.

[49] UNCIO Doc. 597, Committee III/1/30.

the Council was not tied by the specific powers mentioned, and that "The only limitations are the fundamental principles and purposes found in Chapter I of the Charter." [50] The Secretary General had also addressed himself to the question of whether action taken under Article 24 could bind members under Article 25. He answered in the affirmative. At San Francisco there had been rejected an amendment which would have bound States only by decisions taken under the specific powers of Chapters VI, VII, VIII and XII. "The rejection of this amendment is clear evidence that the obligation of the Members to carry out the decisions of the Security Council applies equally to decisions made under Article 24 and to the decisions made under the grant of specific powers." [51] In the ensuing vote, the Security Council, by a vote of 10 in favour and Australia abstaining, approved the three instruments on Trieste and formally accepted the responsibilities devolving upon it under them. The United Kingdom, with the Secretary General's legal advice before it, voted affirmatively. There is nothing in its statement on Namibia to clarify its present position on Article 24 and Article 25, or to relate it to the Trieste precedent.[52]

The Court, in dealing with the Security Council resolutions on Namibia, clearly regarded Chapters VI, VII, VIII and XII as *lex specialis* while Article 24 contained the *lex generalis*. Noting that Article 25 was placed not in Chapter VII, but next to Article 24, the Court asserted that resolutions validly adopted under Article 24 were binding on the membership as a whole.[53] This writer believes that a reading of the Charter, its *travaux* and the limited subsequent practice, testify to the correctness of this conclusion.[54]

7. The Caprivi Strip Incident [r]

The Caprivi Strip, a finger-like piece of territory stretching eastwards from the northern part of South West Africa with Bo-

---

[r] For an account of this incident, see *A Survey of Race Relations in South Africa*, 1971, pp. 96–97.

[50] [1971] I.C.J.Rep. 52.   [51] SCOR 2nd yr., 91st meeting at p. 45.

[52] It can be argued that the two situations are not comparable, as Trieste involved no question of sovereignty, still less of hostility by a sovereign State. In his statement to the Court the Secretary General's representative suggested that in the *Namibia Case*, too, South Africa had no sovereign title which could come between the Security Council and the assumption of powers under Art. 24, C.R. 71/1, p. 52. It is anyway difficult to see that Art. 24 does turn on consent. The issue arose in abortive form in the Palestine question, when further legal advice was given on the Council's ability to accept the General Assembly's Plan A/AC 21/13, Feb. 9, 1948.

[53] [1971] I.C.J.Rep. 54.

[54] Dugard interestingly rejects the Court's position on this, though he is in sympathy generally with the Opinion. He believes that the South African arguments on Arts. 24 and 25 are essentially correct, and that Security Council 276 is recommendatory only. He contends that South Africa's legal obligation to withdraw arises from the combined effect of resolution 2145 (XXI) and the subsequent Security Council resolutions. *Op. cit., supra,* at p. 468.

tswana to the south and Zambia to the north has become the centre of friction between African liberation movements and South African forces. As it forms part of South West Africa politically, the South African Government's legal title to the territory is as dubious as her title to the rest of South West Africa. Legally this has an important drawback. Those States which refuse to recognize the South African Government as the lawful, *de jure,* government of South West Africa can hardly accept any argument that South Africa is acting in lawful self-defence of South West Africa in repulsing guerilla forces, let alone in engaging in reprisal raids against guerilla bases on Zambian territory.

On 5 October 1971, at a National Party Congress, the Prime Minister of South Africa announced that two police vehicles operating in the Caprivi Strip had struck land mines and that one policeman had been killed and four wounded. He then went on to say that South Africa reserved the right to pursue guerilla forces wherever they might flee and that this was being done in this case. This statement was interpreted by the South African press to mean that South African police had crossed the border into Zambia. Later the Prime Minister repudiated this interpretation and denied any crossing into Zambia. The denial came too late, however, as the harm had already been done. Zambia made an official complaint to the Security Council alleging violation of her frontiers and sought a resolution condemning South Africa's violation of her sovereignty. In the absence of real evidence (as opposed to Prime Minister Vorster's ambiguous statement) that any violation of Zambian territory had occurred, the Security Council unanimously adopted a modified resolution which simply called upon South Africa to respect Zambian sovereignty and declared that if she failed to do so the Security Council would "meet again to examine the situation further." [8]

This incident, which occurred during the debate on the Court's Advisory Opinion, was most untimely. It served as a warning, however, of the kind of problems that are bound to occur as long as South Africa retains control over South West Africa.

8. South West African Response to the Opinion and the Ovambo Strike

The South African Government's proposal that the population of South West Africa be consulted in a plebiscite on whether they

---

[8] Resolution 300 of 12 October 1971.

would prefer South African administration to that of the United Nations strongly suggested that the Government was certain of an affirmative answer.[t] The response of the local population groups to the Advisory Opinion, however, suggests that the Government had gravely misjudged local opinion and that a plebiscite might have resulted in a "No" to the South African administration.

Predictably, the Herero (6.6 of the total population), who have consistently opposed South African administration, welcomed the Opinion.[u] The Rehoboth Basters (2.2 of the population) were equally pleased and appealed to the Security Council to implement the Court's decision.[v]

The most significant response, however, came from the Ovambo, the largest group in the territory (45.9 of the population), upon whose support the Government had clearly relied. Following rumours of dissatisfaction on the part of Ovambo students [w] with Chief Councillor Ushona Shiimi's rejection of the Court's Opinion, the leaders of two churches representing over half the population of South West Africa—including the Ovambo—condemned apartheid and appealed to the South African Government for a "separate and independent State" in South West Africa. In an open letter to Mr. Vorster, Bishop Leonard Auala of the Evangelical Lutheran Ovambo Kavango Church [x] and Pastor Paulus Gowaseb of the Evangelical Church in South West Africa [y] declared:

His Honour,

After the decision of the World Court at the Hague was made known on 21st June, 1971, several leaders and officials of our Lutheran Churches were individually approached by representatives of the authorities with a view to making known their views. This indicates to us that public institutions are interested in hearing the opinions of the Churches in this connection. Therefore we would like to make use of the opportunity of informing your Honour of the opinion of the Church Boards of the Evangelical Lutheran Church in SWA and the Evangelical Lutheran Ovambokavango Church which represents the majority of the indigenous population of South West Africa.

---

[t] Before the Advisory Opinion was delivered Mr. Justice Van Wyk stated that "it has been claimed by experts on South West Africa, that possibly 80% of the population might prefer South Africa's administration and all that it entails to that of the United Nations": above, n. d at p. 228.
[u] *The Star*, 6 July 1971.   [v] Ibid.
[w] *The Star*, Johannesburg, 13 August 1971. *Sunday Times*, Johannesburg, 22 August 1971.
[x] Membership estimated at 180,000.   [y] Membership estimated at 110,000.

We believe that South Africa in its attempts to develop South West Africa has failed to take cognizance of Human Rights as declared by U.N.O. in the year 1948, with respect to the non-white population. Allow us to put forward the following examples in this connection:

(1) The government maintains that by the race policy it implements in our country, it promotes and preserves the life and freedom of the population. But in fact the non-white population is continuously being slighted and intimidated in their daily lives. Our people are not free, and by the way they are treated they do not feel safe.

In this regard we wish to refer to Section 3 of Human Rights.

(2) We cannot do otherwise than regard South West Africa, with all its racial groups, as a unit. By the Group Areas Legislation the people are denied the right of free movement and accommodation within the borders of the country. This cannot be reconciled with Section 13 of the Human Rights.

(3) People are not free to express or publish their thoughts or opinions openly. Many experience humiliating espionage and intimidation which has as its goal that a public and accepted opinion must be expressed, but not one held at heart and of which they are convinced. How can sections 18 and 19 of the Human Rights be realised under such circumstances?

(4) The implementation of the policy of the government makes it impossible for the political parties of the indigenous people to work together in a really responsible and democratic manner to build the future of the whole of South West Africa. We believe that it is important in this connection that the use of voting rights should also be allowed to the non-white population.

(Sections 20 and 21 of the Human Rights.)

(5) Through the application of Job Reservation the right to a free choice of profession is hindered and this causes low remuneration and unemployment. There can be no doubt that the "contract" system breaks up a healthy family life because the prohibition of a person from living where he works, hinders the cohabitation of families. This conflicts with sections 23 and 25 of the Human Rights.

The Church Boards' urgent wish is that in terms of the declarations of the World Court and in co-operation with U.N.O. of which South Africa is a member, your government will seek a peaceful solution to the problems of our land and will see to it that Human Rights be put into operation and that South West Africa may become a self-sufficient and independent State.

With high esteem,

Bishop Dr. L. Auala
Chairman of the Church Board
of the Ev. Luth. Ovambokavango Church

Moderator Pastor P. Gowaseb
Chairman of the Church Board
of the Ev. Luth. Church in S.W.A.
(Rhenish Mission Church)

A few weeks later when Mr. Vorster visited Windhoek he took the unprecedented step of arranging a meeting with these two church leaders. According to reports the talks were conducted in a friendly atmosphere but ended in a deadlock.[z]

In December 1971 the Ovambo showed their opposition to the South African administration in more concrete form when 13,000 Ovambo labourers outside the homeland went on strike against labour conditions. The main source of grievance was the contract labour system, which regulated the employment of some 40,000 Ovambo in the southern sector or "police zone." In terms of this system an Ovambo employee entered into a contract for a fixed term (twelve or eighteen months in most cases) with a white employer in the southern sector through the agency of a recruiting body, the South West Africa Native Labour Association (SWANLA). While in the southern sector he was unable to change his employment, as breach of the contract constituted a criminal offence. At the expiry of his contract he was obliged to return to Ovamboland before seeking new employment. This seriously restricted the bargaining power of Ovambo workers, and wages were kept pitifully low. For instance, there was a minimum cash wage for experienced general workers of only R8.25 per month.

In December 1971 Ovambo workers downed tools in a number of industries and were immediately sent home to Ovamboland by the authorities. The strike, however, spread, and by the end of December some 13,000 Ovambo had been "repatriated" and white employers were compelled to rely on white schoolboys, who were paid a minimum wage of R109 per month!

In January 1972, following negotiations between the South African and the Ovambo Governments, SWANLA was abolished as a negotiator of labour contracts, and a new system was introduced. In terms of this the Ovambo Government accepts responsibility for establishing labour employment offices; Ovambo workers are permitted to enter into agreements with employers setting out the full terms of their labour contracts; and workers are given greater freedom to change their employment.[a]

After the conclusion of this agreement Ovambo workers started returning to employment in the southern sector, but the response was not altogether satisfactory from the point of view of the South

[z] *Rand Daily Mail,* 19 August 1971.
[a] *Rand Daily Mail,* 21 January 1972.

African Government. Moreover, there were sporadic acts of violence in the territory. Consequently, on 4 February the Government introduced regulations in Ovamboland which are modelled on the Transkeian emergency proclamations of 1960.[b] These prohibit unauthorized meetings of more than five persons, permit detention without trial, and impose severe restrictions on freedom of political expression.[c] Government spokesmen have vehemently denied that Ovamboland is in a state of emergency, but it is clear that the Government is deeply concerned about developments among what, until recently, were regarded as its most loyal supporters in South West Africa.

9. The Secretary-General's Visit to South Africa and Namibia

In February 1972 the Security Council held a special meeting on African problems in the Ethiopian capital of Addis Ababa at which it adopted two resolutions on Namibia. In Resolution 310 it reaffirmed its previous resolutions on Namibia, condemned "the recent repressive measures against the African labourers in Namibia," called upon the South African Government "to end immediately these repressive measures and to abolish any system of labour which may be in conflict with basic provisions of the Universal Declaration of Human Rights," and called upon "all States whose nationals and corporations are operating in Namibia . . . to use all available means to ensure that such nationals and corporations conform in their policies of hiring Namibian workers to the basic provisions of the Universal Declaration of Human Rights." Resolution 309 was more conciliatory in tone and authorized the new Secretary-General, Dr. Kurt Waldheim, to enter into discussions "with all parties concerned" on the future of South West Africa.
Resolution 309:

   The Security Council,

   Having examined further the question of Namibia, and without prejudice to other resolutions adopted by the Security Council on this matter,
   Recognizing the special responsibility and obligation of the United Nations towards the people and Territory of Namibia,

[b] Proclamations R400 of 1960 (*GGE* 6582 of 30 November 1960) and R413 of 1960 (*GGE* of 14 December 1960) introduced a state of emergency in the Transkei. Despite the subsequent development of this territory towards self-government the regulations have not yet been withdrawn.
[c] Proclamation R17 GG 3377 of 4 February 1972 (*Reg. Gaz.* 1568).

Reaffirming once again the inalienable and imprescriptible right of the people of Namibia to self-determination and independence,

Reaffirming also the national unity and the territorial integrity of Namibia,

1. *Invites* the Secretary-General, in consultation and close co-operation with a group of the Security Council, composed of the representatives of Argentina, Somalia and Yugoslavia, to initiate as soon as possible contacts with all parties concerned, with a view to establishing the necessary conditions so as to enable the people of Namibia, freely and with strict regard to the principles of human equality, to exercise their right to self-determination and independence, in accordance with the Charter of the United Nations;

2. *Calls* on the Government of South Africa to co-operate fully with the Secretary-General in the implementation of this resolution;

3. *Requests* the Secretary-General to report to the Security Council on the implementation of this resolution not later than 31 July 1972.

After it had invited Dr. Waldheim to visit South Africa and Namibia, the South African Government expelled the Anglican Bishop of Damaraland (the name for the diocese of Namibia), the Right Reverend Colin O'Brien Winter, and three of his assistants,[d] from Namibia in an obvious attempt to stifle opposition to the South African administration during the Secretary-General's visit.[e]

Dr. Waldheim visited South Africa and Namibia for five days at the beginning of March. After preliminary discussions in Cape Town with the South African Prime Minister, Mr. B. J. Vorster, he flew to Namibia where he visited Owambo (Ovamboland) and Windhoek. Here he met both supporters and opponents of the South African Government's policies. The former were represented by leaders of the Owambo and Kavango Legislative Assemblies, and by representatives of the Damara people and the Federal Coloured People's Party. The latter were represented by leaders of the National Convention, a united front consisting of the following organizations opposed to South African rule: the two Herero bodies, the National Unity Democratic Organization (NUDO), the South West African National Union (SWANU), the Basters' Volksparty, the Voice of the People (representing the Namas and Damaras), and the Ovambo-controlled South West African Peoples Organization (SWAPO). At its meeting with Dr.

[d] Mr. David de Beer, secretary-general of the Anglican diocese, Rev. Stephen Hayes, and Miss Antoinette Halberstadt.

[e] *The Star,* Johannesburg, 28 February 1972; *Sunday Times,* Johannesburg, 27 February 1972.

Waldheim the National Convention demanded the immediate removal of South African administration from Namibia.[f] After two busy days in Namibia, Dr. Waldheim returned to Cape Town for further talks with Mr. Vorster.

No joint communiqué was issued after these talks, but Dr. Waldheim stated that there was some common ground in the professed aim of both the South African Government and the United Nations to promote self-determination and independence for the people of Namibia.[g] This common ground is illusory. The United Nations is committed to self-determination and independence for Namibia as a whole, as one multi-racial nation. The South African Government is committed to self-determination and independence for the different peoples or "nations" of South West Africa in separate ethnic homelands.[h]

10. The Future

Although there have been several suggestions of ways in which the dispute over Namibia in its present form might be returned to the International Court,[i] it seems unlikely that the Court will again be consulted unless fresh legal difficulties arise. The Court has given its full approval to United Nations action, and it seems probable that the dispute will assume a greater political character, premised of course, upon the legal foundation of the 1971 Advisory Opinion.

Member States of the United Nations appear to be divided on the correct approach to be adopted towards the political resolution of the dispute. Three approaches have emerged: first, uncompromising confrontation with South Africa; second, negotiation and dialogue; third, negotiation backed by coercive measures. The first course will not win the support of the Western Powers and

[f] *Rand Daily Mail,* 8 and 9 March 1972; *The Star,* 10 March 1972.
[g] *The Star,* 9 March 1972.
[h] *The Star,* 11 March 1972; *Sunday Times,* 12 March 1972.
[i] See, for example, the suggestion put forward by Arthur W. Rovine and Anthony A. D'Amato that South Africa's obligations under Chapter XI of the Charter relating to non-self-governing territories continue to apply to her unlawful occupation of Namibia and that "any State that is a member of the United Nations may bring an action against South Africa in the International Court of Justice, under the Court's compulsory jurisdiction, to enforce South Africa's obligations under Chapter XI": "Written Statement of the International League for the Rights of Man filed with the International Court of Justice in the Namibia Question" (1971) 4 *New York University Journal of International Law and Politics* 335 at 402.

the second is clearly unacceptable to most Afro-Asian States. This leaves the third course, which is likely to be pursued, with the emphasis vacillating between coercion and negotiation. This is already apparent from the three Security Council resolutions adopted since the 1971 Advisory Opinion. Two have urged States to take coercive measures against South Africa, but the third has authorized the Secretary-General to enter into talks with the South African Government on the future of Namibia.

The Western Powers, particularly the United States, occupy a pivotal position for the future of Namibia, as ultimately they will determine whether the emphasis is to fall on coercion or negotiation in the resolution of the dispute. The advice given to their decision-makers will vary from suggestions for coercive action to proposals for realistic restraint. This is illustrated by the differing proposals put forward to guide American decision-makers by Dr. Elizabeth Landis, an American expert on Southern African affairs, and by Professor George F. Kennan.

Elizabeth S. Landis: [j]

PROPOSALS OF A GENERAL NATURE

(1) The United States should accept membership on the Council for Namibia.

To establish its *bonafides* vis-à-vis South West Africa the United States should accept membership on the Council for Namibia. However justified originally, the argument is no longer valid that American agreement to become a member would be deemed an act of confrontation, thereby foreclosing a "dialogue" with South Africa on the future of its former mandate. As Ambassador Yost acknowledged, South Africa clearly is unwilling to act voluntarily. Pressure will be necessary to compel it to relinquish its conquest.[57]

Acceptance of Council membership would constitute, however, not merely a symbolic gesture of wholehearted commitment to work for the independence of South West Africa, but also a practical step towards achieving that goal by converting the Council into an effective organ of U.N. policy. It would give new prestige to the Council, which the Great Powers have shunned so far, and might well induce the other permanent Security Council members to accept membership also out of emulation or competition for Third World approbation. A Council with such members would be able to command the

[j] "Namibia: The Beginning of Disengagement" (1970–71) 2 *Studies in Race and Nations* (Denver), 1 at 17–34. These proposals were made before the Court handed down its Opinion, but they are not materially affected thereby. Indeed, they are in most cases endorsed by the Court's ruling.
[57] Press Release USUN-68 (70), 19 May 1970.

respect of the entire U.N. for the measures it proposed. It might also be better able to coordinate its proposals with the action taken by U.N. members to ensure that each reinforced the other.

It should be pointed out, however, that the proposals which follow do not *require* American membership on the Council, desirable as that would be. In view of the apparent lack of American receptivity to the idea of membership, it would be a tragic mistake to assume that the remaining proposals cannot or should not be carried out if the United States continues to adhere to its present attitude towards the Council.

(2) American officials, in all public statements, should consistently refer to South Africa, in relation to its former mandate, as "the (unlawful) occupying power" (or by some equivalent phrase).

Such action would do no more than point out the status that South Africa has attained by refusing to turn over the administration of the Territory to the U.N. after the adoption of resolution 2145; the United States has so described South Africa repeatedly in the U.N. It is important, however, that our government make its position clear under circumstances where its speeches cannot be dismissed as mere harmless rhetoric, designed to appease the opponents of apartheid without substantially discomfiting its proponents.

Moreover, an important function of government is to educate its citizens. In the case of South West Africa, about which most Americans have very little information, the use of such terminology by government spokesmen should arouse public interest and lead to discussion and debate of the South West African question and to coverage of the subject by the media. Ultimately, it may be hoped, this would result in a better informed public which would understand why actions of the sort set forth below should be taken by the government. For those business interests who understandably will invest and/or trade wherever it is profitable, in the absence of a clear indication of government policy to the contrary, such a designation of South Africa would reinforce Ambassador Yost's warning that the United States will no longer encourage investment in South West Africa.

PROPOSALS RELATING TO INTERNATIONAL ACTIVITIES OF SOUTH AFRICA

The proposals under this heading are generally of the type which may be made to protest the annexation of one state by another. American diplomatic history contains many examples of our government's refusal to recognize unlawful incorporation of one state by another.[58]

[58] Most recently the incorporation of the three Baltic states of Latvia, Lithuania, and Esthonia by the Soviet Union. In the nineteen-thirties the League of Nations signaled its disapproval of the Italian conquest of Ethiopia by continuing to recognize the latter country as a League member; as a result, Ethiopia qualified as "another Member of the League of Nations" in order to join with Liberia in bringing the South West Africa Cases in the World Court. For a discussion of some of the possible, but not necessary, effects of non-recognition of a state, see Gould, *An Introduction to International Law* (New York, 1957), pp. 228–29.

Our courts have repeatedly acted to protect the citizens of a country that has been involuntarily merged into another by refusing to recognize the status of the absorbed state as part of the absorbing state.[59] While South West Africa never was an independent *state*, it is a territory with an international status, as both the International Court and the United States have declared. There is good reason for the United States to act in relation to the Territory as it would in relation to a state which had been unlawfully annexed by another.

(1) Accreditation of the American consul in Capetown should be withdrawn insofar as it extends to South West Africa.

The United States already has closed its consulate in Windhoek, but, as far as is known, the American consul in Capetown is still *accredited* to the Cape area *and to South West Africa*. As long as such accreditation continues, it constitutes a recognition of the authority of South Africa over its former mandate, in violation of American duties as spelled out above vis-à-vis South West Africa.

It may be added that withdrawal of accreditation would emphatically underscore our newly announced policy of discouraging American investment in the Territory.

If in the future the Council for Namibia should decide to register and grant corporate franchises and land titles in South West Africa, the United States might accredit an official at its U.N. Mission to undertake consular duties on behalf of Americans interested in such registration and grants from the Council.

(2) The United States should terminate (or, alternatively, treat as automatically terminated by operation of law) the extension to South West Africa of any bilateral treaty between the United States and South Africa. In particular, the United States should terminate the extension to South West Africa of the extradition treaty between the United States and South Africa in accordance with Articles 14 and 15 of that treaty. . . .

(3) The United States should recognize the passports (or equivalent documents) which the Council for Namibia proposes to issue to South West African "nationals" and should refuse to issue American visas to South West Africans travelling on South African passports.

If South Africa is not the legal government in South West Africa, it should not have the power to issue valid passports to the people of the Territory; since the Council is the lawful administering body, it should have (and exercise) such power. The United States should honor documents issued by the lawful administering power only. If this policy penalizes white South West Africans who want to travel in the United States, then that is the price they must pay for their silent or active complicity in the illegal South African occupation of South

---

[59] See, e.g., Application of I.R.O. for the Resettlement or Repatriation of Theresa Strasinkaite (U.S. Court of Allied High Commissioner for Germany, Area Five (1952) (minor Lithuanian child in Germany not to be forcibly repatriated as Soviet citizen since United States does not recognize laws and decrees of Lithuanian S.S.R.; child retains Baltic nationality).

West Africa. It may serve the valuable purpose of making them realize the depth of "outside" disapproval of South African violation of international law.

In practice, recognition of Council documents probably would assist the American government in dealing with refugees from South West Africa. Since the South African government ordinarily refuses to grant passports to nonwhites from the Territory (or South Africa itself), those who wish to leave must do so without papers. It would be helpful for them and for the United States if they could obtain Council passports.[69] White political opponents of the government who are denied passports should also be able to obtain Council passports.

. . . .

(4) The United States should mark all American passports "not valid for travel in Namibia (South West Africa)."

The United States should fulfill its duty not to recognize the legitimacy of the de facto government of South West Africa by prohibiting its citizens from travelling or being in an area where they must accept the authority of the unlawful occupying power. As a practical matter it is not clear what the effect of such a prohibition would be as as far as American law is concerned, for it appears that Americans have violated with impunity similar prohibitions applying to Cuba, North Vietnam, etc. Nevertheless, such a prohibition would have at least great moral and psychological effect and would be a token of American intentions vis-à-vis South West Africa.

If the Council for Namibia assumed the power to issue visas for foreign travel in South West Africa, the American State Department should mark all United States passports "not valid for travel in Namibia (South West Africa) without a visa issued by the U.N. Council for Namibia." While, as far as the United States is concerned, the problem of enforcement would be the same as that raised by a blanket prohibition against travel to or in South West Africa, the cautionary effect of such a prohibition would also be great. That effect could be enhanced by a Council statement that persons violating the prohibition would not be eligible for visas, grants, franchises, etc., issued by a future legitimate Namibian government.

. . . .

(6) The United States should support the right of the Council for Namibia to represent South West Africa in any international organization and in any international activity in or to which South Africa has or might have represented South West Africa.

Since, under U.N. supervision, the Council for Namibia has replaced South Africa as the lawful governing authority for South West

[69] Ambassador Yost stated (Press Release USUN-68 [70], 19 May 1970) that the United States, in accordance with Secretary Rogers' announcement in March 1970, was taking steps to issue travel documents to certain refugees in the United States (including Namibians and others from southern Africa) under the 1951 Geneva Convention on the Status of Refugees. It would probably be far more satisfactory if the Council would issue documents to South West African refugees, which the United States could honor.

Africa, it should be recognized as the successor to South Africa in all international organizations and activities in which South West Africa is entitled to be represented. South Africa's present membership, or lack of it, in such organizations or activities should be irrelevant to the right of the Council to take up membership.

Since, however, the situation of the Territory and the Council is unique, this proposal for Council membership on behalf of the Territory is likely to be opposed because there is no precedent for it. The United States should use its prestige to see that this does not bar the Council from affording South West Africa the representation to which it is entitled in international organizations and activities, representation which can no longer be lawfully given by South Africa.

PROPOSALS RELATING TO DOMESTIC ACTIVITIES OF SOUTH AFRICA

(1) The United States should treat all South African "laws" affecting South West Africa (viz., acts of the South African Parliament; proclamations of the State President, the Prime Minister, other cabinet ministers, or the Administrator of South West Africa; ordinances of the territorial Legislative Assembly; and all sub-legislation) which have come into effect since the adoption of resolution 2145 as invalid insofar as the United States or international law is concerned.

The South African government has been an unlawful occupying power in its former mandate since the termination of its mandate agreement. It follows, therefore, that its laws purporting to affect South West Africa are not valid or binding on either South West Africans or the international community.

Some of the natural consequences of the invalidity of such laws should be: they could not be cited before American courts, administrative officials, or executive officers to justify or support the conduct or objectives of persons appearing before such courts, agencies, or officials; rights granted by such laws or by agencies or officials established by or operating under such laws would not be recognized by American courts, administrative agencies, or officials or, as a result, by banks or other private lending agencies or by auditors and accountants. In particular, rights created by or deriving from such laws should be treated as invalid by the Securities and Exchange Commission in approving prospectuses for security issues by firms claiming land title or other rights under the South African government or its South West African administration.

Conflicting rights obtained from the Council for Namibia under any legislation it might promulgate in connection with the same subject matter should be deemed to supersede rights derived from the invalid South African laws and to permit judicial transfer of property held under such invalid title to the holder of valid title under the Council.

Ambassador Yost's declaration that the American government will not act to protect investments based on rights acquired through the South African government since the adoption of resolution 2145 against the claims of a future lawful government of Namibia has already set basic American policy on at least one aspect of this subject matter. This proposal merely extends the scope of his policy, carries it to its logical conclusion, and suggests how it can be made effective immediately.

(2) American courts should refuse to enforce all judgments of South West African courts and all judgments of South African courts which affect South West Africans, causes of action originating in South West Africa, or property located in South West Africa.

The enforcement of foreign judgments is always a matter of comity and not of right. No American court, as a matter of comity, should enforce a judgment rendered by a court acting as the arm of the unlawful occupying power in an unlawfully occupied territory or by a domestic court of the occupying power when it determines matters related to the unlawfully occupied territory.

.   .   .   .

(6) The President should continue to prohibit the sale of all arms (including replacement parts) to South Africa as long as it continues to occupy South West Africa.

Although the arms ban was imposed under Assembly resolution 1761 (XVII) (1962) and Security Council resolution 191 (1964) in order to exert pressure on South Africa to change its *domestic* (racial) policy, it can serve the dual purpose of inducing the government of the Republic to quit the Territory (as American representatives at the U.N. have tacitly admitted). It should be so used. It is incredible that any government would supply arms to a country so flagrantly in violation of international law, particularly when the violation challenges the authority of the U.N. itself.

(7) The President should prohibit any and all joint planning and training (including anti-insurgency training), joint exercises, and/or military cooperation *of any sort* between American and South African forces as long as South Africa continues to occupy South West Africa. The President should similarly oppose any kind of military cooperation by NATO forces with South Africa under the same circumstances.

Obviously the United States should not engage in any kind of military cooperation with a government which challenges the United Nations in flagrant violation of international law.

.   .   .   .

(12) The government should prohibit investment by Americans in South West Africa; at the very least it should strongly discourage such investment.

Since 20 May it has been the official policy of the United States, according to Ambassador Yost, to discourage American investment in South West Africa. One method of implementing this policy was set forth in the Ambassador's speech as part of the official policy: refusal by the United States to protect against the claims of a future lawful South West African government any rights of American investors in the Territory which are derived from the South African government since the adoption of resolution 2145. Such implementation, however, has future application only, and probably not in the near future.

There is no evidence as of this date that the United States has taken any concrete action to make its policy of discouragement effective.

The longer the United States waits to implement its policy of discouragement, the less likely it is to be effective at all. South Africa is fast generating capital internally for both its own and South-West African needs, making foreign investment ever less necessary for territorial development. Additionally, American domestic opposition to *any* government interference with investment will grow if prohibition or discouragement is attempted only when it is useless. Therefore, logically, the United States should not merely discourage investment now, but prohibit it outright, immediately.

There is no legal bar to such prohibition. Much stronger measures as to investment (and trade) have been applied, quickly and fully, to Communist China, Cuba, and other countries which the U.S. adjudged international miscreants.

If American policy is to be limited to discouragement of investment, it should at least be carried out effectively and immediately. The government should take the following steps at once: change the official literature and advice given by the State and Commerce Departments (as well as by other government officials) to discourage Americans from investing in South West Africa; refuse all government assistance (technical, financial, etc.) to such potential investors and discourage private lending institutions from assisting such investors; use general restrictions on foreign investment and other devices established to deal with the American balance of payments problem to discourage investment in South West Africa.

(13) The government should prohibit or, at the very least, discourage trade with South West Africa.

.   .   .   .

MISCELLANEOUS PROPOSALS

. . . The United States, having acknowledged that conciliation and negotiation have failed to persuade South Africa to relinquish its unlawful occupation of South West Africa, should support the non-violent humanitarian activities of the national liberation movements whose purpose is to free the Territory.

It appears to be established policy that the United States will not engage in any direct confrontation with the dominant white regimes in southern Africa.[87] Such self-imposed restriction should not prevent the United States from giving humanitarian assistance, however, in the form of medical services and supplies, food, and educational grants, to dependents and non-military supporters of the South West African liberation movements, as well as to non-political refugees who have fled the Territory to escape "anti-terrorist" campaigns by the South African armed forces.

[87] Ambassador Yost, Press Release USUN-68 (70), 19 May 1970, also referring to a similar statement by Ambassador Goldberg.

. . . The United States should encourage the U.N. to establish a judicial body ("grand jury") consisting of jurists of the highest and most unimpeachable qualifications, to investigate charges of official maltreatment of South West Africans, to prepare "indictments" of persons responsible therefor, and to give publicity thereto.

Professor Gidon Gottlieb of New York University Law School has already introduced a proposal of this nature, which has the backing of the International Commission of Jurists. The United States should support this or some similar proposal, which would lay the foundation for prosecution, when the Territory attains self-government, of at least the worst offenders against the rights of South West Africans. It is to be hoped that one important side-effect of the establishment of such a judicial body would be to cause South African officials to start acting less oppressively as a general cautionary reaction.

George F. Kennan: [k]

Nowhere is the conflict between the United Nations and the present ruling power in southern Africa so formal, so acute and so complete as in the case of South West Africa. Not just the General Assembly but in this case the Security Council as well has flatly demanded that South Africa withdraw immediately its administration of the territory and hand it over to the authority of the United Nations, and has threatened South Africa with "effective measures in accordance with the appropriate provisions . . . of the United Nations Charter" in the event of noncompliance. The South African rejection of these demands has been no less determined and categoric. The impasse is now complete. It is all the more dangerous because positions have been so formalized on both sides.

Bearing in mind that in international affairs all legal distinctions rest on infirm foundations, one can follow the legal arguments advanced by the United Nations in favor of the termination of the mandate and the establishment of its own authority in South West Africa. It is more difficult to see what the world organization would do with the territory if it had it. This vast arid region, as large as France and the German Federal Republic combined, is inhabited by only 610,000 people. Of these, approximately 96,000 are white South Africans— Afrikaners for the most part—of whom nearly 90 percent live in the administrative center of Windhoek, in the west-central part of the territory. The remaining population is made up of indigenous peoples comprising about half-a-dozen distinct ethnic groups. Of these, nearly 65 percent reside in the northern region of the territory, near the Portuguese border, some 500 miles north of Windhoek, where they are

[k] "Hazardous Courses in Southern Africa" (1971) 49 *Foreign Affairs* 218 at 227–30. (Excerpted by permission from *Foreign Affairs*, January 1971. Copyright by the Council on Foreign Relations, Inc., New York.) This article was also written before the Court's Opinion was delivered, but its relevance is not affected. This article should be contrasted with that of Ernest A. Gross, "The Coalescing Problems of Southern Africa" (1968) 47 *Foreign Affairs* 743.

very little troubled by the proximity or competition of Whites. The majority of these northern natives (the majority, in fact, of the entire indigenous population of South West Africa), in the number of some 300,000, to be exact, are known as the Ovambos. They live in a native homeland—Ovamboland by name—which now enjoys fairly extensive rights of local autonomy. This is perhaps the only native "homeland" under South African control which would seem to have reasonably favorable prospects for progress under the existing concepts of "separate development." Much better watered than most of the rest of the territory, it is relatively ample in area and provides a home for at least 95 percent of the Ovambos. The South African official presence is neither numerous nor burdensome. (Of the territory's 102 policemen, for example, only 50—or about one to each 6,000 inhabitants—are white.) No Whites other than officials are permitted to reside or even normally to travel in the territory. Educational standards at the primary and secondary level compare with the best in Africa. Health and medical services are exemplary. Taxation of the natives, except locally and by their own administration, is negligible.

The overwhelming portion of the expense of maintaining and developing the territory is supplied by the South Africans. Their present contributions of $4,350,000 annually for budgetary expenditures and $12,420,000 in developmental capital run, together, to about $55.00 per capita, as compared with $6.10 in aid from all sources as the average for the black African countries farther north. This is in addition to a bevy of other services—water development, soil research, pest control, public health, meteorological service, etc.—which are extended automatically by virtual inclusion of the territory in the South African state, and could hardly be effectively provided by any other than a highly advanced, and preferably contiguous, country.

Things are not ideal for the Ovambos, and particularly not for those who aspire to higher education or who would like to play a role in public affairs outside their own territory. These, however, are a small minority. As for the remainder: it is difficult to believe that their material condition could be improved, or their capacities for self-government given more extensive scope for development, by any sort of U.N. administration.

This narrows the problem, essentially, to that of the remaining 200,000 non-Whites in the territory. These, for the most part, do not reside in the homelands tentatively marked out for them; most of them probably never will. They suffer indeed from all the restrictions of apartheid, although the atmosphere is perhaps somewhat less tense and cramped than in the Republic proper. If all that was involved in a South African withdrawal and a U.N. takeover was an alleviation of their situation in these respects, there might be much to be said for it, although the effect on the more fortunate Ovambos would still have to be considered. But one is obliged, regrettably, to consider not just the likely positive but also the predictable negative consequences of such a turn of events.

In the event of a forced South African withdrawal, the overwhelming majority of the existing white population of the territory could be expected to withdraw together with the South African authorities. All existing administrative and social services would simply cease to exist. The railways are South African. Their rolling-stock, in its entirety the property of the South African State Railways, would assuredly be removed. Without the railways, the great non-ferrous and diamond mines, employment in which provides a large part of the income of the native population, would close down. In the case of the non-ferrous ones, their pumps would at once cease to function; it would be months before they could be reopened. Agriculture, too, would be largely paralyzed. The territory's only significant port, Walfish Bay, the status of which as a complete South African coastal enclave has never been questioned, would remain under South African administration.

Worst of all, while it is possible to imagine certain of the remaining tribal elements, notably the Ovambos, administering themselves (albeit largely without money), it is not possible to imagine any of these elements collaborating in the administration of any of the others. These tribal entities live, in many instances, hundreds of miles apart; there is no intimacy and little affection among them; none, one suspects, would respond favorably to the appearance in its midst, as would-be administrators, of officials of another tribal affiliation. The United Nations would, in other words, have to create a new administration, largely foreign, to take the place of the South African one. It is easy to believe that such an administration would follow more liberal policies with respect to the status of the native than does the existing one. It is not easy to believe that it would be as efficient, or as well provided with funds; and it would almost certainly be years before it could expect to restore to this vast territory even a semblance of such good order and prosperity as it has now achieved.

One can understand the desire in U.N. circles to remove from South African control at least this one area which was once, and can still be construed to be, an international responsibility. But one wonders whether the practical consequences of such a step have been really thought through. Very few foreigners have visited Sout West Africa in recent years. Senior American officials do not, as a matter of policy, go there. An exchange in 1968 between the South African government and the U.N. Secretary-General about the possibility of the latter's sending a U.N. representative to the territory ended in misunderstanding, confusion and recrimination.

Would it not be better, one must ask, instead of continuing to press the South Africans to take a step which they will not take and cannot be compelled to take, and which, if taken, would only be likely to have unfortunate consequences for the people of the territory anyway —would it not be better for the United Nations to inform itself at first hand on conditions there and then to enter into normal contact with the South African authorities with a view to seeing whether some accommodation could not be found which would relieve the situation of that minority of black African inhabitants of the territory who live outside the homelands, and would at the same time relieve the South Africans of the continued burden of a grievous and dangerous conflict with most of the rest of the international community? This might bring at least limited benefits to the non-white portion of the South West African population; a continuation of the present threats and pressures will bring none at all. That support of the members of the Afro-Asian bloc, not to mention the communists, would not be easily had for such an approach is obvious; but this is no reason why, if it really represents the most hopeful line of possible solution, the Western powers should not support it.

Prima facie the postwar history of South West Africa suggests that all avenues of negotiation have been closed and that coercion remains the only cure. This view is not shared by the present writer. Recent domestic developments, such as the acceleration of the South African Government's "homelands" policy, and international events, such as the Court's 1971 Opinion and the establishment of new independent States in Southern Africa, have provided fresh scope for political manoeuvre. This is reflected in the new approach of white opposition leaders in South Africa.

For years there has been little divergence of opinion between the Government and the two opposition parties—the United Party and the Progressive Party—over the Government's handling of the South West African question. Now, prompted by the Court's latest Opinion and by the new signs of hostility to the Government's policies among the inhabitants of the territory, opposition spokesmen have put forward views which envisage far-reaching changes in the existing order and perhaps the ultimate independence of Namibia. The chief United Party spokesman on foreign affairs, Mr. Japie Basson, who at one stage himself represented a South West African constituency, and the leader of the Progressive Party, Mr. Colin Eglin, have put forward remarkably similar views in recent times. Both have advocated the removal of racial discrimination in South West Africa, the immediate creation of a body representing the leaders of all the peoples of South West Africa to consult with each other [1] and the Government of South Africa on the future of the territory, and the holding of a plebiscite within the foreseeable future (within five years, in the case of Mr. Eglin) to enable the people of South West Africa to exercise their right of self-determination.

[1] Significantly, in February 1972 non-white political leaders representing different population groups and political organizations held their first consultation on the future of the territory: *Rand Daily Mail,* 15 February 1972.

Mr. Japie Basson: [m]

Now I want to mention a few practical steps which I believe we should take.

The first step is one that should be taken at Government level, and it is for the Government to stop making every decision for South West Africa on a party political basis. A consensus should immediately be sought between the main political parties in South Africa over the question of South West Africa, and the Government should take the initiative in this matter by establishing a strong Joint Committee of Parliament to deal with the whole question of South West Africa and its future. This committee should be a permanent committee and should be empowered to do the planning and to act in all matters affecting South West Africa. In other words, South West Africa should, as it were, be set aside, set apart, as a problem and removed from the sphere of National Party politics. In handling the matter, the emphasis would thus fall on Parliament rather than on the political party exercising the power of government.

It follows from this, and this is my second suggestion, that a consultative body of the leaders of all the peoples of South West Africa should be formed immediately and as a matter of urgency. The different groups in South West Africa are, politically speaking, completely isolated from each other. Each may talk separately on a formal and official level with the Government; and we all know how unsatisfactory a means this is of encouraging people to say what they really think. Certainly, Parliament doesn't really know what is going on in the minds of the Non-White peoples in South West Africa. There are six Whites in the House of Assembly, all speaking for the Whites they represent, and, for the rest, Parliament have to depend on what the Government choose to tell them and on statements of individuals published in newspapers from time to time. Even the Legislative Assembly in Windhoek is completely isolated from leading Non-White opinion in South West Africa. They deal with White affairs only and have no political link with other population groups in the Territory with whom they have to work every day. The thin connection which the Non-White councils that have been established, have with the Government in Pretoria are all through civil servants and officials appointed by the Government. This position is as unsatisfactory as it can be; for the first time I have now found in South West Africa and in Windhoek a note of concern among White people, and I found it among politically minded people who are by no means *verlig*,—concern that, by constantly emphasizing and strengthening their own links with the Republic to the total exclusion of the Non-White peoples of South West Africa, the Whites have laid themselves open to the charge that they do not belong where they are and have no concern for other South West Africans. Mr. Kapuuo, the leader of the Hereros, recently gave a hint of the feeling which this state of affairs has created in the minds of

[m] Address to the South African Institute of International Affairs, Johannesburg, 18 November 1971.

many Non-Whites when he said in a statement that "our White brethren in South West Africa who have property here and have made South West Africa their home would be well advised to abandon an outgoing Government, and so win the confidence of the indigenous population. They have been misled by the belief that they must disregard the indigenous population and rely on the strength of South Africa."

As I have said, I have now found for the first time White people who are interested in politics, becoming *concerned* over the total isolation between the different groups. I have already suggested an authoritative joint Parliamentary committee of a permanent nature to start off with, and I wish to add to that the urgent establishment of a consultative committee of leaders of all the population groups as an immediate means of creating frank and honest contact between the different groups of peoples, and between the peoples of South West Africa and Parliament as the ultimate body of control.

. . . .

Mr. Chairman, it is a great pity that, under the present Government, it was considered necessary that the policies and practices they apply here should also be applied to South West Africa. There was never any need for policies applicable to the Republic also to be exported to South West Africa. I think we should stop this and make it clear to all in the Territory, and those interested outside, that apartheid as we know it in the Republic will not be applicable to South West Africa. . . . The dictated apartheid measures, the legalized racial discrimination and discriminatory practices that were introduced in South West Africa in the last couple of years should be systematically removed, and this should be done as soon as possible. We should then declare to the world and to the people of South West Africa that apartheid is not for South West Africa and that we have introduced an open society in the Territory leaving people to be exclusive privately as much as they like. I believe that the vast majority of Whites will adapt themselves easily to the situation which won't differ much from what existed there before. If this were not in fact so, thousands of White South Africans would not today have been working and living with their families in countries like Zambia, Swaziland, Botswana, and many others where no apartheid laws apply.

Finally, sir, these steps I have mentioned should all have one overall goal in mind and that is the goal of self-determination. When I mention self-determination, I mean genuine self-determination. I believe that South Africa should declare itself unequivocally in favour of the principle of self-determination in the accepted sense of the term. I say in the accepted sense of the term, because this is important. There is no other solution, no other ultimate solution, to the South West Africa problem but that the people of South West Africa, the inhabitants of the Territory, should themselves, as soon as possible, decide about their own future, according to the doctrine of self-determination which commands international respect and support.

It is true, South Africa is already theoretically on common ground with the United Nations and with the major nations of the world over the concept of self-determination, but I think the Government is making a mistake by insisting that each little political unit—some of them artificially created by the Government themselves—should formally determine its future separately. Already there is the existing separate position of Owambo and of the southern sector, and I'm not ruling out the right of any group to ask for regional status if they desire this within the whole. Rehoboth, for instance, is such a case in point. But to imagine, for instance, that little Namaland, a completely artificial creation consisting of a grouping of farms around a tiny town called Gibeon where there's a boarding house, a garage and a few shops—to imagine that they have any real prospect of becoming independent, is nonsensical. The choice would amount to choosing between naught and naught.

The same applies to the other artificially created units, although I want to make it clear that I have no objection to more land being bought wherever it is economically necessary for the indigenous groups in South West Africa, and no objection against there being created a political means of expression for any particular group. There are only about 5,000 of the 35,000 Namas living in this new "Namaland". Less than 5,000 of the 50,000 Damaras live in the newly created "Damaraland". And so the question comes up: by what right, in any case, can 90,000 Whites, occupying the best part of the southern sector, legitimately claim that they hold sovereign rights over that part of South West Africa and that they may exclude the rest and refuse to co-operate with them? White South African settlement really started in earnest only about 40 years ago and, even so, nearly one-third of the total White population are civil servants who are there in great numbers on a temporary basis.

The idea is indefensible, and the effort to convince anyone that each little unit must determine its future separately, is, to my mind, bound to fail. In fact, the Government has already defeated its own point by making it clear in its official publications that it is completely impossible for the whole of the Territory to live without contact with South Africa and without being part of the economic life of South Africa. It speaks for itself that a smaller part there would have even less chance to survive on its own.

I say again that I am prepared to exclude Owambo and its associated territories because of the disunity between the north and the south. And let's hope that something that was allowed in the case of Togoland may be applied in the case of South West Africa. In the case of Togoland the principle of a separate plebiscite, or rather, of separate plebiscite areas were conceded by a United Nations mission. And, if I remember correctly, in some areas questions were placed before the voters in different areas; and this could very well be done in the case of a long established separate unit like Owambo.

Self-determination must be our goal, but I think that we shall have to deal with this goal in a mature way. We can work for internal arrangements in South West Africa which will give all groups the right to participate in government without any one dominating the other. But, generally, we should create such internally satisfactory conditions that we can confidently come to an agreement with the world outside to hold a plebiscite under impartial international supervision, and thus to end the dispute finally.

I emphasize again that I am confident that it is within the means of a South African Government to create conditions, to create an order, to create a relationship which will make the vast majority of the people in South West Africa, at a plebiscite, exercise its right of self-determination by voluntarily deciding to have a secure link with the Republic of South Africa.

Mr. Colin Eglin: [n]

On the shoulders of the administering power—whether it be de facto or de jure or both—rests the obligation to give full effect to the purpose of the mandate whether this exists as a legal injunction or as a legacy of responsibility.

From the text of the Mandate and the Covenant of the League of Nations (Article 22, Part 1 of the Treaty of Versailles) it is clear that the primary purpose of the mandate was "to promote to the utmost the material and moral well-being and the social progress of the inhabitants of the territory".

On another issue, often averred to be a purpose—the development of the inhabitants so that they can stand by themselves under the strenuous conditions of the modern world at some stage in the future—the Mandate is not explicit. The International Court of Justice has said that the right of self-determination in due course was implied in the Mandate. The South African Government, supported by many legal authorities, has held that there was no such implication.

I believe that the time has come for South Africa to determine its course of action, not in terms of an implied injunction in the old Mandate—if indeed such an injunction exists—but against the background of the concept of self-determination which has developed in the world in the past 25 years and which has become a pivotal concept in the stated policy of the Nationalist Party Government in South Africa. I believe that the Covenant and the Mandate taken together with the weight which is attached to the concept of self-determination as a national right must lead South Africa to give to the people of South West Africa the right to decide on their own status and form of government at some time in the future.

Indeed Mr. Vorster's government went some way towards conceding this right in offering to the World Court in January of 1971 that the matter of the future status of South West Africa be referred to a plebiscite of the people of the territory. Just to complete the record on this point he was supported in this offer by the United Party—"This is a positive constructive suggestion to find a solution to the problem. It

[n] Address to the South African Institute of International Affairs, Cape Town, 1 February 1972.

has been made before. I hope it finds more favourable consideration on this occasion than in the past" (de Villiers Graaff)—and the Progressive Party—"The offer was a bold attempt by the Government to seize the initiative in the impasse. The offer was an important recognition by South Africa of the quasi-international status of South West Africa" (Colin Eglin). However Mr. Vorster has since, in January of this year, withdrawn the offer.

So much for the background, let me turn to the present and the future. I urge the Government as the administering power to take three steps to discharge its responsibilities towards the people of South West Africa.

Firstly, race discrimination in the sense of the denial of equal opportunity of individual advancement to citizens on the grounds of race can never be compatible with the injunction "to promote to the utmost the material and moral well-being and the social progress of the inhabitants".

That racially discriminatory practices still persist in South West Africa is not in dispute.

.   .   .   .

The Government must start immediately with the elimination of discriminatory practices. The system goes far but the Government could commence by ensuring equal access to education—primary, secondary, and higher—equal access to training and employment opportunities, equal pay for equal work and promotion on merit within Government departments, equal opportunity to enjoy a family life near one's place of employment—this means the end of the wasteful disruptive migrant labour system. These are the first and urgent steps that should be taken.

Secondly, the Government must make it clear that it does envisage the people of South West Africa deciding on their status at some time in the future. The Government itself, before the International Court of Justice in January 1971, offered a plebiscite as a means of making this decision. It has since withdrawn the offer. By doing so it has cast doubt on its own integrity. For if the offer was sincere and meaningful and put forward in the interests of the people of South West Africa, surely having been made the offer must stand unless the people of South West Africa themselves decide that they do not want to express themselves by way of a plebiscite.

I believe that the Government should commit itself to a genuine test of the opinion of the people of South West Africa on the question of the future state of the territory, and in order to remove any uncertainty it should set a date, say within the next five years, by which this exercise in self-determination will be held.

Mr. Vorster has repeatedly declared his Government's intention of granting "independence" to areas of South Africa should the inhabitants at some stage in the future wish this. Surely the Government, especially when it takes into account the background of the Mandate, the very limited extent of integration with South Africa in the field of labour, the size and the relatively separate location of the territory, its relatively buoyant economy and its comparatively brief and qualified constitutional association with South Africa, will not give less opportunity for self-determination to South West Africa than it says it will give to the "Bantu Homelands" of South Africa!

Thirdly, I believe that it is important that the peoples of South West Africa consult with each other and that the Government of South Africa consults with them collectively during the period preceding the test of self-determination.

For this purpose I propose that a South West Africa Council representative of all the groups and communities in the territory be set up without delay.

This Council need not at this stage replace the various legislative and executive bodies which exist at present in the territory. But, the Council could act in an advisory and consultative capacity in relation to the South African Government and could also enable the people of the territory to discuss matters relating to the plebiscite, to the questions to be put, and to the form of government which could emerge.

These three steps which I have outlined could go a long way to resolve the present impasse over the future of South West Africa. They would enable South Africa to discharge with honour the obligations which it undertook in such good faith when the Mandate on South West Africa was conferred on it 53 years ago.

Although the proposals put forward by these two leaders lack the spectacular effect of immediate withdrawal, they do offer a realistic program for social change and self-determination in Namibia. The United Nations might be better advised to support proposals of this kind, which have some prospect of success, rather than to continue to engage in the political rhetoric of immediate, total withdrawal, which offers little amelioration to the position of the indigenous inhabitants of Namibia. The danger of the extremist stance on Namibia is that coercion is seen as a means of altering the political order of Southern Africa as a whole and not as a catalyst for change in Namibia itself. If more limited goals were set, such as those proposed by Mr. Japie Basson and Mr. Colin Eglin, self-determination for the peoples of South West Africa might well be realized during the nineteen-seventies.

The cornerstone of the Basson-Eglin proposals is the plebiscite. Unfortunately, the Afro-Asian States appear to be opposed to any plebiscite co-sponsored by South Africa and prefer, like Sir Muhammad Zafrulla Khan,[°] to insist on South Africa's withdrawal from the territory as a prerequisite to any plebiscite. The mount-

---

[°] Declaration appended to the 1971 Advisory Opinion, 1971 ICJ Reports 65–66.

ing internal opposition to South African administration may have altered this inflexible demand on the part of Afro-Asian States. On the other hand, it has resulted, predictably, in a less enthusiastic approach to a plebiscite on the part of the South African Government. The major Western Powers should, however, use all their influence to induce both parties to accept a plebiscite—held under proper conditions. Any plebiscite agreement should include the following terms:

(1) The people must be permitted to choose between the *status quo*, United Nations trusteeship, and immediate independence.

(2) The plebiscite must take the form of a free vote by all inhabitants of South West Africa above the age of eighteen or twenty-one. This would seem to be acceptable to the South African Government, which has denied [p] that it envisages the type of consultation with the tribal leaders staged by General Smuts for the benefit of the United Nations in 1946.

(3) The United Nations and South Africa must agree to accept the decision of the majority of the voters.

(4) There must be a joint United Nations–South Africa committee charged with the task of supervising the plebiscite.

(5) The plebiscite must not be held immediately but should be set for a date between one and three years hence in order to give both the United Nations and the South African Government ample opportunity to put their views to the people.

(6) All political leaders must be allowed to express their views freely provided this is done without threats or intimidation. (The main task of the joint United Nations–South Africa supervising committee would be to control campaigning.)

(7) All South West African political prisoners must be released and exiles permitted to return, to enable them to participate in the campaigning which would precede the plebiscite.

(8) Consultations must be held between the leaders of all groups in South West Africa to enable them to discuss their future and to formulate the alternatives to be placed before the people. (For instance, if immediate independence is preferred by some leaders, it would be essential to decide in advance whether a federal or a unitary form of government were envisaged.)

The Government of South Africa, the United Nations, and the

---

[p] See South Africa's plebiscite proposal to the International Court of Justice, above, p. 450.

International Court of Justice all profess allegiance to the concept of self-determination. It is difficult to see how this could be better promoted than by a free plebiscite. If the parties involved are genuinely concerned about self-determination and the best interests of the peoples of South West Africa, or Namibia, rather than the promotion of their own ideologies, this surely is the best course.

Bibliography

This bibliography is structured on the lines of the main body of this work and in general follows the sequence of its chapters. No attempt is made to provide a comprehensive bibliography for chapters 1 to 4 covering the pre-United Nations period, as they are introductory to the dispute between the United Nations and South Africa over South West Africa. Here only the standard works are included in a highly selective bibliography. The main focus of the collection of documents and scholarly writings is on the post-1945 period, and here a more comprehensive bibliography of works directed at the international dispute over South West Africa is provided.

The bibliography is limited to books, journal articles, and a selected number of Government publications. The attention devoted to South West Africa by the United Nations is reflected in the volume of United Nations official documentation on South West Africa. Considerations of space and time preclude a bibliography of these official documents, but the most important are included either in the text of the collection or in the footnotes to the text.

My special thanks are due to Mrs. Louise Silver of the library of the University of the Witwatersrand for her assistance in compiling this bibliography.

BIBLIOGRAPHICAL STUDIES

Bielschowsky, Ludwig. *Lists of Books in German on South Africa and South West Africa published up to 1914 in the South African Public Library, Cape Town*. Cape Town: University of Cape Town, 1949.

Both, Ellen Lisa Marianne. *Catalogue of Books and Pamphlets published in German relating to South Africa and South-West Africa as found in the South African Public Library published between 1950–1964*. Cape Town: University of Cape Town, 1966.

Decalo, Samuel. *South West Africa 1960–1968: An Introductory Bibliography*. Rhode Island: University, Occasional Papers in Political Science, no. 5, 1968.

De Jager, Theo. *South West Africa*. Pretoria: State Library, Bibliography, no. 7, 1964.

De Lange, E. J. Roukens. *South West Africa 1946–1960: A Selective Bibliography*. Cape Town: University of Cape Town, 1961.

Douma, J. *Bibliography on the International Court including the Permanent Court 1918–1964* (Being volume IV-C of the series *The Case Law of the International Court* by Edvard Hambro). Leyden: Sijthoff, 1966.

Hoare, Catherine. *United Nations versus South Africa—South Africa's Opinion.* Cape Town: University of Cape Town, 1961.

Loening, I., S. E. *A Bibliography of the Status of South-West Africa up to June 30th, 1951.* Cape Town: University of Cape Town, 1951.

Logan, Richard F. *Bibliography of South West Africa: Geography and Related Fields.* Windhoek: Committee of South West Africa Scientific Society, 1969.

Plaat, A. F. *List of Books and Pamphlets in German on South Africa and South West Africa, published after 1914 as found in the South African Public Library, Cape Town.* Cape Town: University of Cape Town, 1951.

Spohr, Otto Hartung. *Catalogue of Books, Pamphlets and Periodicals published in German relating to South Africa and South West Africa as found in Jagger Library.* Cape Town: University of Cape Town, 1950.

Tötemeyer, Gerhard. *South Africa–South West Africa: A Bibliography 1945–1963.* Freiburg: Arnold-Bergstrasser Institüt für Kulturwissenshaftliche Forschung, 1964.

Welch, F. J. *South-West Africa.* Cape Town: University of Cape Town, 1946.

GENERAL WORKS ON SOUTH WEST AFRICA COVERING THE PERIOD FROM THE START OF EUROPEAN SETTLEMENT TO THE PRESENT

Bruwer, J. P. van S. *South West Africa: The Disputed Land.* Cape Town: Nasionale Boekhandel, 1966.

Carroll, Faye. *South West Africa and the United Nations.* Lexington: University of Kentucky Press, 1967.

First, Ruth. *South West Africa.* Harmondsworth: Penguin Books, Penguin African Library AP10, 1963.

Goldblatt, I. *History of South West Africa from the Beginning of the Nineteenth Century.* Cape Town: Juta, 1971.

Imishue, R. W. *South West Africa: An International Problem.* London: Pall Mall Press, 1965.

Segal, Ronald, and First, Ruth, eds. *South West Africa: Travesty of Trust. The expert papers and findings of the International Conference on South West Africa, Oxford 23–26 March 1966, with a postscript by Iain MacGibbon on the 1966 Judgment of the International Court of Justice.* London: Andre Deutsch, 1967.

Slonim, Solomon. *South West Africa and the United Nations: An International Mandate in Dispute.* Baltimore: Johns Hopkins Press, 1973.

Wellington, J. H. *South West Africa and Its Human Issues.* London: Oxford University Press, 1967.

CHAPTER 1. THE TERRITORY AND ITS PEOPLES

Giniewski, Paul. *Die Styd Om Suidwes-Afrika.* Cape Town: Nasionale Boekhandel, 1966.

Green, Lawrence G. *Lords of the Last Frontier: The Story of South West Africa and Its Peoples of All Races.* Cape Town: Timmins, 1952.

Hahn, C. H. L., Vedder, H., and Fourie, L. *The Native Tribes of South West Africa.* Cape Town: Cape Times, 1928.

Hailey, Lord William Malcolm. *An African Survey*. London: Oxford University Press, 1938 (revised 1957).

Horrell, Muriel. *South West Africa*. Johannesburg: South African Institute of Race Relations, 1967.

Jenny, Hans. *Südwestafrika: Land Zwischen den Extremen*. Stuttgart: W. Kohlhammer, 1967.

Levinson, Olga. *The Ageless Land: The Story of South West Africa*. 2nd ed. Cape Town: Tafelberg, 1964.

Lowenstein, Allard K. *Brutal Mandate: A Journey to South West Africa*. New York: Macmillan, 1962.

Mertens, Alice. *South West Africa and its Indigenous Peoples*. London: Collins, 1966.

Molnar, Thomas S. *South West Africa: The Last Pioneer Country*. New York: Fleet, 1966.

Rhoodie, Eschel. *South West: The Last Frontier in Africa*. Johannesburg: Voortrekkerpers, 1967. Bibliography.

South Africa. Department of Foreign Affairs. *Owambo*. Pretoria: 1971.

South Africa. *Report of the Commission of Enquiry into South West African Affairs, 1962–1963*. R.P. 12 of 1946. Pretoria: Government Printer. [Chairman F. H. Odendaal.]

————. *Report of the Rehoboth Commission. U.G. 41 of 1926*. Pretoria: Government Printer, 1926. [Chairman Jacob de Villiers.]

————. Department of Foreign Affairs. *South Africa's Reply to the Secretary-General of the United Nations*. Pretoria: 1969. [Reprinted in UN Document S/9463 (3 October 1969).]

————. Department of Foreign Affairs. *South West Africa Survey 1967*. Pretoria: 1967.

Steward, Alexander. *South West Africa: The Sacred Trust*. Johannesburg: Da Gama, 1963.

Wellington, J. H. *South West Africa and Its Human Issues*. London: Oxford University Press, 1967. Chapters 1–7.

White, Jon Manchip. *The Land God Made in Anger: Reflections on a Journey through South West Africa*. London: Allen and Unwin, 1969.

CHAPTER 2. HISTORY OF THE TERRITORY UNTIL THE END OF GERMAN RULE

Africanus. *The Prussian Lash in Africa: A Story of German Rule in Africa*. London: Hodder and Stoughton, 1918.

Aydelotte, William Osgood. *Bismarck and British Colonial Policy: The Problem of South West Africa, 1883–5*. Philadelphia: University of Pennsylvania Press, 1967. Bibliography.

Bixler, R. W. *Anglo-German Imperialism in South Africa 1880–1900*. Baltimore: Warwick and York, 1932. Bibliography.

Bley, Helmut. "German South West Africa." *South West Africa: Travesty of Trust*. Edited by Ronald Segal and Ruth First. London: Andre Deutsch, 1967.

————. *South West Africa under German Rule, 1894–1914*. London: Heinemann, 1971.

Bruwer, J. P. van S. *South West Africa: The Disputed Land*. Cape Town, Nasionale Boekhandel, 1966. Chapters 1–6.

Calvert, Albert F. *The German African Empire*. London: Werner Laurie, 1916.

Esterhuyse, J. H. *South West Africa 1880–1894*. Cape Town: Struik, 1968.

Goldblatt, I. *History of South West Africa from the Beginning of the Nineteenth Century*. Cape Town: Juta, 1971. Chapters 1–35.

Great Britain. *Union of South Africa. Report on the Natives of South-West Africa and Their Treatment by Germany. Prepared in the Administrator's Office, Windhoek, South West Africa, January 1918*. Cmd. 9146. London: HMSO, 1918.

Harris, John H. *Germany's Lost Colonial Empire and the Essentials of Reconstruction*. London: Simpkin, Marshall, Hamilton, Kent, 1917.

Headlam, G. "The Race for the Interior," *Cambridge History of the British Empire*. 2nd ed. Vol. 8 (1963), pp. 526–28.

Henderson, W. O. *Studies in German Colonial History*. London: Cass, 1962. Bibliography.

Johnston, Sir Harry H. *A History of the Colonization of Africa by Alien Races*. Cambridge: University Press, 1899.

Lemmer, C. J. C. *Inleiding tot die Geskiedenis van Suidwes-Afrika*. Cape Town: Unie-Volkspers, 1941.

Lewin, Evans. *The Germans and Africa*. London: Cassell, 1939.

Lindley, M. F. *The Acquisition and Government of Backward Territory in International Law: Being a Treatise on Law and Practice Relating to Colonial Expansion*. London: Longmans, Green, 1926.

Louis, Wm. Roger. *Great Britain and Germany's Lost Colonies 1914–1919*. London: Oxford University Press, 1967.

Maclean, Frank. *Germany's Colonial Failure: Her Rule in Africa Condemned on German Evidence*. London: Burrup, Mathieson & Sprague, 1918.

Maclean, Frank. *Towards Extermination: Germany's Treatment of the African Native*. St Albans: Campfield Press, 1918.

O'Connor, J. K. *The Hun in Our Hinterland; or the Menace of GSWA*. Cape Town: Maskew Miller [1915].

Schnee, Heinrich. *German Colonization Past and Future: The Truth about the German Colonies*. London: George Allen & Unwin, 1926.

Steer, G. L. *Judgment on German Africa*. London: Hodder and Stoughton, 1939.

Taylor, A. J. P. *Germany's First Bid for Colonies 1884–1885: A Move in Bismarck's European Policy*. London: Macmillan, 1938.

Townsend, Mary Evelyn. *The Rise and Fall of Germany's Colonial Empire, 1884–1918*. New York: Macmillan Company, 1930.

Valentin, Veit. "The Germans in South West Africa 1883–1914: Civil Administration and Economic Conditions," *Cambridge History of the British Empire,* 2nd ed. Vol. 8 (1963), pp. 731–38.

Vedder, H. "The Germans in South West Africa 1883–1914," *Cambridge History of the British Empire*. 2nd ed. Vol. 8 (1963), pp. 723–31.

Vedder, Heinrich. *South West Africa in Early Times. Being the Story of South West Africa up to the Date of Maherero's Death in 1890*. London: Oxford University Press, 1938.

Wellington, J. H. *South West Africa and Its Human Issues*. London: Oxford University Press, 1967, Chapters 8–11.

Witbooi, Hendrik. *Die Dagboek van Hendrik Witbooi*. Cape Town: Van Riebeeck Society, 1929.

CHAPTER 3. TRANSITION FROM CONQUERED TERRITORY TO MANDATE

Baty, T. "Protectorates and Mandates." *British Year Book of International Law,* 2 (1921–1922):109–21.

Beer, George Louis. *African Questions at the Paris Peace Conference.* New York: Macmillan Company, 1923. Bibliography.

Bentwich, Norman. "Le Système des Mandats." *Recueil des Cours,* 29 (1929):115–86.

———. *The Mandates System.* London: Longmans, Green, 1930. Bibliography.

Chowdhuri, R. N. *International Mandates and Trusteeship Systems: A Comparative Study.* The Hague: Martinus Nijhoff, 1955. Bibliography.

Curry, George. "Woodrow Wilson, Jan Smuts and the Versailles Settlement." *American Historical Review,* 66 (1961):968–86.

Diena, Giulio. "Les Mandats Internationaux." *Receuil des Cours,* 5 (1924):215–65.

Evans, Luther Harris. "Are 'C' Mandates veiled Annexations?" *Southwestern Political and Social Science Quarterly,* 7 (1927):381–400.

———. "The General Principles Governing the Termination of a Mandate," *American Journal of International Law,* 26 (1932):735–58.

———. "Some Legal and Historical Antecedents of the Mandatory System." *Proceedings of the Southwestern Political Science Association,* 5 (1924):143–61.

———. "Would Japanese Withdrawal from the League Affect the Status of the Japanese Mandate?" *American Journal of International Law,* 27 (1933):140–42.

Feinberg, Nathan. "La Juridiction et la Jurisprudence de la Cour Permanente de Justice International en Matière de Mandats et de Minorités." *Recueil des Cours,* 59 (1937):591–708.

Haas, Ernest B. "The Reconciliation of Conflicting Colonial Policy Aims: Acceptance of the League of Nations Mandate System." *International Organization,* 6 (1952):521–36.

Hales, James C. "The Creation and Application of the Mandate System." *Transactions of the Grotius Society,* 25 (1939):185–284.

———. "Some Legal Aspects of the Mandate Systems: Sovereignty—Nationality—Termination and Transfer." *Transactions of the Grotius Society,* 23 (1937):85–126.

Hall, H. Duncan. *Mandates, Dependencies and Trusteeships.* London: Stevens & Sons for Carnegie Endowment of International Peace, 1948. Bibliography.

Keith, A. Berriedale. "Mandates." *Journal of Comparative Legislation and International Law,* 4 (1922):71–83.

League of Nations. *The Mandates System: Origin—Principles—Application.* Geneva: 1945.

Lewis, Malcolm M. "Mandated Territories: Their International Status." *Law Quarterly Review,* 39 (1923):458–75.

Logan, Rayford W. *The African Mandates in World Politics.* Washington: Public Affairs Press, 1948.

———. *The Operation of the Mandate System in Africa, 1919–1927.* Washington, D.C.: The Foundation Publishers, Inc., 1942.

Louis, Wm. Roger. "African Origins of the Mandates Idea." *International Organization,* 19 (1965):20–36.

———. "The Origins of the 'Sacred Trust.'" *South West Africa: Travesty of Trust.* Edited by Ronald Segal and Ruth First. London: Andre Deutsch, 1967.

———. "The South West African Origins of the 'Sacred Trust,' 1914–1919." *African Affairs,* 66 (1967):20–39.

———. "The United States and the African Peace Settlement: The Pilgrimage of George Louis Beer." *Journal of African History,* 4 (1963):413–33.

McNair, Arnold D. "Mandates." *Cambridge Law Journal,* 3 (1928):149–60.

Miller, David Hunter. "The Origin of the Mandates System." *Foreign Affairs,* 6 (1928):276–89.

Mills, Mark Carter. "The Mandatory System." *American Journal of International Law,* 17 (1923):50–62.

Potter, Pittman B. "Origin of the System of Mandates under the League of Nations." *American Political Science Review,* 16 (1922):563–83.

Rolin, H. "La Pratique des Mandats Internationaux." *Recueil des Cours,* 19 (1927):493–628.

Slonim, Solomon. "The Origins of the South West Africa Dispute: The Versailles Peace Conference and the Creation of the Mandates System." *Canadian Year Book of International Law,* 6 (1968):115–43.

———. *South West Africa and the United Nations: An International Mandate in Dispute.* Baltimore: Johns Hopkins Press, 1973. Chapter 1.

Smuts, J. C. *The League of Nations: A Practical Suggestion.* London: Hodder and Stoughton, 1918.

Stoyanovsky, J. *La Théorie Générale des Mandats Internationaux.* Paris: Les Presses Universitaires de France, 1925.

Van Maanen-Helmer, Elizabeth. *The Mandates System in Relation to Africa and the Pacific Islands.* London: P. S. King, 1929. Bibliography.

Van Rees, D. F. W. *Les Mandats Internationaux: le control international de l'administration.* Paris: Rousseau, 1927.

White, Freda. *Mandates.* London: Jonathan Cape, 1926.

Wright, Quincy. *Mandates under the League of Nations.* Chicago: University of Chicago Press, 1930. Bibliography.

CHAPTER 4. SOUTH WEST AFRICA
UNDER THE LEAGUE OF NATIONS

Davey, A. M. *The Bondelzwarts Affair: A Study of the Repercussions, 1922–1959.* Pretoria: University of South Africa, Communication no. 31, 1961.

Dundas, Sir Charles. *South-West Africa: The Factual Background.* Johannesburg: South African Institute of International Affairs, 1946.

Emmett, E. "The Mandate over South-West Africa." *Journal of Comparative Legislation and International Law,* 9 (1927):111–22.

Freislich, Richard. *The Last Tribal War.* Cape Town: Struik, 1964.

Goldblatt, I. *History of South West Africa from the Beginning of the Nineteenth Century.* Cape Town: Juta, 1971. Chapters 36–44.

Hofmeyr, J. H. "Germany's Colonial Claims: A South African View." *Foreign Affairs,* 17 (1939): 788–798.

Keith, Arthur Berriedale. *The Constitutional Law of the British Dominions.* London: Macmillan, 1933.

————. *The Dominions as Sovereign States: Their Constitutions and Governments.* London: Macmillan, 1938.

Kennedy, William Paul McClure, and Schlosberg, Herzl Joshua. *The Law and Custom of the South African Constitution. A Treatise on the Constitutional and Administrative Law of the Union of South Africa, the Mandated Territory of South-West Africa, and the South African Crown Territories.* London: Oxford University Press, 1935.

Mathews, E. L. "International Status of Mandatory of League of Nations: High Treason against Mandatory Authority." *Journal of Comparative Legislation and International Law,* 6 (1924):245–50.

————. "The Grant of a Constitution to the Mandated Territory of South-West Africa." *Journal of Comparative Legislation and International Law,* 8 (1926):161–83.

"The Sovereignty of South-West Africa." *Round Table,* 18 (1927–28):217–22.

South Africa. *Report of the South West Africa Commission.* U.G. 26 of 1936. Pretoria: Government Printer, 1936. [Chairman H. S. van Zyl.]

"South West Africa." *Round Table,* 23 (1932–1933):207–11.

"The South-West Africa Commission." *Round Table,* 26 (1935–1936):772–83.

"The South West Africa Mandate." *Round Table,* 15 (1924–1925):610–16.

Toynbee, Arnold J. *Survey of International Affairs 1920–1923.* London: Oxford University Press, 1927.

Wellington, J. H. *South West Africa and Its Human Issues.* London: Oxford University Press, 1967. Chapters 13–14.

Wessels, Louis Herman. *Die Mandaat vir Suidwes-Afrika.* 'S-Gravenhage, Netherlands: Martinus Nijhoff, 1938. [Summary in English.]

CHAPTER 5. THE MANDATE, THE DISSOLUTION OF THE LEAGUE OF NATIONS, AND THE CREATION OF THE UNITED NATIONS, 1945–1949

Ballard, Brook B. *South West Africa, 1945–50: Union Province or United Nations Trusteeship.* Chicago: Library Department of Photographic Reproduction, University of Chicago, 1955.

Ballinger, Ronald B. *South-West Africa: The Case against the Union.* Johannesburg: South African Institute of Race Relations, 1961.

Bentwich, Norman. "Colonial Mandates and Trusteeships." *Transactions of the Grotius Society,* 32 (1947):121–34.

Bowett, D. W. *The Law of International Institutions.* 2nd ed. London: Stevens & Sons, 1970.

Brookes, Edgar H., Rheinallt Jones, J. D., and Webb, Maurice. *South Africa Faces UNO.* Johannesburg: South African Institute of Race Relations, 1947.

Chowdhuri, R. N. *International Mandates and Trusteeship Systems: A Comparative Study.* The Hague: Martinus Nijhoff, 1955. Bibliography.

Dale, Richard. "The Evolution of the South West African Dispute before the United Nations, 1945–1950." Unpublished PhD dissertation, Princeton University, 1962. (University Microfilms, Ann Arbor, Michigan.)

"A Fifth Province of the Union?" *Round Table,* 35 (1945–1946):337–39.

Gey Van Pittius, E. F. W. "Whither SouthWest Africa?" *International Affairs,* 23 (1947):202–9.

Gilchrist, H. "Trusteeship and the Colonial System." *Proceedings of the Academy of Political Science,* 22 (1947):203–17.

Gilchrist, H. "The United Nations: Colonial Questions at the San Francisco Conference." *American Political Science Review*, 39 (1945):982–92.

Haas, Ernest B. "The Attempt to Terminate Colonialism: Acceptance of the United Nations Trusteeship System." *International Organization*, 7 (1953):1–21.

Hailey, Lord. "South-West Africa." *African Affairs*, 46 (1947):77–86.

Hales, James C. "The Reform and Extension of the Mandate System: A Legal Solution to the Colonial Problem." *Transactions of the Grotius Society*, 26 (1941):153–210.

Hall, H. Duncan. *Mandates, Dependencies and Trusteeships*. London: Stevens & Sons for Carnegie Endowment of International Peace, 1948. Bibliography.

———. "The Trusteeship System." *British Year Book of International Law*, 24 (1947):33–71.

———. "The Trusteeship System and the Case of South-West Africa." *British Year Book of International Law*, 24 (1947):385–89.

Hunton, W. A. *Stop South Africa's Crimes: No Annexation of S. W. Africa*. New York: Council on African Affairs, Inc., 1946.

Kahn, E. "South West Africa." *Annual Survey of South African Law*, 1949, pp. 19–27.

Mockford, Julian. *South-West Africa and the International Court*. London: Diplomatic Press and Publishing Company, 1950.

Murray, James N. *The United Nations Trusteeship System*. Urbana: University of Illinois Press, 1957.

Parry, Clive. "The Legal Nature of the Trusteeship Agreements." *British Year Book of International Law*, 27 (1950):164–85.

Rappard, William E. "The Mandates and the International Trusteeship Systems." *Political Science Quarterly*, 61 (1946):408–19.

Rheinallt Jones, J. D. *The Future of South-West Africa*. Johannesburg: South African Institute of Race Relations, 1946.

Sayre, Francis B. "Legal Problems Arising from the United Nations Trusteeship System." *American Journal of International Law*, 42 (1948):263–98.

Scott, Michael. "The International Status of South West Africa." *International Affairs*, 34 (1958):318–29.

———. *The Orphans' Heritage: The Story of the South West Africa Mandate*. London: Africa Bureau, 1958.

———. "The Sacred Trust of South West Africa." *Africa South*, 5 (1960):46–49.

———. *Shadow Over Africa*. London: Union of Democratic Control, 1950.

———. "South West Africa and the Union: How the Natives voted for the Union." *British Africa Monthly*, 1 (1948):13–15.

———. *A Time to Speak*. New York: Doubleday, 1958.

South Africa. Government Information Office. *South West Africa and the Union of South Africa: The History of a Mandate*. New York: 1946.

Steyn, L. C. "Suid-Afrika en die Verenigde Volke." *Tydskrif vir Hedendaagse Romeins-Hollandse Reg*, 12 (1949):1–18.

Toussaint, Charmian Edwards. *The Trusteeship System of the United Nations*. London: Stevens & Sons, 1956.

Troup, Freda. *In Face of Fear: Michael Scott's Challenge to South Africa*. London: Faber and Faber, 1950.

Webb, M. "South-West Africa and the Union." *World Today*, 6 (1950):459–69.

Wight, Martin. "Note." *International Affairs*, 23 (1947):209–12.

Xuma, Alfred Bitini. *South West Africa: Annexation or United Nations*

Trusteeship? Durban: H. A. Naidoo and Sorabjee Rustomjee, Delegates of the South African Passive Resistance Council, 1946.

CHAPTER 6. THE DISPUTE GROWS, 1950–1960

Arden-Clarke, Charles. "South West Africa, the Union and the United Nations." *African Affairs,* 59 (1960):26–35.

Ballinger, Ronald B. *South-West Africa: The Case against the Union.* Johannesburg: South African Institute of Race Relations, 1961.

Biermann, H. H. H., ed. *The Case for South Africa as Put Forth in the Public Statements of Eric H. Louw, Foreign Minister of South Africa.* New York: Macfadden, 1963.

Brinton, J. Y. "The International Court of Justice: Advisory Opinion on Voting Procedure." *Revue égyptienne de droit international,* 11 (1955):182–89.

———. "Mandates, Trusteeship and South-West Africa." *Revue égyptienne de droit international,* 6 (1950):82–102.

Bunting, B. "Windhoek Diary." *Africa South,* 4 (1960):76–83.

Colliard, Claude-Albert. "Le Statut International du Sud-Ouest Africain." *Revue juridique et politique de l'Union française,* 5 (1951):94–112.

Goldblatt, I. *The Conflict between the United Nations and the Union of South Africa in regard to South West Africa.* Windhoek: by the author, 1960.

———. *The Mandated Territory of South West Africa in Relation to the United Nations.* Cape Town: Struik, 1961.

Green, L. C. "United Nations General Assembly, 1950: South West Africa." *International Law Quarterly,* 4 (1951):219–21.

Homont, André. "L'application du régime de la tutelle aux territoires sous mandat." *Revue juridique et politique de l'Union française,* 6 (1952):149–88.

Hudson, Manley O. "The Common Interpretation of the Mandates of International Law." *Proceedings of the American Society of International Law,* 45 (1951):44–55.

———. "The Thirty-Fifth Year of the World Court." *American Journal of International Law,* 51 (1957):1–4.

———. "The Thirty-Fourth Year of the World Court." *American Journal of International Law,* 50 (1956):5–9.

———. "The Twenty-Ninth Year of the World Court." *American Journal of International Law,* 45 (1951):11–19.

Jennings, R. Y. "The International Court's Advisory Opinion on the Voting Procedure on Questions Concerning South-West Africa." *Transactions of the Grotius Society,* 42 (1956):85–97.

Jully, Laurent. "La Question du Sud-Ouest Africain devant la Cour Internationale de Justice." *Die Friedens-Warte,* 50 (1950–1951):207–26.

Kahn, Ellison. "The International Court's Advisory Opinion on the International Status of South West Africa." *International Law Quarterly,* 4 (1951):78–99.

Kerina, Mburumba A. "South West Africa and the United Nations." *Africa South,* 3 (1958):8–15.

Kerno, Ivan S. "Court's Opinion on International Status of South-West Africa." *United Nations Bulletin,* 9 (1950):100–101.

Kozonguizi, Jariretundu. "Background to Violence." *Africa South,* 4 (1960):71–75.

Kozonguizi, Jariretundu. "South West Africa." *Africa South*, 2 (1957):64–72.

Lacharrière, R. De. "Admissibilité de l'audition de pétitionnaires par le Comité du Sud-Ouest Africain." *Annuaire français de droit international*, 2 (1956):379–82.

Lalive, F. J. "Statut international du Sud-Ouest Africain." *Journal du droit international*, 77 (1950):1252–71.

Leeper, Donald S. "Trusteeship Compared with Mandate." *Michigan Law Review*, 49 (1951):1199–1210.

Nisot, Joseph. "The Advisory Opinion of the International Court of Justice on the International Status of South-West Africa." *South African Law Journal*, 68 (1951):274–85.

Rheinallt Jones, J. D. "Administration of South West Africa: Welfare of the Indigenous Population." *Race Relations Journal*, 19 (1952):3–21.

Roberts, E. D. "World Court and South-West Africa." *South African Outlook*, 80 (1950):118–19.

Rosenne, Shabtai. "The International Court and the United Nations: Reflections on the Period 1946–1954." *International Organization*, 9 (1955):244–56.

———. "Sir Hersch Lauterpacht's Concept of the Task of the International Judge." *American Journal of International Law*, 55 (1961):825–62.

South Africa. *Report of the Commission of Enquiry into the Occurrences in the Windhoek Location on the Night of the 10th to the 11th December, 1959, and into the Direct Causes which led to those Occurrences*. U.G. 23 of 1960. Pretoria: Government Printer, 1960. [Chairman C.G. Hall]

"South West Africa before the United Nations." *World Today*, 16 (1960):334–45.

Steinberg, K. "The International Court's Advisory Opinion on South-West Africa." *South African Law Journal*, 67 (1950):422–26.

Themaat, J. P. Verloren van. "Kan die Komitee oor Suidwest-Afrika van die Algemene Vergadering van die Verenigde Volke mondelinge vertöe en getuienis aanhoor?" *Tydskrif vir Hedendaagse Romeins-Hollandse Reg*, 21 (1958):176–80.

Van Essen, J. F. L. "Zuid-West Afrika voor het Internasionale Hof van Justisie." *Tydskrif vir Hedendaagse Romeins-Hollandse Reg*, 13 (1950):187–203.

Van Rensburg, Helgard Michael Janse. *Die Internasionale Status van Suidwes-Afrika: 'n Kritiese Beskouing van die Internasionale Hof van Justisie se Raadgewende Mening van 11 Julie 1950*. Leiden: Drukkerij Luctor et Emergo, 1953. [Summary in English.] Bibliography.

Verzijl, J. H. W. "The International Court of Justice: Admissibility of Hearings of Petitioners by the Committee on South-West Africa." *Nederlands Tydschrift voor Internationaal Recht*, 3 (1956):315–23.

———. *The Jurisprudence of the World Court*. Vol. 2. Leyden: Sijthoff, 1966.

Wood, Vivian C. "South West Africa: Land of Promise." *Lantern*, 7 (1957):35–71.

Yankson, J. Ackah. *South West Africa in the International Scene*. London: Blackwood, 1953.

CHAPTER 7. POLITICAL DEVELOPMENTS, 1960–1966

"Apartheid in South West Africa." *International Commission of Jurists Bulletin*, no. 30 (June 1967):26–37.

Austin, Dennis. *Britain and South Africa.* London: Oxford University Press, 1966.

Ballinger, R. B. *South Africa and the United Nations: Myth and Reality.* Johannesburg: South African Institute of International Affairs, 1963.

———. "The Territory of South West Africa." *Current History,* 45 (1963):361–65.

Blom-Cooper, L. J. "Republic and Mandate." *Modern Law Review,* 24 (1961):256–60.

Brooks, Angie. "South West Africa: The United Nations Position and a Projection for the Future." *Southern Africa in Transition.* Edited by John A. Davis and James K. Baker. New York: Praeger, 1966. Pp. 59–73.

Calvocoressi, Peter. "South-West Africa." *African Affairs,* 65 (1966):223–32.

D'Amato, Anthony. "Apartheid in South West Africa: Five Claims of Equality." *Portia Law Journal,* 1 (1967):1–18.

———. "The Bantustan Proposals for South-West Africa." *Journal of Modern African Studies,* 4 (1966):177–92.

Dugard, John. "The Legal Effect of United Nations Resolutions on Apartheid." *South African Law Journal,* 83 (1966):44–59.

———. "Naciones Unidas, derechos humanos y el 'apartheid.' " *Foro Internacional,* 11 (1970):286–307.

Horrell, Muriel. *South-West Africa.* Johannesburg: South African Institute of Race Relations, 1967.

Kahn, Ellison. "South-West Africa and the United Nations." *Annual Survey of South African Law,* 1960, pp. 54–59.

———. "South West Africa." *Annual Survey of South African Law,* 1964, pp. 41–43.

Kerina, Mburumba. "South-West Africa, the United Nations, and the International Court of Justice." *African Forum,* 2 (1966), no. 2, pp. 5–22.

Kozonguizi, Jariretundu. "South West Africa: Historical Background and Current Problems." *Southern Africa in Transition.* Edited by John A. Davis and James K. Baker. New York: Praeger, 1966. Pp. 45–58.

Lawrie, Gordon. "New Light on South West Africa: Some extracts from and Comments on, the Odendaal Report." *African Studies,* 23 (1964):105–19.

Legum, Colin and Margaret. *South Africa: Crisis for the West.* London: Pall Mall, 1964.

Mason, Philip. "Separate Development and South West Africa: Some Aspects of the Odendaal Report." *Race,* 5 (1964):83–97.

"The Mystery of South West Africa." *World Today,* 18 (1962):315–17.

Olivier, M. J. "Carpio: Persmenings oor sy jongste uitlatinge." *Journal of Racial Affairs,* 13 (1962):133–37.

Segal, Ronald, ed. *Sanctions Against South Africa.* Harmondsworth: Penguin Books, Penguin Special S212, 1964.

Segal, Ronald, and First, Ruth, eds. *South West Africa: Travesty of Trust. The expert papers and findings of the International Conference on South West Africa, Oxford 23–26 March 1966, with a postscript by Iain MacGibbon on the 1966 Judgment of the International Court of Justice.* London: Andre Deutsch, 1967.

"Selfstandige ontwikkeling vir Suidwes-Afrika." *Journal of Racial Affairs,* 13 (1962):249–54.

South Africa. *Report of the Commission of Enquiry into South West African Affairs,* 1962–1963. R.P. 12 of 1946. Pretoria: Government Printer. [Chairman F. H. Odendaal.]

"South West Africa: The Crisis and Its Background." *Round Table,* 52 (1961–1962):155–61.

Spence, J. E. *Republic under Pressure: A Study of South African Foreign Policy*. London: Oxford University Press, 1965.
Wellington, J. H. "South West Africa: The Facts about the Disputed Territory." *Optima*, 15 (1965):40–54.

CHAPTER 8. LEGAL PROCEEDINGS, 1960–1966

Alexandrowicz, Charles H. "The Juridical Expression of the Sacred Trust of Civilization." *American Journal of International Law*, 65 (1971):149–59.
Anand, R. P. *Studies in International Adjudication*. Dobbs Ferry, N.Y.: Oceana Publications, 1969. Chapter 5.
Arkadyev, Y., and Yakovlev, I. "International Court of Justice against International Law." *International Affairs*, Moscow, 9 (1966):37–71.
Ballinger, Ronald B. "Grounds for Revision Revised: An Examination of Mr. Justice Wynne's Argument Concerning the International Court of Justice and the South West Africa Cases." *South African Law Journal*, 82 (1965):26–30.
———. "The International Court of Justice and the South West Africa Cases: Judgment of 21st December, 1962." *South African Law Journal*, 81 (1964):35–62.
———. "South West Africa after the Judgment." *Optima*, 14 (1964):142–54.
Bastid, Suzanne. "L'affaire du Sud-Ouest africain devant la Cour Internationale de Justice." *Journal du droit international*, 94 (1967):571–83.
———. "Les Problèmes Territoriaux Dans la Jurisprudence de la Cour Internationale de Justice." *Recueil des Cours*, 107 (1962):361–492.
Brinton, J. Y. "The South West Africa Decision." *Revue égyptienne de droit international*, 22 (1966):147–160.
Carey, John, ed. *Race, Peace, Law and Southern Africa: Background Paper and Proceedings of the Tenth Hammarskjold Forum*. Dobbs Ferry, N.Y.: Oceana Publications, 1968.
Carillo Salcedo, Juan Antonio. "Uno Caso de Descolonización: El Territoria del Sudoeste Africano." *Revista Española de Derecho Internaciónal*, 20 (1967):417.
Cheng, Bin. "The 1966 South-West Africa Judgment of the World Court." *Current Legal Problems*, 20 (1967):181–212.
Cilliers, A. C. "Die Suidwes-Afrika-saak en die Volkereg." *Tydskrif vir Hedendaagse Romeins-Hollandse Reg*, 34 (1971):25–44 [English summary].
Dale, Richard. "South Africa and the International Community." *World Politics*, 18 (1966):297–313.
D'Amato, Anthony A. "Legal and Political Strategies of the South West Africa Litigation." *Law in Transition Quarterly*, 4 (1967):8–43.
De Brody, Olga Pellicer. "Africa Sud-occidental en la Corte de la Haya: una interpretación errónea del derecho internaciónal." *Foro Internaciónal*, 7 (1966):46–67.
De Villiers, D. P. "The South West Africa Cases: The Moment of Truth." *Ethiopia and Liberia vs South Africa: The South West Africa Cases*. Symposium. Los Angeles: African Studies Center, University of California, Occasional Paper no. 5, 1968, pp. 13–19.
De Villiers, D. P., and Grosskopf, E. M. "The South West Africa Case: A Reply from South Africa." *International Lawyer*, 1 (1967):457–74.
Dugard, John. "Objections to the Revision of the 1962 Judgment of the International Court of Justice in the South West Africa Case." *South African Law Journal*, 82 (1965):178–91.

———. "The South West Africa Cases, Second Phase, 1966." *South African Law Journal,* 83 (1966):429–60.

———. "South West Africa: 1966 and All That." *Annual Survey of South African Law,* 1966, pp. 39–48.

Emanuel, P. A. "De Inwoners van Zuidwes-Afrika en hun welsijn." *Internationale Spectator,* 19 (1965):854–67.

Ethiopia and Liberia vs South Africa: The South West Africa Cases. Symposium. Los Angeles: African Studies Center, University of California, Occasional Paper no. 5, 1968.

Falk, Richard A. "South West Africa Cases: An Appraisal." *International Organization,* 21 (1967):1–23.

———. "The South West Africa Cases: The Limits of Adjudication." *Ethiopia and Liberia vs South Africa: The South West Africa Cases.* Symposium. Los Angeles: African Studies Center, University of California, Occasional Paper no. 5, 1968, pp. 31–41.

———. *The Status of Law in International Society.* Princeton: Princeton University Press, 1970. Chapters 5, 12.

Favoreu, Louis. "Affaires du Sud-Ouest africain." *Annuaire français de droit international,* 12 (1966):123–44.

———. "L'arrêt du 21 décembre 1962 sur le Sud-Ouest africain et l'évolution du droit des organisations internationales." *Annuaire français de droit international,* 9 (1963):303–57.

———. "Récusation et administration de la preuve devant la Cour internationale de Justice. A propos des affaires du Sud-Ouest africain." *Annuaire français de droit international,* 11 (1965):233–77.

Feder, Gerald M.; Rice, David A.; and Etra, Aaron. "The South West Africa Cases: A Symposium." *Columbia Journal of Transnational Law,* 4 (1965):47–118.

Fischer, G. "Les réactions devant l'arrêt de la Cour internationale de Justice concernant le Sud-Ouest africain." *Annuaire français de droit international,* 12 (1966):144–54.

Flemming, Brian. "The South West Africa Cases: Ethiopia v South Africa; Liberia v South Africa: Second Phase." *Canadian Year Book of International Law,* 5 (1967):241–52.

Friedmann, Wolfgang G. "The Jurisprudential Implications of the South West Africa Case." *Columbia Journal of Transnational Law,* 6 (1967):1–16.

Gormley, W. P. "Elimination of the Interstate Complaint: South West Africa Cases and resulting procedural deficiencies in the International Court of Justice." *Texas International Law Forum,* 3 (1967):43–82.

Green, L. C. "South West Africa and the World Court." *International Journal,* 22 (1966):39–67.

———. "The United Nations, South-West Africa and the World Court." *Indian Journal of International Law,* 7 (1967):491–515.

Gross, Ernest A. "The South West Africa Cases: On the Threshold of Decision." *Columbia Journal of Transnational Law,* 3 (1964):19–25.

———. "The South-West Africa Case." *International Lawyer,* 1 (1967):256–70.

———. "The South West Africa Cases: An Essay on Judicial Outlook." *Ethiopia and Liberia vs South Africa: the South West Africa Cases.* Symposium. Los Angeles: African Studies Center, University of California, Occasional Paper no. 5, 1968, pp. 1–12.

———. "The South West Africa Case: What Happened? *Foreign Affairs,* 45 (1966):36–48.

Hidayatullah, M. *The South-West Africa Case*. London: Asia Publishing House, 1967.

Higgins, Rosalyn. "The International Court and South West Africa: The Implications of the Judgment." *International Affairs*, 42 (1966):573–99.

———. "The International Court and South West Africa: The Implications of the Judgment." *Journal of the International Commission of Jurists*, 8 (1967):3–35.

———. "Policy Considerations and the International Judicial Process." *International and Comparative Law Quarterly*, 17 (1968):58–84.

Highet, Keith. "The South West Africa Cases." *Current History*, 52 (1967):154–61.

International Commission of Jurists. Staff Study. "Judgment of the International Court of Justice on South West Africa." *Journal of the International Commission of Jurists*, 7 (1966):163–213.

"International Law and the South West Africa Case." *Howard Law Journal*, 13 (1967):120–54.

Januta, Donatas. "International Law: Enforceability of Administrative Provisions of a League of Nations Mandate: *South West Africa Cases.*" *California Law Review*, 55 (1967):351–65.

Johnson, D. H. N. "The South-West Africa Cases (Second Phase)." *International Relations*, 3 (1967):157–76.

———. "South West Africa Issue in International Law." *Optima*, 11 (1961):118–24.

Johnson, O. "Contribution of the International Court to International Law through the South West Africa Case." *Nigerian Bar Journal*, 4 (1963):46.

Kahn, Ellison. "The International Court and the South-West Africa Case." *Annual Survey of South African Law*, 1962, pp. 66–71.

Katz, Milton. *The Relevance of International Adjudication*. Cambridge: Harvard University Press, 1968. Chapters 4, 5.

Kerina, Mburumba. "South-West Africa, the United Nations, and the International Court of Justice." *African Forum*, 2 (1966), no. 2, pp. 5–22.

Knitel, H. G. "Das Mandat uber Südwestafrika." *Juristische Blätter*, 89 (1967):8–14.

Kozonguizi, Jariretundu. "South-West African Nationalism and the International Court of Justice." *African Forum*, 2 (1966), no. 2, pp. 23–32.

Landis, Elizabeth S. "South West Africa in the International Court: Act II, Scene 1," *Cornell Law Quarterly*, 49 (1964):179–227.

———. "The South West Africa Cases: Remand to the United Nations." *Cornell Law Quarterly*, 52 (1967):627–71.

Leiss, Amelia C., ed. *Apartheid and United Nations Collective Measures*. New York: Carnegie Endowment for International Peace, 1965.

Louw, M. M. H. "Some Political Implications of the ICJ Decision on SWA." *Codicillus*, Special edition, October 1966, pp. 40–43.

MacGibbon, Iain. "The Legal Case" and "Postscript: the International Court Decides." *South West Africa: Travesty of Trust. The expert papers and findings of the International Conference on South West Africa, Oxford 23–26 March 1966, with a postscript by Iain MacGibbon on the 1966 Judgment of the International Court of Justice*. London: Andre Deutsch, 1967, pp. 288–306, 329–46.

McKay, Vernon. "South African Propaganda on the International Court's Decision." *African Forum*, 2 (1966), no. 2, pp. 51–64.

McKean, W. A. "The South West Africa Cases (1966): Two Views." *Australian Year Book of International Law*, 1966, pp. 135–48.

Makonnen, Endalkachew. "The South West Africa Cases: the Case for Rectification." *Ethiopia and Liberia vs South Africa: The South West Africa Cases.* Symposium. Los Angeles: African Studies Center, University of California, Occasional Paper no. 5, 1968, pp. 21–29.

Manning, C. A. W. "The South West Africa Cases: A Personal Analysis." *International Relations,* 3 (1966):98–110.

Marshall, Charles Burton. "Justice and the International Court." *World View,* 9 (1966):7–11.

Monroe, Malcolm W. "Namibia—the Quest for the Legal Status of a Mandate: An Impossible Dream?" *International Lawyer,* 5 (1971):549–57.

Murphy, Cornelius F., Jr. "The South West Africa Judgment: A Study in Justiciability." *Duquesne University Law Review,* 5 (1967):477–86.

Nisot, Joseph. "La Question du Sud-Ouest africain devant la Cour Internationale de Justice." *Revue Belge de Droit International,* 3 (1967):24–36.

Nordau, R. N. "The South West Africa Case." *World Today,* 22 (1966):122–30.

Pérez, Vera E. "La Sentencia de T I J sobre el Sudoeste Africano y la XXI Asamblea General de las Naciones Unidas." *Revista Española de Derecho Internaciónal,* 20 (1967):247–68.

Pollock, Alexander J. "The South West Africa Cases and the Jurisprudence of International Law." *International Organization,* 23 (1969):767–87.

Prott, Lyndel V. "Some Aspects of Judicial Reasoning in the South West Africa Case of 1962." *Revue Belge de Droit International* 3 (1967):37–51.

Rao, P. Chandrasekhara. "South West Africa Cases: Inconsistent Judgments from the International Court of Justice." *Indian Journal of International Law,* 6 (1966):383–94.

Reisman, William M. "Revision of the South West Africa Cases: An Analysis of the Grounds of Nullity in the Decision of July 18th 1966, and Methods of Revision." *Virginia Journal of International Law,* 7 (1966):1–90.

Roskam, K. L. "Het Mandaat Zuid-West-Afrika: 'A Sacred Trust.' " *Volkerechtelijke Opstellen,* 1962, pp. 111–22.

Rothensberg, Leslie. "The [American Society of International Law's] meeting on South West Africa at University of California at Los Angeles." *American Journal of International Law,* 61 (1967):1053–57.

Rubin, Neville. "South West Africa: From Courtroom to Political Arena." *Africa Report,* 11 (December 1966):12–15.

Schmidt, C. W. H. "The 1950 Advisory Opinion: The Status of S W A and the Powers of the U N." *Codicillus,* special edition, October 1966, pp. 23–27.

Scrivner, Robert W. "The South-West Africa Case: 1962 Revisited." *African Forum,* 2 (1966), no. 2, pp. 33–50.

South Africa. Department of Foreign Affairs. *South West Africa Survey 1967.* Pretoria: 1967.

South Africa. Department of Information. *Ethiopia and Liberia versus South Africa: An Official Account of the Contentious Proceedings on South West Africa before the International Court of Justice at the Hague 1960–1966.* Pretoria: 1966.

"South West Africa Cases (Ethiopia v South Africa; Liberia v South Africa), Preliminary Objections." Digested and excerpted by Wm. W. Bishop, Jr. *American Journal of International Law,* 57 (1963):640–59.

"South West Africa Cases (Ethiopia v South Africa; Liberia v South Africa), Second Phase." Digested and excerpted by Wm. W. Bishop, Jr. *American Journal of International Law,* 61 (1967):116–210.

"South West Africa Cases." *Washington University Law Quarterly,* 1967, pp. 159–205.

"South West Africa: A Case Reviewed." *Codicillus,* Special edition, October 1966.

"The South West Africa Cases: *Ut Res Magis Pereat Quam Valeat.*" *University of Pennsylvania Law Review,* 115 (1967):1170–94.

Steyn, R. S. "Has the Mandate for South West Africa Survived the Demise of the League of Nations?" *Responsa Meridiana,* 1 (1965):51–55.

Stone, Julius. "Reflections on Apartheid after the South West Africa Cases." *Washington Law Review,* 42 (1967):1069–82.

———. "South West Africa and the World Court." *The Australian,* 1966, September 26, 27, 28.

Suy, E. "Een Nieuw Arrest van het International Gerechtshof over Zuid-West-Afrika." *Rechtskundig Weekblad,* 26 (1963):1982–94.

Taubenfeld, Rita F. and Howard J. "Working Paper." *Race, Peace, Law and Southern Africa. Background Paper and Proceedings of the Tenth Hammarskjold Forum.* Edited by John Carey. Dobbs Ferry, N.Y.: Oceana Publications, 1968.

Van Raalte, E. "Een belangrijk, maar teleurstellend internationaal arrest." *Internationale Spectator,* 20 (1966):1259–77, 1483–1502.

———. "De Rechtsstrijd over Zuid-West Afrika." *Internationale Spectator,* 19 (1965):325–38.

Van Wyk, J. T. "The International Court of Justice at the Cross-Roads." *Acta Juridica,* 1967, pp. 201–213.

———. "The United Nations, South West Africa and the Law." *Comparative and International Law Journal of Southern Africa,* 2 (1969):48–72.

———. *The United Nations, South West Africa and the Law.* Cape Town: University of Cape Town, 1968.

Verzijl, J. H. W. "International Court of Justice: South West Africa and Northern Cameroons Cases (Preliminary Objections)." *Nederlands Tijdschrift voor Internationaal Recht,* 11 (1964):1–33.

———. "The South West Africa Cases (Second Phase)." *International Relations,* 3 (1966):87–97.

Von Imhoff, Christoph. "Sud west afrika und das Haager Urteil." *Aussenpolitik,* 17 (1966):552–59.

Wiechers, Marinus. "The Judgment of 18 July 1966: The Legal Implications." *Codicillus,* Special edition, October 1966, pp. 6–11.

———. "South West Africa: The Decision of 18 July 1966 and Its Aftermath." *Comparative and International Law Journal of Southern Africa,* 1 (1968):408–46.

———. "Die Suidwes-Afrika-Saak: Enkele Aspekte van die Uitspraak van die Internasionale Geregshof van 18 Julie 1966." *Tydskrif vir Hedendaagse Romeins-Hollandse Reg,* 29 (1966):297–319.

"The World Court's Decision on South-West Africa." A Symposium of the Section of International and Comparative Law of the American Bar Association. Moderator: Harry Inman. Panelists: John Carey and Clifford J. Hynning. *International Lawyer,* 1 (1966):12–38.

Wynne, George. "Grounds for Revision of the Judgment of the International Court of Justice of 21st December, 1962, that it had Jurisdiction to adjudicate upon the South West Africa case: *Ad Hoc* Judge Improperly Chosen as Liberia had no *Locus Standi.*" *South African Law Journal,* 81 (1964):449–57.

De Zaak Suid-West Afrika: het vonnis van het Internationaal Gerechtshof critisch bezien: symposium gehouden te Leiden op 17 december, 1966 op initiatief van Cornelis van Vollenhoven Stichting met inleidingen van Professor Mr. M. Bos, Professor Mr. W. L. Haardt en Professor Jhr Mr. H. F. van Panhuys. With summary in English. Leiden: Sijthoff, 1967. Bibliography.

CHAPTER 9. THE REVOCATION OF THE MANDATE AND ITS AFTERMATH, 1966–1970

Cilliers, A. C. *Whither the International Court?* Port Elizabeth: University, inaugural address D1, 1971.

Cockram, Gail-Maryse. *Vorster's Foreign Policy.* Pretoria: Academica, 1970.

Crawford, John F. "South West Africa: Mandate Termination in Historical Perspective." *Columbia Journal of Transnational Law,* 6 (1967):91–137.

Dugard, John. "The Revocation of the Mandate for South West Africa." *American Journal of International Law,* 62 (1968):78–97.

———. "South West Africa and the Supremacy of the South African Parliament." *South African Law Journal,* 86 (1969):194–204.

———. "South West Africa and the 'Terrorist Trial.' " *American Journal of International Law,* 64 (1970):19–41.

———. "Termination of the Mandate for South West Africa." *Annual Survey of South African Law,* 1966, pp. 44–48.

———. "South West Africa." *Annual Survey of South African Law,* 1967, pp. 37–43, 45–48.

———. "South West Africa: Same Dispute, New Name." *Annual Survey of South African Law,* 1968, pp. 49–52.

———. "South-West Africa." *Annual Survey of South African Law,* 1969, pp. 48–51, 58–62.

———. "South West Africa Returns to the International Court of Justice." *Annual Survey of South African Law,* 1970, pp. 69–72, 79–80.

Engers, J. F. "The United Nations Travel and Identity Document for Namibians." *American Journal of International Law,* 65 (1971):571–78.

Falk, Richard A. "Observers Report: The State v Eliaser Tuhadeleni and Others." *Erosion of the Rule of Law in South Africa.* Geneva: International Commission of Jurists, 1968.

Hall, Richard, ed. *South-West Africa (Namibia): Proposals for Action* [Papers by Randolph Vigne, Jennifer Bray, Richard Plender and Michael Scott]. London: Africa Bureau, 1970.

Kahn, Ellison. "South West Africa." *Annual Survey of South African Law,* 1968, pp. 43–47.

———. "South West Africa." *Annual Survey of South African Law,* 1969, pp. 43–46.

———. "South West Africa." *Annual Survey of South African Law,* 1970, pp. 64–67.

Katz, Milton. *The Relevance of International Adjudication.* Cambridge: Harvard University Press, 1968. Chapter 5.

Khan, Rahmatullah, and Kaur, Satpa. "Deadlock over South West Africa." *Indian Journal of International Law,* 8 (1968):179–200.

Manning, C. A. W. *The United Nations and South West Africa.* London: South Africa Society Papers, no. 6, 1970.

Marston, Geoffrey. "Termination of Trusteeship." *International and Comparative Law Quarterly,* 18 (1969):1–40.

South Africa. Department of Foreign Affairs. *South Africa and the Rule of Law.* Pretoria, Government Printer, 1968.

Spence, Jack. "South Africa and the Modern World." *Oxford History of South Africa*. Edited by Monica Wilson and Leonard Thompson. London: Oxford University Press, 1971. Pp. 477–527.

Umozurike, U. O. "International Law and Self-determination in Namibia." *Journal of Modern African Studies*, 8 (1970):585–603.

Van der Westhuizen, W. M. "Die Bevoegdheid van die Verenigde Volke om die Mandaat vir Suidwes-Afrika te Beëindig." *Tydskrif vir Hedendaagse Romeins-Hollandse Reg*, 31 (1968):330–45.

Venter, F. "Suidwes-Afrika: 'n Dominium van die Republiek?" *Speculum Juris*, 6 (1970):70–78.

Wiechers, Marinus. "South West Africa: The Decision of 18 July 1966 and Its Aftermath." *Comparative and International Law Journal of Southern Africa*, 1 (1968):408–46.

CHAPTER 10. THE COURT'S OPINION OF 1971 AND THE FUTURE

Acheson, Dean. "United States Involvement in South West Africa." *South Africa International*, 1 (1971):207–12. [Reproduced from *The Washington Post*, 2 January 1971.]

Acheson, Dean, and Marshall, Charles Burton. "Applying Dr. Johnson's Advice." *South Africa International*, 2 (1972):129–39.

De Beer, David. "South West African Churches versus South African State." *Sash: the Black Sash Magazine*, 15 (1971), no. 2, pp. 18–19.

Dugard, John. "The Advisory Opinion on South-West Africa." *Annual Survey of South African Law*, 1971, pp. 35–45.

―――. "Namibia: the Court's Opinion, South Africa's Response, and Prospects for the Future." *Columbia Journal of Transnational Law*, 11 (1972): 14–49.

―――. "The Opinion on South-West Africa ('Namibia'): The Teleologists Triumph." *South African Law Journal*, 88 (1971):460–77.

Falk, Richard A. "Realistic Horizon for International Adjudication." *Virginia Journal of International Law*, 11 (1971):314.

"The Future of South West Africa (Namibia)." Symposium. Chairman: Francis O. Wilcox. Panelists: Clifford J. Hynning, Ernest A. Gross, J. Adriaan Eksteen, Allard K. Lowenstein. *Proceedings of the American Society of International Law*, 1971, pp. 143–167.

Gordon, Edward. "Old Orthodoxies amid New Experiences: The South West Africa (Namibia) Litigation and the Uncertain Jurisprudence of the International Court of Justice." *Denver Journal of International Law and Policy*, 1 (1971):65–92.

Gross, Ernest A. "The Coalescing Problems of Southern Africa." *Foreign Affairs*, 46 (1968):743–57.

Grosskopf, E. M. "South West Africa and the World Order." *South Africa International*, 2 (1971):73–81.

Higgins, Rosalyn. "The Advisory Opinion on Namibia: Which UN Resolutions Are Binding under Article 25 of the Charter?" *International and Comparative Law Quarterly*, 21 (1972):270–86.

Howe, Russell Warren. "War in Southern Africa." *Foreign Affairs*, 48 (1969):150–65.

Kane-Berman, John. *Contract Labour in South West Africa*. Johannesburg: South African Institute of Race Relations, 1972.

Kennan, G. F. "Hazardous Courses in Southern Africa." *Foreign Affairs,* 49 (1971):218–36. Reprinted in *South Africa International,* 1 (1971):176–95.

Landis, Elizabeth. "Namibia: The Beginning of Disengagement." *Studies in Race and Nations* (Denver), 2 (1970–1971), no. 1, pp. 1–45.

Lejeune, Anthony. *The Case for South West Africa.* London: Tom Stacey, 1971.

"The Ovambo Workers' Strike." *Nusas Press Digest.* Cape Town: National Union of South African Students, 1972.

Rovine, Arthur W., and D'Amato, Anthony. "Written Statement of the International League for the Rights of Man filed with the International Court of Justice in the Namibia Question." *New York University Journal of International Law and Politics,* 4 (1971):335–402.

Sanders, A. J. G. M. "Palace of Peace Revisited." *Codicillus,* 11 (1970), no. 2, pp. 22–24.

Schreve, P. K. "Die Gelding van Wette in die Caprivi-Zipfel." *Tydskrif vir Hedendaagse Romeins-Hollandse Reg,* 29 (1966):62–66.

Schwelb, Egon. "The International Court of Justice and the Human Rights Clauses of the Charter." *American Journal of International Law,* 66 (1972):337–51.

South Africa. Department of Foreign Affairs. *South West Africa Advisory Opinion 1971.* Cape Town: Cape and Transvaal Printers, 1972.

Stevenson, J. R. "United States Oral Statement on Continued Presence of South Africa in Namibia Presented before the International Court of Justice." *Department of State Bulletin,* 64 (1971):542–49.

Van Wyk, J. T. "The Request for an Advisory Opinion on South West Africa." *Acta Juridica,* 1970, pp. 219–29.

Wiechers, Marinus. "South West Africa: The Background, Content and Significance of the Opinion of the World Court of 21 June 1971." *Comparative and International Law Journal of Southern Africa,* 5/(1972):123–70.)

———. "South West Africa and the International Court of Justice." *Codicillus,* 12 (1971), no. 2, pp. 46–50.

Bibliography, 1972-1973

Acheson, Dean, and Marshall, Charles Burton. "Applying Dr. Johnson's Advice." *Columbia Journal of Transnational Law*, 11 (1972): 193.

Brown, P. "1971 Advisory Opinion on South West Africa (Namibia)." *Vanderbilt Journal of Transnational Law*, 5 (1971): 213.

Dale, Richard. "The Political Futures of South West Africa and Namibia." *World Affairs*, 134 (1972): 325–343.

Dugard, John. *South West Africa/Namibia: Review of the International Dispute*. Johannesburg: South African Institute of Race Relations, 1973 (RR/4/73).

Hamutenya, H. L. and Geingob, G. H. "African Nationalism in Namibia." In *Southern Africa in Perspective*, ed. Christian P. Potholm and Richard Dale. New York: Free Press, 1972. Pp. 85–94.

Holder, William E. "1971 Advisory Opinion of the International Court of Justice on Namibia (South West Africa)." *Federal Law Review*, 5 (1972): 115–124.

Iwanejko, M. E. and Rysiak, Gwidon. "The Problem of Namibia" [in Polish]. *Sprawy Miedzynarodowe*, 25 (1972): 52.

Kane-Berman, John. *The Labour Situation in South West Africa*. Johannesburg: South African Institute of Race Relations, 1973 (RR/10/73).

Kapuuo, Clemens. *The Internal Situation in South West Africa*. Johannesburg: South African Institute of Race Relations, 1973 (RR/12/73).

Lissitzyn, Oliver J. "International Law and the Advisory Opinion on Namibia." *Columbia Journal of Transnational Law*, 11 (1972): 50–73.

Manning, C. A. W. "Political Justice at the Hague." *Cambrian Law Review*, 1972: 64.

"Namibia" [Ovambo strike]. *Review of International Commission of Jurists*, 1972 (no. 8): 12–13.

O'Linn, Brian. *The Internal Situation in South West Africa*. Johannesburg: South African Institute of Race Relations, 1973 (RR/13/73).

Potholm, Christian P. and Dale Richard, eds. *Southern Africa in Perspective*. New York: Free Press, 1972.

Rovine, Arthur W. "The World Court Opinion on Namibia." *Columbia Journal of Transnational Law*, 11 (1972): 203.

Van der Merwe, Paul. "South Africa and South West Africa." In *Southern Africa in Perspective*, ed. Christian P. Potholm and Richard Dale. New York: Free Press, 1972. Pp. 69–84.

Voipio, R. *Die Arbeidsituasie in Suidwes-Afrika*. Johannesburg: South African Institute of Race Relations, 1973 (RR/2/73).

Wiechers, Marinus. *South West Africa/Namibia: Review of the International Dispute*. Johannesburg: South African Institute of Race Relations, 1973 (RR/5/73).

South African and
South West African
Statutory Instruments

Table of Cases

MUNICIPAL COURTS

Australia

Israel

New Zealand

South Africa and South West Africa

United Kingdom

Resolutions of the
General Assembly and the
Security Council

GENERAL ASSEMBLY

566

Author Index

Subject Index